THE AGE OF JACKSON

THE AGE OF
JACKSON

By Arthur M. Schlesinger, Jr.

KONECKY&KONECKY

KONECKY & KONECKY
72 AYERS POINT RD,
OLD SAYBROOK, CT 06475

THIS EDITION PUBLISHED BY ARRANGEMENT WITH
LITTLE, BROWN AND COMPANY, NEW YORK, NY

ISBN: 1-56852-436-6

PRINTED AND BOUND IN THE USA

TO
MARIAN

The feud between the capitalist and laborer, the house of Have and the house of Want, is as old as social union, and can never be entirely quieted; but he who will act with moderation, prefer fact to theory, and remember that every thing in this world is relative and not absolute, will see that the violence of the contest may be stilled.

— GEORGE BANCROFT

FOREWORD

THE WORLD crisis has given new urgency to the question of the "meaning" of democracy. If democracy is indeed to be the hope of the future, we know now that we must have its lineaments clearly in mind, so that we may the more surely recognize it and the more responsibly act upon it. For some the questioning has taken the form of a search for the immutable moral abstractions of the democratic faith. Such an inquiry meets profound human needs, even if it rarely succeeds in getting far along its own path. But, for the student of history, the "meaning" of democracy is likely to assume a form at once far more simple and far more complex. The key to that meaning is rather to be sought in the concrete record of what democracy has meant in the past. What range of possibilities has it, in fact, unfolded? What methods has it found legitimate? What have been its values and its resources?

The world after victory will contain internal, as well as external, perplexities of the utmost difficulty and importance. We do not yet know how in detail the American democracy will move to meet them; but this we do know, that, if it is to remain a democracy, its moods, methods and purposes will bear a vital relation to its attack on similar (if less intense) crises of its past.

Democracy has recommended itself above all other modes of organizing society by its capacity for the peaceable solution of its internal problems. Its flexible political and social structure, with the premium placed on tolerance, bargaining and compromise, has on the whole kept alive enough hope for discontented minorities to deter them from taking up the option of revolution. The great exception in our history was a question so crucial that perhaps it could have been solved in no other way. (We know now that it is an illusion that wars have always been unnecessary.)

But the crisis of the second order — the time of bitter social tension which somehow escapes the final flare-up — constitutes democracy's great triumph. The resources which have enabled the American democracy to surmount such crises in the past will be drawn on to the full in the near and shadowed future. The actual issues, political and economic, of Jackson's day have now an almost Arcadian simplicity. Nonetheless they went to the roots of many of the democratic ambiguities, opening up and probing questions whose recurrence a century later testifies to their continuing significance for a free society.

The heritage of Andrew Jackson, as President Roosevelt has said, is "his unending contribution to the vitality of our democracy. We look back on his amazing personality, we review his battles because the struggles he went through, the enemies he encountered, the defeats he suffered and the victories he won are part and parcel of the struggles, the enmities, the defeats and the victories of those who have lived in all the generations that have followed." [1]

In the days of Jackson, as in all periods of rapid social adjustment, there was a close correspondence between the movement of politics and the movement of ideas. This work attempts to examine the politics more or less in terms of the ideas; and, in the course of the study, it has seemed that Jacksonian democracy, which has always appeared an obvious example of Western influence in American government, is not perhaps so pat a case as some have thought; that its development was shaped much more by reasoned and systematic notions about society than has been generally recognized; and that many of its controlling beliefs and motives came rather from the East and South than from the West.

The clash of ideas in these years reveals, moreover, a number of characteristics of democracy in transition. It may help perhaps in building up a conception of the peaceable "revolution" by which our democracy has, save for the tragic exception, thus far avoided the terror of violent revolution.

History can contribute nothing in the way of panaceas. But it can assist vitally in the formation of that sense of what is democratic, of what is in line with our republican traditions, which alone can save us.

ARTHUR M. SCHLESINGER, JR.

May 7, 1944
Washington, D.C.

[1] Franklin D. Roosevelt, *Public Papers and Addresses*, S. I. Rosenman, arr., VII, 41.

ACKNOWLEDGMENTS

THIS book is the outgrowth of a series of lectures entitled "A Reinterpretation of Jacksonian Democracy" delivered at the Lowell Institute in Boston in the fall of 1941. I am profoundly indebted to my father, Arthur M. Schlesinger, for his wise counsel and keen criticism. Bernard DeVoto, Frederick Merk and my mother, Elizabeth Bancroft Schlesinger, have contributed to my understanding of the pre-Civil War period. I wish also to express my gratitude to the Society of Fellows of Harvard University, which made my researches possible, and in particular to Lawrence J. Henderson and to A. Lawrence Lowell, who greatly enriched my insight into the interplay of historical forces. Although I cannot believe they would altogether have liked my conclusions, I hope that they would have respected the methods by which they were reached. I am grateful to Charles A. Beard, who generously placed at my disposal his notes on the Jacksonian era. The librarians of the Harvard College Library, the Massachusetts Historical Society, the Library of Congress and the New York Public Library were of great assistance. My wife, Marian Cannon Schlesinger, has been a source of inestimable help and encouragement at all times.

A. M. S., Jr.

CONTENTS

THE AGE OF JACKSON

I PROLOGUE: 1829

FOR THE White House the new year began in gloom. The President's wife spent a sleepless and painful night, and Mr. Adams, waking at daybreak, found the dawn overcast, the skies heavy and sullen. He prayed briefly, then fumbled for his Bible and turned to the Book of Psalms, reading slowly by the yellow light of his shaded oil lamp. "Blessed *is* the man that walketh not in the counsel of the ungodly, nor standeth in the way of sinners, nor sitteth in the seat of the scornful." On he read to the ultimate assurance. "For the Lord knoweth the way of the righteous: but the way of the ungodly shall perish."

The familiar words assuaged disappointments of four years. To an Adams, the first psalm seemed almost a personal pledge. "It affirms that the righteous man is, and promises that he shall be, blessed," he noted with precise gratification in his journal, and went to his desk for his usual early-morning work. As his pen began to scratch across the paper, the lamp, its oil low, flared for a moment, then flickered out. Mr. Adams sat in the gray light.[1]

It was no year for righteous men: everywhere they sat in darkness. Two months before, General Andrew Jackson had been elected President of the United States. The ungodly were now in the ascendancy, and those who walked not in their counsels had little but Scriptures for consolation. "There is more effrontery," Samuel Clesson Allen, retiring Congressman from Massachusetts, had exclaimed, ". . . in putting forward a man of his bad character — a man covered with crimes . . . than ever was attempted before upon an intelligent people." The good Reverend Robert Little, pastor of the Unitarian Society of Washington, sadly chose his text: "When Christ drew near the city he wept over it."[2]

The retiring President put on a brave front at his last reception; but, too weary for his walks along the Potomac, he now sought his

---

[1] J. Q. Adams, *Memoirs*, C. F. Adams, ed., VIII, 89.
[2] S. C. Allen to Samuel Lathrop, May 14, 1828, Miscellaneous Papers, Pennsylvania Historical Society; anon., *William Winston Seaton of the "National Intelligencer,"* 210.

exercise on horseback, while his wife prepared to move from the executive mansion. The appearance of Mr. Clay, the Secretary of State, shocked the capital. One visitor, on a January afternoon, found the small drawing room in the Clay house bright with lamps and blazing fire, but its inhabitants deep in melancholy. Mrs. Clay, mournfully pacing the room, whispered, "He sleeps." Stretched full length on the sofa lay Henry Clay, thin and white, covered from head to foot with a dark cloak, which looked like "a black pall." Through the parties of January and February he masked his dejection under frigid smiles.[3]

Uncertainty about the future increased the official gloom. Mr. Webster, the distinguished Senator from Massachusetts, scrawled a memorandum for friends at Boston: —

Gen. J. will be here abt. 15 Feb. —
Nobody knows what he will do when he does come. . . .
My opinion is
That when he comes he will bring a breeze with him.
Which way it will blow, I cannot tell. . . .
My *fear* is stronger than my *hope*.[4]

*   *   *

From faraway states the people came to Washington — local politicians, newspaper editors, war veterans, curiosity seekers, enthusiasts for Jackson, and just the people. *Their* hope was stronger than their fear.

They found a scattered, straggling city. The 91,665 feet of brick pavement, of which the old citizens boasted, was inadequate to the mud of February, and the boots of the mob slogged excitedly, patiently, wearily about the town, to snatch at the rumors and gawk at the sights and plague the friends of Jackson. Hospitable taverns served them endless draughts of gin slings, gin cocktails, sherry cobblers, mint juleps, snakeroot bitters, timber doodle and eggnog. Local theaters entertained them with rare divertissement. Some went to the Amphitheatre to watch George Washington Dixon, "the celebrated Buffo Singer," first of the great black-face artists, who sang "Push-a-Long Keep Moving" or "The Hunters of Kentucky" and soon would delight the land with "Zip Coon" and the haunting "Coal Black Rose," twanging his banjo and breathing out his insistent strains. The more "high-toned" preferred bewitching Clara Fisher at the

---

[3] Margaret B. Smith, *The First Forty Years of Washington Society*, Gaillard Hunt, ed., 256–257.
[4] Note by Webster, February, 1829, Daniel Webster, *Letters*, C. H. Van Tyne, ed., 142.

Theatre, the girl who had won all London before she was twelve and now, an enchanting seventeen, was winning America. Steamboats were named after her, and racehorses, drinks and Negro babies. Soon there would appear the great Edwin Forrest, mightiest actor of the day, whose swelling muscles and rumbling voice and heroic passion as Brutus and Virginius thrilled the galleries in dramas of democratic martyrdom in ancient Rome.

The crowd drifted to inspect Mr. Jefferson's library, on exhibition at the auctioneer's before it went on sale to pay the debts of his estate. It admired the elegant "Transparent Panoramic View of West Point and the adjacent scenery" at the Rotundo on the corner of Pennsylvania Avenue and Thirteenth Street. It peered through the celebrated solar microscope. It looked with amazement on the cat with the face of a Greek hero.

Gossip was incessant. Had you heard about Frances Wright, of Scotland and Nashoba, Tennessee, and her alarming views on religion and society? New York, Philadelphia and now neighboring Baltimore quivered with indignation at her presence. And there was always the latest quip about Major Eaton of Tennessee, and his New Year's Day bride, the notorious Margaret O'Neale Timberlake. ("There is a vulgar saying of some vulgar man, I believe Swift, on such unions," the ribald New York Congressman, C. C. Cambreleng, had written to his intimate friend Martin Van Buren, " — about using a certain household . . . and then putting it on one's head.")

If other entertainment languished, Congress was inexhaustible: the Senate, dignified and decorous, and the House, with members lolling back in armchairs, laughing, coughing, spitting, rattling newspapers, while some poor speaker tried to talk above the din. For a few there were the formal banquets, beginning as late as five-thirty or six, with rich courses served in quick succession — soup, bass, turkey, beef smothered in onions, mutton, ham, pheasant, ice cream, jelly, fruit — washed down by a steady flow of sherry, pale and brown, madeira and champagne.[5]

But, above all, there were the reports on the progress of General

[5] For Cambreleng's remark (the elisions are his own), Cambreleng to Van Buren, January 1, 1829, Van Buren Papers (Professor Bassett has noted that Cambreleng probably meant Montaigne, J. S. Bassett, *Life of Andrew Jackson,* 459 n.). For Washington early in 1829, see the *National Intelligencer, United States Telegraph* and *Niles' Register* for these months. For Congress, see, e.g., Robert Dale Owen in the *Free Enquirer,* May 12, 1832; John Fairfield to his wife, December 15, 1835, John Fairfield, *Letters,* A. G. Staples, ed., 33; George Combe, *Notes on the United States of North America, during a Phrenological Visit in 1838-9-40,* I, 271. For a typical banquet, see Fairfield to his wife, January 24, 1836, Fairfield, *Letters,* 81–83.

Jackson. For one terrible day in January, Washington had trembled at the rumor of his death, till Duff Green printed an authoritative denial in the *United States Telegraph,* the Jackson organ; and on February 11 the President-to-be finally arrived. People noted him as a tall, gaunt man, his face wrinkled with pain and age, his thick gray hair turning snow-white. His eyes were sad and heart empty from the recent death of his wife, and his right hand ached from the hard grips of admirers along the way. Through the three weeks before inauguration he quietly consulted with advisers and chose his cabinet.

The skies were clouded on the fourth of March, but the sun broke through as General Jackson left for the Capitol, and a soft southwest wind played over the noisy crowd awaiting him. The old man, wearing a plain black suit and a black cravat, stiffly delivered his inaugural address to the excited gathering. A shrewd Kentucky newspaperman, on from Frankfort for a job in the new government, reported the mood of the crowd. "It was a proud day for the people," Amos Kendall wrote his paper. "General Jackson is *their own* president." But Justice Story, John Marshall's close friend and disciple on the Supreme Court, reported another mood in accents of despair. "The reign of King 'Mob' seemed triumphant." [6]

The friends of Mr. Adams had no monopoly on pessimism. Martin Van Buren, just resigned as Governor of New York to become Jackson's Secretary of State, made his way to the capital amidst discouraging tidings. Levi Woodbury of New Hampshire roused him from bed, late on a March night, in New York, to pour glum prophecies in his ear. At Philadelphia he had a cheerless talk with Edward Livingston and his wife, both old friends of the President. At Newcastle, Louis McLane of Delaware, who had expected a cabinet post, met his steamboat, every line of his face stamped with disappointment. Rushing to take Van Buren's arm, he harangued him over the feebleness of the administration and hinted that he had better get out before becoming involved in its wreck.

It was after dark when Van Buren reached Washington. His coach hardly arrived at the hotel before office-seekers surrounded it. They pursued him inside, flocking relentlessly into the room where he lay on a sofa, weary from the journey. The Secretary of State listened to them patiently for an hour, then dismissed them to go to the White House.

[6] *Argus of Western America* (Frankfort), March 18, 1829; Story to Sarah Waldo Story, March 7, 1829, W. W. Story, *Life and Letters of Joseph Story,* I, 563.

A solitary lamp shone in the vestibule, and a single candle flickered in the President's office, where the old General sat with his intimate from Tennessee, Major Lewis. Jackson was in bad health, tired, uncertain where to turn for loyalty or support. "His friends have no common principle," Daniel Webster had written back to New England, " — they are held together by no common tie." But when Van Buren entered the room, his face brightened and his eye flashed. He rose invincibly to offer his cordial greeting. Van Buren's doubts dropped away in a surge of warmth and confidence in the resolute old man.[7]

The young republic faced its critical test. Could it survive the rule of the people? Or were Webster, Clay, Adams and the friends of Van Buren right in their anticipations of disaster?

John Randolph of Roanoke spoke a prevailing mood with wild intensity. "The country is ruined past redemption," he cried; "it is ruined in the spirit and character of the people." Was there any hope for the future? "There is an abjectness of spirit that appals and disgusts me," he declared in despair. "Where now could we find leaders of a revolution?"[8]

[7] Martin Van Buren, *Autobiography*, J. C. Fitzpatrick, ed., 229–231; Webster to Ezekiel Webster, February 23, 1829, Webster, *Letters*, 142; Emily Donelson to Polly Coffee, March 27, 1829, Pauline W. Burke, *Emily Donelson of Tennessee*, I, 164, 178.

[8] Randolph to J. Brockenbrough, January 12, February 9, 1829, H. A. Garland, *Life of John Randolph of Roanoke*, II, 317–318.

II END OF ARCADIA

THE AMERICA of Jefferson had begun to disappear before Jefferson himself had retired from the presidential chair. That paradise of small farms, each man secure on his own freehold, resting under his own vine and fig-trees, was already darkened by the shadow of impending change. For Jefferson, Utopia had cast itself in the form of a nation of husbandmen. "Those who labor in the earth," he had said, "are the chosen people of God, if ever He had a chosen people"; and the American dream required that the land be kept free from the corruptions of industrialism. "While we have land to labor then, let us never wish to see our citizens occupied at a work-bench, or twirling a distaff." Far better to send our materials to Europe for manufacture, than to bring workingmen to these virgin shores, "and with them their manners and principles." "The mobs of great cities," he concluded ominously, "add just so much to the support of pure government, as sores do to the strength of the human body." [1]

1

But actuality was betraying the dream. The "Notes on Virginia" furnished imperfect texts for the energies of a bustling nation. Jefferson's own administration became a series of notations on the doom of his Utopia. However wiser it might have been to leave the workshops in Europe, it slowly became more profitable to bring them to the materials. Jefferson himself helped nourish the serpent in his Eden with one of his favorite measures, the Embargo of 1807, which set on firm footing manufacturing establishments started experimentally along the Atlantic coast during the twenty years preceding. The War of 1812 and the British blockade further stimulated domestic manufactures. A protective tariff followed the war, and behind its wall yet more undertakings sprang up.

The farm remained the statistical center of American life, but business enterprise was exerting stronger and stronger claims on the

[1] Thomas Jefferson, "Notes on Virginia," *Writings* (Memorial Edition), II, 229–230.

imagination of the people and the action of the government. The number of persons engaged in manufactures increased 127 per cent between 1820 and 1840, while agricultural labor increased only 79 per cent. The number of city dwellers rose similarly. In 1820 less than a twentieth of the nation lived in communities of eight thousand or over; but two decades later more than a twelfth lived in such places, and more than a ninth in towns larger than two thousand.[2]

The new economic life acquired its appropriate institutions. The private business association was reshaped into an effective agency of capitalist enterprise; and by its side the chartered corporation, created by special act of the state legislature, began its rise to dominance, first in banking, then in insurance and inland transportation, soon in manufacturing.

Paper money underwrote and stimulated the contagion of enterprise. Banking privileges, jealously guarded in the early days of the republic and held in deep suspicion by strict Jeffersonians, were extended liberally by state legislatures, especially in the financial stringency during the War of 1812. Wildcat paper may not have been the most reliable form of capital, but the turnover was quick, expansion would take up the slack, and what merchant, whether bankrupt or wealthy, would not prefer a ready-flowing supply of money, however imperfect, to a limited quantity of specie currency? The evident usefulness and frequent profitability of state banks wiped away many of the remaining Jeffersonian scruples. So essential did they speedily become to the new economic fabric that an important argument in 1816 for establishing a second Bank of the United States was its indispensability in controlling them. In the meantime, the nation's thrust to the westward, laying out new fringes of settlement where money was necessary and specie scarce, generated further demands for fluid capital.

2

Alexander Hamilton, the brilliant and ambitious aide of General Washington, gave the new industrialism its political philosophy. The precarious days of the Revolution had convinced him that social stability rested on the firm alliance of government and business. No society, he believed, could succeed "which did not unite the interest and credit of rich individuals with those of the state." As early as 1780, he was turning over in his mind plans which would "make it the

[2] George Tucker, *Progress of the United States*, 135, 128; J. R. Commons and associates, *History of Labour in the United States*, I, 176.

immediate interest of the moneyed men to co-operate with govern-ment in its support."

To his conviction of the essential wisdom of the wealthy classes, he added a deep skepticism as to the capacity of the masses for self-government. "All communities," he told the men gathered in Phila-delphia to ponder a constitution for the thirteen states, "divide them-selves into the few and the many. The first are rich and well-born, the other the mass of the people. . . . The people are turbulent and chang-ing; they seldom judge or determine right." The formula for govern-ment was simple. "Give, therefore, to the first class a distinct, perma-nent share in the government. They will check the unsteadiness of the second, and, as they cannot receive any advantage by a change, they therefore will ever maintain good government." [3]

For Hamilton, then, the problem reduced itself to the invention of means which would secure to the "rich and well-born" their "distinct, permanent share in the government." He first hoped to imbed his scheme in the Constitution; but his failure in the convention taught him that the marriage of the wealthy classes and the state must come after the Constitution, and on grounds which would not shake the loyalty of the masses.

Thus he cheerfully conceded the republican frame of government, and even defended it powerfully in the *Federalist* papers. Then, as Secretary of the Treasury, he saw his chance and proposed a financial program which not only was a statesmanlike solution of pressing financial difficulties, but was brilliantly designed to give the business community its enduring stake in the government. He offered as im-mediate bait the assumption of the state debts and the funding system. He projected, as the keystone of a durable alliance, the Bank of the United States — a profit-making institution to be privately owned and to enjoy special access to the public funds — which, as he had earlier observed, would link "the interest of the State in an intimate con-nection with those of the rich individuals belonging to it." [4] And in his celebrated Report on Manufactures he made a classic statement of the long-run possibilities for business in an alliance with the govern-ment.

The Report on Manufactures was the first great expression of the industrial vision of the American future. Astutely conceding to the Jeffersonian dream that agriculture has "intrinsically a strong claim to pre-eminence over every other kind of industry," Hamilton pro-

---

[3] Hamilton to Robert Morris, 1780, *Works of Alexander Hamilton*, H. C. Lodge, ed., III, 332; "Speeches in the Federal Convention," *ibid.*, I, 401.
[4] Hamilton to Robert Morris, 1780, *Works*, III, 338.

posed to show that its *real* interests "will be advanced, rather than injured, by the due encouragement of manufactures." [5] From this premise the Report marched unconquerably on to its conclusion: the plea for government protection of industry. For all its deference to Jeffersonian sensibilities, for all its silence about the political implications of this scheme to build up the business classes, the drift of the Report was unmistakable, and enterprising capitalists could hardly miss it. Though it caused no immediate action, the Report in the long run was supremely successful, serving as an arsenal of argument and inspiration for later generations of Hamiltonians. Its progressive enactment became the index of the rising power of the business community.

The victory of Jefferson in 1800 rebuked the comparative candor with which Hamilton and the early Federalists had sought to orient society around the business classes. But the energies of industrialism were irresistible, and now they began to work through the Republican party, giving the economic program of Hamilton a kindlier aspect and a more ingratiating vocabulary.

Its most persuasive champion after the War of 1812 was Henry Clay of Kentucky, a former Jeffersonian Republican, who reshaped it to appeal to the West, from which he had emerged as the first great political leader. He amplified Hamilton's case for the tariff by expanding the "home market" argument, with its assurance that industrialism would buy everything the farmers could raise; and he rounded out the general program by adding to it the policy of government support of internal improvements, which further won the West.[6]

The various measures dovetailed neatly in a compact system, based in large part on the debt created by Hamilton's funding plan. The debt made the Bank indispensable as a financial agent, and the tariff indispensable as a source of revenue. The internal-improvements policy promised a future of steady spending which would save the debt from extinction. And the debt itself, by its very existence, bound the government to its creditors, the business and financial groups. "A national debt," Hamilton had written, "if it is not excessive, will be to us a national blessing." [7]

Henry Clay adorned the Federalist program with all the fascination of his personality, the fire of his rhetoric and the daring of his political management. It acquired a broad emotional significance which the

[5] Hamilton, "Report on Manufactures," *Works*, IV, 74.
[6] Hamilton had even foreseen the need and value of the internal-improvements policy, though he never broached it publicly. See his letter to Jonathan Dyer, 1799, *Works*, VIII, 519.
[7] Hamilton to Robert Morris, April 20, 1781, *Works*, III, 387.

colder Hamilton had never succeeded in giving it. No man in America had a greater gift for exciting intense personal enthusiasm than Clay. A splendid orator, with a sure understanding of the crowd, he was endowed with a magnificent and garish imagination, which caught up and expressed the inarticulate popular feelings in their vague longing, their vulgarity and their wonder. He made Federalism a living vision, replacing the dry logical prose of Hamilton with thrilling pictures of a glorious future. The blaze of nationalism suggested a new and disarming name — the American System — and under Clay's solicitous care, this rebaptized Federalism slowly won its way to the inner councils of the government.

3

Yet the economic program of Hamilton, which Clay took over, was but part of a general social philosophy, the object of which was much less to distribute profits than power. Hamilton's distinction between the "rich and well-born" and the "mass of the people" had formulated concisely the problem of government for Federalists. While the spirit of Federalism on the national scene tended increasingly to appropriate the language, the principles and the party of Jefferson, this distinction remained very much alive within the states. The conventions to revise the state constitutions provided ample evidence of its vigor in the years after the second war with Britain.

Discontent had welled up with sufficient force in three leading states to compel a scrapping of old constitutions: Massachusetts in 1820, New York in 1821, Virginia in 1829. The delegates included many of the statesmen of the day — John Adams, Daniel Webster, Joseph Story, James Kent, Martin Van Buren, John Marshall, James Madison, James Monroe, John Randolph, Benjamin Watkins Leigh, John Tyler — and their sessions gave a vivid picture of the conflicts which were unsettling the social order. In particular, the debates over property qualifications for suffrage, over religious qualifications for officeholding, and over the judiciary, placed Federalism in the full fire of the democratic attack, eliciting some of the frankest expositions of its underlying principles.

The rock on which Alexander Hamilton built his church was the deep-seated conviction that society would be governed best by an aristocracy, and that an aristocracy was based most properly and enduringly on property. Daniel Webster put the argument in its most massive form in his famous speech in the Massachusetts convention. "Power *naturally* and *necessarily* follows property," he declared; and again, "A republican form of government rests not more on political constitutions than on those laws which regulate the descent and transmission of property." "It would seem, then," he concluded, "to be the part of political wisdom to found government on property; and to establish such distribution of property, by the laws which regulate its transmission and alienation, as to interest the great majority of society in the protection of the government." "Power and property," as Benjamin Watkins Leigh observed in the Virginia convention, "may be separated for a time by force or fraud — but divorced, never. For, so soon as the pang of separation is felt, . . . property will purchase power, or power will take over property. And either way, there must be an end of free Government." [8]

If power and property belonged together, and if they were in fact together by virtue of restricting the franchise to those who could satisfy a property qualification, the task of neo-Federalism was to prevent their separation — that is, to prevent the flight of political power from men of property.

The crucial struggle, then, centered on the extension of the vote to the propertyless masses. "The notion that every man that works a day on the road, or serves an idle hour in the militia," declared the jurist Chancellor Kent with vehemence in the New York convention, "is entitled as of right to an equal participation in the whole power of government, is most unreasonable, and has no foundation in justice." He invoked a favorite image. "Society is an association for the protection of property as well as of life, and the individual who contributes only one cent to the common stock, ought not to have the same power and influence in directing the property concerns of the partnership, as he who contributes his thousands." This was a cherished argument. "It was a principle admitted in all private corporations," another speaker pointed out triumphantly, "that all persons who have a larger share should have a larger vote. So in the community." [9]

The implications of this principle were plain, and the tougher Federalists did not flinch from them. "As the wealth of the commercial and manufacturing classes increases," wrote Jeremiah Mason, whom Daniel Webster considered the best lawyer in the country, "in the same degree ought their political power to increase. . . . I know this

[8] *Journal of Debates and Proceedings in the Convention of Delegates, Chosen to Revise the Constitution of Massachusetts*, 309, 312; *Proceedings and Debates of the Virginia State Convention*, 156.

[9] N. H. Carter and associates, *Reports of the Proceedings and Debates of the Convention of 1821, assembled for the Purpose of amending the Constitution of the State of New-York*, 221; Samuel S. Wilde in the Massachusetts Convention, *Journal*, 272.

aristocracy of wealth is apt to be evil spoken of. But in a country where wealth greatly abounds, I doubt whether any other foundation for a stable free government can be found." [10]

Having justified their political supremacy by expounding the pre-rogatives of concentrated wealth, they justified concentrated wealth by expounding the virtues of inequality. "The diversity of poverty and riches," in the words of Peter Oxenbridge Thacher, a Boston judge and classical conservative, "is the order of Providence. . . . Why are not all the flowers of the field equally beautiful and fragrant? Why are not all the fruits of the earth equally rich and wholesome? And why," he continued, warming to the subject, "towers the oak in grandeur to heaven, while the shrub at its base is trodden under feet? Will vain regrets, and still vainer discontent change the course of nature?" [11]

The gradation of values was clear, with honor reserved for the towering oak and vice and indolence assigned to the shrub. "The lowest orders of society ordinarily mean the poorest — and the highest, the richest," was the comfortable judgment of the *American Quarterly Review*. "Sensual excess, want of intelligence, and moral debasement, distinguished the former — knowledge, intellectual superiority, and refined, social, and domestic affections, the latter." Property, in Feder-alist reflexes, became almost identified with character; and remarks like Nicholas Biddle's petulant complaint about "men with no prop-erty to assess and no character to lose" rolled easily off the tongue. [12]

But all the logic of neo-Federalism was in vain. Inexorably, the vote passed on to the propertyless classes. And this divorce of political power from property left Federalist logic itself in a perilous position. For if, as Webster had observed, universal manhood suffrage "could not long exist in a community where there was great inequality of

[10] Mason to George Ticknor, April 3, 1836, G. S. Hillard, *Memoir and Corre-spondence of Jeremiah Mason*, 359–360. Mason was the man whose conduct as president of the Portsmouth Branch of the United States Bank enraged the New Hampshire Democrats and contributed to Jackson's campaign against the Bank. However partisan Mason may have been, he was at least acting in accordance with a considered belief.

James Fenimore Cooper later ridiculed this general Federalist theory rather ex-tensively in *The Monikins* under the name of the "social stake system." See *The Monikins*, 74 and *passim*.

[11] P. O. Thacher, *A Charge to the Grand Jury of the County of Suffolk* (1834), 17.

[12] "Results of Machinery," *American Quarterly Review*, XII, 307 (December, 1832); Biddle at the Tide Water Canal celebration, *Niles' Register*, August 29, 1840. The opinions of the *American Quarterly* were fortified by cash payments from the United States Bank. It was detested by the Democrats. On the appearance of one number, William Leggett observed, "It fully sustains the long established character of the work for ignorance, prejudice and malignity." *New York Evening Post*, December 16, 1834

property," and if the states were moving constitutionally toward manhood suffrage, did it not become the obligation of faithful Websterians to strive to reduce economic inequality? [13]

4

The Federalist logic of power thus became a casualty of history, for the neo-Federalists would move neither to redistribute their property nor to reopen the question of manhood suffrage. But they were not at all deflected from their basic purposes; and the American System, already fairly well emancipated by Clay from Hamiltonian premises, was admirably designed to continue the struggle toward Hamiltonian objectives. The aristocracy of property, moreover, attracting whatever in society bestowed prestige, could count on the authority of law and religion to buttress its influence.

At first, the Federalists had drastically underrated the power of the courts. In complete possession of the executive, they had no need of seeking power elsewhere. Even Hamilton dismissed the judiciary as "beyond comparison the weakest of the three departments." Jefferson's victory in 1800 changed the situation. Plunged in despondency, Hamilton now despaired of the Constitution and pronounced it a "frail and worthless fabric." But a more resourceful statesman appeared to take up the standard of conservatism. If the Federalists were expelled from the executive and legislative branches, at least they still had the judiciary, and John Marshall proposed to make it an impregnable fortress. The Federalist party, in Van Buren's phrase, was "conducted to the judicial department of the Government, as to an ark of future safety which the Constitution placed beyond the reach of public opinion." [14]

Marshall proceeded brilliantly to fortify the new battle line. During the next quarter of a century, in spite of the hatred of Jefferson, the indignation of the Virginia school, the occasional raids of men like Richard M. Johnson and Martin Van Buren in the Senate, he invincibly expanded the power of the Supreme Court and indirectly the prestige of the whole judiciary. The courts promised to become a perpetual check on popular government, so long as the judges themselves were safe from the penalties of popular disapproval. A conflict thus arose in the state conventions over what was variously called the "inde-

[13] Webster's remark was made in the Massachusetts convention, *Journal*, 312.

[14] Federalist No. 78, *The Federalist*, E. M. Earle, ed., 504; Hamilton to Gouverneur Morris, February 27, 1802, Hamilton, *Works*, VIII, 591; Martin Van Buren, *Inquiry into Origin and Course of Political Parties in the United States*, 278; see also 274–280, 302.

pendence" or "irresponsibility" of the judiciary. As Justice Story frankly admitted in the Massachusetts convention, "It is the minority who are interested in the independence of the judges." [15] Backed by British traditions of a free judiciary, the Federalists succeeded pretty well in entrenching themselves in the courts.

In the same spirit they worked to preserve the English common law in all its sanctity and mystery. To their opponents, the common law seemed an infinite morass of judicial precedent which would always result practically in "judge-made" law; and it is true that in the hands of judges like Peter Oxenbridge Thacher the common law became a bottomless reservoir of reasons why no one should do anything. The democratic movement to revise and codify the laws thus produced another heated battle line.

Federalism similarly mobilized religion to support its views of society. At the very start, many conservatives, with the discreet skepticism of eighteenth-century gentlemen, considered religion indispensable to restrain the brute appetites of the lower orders but hardly necessary for the upper classes. As the polite doubts of the eighteenth century passed away, and particularly as the clergy loudly declared Jefferson's deism to be a threat, not only to themselves, but to the foundations of social order, conservatism grew more ardent in its faith. In 1802 Hamilton, seeking desperately to rejuvenate the Federalist party, suggested the formation of a Christian Constitutional Society with the twofold purpose of promoting Christianity and the Constitution. [16]

Though Hamilton's particular scheme never came to anything, the alliance he had in mind was rapidly consummated. Religion, in exchange for protection against Jeffersonian anticlericalism, would hedge the aristocracy of wealth with divinity. To the clergy were assigned the essential functions of reconciling the lower classes to inequality and binding them to absolute obedience to the laws. "Christian morality and piety, in connexion with the intelligence of the common people," declared Calvin Colton, Episcopalian preacher, later Whig pamphleteer, great friend and official biographer of Henry Clay, "are the last hope of the American Republic, and the only adequate means of bridling and holding in salutary check that rampant freedom, which is so characteristic of the American people." [17]

Some clergymen went very far indeed in certifying to the divine origin of Federalism. As Jonathan M. Wainwright, not yet Episcopalian bishop of New York, assured the Massachusetts legislature in

[15] *Journal*, 525.
[16] Hamilton to J. A. Bayard, April, 1802, Hamilton, *Works*, VIII, 598.
[17] Calvin Colton, *A Voice from America to England*, 60.

1835, religion "recognizes and sanctions the principle of inequality in the distribution of wealth amongst men . . . to be acquiesced in as a permanent condition of society." [18] Opponents of Federalism were denounced from the pulpit as enemies of the cosmic scheme. "That there should be an inequality in the conditions of men, as there is in all the other works of providence, is clearly a wise and benevolent ordinance of heaven," said the Reverend Hubbard Winslow, who went on to point out ominously that "it was the levelling disposition, that cast down the shining angels from their starry heights"; and Winslow's friend and idol Daniel Webster did his best to read the minister's interpretation of divine intention into the laws of the land.[19]

The support of law and religion strengthened Federalism incalculably by identifying the deepest desires of man — toward social stability and religious salvation — with a particular political order. It guaranteed Federalism, moreover, the loyalty of the only groups in the population with an authority not dependent on property. It meant that whatever there was of an aristocracy of status would surely be on the side of the aristocracy of wealth. The combination of judges, clergymen and men of property seemed invincible.[20]

Only the defection of the Southern planters and the rise of new applicants for the aristocracy of status — generals, editors and literary men — whose claims were resisted by the old Federalism, could provide the great mass with leadership in their struggle for political power.

[18] J. M. Wainwright, *Inequality of Individual Wealth the Ordinance of Providence, and Essential to Civilization*, 6, 7. Four years before, Wainwright had told Tocqueville that he never interfered with politics, even refusing to vote at elections. G. W. Pierson, *Tocqueville and Beaumont in America*, 138.

[19] Hubbard Winslow, *An Oration delivered . . . July 4, 1838*, 16–17. In face of this type of exegesis, it is easy to understand the bewilderment of Ichabod Emmons of Hinsdale, a simple-minded Whig member of the Massachusetts House of Representatives, who declared frantically, "I'm in favor of all Corporations, and those who would oppose them would also oppose the Christian Religion." *Boston Post*, January 26, 1836.

[20] Cf. Richard Hildreth's acute account of the "natural aristocracy" of the United States as of 1792. "The body of lawyers . . . a sort of separate and superior order in the state," "the clergy and the leading members of the great religious sects," "the merchants and capitalists," "the large landed proprietors of the Middle States and the slave-holding planters of the South" — "The classes above enumerated might be considered as constituting the natural aristocracy of the Union." *History of the United States*, IV, 346–347. On the law as aristocracy, see A. de Tocqueville, *Democracy in America*, I, 297–306. Cf. also Martin Van Buren's heartfelt remark: "There are two classes in every community, whose interference in politics is always and very naturally distasteful to sincere republicans, and those are judges and clergymen." *Political Parties*, 365.

III KEEPERS OF THE
JEFFERSONIAN CONSCIENCE

THE ECONOMIC changes of the early years of the nineteenth century, blasting the dream of an agricultural Utopia, raised up problems for government hardly contemplated by the Arcadian philosophy of Virginia. Jefferson himself, in whom keen sensitivity to national needs always overcame loyalty to abstractions, steadily revised his views on industrialism during his presidency. "As yet our manufacturers are as much at their ease, as independent and moral as our agricultural inhabitants," he exclaimed in 1805, apparently with surprise. Four years later he conceded that an equilibrium of agriculture, manufacturing and commerce had become essential to American independence. In 1813 he recanted explicitly: events "have settled my doubts." In 1816, at the first serious attempt to enact Hamilton's Report on Manufactures, Jefferson remarked contritely, "Experience has taught me that manufactures are now as necessary to our independence as to our comfort." Eight years of responsibility had made certain the triumph of the statesman over the philosopher.[1]

1

If Jefferson's presidency was a set of compromises with necessity, those of his immediate successors took on the aspect almost of surrender. The War of 1812 clearly exposed the inadequacy of simple Jeffersonian solutions for complex questions either of finance or of administration. The postwar economic chaos made the government especially vulnerable to the cogent and specific demands of the business community; and Madison and Monroe, the Virginia Presidents who occupied the White House from 1809 to 1825, lacking either the will or the capacity to work out a program in terms of their own social philosophy, were forced to beat a faltering but unmistakable retreat from the original Jeffersonian positions.

[1] Jefferson to J. Lithgow (or Lithson), January 4, 1805, *Writings* (Memorial Edition), XI, 55; Jefferson to John Jay, April 7, 1809, *ibid.*, XII, 271; Jefferson to John Melish, January 13, 1813, *Writings*, P. L. Ford, ed., IX, 373; Jefferson to Benjamin Austin, January 9, 1816, *ibid.*, X, 10.

The approval of the Second Bank of the United States in 1816 by the man who twenty-five years before had been the ablest opponent of the First Bank was an appropriate commentary on the breakdown of the Jeffersonian idyl. Madison went on to endorse the tariff of 1816; and then, while refusing to concede the constitutionality of internal improvements, he urged their importance, and, like Jefferson himself, advised amending the Constitution in order to sanctify them. Monroe yielded still more ground. Before his second term was over, he signed a bill for internal improvements whose constitutional latitudinarianism appalled many Jeffersonians, and in 1824 he allowed the tariff duties to be increased once again. The last days of the Virginia dynasty turned into a confession of the impotence of Virginia doctrines.

The Federalist party itself had been largely destroyed by its resistance to the War of 1812. With Madison adopting so much of its program, revival was superfluous. Certain local vestiges of the Federalist organization were without much significance in national politics. By 1820, the bitter enmities of 1800 had dissolved into the benign atmosphere of the Era of Good Feelings. The single electoral vote dissenting to Monroe's re-election was occasioned by no more urgent a motive than personal dislike.

Four years later, in 1824, the election was indeed a contest, but it dealt much more in personalities than in issues. Henry Clay was the most outspoken champion of the American System, while John Quincy Adams was suspected of being a Federalist in sheep's clothing; William H. Crawford stood in the strict Jeffersonian school, and Andrew Jackson occupied a vague and intermediate position. But all the candidates were nominally Jeffersonian Republicans, and all were presumed pretty much to accept the drift of the decade preceding.

When no one obtained a majority of electoral votes, the choice fell to the House of Representatives. There, a union of Adams and Clay men elected Adams, and soon after Clay became Secretary of State. The avowed defenders of the American System were now in frank control of the government. The rout of the Jeffersonians was complete.

2

Jefferson's compromises were necessary, but the surrender of Madison and Monroe was not. The drive to the West had helped preserve the power of agriculture in the nation. These years saw the purchase of Louisiana and the acquisition of Florida, while new states carved from the beckoning frontier steadily enlarged the Union. By 1830 the original thirteen had grown to twenty-four. Farming remained the chief occupation of the people and the principal source of the national income.

Yet politically agriculture lacked the power its economic importance merited. The business community enjoyed the vital advantage of compactness and unity. Only in the planting South did agriculture possess concentrated holdings, alert leadership and a compulsion to run the state. To the Southern planters thus fell the main responsibility of opposing the Hamiltonian tendencies in the government.

In Virginia especially, the course of appeasement was watched with deepening gloom. Jefferson's genial remark at his inaugural — "We are all Republicans, we are all Federalists" [2] — had been shocking enough. His administration swiftly convinced some of his radical followers that he was taking this declaration altogether too seriously. Misgivings boiled up toward revolt when he named James Madison for the succession. Madison had a long record of Republicanism. Yet at one time he had collaborated sufficiently well with Alexander Hamilton to make it still doubtful which of them wrote certain of the *Federalist* papers, and his personal caution was rightly supposed to equip him badly to resist the pressure behind Federalism. For their own candidate in 1808, the "Tertium Quids," as the doctrinaires called themselves, settled rather desperately on James Monroe, who had been a fiery and radical Republican in the seventeen-nineties. But Monroe eventually calculated that his best chance for the White House lay in sticking with the party, and the schismatic movement collapsed.

The Quids now awaited further betrayal. The addition of John Quincy Adams to the Republican party failed to increase their confidence in Madison. "That both the Adams' are monarchists," observed John Taylor of Caroline, "I never doubted. Whether monarchists, like pagans, can be converted by benefices, is a problem the solution of which I always feared Mr. Madison would attempt." The War of 1812 made them further uneasy, and the events of 1816 vindicated their pessimism. Jefferson himself seemed almost an apostate. In the sneer of John Randolph of Roanoke, the father of the faith had declined into "that prince of projectors, St. Thomas of Cant*ing*bury." [3]

Randolph led the bitter fight in Congress against the Madisonian surrender. Always the leader of the Quids in debate and political manipulation, he would too often weaken his case by the indiscriminate ferocity of his attack. But his conviction of the gravity of the cause raised him to new heights in 1816. Executing raids on the Madison

[2] J. D. Richardson, comp., *Messages and Papers of the Presidents*, I, 322.
[3] Taylor to Monroe, November 8, 1809, "Letters of John Taylor," *John P. Branch Historical Papers*, II, 302; Garland, *Randolph*, II, 346.

position with a withering cruelty of invective and stunning brilliance of language, this remarkable man, with his lanky, disordered figure and arrogant bearing, made himself feared and hated by the administration. Sometimes his shrill, piercing voice drove tormented opponents to unwise reflections on his virility, but not often. Randolph's retort, as reproduced by folklore, was concise and crushing: "You pride yourself upon an animal faculty, in respect to which the negro is your equal and the jackass infinitely your superior."

But all his wit and savagery were vain. "Until the present session," he cried in despair after weeks of debate, "I had not a conception of the extent of the change wrought in the sentiments of the people of this country by the war." The doctrines of Republicanism seemed to have lost their power, and the unreconstructed Jeffersonians stood helpless in negligible minority.[4]

3

While Randolph waged his desperate war in Congress, John Taylor of Caroline, the best farmer in lower Virginia, was mulling and ruminating over the broad implications of the economic changes.[5] Most of his years had been passed, not in public life, but on this plantation on the shady Rappahannock. Taylor's love for the countryside, his passion for the improvement of agricultural methods, his deep belief in rural virtue, had been poured lavishly into his *Arator*, which became the bible of farming Virginia.

Yet, like a true Jeffersonian, he fully acknowledged the claims of public service. From time to time he would leave his plow, like Cincinnatus, and go up to Richmond or Washington to serve his people and his principles. His pamphlet of 1794, *Definition of Parties, or the Political Effects of the Paper System Considered*, a penetrating attack on the measures of Hamilton, did much to lay down the main lines of Jeffersonian polemics. In 1798 he presented the famous Virginia Resolutions, conceived by Jefferson, drawn up by Madison, and soon to become the Thirty-nine Articles of Republicanism. In the eighteen-twenties he served in the Senate. A venerable man, plain and solid in manner, wise and courteous in debate, simply clothed in coat, waistcoat and pantaloons of uniform "London brown," cut according to the fashion of an earlier age, he deeply impressed the young politicians of the day. "I can hardly figure to myself the ideal of a republican

[4] W. C. Bruce, *John Randolph of Roanoke*, II, 321; Garland, *Randolph*, II, 73.
[5] For new testimony on Taylor as a farmer, see Frank G. Ruffin to George Bancroft, August 12, 1841, Bancroft Papers.

statesman," declared Thomas Hart Benton, "more perfect and complete than he was in reality." [6]

As Taylor worked his fields, talked to friends stopping a night at Caroline and corresponded with acquaintances, he turned over unceasingly in his mind the doctrines of Virginia, and probed anxiously into the forces which threatened them. He early discerned the tendencies of Jefferson's presidency. "Federalism," he wrote, ". . . has gained a new footing, by being taken into partnership with republicanism." His pen scratched on, "in a wild, careless, and desultory way," and the pages, written in fits and starts, blotted and interlined, finally grew into a book.[7]

In 1814, the great work was finally published at Fredericksburg, a volume of seven hundred pages entitled *An Inquiry into the Principles and Policy of the Government of the United States*. It was meandering and unsystematic in form, strolling up to a subject, regarding it from one side, glancing at it from behind, and sometime later looking at it from a hilltop or using it as a familiar landmark. "For heaven's sake," exclaimed the impatient Randolph, "get some worthy person . . . to do the second edition into *English*. . . . it is a monument of the force and weakness of the human mind; forcible, concise, perspicuous, feeble, tedious, obscure, unintelligible." [8]

Yet Randolph was unjust to the essential quality of the work. Its style was one of unusual distinction, a kind rare in America and ignored by literary historians, but extraordinary in its ease and pliancy, its richness of texture and its mastery of elaborate and illuminating metaphor. It was seventeenth-century in character, a "quaint Sir Edward Coke style," in Benton's phrase, filled with involutions and conceits, with an almost "metaphysical" body and force in its diction.[9] The defects were obvious: garrulity, repetitiousness, frequent obscurity. But the complexity, wit and penetration did full justice to the remorseless subtlety of the analysis.

The *Inquiry* explored with great comprehensiveness the basic meanings of Jefferson's agricultural paradise. Like Jefferson, Taylor was possessed by a vision of free society; and like Jefferson, he was profoundly aware of the material conditions of freedom. In his own emphatic words, "Wealth, like suffrage, must be considerably distributed,

[6] T. H. Benton, *Thirty Years' View*, I, 45.

[7] Taylor to Monroe, October 26, 1810, "Letters of John Taylor," *Branch Historical Papers*, II, 310; Taylor to Aaron Burr, March 25, 1803, M. L. Davis, *Memoirs of Aaron Burr*, II, 236; Taylor to Monroe, November 8, 1809, "Letters of John Taylor," *Branch Historical Papers*, II, 301.

[8] Randolph to J. M. Garnett, February 14, 1814, Bruce, *Randolph*, II, 622.

[9] Benton, *Thirty Years' View*, I, 46.

to sustain a democratick republic; and hence, whatever draws a considerable proportion of either into a few hands, will destroy it. As power follows wealth, the majority must have wealth or lose power." [10]

In the continuing supremacy of agriculture — "the guardian of liberty as well as the mother of wealth" — he saw the best promise for a wide distribution of property. Agriculture dealt in what he called "natural" or "substantial" property, that is, property directly gained in productive labor. It was his central thesis that the preservation of a free democracy depended on the preservation of the order of "natural" private property, where each man was secure in the fruits of his own labor, against depredations by force or by fraud. [11]

Taylor named two threats to the natural economic order, "two modes of invading private property; the first, by which the poor plunder the rich, . . . sudden and violent; the second, by which the rich plunder the poor, slow and legal." The first he dismissed as irrelevant to the American circumstance. Here the poor could not become dangerous until the concentration of wealth greatly increased their number. The real peril, he believed, lay in the second mode: plunder from above, orderly and legalized. The succession of privileged orders through history — the priesthood, the nobility, now the banking system — showed how every age had known its own form of institutionalized robbery by a minority operating through the state. [12]

Priesthood and nobility had been overthrown in America; but no one, he warned, should think that America had thereby won immunity from tyranny. The invention of a second form of property, which he called "artificial" or "fictitious," now enabled the aristocracy to prey systematically upon the hardworking farmer and mechanic. The original error, of course, had been the Hamiltonian policy. A financial program modeled on the caste system of Britain seemed to Taylor thoroughly vicious in the New World. "In my eyes," he wrote in a characteristic passage, "this beauty of theirs, appears to be a painted courtezan, who corrupts and plunders her admirers; and though we cannot account for different tastes, that especially called love, it seems impossible to discern even a probability that the United States will gain an addition of present or future happiness, by divorcing the healthy and chaste country girl whom they first espoused . . . to marry a second-hand town lady, so diseased and ulcerated, that the English people are heartily willing to part with her." [13]

[10] Taylor, *Inquiry*, 274–275.
[11] Taylor, *Arator*, fifth edition, vi.
[12] Taylor, *Inquiry*, 280.
[13] Taylor, *Tyranny Unmasked*, 163–164.

He examined in sardonic detail the workings of the funding system, of paper-money banking and of the protective tariff, showing how they all benefited the financial aristocracy at the expense of the honest and virtuous agriculturist. "The property-transferring policy," he declared, "invariably impoverishes all labouring and productive classes." These Federalist measures, insuring the payment of a steady indemnity by "natural" property to "artificial" property, would conclude in the establishment of despotism. "Taxation, direct or indirect, produced by a paper system in any form, will rob a nation of property, without giving it liberty; and by creating and enriching a separate interest, will rob it of its liberty, without giving it property." [14]

The aristocracy, moreover, as Taylor pointed out in some of his most striking passages, fortified itself by an exploitation of psychological resources as effective as its exploitation of wealth. "The hooks of fraud and tyranny," he observed, "are universally baited with melodious words. . . . There is edification and safety in challenging political words and phrases as traitors, and trying them rigorously by principles, before we allow them the smallest degree of confidence. As the servants of principles, they gain admission into the family, and thus acquire the best opportunities of assassinating their masters." Like the priesthood and the nobility, the financial aristocracy had its psychological allies, "using force, faith and credit, as the two others did religion and feudality." [15]

He attacked in particular the attempt to distract the people from the real danger by starting a hullabaloo over freedom of religion and the prohibition of a titled nobility. A serpent "is silently and insidiously entwining liberty; and to divert our attention from the operation we are terrified by the dead skeletons of ancient aristocratical mamoths." Or, as he compressed it into one of his brilliant images, "We know death very well, when killing with one sythe, but mistake him for a deity, because he is killing with four." [16]

But the aristocracy's greatest source of strength lay in its success in cloaking "fictitious" property — bank paper and stocks — with the prestige of honest private property. By pretending to protect land and labor from redistribution from below, the aristocracy was enabled to maintain its own institutions of redistribution from above. Taylor desperately fought this unnatural alliance. "If the fruit of labour is private property, can stealing this fruit from labour, also make private property? By calling the artillery property, which is playing on prop-

---

[14] Taylor, *Tyranny Unmasked*, 348; *Inquiry*, 286.
[15] Taylor, *Inquiry*, 558–559, 275.
[16] Taylor, *Inquiry*, 276; *Arator*, 36.

erty, the battery is masked. Tythes and stocks, invented to take away private property, are as correctly called private property, as a guillotine could be called a head." [17]

What was to be done? Taylor's writing had an undercurrent of pessimism, occasionally almost an elegiac note, as if he were lamenting a world mortally wounded by change. The *Inquiry* was, in a sense, an elaborate obituary on the lost paradise. He had begun to feel that even his own party in power would inevitably fall from true principles. "The moment you are elected," he told Monroe, "though by my casting vote, carried an hundred miles in a snow storm, my confidence in you would be most confoundedly deminished, and I would instantly join again the republican minority."

Could any party resist the temptations of power? "Majority republicanism," he said, "is inevitably, widely (but not thoroughly) corrupted with ministerial republicanism, and it is also tinctured with the folly of certain sympathies, towards strong parties, popularity, and noise. Now the business and view of a true minority man is to unveil ministerial republicanism, when it is riding with its eyes shut directly from its own object, on one of these jack asses." A pure Jeffersonian thus was doomed to perpetual dissent. This announcement of the futility of Jeffersonianism by its keenest analyst showed how deeply the conviction of failure had entered the interstices of thought in Virginia.[18]

Taylor continued to issue his warnings, but events passed on, hardly pausing to refute him. He thought the indifference of the people responsible for their bondage. "We farmers and mechanics have been political slaves in all countries," he declared bitterly, "because we are political fools." [19] In 1820, he published perhaps his most influential book, *Construction Construed, and Constitutions Vindicated*, an attack on the Marshallian exegesis of the Constitution. In 1822 came *Tyranny Unmasked*, a mordant and inclusive review of almost every argument then advanced for the protective tariff. A year later he sent forth *New Views of the Constitution*, another attempt to expose the heresies of Marshall.

He wrote endlessly, unraveling his complicated thought, strangling Federalism in the coils of his rhetoric; but the American System kept rising toward dominance. Taylor's own program? "Return to frugality; restore a free trade; abolish exclusive privileges; retract unjust

---

[17] Taylor, *Inquiry*, 280.
[18] Taylor to Monroe, January 31, 1811, "Letters of John Taylor," *Branch Historical Papers*, II, 316, 317.
[19] Taylor, *Arator*, 35.

pensions; surrender legislative patronage; surrender, also, legislative judicial power; and vindicate the inviolability of property, even against legislatures, except for genuine national welfare." Also deflate the Supreme Court; restrain manufacturing; abolish paper money; revive the militia; and produce a government which would be "fair, free, mild, and cheap." In a sentence, decree Utopia. In a word, despair.[20]

4

Gloom settled deep on the Jeffersonians in the twenties. Jefferson himself, when he greeted amiably the rise of manufacturing in 1816, had forgotten those evils which in 1782 he had warned manufacturing would bring. Now, as some of his first predictions began to come true, he reverted to his original pessimism. (Long before, John Taylor had prophesied that Jefferson would resume his old opinions, "none of which I have yet seen satisfactorily exploded even by himself.") The growing power of his ancient enemy John Marshall increased his despondency. Federalism, as he told Albert Gallatin in 1823, has "changed its name and hidden itself among us"; it was "as strong as it ever has been since 1800. . . . The judges, as before, are at their head and are their entering wedge." In 1821 he welcomed *Construction Construed* with enthusiasm, but when *New View of the Constitution* appeared three years later, he could only say sadly, "I fear it is the voice of one crying in the wilderness." In some moods, his agricultural paradise seemed but "the dreams of an old man," the American opportunity had perhaps "passed away without return." He lived on at quiet Monticello, watching sorrowfully the strides of aristocracy, mourning the collapse of his hopes.[21]

The eighteen-twenties found those others who had so strongly shared these hopes — Randolph, Taylor, Nathaniel Macon of North Carolina — active in Washington. Randolph still performed in the House of Representatives; but he was incapacitated for leadership by his ever more frequent outbursts into dazzling, pathetic and uncontrollable tirades. He lived now in constant dread of insanity. John Taylor returned briefly from Caroline and the shady Rappahannock to the strife of the Senate in 1823. For a session the younger men saw him, often with Macon, the two talking earnestly, "looking like two

[20] Taylor, *Tyranny Unmasked*, 100, 346.
[21] Taylor to Monroe, November 8, 1809, "Letters of John Taylor," *Branch Historical Papers*, II, 303; Jefferson to Gallatin, August 2, 1823, Albert Gallatin. *Writings*, Henry Adams, ed., II, 273; Jefferson to Robert J. Garnett, February 14, 1824, *Writings*, P. L. Ford, ed., X, 294; Jefferson to W. H. Crawford, June 20, 1816, *ibid.*, X, 36.

on the frontier ran at first into Jeffersonian prejudices against moneyed monopolies. But the scarcity of money during the War of 1812, and the inflationary policies of the Second United States Bank in the first few years after 1816, caused banks to spread fairly indiscriminately through Kentucky, Tennessee and other Western states. Then, with the depression of 1819, the big Bank, reversing its policy, began a peremptory contraction. Specie flowed out of the West, leaving in its wake a trail of bankruptcies and a large debtor population unable to meet obligations.

Under strong popular pressure many of the states passed "relief" legislation, in the form of stop laws, stays of execution, replevin acts and the establishment of state banks licensed to issue millions in paper. "Relief," of course, simply produced further inflation, bringing back those happy times when "creditors were seen running away from their debtors, and debtors pursuing them in triumph, and paying them without mercy." [1] In 1823 the Kentucky Court of Appeals, expressing the heartfelt convictions of the creditor class, declared the relief system unconstitutional.

This decision was based on doctrines set forth by Chief Justice Marshall in *Sturges v. Crowninshield* (1819): that bankruptcy laws were invalid when they impaired the obligation of contracts, and that the legal remedies laid down for the collection of debts formed part of the total contract and were therefore safe from legislative control. [2]

Nothing daunted by the courts, or even by the opposition of Henry Clay and most of upper-class Kentucky, the Relief party, after winning a substantial victory at the polls in 1824, tried to remove the state court and, this failing, set up a court of its own. The new Chief Justice was an eloquent lawyer named William T. Barry; the Clerk

[1] Dr. Witherspoon quoted by W. M. Gouge, *A Short History of Paper Money and Banking in the United States,* part ii, 234.

[2] The array of opinions in the similar case of *Ogden v. Saunders* (1827) showed that the Court was much more divided over these questions than the decision in *Sturges v. Crowninshield* had suggested. A subsidiary problem had been whether the general principle applied to all debts, or just to those contracted before the passage of the law, which would make relief legislation perfectly valid for debts contracted *after* its enactment. Marshall believed that it applied to all debts, but the Court rebelled in *Ogden v. Saunders* and ruled that it applied only to debts contracted before enactment. See the stimulating discussion in Louis Boudin, *Government by Judiciary,* chs. xii, xiv; also A. M. Stickles, *The Critical Court Struggle in Kentucky, 1819–1829.*

Sturges v. Crowninshield had been followed by another decision supposedly hostile to the interests of Kentuckians in the case of *Green v. Biddle* (1823). These judgments led to attacks on the Court in the Senate by Colonel Richard M. Johnson of Kentucky, hero of the War of 1812, champion of the abolition of imprisonment for debt, and ally of the debtor party in the state.

was a fiery newspaperman named Francis Preston Blair; the leading pamphleteer, as well as ghostwriter for the relief Governor, was an earnest Yankee named Amos Kendall; we have not heard the last of these names.

The Old Court and New Court parties contended bitterly for jurisdiction, to the accompaniment of newspaper invective, brawls and general confusion. As times improved and economic urgency slackened, the issue of the battle changed from the expediency of the relief system to its constitutionality; and, in the end, with prosperity steadily diminishing their real grievances, the New Court party collapsed. By 1827 the battle was over. Yet the resentments excited in the conflict still lived, and awaited only new opportunities for expression. The struggle for power was but in abeyance.

2

The impact of the new industrialism in the Northern and Middle states, and particularly of the capitalist organization of what had been journeyman industries, produced another contagion of discontent. Some workingmen were disquieted by the gradual loss of ownership over their means of production, others by their separation from direct contact with the market, others by the disappearance of any feeling of social or economic equality with the moneyed groups, still others simply by the physiological strain of adjusting to new habits of work and discipline. With a class neither so relatively numerous as the Western debtors nor so intellectually confident as the Southern planters, discontent caused no comparable outbursts, leading rather to a decade of stirrings and mutterings among the laboring men.

Shut off from the rest of society, they began to develop a consciousness of class, which helped them recover a sense of human function in a social order that baffled them by its growing impersonality. They held conventions, published addresses, founded labor newspapers and trade-unions. Their main effort was to vindicate their social status, to regain a feeling of self-respect and security. Thus their demands centered around education, abolition of imprisonment for debt, reform of the militia system — measures intended to check the tendencies which they felt were turning the working classes into the outcasts of the land.

The rising prices of 1824 and 1825 encouraged the workers to undertake fairly aggressive organizing activity, and in 1828 the Mechanics' Union of Trade Associations in Philadelphia sponsored the first workingmen's party. There were several other such parties before the decade was over, some mainly rural in character, some urban.[3]

National allegiances were vague. When John Quincy Adams was elected President by the House of Representatives, Washington learned with relief that a heavy snow had dispersed the crowds of "the lower citizens" who had prepared an effigy to burn and might have committed "some foolish violence."[4] But such outbreaks had little significance. National political organizations, such as they were, made only sporadic appeals to the laboring classes. For most of these years, the cultivation of the awakening class consciousness was left to intellectuals, like Robert Dale Owen, George H. Evans and Frances Wright in New York.

The absence of direction was less important than the presence of discontent. The working classes in the North were rendered explosive by a variety of broad frustrations and particular grievances, all of which, more or less, stemmed from the American System and the social philosophy which lay behind it. The depression of 1828–1829, and the grim winter it brought to the larger cities, fanned this discontent into an imperative demand for action.

3

The Southern planters, as the ruling class in their own section, were burdened with responsibilities which prevented them from meddling with government as casually as the poor debtors of Kentucky, or from burning Presidents in effigy like the workingmen of Washington. Yet, they were no less anxious; and their gestures of defiance, while chiefly on an intellectual plane, would in the end threaten the Union more profoundly than all the noise and violence in the North.

Declining profits in cotton were causing the South to think a second time about the American System and the loose interpretation of the Constitution which made it possible. Virginia was working out the polemics of strict construction more elaborately and insistently than ever before; Randolph and Taylor raised the pitch of argument to a new intensity; and red ink in plantation ledgers verified all charges against the North. Gradually the South bent back from its nationalism of the War of 1812.

John C. Calhoun traced the full circle of change. An ardent advocate of the Bank, tariff and internal improvements in 1816, he became

---

[3] Commons and associates, *History of Labour*, I, 108–231.
[4] Margaret B. Smith, *The First Forty Years of Washington Society*, 186.

the strictest of strict constructionists by 1828. In 1823 he had visited the venerable Taylor at Caroline.[5] No one knows what took place, but there should have been a laying on of hands. After Taylor's death Calhoun, temporarily removed from active politics by the vice-presidency, quietly began to formulate his great, comprehensive and interminable rationale of State rights. With the adoption of the "Tariff of Abominations" in 1828, he felt driven to explore to the uttermost the development of guarantees which would set effective bounds on constitutional interpretation.

"You may cover whole skins of parchment with limitations," John Randolph had cried, "but power alone can limit power." [6] Calhoun, whose philosophy systematized the penetrating intuitions of Randolph, saw that the states must recapture their sovereignty in order to protect themselves against the federal government, and his solution was the doctrine of nullification. A single state, Calhoun argued in his South Carolina Exposition of 1828, might suspend a federal law which it regarded as unconstitutional (that is to say, as injurious to its own interests), until three quarters of the states had justified the law through the amending power.

This doctrine signaled a new stage in the slavery controversy, with leadership passing from the moderation of Virginia to the extremism of South Carolina. It gave ominous expression in another area of the growing sense of cramp the American System inflicted on the nation.

4

South Carolina's peculiar situation regarding the tariff, and the peculiar brooding cast of Calhoun's mind with its intense and abstract logical force, account for the cutting edge which South Carolina gave to the doctrine of State rights. Yet, all the groups which shared misgivings over the American System recognized the protective value of strict construction, and for most of them Jeffersonianism constituted the only available tradition of democracy and equality. The South drew particularly on the State-rights strain in the Jeffersonian tradition, the North and West particularly on the equalitarian strain; but the two were then inextricable, and the dissatisfied classes everywhere thus found themselves gathering behind the doctrines sustained so long by the lonely devotion of the Macons and Taylors. In 1824

[5] Taylor to Monroe, April 29, 1823, "Letters of John Taylor," *Branch Historical Papers*, II, 352.
[6] Bruce, *Randolph*, II, 211.

the leaders of this growing opposition tended to support William H. Crawford of Georgia, the candidate most clearly committed against the American System.

The victory of John Quincy Adams gave the business community its last chance. If his administration could solve the urgent problems of discontent, the leadership of the commercial classes would be unchallenged, and the American System, with Bank, tariff and internal improvements, remain secure.

The new President had been instructed in the nature of the problem. On a warm day in May, 1820, Adams, then Secretary of State under Monroe, took a long ride through the green sweep of the countryside around Washington with Calhoun, Secretary of War and still in his nationalist period. Calhoun spoke gloomily of the depression of 1819. It had, he said, produced "a general mass of disaffection to the Government, not concentrated in any particular direction, but ready to seize upon any event and looking out anywhere for a leader." The excitement over the Missouri question and over the tariff seemed to him but the expression of this deeper anxiety. "It was a vague but wide-spread discontent," he repeated, "caused by the disordered circumstances of individuals, but resulting in a general impression that there was something radically wrong in the administration of the Government."

Adams pondered Calhoun's remarks. The cause of the economic collapse was clear enough — the overexpansion of the paper-money system — but the remedy? "Not discernible," he mused sadly. ". . . Government can do nothing, at least nothing by any measure yet proposed, but transfer discontents, and propitiate one class of people by disgusting another." [7] But if discontent grew intense and fiery, might it not be necessary to "propitiate" the dissatisfied classes, even at the cost of "disgusting" the class in possession?

If Adams's diary was not clear on this point, his administration settled any doubts. When the classes to be propitiated were outside the experience of an Adams, and the class to be disgusted was his own, he could not bring himself to see any advantage in changing the original policy. For all his real abilities, Adams as President showed few evidences of statesmanship. His immobility in the face of crisis allowed the impression to harden through the land "that there was something radically wrong in the administration of the Government." His overthrow in 1828 resulted directly from his failure to meet the problem outlined by Calhoun. In his place, the people thrust forward the man whom they had made their favorite in 1824, and to whom

[7] Adams, *Memoirs*, V, 128–129.

the leaders of the fight against Adams turned after a paralytic stroke eliminated Crawford.

5

Who was General Andrew Jackson, the new popular favorite? To the nation he was known primarily as a military hero. In the Revolution, an English officer had slashed him with a saber for refusing to clean a pair of boots. In the War of 1812 he had shown great energy and resource in putting down some Indian uprisings, and in 1815, after the treaty of peace had been signed, he won at New Orleans the greatest American victory of the war. His nominal profession was the law, and he had served in the House of Representatives and Senate of the United States, as well as on the Tennessee Supreme Court. For the decade past, his life had been mainly that of a Tennessee gentleman, living on a fine plantation near Nashville, entertaining his friends, racing his horses and heatedly talking politics. In 1828 he was sixty-one years old.

His immense popular vote in 1824 came from his military fame and from the widespread conviction of his integrity.[8] His actual politics were somewhat vague. In 1808 he had sympathized with the schismatic movement of Randolph and Macon, but in a letter to President Monroe in 1816 he recommended a policy of reconciliation with the war Federalists (accompanied by characteristic regrets that the leaders of the Hartford Convention had escaped hanging). Seven years later in the Senate, his votes indicated an attitude of at least tolerance toward the American System. He favored what he called enigmatically a "judicious" tariff in order to end dependence on foreign nations for war materials, but at the same time he committed himself definitely against the premises of Federalism. "I am one of those who do not believe that a national debt is a national blessing," he said, "but rather a curse to a republic; inasmuch as it is calculated to raise around the administration a moneyed aristocracy dangerous to the liberties of the country." [9]

In Tennessee, he normally acted with the landholding aristocracy both against the financial aristocracy and the canebrake democracy. When the depression of 1819 gave Tennessee a relief system similar to Kentucky's, Jackson vainly opposed it, not in order to protect the banks, but on the correct conviction that inflation would not solve the

---

[8] Van Buren, *Autobiography*, 449.
[9] Jackson to L. H. Colman, April 26, 1824, James Parton, *Life of Andrew Jackson*, III, 35–36.

problems of the debtors. Yet he also supported a dubious adventure which would have despoiled many small farmers of their lands for the benefit of speculators. His experience neither in national nor in state politics afforded any clear indication of what could be expected from him once in power.[10]

Nor could much be inferred from the nature of his backing in 1824. Persons of every political faith endorsed him, including even many former Federalists who never forgave John Quincy Adams for deserting the party; and he was specifically opposed by the guardians of Virginia orthodoxy. Jefferson himself is supposed to have told Daniel Webster, "He is one of the most unfit men I know of for such a place. . . . he is a dangerous man."[11] John Taylor (who rather desperately favored Adams) and James Madison shared this mistrust. Martin Van Buren, the chief Crawford manager in 1824, brought the Virginians timidly into the Jackson fold by 1828. There they remained in constant fear of his indiscretion. According to Van Buren, Thomas Ritchie of the *Richmond Enquirer* "scarcely ever went to bed . . . without apprehension that he would wake up to hear of some *coup d'état* by the General."[12]

Jackson did indeed bear the reputation of being intemperate, arbitrary and ambitious for power. As a general he had tended to do necessary things with great expedition and to inquire afterward into their legality. His political opponents, building ardently upon incidents of his military past, managed almost to read into the records of history a legend of his rude violence and uncontrolled irascibility.

[10] For Jackson in Tennessee, Gouge, *Paper Money*, part ii, 135; St. G. L. Sioussat, "Some Phases of Tennessee Politics in the Jackson Period," *American Historical Review*, XIV, 60–61; T. P. Abernethy, "Andrew Jackson and the Rise of Southwestern Democracy," *ibid.*, XXXIII, 64–77.

[11] Webster, *Private Correspondence*, Fletcher Webster, ed., I, 371. Cf. also George Ticknor to George Bancroft, December 26, 1824, Bancroft Papers: Mr. Jefferson "expressed his unwillingness to see Genl. Jackson in the chair of state, as decidedly as any New-Englander of us all." When Monroe asked Jefferson whether it would be a good idea to appoint Jackson to the Russian mission, Jefferson burst out, "Why, good God! he would breed you a quarrel before he had been there a month!" Adams, *Memoirs*, IV, 76.

On the other hand, it is fair to state that Webster's original notes of his conversation with Jefferson, which Senator Hoar republished with the flat comment that Webster's record of the talk was "published in full from these *memoranda*," do not include any mention of Jefferson's attack on Jackson; and Webster failed to make public his account of the conversation till after Jefferson's death, when it served his political purpose. George F. Hoar, "Daniel Webster," *Scribner's Magazine*, XXVI, 215 (August, 1899). Professor Bassett points out that Webster's statement is hard to reconcile with the tone and content of Jefferson's letter to Jackson of December 18, 1823. Bassett, *Jackson*, 329.

[12] Van Buren, *Political Parties*, 322.

In the republic's early years, martial reputation had counted little for future political success. But the broadening of the suffrage, the thrill of surging nationalism and the declining glamour of the old ruling class created a favorable atmosphere for new idols, and the War of 1812 promptly produced the military hero. The old aristocracy resented such vulgar and *parvenu* prestige, and a man with Jackson's credentials was almost forced into the opposition. Moreover, while the newly enfranchised and chauvinistic masses regarded the military hero with wild enthusiasm, to the old aristocracy, raised on classical analogies, no figure could seem more dangerous to the republic. The warnings of Cicero and the example of Caesar supplied ample documentation for their worst misgivings. This background, in addition to Jackson's own record, accounted for the singular consternation which greeted his candidacy.

Yet, in actual fact, virtually all the direct testimony agrees in describing the Jackson of these later years as a man of great urbanity and distinction of manner. His presence in Washington as Senator in the winter of 1823–1824 did much to dispel the impression that he was some kind of border savage. As the elegant wife of the editor of the *National Intelligencer* put it, the General "appears to possess quite as much *suaviter in modo* as *fortiter in re*." Even Daniel Webster, later to become a sedulous promoter of the Jackson legend, commented in 1824, "General Jackson's manners are more presidential than those of any of the candidates. . . . My wife is for him decidedly." [13]

Tall and thin, his white hair pushed straight back from his forehead, his long face reamed with wrinkles, his eyes sharp and commanding, Jackson was a noble and impressive figure. On foot, with firm military step, compressed lips and resolute expression, or on horseback, where his seat was excellent, his hand light and his carriage easy, he had a natural grandeur which few could resist. Many in this bitter day shared the emotions of the conservative Boston merchant who watched out of his window to catch a glimpse of the old General, "regarding

[13] Letter of Sarah Gales Seaton, December, 1823. She continues, "He is, indeed, a polished and perfect courtier in female society, and polite to all." *William Winston Seaton,* 161. Webster's comment appeared in a letter to Ezekiel Webster, February 22, 1824, Webster, *Private Correspondence,* I, 346. Cf. the remarks of Elijah H. Mills, an old Massachusetts Federalist, in a letter to his wife, January 22, 1824, *Proceedings of the Massachusetts Historical Society,* XIX, 40–41: "He was considered extremely rash and inconsiderate, tyrannical and despotic, in his principles. A personal acquaintance with him has convinced many who held these opinions that they were unfounded. He is very mild and amiable in his disposition, of great benevolence, and his manners, though formed in the wilds of the West, exceedingly polished and polite. Everybody that knows him loves him. and he is exactly the man with whom *you* would be delighted."

him very much as he might have done some dangerous monster which was being led captive past his house." When Jackson finally appeared, his hatred abruptly collapsed. Exclaiming, "Do some one come here and salute the old man!" he thrust his small daughter forward to wave her handkerchief. Jackson, as Josiah Quincy said, "wrought a mysterious charm upon old and young." [14]

By 1829 he was technically a sick man — many thought dying. His head throbbed with splitting pains apparently produced by years of tobacco chewing, and his lean frame shook with a hacking consumptive cough. Yet, while his face grew whiter and more haggard, his spirit was grim and indomitable.

At White House receptions he remained urbane, though reserved and somewhat formal. Among his intimates he cast off his gravity, becoming sociable and sympathetic. He smoked with fierce energy, usually an old Powhatan bowl pipe with a long stem which he rested on his crossed legs, while he puffed out great white clouds until the whole room was "so obfuscated that one could hardly breathe." Or, after the Tennessee custom, he would chew and spit at regular intervals, while carrying on conversation or even conducting the affairs of state.[15]

He spoke quickly and forcibly, often emphasizing his points by raising a clenched hand in a brief, sharp gesture. "He obviously had a hidden vein of humor," reported Henry A. Wise, for many years a bitter foe, "loved aphorism, and could politely convey a sense of smart travesty. If put upon his mettle, he was very positive, but gravely respectful." When his mind was made up, he would draw down the left corner of his mouth, giving his face, as one observer noted, "a peculiar 'G—d damn me' expression." [16]

But he was not particularly dogmatic. Though accustomed to maintain his own position with pertinacity, he yielded gracefully when convinced of his error. No man, as Benton said, knew better the difference between firmness and obstinacy. "Of all the Presidents who have done me the honor to listen to my opinions, there was no one to whom I spoke with more confidence when I felt myself strongly to be in the right." The testimony on this point is fairly conclusive. "I never knew a man," commented Van Buren, "more free from con-

[14] The merchant was Daniel P. Parker; Josiah Quincy, *Figures of the Past*, 363. This essay contains an attractive account of Quincy's own surrender to Jackson's magnetism.

[15] The quotation is from Henry A. Wise, *Seven Decades of the Union*, 110–111. See also Edward Everett to his wife, January 1, 1834, Everett Papers, and Theodore Sedgwick, Jr., to Theodore Sedgwick, February 6, 1835, Sedgwick Papers.

[16] The quotations are from Wise, *Seven Decades*, 98–99, and J. B. Derby, *Political Reminiscences, including a Sketch . . . of the "Statesman Party" of Boston*, 57.

ceit, or one to whom it was to a greater extent a pleasure, as well as a recognized duty, to listen patiently to what might be said to him upon any subject. . . . Akin to his disposition in this regard was his readiness to acknowledge error." [17]

In fact, far from exacting uniformity of opinion, Jackson so indulged disagreement that he exasperated his more radical followers, like Amos Kendall and Roger B. Taney. "If he be censurable on this score," wrote Kendall, "it is for too much forbearance." "Frank himself (perhaps almost to a fault in a public man)," observed Taney, "he loved frankness in others; and regarded opposition to his opinions, by one who held office under him, as evidence of firmness as well as of honesty of purpose." [18]

In his military campaigns he would consult his council of war, but never submit a question to vote. Similarly as President, he would open up problems to the full discussion of the cabinet; but when the moment for action came, he always made up his own mind. "I have accustomed myself to receive with respect the opinions of others," he explained, "but always take the responsibility of deciding for myself." Once his mind was made up, no threats, no warnings of catastrophe, no dictates of prudence, could sway him. "I care nothing about clamors, sir, mark me! I do precisely what I think just and right." [19]

So superb a self-sufficiency could be effective only when matched by an equally superb self-control. Again contrary to the Jackson myth, there was small basis for the picture of uncontrolled irascibility. Jackson, who knew his reputation, never hesitated to exploit it. "He would sometimes extemporize a fit of passion in order to overwhelm an adversary, when certain of being in the right," said one observer, "but his self-command was always perfect." His towering rages were actually ways of avoiding futile argument. To committees which called on him to protest his financial policy, he would fly into vehement denunciations of the moneyed monopoly. When they left in disgust, he would coolly light his pipe and, chuckling "They thought I was mad," remark blandly on the importance of never compromising vital issues; one always lost friends and never appeased enemies.

Once Van Buren, before he knew Jackson well, watched with disapproval while he stormed before a delegation. As soon as the door was closed behind them, Jackson commented mildly, "I saw that my re-

---

[17] Benton, *Thirty Years' View*, I, 738; Van Buren, *Autobiography*, 312.

[18] Amos Kendall, "Anecdotes of General Jackson," *Democratic Review*, XI, 272 (September, 1842); R. B. Taney, Bank War Manuscript, 90.

[19] Jackson's two remarks were quoted by J. A. Hamilton in a letter to Timothy Pickering, July 3, 1828, J. A. Hamilton, *Reminiscences*, 77, and by N. P. Trist in a communication to James Parton, Parton, *Jackson*, III, 605.

marks disturbed you." Van Buren admitted that they had. "No, my friend," his chief replied, "I have great respect for your judgment, but you do not understand these gentlemen as well as I do"; and the sequel vindicated Jackson. "This was but one of numerous instances," Van Buren wrote later, "in which I observed a similar contradiction between his apparent undue excitement and his real coolness and self-possession in which, I may say with truth, he was seldom if ever wanting." Amos Kendall reported flatly, "I never saw him in a passion." N. P. Trist, his private secretary, was equally emphatic: "I never witnessed any thing of the sort." [20]

Jackson's intelligence expressed itself in judgment rather than in analysis. "He had vigorous thoughts," as Benton put it, "but not the faculty of arranging them in a regular composition." "Possessed of a mind that was ever dealing with the substance of things," said Van Buren, "he was not very careful in regard to the precise terms." "He had never studied the niceties of language," said Taney, "— and disliked what he was apt to regard as mere verbal criticisms." He certainly could never have written Benton's erudite discourses, or Van Buren's thoughtful recollections, or the masterly arguments of Taney, or the treatises of Edward Livingston, or the polemics of Amos Kendall. Yet he dominated them all.

In after years, the friends of Jackson wrestled with the problem of what gave his judgment a specific gravity which exposed their facile verbalizations or quick syllogisms and far outran their logical analysis. ("Beware of your metaphysics," Jackson would exclaim. ". . . Hair-splitting is dangerous business.") "The character of his mind," remarked Benton, "was that of judgment, with a rapid and almost intuitive perception, followed by an instant and decisive ac-

---

[20] The first quotation is from T. N. Parmalee, "Recollections of an Old Stager," *Harpers*, XLV, 602 (September, 1872); the anecdotes are from Wise, *Seven Decades*, 106–107, and Van Buren, *Political Parties*, 324; the last two quotations from Amos Kendall, *Autobiography*, William Stickney, ed., 635, and Parton, *Jackson*, III, 603.

There is abundant evidence of the calculation which lay beneath Jackson's famous rages. Cf. Wise's statement: "He knew that the world . . . counted him of a temperament weak, impassioned, impulsive, and inconsiderate in action; and he often turned this mistake as to character into a large capital of advantage. He was a consummate actor, never stepped without knowing and marking his ground, but knew that most men thought he was not a man of calculations. This enabled him to blind them by his affectation of passion and impulse." *Seven Decades*, 106. George Bancroft described Jackson to Goldwin Smith as "mild by nature and putting himself into a rage only when it would serve a purpose." Goldwin Smith, *Reminiscences*, Arnold Hautain, ed., 332. See also B. F. Perry, *Reminiscences of Public Men*, 29; and Marquis James *Andrew Jackson: Portrait of a President*, 366, 368.

tion." "General Jackson is the most rapid reasoner I have ever met with," declared Louis McLane. "He jumps to a conclusion before I can start on my premises." "He was indeed an extraordinary man," wrote the author James Kirke Paulding; "the only man I ever saw that excited my admiration to the pitch of wonder. To him knowledge seemed entirely unnecessary. He saw intuitively into everything, and reached a conclusion by a short cut while others were beating the bush for the game." [21]

One hot Sunday evening in July of 1858, while the Italian sun lingered over the house tops of Florence, two Americans discovered a mutual reverence for Jackson. Nathaniel Hawthorne had seen him but once, in 1833, when the old General visited Salem. The haunted young recluse had walked to the edge of town to catch a glimpse of the Old Hero. He never forgot the grim, majestic visage. Years later, when he saw Raphael's painting of Pope Julius II, "the best portrait in the whole world," his instant wish was that Raphael could have painted General Jackson.

Hiram Powers, the famous sculptor, had met Jackson and talked to him. "He thinks," Hawthorne reported, "that General Jackson was a man of the keenest and surest intuitions, in respect to men and measures, but with no power of reasoning out his conclusions, or of imparting them intellectually to other persons." Hawthorne mused over what others, Franklin Pierce and James Buchanan, had told him about Jackson. "Men who have known Jackson intimately, and in great affairs, would not agree as to this intellectual and argumentative deficiency, though they would fully allow this intuitive faculty." His conclusion was positive: "Surely he was a great man, and his native strength, as well of intellect as of character, compelled every man to be his tool that came within his reach; and the more cunning the individual might be, it served only to make him the sharper tool." [22]

Yet, as Jackson paused on the threshold of achievement in 1829,

[21] The quotations are from Benton, *Thirty Years' View*, I, 738; Van Buren, *Political Parties*, 313; Taney, Bank War Manuscript, 88; Parton, *Jackson*, III, 610; Benton, *Thirty Years' View*, I, 737; Kendall, *Autobiography*, 634; W. I. Paulding, *Literary Life of James K. Paulding*, 287–288.

[22] Hawthorne thought that Powers's assertion would be inherently plausible, "were there not such strong evidence to the contrary. The highest, or perhaps any high administrative ability, is intuitive, and precedes argument, and rises above it. It is a revelation of the very thing to be done, and its propriety and necessity are felt so strongly that very likely it cannot be talked about; if the doer can likewise talk, it is an additional and gratuitous faculty, as little to be expected as that a poet should be able to write an explanatory criticism on his own poem." "French and Italian Note-books," *Writings of Nathaniel Hawthorne* (Manse Edition), XXII, 158–160.

no one could have predicted that crisis would transform him into greatness. The challenge of events, the responsibilities of leadership, the stimulus of popular confidence, the intuitive grasp of the necessities of change: these shaped the man and drew out his finest possibilities. Like Washington, Lincoln, Wilson, Franklin Roosevelt, he gave small promise in his earlier career of the abilities he was to exhibit as Chief Magistrate. All were educated by the urgencies of the moment.[23]

Jackson grew visibly from the day of his inauguration. His leadership gained steadily in confidence and imagination. He grew stronger after every contact with the people. In last analysis, there lay the secret of his strength: his deep natural understanding of the people. "They were his blood relations," said Van Buren, " — the only blood relations he had." He believed that "to labour for the good of the masses was a special mission assigned to him by his Creator and no man was ever better disposed to work in his vocation in season and out of season." [24] The people called him, and he came, like the great folk heroes, to lead them out of captivity and bondage.[25]

[23] Van Buren perhaps had Jackson in mind when he described the process: "that which similar crises in all countries and times, have brought about, namely, the production of great men by great events, developing and calling into action upon a large scale intellects the power of which, but for their application to great transactions, might have remained unknown alike to their possessors and to the world." Van Buren, *Political Parties*, 171–172.

[24] Van Buren, *Autobiography*, 255.

[25] Few modern historians hold to the Whig-Republican legend of Jackson in its literal form, but there is a visible tendency to revive it in somewhat more sophisticated version, led especially by Professor T. P. Abernethy in an article, "Andrew Jackson and the Rise of Southwestern Democracy," *American Historical Review*, XXXIII, 64–77, in his excellent book, *From Frontier to Plantation in Tennessee*, and in his sketch of Jackson in the *Dictionary of American Biography*, IX, 526–534.
Professor Abernethy's thesis seems to be that Jackson, not having been a great democratic leader in Tennessee politics, could not therefore have been a genuine champion of the people, but was an unprincipled opportunist, who happened through a set of accidents to head a democratic movement. Jackson was basically a conservative, Abernethy argues, but he and his backers "had no very strong convictions and were willing to make friends with the times. It is not the greatest men who go to the top in politics." (This aside is typical of the animus against Jackson which runs through Professor Abernethy's work.) "Not only was Jackson not a consistent politician, he was not even a real leader of democracy . . . he always believed in making the public serve the ends of the politicians. Democracy was good talk with which to win the favor of the people and thereby accomplish ulterior objectives. Jackson never really championed the cause of the people." (*From Frontier to Plantation*, 241, 248, 249; *passim*, especially chapter iv.) "No historian has ever accused Jackson, the great Democrat, of having had a political philosophy. It is hard to see that he even had any political principles. . . . He thought he was sincere when he spoke to the people, yet he never really championed their cause. He merely encouraged them to champion his." (*American Historical Review*, XXXIII, 76–77.) "He had little understanding of the democratic

movement which bears his name and he came to support it primarily because it supported him." (*Dictionary of American Biography*, IX, 534.)

The point about Professor Abernethy's thesis is that his conclusion is one to be established by evidence, not by deductive logic. A judgment on the character of Jackson's democracy must be founded on an examination of what Jackson did as President, and on nothing else; certainly not on an extrapolation made on the basis of his career before he became President.

No amount of inference based on what Jackson was like before 1828 can be a substitute for the facts after 1828. Yet Abernethy's own published work was concerned almost exclusively with Jackson in Tennessee. His bias is sufficiently betrayed by the odd and otherwise baffling proportions of his article in the *Dictionary of American Biography*, which devotes over two thirds of its space to Jackson before he became President. If Abernethy were to use the same method on Lincoln, or Wilson, or Franklin Roosevelt — that is, to dogmatize on their presidencies on the basis of their pre-presidential records — his results would be self-evidently absurd.

V THE FIRST YEAR

THE SHOUTING crowd on Inauguration Day, Daniel Webster noted sarcastically, really seemed to think "the country is rescued from some dreadful danger." [1] Yet where was this danger? It was clear that Jackson had an impressive mandate, but it was not so clear what the mandate was for. Through the land, an excitement for change had welled up from profound frustration. But its concrete expressions were only slogans, epithets, meaningless phrases, the shout of crowds — not issues, programs, policies.

1

The new President's supporters in Congress had conspicuously failed to develop measures to meet the discontents which had toppled the previous administration. Their opposition to Adams and Clay had been confused and opportunistic, hiding a basic lack of ideas behind a smoke-screen of parliamentary obstruction and campaign invective. The campaign had reflected its shallowness. Hardly an issue of policy figured in the canvass, and, when Jackson triumphed, no one could be certain that his administration would not duplicate that of Madison or Monroe or even of Adams.

As for the new President, he was not only tired, sick and depressed by grief, but politically inexperienced. The problems he faced were new to him; and for a man who learned by dealing with actualities rather than by intellectual analysis this was a serious handicap. He had to feel his way and let things seep in before he could move with decision. In the meantime the demand for "reform" had to be met. The common man, too long thwarted by official indifference, had to be given a sense that the government was in truth the people's government. Jackson's answer was shrewd and swift: a redistribution of federal offices.

This measure served obvious political needs. It adapted to national purposes methods of political reward, long employed in some of the

[1] Webster to Mrs. Ezekiel Webster, March 4, 1829, Webster, *Private Correspondence*, I, 473.

states, and became an invaluable means of unifying administration support. A party formed to aid special moneyed interests could depend on private contributions to pay the bills and keep the organization alive; but a party formed in the popular interest had no other resources save the offices at its disposal. "If you wish to keep up the party," a Pennsylvania politician told Van Buren, "you must induce them to beleive that it is their interest — Some few may adhere to the party from mere consciencious conviction of doing right but interest is a powerful stimulus to make them act energetically and efficiently." [2]

But, while helping to build the party, the spoils system also contributed to the main objective of helping restore faith in the government. In the eyes of the people, the bureaucracy had been corrupted by its vested interests in its own power. "Office is considered as a species of property," as Jackson told Congress, "and government rather as a means of promoting individual interests than as an instrument created solely for the service of the people." Jackson believed that official duties could be made "so plain and simple that men of intelligence may readily qualify themselves for their performance." His quick action on this principle meant that the government was no longer "an engine for the support of the few at the expense of the many." [3]

The doctrine of rotation-in-office was thus in large part conceived as a sincere measure of reform. Many professional reformers so regarded it. Robert Dale Owen hailed it enthusiastically in his radical New York sheet, the *Free Enquirer*, and Jeremy Bentham, the great English reformer, confided to Jackson, as one liberal to another, that he had held the doctrine of rotation himself since 1821. [4]

In a larger context, which contemporary Americans could only have dimly apprehended, rotation-in-office possessed another significance. The history of governments has been characterized by the decay of old ruling classes and the rise of more vigorous and intelligent ones to replace them. This process had already begun in America. The "natural aristocracy" of Richard Hildreth — the class composed of merchant, banker, planter, lawyer and clergyman — had started to decline after the War of 1812. The rise of the military hero, a new "natural" aristocrat, hastened the time for a general breaking-up of the old governing elite. In extreme cases one ruling order succeeds another by violent revolution, but a democracy which preserves suffi-

[2] David Petrikin to Van Buren, November 18, 1836, Van Buren Papers.
[3] Richardson, comp., *Messages and Papers of the Presidents*, II, 448-449.
[4] *Free Enquirer*, January 2, 1830; Bentham to Jackson, April 26, 1830, *Jeremy Bentham, Works*, John Bowring, ed., XI, 40.

cient equality of opportunity may escape so drastic a solution. The spoils system, whatever its faults, at least destroyed peaceably the monopoly of offices by a class which could not govern, and brought to power a fresh and alert group which had the energy to meet the needs of the day.

Modern research has shown that legend, invented and fostered for partisan purposes, has considerably exaggerated the extent of Jackson's actual removals. The most careful estimate is that between a fifth and a tenth of all federal officeholders were dismissed during Jackson's eight years, many for good reason. Frauds to the amount of $280,000 were discovered in the Treasury Department alone. Jackson ousted no greater a proportion of officeholders than Jefferson, though his administration certainly established the spoils system in national politics.[5]

Until recent years, the study of the spoils system has been marred by a tendency to substitute moral disapproval for an understanding of causes and necessities. There can be small doubt today that, whatever evils it brought into American life, its historical function was to narrow the gap between the people and the government — to expand popular participation in the workings of democracy. For Jackson it was an essential step in the gradual formulation of a program for democratic America.

2

As the Jackson administration moved through its first year, two hostile factions began to emerge within the party, one pressing Vice-President John C. Calhoun's claims for the presidency in 1832, the other supporting Martin Van Buren, the Secretary of State.

Van Buren had been born forty-six years before at Kinderhook, a small village of old New York, the son of a farmer and tavern-keeper of Dutch stock. After scant schooling, he entered a law office at the age of fourteen. For six years, in between sweeping the floor, lighting fires in winter and copying legal papers, he pored over law books and prepared himself for a career at the bar. Successful in practice, he soon went into politics where his talents for intrigue and leadership won him rapid promotion. He played a dominant role in the state

[5] E. M. Eriksson, "The Federal Civil Service under President Jackson," *Mississippi Valley Historical Review*, XIII, 517–540. Petrikin's letter, cited above, blamed reduced Democratic majorities in Pennsylvania in part on "the course pursued by the Post office Department ever since Gen¹ Jackson was elected in refusing to remove postmasters who were and always have been opposed to the Democratic party." This complaint was not uncommon among Democratic politicians.

constitutional convention of 1821 and the same year he was sent to the Senate. There he remained until elected Governor in 1828, from which office Jackson called him to the State Department.

Van Buren was an active little man with a tendency toward stoutness, his eyes sharp, his perceptions quick, and his manner charming. Fanny Elssler, the dancer, was surprised to discover his bearing as distinguished as Metternich's; and the French Minister remarked in 1840 that this man, "*fils d'un cabaretier,*" had attained "*une certaine aisance qui le rend supérieur, comme homme du monde, à ceux de ses compatriotes que j'ai vus jusqu'ici.*" He had a keen wit — Jackson, who delighted in the newspaper humorist, Major Jack Downing, would exclaim after some particularly telling quip, "Depend upon it, Jack Downing is only Van Buren in masquerade" — but his tongue was kept constantly in leash by his politic temperament. Self-control, indeed, was almost his outstanding characteristic. At an early age, he jotted down in a notebook, "To yield to necessity is the real triumph of reason and strength of mind," and this became the rule of his life. When disappointed, he would say, "Well, after all, I have made up my mind, that it is *the best thing that could have happened.*" [6]

In public office Van Buren pursued a steady Jeffersonian policy. He was one of the first in the nation to introduce bills against imprisonment for debt. He marshaled the liberal forces in the New York constitutional convention and delivered the most crushing reply to the neo-Federalist arguments of Chancellor Kent on the question of the suffrage. In the United States Senate he continued his fight against debt imprisonment, opposed federal expenditures for internal improvements, favored settlement of the Western lands and led the assault on the Supreme Court.

He spent his brief term as Governor mainly in an attack on the banking problem, proposing to protect the public "and more particularly the laboring classes" from losses through the reckless issue of paper money and, at the same time, to move toward the abolition of the state banking monopoly. As early as 1817, he had recommended a law to end the system of special charters and throw banking open to general competition, but this measure was ahead of its time even in 1829. The chief result of his three-month term was the so-called safety-fund plan. Since the chartered banks enjoyed the exclusive and highly profitable privilege of issuing paper money, the statute sought to guarantee the soundness of their currency by requiring each institution to contribute a proportion of its capital to a general fund,

---

[6] Adolph de Bacourt, *Souvenirs d'un Diplomate*, 94, 83; Josiah Quincy, *Figures of the Past*, 359; Notebook, Van Buren Papers; G. A. Worth to W. L. Marcy, November 7, 1846, Marcy Papers.

which could be drawn upon to redeem the notes of any bank becoming insolvent. A board of commissioners was to supervise banking operations. Though essentially a stopgap system, the safety-fund plan brought banks much more under state control and distinctly improved the condition of the currency.[7]

Yet the fact remains that, in spite of his known convictions and his record of forceful leadership, Van Buren enjoyed a name for noncommittalism that survived when most other things about him were forgotten. His nicknames — the Little Magician, the American Talleyrand, the Red Fox of Kinderhook — suggest his popular reputation. They were certainly confirmed by the almost systematic obscurity of some of his public utterances. Once he had reached a decision, his stand would probably be unequivocal and aggressive; but in the course of a long political career he encountered many questions on which he had not yet made up his mind. For these contingencies he became the master of an enormously complicated and diffuse style, which enabled him to say many intelligent things for and against a policy without conveying a very clear idea of his own sentiments. "Mr. Knower! that was a very able speech!" an Albany wool buyer exclaimed to a friend after hearing Van Buren explain his views on the tariff in 1827. "Yes, very able!" was the answer. "Mr. Knower!" said the wool buyer, after a considerable pause, "on what side of the Tariff question was it?"[8]

Even after deciding on a course of action, Van Buren might move with an air of evasiveness. As John Randolph said, he "rowed to his object with muffled oars." And even when embarked in open opposition, Van Buren sought to keep party antagonisms from souring social relations, partly from genuine good nature, partly from a conviction that it was bad tactics to turn a political opponent into a personal enemy. In an era of fiery partisanship, Washington would marvel at the spectacle of Van Buren cheerfully exchanging handshakes, jokes and pinches of snuff with his harshest foes. His unruffled amiability forced the opposition to resort to the distinction made by Henry Clay: "An acquaintance with him of more than twenty years' duration has inspired me with a respect for the man, although I regret to be compelled to say, I detest the magistrate."[9]

Intellectually he suffered from a surprising sense of inferiority. His writings reveal an acute and reflective mind, shrewd in judging men and analyzing events. William Cullen Bryant was much impressed that

[7] Van Buren, *Autobiography*, 221; George Bancroft, *Martin Van Buren*, 53; R. G. Chaddock, *The Safety Fund Banking System in New York, 1829–1866*.

[8] Van Buren, *Autobiography*, 171. It was characteristic that Van Buren should enjoy telling this story on himself.

[9] Bruce, *Randolph*, II, 203; E. M. Shepard, *Martin Van Buren*, 339.

Van Buren could "so steadily command resources beyond the occupations in which so large a part of his life had been engaged." His legal ability prompted John Quincy Adams to urge his appointment to the Supreme Court; and the veteran Federalist, Rufus King, agreed that no man was "better qualified for a high and difficult judicial station." Yet, Van Buren always felt the lack of college training "to sustain me in my conflicts with able and better educated men." "My mind might have lost a portion of its vivacity, in the plodding habits formed by such a course," he wrote, "but it could not have failed to acquire in the elements of strength supplied by a good education much more than it lost." [10]

He sought reassurance in many ways. He carefully practised intellectual humility. "Whatever weaknesses I may be subject to, — and doubtless they are numerous, — dogmatism, I am very sure, is not one of them." [11] He cultivated the companionship of intellectuals and men of letters. Bryant was for some years a close friend, Washington Irving another. He numbered Frances Wright and Robert Dale Owen among his acquaintances. As President he gave government posts to Hawthorne, George Bancroft, J. K. Paulding, Orestes A. Brownson and William Leggett.

His lack of intellectual confidence made him tame and unoriginal as a political thinker. A pious Jeffersonian, he rarely ventured to do more than annotate the gospel. His posthumous work on political parties is a classic of Virginia fundamentalism. He took the strict-construction dogma much more seriously than Jackson himself, or most others of the inner circle. He more than once counseled new kinds of governmental action, but he justified them always in terms of the sacred texts.

3

Yet, for all his reluctance to abandon dogma, Van Buren was fertile in introducing new methods. Endowed with practical political intuitions of the highest order, he was the first national leader really to take advantage of the growing demand of the people for more active participation in the decisions of government. Political bosses had existed before Van Buren, and he invented no important technical device of party organization. Yet his management of the Albany

[10] Bryant in the *New York Evening Post*, September 18, 1841, quoted by Parke Godwin, *Biography of William Cullen Bryant*, I, 390; Charles Warren, *The Supreme Court in United States History*, revised edition, I, 591–594; Van Buren, *Autobiography*, 11–12.

[11] Van Buren, *Political Parties*, 309.

Regency, as his own group was called, raised the methods of Aaron Burr in New York, the Essex Junto in Massachusetts, the Richmond Junto in Virginia, to a new efficiency; and his own career, especially after the lessons taught him by the outcry against the caucus system in 1824, was based on a thorough understanding of the importance of the press, city machines, county committees, nominating conventions, stump speaking, monster mass meetings and all other expedients reaching out to the people.

The growing importance of the common man was accompanied by a declining importance of Congress. The function of the legislature was now rather to elicit, register and influence public opinion than to assert its independent will. The great party leader was no longer the eloquent parliamentary orator, whose fine periods could sweep his colleagues into supporting his measures, but the popular hero, capable of bidding directly for the confidence of the masses. Van Buren thought Voltairean conceptions of politics fatally underestimated the power of public opinion. "Those who have wrought great changes in the world," he wrote, "never succeeded by gaining over chiefs; but always by exciting the multitude. The first is the resource of intrigue and produces only secondary results, the second is the resort of genius and transforms the face of the universe." [12]

He protested repeatedly against romantic views of the magic of oratory. When Macaulay declared grandly, in the well-known passage on Pitt, "Parliamentary Government is Government by speaking," Van Buren begged to differ. True parliamentary leadership, he declared, involved "powers of the mind more humble in pretension and less dazzling in appearance but, as experience has often proved, far more effective in the end than the most brilliant oratory when not sustained by them." Good judgment in timing measures, the capacity to strike directly at the opposition's weakest point without wasting time in "mere oratorical" disquisition, skill in guiding the debate so as to capitalize on "latent diversities of feeling and opinion on points either not at all or only remotely bearing upon the principal subject," and good sense to strive for objects not beyond practical reach — oratory was useless without these technical skills and without, in the end, "the deep seated and habitual confidence" of a majority of the assembly and of the people in general. [13]

Van Buren's point was fully borne out by the party struggles of the

[12] The new leader, Van Buren went on, would never make "overtures to leaders to gain over parties," but would win over "the mass of the parties that he might be in a situation to displace the leaders." Notebook, Van Buren Papers.
[13] Van Buren, *Autobiography*, 466–471. Hawthorne commented similarly: "It is only tradition and old custom, founded on an obsolete state of things, that assigns

thirties. The two greatest orators of the day, Webster and Clay, were almost invariably on the losing side. Their speeches won the highest praise from others brought up on traditional values, and this praise has descended into the popular consciousness through schoolbook history. Yet, the majesty of Webster and Clay was highly vulnerable to the tireless labors on the floor and in the cloakrooms of party whips like Felix Grundy and Silas Wright in the Senate, Polk and Cambreleng in the House; and in case of doubt Jackson's appeals to the people always proved decisive.

The new parliamentary style — intimate and conversational, with low-pitched voice and clear enunciation — tended by itself to deflate the resounding declamation of the classical school. John Quincy Adams, former professor of rhetoric at Harvard and a great admirer of the elaborate periods of Edward Everett, perfectly expressed the baffled exasperation of the old school in an outburst against James K. Polk: "He has no wit, no literature, no point of argument, no gracefulness of delivery, no elegance of language, no philosophy, no pathos, no felicitous impromptus; nothing that can constitute an orator, but confidence, fluency, and labor." [14]

Van Buren's understanding of the new functions of public opinion, as well as of Congress, furnished the practical mechanisms which transformed Jackson's extraordinary popularity into the instruments of power. Most of the devices he developed to increase governmental responsiveness to the popular will could become devices for frustrating the popular will. Yet without them the gains of Jacksonian democracy would have been impossible.

4

Van Buren's rival, John Caldwell Calhoun, though but a few months older, had been much longer on the national stage. A graduate of Yale and of Judge Tapping Reeve's law school at Litchfield, he

---

any value to parliamentary oratory. The world has done with it, except as an intellectual pastime. The speeches have no effect till they are converted into newspaper paragraphs; and they had better be composed as such, in the first place, and oratory reserved for churches, courts of law, and public dinner tables." Hawthorne, *Writings*, XXII, 160.

[14] Adams, *Memoirs*, IX, 64. Van Buren was capable, while presiding over the Senate, of deliberately puncturing the effects of full-blown oratory. Clay once delivered a classical apostrophe to the chair, charging the Vice-President with a plea to Jackson to relax his financial policy. Van Buren, "looking respectfully, and even innocently at the speaker," appeared to treasure every word; but at the conclusion Van Buren simply strolled over to Clay, asked for a pinch of his fine maccoboy snuff, as he often did, and walked placidly away when he received it, leaving the collapsed eloquence behind him. Benton, *Thirty Years' View*, I, 420.

entered Congress at the age of twenty-nine and won countrywide prominence for his zeal in whipping up enthusiasm for the War of 1812. After the peace he emerged as the leader in converting the party of Jefferson to the policy of Hamilton, championing the national bank, internal improvements and a protective tariff. John Quincy Adams declared him in 1821 to be "above all sectional and factious prejudices more than any other statesman of this Union with whom I have ever acted." [15]

Elected Vice-President in 1824, Calhoun was expected to work harmoniously with Adams and Clay in extending the American System. But this calculation did not allow for South Carolina. In 1826, after many years' residence in Washington, Calhoun bought Fort Hill, an upcountry plantation at Pendleton, and returned to live in his native state. He found a changed South. In 1816 nearly everyone but the Virginia doctrinaires had accepted the Hamiltonian tendencies, but disillusion ran now at full tide. Rendered sensitive by intense devotion to his state, as well as by a consuming ambition for the presidency, Calhoun lost his old enthusiasms. By 1828, after a period of silent recantation, he became the secret author of the South Carolina Exposition. In the election he supported Jackson, probably in the belief that the old General would be easy to dominate, and in return retained his seat as heir-apparent.

He was an impressive figure, sitting bolt upright in the vice-presidential chair, with his harsh, consecrated face, his head covered with a mass of stiff iron-gray hair, his eyes so black and piercing that they almost seemed to give out light in the dark. Often he would pace the corridors of the Capitol, his spare body bent in a slouching walk, one hand behind his back, the other crushing a huge East India handkerchief. Young men found him fascinating and listened raptly as he poured out his political ideas in abrupt, emphatic phrases; but his contemporaries were just beginning to find him overbearing, almost arrogant. Yet political considerations still tempered his fervor. He was not yet the cast-iron man of Miss Martineau, and men like Van Buren and Webster respected the South Carolinian much more than they did each other or Clay.[16]

[15] Adams, *Memoirs*, V, 361.
[16] W. H. Milburn, *Ten Years of Preacher-Life: Chapters from an Autobiography*, 152–153; Oliver Dyer, *Great Senators of the United States Fifty Years Ago*, 148–187; T. N. Parmalee, "Recollections of an Old Stager," *Harpers*, XLVII, 757 (October, 1873); Sarah M. Maury, *The Statesmen of America in 1846*, 181. For Van Buren on Calhoun, see Lord Morpeth's Diary, manuscript transcript, November 15, 1841, p. 61; for Webster, see Peter Harvey, *Reminiscences and Anecdotes of Daniel Webster*, 219.

Calhoun, who felt he had waited long enough, realized that the bland and cheerful Secretary of State was the main obstacle in the path toward the White House. Yet, early in 1829, he must have found the future promising. He had triumphed signally in the making of the cabinet. The Secretaries of the Treasury and the Navy, and the Attorney General, strongly preferred him, while Van Buren could count only on John H. Eaton, the Secretary of War, and William T. Barry (of the Kentucky Relief War), the Postmaster General. Moreover, Barry was negligible, and Eaton's marriage, which had provoked C. C. Cambreleng to such coarse hilarity, made him highly vulnerable to attack.

Accordingly, the partisans of Calhoun took advantage of the ambiguous social position of Peggy Eaton to set in motion a complicated intrigue with the eventual aim of driving her husband from the cabinet. The wives of cabinet members friendly to Calhoun began to snub her. Men like Attorney General John M. Berrien and Justice McLean of the Supreme Court, both of whom had actually attended her wedding, now ostentatiously withheld all civilities. Through the country, Calhoun's followers, and soon all enemies of the administration, worked up an indignation out of all proportion to the episode. Barry was probably right in asserting that, if her husband were not in the cabinet, "Mrs. Eaton would be unmolested." Peggy herself, writing years later, was convinced she was the victim of a political frame-up.[17]

In any event, the plot backfired. Jackson, who believed that his own wife's death had been hastened by the campaign of vilification directed against her in 1828, now intervened on Mrs. Eaton's behalf. In the end, the friends of Calhoun, instead of forcing Jackson to get rid of Eaton, only succeeded in entrenching Eaton and Van Buren more solidly than ever in the President's confidence.

The wedge between Calhoun and Jackson was soon driven home. Duff Green's calm assumption, forever between the lines of the *United States Telegraph*, that Calhoun would be the candidate in 1832, began to get on the nerves of the White House. The nullification issue proved further irritating, and Jackson flatly rebuked Calhoun's new doctrines in his famous toast at the Jefferson birthday dinner on April 15, 1830: "Our Federal Union: it must be preserved!" The President was finally infuriated by the disclosure that Calhoun,

[17] W. T. Barry to Mrs. Susan Taylor, February 25, 1830, "Letters of William T. Barry," *William and Mary College Quarterly*, XIV, 19–20; Margaret Eaton, *Autobiography of Peggy Eaton*, C. F. Deems, ed., 65 and *passim*. The facts are inconclusive, however, and it may be plausibly argued that it was simply a social issue.

who had always given the impression of having supported Jackson's adventures in Florida in 1818, had really denounced them in the privacy of Monroe's cabinet. Calhoun sought to justify himself in a lengthy and bitter pamphlet. With this act the fight came into the open, and Jackson coldly terminated relations.

Friends of Van Buren had been indispensable in engineering the break with Calhoun, but the Secretary of State himself remained in careful ignorance of what was going on. With the split irrevocable, he ingeniously proposed his own resignation and a dissolution of the cabinet, which could lead to a reorganized government totally purged of the Calhoun influence. Van Buren then accepted the British ministry and departed for London, confident that his interests were safe in the President's hands.

The Vice-President, burning with resentment, planned for revenge. While Van Buren moved coolly in the court circles of London, conversed with Palmerston, flattered the aged Talleyrand, Calhoun bided his time, proud and silent on the bench above the Senate, waiting for the President to submit Van Buren's name. On a bitter, cold night late in January, 1832, a contrived tie gave Calhoun the pleasure of casting the deciding vote for rejection. "It will kill him, sir, kill him dead," the Vice-President exulted. "He will never kick, sir, never kick." [18] But there were other diagnoses, perhaps more expert. "You have broken a minister, and elected a Vice-President," Thomas Hart Benton triumphantly exclaimed. G. C. Verplanck, Congressman from New York, looking farther into the future, observed to William Cullen Bryant, "That makes Van Buren President of the United States." [19]

Van Buren learned the outcome as he lay sick in his bedroom in London. "Altho' I had ardently desired it," wrote Cambreleng, "I could not persuade myself to believe that their passions would drive them into a measure the inevitable results of which might have been seen by a schoolboy." Much invigorated, Van Buren went down to breakfast. There he found Washington Irving, Secretary of the Legation, delighted by the news and predicting that Van Buren would be Vice-President. ("The more I see of Mr. V. B., the more I feel confirmed in a strong personal regard for him," Irving was shortly to write. "He is one of the gentlest and most amiable men I have ever met with.") In the afternoon, Van Buren made his usual composed appearance at the Queen's first drawing room, and he dined at

[18] Benton, *Thirty Years' View*, I, 219; C. J. Ingersoll, *Historical Sketch*, II, 266.
[19] Benton, *Thirty Years' View*, I, 215; W. C. Bryant, *Prose Writings of William Cullen Bryant*, Parke Godwin, ed., II, 410.

Talleyrand's. In June he made a triumphal return to America. The next March he became Vice-President.[20]

John C. Calhoun sank into icy bitterness. For four years he could hardly mention Van Buren without biting and contemptuous epithets. "Calhoun, by this time, must be in Hell," observed John Randolph. ". . . He is self mutilated like the Fanatic that emasculated himself." [21]

[20] Cambreleng to Van Buren, January 27, 1832, Van Buren, *Autobiography*, 454; Irving to Peter Irving, March 16, 1832, Pierre M. Irving, *Life and Letters of Washington Irving*, II, 482. See also Irving to Van Buren, January 2, 1833, Van Buren Papers.
[21] Randolph to Jackson, March 28, 1832, Andrew Jackson, *Correspondence*, J. S. Bassett, ed., IV, 429.

VI THE MEN AROUND THE PRESIDENT

THE BATTLE against the American System was relying increasingly on the political and intellectual resources of the Jeffersonian tradition; and the break with Calhoun made certain that Jackson's interpretation of the Jeffersonian heritage would not stem from men for whom Jeffersonianism was hardening into a sectional philosophy. In the later writings of Virginia, deep solicitude for slavery had diluted the old republican faith in liberty and equality; and, with Calhoun, the State-rights strain was growing to a degree that threatened to smother the democratic strain. While this Southern version opposed the American System with all vigor, it hardly did so for the benefit of the common man. Now it had lost its power in the administration. The men who remained stood for a different reading of the Jeffersonian creed. Inspired by the democratic, rather than by the sectional, utterances of Taylor, Randolph and Macon, they conceived of Jeffersonianism in terms of equality rather than of provincial security.

1

Yet Jeffersonian equality itself was open to two interpretations: the emphasis of the Declaration of Independence on political equality and home rule; and the emphasis which matured during the conflicts with Federalism, on economic equality as well.

Here again there were sectional divergences. The Western Jeffersonians, living amidst conditions of substantial equality with limitless vistas of economic opportunity before them, aimed more at establishing local self-government and majority rule than at safeguarding the material foundations of political democracy. Where approximate equality of economic opportunity existed, there was no pressure to defend it. The Jeffersonians of the East, on the other hand, made keenly aware, by direct experience, of growing inequality and declining opportunity, were much more sensitive to the economic issues.

The American System awoke the first intimations of divergence.

While it certainly did not violate principles of political equality, yet its tendency was widely felt to be destructive of economic equality. It was thus much more heartily abhorred by the dispossessed classes of the East, grimly fighting against further exploitation, than it was by the West, where classes hardly existed.

In the campaign of 1828 Jackson's supporters had to take great pains to represent him through the West as a friend of the American System. Amos Kendall repeatedly assured the reader of the *Argus of Western America* that these favorite projects of Mr. Clay were perfectly safe, challenging the Adams party "to produce even a *newspaper paragraph* advocating Jackson's election on the ground of his opposition to 'the present American system.' It cannot be done." This impression was so widespread that Hezekiah Niles, veteran protectionist and editor of the nation's favorite newsweekly, *Niles' Register,* could console himself after the election with the belief that "the *whole* 'American system,' if it shall not *advance* under the new administration, will, at least, maintain its ground, as to principle." [1]

But the Eastern Jacksonians begged to differ. "We know our enemies," wrote C. C. Cambreleng, to Van Buren, from Washington three days before Jackson's inauguration, "and our motto should be those who are not for us are against us. . . . You stand between Clays aristocratic and prohibitory American system on the one hand — and Calhouns anti-constitutional and anti-union doctrines on the other." [2] When in April, 1830, a bill was passed authorizing the government to subscribe to the stock of a Kentucky company for a turnpike from Maysville to Lexington, Jackson, moving into increasingly radical positions, willingly accepted Van Buren's argument that the policy of government aid to private corporations should, once and for all, be ended.

Yet Jackson's Western supporters trembled at the possibility of veto. As Richard M. Johnson of Kentucky exclaimed heatedly to the President, with a flourish of his open hand, "General! If this hand were an anvil on which the sledge hammer of the smith was descending and a fly were to light upon it in time to receive the blow he would not crush it more effectually than you will crush your friends in Kentucky if you veto that Bill!" The chief Western advisers — William B. Lewis, John H. Eaton, Felix Grundy and William T. Barry — gathered for a despondent breakfast at the White House on the morning the rejection was to go to Congress. Van Buren, calm and confident, remarked privately to Jackson that their friends were fright-

[1] *Argus of Western America* (Frankfort), September 10, 1828; *Niles' Register,* December 20, 1828, Supplement.
[2] Cambreleng to Van Buren, March 1, 1829, Van Buren Papers.

ened. "Yes," answered the General, "but don't mind that! The thing is here" — he tapped his breast-pocket — "and shall be sent up as soon as Congress convenes." [3]

"A half reformation, like a half revolution never produces lasting benefits; it leaves half the bad seed, to sprout & produce an unprofitable crop, & the cockle if not destroyed ruins the wheat." Nathaniel Macon well knew the dangers of faintheartedness, and his warning to Van Buren not to stop with the Maysville veto came from bitter memories. "Some of the friends of Mr. Jefferson were alarmed & afraid of too much reform, & their unwillingness to do more stopped his administration at the point at which it ceased to go on." [4]

If the Jacksonian drive were to continue, the President required followers who would keep fighting on the economic front. His close counselors from Tennessee days were increasingly out of place in the great democratic surge. For years, Major Eaton, Major Lewis and Judge John Overton had stood at Jackson's elbow, helping write his public letters, building up his organization, and plotting eternally for his advancement. Eaton and Lewis accompanied him to Washington and received posts in the government. But they were not the men for the new battle lines. By 1840 Eaton would become a vehement opponent of Jacksonian democracy. Lewis remained on warm personal terms with the President and attended to business matters for him, but he had no political importance save as a party fixer; he supported the United States Bank, favored John Bell over James K. Polk in the contest for Speaker of the House in 1834 and otherwise departed from the strict Jacksonian line. Neither Van Buren nor Polk had much confidence in him. [5] As for Jackson's more democratic Western followers, many of them, like Richard M. Johnson, were indifferent to the economic issues involved in the American System.

The President needed men who shared fully his deepening belief that the economic problem, the balance of class power, overshadowed all other questions of the day. There were such men. In the Senate, he could rely on Thomas Hart Benton of Missouri. A native of North Carolina, Benton had moved West as a young man, first to Tennessee, where he and Jackson had mixed in an angry frontier brawl, then to Missouri. In 1820 he entered the Senate, and four years later he and Jackson were reconciled. Now forty-eight years old, he was a striking figure, not tall but large-boned, with broad shoulders, a deep

[3] Van Buren, *Autobiography*, 312–338.
[4] Macon to Van Buren, October 1, 1830, Van Buren Papers.
[5] Lewis to Jackson, October 6, 1839, Lewis to the editor of the *Nashville Banner*, July, 1845, Jackson-Lewis Papers.

chest and a fine and massive head. In most things he was built on a scale somewhat larger than life. Vanity was his most obvious trait, but it was so vast and towering that it rarely offended. He had a giant conviction that he and the people were one. "Nobody opposes Benton," he would roar, pronouncing it "Bane-ton," "but a few blackjack prairie lawyers; these are the only opponents of Benton. Benton and the people, Benton and Democracy are one and the same, sir; synonymous terms, sir; synonymous terms, sir."

Nothing chastened him. After Calhoun's death, a friend said, "I suppose, Colonel, you won't pursue Calhoun beyond the grave?" Benton replied majestically, "No, sir. When God Almighty lays his hand upon a man, sir, I take mine off, sir." As an appreciative newspaperman put it, "One could not help feeling that the old ironclad's egotism was a sort of national institution, in which every patriotic American could take a just pride." [6]

For all his vanity, Benton could be most gracious and urbane. The fastidious French Ambassador, who, in 1840, thought that Clay looked like an English farmer and found Webster *"Pompous au dernier point"* except when drunk, declared Benton to be *"instruit, éloquent et habile."* N. P. Willis shrewdly noted the difference between his public formidability and his private charm: "His lower features are drilled into imperturbable suavity, while the *eye*, that undullable tale-teller, twinkles of inward slyness as a burning lamp wick does of oil." Charles Sumner, brought up on Whig legends, reported himself glad to be undeceived: "I was not prepared to find him as much of a courtier in his manners, and as full of the stores of various learning." Even that grizzled warrior John Quincy Adams confessed himself disarmed by Benton's delight in his children. [7]

Domestic life, indeed, revealed Benton's most winning qualities. His children long remembered their rich happiness in the old family home at Washington, with its thick walls and spacious rooms, and the green lawn in back, framed by growths of ivy and the scarlet trumpet creeper along the garden walls. In the evening, when supper was over, Benton would leave his work to join the animated group by the fireplace, his wife knitting woolen garments, and his four daughters breathlessly discussing the events of the day, or working at their portfolios, or listening to music. One of them would someday play Beethoven to Rossini in Paris.

[6] W. M. Meigs, *Life of Thomas Hart Benton*, 451–455; Oliver Dyer, *Great Senators*, 207–213.

[7] Adolph de Bacourt, *Souvenirs*, 69, 72, 236, 368; N. P. Willis, *Hurry-Graphs: or, Sketches of Scenery, Celebrities and Society*, 179; Sumner to Bancroft, April 22, 1846, Bancroft Papers; J. Q. Adams, *Memoirs*, X, 257.

Jessie, five years old in 1829, with red-brown curls and brown eyes and bright eager face, was Benton's favorite. In Washington they took daily walks together, Benton often "pasturing" her at the Congressional Library while he went on to the Capitol; but Jessie's greatest joy was to return to Missouri, which Benton did seldom enough, and go quail shooting with her father on brown October days. Soon she would grow up, a charming and clever girl, whose "pleasant wild strawberry flavor" would capture even the frigid Sumner and would bewitch a young army lieutenant named John Charles Frémont.[8]

Benton's intellectual abilities were of a high order. Horace Mann considered him the best constitutional lawyer in the country. By common consent, only Adams could rival him in general erudition. His memory for detail was prodigious, and his speeches bristled with facts. He was not in these days an effective orator. When he rose in the Senate, his colleagues turned to their correspondence or fled the chamber. Yet, when aroused to anger, he was powerful. His personal appearance was more commanding than that of any Senator, save possibly Webster, and his face and eyes could express withering disgust and contempt. The more furious he was, the more icy he became till he was like "a brazen statue, his flesh all solidified and every muscle strongly drawn and fixed." He would speak more and more slowly, his voice dragging into an intolerable rasp, while he poured out his taunts in hard, cold tones and his opponents cowered and begged for mercy.[9]

His early years in the Senate brought him into intimate contact with Randolph and Macon. From them he imbibed the Jeffersonian faith undefiled. From the first he showed ability in making it an affirmative social philosophy instead of the melancholy and defeatist creed it had become in the hands of the doctrinaires. He would prove of the greatest assistance in developing a constructive policy for the new administration.

2

In the House, Jackson could count on the unfaltering support of a young friend from Tennessee, James K. Polk. Like Benton, a

---

[8] Jessie Benton Frémont, *Souvenirs of My Time*, especially 57–60; Catherine C. Phillips, *Jessie Benton Frémont*, 32–43; Sumner to George Bancroft, April 22, 1846, Bancroft Papers.

[9] Mary P. Mann, *Life of Horace Mann*, 45; John Wentworth, *Congressional Reminiscences*, 48–49; John Fairfield to his wife, January 12, 1836, Fairfield, *Letters*, 71; Dyer, *Great Senators*, 202–203; H. S. Foote, *Casket of Reminiscences*, 330–339.

native of North Carolina, Polk had attended the University of North
Carolina, moved West and in 1820 settled as a lawyer in Columbia,
Tennessee. Five years later he was elected to Congress. Only thirty-
four years old in 1830, he was already a leading figure in the House.
Of middle height, he had a high, broad forehead, penetrating dark
eyes and a somewhat serious cast of countenance, occasionally light-
ened by an exceptionally winning smile. His slender frame gave the
impression of delicacy, but he was extremely hardworking and
capable of great endurance. If his calm, incessant voice, setting forth
a long array of facts and close argument, exasperated persons like
Adams, it ordinarily impressed his audiences.[10]

Like Benton, Polk steadfastly opposed what he considered to be
the conspiracy to pauperize agriculture and labor for the benefit of
the business community. "Since 1815," he declared, "the action of
the Government has been . . . essentially vicious; I repeat, sir, essentially vicious." He gave a careful and comprehensive definition of
the American System: "it is a tripod, it is a stool that stands upon
three legs; first, high prices of the public lands. . . . the policy of
this branch of the system is, to sell your lands high, prevent thereby
the inducements to emigration, retain a population of paupers in the
East, who may, of necessity, be driven into manufactories, to labor at
low wages for their daily bread. The second branch of the system is
high duties . . . first, to protect the manufacturer, by enabling him
to sell his wares at higher prices, and next to produce an excess of
revenue. The third branch of the system is internal improvements,
which is the sponge which is to suck up the excess of revenue."[11]

C. C. Cambreleng, the crony of Van Buren and Representative from
the city of New York, gave Polk active support. Another North
Carolinian, now in his early forties, Cambreleng had left school at the
age of twelve, gone to New York at sixteen and entered a highly
successful business career. For a dozen years or so, he lived an adven-
turous life, roaming around Europe in the midst of the Napoleonic
wars, part of the time as agent for John Jacob Astor, and finally settling in New York. His curiosity always had an intellectual bent,

[10] "James K. Polk," *Democratic Review*, II, 208 (May, 1838); Ben: Perley Poore,
Perley's Reminiscences of Sixty Years in the National Metropolis, I, 328–330; Anne
Royall, *Letters from Alabama on Various Subjects*, 182; O. P. Temple, *Notable
Men of Tennessee from 1833 to 1875*, 253–254.
[11] Polk in the House, March 29, 1830, *Register of Debates*, 21 Congress 1 Session,
698–699. John Bell, Polk's main competitor for the speakership of the House and
the leadership of the Jackson party in Tennessee, had different views on the
American System. For the struggle between Polk and Bell, see T. P. Abernethy,
"The Origin of the Whig Party in Tennessee," *Mississippi Valley Historical Review*, XII, 504–522.

and reflection and experience combined to make him a militant free trader. In 1821 he drifted into politics, probably with the encouragement of Van Buren, and won a seat in Congress. From the outset he was opposed by the mercantile community. "How violent and embittered that hostility has been made of late years," someone said in 1839, ". . . is too well known to require comment." The bonds with Van Buren strengthened through the years. "As honest as the steelyard and as direct in the pursuit of his purpose as a shot from a culverin," Van Buren said of his friend. ". . . I have never known a man to whose statements I would more readily trust my own interests."

Cambreleng had great influence in the House. A small man, inclining toward portliness, alert in expression, friendly in manner, he would be in his seat early, deep in perusal of a huge mass of documents, or tirelessly answering letters from constituents. When the Speaker called the House to order, he would apply a double quizzing glass to his eye, gaze around the hall and then return to work. Though always seemingly immersed in his papers, he was ever ready to leap to his feet for the heated exchanges which frequently enlivened the House. He excelled on economic questions — his Report from the Commerce and Navigation Committee in 1830 was an early classic of American free-trade literature — but he spoke on all issues of human liberty. His rebuke of Edward Everett's gratuitous defense of slavery in 1826 — the handsome New Englander, ex-minister, ex-college professor, had announced, "There is no cause in which I would sooner buckle a knapsack on my back and put a musket on my shoulder than that of putting down a servile insurrection at the South" — was not soon forgotten.[12]

3

The reorganized cabinet should have provided further aid for the common cause, but political necessities and Jackson's own amiability intervened. The new set of ministers turned out to be only slightly more concerned with executing the presidential policy than the old.

The Secretary of State, Jackson's old friend, Edward Livingston, of Louisiana, was a charming, scholarly gentleman, devoted to literature, historical research, legal reform and his lovely wife, but with-

[12] Quotations from "Churchill Caldom Cambreleng," *Democratic Review*, VI, 151 (August, 1839); Van Buren, *Autobiography*, 655; Henry Wilson, *History of the Rise and Fall of the Slave Power in America*, I, 329. See also "Walter Barrett" (Joseph A. Scoville), *The Old Merchants of New York City*, III, 115–126; Royall, *Letters from Alabama*, 192; "Glances at Congress," *Democratic Review*, I, 80 (October, 1837).

out much interest in broad social questions or much zest for controversy. "His faults," said Justice Catron of the Supreme Court, "lay in a kindly nature, and an easy credulity." "He is a polished scholar, an able writer, and a most excellent man," said Jackson himself, "but he knows nothing of mankind." His memory was beginning to fail by 1831, and, absorbed by the affairs of his department, he took small part in the other matters of government.[13]

Louis McLane, the Secretary of the Treasury, was a bold, ambitious man of Federalist antecedents who was aiming systematically for the presidency. He had, as Roger B. Taney put it, "great tact, and always knew whether he should address himself to the patriotism, the magnanimity, the pride the vanity, the hopes or the fears of the person on whom he wished to operate." Even Van Buren was inveigled for a time into helping promote McLane; but, as McLane worked himself up from Minister to England to head of the Treasury and in 1833 to Secretary of State, Van Buren came to recognize a dangerous rival. McLane was no trifling opponent. Jackson liked him, and he exerted great influence over the indecisive members of the cabinet, particularly Livingston and Lewis Cass.[14]

Cass, Secretary of War, a grave, lazy, dark-faced man, almost fifty years old, had been Governor of the Michigan Territory. Jackson and Taney provided almost identical testimony on his main weakness. "It is hard for him to say no," remarked the President, "and he thinks all men honest." Or, as Taney put it, Cass was virtually "unwilling to say *no* to any proposition not morally wrong, when earnestly pressed upon him by one whom he esteems." He always tried to offend no one. A temperance man, he would yet sit at Washington banquets with wine before him and every few minutes raise the glass to his lips, going elaborately through the motions, but not drinking. His political views were those of a Western Jeffersonian. Caring deeply about home rule and political democracy, he was quite indifferent to economic questions. McLane understood him perfectly and fairly well controlled his opinions.[15]

Levi Woodbury, Secretary of the Navy, was a truly noncommittal man beside whom even Van Buren might seem a chatterbox. A per-

[13] Catron to H. D. Gilpin, October 8, 1844, Gilpin Papers; Jackson to Van Buren, December 17, 1831, Jackson, *Correspondence*, IV, 385; R. B. Taney, Bank War Manuscript, 75.

[14] Taney, Bank War Manuscript, 77–79; Van Buren, *Autobiography, passim*, especially 566–617.

[15] Jackson to Van Buren, December 17, 1831, Jackson, *Correspondence*, IV, 385; Taney, Bank War Manuscript, 81–82; John Fairfield to his wife, February 6, 1836, Fairfield, *Letters*, 96; W. C. Bryant to his wife, January 29, 1832, Parke Godwin, *Bryant*, I, 269.

son of strong and shrewd mind, he undoubtedly held definite ideas of his own; but he was singularly wary, never committing himself to a position upon which he was not immediately obliged to act, and then never further than that action required. In the heated cabinet meetings, Woodbury usually tried to mediate between McLane and Taney without ever indicating his own views. "If he expressed an opinion upon a measure," commented Taney with some irritation, "he most commonly added to it many qualifications and hesitations and doubts, that sometimes appeared to take it back again." Woodbury probably feared to embarrass his future by acting too heroically in the present. As Cambreleng put it, "Woodbury keeps snug and plays out of all the corners of his eyes." [16]

Roger B. Taney, Attorney General, was the spearhead of radicalism in the new cabinet. A Maryland lawyer, fifty-four years old in 1831, he had once, like McLane, been a Federalist; but he left the party during the War of 1812 and by 1824 was a Jackson leader in Maryland. A tall, sharp-faced man, with nearsighted eyes, a large mouth and irregular yellow teeth, generally clamped on a long black cigar, he made a bad first impression. He was ordinarily dressed in ill-fitting black clothes; and his voice, still bearing traces of an impediment, was flat and hollow. But people soon forgot his appearance. He would speak in low tones, sincerely and without gestures, relying on the lucidity of the argument and his own quiet conviction. His performances before the Supreme Court impressed both Marshall and Story, and his appointment as Attorney General was widely applauded.

While not a dominating personality, like McLane, Taney was a man of unshakable determination. His experience as a lawyer had deepened his feeling against the unnecessary concentration of power in the hands of the business community; and from the first, the radicals, somewhat to their surprise, found him their spokesman in the inner council. Cambreleng wrote to Van Buren early in 1832 that Taney was "the only efficient man of sound principles in the Cabinet." [17]

William T. Barry, Postmaster General, alone survived the reorganization, largely because neither he nor his position was considered important. He had shown his radical leanings in the Kentucky Relief

[16] Taney, Bank War Manuscript, 83–84; Cambreleng to Van Buren, January 4, 1832, Van Buren Papers.

[17] Cambreleng to Van Buren, February 5, 1832, Van Buren Papers. C. B. Swisher, *Roger B. Taney*, is an admirable biography. See also Samuel Tyler, *Memoir of Roger Brooke Taney, LL.D.*, especially 212; W. W. Story, *Life and Letters of Joseph Story*, I, 493, II, 122; J. E. Semmes, *John H. B. Latrobe and His Times, 1803–1891*, 202–203; J. W. Forney, *Anecdotes of Public Men*, II, 226.

War; but he lacked both firmness and intellectual conviction. He would declaim "eloquently and beautifully," Taney dryly commented, in a manner "particularly impressive before a jury or a public assembly," which was to say he "thought loosely and reasoned loosely and without point." His administration of the post office was wretched. Friends exploited his geniality for their own profit, and he was incapable of preserving order or even knowing what was going on. William Cullen Bryant thought him in 1832 "apparently the wreck of a man of talents." [18]

The cabinet, then, promised Jackson highly uncertain support for a radical program. Far from being an effective instrument of the executive, it was a group of squabbling men, some in basic disagreement with the President, and one at least intent on defeating his policy. The radicals severely criticized Jackson's tolerance of dissent. "By forming his cabinets upon these principles," Taney said later, "he undoubtedly embarrassed his administration and endangered its success. . . . he raised up obstacles to the execution of his own measures: and then found himself compelled to remove them. This was always unpleasant; made new enemies: and weakened his strength." [19]

Jackson had great respect for men who differed with him, so long as they conducted their opposition honestly. Moreover, like more recent Presidents, he found it difficult to fire people no matter how fully they demonstrated their incompetence or disloyalty. He kept McLane in the cabinet, for example, long after his usefulness had ceased, and only the strongest pressure led him to get rid of Barry. His complaisance may further have been prompted by a desire to conciliate conservatives within the party. As long as men like McLane and Livingston had the President's ear, he had a much better chance of retaining the confidence of the respectable classes.

It should be remembered, too, that the conception of the function of the cabinet was in process of change. Washington, thinking of the cabinet as a council for reconciling antagonistic interests, had appointed a Jefferson to one post and a Hamilton to another. John Quincy Adams retained somewhat this conception as late as 1825, when he considered inviting his defeated opponents into his official family. Under Jackson the cabinet was in transition, and the debate over the dismissal of Duane in 1833 would show the confusion of ideas; but the imperatives of the party system were slowly requiring the cabinet to be an efficient arm of the executive.[20]

[18] Taney, Bank War Manuscript, 85; Bryant to his wife, January 29, 1832, Godwin, *Bryant*, I, 290; Van Buren, *Autobiography*, 588–589.

[19] Taney, Bank War Manuscript, 91.

[20] For an acute analysis of some aspects of this change, see Pendleton Herring, *The Politics of Democracy*, 69–81.

4

The driving energy of Jacksonian democracy, like that of any aggressive reform movement, came from a small group of men, joined together by essential sympathies in a concerted attempt to transform the existing order. Communion among these men was frank and free, and the men themselves were utterly loyal to the cause. Few nationally known politicians, available for cabinet posts, could meet the necessary standards of selflessness and candor. As a result, Jackson had to turn away from his cabinet for his most confidential counsel to men more basically dissatisfied with the existing order. There thus sprang into existence the celebrated Kitchen Cabinet, "an influence, at Washington," as one member of the official cabinet ominously described it, "unknown to the constitution and to the country." [21]

Such an influence naturally drew to a considerable degree on rising social groups as yet denied the prestige to which they felt their power and energies entitled them. One such class was, of course, that of the military hero, of which Jackson himself was the outstanding example. Another consisted of the literary man in general and of the newspaperman in particular. The journalist had hitherto been indulgently accepted as the friend or servant of the governing class, but never as an equal. William Cullen Bryant wryly described the attitude toward his profession: "Contempt is too harsh a word for it, perhaps, but it is far below respect." [22]

Many newspapermen rankled under this disdain. When the election of Jackson cracked the old aristocracy wide open, they tried to flock through the breach; and Jackson proceeded to fill many offices with newspaper editors. This act instantly turned the status of the press into a live issue. The old governing class, having lost temporarily to the military hero, hoped at least to avoid the final humiliation of bowing to the journalist, and the furor over the spoils system centered particularly on the appointment of editors. Jackson boldly defended his course: "why should this class of citizens be excluded from offices to which others, not more patriotic, nor presenting stronger claims as to qualification may aspire?" [23] But even he dared not give them important positions. Their substantial influence had to be exerted in other ways.

The two leading members of the Kitchen Cabinet, both ex-newspapermen, were Amos Kendall and Francis Preston Blair. Kendall was

[21] William J. Duane, *Narrative and Correspondence Concerning the Removal of the Deposites*, 9.

[22] W. C. Bryant, "William Leggett," *Democratic Review*, VI, 18 (July, 1839).

[23] Jackson to Z. I. Miller, May 13, 1829, Bassett, *Jackson*, 450.

born in 1789 on a barren farm at Dunstable, Massachusetts. His poor health and studious disposition singled him out early as the scholar of the family, and, in between periods of labor on the farm, he attended country school and then Dartmouth. At college he was a reserved, priggish boy; a classmate observed dryly in 1835 that if he had become "an intriguing, managing, artful politician," with an ingratiating personality and a capacity to manipulate people, "he has entirely changed his character." [24]

After Dartmouth Kendall went to Groton where he taught in the Academy and studied law. This later seemed to him an especially happy time, "but my happiness was too irregular and tumultous" (he was unrequitedly in love), and openings for a young lawyer without connections seemed scant in New England. At the age of twenty-five he emigrated to Kentucky. At Lexington he met a pleasant law student, who turned out to be Henry Clay's brother, and soon he was introduced to Mrs. Clay, who asked him to tutor her children. The stiff New Englander, with his intolerable gravity, relentless conscience and yet shy charm, delighted easy-going Lucretia Clay, the mistress of Ashland. She tutored Kendall, polishing his manners, brightening his conversation and making him fit for society. [25]

After staying at Ashland for about a year, Kendall left to begin law practice, with Clay still in Europe helping negotiate peace with Britain. Early in 1816, while revisiting Lexington, he fell seriously sick. As soon as he could be moved, Mrs. Clay had him brought out to Ashland, nursing him, as Kendall said later, "with the kindness of a mother." Years after, when Lucretia Clay was long dead and her Yankee protégé Jackson's chief adviser, this episode flowered into a tale of Kendall as a monster incapable of gratitude or loyalty. He had come to Lexington, a friendless youth, the story went, and Mrs. Clay had taken him ill into her home and nursed him to recovery. Henry Clay then treated him like a son, set him up with a newspaper — only to have Kendall betray his benefactor and become the hireling of his worst enemy. [26]

The man who actually started Kendall as an editor was Colonel Richard M. Johnson. Kendall plunged into Kentucky journalism with celerity, quickly adapting himself to its rugged ways. At one period,

[24] "Spectator" in the *Boston Post*, December 30, 1835; see also *Argus of Western America*, May 21, 1828; Amos Kendall, *Autobiography*, 1–68.

[25] Kendall to Caleb Butler, May 13, 1835, Miscellaneous Letters, Library of Congress; Kendall, *Autobiography*, 131.

[26] *Argus of Western America*, May 21, 1828; *Kendall's Expositor*, December 16, 1841; Kendall, *Autobiography*, 115–149; Harriet Martineau, *Retrospect of Western Travel*, I, 259–260.

as editor of the *Argus of Western America* at Frankfort, he had to carry a dirk, at another a pistol, and he always made his pen do the service of both. His trenchant intelligence, his honesty and pertinacity, his facility both at lofty exhortation and at coarse invective, quickly made the *Argus* the best paper in the state and soon one of the most influential in the West.

In the Kentucky struggle over banking, Kendall at first opposed the relief measures, considering that salvation for the lower classes lay in the direction of hard money rather than inflation. But with Johnson and W. T. Barry, another of his patrons, leading the Relief party, and the issue so formulated as to make an alliance with the aristocracy the only alternative, Kendall had small choice but to support their program. Eventually he became a director of the Commonwealth Bank and later claimed to have been responsible for restraining its policy of note issue.

When the struggle shifted from the expediency to the constitutionality of the relief system, he took a happier part, vehemently attacking the Supreme Court and judicial legislation, both as editor of the *Argus* and as ghostwriter for the Governor. In national politics, Kendall, like all Kentucky, supported its favorite son, and for Kendall, of course, personal obligations confirmed the loyalty. After backing Clay in 1824, he proposed to remain neutral during the Adams administration rather than turn on the husband of his benefactress; but the Jacksonians insisted that the *Argus*, as the organ of Kentucky progressivism, speak out for their candidate, even threatening to start a rival sheet. Clay's continuing support of the Old Court party finally pushed Kendall into the opposition.[27]

Jackson's election gave Kendall his great opportunity to leave Kentucky. He was at first somewhat appalled by the excesses of the national capital. The ladies laced too tightly and exposed their shoulders too brazenly for his Yankee sensibilities, while the "ridiculous English custom" of dining after dark irritated him. A picture is preserved of Kendall at a Washington reception, snatching a cup of coffee from a Negro waiter, and watching with glum disapproval the men crowding around the wine and spirits on the sideboard.

But he impressed the right people. Van Buren remarked, "Kendall is to be an influential man. I wish the President would invite him to dinner." Kendall was not only invited, but soon received appointment

[27] *Argus of Western America*, May 28, 1828; Kendall to Joseph Desha, April 9, 1831, Desha to Kendall, May 6, 1831, "Correspondence between Governor Joseph Desha and Amos Kendall — 1831–1835," James A. Padgett, ed., *Register of the Kentucky State Historical Society*, XXXVIII, 8–10, 13; "Amos Kendall," *Democratic Review*, I, 408–409 (March, 1838).

as fourth auditor of the Treasury. There he went conscientiously to work and discovered large frauds in the accounts of his predecessor, Tobias Watkins, a close friend of John Quincy Adams. This feat, which gave the spoils system a temporary odor of sanctity, especially endeared him to the President. Kendall himself found rotation-in-office less inspiring in practice than in theory: "I turned out six clerks on Saturday. . . . It was the most painful thing I ever did." [28]

Bent, nearsighted, badly dressed, with premature white hair, sallow complexion and a hacking asthmatic cough, Kendall was an unprepossessing figure. On a blazing July day he would wear a white broadcloth greatcoat, buttoned to the throat. If he were suffering from one of his piercing headaches, he would bind a white handkerchief about his head. "Poor wretch," exclaimed Henry A. Wise, "as he rode his Rosinante down Pennsylvania Avenue, he looked like Death on the pale horse." [29]

His chronic bad health may have created a special bond of sympathy with the President, and Jackson soon began to rely on Kendall for aid in writing his messages, first on the Indian question and then on general policy. Gradually, Kendall's supreme skill in interpreting, verbalizing and documenting Jackson's intuitions made him indispensable. The President would lie on his bed beneath the picture of his Rachel, smoking away and pouring out his ideas in vigorous but imprecise language. Kendall would smooth out a paragraph and read it back. The old General, shaking his head, would try again, and Kendall would revise and work it over, getting closer and closer, till his chief would relax satisfied, and Kendall himself be surprised at the full force of the point. [30]

When he first went to Washington, Kendall favored Calhoun for the succession, but he soon saw that the future of the radical program rested with Van Buren. [31] During the early months of 1830, as the feud with Calhoun developed, the Kentucky group began to discuss the need for superseding Duff Green and the *United States Telegraph* with a new administration organ. Barry suggested Francis Preston Blair, Kendall's successor on the *Argus*, as editor.

Blair, a native-born Virginian taken to Kentucky as a child, was

[28] Kendall, *Autobiography*, 278–292; J. A. Hamilton, *Reminiscences*, 130.

[29] H. A. Wise in the House, December 21, 1838, *Congressional Globe*, 25 Congress 3 Session, Appendix, 386. See also J. B. Derby, *Political Reminiscences*, 58–59; Colonel Claiborne's recollections of the Washington press, from the *New Orleans Delta*, Frederic Hudson, *Journalism in the United States from 1690 to 1872*, 245.

[30] H. A. Wise, *Seven Decades*, 117; Kendall, *Autobiography*, 686.

[31] T. P. Moore to F. P. Blair, October 30, 1833, Blair-Rives Papers.

thirty-nine years old in 1830. As a young man, he was so delicate that his prospective father-in-law tried to discourage his daughter from marriage: "You will be a widow in six months." "I would rather be Frank's widow than any other man's wife," the girl replied, and Blair's vitality amazed everyone who knew him for the next fifty years. Like Kendall, Blair supported Clay in 1824, but the Relief War drove a wedge between them, and Blair drifted to his more natural alliance with the Jackson party. "I never deserted your banner," he told Clay, "until the questions on which you and I so frequently differed in private discussion — (State rights, the Bank, the power of the Judiciary, &c.) — became the criterions to distinguish the parties." He was a fiery pamphleteer during the Relief War, entering the lists with much more enthusiasm than Kendall, becoming Clerk of the New Court and later president of the Commonwealth Bank. After Kendall's departure he was the logical man to edit the *Argus*.[32]

Though Van Buren's friends had been suspicious of Duff Green since 1828, the initiative toward a new press was taken mainly by the Kentucky group. Kendall seems to have broached the subject to Blair in July, 1830. Blair, who was $40,000 in debt, required certain preliminary financial arrangements, which Kendall took care of, and late in the year Blair was called to Washington. The inner circle anxiously awaited this new champion, who was to chastise Duff Green, whittle down Calhoun and defend the administration. There appeared an insignificant-looking man, weighing slightly over one hundred pounds, sandy-haired and hatchet-faced, with a black patch covering a head wound he had got when the stage overturned near Washington. Major Lewis observed pointedly, "Mr. Blair, we want stout hearts and sound heads here." But a glance at Blair's clear, blue, unblinking eyes, and a few minutes of his keen and sensible conversation, wiped out the initial misgivings.[33]

The first number of the *Washington Globe*, as it was called, came out in December. Its editor meanwhile plunged more zestfully than Kendall into Washington life, attending parties and receptions, drinking sherry and champagne, and awaking in the morning with feelings which, as he sadly noted, "make a man fashionable and miserable." His wife vigilantly watched over his health, making him ride horse-

[32] Blair to Clay, October 3, 1827, W. E. Smith, *The Francis Preston Blair Family in Politics*, I, 46–47, also 21, 31.

[33] Parton, *Jackson*, III, 335–337; Hudson, *Journalism*, 252; G. C. Verplanck to Van Buren, December 6, 1828, Silas Wright to Van Buren, December 9, 1828, Blair to Kendall, December 24, 1842, Van Buren Papers; Kendall to Virgil Maxcy, November 12, 1830, Miscellaneous Letters, New York Public Library; Kendall, *Autobiography*, 372–374.

back daily, work in the garden and down a tumbler of rye whisky after every meal.

Blair was profoundly impressed with the President. "I can tell you that he is as much superior here as he was with our generals during the war," he wrote after a few months. Jackson on his part warmed to Blair as he had to Van Buren and Kendall. "Give it to Blair," he would say when he wanted to reach the public (he pronounced it *Blar*), and Blair would convert the President's suggestions into fighting editorials, ordinarily penciled on scraps of paper held on his knee, sometimes at such furious speed that two boys were kept busy carrying copy to the typesetters. In 1832 John C. Rives, a huge, shaggy man, nearly six and a half feet tall and weighing two hundred and forty pounds, joined the *Globe*, becoming Blair's partner in 1834 and relieving him of the business end. The two worked together in perfect harmony. As Rives liked to say, they made "the ugliest looking pair in the country." [34]

Like Kendall, Blair went to Washington with predilections for Calhoun; but, as he participated in the conferences about the President, he came to see that Van Buren, Benton and Taney had the welfare of the common man much more at heart. His affectionate nature led him to warm personal attachments with all three, and particularly with Van Buren.

In a time of vague but intense apprehension any group so obscure in its workings as the Kitchen Cabinet became inevitably an object of deep suspicion, increased in Kendall's case by the fact that bad health kept him from appearing often in public. One Congressman told Harriet Martineau that he waited for four sessions before catching a glimpse of Kendall, and William Duane, in three months as Secretary of the Treasury, saw Kendall only four times and never for longer than ten minutes. "He is supposed to be the moving spring of the whole administration; the thinker, planner, and doer," wrote Miss Martineau; "but it is all in the dark. Documents are issued of an excellence which prevents their being attributed to persons who take the responsibility of them; a correspondence is kept up all over the country for which no one seems to be answerable; work is done, of goblin extent and with goblin speed, which makes men look about them with a superstitious wonder; and the invisible Amos Kendall has the credit of it all." As Henry A. Wise shrilled in the House in

[34] T. H. Clay, "Two Years with Old Hickory," *Atlantic Monthly*, LX, 187–190 (August, 1887); Van Buren, *Autobiography*, 323; Smith, *Blair Family*, I, 77, 100; J. C. Rives to Kendall, December 21, 1842, Van Buren Papers; Hudson, *Journalism*, 238–253.

1838, "He was the President's *thinking* machine, and his *writing* machine — ay, and his *lying* machine! . . . he was chief overseer, chief reporter, amanuensis, scribe, accountant general, man of all work — nothing was well done without the aid of his diabolical genius."

Dr. Robert Mayo, a frustrated brain truster, revenging himself in the modern manner by writing a book against the administration which refused to follow his advice, set forth the thesis that Kendall was bent on revolution. This vile purpose was expounded, according to Mayo, in an unpublished manuscript, "the great principle of which was, that all the burthen of supporting the government and supporting schools, colleges, roads, internal improvements, city expenses, generally, should be laid upon those, and those only, who had property above the value of $6,000. . . . All above 6,000 dollars, would thus, in time, be *razed* down to that amount."

The theory of Kendall's ascendancy was accepted in less hysterical form by other enemies of the administration, including John Quincy Adams, who observed in 1840 of Jackson and Van Buren, "Both . . . have been for twelve years the tool of Amos Kendall, the ruling mind of their dominion." But there can be no doubt that Jackson dominated the Kitchen Cabinet and used it for his own purposes.[35]

[35] Martineau, *Retrospect*, I, 257–258; Duane, *Narrative*, 130; H. A. Wise in the House, December 21, 1838, *Congressional Globe*, 25 Congress 3 Session, Appendix, 386; Robert Mayo, *A Chapter of Sketches on Finance*, especially 110–111; Adams, *Memoirs*, X, 366; see also Adams to Edward Everett, November 14, 1837, Everett Papers.

VII BEGINNINGS OF THE
BANK WAR

IN 1836 the charter of the Second Bank of the United States was to expire. This institution was not in the later sense a national bank. It was a banking corporation, located in Philadelphia, privately controlled, but possessing unique and profitable relations with the government. To its capital of thirty-five million dollars, the government had subscribed one fifth. It served as repository of the public funds, which it could use for its own banking purposes without payment of interest. It could issue bank notes up to the physical ability of the president and cashier to sign them; after 1827 it evaded this limitation by the invention of "branch drafts," which looked and circulated like notes but were actually bills of exchange. The Bank was not to be taxed by the states and no similar institution was to be chartered by Congress. In return for these privileges the Bank paid a bonus of one and a half million dollars, transferred public funds and made public payments without charge, and allowed the government to appoint five out of the twenty-five directors. The Secretary of the Treasury could remove the government deposits provided he laid the reasons before Congress.

1

Even advocates of the Bank conceded that this charter bestowed too much power. That staunch conservative Hezekiah Niles, writing in the heat of the fight for renewal, declared he "would not have the present bank re-chartered, with its present power . . . for the reason that the bank has more power than we would grant to any set of men, unless responsible to the people" (though he ultimately supported the Bank). Nathan Appleton, who had tried vainly to modify the charter in 1832, wrote carefully but emphatically in 1841: "A great central power, independent of the general or state governments, is an anomaly in our system. Such a power over the currency is the most tremendous which can be established. Without the assur-

ance that it will be managed by men, free from the common imperfections of human nature, we are safer without it." [1]

There could be no question about the reality of the Bank's power.
It enjoyed a virtual monopoly of the currency and practically complete control over credit and the price level. Biddle's own testimony
disclosed its extent: —

> Q.3. Has the bank at any time oppressed any of the State banks?
> A. Never. There are very few banks which might not have been
> destroyed by an exertion of the powers of the bank. None have
> ever been injured.

To radical Democrats like Taney, Biddle's tone implied that he
thought himself entitled to credit for his forbearance. "It is this power
concentrated in the hands of a few individuals," Taney declared,
" — exercised in secret and unseen although constantly felt — irresponsible and above the control of the people or the Government for the 20
years of its charter, that is sufficient to awaken any man in the country if the danger is brought distinctly to his view." [2]

There could be no question either about the Bank's pretensions to
complete independence of popular control. Biddle brooked no opposition from within, and the government representatives sat through
the directors' meetings baffled and indignant. "I never saw such a
Board of *directors*," raged Henry D. Gilpin, " — it is a misuse of terms
of *directed*. . . . We know absolutely nothing. There is no consultation, no exchanges of sentiments, no production of correspondence, but
merely a rapid, superficial, general statement, or a reference to a Committee which will probably never report." He added, "We are perfect
cyphers." [3]

Biddle not only suppressed all internal dissent but insisted flatly that
the Bank was not accountable to the government or the people. In
1824 the president of the Washington branch had written Biddle,
"As . . . there are other interests to be attended to [besides those of
the Bank], especially that of the Government, I have deemed it proper
to see and consult with the President." Biddle hotly replied, "If . . .
you think that there are other interests to be attended to besides those
with which you are charged by the administration of the bank, we

[1] *Niles' Register*, May 12, 1832; Nathan Appleton, *Remarks on Currency and Banking*, 36.

[2] *Register of Debates*, 21 Congress 1 Session, Appendix, 103; Taney to Thomas Ellicott, February 20, 1832, Taney Papers. See also Taney, Bank War Manuscript, 14–15.

[3] Gilpin to G. M. Dallas, January 26, 1833, to J. K. Kane, January 27, 1833, Gilpin Letterbooks.

deem it right to correct what is a total misapprehension. . . . The moment this appointment [of the five government directors] takes place the Executive has completely fulfilled its functions. The entire responsibility is thenceforward in the directors, and no officer of the Government, from the President downwards, has the least right, the least authority, the least pretence, for interference in the concerns of the bank. . . . This invocation of the Government, therefore . . . is totally inconsistent with the temper and spirit which belong to the officers of the bank, who should regard only the rights of the bank and the instructions of those who govern it, and who should be at all times prepared to execute the orders of the board, in direct opposition, if need be, to the personal interests and wishes of the President and every officer of the Government." [4]

In Biddle's eyes the Bank was thus an independent corporation, on a level with the state, and not responsible to it except as the narrowest interpretation of the charter compelled. Biddle tried to strengthen this position by flourishing a theory that the Bank was beyond political good or evil, but Alexander Hamilton had written with far more candor that "such a bank is not a mere matter of private property, but a political machine of the greatest importance to the State." [5] The Second Bank of the United States was, in fact, as Hamilton had intended such a bank should be, the keystone in the alliance between the government and the business community.

2

Though conservative Jeffersonians, led by Madison and Gallatin, had come to accept Hamilton's Bank as necessary, John Taylor's dialectics and Randolph's invective kept anti-Bank feeling alive, and men in the old radical tradition remained profoundly convinced of the evil of paper money. Jackson's hard-money views prompted his opposition to the Tennessee relief system in 1820. "Every one that knows me," as he told Polk in 1833, "does know, that I have been always opposed to the U. States Bank, nay all Banks." [6] Benton, from

[4] Biddle to Thomas Swann, March 17, 1824, *Senate Document*, 23 Congress 2 Session, no. 17 (Tyler Report), 297–298.

[5] "Report on a National Bank," Hamilton, *Works*, III, 424.

[6] Jackson to Polk, December 23, 1833, Jackson, *Correspondence*, V, 236. Jackson told Nicholas Biddle late in 1829, "I do not dislike your Bank any more than all banks." Bassett, *Jackson*, 599. Cf. C. J. Ingersoll to Biddle, February 2, 1832: "General Jackson's antipathy is not to the Bank of the United States in particular, but to all banks whatever. He considers all the State Banks unconstitutional and impolitic and thinks that there should be no Currency but coin." R. C. H. Catterall, *Second Bank of the United States*, 185 n. All serious students of the Bank

talks with Macon and Randolph and his observations of the collapse of the paper system in 1819, similarly concluded that the only safeguard against future disaster lay in restricting the system; and that, to this end, the government should deal only in gold and silver, thus withdrawing support from the issues of privately owned banks.[7] Van Buren, Cambreleng, Taney and Polk more or less shared these views.

The ordinary follower of Jackson in the West also regarded the Bank with strong latent antagonism, but for very different reasons. Its policy in 1819 of recalling specie and checking the note issue of state banks had gained it few friends in any class, and, in Kentucky especially, the Relief War kept resentments alive. But this anti-Bank feeling owed little to reasoned distrust of paper money or to a Jeffersonian desire for specie. As a debtor section the West naturally preferred cheap money; and Kentucky, for example, which most vociferously opposed the United States Bank, also resorted most ardently to wildcat banking of its own. The crux of the Kentucky fight against the Bank was not the paper system, but outside control: the Bank's sin lay not in circulating paper money itself, but in restraining its circulation by Kentucky banks. Almost nowhere, apart from doctrinaires like Jackson and Benton, did Westerners object to state banks under local control.

Indeed, during the eighteen-twenties, even the Philadelphia Bank to a considerable degree overcame the Western prejudices against it.[8] In Tennessee, for example, until 1829 "both [Governor William] Carroll and the legislature favored federal as well as state banks, nor does anything in the history of the state indicate that there was any general feeling against such institutions before Jackson became President."[9]

War agree that Jackson's hostility to the Bank was of long standing and based on principle, not the result of a burst of temper over the conduct of a branch at Portsmouth, New Hampshire, or elsewhere. Cf. *ibid.*, 183, 195; Bassett, *Jackson*, 589–593.

[7] For Benton's account of the origin of his economic views, see his speeches in the Senate, March 14, 1838, *Congressional Globe*, 25 Congress 2 Session, Appendix, 216, and January 16, 1840, *Congressional Globe*, 26 Congress 1 Session, Appendix, 118–119.

[8] This was less true in Missouri, where there was considerable hard-money sentiment which the most careful student of the question ascribes in large part to Benton's personal influence. C. H. McClure, *Opposition in Missouri to Thomas Hart Benton*, 23 n.

[9] T. P. Abernethy, "Andrew Jackson and the Rise of Southwestern Democracy," *American Historical Review*, XXXIII, 70. Cf. St. George L. Sioussat, "Some Phases of Tennessee Politics in the Jackson Period," *ibid.*, XIV, 69: "though originally predisposed to hostility against the Bank of the United States, Tennessee, or rather the dominant western portion of the state, was yet quite willing to accept the

Caleb Atwater, a lusty Jackson man from Ohio and something of a professional Westerner, expressed a widespread feeling when he wrote in 1831, "Refuse to re-charter the bank, and Pittsburgh, Cincinnati, Louisville, St. Louis, Nashville, and New Orleans, will be crushed at one blow." Even Frank Blair's first large-scale blast against the Bank in the *Argus of Western America* after Jackson's election did not come until December 23, 1829, many months after Eastern groups had begun to agitate the question. This editorial — actually prefaced by an anti-Bank quote from a Van Buren paper in New York — appealed to the Kentucky fear of Eastern control; and all through 1830 the *Argus* continued to focus on the power and privileges of the Bank and the consequent peril to the Commonwealth Bank of Kentucky, never on the general implications of the paper system.[10]

Some writers have talked of frontier life as if it bred traits of "individualism" and equality which made Westerners mystically opposed to banks. Actually, like all other groups in the population, Westerners favored banks when they thought they could profit by them and fought them when they thought others were profiting at their expense. The Western enthusiasm for an assault on the Bank came, not from an intuitive democratic *Weltschmerz* born in the American forest, nor from a Jeffersonian dislike of banks, but from a farmer-debtor desire to throw off restraints on the local issue of paper money.

Similar objections to control from Philadelphia ranged many Easterners against the Bank. State institutions hoped, by falling heir to the government deposits, to enlarge their banking capital, at no expense to themselves. Special grievances multiplied the motives. The state banks of New York, for example, envied the United States Bank because its loan operations were not restricted by Van Buren's safety-fund system. New York City had long resented the choice of Philadelphia as the nation's financial capital. Thus in a fight against the Bank Jackson could expect the backing of a decent minority of the local banking interests.

But there was still another and more reliable source of support. In March, 1829, after the grim depression winter, a group of Philadelphia workingmen, under the very shadow of the Bank, called a

---

benefits of a branch of the great bank, as long as times were good and credit was easy, and only gradually listened to and joined in the attack on that institution, which was begun in the year of Jackson's inauguration."

[10] Caleb Atwater, *Remarks Made on a Tour to Prairie du Chien; Thence to Washington City, in 1829*, 281; *Argus of Western America*, December 23, 1829, March 3, May 19, 1830, etc.

meeting "opposed to the chartering of any more new banks." The hard times were blamed upon the "too great extension of paper credit," and the gathering concluded by appointing a committee, "without confining ourselves to the working classes," to draw up a report on the banking system. The committee, which was dominated by intellectuals, included two leading economists, William M. Gouge, editor of the *Philadelphia Gazette*, and Condy Raguet, editor of the *Free Trade Advocate*, as well as William Duane, the famous old Jeffersonian journalist, his son William J. Duane, a lawyer, Roberts Vaux, the philanthropist, Reuben M. Whitney, a disgruntled businessman and former director of the Bank, and William English and James Ronaldson, two trade-union leaders. A week later the committee pronounced its verdict on the paper system: —

> That banks are useful as offices of deposit and transfer, we readily admit; but we cannot see that the benefits they confer in this way are so great as to compensate for the evils they produce, in . . . laying the foundation of *artificial* inequality of wealth, and, thereby, of *artificial* inequality of power. . . . If the present system of banking and paper money be extended and perpetuated, the great body of the working people must give over all hopes of ever acquiring any property.[11]

This view was spreading rapidly through the Middle and Northern states of the East in the late eighteen-twenties. The working class was no more affected by an instinctive antipathy toward banking than the backwoodsmen beyond the Alleghenies; but they never enjoyed the Western opportunity of having banks under their own control. Their opposition, instead of remaining fitful and capricious, began slowly to harden into formal anti-banking principle. Their bitter collective experience with paper money brought them to the same doctrines which Jackson and Benton gained from the Jeffersonian inheritance.

3

The war against the Bank thus enlisted the enthusiastic support of two basically antagonistic groups: on the one hand, debtor interests of the West and local banking interests of the East; on the other, Eastern workingmen and champions of the radical Jeffersonian tradition. The essential incompatibility between cheap money and hard could be somewhat concealed in the clamor of the crusade. Yet that incompatibility remained, and it came to represent increasingly a dif-

[11] *Free Trade Advocate*, May 9, 16, 1829.

ference between the Western and Eastern wings of the party, as the state banking group gradually abandoned the Jackson ranks. It was, indeed, a new form of the distinction between Western and Eastern readings of "equality." The West, in its quest for political democracy and home rule, did not object to paper money under local control, while the submerged classes of the East, seeking economic democracy, fought the whole banking swindle, as it seemed to them, root and branch.

The administration took care not to offend its cheap-money adherents by openly avowing hard-money ideas. Yet, the drift was unmistakable, and it rendered ineffective some of Jackson's Western followers for whom the battle was being pressed on lines they could not understand. Richard M. Johnson, for example, a staunch relief man and ancient foe of the Bank, served on the House committee which investigated the Bank in 1832; but he could take no real part in a hearing dominated by Cambreleng's hard-money views, and, though he signed Cambreleng's report, he confessed later that he had not asked a question or looked at a Bank book.[12] In general, the Western politicians, torn between the hard-money leanings of the White House and the cheap-money preferences of the folks back home, tended to pursue an erratic course.

Only the intellectuals, who did not have to think about re-election, effected a quick adjustment. Amos Kendall, who had been originally a hard-money man, perhaps from his Eastern upbringing, found no difficulty in reverting to his earlier opinions. Frank Blair also rapidly shifted his ground after coming to Washington. These were not basic reversals of position. Their allegiance, after all, had been primarily to a social class, not to a set of financial theories. The experience of the Kentucky relief system taught that salvation was not to be bought so cheaply: however much inflation might temporarily benefit a frontier state with a large debtor element, it was at best a risky expedient, imposed by political necessity; it never could serve as the basis of a national economic policy. Kendall and Blair, liberated from their local obligations, naturally turned to hard-money ideas as affording the only permanent solutions for the financial problems in favor of the non-business classes.

Thomas Hart Benton had long awaited the opportunity to fight for this solution. In the eighteen-twenties, when he fumed about the paper system, Nathaniel Macon would remark that it was useless to attempt reform unless the administration was with you. Now, at last, the administration seemed to be with him. Jackson's first message had ex-

---

[12] Benton, *Thirty Years' View*, I, 241.

pressed grave doubts about the constitutionality and expediency of the Bank. In 1830 the President continued to make ominous allusions to the subject of recharter. But the administration position was still not clear. Jackson's views were widely regarded as the expressions of private prejudice, not of party policy. Few people interpreted the Maysville veto as opening a campaign which might end by involving the Bank.[13] Even now, the Bank was confidently conducting backstairs negotiations with Secretary McLane to work out a formula for recharter, and it had inspired an effective press campaign to counteract Jackson's pronouncements. Benton, watching impatiently, concluded that someone (who else but Benton?) would have to set forth the hard-money case.

He tried several times to get the floor in the Senate, but the friends of the Bank succeeded always in silencing him by parliamentary technicalities. Finally, on February 2, 1831, he outmaneuvered the opposition and launched his comprehensive indictment: —

> First: Mr. President, I object to the renewal of the charter . . . because I look upon the bank as an institution too great and powerful to be tolerated in a Government of free and equal laws. . . . Secondly, I object . . . because its tendencies are dangerous and pernicious to the Government and the people. . . . It tends to aggravate the inequality of fortunes; to make the rich richer, and the poor poorer; to multiply nabobs and paupers. . . .
> Thirdly. I object . . . on account of the exclusive privileges, and anti-republican monopoly, which it gives to the stockholders.

And his own policy? "Gold and silver is the best currency for a republic," he thundered; "it suits the men of middle property and the working people best; and if I was going to establish a working man's party, it should be on the basis of hard money; a hard money party against a paper party." [14] The words reverberated through the hall

---

[13] Nicholas Biddle's statement in 1830 that opposition to recharter was "not . . . a cabinet measure, nor a party measure, but a personal measure" was accurate. Biddle to Samuel Smith, January 2, 1830, Biddle, *Correspondence*, R. C. McGrane, ed., 94. Few anticipated the emergence of the Bank as the crucial issue. Webster wrote to Clay on May 29, 1830, "The great ground of difference will be Tariff and Internal Improvements." Clay, *Private Correspondence*, Calvin Colton, ed., 276. Cf. Hezekiah Niles's comment on a letter by A. L. Dabney of Virginia: "His remark that it is the tariff and internal improvement policy that now divides the parties in the United States, is certainly true." *Niles' Register*, August 14, 1830. As late as 1831, Tocqueville was told repeatedly, among others by Biddle, that no real issues divided the parties. G. W. Pierson, *Tocqueville and Beaumont in America*, 49, 399, 495, 536. Tocqueville, who was a surprisingly poor political reporter, later incorporated this theory in his famous work.

[14] Benton in the Senate, February 2, 1831, *Register of Debates*, 21 Congress 2 Session, 50–75; Benton, *Thirty Years' View*, I, 187–205.

— "a hard money party against a paper party" — as Mr. Webster of Massachusetts hastily rose to call for a vote which defeated Benton's resolution against recharter.

But the words also reverberated through the country. The *Globe* speedily reprinted the speech, the party press took it up, and pamphlets carried it through the land, to be read excitedly by oil lamp and candlelight, talked over heatedly in taverns and around fireplaces, on steamboats and stagecoaches, along the crooked ways of Boston and the busy streets of New York and on isolated farms in New Hampshire, Missouri, Iowa, Michigan, Arkansas. Nathaniel Macon read it with deep pleasure in North Carolina. "You deserve the thanks of every man, who lives by the sweat of his face," he told Benton, adding with sturdy candor, ". . . I observe some bad grammar, — you must pardon my freedom." [15]

4

Nicholas Biddle, in his fine offices on Chestnut Street, was disturbed by much more than Benton's grammar. This able, suave and cosmopolitan Philadelphian was only thirty-seven when he became president of the Bank in 1823. He had been known mainly as a literary man — an early training which instilled a weakness for writing public letters that would often prove embarrassing. One English traveler pronounced him "the most perfect specimen of an American gentleman that I had yet seen" and commended his "exemption from national characteristics." [16]

As head of the Bank, he inclined to pursue an active policy; but up to 1830 all his ventures had succeeded, he had taken no unnecessary risks (except perhaps for the "branch draft" device), and his judgment was universally respected. Yet, for all his ability, he suffered from a fatal self-confidence, a disposition to underrate his opponents and a lack of political imagination. He sought now to make a deal with the administration, while working on public opinion by newspaper articles, loans to editors and personal contacts. But his ultimate reliance was on two of the nation's giants, Henry Clay and Daniel Webster.

Henry Clay was the most beloved politician of the day. He was tall and a little stooped, with a sandy complexion, gray, twinkling eyes, and a sardonic and somewhat sensual mouth, cut straight across the face. In conversation he was swift and sparkling, full of anecdote and swearing freely. Reclining lazily on a sofa, surrounded by friends,

[15] Macon to Benton, March 7, 1831, *Washington Globe*, June 17, 1831.
[16] J. S. Buckingham, *America, Historical, Statistic, and Descriptive*, II, 214.

snuffbox in hand, he would talk on for hours with a long, drawling intonation and significant taps on the snuffbox as he cracked his jokes. John Quincy Adams called him only half-educated, but added, "His school has been the world, and in that he is a proficient. His morals, public and private, are loose, but he has all the virtues indispensable to a popular man."

Brilliant, reckless, fascinating, indolent, Clay was irresistibly attractive. Exhilarated by his sense of personal power, he loved to dominate his human environment everywhere, in Congress and at party councils, at dinner and in conversation; but he was not meanly ambitious. If he possessed few settled principles and small analytical curiosity, he had broad and exciting visions, which took the place of ideas.

It was these rapt visions which made him so thrilling an orator. His rich and musical voice could make drama out of a motion for adjournment, and Clay took care that it ordinarily had much more to occupy itself with. His brilliance of gesture — the sharp nods of the head, the stamp of the foot, the pointed finger, the open palm, the tight-clenched fist — made the emotion visible as well as audible. He carried all, not by logic, not by knowledge, but by storm, by charm and courage and fire. His rhetoric was often tasteless and inflated, his matter often inconsequential. "The time is fast approaching," someone remarked in 1843, "when the wonder will be as great, how his speeches could have been so thrilling, as it now is, how Mr. Burke's could have been so dull." Yet he transfixed the American imagination as few public figures ever have. The country may not have trusted him, but it loved him.[17]

Daniel Webster lacked precisely that talent for stirring the popular imagination. He was an awe-inspiring figure, solid as granite, with strong shoulders and an iron frame. His dark, craggy head was unforgettable; strangers always recognized the jet-black hair, the jutting brow, the large smoldering eyes, and the "mastiff-mouth," as Carlyle saw it, "accurately closed." Yet, he inclined to be taciturn in public,

[17] The quotations are from Adams, *Memoirs*, V, 325, and "Mr. Clay and the Restrictive System," *Democratic Review*, XII, 302 (March, 1843). See also G. W. Bungay, *Off-hand Takings; or, Crayon Sketches of the Noticeable Men of Our Age*, 21–24; T. C. Grattan, *Civilized America*, I, 172, II, 395–396; H. W. Hilliard, *Politics and Pen Pictures*, 3; C. C. Baldwin, *Diary of Christopher C. Baldwin, 1829–35*, 244; Martineau, *Retrospect*, I, 242, 275, 290; Lord Morpeth, Diary, manuscript transcript, 128, 141; "A Peep at Washington," *Knickerbocker Magazine*, III, 443 (June, 1834). I am also indebted to Leonard Woolf's brilliant sketch of Brougham for some suggestions on the interpretation of Clay: *After the Deluge*, II, 122. The resemblance between Clay and Brougham was noted by English visitors; see Tyrone Power, *Impressions of America, during the Years 1833, 1834, and 1835*, I, 270.

except when he worked up, with the aid of brandy, a heavy geniality for social purposes. He loved his comfort too much: liquor and rest, duck-shooting at Marshfield and adulation in Boston. His intellectual ability was great, but he used it only under the spur of crisis. In his great speeches inspiration would take charge of his deep booming voice, and he would shake the world. Then he was, as Emerson remembered him, "the great cannon loaded to the lips." But when inspiration lagged he became simply pompous.

The nation never gave its heart to Webster. The merchants of Boston did, along with a share of their purses, and also the speculators of Wall Street and rich men everywhere. But the plain man did not much respond to him, except for a few Yankee farmers in New Hampshire, who liked to hobnob with statesmen. "He gives the idea of great power," said one English observer, "but does not inspire 'abandon.'" The people, who trusted Jackson and loved Clay, could neither trust nor love Webster. He never won the people simply because he never gave himself to them. He had, as Francis Lieber said, "no instinct for the massive movements."

Clay fought for Biddle and his Bank because it fitted in with his superb vision of America, but Webster fought for it in great part because it was a dependable source of private revenue. "I believe my retainer has not been renewed or *refreshed* as usual," he wrote at one point when the Bank had its back to the wall. "If it be wished that my relation to the Bank should be continued, it may be well to send me the usual retainers." How could Daniel Webster expect the American people to follow him through hell and high water when he would not lead unless someone made up a purse for him? [18]

In the House, Biddle could count on aid almost as formidable. John Quincy Adams, the ex-President, had come out of retirement to defend the American System in this moment of its peril. Adams, as Emerson noted, was no gentleman of the old school, "but a bruiser

---

[18] The quotations are from Carlyle to Emerson, June 24, 1839, *Correspondence of Thomas Carlyle and Ralph Waldo Emerson, 1834–1872*, C. E. Norton, ed., I, 247–248; R. W. Emerson, *Journals*, E. W. Emerson and W. E. Forbes, eds., VII, 87; Lord Morpeth, Diary, manuscript transcript, 102; Lieber to G. S. Hillard, December, 1852, T. S. Perry, *Life and Letters of Francis Lieber*, 256; Webster to Biddle, December 21, 1833, Biddle, *Correspondence*, 218.

Stephen Vincent Benét's recent skillful attempt to make Webster a hero of myth would have surprised many of Webster's contemporaries. The real Webster lacked the generosity and warm humanity of Mr. Benét's hero, and would have opposed many of the things which Mr. Benét himself has stood for today. In fact, the least plausible part of Mr. Benét's charming tale is not that a New Hampshire man should sell his soul to the devil, or that Benedict Arnold and Simon Girty should be on tap for jury service, but that Daniel Webster should be found arguing against the sanctity of contract.

. . . an old roué who cannot live on slops but must have sulphuric acid in his tea!" He loved the rough-and-tumble of debate and neither asked quarter nor gave any. Sometimes he would lash himself into a rage, his body swaying with anger, his voice breaking, and the top of his head, usually white as alabaster, flushing a passionate red. Old age made him majestic and terrifying, with that bald and noble head, the cracked voice, the heavy figure clad in a faded frock coat. "Alone, unspoken to, unconsulted, never consulting with others, he sits apart, wrapped in his reveries," reported a Washington correspondent in 1837, ". . . looks enfeebled, but yet he is never tired; worn out, but ever ready for combat; melancholy, but let a witty thing fall from any member, and that old man's face is wreathed in smiles." [19]

Adams's protégé, Edward Everett, the great rhetorician, could also be relied on to embellish Biddle's case with splendid exordiums and perorations; and George McDuffie, an experienced politician from South Carolina, was entrusted with the actual charge of the bill in the House. To strengthen the Bank forces, Biddle induced Horace Binney, the noted Philadelphia lawyer, to run for Congress. Binney had served as Bank lobbyist in Washington in the spring of 1832, and the next year took his seat as legislator.

In Clay, Webster, Adams, Everett, McDuffie and Binney, Biddle had a team whose personal following, abilities and oratory promised to overwhelm the best efforts of the administration. As the skirmishes began, he might be pardoned if he failed to regard Jackson, Benton and the Kitchen Cabinet as constituting a serious threat.

5

In the spring of 1830 a House committee, directed by George McDuffie, had brought in a report clearing the Bank of the charges made by Jackson in his first message to Congress. Jackson returned to the subject in more detail in his second message, and Benton's speech in 1831 thrust the question vigorously to the fore.

Biddle would have much preferred to keep the Bank out of politics altogether. His one interest was in renewing the charter. This he would do with Jackson's help, if possible; with Clay's, if necessary. Thus, during 1830 and 1831 he carefully explored the chances of winning over the President. The active co-operation of McLane and Livingston

---

[19] The quotations are from Emerson, *Journals*, VI, 349, and "Glances at Congress," *Democratic Review*, I, 78–79 (October, 1837). See also "A Peep at Washington," *Knickerbocker Magazine*, III, 440 (June, 1834); John Fairfield to his wife, December 31, 1835, Fairfield, *Letters*, 47.

and the evident division in Jackson's party raised Biddle's hopes. The President, in the meantime, while saying quietly that his views had not changed, allowed McLane to recommend recharter in his Treasury report and barely mentioned the Bank question in his message of 1831.

But for all his amiability Jackson remained unyielding, while the Van Buren group seemed irrevocably hostile. Henry Clay, fearful lest so good an issue slip through his fingers, kept pressing Biddle to let him make recharter a party question. Biddle hesitated, considered, stalled, watched the National Republican convention nominate Clay, with John Sergeant, a lawyer for the Bank, as running mate, read the party address denouncing Jackson's views on the Bank — and on January 9, 1832, petitions for recharter were presented in each House of Congress.[20]

Benton, certain that the Bank could carry Congress, realized that the administration's only hope lay in postponement. Accordingly he had a good many obstructionist amendments prepared for the Senate, and in the House he set in motion plans for an investigating committee. Late in February, A. S. Clayton of Georgia moved the appointment of such a committee, defending the proposal from unexpectedly hot attacks by reading from hasty notes provided by Benton, twisting the paper around his finger so that no one would recognize the handwriting.[21]

The Bank forces could hardly refuse this request without raising strange suspicions. Yet, they first resisted it, then tried to keep it in their own hands, then tried to restrict its scope — overruling McDuffie who understood perfectly the futility of these tactics — with the result that by the time the committee was appointed the Bank had lost considerable prestige through the country. McDuffie, John Quincy Adams and J. G. Watmough, Biddle's vestpocket representative, served on the committee as friends of the Bank, with Cambreleng, Clayton, Richard M. Johnson and Francis Thomas of Maryland as opponents. After six weeks in Philadelphia, examining records and questioning witnesses, it issued three reports: a majority report against the Bank, and two minority dissents, one by Adams.[22]

---

[20] The best account of the Bank War is in Swisher, *Taney*, 160–326.

[21] Benton, *Thirty Years' View*, I, 232–241.

[22] The operations of this committee confound naïve theories of economic determinism. All the opponents of the Bank were in debt to it (Clayton, $400; Johnson, $650; Thomas, $650; Cambreleng, $400), while the friends of the Bank owed it much less (McDuffie, $500; Watmough, $300; Adams, nothing). Though the Jacksonians made a good deal of the Bank's loans to Congressmen, there was not much correlation between the size of the loans and the intensity of the devotion to the Bank; see *House Report*, 22 Congress 1 Session, no. 460, "Bank of the United States," especially 569–570.

This statement does not apply at all, however, to loans to newspaper editors;

In May the fight began in earnest. Biddle had already sent an advance guard of crack lobbyists, but, with the crucial struggle about to start, he took personal command. By now he was growing drunk with power. When Nathan Appleton, Massachusetts mill owner and member of the House, proposed the charter be modified, Biddle scorned the suggestion, and Clay interceded with Appleton, begging him to vote for the measure as it stood. "Should Jackson veto it," exclaimed Clay with an oath, "I shall veto him!" [23]

On June 11 the bill passed the Senate, 28–20, and on July 3 it passed the House, 107–85. When Biddle made a smiling appearance on the floor after the passage, members crowded round to shake his hand. A riotous party in his lodgings celebrated the victory late into the night. [24]

---

and Taney's analysis of one Congressman's change of opinion after a large loan was certainly true for a small number of individual cases. "Now I do not mean to say," wrote Taney, "that he was directly bribed to give this vote. From the character he sustained and from what I knew of him I think he would have resented any thing that he regarded as an attempt to corrupt him. But he wanted the money — and felt grateful for the favor: and perhaps he thought that an institution which was so useful to him, and had behaved with so much kindness, could not be injurious or dangerous to the public, and that it would be as well to continue it. Men under the influence of interest or passion . . . do not always acknowledge even to themselves the motives upon which they really act. They sometimes persuade themselves that they are acting, on a motive consistent with their own self-respect, and sense of right, and shut their eyes to the one which in fact governs their conduct." Bank War Manuscript, 113–114.

[23] Robert C. Winthrop, "Memoir of Hon. Nathan Appleton," *Proceedings of the Massachusetts Historical Society*, V, 279.

[24] Taney, Bank War Manuscript, 116.

VIII VETO

JESSIE BENTON knew she must keep still and not fidget or squirm, even when General Jackson twisted his fingers too tightly in her curls. The old man, who loved children, liked to have Benton bring his enchanting daughter to the White House. Jessie, clinging to her father's hand, trying to match his strides, would climb breathlessly up the long stairs to the upper room where, with sunshine flooding in through tall south windows, they would find the General in his big rocking chair close to the roaring wood fire. The child instinctively responded to the lonely old man's desire for "a bright unconscious affectionate little life near him," and would sit by his side while his hand rested on her head. Sometimes, in the heat of discussion, his long bony fingers took a grip that made Jessie look at her father but give no other sign. Soon Benton would contrive to send her off to play with the children of Andrew Jackson Donelson, the President's private secretary. Then the talk would resume. In the latter days of 1831 the discussions grew particularly long and tense.[1]

1

Jackson's grim calm during that year cloaked no basic wavering of purpose. With characteristic political tact he presented an irresolute and amenable face to the world in order to hold the party together.[2] Benton and Kendall were in his confidence, but very few others. His apparent moderation deceived not only Biddle but many of the Bank's enemies. James A. Hamilton considered making a hurried trip to London to discuss Jackson's vacillations with Van Buren; and William Dunlap, the artist, voiced the misgivings of many liberals in his remark to Fenimore Cooper that Jackson had "proved weaker than could have been anticipated; yet those who hold under him will hold to him and strive to hold him up."[3]

[1] Jessie Benton Frémont, *Souvenirs*, 88–89.
[2] The evidence for this view is set forth in Bassett, *Jackson*, 610–616.
[3] Bassett, *Jackson*, 612; Dunlap to Cooper, September 20, 1831, J. F. Cooper, *Correspondence*, J. F. Cooper, ed., I, 241.

In particular, Jackson's cabinet misinterpreted his pose. McLane, Livingston and Taney were all convinced that compromise was possible, greatly to the relief of the two and the despair of the third. Taney was coming to believe that he stood alone in the cabinet and almost in the country in opposing recharter. In the meantime, the Bank's alacrity in opening new offices and making long-term loans, though its charter was soon to expire, seemed "conclusive evidence of its determination to fasten itself by means of its money so firmly on the country that it will be impossible . . . to shake it off without producing the most severe and extensive public suffering. — And this very attempt," he cried, "calls for prompt resistance — for future resistance will be in vain if the charter is renewed." [4]

But who would lead the resistance? He watched the debates drag on and the votes pile up through the spring of 1832 with mounting apprehension. In the late spring, having to attend the Maryland Court of Appeals, he decided to prepare a memorandum setting forth his conviction that recharter should be vetoed. He finished it the night before his departure and notified the President that the opinion would be delivered as soon as the bill was passed.

On July 3 Jackson received the bill. Hearing the news, Martin Van Buren, just back from England, went straight on to Washington, arriving at midnight. The General, still awake, stretched on a sick-bed, pale and haggard and propped up by pillows, grasped his friend's hand. Passing his other hand through his snow-white hair, he said firmly but without passion, "The bank, Mr. Van Buren, is trying to kill me, *but I will kill it!*" [5]

A day or two later, Taney, busy in Annapolis, received word to hurry back to Washington. He found the President out of bed and eager for action. He had read Taney's memorandum with emphatic agreement and then had heard the arguments of the rest of the cabinet. While disapproving the bill, they wanted him to place his rejection on grounds which would allow the question to be reopened in the future. Jackson, unwilling to compromise, then turned to Amos Kendall for a first draft of the veto message. Andrew J. Donelson was now revising Kendall's draft in the room across the hall. Would Taney help? The lean, determined face of the Attorney General expressed no reservations.

It took three days to finish the document. The first day Taney and Donelson worked alone, except for Jackson and Ralph Earl, an artist

[4] Taney to Thomas Ellicott, December 15, 23, 1831, Taney Papers; Taney, Bank War Manuscript, 104.

[5] Van Buren, *Autobiography*, 625; *Political Parties*, 314.

who lived at the White House and used this room as a studio, painting away, oblivious of the tense consultations, the hasty scribbles, the
words crossed out, the phrases laboriously worked over, the notes
torn up and discarded. On the second day Levi Woodbury, having
decided to change his stand, made an unabashed appearance and
assisted till the job was done. Jackson meanwhile passed in and out
of the room, listening to the different parts, weighing the various
suggestions and directing what should be inserted or altered.[6]

2

The message, dated July 10, burst like a thunderclap over the
nation. Its core was a ringing statement of Jackson's belief in the
essential rights of the common man. "It is to be regretted, that the
rich and powerful too often bend the acts of government to their
selfish purposes," Jackson declared. "Distinctions in society will always exist under every just government. Equality of talents, of education, or of wealth can not be produced by human institutions. In
the full enjoyment of the gifts of Heaven and the fruits of superior
industry, economy, and virtue, every man is equally entitled to protection by law; but when the laws undertake to add to these natural
and just advantages artificial distinctions . . . to make the rich richer
and the potent more powerful, the humble members of society — the
farmers, mechanics, and laborers — who have neither the time nor the
means of securing like favors to themselves, have a right to complain
of the injustice of their Government." [7]

But the case against the Bank could not rest simply on generalities.
Jackson's real opposition, of course, and that of Benton, Taney and
Kendall, arose from their hard-money views. Yet, a great part of their
backing came from cheap-money men. Thus powerful hard-money arguments — the economic argument that the paper system caused
periodic depressions, and the social argument that it built up an
aristocracy — were unavailable because they were as fatal to the debtor
and state banking positions as to the Bank itself.

The veto message was brilliantly successful in meeting this dilemma.
It diverted attention from the basic contradiction by its passages of
resounding and demagogic language; it played down the strictly
economic analysis; and it particularly sought to lull Western fears
by dwelling on the hardships worked by the long arm of the Bank
in the Mississippi Valley. Its main emphasis fell, first, on the case

[6] Taney, Bank War Manuscript, 118–126.
[7] Richardson, comp., *Messages and Papers*, II. 590.

against the Bank as unconstitutional, and then on the political argument that the Bank represented too great a centralization of power under private control. The stress on the "great evils to our country and its institutions [which] might flow from such a concentration of power in the hands of a few men irresponsible to the people" sounded good to the state banks and to the West, both of which had chafed long enough at the ascendancy of Chestnut Street.[8] The message thus thrust to the foreground the issues on which all enemies of the Bank could unite, while the special aims of the hard-money school remained safely under cover.[9]

The distinction between "the humble members of society" and "the rich and powerful" drew quick reactions from both classes. The common man through the land responded enthusiastically to his leader's appeal. "The veto works well everywhere," Jackson could report from the Hermitage in August; "it has put down the Bank instead of prostrating me."[10]

But men who believed that the political power of the business community should increase with its wealth were deeply alarmed. When Jackson said, "It is not conceivable how the present stockholders can have any claim to the special favor of the Government," did he mean that the common man had the same rights as the rich and wellborn to control of the state?[11] The Bank of the United States, according to the plan of Hamilton, would serve as the indispensable make-weight for property against the sway of numbers. Did not the veto message attack the very premises of Federalism, rejecting its axioms, destroying its keystone and rallying the groups in society bent on its annihilation?

No wonder Nicholas Biddle roared to Henry Clay, "It has all the fury of a chained panther, biting the bars of his cage. It is really a manifesto of anarchy, such as Marat or Robespierre might have issued to the mob of the Faubourg St. Antoine." Or, as Alexander H. Everett wrote in Boston's conservative daily, the *Advertiser*, "For the first

---

[8] Richardson, comp., *Messages and Papers*, II, 581.

[9] The Bank controversy elicited a few examples of what would be a natural modern argument: that the Bank was clothed with the public interest. Henry D. Gilpin, a former government director of the Bank and Attorney General under Van Buren, suggested somewhat this argument in 1836: "I am not sure that Dallas has put the argument [against the Bank] in its strongest form — that such an institution is essentially *public*, affecting the general value of property and exercising powers too broad to be regarded as private acts — and that whether public or private the chief legislative body have a right to rescind a franchise, as they have to take private property, when the public welfare requires it." Gilpin to Van Buren, September 14, 1836, Van Buren Papers.

[10] Jackson to W. B. Lewis, August 18, 1832, Jackson–Lewis Letters.

[11] Richardson, comp., *Messages and Papers*, II, 577.

time, perhaps, in the history of civilized communities, the Chief Magistrate of a great nation . . . is found appealing to the worst passions of the uninformed part of the people, and endeavoring to stir up the poor against the rich." Webster, rising gravely in the Senate, summed up the indictment: "It manifestly seeks to influence the poor against the rich. It wantonly attacks whole classes of the people, for the purpose of turning against them the prejudices and resentments of other classes. It is a State paper which finds no topic too exciting for its use, no passion too inflammable for its address and its solicitation." For Webster, as for Jackson, it was becoming a battle between antagonistic philosophies of government: one declaring, like Webster at the Massachusetts convention, that property should control the state; the other denying that property had a superior claim to governmental privileges and benefits.[12]

3

The veto struck consternation through some parts of the Democratic party. The summer and fall of 1832 saw a hasty recasting of party lines. In Boston, the ex-Federalist silk-stocking Democrats scurried back to their natural political allegiances, even at the cost of associating once again with John Quincy Adams. In New York, conservative politicians like G. C. Verplanck and businessmen like Moses H. Grinnell abandoned the radicals. Almost every city had its meeting of "original Jackson men" to disown the administration and renounce its works.

Two thirds of the press, largely perhaps because of advertising pressure, supported the Bank.[13] Even such a theoretically unpolitical

[12] Biddle to Clay, August 1, 1832, Clay, *Private Correspondence*, 341; A. H. Everett, *The Conduct of the Administration*, 60, 74–75; Webster in the Senate, July 11, 1832, *Register of Debates*, 22 Congress 1 Session, 1240.

[13] Two thirds was the estimate of W. M. Holland in 1835, *Life and Political Opinions of Martin Van Buren*, 365; Van Buren's own estimate was three fourths, *Autobiography*, 746. As for the cause, as a discerning English traveler pointed out, "Relying chiefly, if not entirely, on their advertisements for support, and these being furnished by persons engaged in the mercantile and trading operations, they can hardly dare offend those on whom they are so dependent. . . . Hence they are almost all Whigs." Buckingham, *America*, III, 332. The report of the Philadelphia workingmen's committee of 1829, largely the work of two editors, W. M. Gouge and Condy Raguet, charged: "Even now it is impossible to obtain entrance into many papers for free disquisitions of the [banking] system. The conductor of a public journal who ventures on so bold a step, risks his means of subsistence." *Free Trade Advocate*, May 9, 16, 1829. Biddle's newspaper loans were notorious. The most celebrated example was the reversal of the policy of the *New York Courier and Enquirer*, formerly a strong Jackson paper, on receiving loans which aggregated to nearly $53,000 and were very risky business ventures.

family magazine as the *Saturday Evening Post* had opinions which led the *Washington Globe* to denounce it, in terms which would appeal to later generations, for conveying "its stealthy political influence into the bosom of such *families* as avoided the contests of politics." [14] Biddle also hired such august journals as Robert Walsh's *American Quarterly Review* to print pro-Bank articles.

A part of the business community stuck by Jackson. Some merchants opposed the concentration of power in the Bank. Some distrusted Biddle. Some hoped the Bank would be replaced by a Democratic Bank of the United States in which they might hold stock. Some were investors or officers in state banks with an eye on the government deposits. But they made up a small part of the whole. "Since landing in America," noted young Tocqueville, "I have practically acquired proof that all the enlightened classes are opposed to General Jackson." [15]

As the day of election drew near, the universal debate went on with increasing acrimony, from the shacks of Maine fishermen to the parlors of Philadelphia and the plantations of Alabama. An epidemic of cholera swept through the North in the first months of summer. "If it could only carry off Jackson and a few other of our politicians by trade," wrote Henry C. Carey, Philadelphia publisher and economist, "I would submit to all the inconveniences of it for a month or two." The din of politics, filling the cabin of a ship bound for America, wearied a charming British actress: "Oh, hang General Jackson!" cried Fanny Kemble.[16]

August gave way to September, September to October, and the clamor grew increasingly furious. Jackson men paraded the streets in the glare of torches, singing campaign songs, carrying hickory poles, gathering around huge bonfires blazing high into the night. Late in October, Horace Binney solemnly told a Philadelphia audience that "the preservation of the Constitution itself" depended on the defeat of Jackson, congratulating them that the right of a free election could still be exercised with safety. "How long it will continue so, or how long the enjoyment of it will be of any value to you, are questions upon which the short remainder of the present year will probably furnish materials for a decisive judgment." Fanny Kemble, resting in Philadelphia after her successes in Washington (where she had dazzled Chief Justice Marshall and Justice Story as well as Frank Blair of the

[14] *Washington Globe*, November 7, 1833.
[15] Pierson, *Tocqueville and Beaumont*, 484. For Tocqueville the "enlightened classes" were the merchants and lawyers, as Dr. Pierson points out, *ibid.*, 151.
[16] Carey to J. F. Cooper, July 13, 1832, Cooper, *Correspondence*, I, 269; Parton, *Jackson*, I, v.

Globe), was assured by her friends that Henry Clay, "the leader of the aristocratic party," was already certain of election.[17]

But the people had not spoken. Soon their time came: "The news from the voting States," Rufus Choate wrote to Edward Everett, "blows over us like a great cold storm." [18] The results rolled in: Jackson, 219, Clay, 49, John Floyd, 11, William Wirt, 7.[19] The bitterness with which conservatism faced the future flared up briefly in a post-election editorial in Joseph T. Buckingham's *Boston Courier*. "Yet there is one comfort left: God has promised that the days of the wicked shall be short; the wicked is old and feeble, and he may die before he can be elected. It is the duty of every good Christian to pray to our Maker to have pity on us." [20]

4

Mr. McDuffie was addressing the House. He stammered, he shouted and screamed, he banged his desk and stamped the floor. The crowded galleries listened with fascination.

> Sir, [a thump on desk upon a quire of paper heavy enough to echo over the whole hall] sir, South Carolina is oppressed, [a thump.] A tyrant majority sucks her life blood from her, [a dreadful thump]. Yes, sir, [a pause] yes, sir, a tyrant [a thump] majority unappeased,

[17] C. C. Binney, *Life of Horace Binney*, 98; Frances A. Kemble, *Records of a Girlhood*, 549.

[18] Choate to Everett, November 10, 1832, Samuel G. Brown, *Life of Rufus Choate*, 61.

[19] A later President's judgment on Jackson's opposition has bearing on both their experiences. "An overwhelming proportion of the material power of the Nation was against him. The great media for the dissemination of information and the molding of public opinion fought him. Haughty and sterile intellectualism opposed him. Musty reaction disapproved him. Hollow and outworn traditionalism shook a trembling finger at him. It seemed sometimes that all were against him — all but the people of the United States." Franklin D. Roosevelt, Jackson Day Address, January 8, 1936, *Public Papers and Addresses of Franklin D. Roosevelt*, Samuel I. Rosenman, ed., V, 40.

[20] Reprinted in the *Washington Globe*, November 27, 1832. It continues in similar vein, declaring that the works of Paine "do not furnish Atheists with a single argument against the existence of a benign Providence, half so strong as the continuance of the misrule of Andrew Jackson. . . . We are constrained to acknowledge that the experiment of an absolutely liberal government has failed. . . . Heaven be praised that Massachusetts and Connecticut have escaped the moral and political contagion! As for the rest, they have proved themselves slaves, born to be commanded — they have put the whip into the hands of one who has shown every inclination to be absolute master, and it is some consolation to think that he will probably ere long lay it upon their backs till they howl again. . . . Who doubts that if all who are unable to read or write had been excluded from the polls, Andrew Jackson could not have been elected?"

[arms aloft] unappeasable, [horrid scream] has persecuted and persecutes us, [a stamp on the floor.] We appeal to them, [low and quick,] but we appeal in vain, [loud and quick.] We turn to our brethren of the north, [low with a shaking of the head] and pray them to protect us, [a thump] but we t-u-r-n in v-a-i-n, [prolonged and a thump.] They heap coals of fire on our heads, [with immense rapidity] — they give us burden on burden; they tax us more and more [very rapid, slam-bang, slam — a hideous noise.] We turn to our brethren of the south, [slow with a solemn, thoughtful air.] We work with them; we fight with them; we vote with them; we petition with them; [common voice and manner] but the tyrant majority has no ears, no eyes, no form, [quick] deaf, [long pause] sightless, [pause] inexorable, [slow, slow.] Despairing, [a thump] we resort to the rights [a pause] which God [a pause] and nature has given us, [thump, thump, thump] . . .[21]

They listened to more than just the ferocity of McDuffie: behind his hot periods raged the anger of a whole state, and behind his violent gesticulations stood the cold, consecrated figure of Calhoun, no longer Vice-President, now Senator from South Carolina. In July, 1832, Jackson had signed a new tariff bill, lowering the duties but leaving them still clearly protective. South Carolina, unsatisfied, prepared to object. The complex abstractions of the Exposition of 1828 were now seen to be tipped with steel, and nullification marched out of the study into the battlefield. Late in November, a state convention declared the tariffs of 1828 and 1832 void within the state after February 1, 1833.

Jackson met the South Carolina ordinance with a ringing proclamation on the nature of the Union, drawn up in large part by Edward Livingston. As the crisis approached, a "force bill," authorizing the President to use force to execute the laws, was introduced in the Senate. At the same time, however, the President acted to abate the actual grievance by furthering a compromise on the tariff. Late in December friends of Van Buren sponsored a much lower tariff bill in the House. Henry Clay, aware of the nation's peril but reluctant to enhance Van Buren's prestige or to reduce rates unduly, countered with a somewhat more protectionist compromise. By some parliamentary sleight-of-hand the Clay bill replaced the first bill in the House; and it also quickly passed the Senate with the support of Calhoun, who thought higher duties a small price to pay for the pleasure of thwarting Van Buren and the administration.

[21] As seen by a correspondent for the *Portland Daily Advertiser*, reprinted in *Niles' Register*, August 17, 1833.

With compromise achieved, South Carolina now rescinded the ordinance nullifying the tariff, but, to score a final victory for its logic, it passed another, nullifying the now unnecessary force bill. This was a hollow triumph, for the episode had shown that in practice nullification was indistinguishable from rebellion and would call down the force of the government. Though nullification had paid its way this time, everyone knew it never would again.

By his masterly statesmanship Jackson had maintained the supremacy of the Union. But, in so doing, he had committed himself to doctrines on the nature of the Union which frightened the State-rights fundamentalists among his supporters. The spectacle of Daniel Webster and John Quincy Adams defending Jackson in Congress, and of Justice Story remarking that he and Marshall had become the President's "warmest supporters," deepened Jeffersonian misgivings. Van Buren, ever cautious, was gravely concerned. C. C. Cambreleng objected to "the metaphysics of the Montesquieu of the Cabinet," as he labeled Livingston, but consoled himself that "happily the mass of the people sleep over such parts of it and dwell only on those which make them think and feel like men." Benton was without enthusiasm. Many years later, after guns had boomed over Sumter, Taney declared that he had not seen the proclamation until it was in print and that he disapproved some of its principles. Young Theodore Sedgwick, Jr., of Massachusetts asked the essential question: could Jeffersonians "endure from any other man the profession of the same sentiments which they received with acclamation from General Jackson? Would these Doctrines be as safe in any other hands as they are in his?" [22]

Yet, only a few politicians and intellectuals worried about constitutional hairsplitting. The mass of the people, as Cambreleng observed, slept over such passages while responding unreservedly to the central appeal — the preservation of the Union. Party lines faded as men who had cursed Jackson a few months before now rushed to praise him. "It is amusing to witness the unanimity of public opinion at this moment," commented the popular novelist, Catharine Maria Sedgwick, " — to hear the old sober standard anti Jackson men, who tho't the republic was lost if he were reëlected say 'well: I really believe it is all for the best that Jackson is president.' " [23] It would not be the last time that conservatism, scared by national crisis, would

[22] Story to Sarah Waldo Story, January 27, 1833, Story, *Story*, II, 119; Cambreleng to Van Buren, December 18, 1832, Van Buren Papers; Samuel Tyler, *Taney*, 189; Theodore Sedgwick, Jr., to Van Buren, January 22, 1833, Sedgwick Letterbooks.

[23] Catharine M. Sedgwick to Theodore Sedgwick, January 20, 1833, Sedgwick Papers.

shelter itself gratefully behind the vigorous leadership of a Democratic President it had previously denounced.

Jackson became for the moment the country's hero. It was whispered that even Daniel Webster, dissatisfied with a junior partnership in the opposition, would join the administration. Webster himself was reported to regard Jackson's anti-Bank attitude as the only obstacle — which led Louis McLane to remark, "I consider this only the last qualm of a frail lady, who notwithstanding, finally falls into the arms of the seducer." But why, in any case, should Jackson not forget the Bank? As McLane added, "If he devote the remainder of his term to tranquilize the public mind, he will go into retirement with greater fame than any other man in our history." [24]

But these calculations omitted General Jackson, who cared less for his popularity than for his program. Early in December, Amos Kendall made one of his rare public speeches to the Central Hickory Club. "In all civilized as well as barbarous countries," he declared, "a few rich and intelligent men have built up *Nobility Systems;* by which, under some name, and by some contrivance, the few are enabled to live upon the labor of the many." These ruling classes, he said, have had many names — kings, lords, priests, fundholders, but all "are founded on deception, and maintained by power. The people are persuaded to permit their introduction, under the plea of public good and public necessity. As soon as they are firmly established, they turn upon the people, tax and control them by the influence of monopolies, the declamation of priestcraft and government-craft, and in the last resort by military force." Was America immune from this universal pattern? "The United States," said Kendall ominously, "have their young *Nobility System.* Its head is the Bank of the United States; its right arm, a protecting Tariff and Manufacturing Monopolies; its left, growing State debts and States incorporations." [25] The friends of Daniel Webster might well ponder these quiet words.

5

Jackson's re-election and the popular acclaim following the nullification crisis only reinforced the administration's resolve to press the offensive against the American "Nobility System." The first necessity was to destroy its "head," the Bank. But the charter still had well over three years to run. The Bank was still backed by the

[24] McLane to Buchanan, June 20, 1833, G. T. Curtis, *Life of James Buchanan,* I, 191–192.
[25] *Washington Globe,* December 13, 1832.

National Republican party, most of the press and many leading citizens. And the custody of the government deposits, the radicals feared, provided the Bank with campaign funds for recharter. Generous loans, subsidies and retainers, strategically distributed, might substantially change public opinion before 1836. Moreover, the government deposits, by enabling the Bank to take most of the specie out of circulation in exchange for its bank notes, might place Biddle in a position, just before the election of 1836, to create a financial panic and insure the success of Bank candidates and the recharter of the Bank.[26]

The solution lay in withdrawing the deposits. This would cripple the Bank's attempt to convulse the money market and probably provoke it into an all-out fight against the only man who could whip it, thus foreclosing the issue once and for all. Jackson seems to have decided on this course shortly after his re-election.[27] It was his own plan, "conceived by him," as Benton later wrote, "carried out by him, defended by him, and its fate dependent upon him." [28] Taney, Kendall and Blair actively supported him while Barry added his crumbling influence. Benton, vastly pleased, for some reason played little part in working out the details. Woodbury remained inscrutable, with McLane, Livingston and Cass all hostile.

McLane and Biddle, indeed, went quickly to work to forestall the President. A special Treasury investigator reported early in 1833 that the Bank was sound, and in March the House upheld a majority report of the Ways and Means Committee declaring the funds perfectly safe in the Bank's custody. These incidents only confirmed the radicals' conviction of the extent of Biddle's power.

The campaign for removal slowed down in May and June, during the President's trip to New York and New England. No overt act had yet destroyed his almost universal popularity, and the tour proved a long triumphal procession, marked by the thunder of cannon, the cheering of crowds, pompous reception committees and interminable banquets. General Jackson, though tormented by a throbbing pain in his side and the bleeding of his lungs, remained resolute and erect through it all.

[26] Evidence of the Bank's intention to use its funds for political activity was marshaled by Taney in his "Report on the Removal of the Public Deposites," *Register of Debates*, 23 Congress 1 Session, Appendix, 66–67. For the fears of the radicals, see Kendall, *Autobiography*, 375; J. A. Hamilton to Jackson, February 28, 1833, Jackson, *Correspondence*, V, 22–23; Taney's speech of August 6, 1834, *Washington Globe*, August 25, 1834; Benton's speech of July 18, 1835, *ibid.*, August 8, 1835; etc.

[27] Marquis James effectively disposes of the story that Jackson believed the Bank insolvent, *Portrait of a President*, 334–335 and note.

[28] Benton, *Thirty Years' View*, I, 374.

As he rode through the streets of New York on a fragrant summer morning, a boy in the crowd turned devoted eyes on the President. The fine old man, with his weatherbeaten face, snow-white hair and penetrating eyes, waving his big-brimmed beaver hat gravely to the throng, formed a picture fixed indelibly in the mind of young Walter Whitman. (From such experiences, endlessly mulled, meditated, distilled, sinking deep into the reflexes of consciousness, and rising again to liberate language for the new spaciousness of democratic living, there would emerge Walt Whitman, free and unconquerable, poet and seer of democracy.) Jackson carried Manhattan by storm. Philip Hone, portly ex-auctioneer, pillar of New York's parvenu society, commented ruefully that the President was "certainly the most popular man we have ever known. Washington was not so much so. . . . He has a kind expression for each — the same to all, no doubt, but each thinks it intended for himself. His manners are certainly good, and he makes the most of them. . . . Adams is the wisest man, the best scholar, the most accomplished statesman; but Jackson has most tact. So huzza for Jackson!" [29]

So huzza for Jackson, and on to New England, ancient stronghold of Federalism, and to Boston, citadel of Mr. Webster — everywhere, huzza for Jackson! At the Massachusetts border the General was greeted by young Josiah Quincy, a relative of ex-President Adams, bred on Boston notions of Jackson, and to his dismay appointed official escort for the President. But a single day converted Mr. Quincy: this Tennessean was no ignorant savage, but "a knightly personage," a man worthy to be President, in fact, even worthy of a Harvard degree. The elder Josiah Quincy, president of the college, called a sudden meeting of the overseers for that very purpose. Thus Jackson, his health growing steadily worse, found himself a Doctor of Laws (a courtesy which infuriated John Quincy Adams). Dr. Jackson moved on, to Charlestown, Lynn and up the North Shore. Outside Salem the dim figure of Nathaniel Hawthorne watched eagerly through the falling dusk for a glimpse of the old hero. That night, Jackson was prostrated by a hemorrhage of his lungs, but the next day he continued indomitably toward New Hampshire. At Concord he finally collapsed and was hurried back to Washington.[30]

In the meantime the transfer of Livingston to the French ministry and of McLane to the State Department had created a vacancy in the

---

[29] "Andrew Jackson," *Brooklyn Eagle*, June 8, 1846, Walt Whitman, *Gathering of the Forces*, Cleveland Rodgers and John Black, eds., II, 178–179; Philip Hone, *Diary of Philip Hone, 1828–1851*, Allan Nevins, ed., 96–97.

[30] Josiah Quincy, *Figures of the Past*, 352 ff.

Treasury for which McLane proposed William J. Duane, the Philadelphia lawyer who had signed the anti-Bank report of the workingmen's meeting in March, 1829. Jackson approved, and Duane took
office on June 1. This appointment raised fresh difficulties. Though
Duane could hardly have been much surprised on learning Jackson's
sentiments about removal, he played an equivocal part, neither accepting nor opposing the President's views, but stalling and obstructing.
Kendall and Reuben M. Whitney, another veteran of the workingmen's
meeting in 1829, were working out the details of a system of deposit in
selected state banks, and Duane finally agreed to resign if, after Kendall's report, he still found himself unable to take the desired action.

July, as usual, was unbearable in Washington. Jackson, sick and
weary, prepared to go to Ripraps in Virginia for a rest. Where, in
this moment of loneliness, stood the Vice-President? Van Buren at
first had opposed immediate removal. The imminence of 1836, and his
role as heir-apparent, had probably intensified his natural caution.
Sometime in the spring, during a heated discussion with Van Buren,
Amos Kendall, rising from his seat in excitement, warned that a
Bank victory in 1836 was certain unless it were stripped of the power
it gained from managing the public money: "I can live under a
corrupt despotism, as well as any other man, by keeping out of its
way, which I shall certainly do." Impressed by Kendall's vehemence,
Van Buren changed his attitude, though he never allowed himself to
become identified with the measure. His own private council, the
Albany Regency, was divided, Silas Wright favoring delay, while
A. C. Flagg and John A. Dix supported the President. During August
and September Van Buren traveled around New York, first to Saratoga, then, with Washington Irving, taking a four-week tour of the
Dutch settlements on Long Island and the North River, always one
step ahead of the Washington mail. For once he was living up to his
reputation.[31]

Frank Blair accompanied Jackson to the seaside, where the two
households spent a pleasant month, the invigorating salt air restoring
Jackson's appetite and improving his health. Letters bombarded the
President, pleading with him not to disturb the deposits. What seemed
an organized campaign only strengthened his purpose: "Mr. Blair,

[31] Kendall, *Autobiography*, 376; Hamilton, *Reminiscences*, 258; Van Buren,
Autobiography, 601–604; correspondence between Jackson and Van Buren, August–
September, 1833, Jackson, *Correspondence*, V; Silas Wright to Polk, January 21,
1845, R. H. Gillet, *Life and Times of Silas Wright*, II, 1644; Wright to Flagg,
August 8, 1833, Flagg Papers (Wright added as another argument against removal
the fear that "such men and mausers as Jas. A. Hamilton and Jesse Hoyt" might
try to benefit in stock speculation by prior knowledge of removal).

Providence may change me but it is not in the power of man to do it." [32] In spare moments, he shaped his notes into a militant and uncompromising document. Returned to the White House late in August, he resolved to end the matter before Congress convened.

On September 10 he presented Kendall's report on the state banks to the cabinet. Taney and Woodbury backed the proposal to discontinue placing funds with the Bank on October 1, while McLane, Cass and Duane vigorously opposed it. Duane's assent as Secretary of the Treasury was necessary for the action. By September 14 Jackson, having tortuously overcome his scruples against discharging persons who disagreed with him, suggested to Duane that he resign; perhaps he might be named Minister to Russia. Duane refused. The next day Jackson handed Taney for revision the fiery paper he had dictated at Ripraps. On the eighteenth he read this paper to the cabinet. Two days later the *Globe* announced the plan to cease deposits in the Bank after October 1. Duane continued in frightened obstinacy, agreeing to the removal of neither the deposits nor himself. "He is either the weakest mortal, or the most strange composition I have ever met with," Jackson wrote in exasperation. [33] The next five days exhausted even the President's patience. He dismissed Duane and appointed Taney to the place. [34]

He now faced the threatened resignations of McLane and Cass. A friend of the Secretary of War told Blair that Cass would remain if a paragraph in the President's statement would exempt him from responsibility. Jackson, amused at the suggestion that Cass might be held responsible, said, "I am very willing to let the public know that I take the whole responsibility," and conceded the point. The amended message went off to the *Globe* for publication, and the next morning Blair took Taney the proofs. Taney, black cigar in mouth and feet on table, listened as Andrew J. Donelson read the message aloud. "How under heaven did that get in?" exclaimed Taney on hearing the inserted passage. When Blair explained, Taney observed, "This has saved Cass and McLane; but for it they would have gone out and have been ruined — as it is, they will remain and do us much mischief." [35]

The radical Jacksonians exulted at the removal. "This is the crown-

---

[32] Blair to Van Buren, November 13, 1859, Van Buren, *Autobiography*, 607.

[33] Jackson to Van Buren, September 22, 1833, Jackson, *Correspondence*, V, 206.

[34] Duane published in 1838 a plaintive defense of his odd behavior, called *Narrative and Correspondence Concerning the Removal of the Deposites*, and correctly described by the *New York Evening Post*, May 14, 1839, as a work of "feeble bitterness."

[35] Blair to Van Buren, November 13, 1859, Van Buren, *Autobiography*, 608.

ing glory of A. J.'s life and the most important service he has ever rendered his country," cried Nicholas P. Trist, the intelligent young Virginian who served as the President's secretary. "Independently of its misdeeds, the mere *power*, — the bare existence of such a power, — is a thing irreconcilable with the nature and spirit of our institutions." Benton pronounced it "the most masterly movement in politics which the age had witnessed." The *Boston Post* put it in the same class as Christ's expelling the money-changers from the Temple. The sturdy and rebellious William Cobbett, in England, called it "one of the greatest acts of his whole wonderful life." Jovial Charles Gordon Greene, editor of the *Boston Post*, even composed an epitaph for the Bank: "BIDDLED, DIDDLED, and UNDONE." [36]

But Biddle was not yet convinced that it was the Bank which needed the epitaph.

[36] Trist to H. D. Gilpin, October 21, 1833, Gilpin Papers; Benton in the *Washington Globe*, August 8, 1835; *Boston Post*, October 15, 1833; William Cobbett, *Life of Andrew Jackson*, 120; *Boston Post*, October 18, 1833.

IX COUNTERATTACK

THE NEW storm of denunciation made the attack on the veto seem a model of good temper. Biddle, convinced by midsummer that the deposits were doomed, began in August to fight back. Employing to the full his power over the state banks, he commenced to present their notes for redemption, reduce discounts and call in loans. While claiming to be simply winding up business in preparation for the expiration of the charter, he was in fact embarked on the campaign the radicals above all had feared: the deliberate creation of a panic in order to blackmail the government into rechartering the Bank. "Nothing but the evidence of suffering abroad will produce any effect in Congress," he wrote privately to a friend. ". . . if . . . the Bank permits itself to be frightened or coaxed into any relaxation of its present measures, the relief will itself be cited as evidence that the measures of the Govt. are not injurious or opressive, and the Bank will inevitably be prostrated." "My own course is decided," he informed another, " — all the other Banks and all the merchants may break, but the Bank of the United States shall not break." [1]

1

The strategy was at first brilliantly successful. The business community, already incensed by Jackson's measures, was easily persuaded that deflation was the inevitable consequence of removal. The contraction of loans by the Bank tightened credit all along the line. Businesses failed, men were thrown out of work, money was unobtainable. Memorials, petitions, letters, delegations and protests of every kind deluged Congress.

The friends of the administration now needed all their skill. Thomas Hart Benton still swaggered through the Capitol, a host in himself, and still rose to make his crushing speeches, pausing only to apply a double glass to his eye as he read the tedious, yet essential, statistics. But his footwork was slow, and the brunt of the defense in Senate de-

[1] Biddle to William Appleton, January 27, 1834, to J. G. Watmough, February 8, 1834, Biddle, *Correspondence*, 219, 221.

bates fell rather on the shoulders of John Forsyth of Georgia, a good Southern politician, talented, facile and endowed with strong political loyalties which served him in place of principles. No one excelled Forsyth in the guerrilla aspects of debate, in reconnoitering and skirmishing, in leading the assault and covering the retreat.

In Isaac Hill of New Hampshire, Andrew Jackson had another firm defender. Coming from a poverty-stricken Yankee family, Hill before his twenty-first birthday had become the owner, editor, clerk, printer and newsboy of the *Concord Patriot,* then a small weekly sheet. During the next two decades he threw all his energies into a war against the New Hampshire aristocracy. Jackson rewarded his powerful aid by an appointment in 1829, but the Senate voted his rejection, and Hill decided to avenge the humiliation by entering the Senate himself and on equal terms. He was a short, small man, lame, thin and cadaverous, humble in dress, with eyes sharp as needles and an intentness of expression his opponents found fanatical. Tradition has assigned him a place in the Kitchen Cabinet, but this is not confirmed by contemporary evidence. Actually Hill was a radical more out of a sense of personal injury than out of intellectual conviction. The world had hurt him, and he intended to strike back. When prosperity assuaged his sores, he retreated from his early views. It could not have much surprised the friends of Van Buren, who never fully accepted Hill, to watch him join the Tyler party in 1842, support Calhoun for 1844 and by 1850 become a genial dining companion of Daniel Webster.[2]

The special representative of Van Buren was Silas Wright, the Senator from New York. Thirty-eight years old in 1833, he had been born in Massachusetts, grew up in Vermont, graduated from Middlebury and entered law practice at Canton in St. Lawrence County, New York State. He was a stout, ruddy-faced man, square-built and muscular, with dark-brown hair, gentle blue eyes and an open countenance often lit up by a singularly pleasing smile. His manner was winning and honest, and in the Senate his plain, earnest words carried great weight. He rarely spoke unless he had something to say, and when he had said it, he sat down. If he slipped into rhetoric, he would apologize later; "the speech was rather more for Bunkum than I am accustomed to make," he once wrote. Even such a partisan editor as Horace Greeley conceded him to be the "keenest logician in the Senate."

Wright was oddly lacking in ambition at a time when it dominated the lives of most public figures. Of him it could be said with truth

---

[2] [Cyrus P. Bradley], *Biography of Isaac Hill, passim;* B. P. Shillaber, "Experiences during Many Years," *New England Magazine,* VIII, 626 (July, 1893).

that he would rather be Wright than President. Though a brigadier-general in the New York militia, he was always known as plain *Mr.* Wright in a day when few politicians were seen in daylight without a military title. "My deference to his judgment in many things and especially in such as had political relations, was all but absolute," Van Buren later wrote; ". . . in that important attribute of a truly admirable statesman, perfect disinterestedness — he stood above any man I ever knew." For personal ambition, Wright substituted deep party loyalty. Sincerely believing the triumph of the Democrats essential for popular liberty, he tended to condone dubious political usages which, by keeping the Democracy in power, would supposedly aid the people in their battle against special privilege.

Wright's main weakness, which comported strangely with his general strength of character, was intemperance. No doubt his natural floridity of face encouraged whispers, and partisan malice exaggerated them; but during the eighteen-thirties he certainly drank enough to invite the solicitude of his friends and the gibes of his enemies. If the failing was not unusual in those lustier days, it was much more to be sought in a Webster or a Clay or a Franklin Pierce. It proved a blessing for hostile wits.

> The sun retires in deep and sad disgrace,
> Outshone by Silas' round effulgent face.
> Like some great lamp with *spirit*-gas well fed,
> He burns the brightest when he fires his head.[3]

2

Roger B. Taney set forth the issue in the report he rendered to the House early in the session. "It is a fixed principle of our political institutions," he declared, "to guard against the unnecessary accumulation of power over persons and property in any hands. And no hands are less worthy to be trusted with it than those of a moneyed corporation." What would be the future of American democracy if the course of the government was to be regulated by fear of the Bank? "They may now demand the possession of the public money, or the

[3] The quotations are from Wright to A. C. Flagg, August 28, 1841, Flagg Papers; James Parton, *Life of Horace Greeley*, 220; Van Buren, *Autobiography*, 728; Eustacius Swammerdam, *The Lash; or Truths in Rhyme*, 27. See also the biographies of Wright by J. D. Hammond and R. H. Gillet; John Fairfield to his wife, February 17, 1838 [1836?], Fairfield, *Letters*, 198; "Silas Wright, Jr.," *Democratic Review*, V, especially 416–417 (April, 1839); *Boston Post*, March 25, 1834; Ben: Perley Poore, *Perley's Reminiscences*, I, 83–85; B. F. Perry, *Reminiscences of Public Men, Second Series*, 186.

renewal of the charter; and if these objects are yielded to them from apprehensions of their power, or from the suffering which rapid curtailments on their part are inflicting on the community, what may they not next require? Will submission render such a corporation more forbearing in its course?" [4]

This was indeed the question: if Mr. Biddle's panic could coerce the Congress into restoring the deposits, would not the Bank, strengthened by the deposits, in the same manner coerce the Congress into recharter; and as its power grew, would not its demands become more exigent, until democracy was dead? "For, rely upon it," as Taney warned again in a speech in Maryland the next summer, "if the deposits are restored, the Bank is surely rechartered. And if, after all its enormities, it obtains an extension of its charter for a single year, the contest is over, and we may quietly resign ourselves to the chains with which it is prepared to bind us." [5]

The Bank forces were now reinforced by the support, under complex and tenuous conditions, of John C. Calhoun. The philosopher from South Carolina proved helpful in lifting the issue to more elevated planes of discussion. He sharply denied that the struggle was over the question of Bank or no Bank. If it were, "if it involved the existence of the banking system, . . . I would hesitate, long hesitate, before I would be found under the banner of the system." What then was it all about? "I answer, it is a struggle between the executive and legislative departments of the Government; a struggle, not in relation to the existence of the bank, but which, Congress or the President, should have the power to create a bank, and the consequent control over the currency of the country. This is the real question." [6]

While this was hardly the real question, it was certainly a far nobler question than the discredited plea for recharter. It fitted neatly into the ancient picture of Jackson as a backwoods Caesar, bent on establishing a military dictatorship; and it supplied an issue on which the friends of the Bank and the friends of nullification could unite in an anti-Jackson front. Clay sounded the new keynote before a hushed Senate and packed galleries on the day after Christmas. "We are in the midst of a revolution," he declared, "hitherto bloodless, but rapidly tending towards a total change of the pure republican character of the Government, and to the concentration of all power in

[4] Taney's report on the removal of the deposits, *Register of Debates*, 23 Congress 1 Session, Appendix, 68.

[5] *Washington Globe*, August 25, 1834.

[6] Calhoun in the Senate, January 13, 1834, *Register of Debates*, 23 Congress 1 Session, 217–218.

the hands of one man." The currency had been undermined, the re-charter vetoed against the will of the Congress, the system of internal improvements crushed, the tariff imperiled, and now liberty and the Constitution were themselves in danger. "If Congress do not apply an instantaneous and effective remedy, the fatal collapse will soon come on, and we shall die — ignobly die — base, mean, and abject slaves; the scorn and contempt of mankind; unpitied, unwept, un-mourned!" [7]

Webster took up the attack, arguing the imminence of despotism with massive logic; Silas Wright replied, and Webster slashed back at Wright. (The two men disliked each other. Webster thought Wright "the most over-rated man" he had ever met, while Wright, regarding Webster as the Bank's henchman, had only contempt for his views "as far as he is competent to entertain views today which will govern his action tomorrow.")[8] For a moment in his rejoinder, Webster glanced from the fictitious issue to the real one. "Sir," he exclaimed, holding a newspaper clipping in his hand and turning his great, stern, dark face on Wright, "I see . . . plain declarations that the present controversy is but a strife between one part of the com-munity and another. I hear it boasted as the unfailing security, the solid ground, never to be shaken, on which recent measures rest, that the poor naturally hate the rich." The great voice throbbed with indigna-tion. Whoever was wicked enough thus to attack the Bank, "by array-ing one class against another . . . deserves to be marked especially as the poor man's curse!" [9]

But the Bank forces took care most of the time to avoid such issues, and the debates turned more and more on constitutionality. On Feb-ruary 5 a resolution passed declaring Taney's reasons for removal unsatisfactory, and on March 28 came another charging Jackson with having acted in derogation of the Constitution. When Jackson replied by a long protest, the Senate refused to enter it in its records, and the session came to a bitter end.

Events moved more favorably in the House. The quiet, remorseless leadership of James K. Polk kept the discussion to the point. "The Bank of the United States has set itself up as a great irresponsible rival power of the Government," he declared; and if it won this fight, no man thereafter could expect "to arrive at the first station in this great

[7] Clay in the Senate, December 26–30, 1833, *Register of Debates*, 23 Congress 1 Session, 59–94.
[8] Peter Harvey, *Reminiscences of Webster*, 233; Wright to A. C. Flagg, Janu-ary 31, 1836, Flagg Papers.
[9] Webster in the Senate, January 21, 1834, *Register of Debates*, 23 Congress 1 Session, 439–442.

republic, without first making terms with the despot." He assailed the attempt to divert the debate into quibbles about constitutionality. "The present is, in substance and in fact, the question of recharter or no recharter. The question is, in fact, whether we shall have the republic without the bank, or the bank without the republic." [10]

Horace Binney replied in a three-day attack on the removal; but it was in terms of argument rather than invective, and Jackson, amiably inviting him to dinner, showed him, as Binney wrote back to an amazed Philadelphia, "a succession of the most obliging civilities, of the most marked and striking kind, from the beginning to the end of a really excellent dinner in every possible sense." [11] Cambreleng responded to Binney, and Samuel Beardsley, a rather conservative New York Democrat, added, in words which seemed to unveil the secret purposes of Jackson and Amos Kendall, that, if the credit and commerce of the country depended upon the Bank, "I, for one, say perish credit; perish commerce; . . . give us a broken, a deranged, and a worthless currency, rather than the ignoble and corrupting tyranny of an irresponsible corporation." [12]

Perish credit; perish commerce: these chilling words struck terror in the hearts of the more apprehensive conservatives. Was not this the whole drift of the administration policy? First, the Maysville veto, then the Bank veto, then the removal of the deposits — who knew what would follow? "How far this Catilinarian conspiracy has been carried, who but the miscreants concerned in the plot can now disclose to the nation?" snarled fiery Tristram Burges, of Rhode Island. "Have they already parcelled out our cities and villages, and appointed some Lentulus to superintend their conflagration?" [13] But Polk steered straight to his objectives, through all these furious gales, carrying through the House forthright resolutions against recharter, against restoration of the desposits, and in favor of a new deposit system employing state banks.

The President meanwhile remained unshaken by all the uproar. James Fenimore Cooper began to believe that "hickory will prove to be stronger than gold," and he need never have doubted. One day it was reported in Washington that a Baltimore mob was threatening to camp on Capitol Hill till the deposits were restored. A group of

[10] Polk in the House, January 2, 1834, *Register of Debates*, 23 Congress 1 Session, 2289.

[11] Binney to his son, January 10, 1834, Binney, *Binney*, 111.

[12] Beardsley in the House, January 16, 1834, *Register of Debates*, 23 Congress 1 Session, 2450.

[13] Burges in the House, March 26, 1834, *Register of Debates*, 23 Congress 1 Session, 3166.

quaking administration Congressmen beseeched Jackson to say what was to be done. "Gentlemen," the old General reassured them with grim humor, "I shall be glad to see this federal mob on Capitol Hill. I will fix their heads on the iron palisades around the square to assist your deliberations. The leaders I will hang as high as Haman to deter forever all attempts to control the legislation of the Congress by intimidation and design." [14]

Delegations of businessmen, from New York, Baltimore and Philadelphia, also beset the President. Jackson, disliking to argue with people who were either fools enough to believe Nicholas Biddle or knaves enough to work for him, would make his unshakable determination clear by launching into fearful tirades against the Bank. A deputation from New York found him writing at his desk, smoking fiercely away at his long pipe. He excused himself, finished the paper and rose. "Now gentlemen, what is your pleasure with me?" James G. King, son of Rufus King, had hardly spoken a few sentences of a prepared address asking for relief when Jackson interrupted angrily: "Go to Nicholas Biddle. We have no money here, gentlemen. Biddle has all the money. He has millions of specie in his vaults, at this moment, lying idle, and yet you come to *me* to save you from breaking." And so on, with mounting vehemence, until the visitors departed. The man who had introduced them was overtaken by a messenger on the White House stairs and asked to return to the President's office. He found Jackson chuckling over the interview: "Didn't I manage them well?" [15]

A Philadelphia delegation barely announced its mission when Jackson broke in with an excited speech. "*Andrew Jackson* never would restore the deposites to the bank — *Andrew Jackson* would never recharter that monster of corruption. . . . sooner than live in a country where such a power prevailed, he would seek an asylum in the wilds of Arabia." (Biddle, on hearing this, observed that he might "as well send at once and engage lodgings.") A Baltimore deputation, waiting on Taney, declared that, unless the government changed its policy, a large part of the business community would fail, and understood Taney to reply, "If *all* did fail, the policy of the government would not be changed." Jackson provided little more sympathy. "The failures that are now taking place," he told them, "are amongst the stock-jobbers, brokers, and gamblers, and would to God, they were all swept from the land!" *Go to Nicholas Biddle* was Jackson's refrain,

[14] Cooper to Dr. De Lancey, December 20, 1833, Cooper, *Correspondence*, I, 331; Blair to George Bancroft, June 24, 1845, Jackson, *Correspondence*, V, 238 n.
[15] Parton, *Jackson*, III, 549–550.

until he felt that his interviews had been so deliberately misquoted that he would receive no more committees.[16]

"THE NATION STANDS ON THE VERY BRINK OF A HORRIBLE PRECIPICE," exclaimed Hezekiah Niles, in March, on behalf of the business community. A month later he announced with alarm that it is later than you think: "*Things cannot remain and stand still. . . .* Wives, children and property — liberty and peace — are the things which are under consideration. . . . A worse or better state must soon happen." Fanny Kemble turned a moment from her army of admirers to note that everything threatened "change and disintegration." While playing "The Inconstant" in Philadelphia, she toasted "*Here's the deposites back again*" in one scene, and the audience roared its approval. Late in the summer another English lady, sharp-eyed, spinsterish and deaf, arrived in America. The first person Harriet Martineau met was quick to inform her that the nation was on the verge of a military despotism.[17]

The "natural aristocracy" was everywhere shocked into fantasies of collapse. Chancellor Kent departed from judicial calm to proclaim comprehensively: "I look upon Jackson as a detestable, ignorant, reckless, vain & malignant tyrant." Justice Story was sufficiently under the influence of Clay's rhetoric to observe, "Though we live under the form of a republic we are in fact under the absolute rule of a single man." He felt himself called back as in a dream to the last days of the Roman republic, when the mob shouted for Caesar, and liberty expired with the dark and prophetic words of Cicero. "It has been remarked with much justice and truth," a Missouri businessman wrote Frank Blair, "that the merchants through the United States, as a class, are opposed to our present Administration."[18]

On the very day that Story was delivering himself of his classical vision, Edward Everett told an English banker, "The present contest is nothing less than a war of Numbers against Property." He reported the rise of the mob with horror. "In Philadelphia, after the powerful expression of sentiment proceeding from the merchants and men of business, [Congressman] Southerland coolly observed that this was only the view of Chestnut Street and Market Street; that he went to

---

[16] *Niles' Register*, March 1, 8, 15, 22, 1834; Biddle to Joseph Hopkinson, February 21, 1834, Biddle, *Correspondence*, 222.

[17] *Niles' Register*, March 8, April 19, 1834; Frances A. Kemble, *Records of a Girlhood*, 568; *Boston Post*, March 22, 1834; Harriet Martineau, *Society in America*, I, 8.

[18] Kent to Story, April 11, 1834, *Proceedings of the Massachusetts Historical Society*, xxxiv, 418; Story to S. P. Fay, February 18, 1834, Story, *Story*, II, 154; *Washington Globe*, December 5, 1834.

the lanes and alleys, where they held a different language." Appalling
— and only one man, Daniel Webster, could save the nation, though
this, of course, required certain preliminaries! Everett was candid: "If
our friends in Boston mean that their houses, their lands, their stocks
shall really be their own much longer, they must make the effort;
they must make it at once. It is but $1000 each for one hundred gen-
tlemen." [19]

3

But Biddle could not hope to fool the business community
indefinitely. More and more merchants were coming to believe that he
was carrying the money pressure farther than necessary, and few
would agree that it was worth breaking "all the other Banks and all
the merchants" to restore Nicholas Biddle to power. Late in February,
Governor George Wolf of Pennsylvania, hitherto a leading Bank
Democrat, came out against the Bank. Clay probably sensed the reaction in March when Van Buren offered to bet him a suit of clothes
on the elections in Virginia and New York City. The Senator responded gallantly that if the people did support the administration,
he would fear self-government had failed; but it is noticeable that
he did not take up the Vice-President's wager.[20]

In the same month, the leading merchants of Boston gathered at
Faneuil Hall to appoint a committee to go to Washington with another
petition. When Nathan Appleton, the chairman, reached New York,
he discovered his old suspicion of Biddle's motives confirmed by
James G. King and Albert Gallatin. King, as chairman of a New York
committee, had already threatened the Bank with exposure if it did
not change its policy. (*Go to Nicholas Biddle*, the old General had
said; James G. King was quick to get the point.) Though Biddle had
ignored earlier attempts at persuasion, this threat spoke in another
tone, and he hurried to New York for personal consultations. Appleton and others of the Boston committee backed up King and Gallatin,
informing Biddle that he knew very well the contraction was not
necessary for the safety of the Bank, and that his whole object was
to extort a charter from the government. Biddle could not talk himself out of the hole, and he knew that repudiation by Gallatin, an
honored champion of the Bank, would be fatal. "Hence the Bank
had to do something," as he explained to Watmough, the Bank lackey,
"for the evil of such an announcement would have been enormous."

[19] Everett to T. W. Ward, February 18, 1834, *Boston Herald*, February 24, 1913.
[20] Clay to Francis Brooke, March 23, 1834, Clay, *Private Correspondence*, 383.

So during April the pressure relaxed, but in May it resumed with greater violence than before, though even Webster now counseled prudence.[21]

On returning to Boston, Appleton found that, though the politicians proposed to support Biddle at any cost, the business community had lost all patience. When the contraction continued into June, he wrote a long letter to the directors of the Boston branch for transmission to Biddle. Signed by many of the solidest and most conservative merchants — such men as George Bond, Henry Lee, Warren Dutton, Amos Lawrence, G. W. Lyman, W. P. Eustis — and also approved by Abbott Lawrence and William Appleton, it abundantly documented the Jacksonian indictment from a quarter whose every predilection was on the side of Nicholas Biddle.

> It is well understood that the Bank is pursuing a regular system of contraction apparently at the rate of about a million of Dollars per month, — the effects of which have been a renewal, since the first of May, of the pressure on the money market, and which threatens to Paralize business for the future, indefinitely, so long as it shall be continued. At the same time the Statement of the Bank for the month of June shows a degree of strength wholly unprecedented in the history of the Bank, and its ability, with perfect safety to itself, not merely to relieve the pressure, but to make discounts far beyond the present actual wants of the community.
>
> No satisfactory reason has been assigned for this course. It has sometimes been put forward, that it is necessary for the Bank, preparatory to winding up its concerns on the expiration of its charter — but however good a reason that may be for reducing the amount of pure accommodation loans, it cannot be considered any reason for refusing to employ its funds in discounting business paper in the commercial cities, or on the pledge of its own on other stocks. — It is not supposed that this ground of the necessity of this course preparatory to winding up its concerns, has been taken by the Bank, since if it were sound it would go far to justify the government, in the removal of the deposites. . . .
>
> Under these circumstances it is not perhaps surprising that public opinion, even amongst the most intelligent of our commercial men of the Whig Party, should attribute to the Bank the design, unnecessarily if not wantonly to continue the pressure, for the purpose of operating upon the fall elections. And it is quite apparent, that the general diffusion of this opinion, must operate most

[21] Appleton to George Ticknor, February 4, 1853, Appleton Papers; Winthrop, "Nathan Appleton," *Proceedings of the Massachusetts Historical Society*, V, 287-288; Biddle to Watmough, March 17, 1834, Catterall, *Second Bank*, 341.

unfavourably upon the Bank, and in some measure upon the party which supports it. — It may even create a necessity for the Whigs in self-defence to separate themselves entirely from that institution. — In this state of things the subscribers are of opinion, that the interest of the Bank, of the country and of the party, requires a change of measures, and that no time should be lost in adopting it, as the only mode of averting a most dangerous crisis.

Biddle responded evasively and desperately, apparently even denying that there was any systematic curtailment of discounts. In a second letter Appleton blasted Biddle's claims with a grim array of evidence, mostly taken from the Bank's own statements, concluding with the harsh but essential question: "what is the policy of the Bank? why is it pursuing a course of policy so utterly irreconcilable with the ordinary principles of Banking?" [22]

4

Biddle acknowledged the answer himself on September 16 when he gave the lie direct to the case for curtailment by suddenly entering on a policy of expansion. After reducing its loans by well over eighteen million dollars from August 1, 1833, to November 1, 1834, under the plea of winding up its affairs, the Bank in the next five months *increased* its loans by almost fourteen and a half million. On June 1, 1835, the loans were almost what they were when Biddle's campaign began in August, 1833, and the note circulation was actually greater than ever before.[23] The panic was over, and the Bank had not recovered the deposits.

Somewhere along the way, Biddle had lost his grip on reality. Ambition, vanity and love of power had crossed the thin line to megalomania. So little had he understood the American people that he ordered the circulation of thirty thousand copies of the Bank veto as a campaign document for Henry Clay. He completely misconceived the grounds of the Jacksonian attack; and, when the President stated

[22] Appleton, *et al.*, to the Board of Directors of the United States Branch Bank at Boston (draft), June 21, 1834, Appleton to Biddle (draft), July, 1834, Appleton Papers. Appleton's opinion of Biddle did not improve with time. "The case of the U. States Bank," he wrote in 1853, ". . . was the result of Mr. Biddle's wanton abuse of the power intrusted to him. He pursued a course of unnecessary contraction under the pretence that it was necessary to the winding up of the Bank, until after the rising of Congress, when finding that he could not coerce them into a renewal of the charter he most wantonly and recklessly increased his discounts." Appleton to Samuel Hooper, February 21, 1853, Appleton Papers; cf. Appleton, *Remarks on Currency*, 38–39.

[23] *Washington Globe*, April 13, June 10, 1835.

them, Biddle brushed the explanation aside as mere demagogy. As late as the summer of 1833, he still believed that Jackson's secret purpose was to found a new national bank of his own.[24]

Senator Theodore Frelinghuysen of New Jersey, his friend and defender, found the exact image for such a man. "There," Frelinghuysen observed with satisfaction, speaking on the effects of the panic, "sits Mr. Biddle, in the presidency of the Bank, as calm as a summer's morning, with his directors around him, receiving his salary, with everything moving on harmoniously: and has this stroke reached him? No, sir. The blow has fallen on the friends of the President [Jackson] and the country." What a touching picture of innocent virtue! (Roger B. Taney muttered ungraciously, "Nero is said to have fiddled while Rome was burning, but I have not learned from history that even his courtiers praised him for doing so.") [25]

Biddle continued to console himself by fantasy. "My theory in regard to the present condition of the country is in a few words this," he wrote in 1835. "For the last few years the Executive power of the Govt. has been weilded by a mere gang of banditte. I know these people perfectly — keep the police on them constantly — and in my deliberate judgment, there is not on the face of the earth a more profligate crew." He warned the alumni of Princeton of the insolent ambitions of "some frontier Cataline." "It cannot be," he concluded with a flash of bravado, "that our free nation can long endure the vulgar dominion of ignorance and profligacy. You will live to see the laws re-established — these banditti will be scourged back to their caverns — the penitentiary will reclaim its fugitives in office, and the only remembrance which history will preserve of them, is the energy with which you resisted and defeated them." [26]

[24] Catterall, *Second Bank*, 241; Biddle to J. S. Barbour, July 11, 1833, Biddle, *Correspondence*, 210.

[25] Frelinghuysen in the Senate, January 27, 1834, *Congressional Globe*, 23 Congress 1 Session, 129; for variant version, see *Register of Debates*, 23 Congress 1 Session, 340; Taney, Bank War Manuscript, 29.

[26] Biddle to Herman Cope, August 11, 1835, Biddle, *Correspondence*, 255; Biddle, *Address before the Alumni Association of Nassau Hall*, 22, 23.

X HARD MONEY

THE DETERMINATION which enabled Jackson to resist the hysteria of panic came basically from the possession of an alternative policy of his own. Madison had surrendered to a corresponding, though less intense, pressure in 1816 because he had no constructive program to offer. But, for Jackson, the emotions and ideas which underlay the hard-money case against the Bank were crystallizing into a coherent and concrete set of measures, designed to capture the government for "the humble members of society," as Hamilton's system had captured it for "the rich and powerful."

1

The Jeffersonian tradition provided the main inspiration for this program. The Virginia condemnation of paper money, pronounced by Jefferson, formulated profoundly by Taylor, kept pure and uncompromising by Macon and Randolph, had passed on as a vital ideological legacy to Jackson, Benton, Van Buren, Polk, Cambreleng. Yet it was handed down as a series of keen but despairing criticisms delivered in the shadow of an invincible industrialism. The creative statesmen of the Jackson administration now proposed to transform it into a positive governmental policy.

The Bank War played an indispensable role in the precipitation of hard-money ideas. It dramatized currency questions in a way which captured the imagination of the people and excited their desire for further action on the financial front. It enlisted the enthusiasm of intellectuals, stimulating them to further analysis, widening the range and competence of economic theory. It tightened class lines, and the new bitterness of feeling sharpened the intellectual weapons.

Above all, the Bank War triumphantly established Jackson in the confidence of the people. Their faith in him had survived ordeals and won vindication: thereafter, when faced by a choice between Jackson and a cherished policy, most of them would choose Jackson. The effect of this mandate was particularly to sell the West on an intricate economic program, which many Westerners did not understand and which ran counter to their preconceptions.

The uncertainty about the West had postponed the avowal of the hard-money system.[1] The veto message, written by three men of known hard-money convictions, Jackson, Taney and Kendall, suppressed mention of the doctrine, as if by main force. But the election of 1832 increased Jackson's confidence. He could have lost the entire West and still have broken even with Clay, but he carried the whole West except for Kentucky.[2] He now felt certain of vigorous national support, and also of probable Western support, even for his economic ideas. Not all the West would follow, of course, and even three leaders from his own state turned against him on the currency question: his old friend Hugh Lawson White, young and able John Bell, and the picturesque if somewhat phony frontiersman, Davy Crockett. Others of his Western supporters, like Robert J. Walker of Mississippi, were careful to disclaim any hard-money leanings.[3] But, on the whole, the magic of Jackson's name was fairly certain to win Western approval for almost anything.

He thus was emboldened to come out publicly for the hard-money policy, expressing himself first in his interview with the Philadelphia delegation a few days before his second inaugural. His objective, he said, was gradually to reduce the circulation of paper, by forbidding deposit banks to issue small notes and by refusing such notes in payment for taxes, until all notes under twenty dollars would be eliminated

[1] Orestes A. Brownson later declared that he had been urged in 1831 by "men high in the confidence of the party . . . to support the administration of that day, on the ground that it was opposed to all corporate banking, whether state or national." This was, of course, long before any such purpose was avowed as party policy. *Boston Reformer*, August 4, 1837.

[2] The "West" here includes Alabama, Mississippi, Louisiana, Kentucky, Tennessee, Ohio, Indiana, Illinois and Missouri. Jackson had only to carry one Western state to get a majority of the electoral votes.

[3] "God save us from the wild, visionary, ruinous, and impracticable schemes of the senator of Missouri," Walker cried in 1837. ". . . Sir, in resistance to the power of the Bank of the United States, in opposition to the re-establishment of any similar institution, the Senator from Missouri would find Mr. W. with him; but he could not enlist as a recruit in this new crusade against the banks of his own and every other State in the Union. . . . [It] was not, he believed, anticipated by any one of his constituents." Walker in the Senate, January 28, 1837, *Register of Debates*, 24 Congress 2 Session, 621–622. Note Walker's emphasis on "resistance to the power of the Bank" as his main motive in fighting it. In 1840, when Walker, now a strong hard-money man, undertook to explain the origins of the hard-money policy, he correctly declared: "The workingmen of the city of New York, next, perhaps to the patriot Jackson and the Senator from Missouri, may be justly considered the original Loco Focos and hard money men of the Union." Walker in the Senate, January 21, 1840, *Congressional Globe*, 26 Congress 1 Session, Appendix, 140.

and "thus a metallic currency be ensured for all the common purposes of life, while the use of bank notes would be confined to those engaged in commerce." [4]

Soon after, he reorganized his cabinet, turning it for the first time into an effective unit. McLane and Duane, both evidently hostile to a radical economic policy, were replaced by John Forsyth in the State Department and Roger B. Taney in the Treasury. William T. Barry, whose incompetence as Postmaster General finally drove even Jackson to despair, was succeeded by Amos Kendall. Benjamin F. Butler of New York, Van Buren's former law partner, followed Taney as Attorney General, and, after Taney's eventual rejection by the Senate, Levi Woodbury was promoted to the Treasury. In this circle of staunch hard-money men Lewis Cass could only relapse into mournful silence. The administration was now streamlined for action.

2

The hard-money system owed many of its maxims and dogmas to the Jeffersonians, and much of its vitality to the Northern workingmen who backed it so warmly; but the man to whom, after Jackson, Benton and Taney, it perhaps owed most for its emergence as a constructive policy was William M. Gouge, the Philadelphia editor and economist. Gouge put the hard-money doctrines in the clearest form, furnished the most cogent indictment of the paper system, stated the general problems in a way (unlike the Jeffersonian) relevant to a society where finance capitalism was well entrenched, and proved unfailingly resourceful in working out the practical measures to realize his policy. Thirty-seven years old in 1833, he had been from 1823 to 1831 editor and part proprietor of the *Philadelphia Gazette*. For the next two years, he busied himself with a treatise on the banking system, published in Philadelphia in February, 1833, under the title *A Short History of Paper Money and Banking in the United States*.[5]

The work consisted of an analysis of the social consequences of the paper system, followed by a detailed account of the history of paper money in America. The first section set forth the broad theoretical case, while the second provided the crushing documentation. Facts were Gouge's most powerful weapons; and in a plain, circumstantial way, occasionally flavored by irony, constantly buttressed by names, dates and citations, he supplied a crisp and comprehensive statement of the hard-money position.

[4] *Niles' Register*, March 1, 1834.
[5] Gouge's own copy, with interleaved notes, is in the Harvard College Library.

The book became an instant success. Probably no work in economics had ever circulated so widely in the United States. The first edition was nearly exhausted by the fall of 1834, and, in 1835, it was reprinted in cheap stereotyped form to sell for twenty-five cents. By 1837 it had gone into a third edition. It was serialized in the *New York Evening Post* in 1834, and later in the *Washington Globe* and many other papers. William Cobbett published an English edition, and an abridged version was translated into French and printed at Brussels. All the radicals of the day read it voraciously — William Leggett, Theophilus Fisk, Orestes A. Brownson, William Cullen Bryant — and paid cordial tribute to the author. It delighted Frank Blair, was passed from hand to hand in the inner circle of the government; and early in 1835 Gouge was called down to Washington to take a job under Levi Wood-bury in the Treasury Department. There his terse and hard-hitting memoranda were to exert for many years an important influence on financial policy.[6]

. The book's success was deserved. Its historical sections went un-challenged, even by the most ardent defenders of the system; and Gouge's keenness of analysis, as well as his accuracy, has won the approval of our ablest historians of banking. When it was first pub-lished Condy Raguet called it "decidedly the best work on Banking that we have ever met with." Modern students have treated it with similar respect. As William Graham Sumner, no friend of Jacksonian de-mocracy, put it, Gouge "studied this system [of paper money] in its operation more thoroughly and with more intelligence than anybody else." A popular jingle expressed contemporary appreciation: —

> Of modern books, the best I know —
>   The author all the world is thanking —
> One written more for use than show,
>   Is quaintly titled, "*Gouge* on Banking."
>
> But still improvements might be made,
>   Whilst books on books the world is scrouging,
> Let *Biddle* try to help the trade,
>   And write one titled, "Banks on *Gouging*."[7]

---

[6] *Journal of Banking*, July 7, 1841; *New York Evening Post*, September 15, 1834, June 29, 1837.

[7] *The Examiner, and Journal of Political Economy*, October 30, 1833; W. G. Sumner, *History of Banking in the United States*, 181; *Journal of Banking*, August 18, 1841. The leading modern historian of early banking theories remarks: "Gouge was one of the most thorough students of our early banking and also one of its keenest and most influential critics." Miller, *Banking Theories in the United States*

3

The hard-money policy was conceived by Gouge and its other champions as a total alternative to the Hamiltonian system. Its central point was the exclusion of banks from control over the currency. It was not, as its opponents persisted in describing it, a demand for the annihilation of the banking system and the establishment of an exclusively metallic currency. It proposed merely to limit bank paper to commercial transactions, and to confine banks to the functions of deposit and discount, slowly withdrawing from them the privilege of note issue.[8]

The main purposes were three. One was essentially economic: to prevent periodic depressions; another essentially political: to prevent the rise within the state of independent powers, not responsible to the people and able to defy the government; and the third essentially social: to prevent the rule of a moneyed aristocracy systematically exploiting the "humble members of society."

The economic argument was brought to public attention largely by Benton and Gouge, and it drew somewhat on the reports of the English bullionists. The political was, of course, central in the American tradition; it was perhaps the particular contribution of the frontier to this controversy, and had been thrust forward during the Kentucky Relief War. The social argument represented the Jeffersonian legacy and was indebted considerably in its details to John Taylor of Caroline. As political expediency dictated, one could be stressed at certain times and others concealed. The Bank veto, for example, confined itself mainly to the second argument, with some suggestions of the third. But, after the election of 1832 had demonstrated the national confidence in Jackson, the administration began to urge all three. Gouge's book stated them conveniently, and Jackson's Farewell Address provided an excellent brief summary.

The economic argument turned ultimately on varying attitudes toward the concrete economy as an environment for living, rather than on disagreement over abstract principles. Alexander Hamilton in his eagerness to make out a case for paper money had once argued that note issue constituted "an absolute increase of capital," but this obviously

---

before 1860, 86 n. For Nicholas Biddle's characteristic misjudgment of Gouge's work and its significance, see Biddle to J. S. Barbour, July 11, 1833, Biddle, *Correspondence*, 211. For the impact of Gouge on an ordinary intelligent and untutored young man, see Lucian Minor, "Diary of a Journey to the West in 1836," *Proceedings of the Massachusetts Historical Society*, XXVII, 284, 286.

[8] See Appendix.

untenable view was pretty well abandoned by 1830.[9] Even the most
fervent admirers of paper money acknowledged the value of increasing
the proportion of specie in the circulating medium. Nicholas Biddle
himself in some moods was a hard-money man.[10] Daniel Webster
loudly and constantly proclaimed the evils of overissue, except when
he had to vote on a measure intended to prevent it.

Yet men like Biddle and Webster plainly preferred in last analysis
a speculative economy, with quick expansion, huge gains and huge
risks. During the investigation of the Bank by the Clayton Committee,
when Cambreleng asked whether the existing banking system did not
encourage speculation, Biddle replied: "Until the nature of man is
changed, men will become speculators and bankrupts — under any
system — and I do not perceive that our own is specially calculated to
create them." Cambreleng became more specific. Would not the system be more healthy if note issue were forbidden? Biddle hedged: "I
fear I do not comprehend all this. . . . That banks do occasional mischief there can be no doubt; but until some valuable improvement is
found which supplies unmixed good, this is no objection to them.
And constituted as they now are, the banks of the United States may
be considered safe instruments of commerce." [11]

Biddle and men like him were willing to take the chance of depression in exchange for the thrills and opportunities of boom. But
others confronted a speculative situation with much less confidence.
Men of small and fairly fixed income — farmers, laborers, mechanics,
petty shopkeepers, many of the Southern planters — felt themselves
the victims of baffling and malevolent economic forces which they
could not profit by or control.

On the most obvious level, the working classes believed that they
were regularly cheated by paper money. A good portion of the small
notes they received in wages were depreciated, worthless or counterfeit.
Unscrupulous employers even bought up depreciated notes and palmed
them off on their workingmen at face value. And, in the larger
economic picture, all the stable-income classes had to stand by helpless

[9] Miller, *Banking Theories*, 30–34.

[10] In 1832 Biddle recommended the following reforms: "First, to widen the basis
of the metallic circulation, by abolishing the use of small notes. . . . And second,
to annex to the non-payment of specie by the banks, so heavy a penalty . . . as
would deprive the banks of all temptation to incur the risk of insolvency." *House
Report*, 22 Congress 1 Session, no. 460, "Bank of the United States," 367. For a
typical expression of a theoretical preference for hard money hedged round by
practical arguments against it, see Edward Everett, "Address to the Legislature,"
Massachusetts *House Document*, no. 6 (1836), 16–18.

[11] *House Report*, 22 Congress 1 Session, no. 460, "Bank of the United States,"
362, 364, 365, 367.

and impotent during the unpredictable rise and fall of prices or ebb and flow of credit. Their reaction to a gambling economy was not delight at the opening up of chances for gain, but an intense feeling of insecurity. Jackson expressed their pent-up exasperation in his exclamation to the Baltimore committee on stock-jobbers, brokers and gamblers — "would to God, they were all swept from the land!" [12]

The administration proposed to rescue the working classes from this treacherous economic order. "It is time," declared Taney, "that the just claims of this portion of society should be regarded in our legislation in relation to the currency. So far we have been providing facilities for those employed in extensive commerce, and have left the mechanic and the laborer to all the hazards of an insecure and unstable circulating medium." Jackson pronounced it "the duty of every government, so to regulate its currency as to protect this numerous class, as far as practicable, from the impositions of avarice and fraud." [13]

Prompted by these aims, the Jacksonians began to sketch out fairly coherent theories of self-generating business cycles. Condy Raguet was perhaps the first to adumbrate the general theory, and Gouge set forth the classic description in his *Paper Money*.

In its simplest outline the theory was this: Banks incline to over-issue their notes. Prices then rise, and a speculative fever begins to spread. Excited by the appearance of prosperity that accompanies boom, people spend freely. The general expansion of credit leads to overtrading and inflation. Every new business operation on credit creates more promissory notes, and these increase the demand for discounts, till finally the currency depreciates so greatly that specie is required for export in order to pay foreign debts. With specie at a premium, contraction sets in. Banks call in their loans, timid people start runs on banks, contraction turns to panic, and panic to collapse. "One man is unable to pay his debts," wrote Gouge. "His creditor depended on him for the means of paying a third person to whom he is himself indebted. The circle extends through society. Multitudes become bankrupt, and a few successful speculators get possession of the earnings and savings of many of their frugal and industrious neighbors." [14]

[12] See also his remark to the Philadelphia delegation that "*brokers* and *stock speculators*, and *all who were doing business upon borrowed capital* . . . all such people ought to break." *Niles' Register*, March 1, 8, 1834.

[13] Taney, "Letter to the Ways and Means Committee," April 15, 1834, *Register of Debates*, 23 Congress 1 Session, Appendix, 161; Richardson, comp., *Messages and Papers*, III, 302.

[14] Gouge, *Paper Money*, Part I, 24–25. See also Condy Raguet in the *Free Trade Advocate*, July 4, 1829, and the admirable discussion in Miller, *Banking Theories*. 192–205.

The more careful analysts pointed out the complex interdependence of bank credit and general business activity, but political pamphleteers skipped the subtleties and blamed depressions on the paper-money system alone. Bank paper, they argued, stimulated the original boom psychology by beguiling businessmen into overtrading at times of rising prices. It linked the whole system so intimately that the failure of one merchant might prevent a dozen others from meeting their obligations. And most particularly, the expansion or contraction of paper in circulation bore only a perverse and futile relation to actual business needs. In the words of George Bancroft, it "expands when rising prices require a check to enterprise, and contracts when falling prices make credit most desirable." Or, as Theophilus Fisk put it with more venom, "The moment a spirit of speculation can be excited, the banks increase the flame by pouring oil upon it; the instant a reaction takes place, they add to the distress a thousand fold." [15]

If by modern standards highly inadequate, this currency theory of depression yet represented a considerable advance over no theory at all. Very little was then said of general overproduction as a cause of depression. Some men, like Robert Rantoul, Jr., laid special stress on the glutting of markets as a factor in crisis; but many would agree with Gouge's note on such arguments, that "if the real wants of the community, and not their ability to pay, be considered, it will not, perhaps, be found that any one useful trade or profession has too many members," and accept his emphasis on the problem of "ability to pay." In 1843 Orestes A. Brownson in a brilliant passage placed the blame squarely on "our vicious method of distributing the products of labor." "More can be produced, in any given year," he wrote, "with the present productive power, than can be sold in any given five years." The fault lies in distribution.

> We create a surplus — that is a surplus, not when we consider the wants of the people, but when we consider the state of the markets — and then must slacken our hand till the surplus is worked off. During this time, while we are working off the surplus, while the mills run short time, or stop altogether, the workmen must want employment. The evil is inherent in the system.

But this line of thought evidently failed to strike much response and was carried no farther.[16]

[15] George Bancroft, *Address at Hartford, . . . Feb. 18, 1840*, 14; Theophilus Fisk, *The Banking Bubble Burst; or the Mammoth Corruptions of the Paper Money System Relieved by Bleeding*, 25.

[16] Robert Rantoul, Jr., speech at Salem, March 31, 1834, Luther Hamilton, *Memoirs, Speeches and Writings of Robert Rantoul, Jr.*, 537; Gouge, *Paper Money*,

4

The political argument — opposition to the rise of independent powers within the state — had general premises deeply entrenched in the national consciousness. Everyone, from right to left, believed, with more or fewer qualifications, that sovereignty belonged to the people. It was but one step from this to declare that the people's government, therefore, should not be defied by private institutions; and it was easy to extend this proposition to economic institutions, as well as political.

In their nature as corporations, banks gave rise to one set of objections, springing from their monopoly of financial prerogative through special charter. Indeed, they provided so much the most flagrant instances of abuse of corporate privilege that they were mainly responsible for fixing national attention on the problem.

Their power over the currency was viewed as an especially grave encroachment on the domain of government. The regulation of the currency, in the words of Benton, was "one of the highest and most delicate acts of sovereign power . . . precisely equivalent to the power to create currency"; and he considered it "too great a power to be trusted to any banking company whatever, or to any authority but the highest and most responsible which was known to our form of Government." Commercial credit was another matter, "an affair of trade," as Cambreleng put it, "and not of government"; and the logic of this position pointed to the abolition of banks of note issue, on the one hand, and the establishment of free competition among banks of discount and deposit, on the other. The crucial error of the federal government, according to the hard-money advocates, lay in accepting bank notes in the payment of federal dues, by which it thus extended and virtually underwrote the credit of the banks. The remedy was to exclude bank notes from government payments.[17]

The behavior of banks in practice, moreover, violated the national faith in popular rule. The most powerful argument against Biddle's Bank was always its calm assumption of independence. "The Bank of the United States," Jackson charged, "is in itself a Government which has gradually increased in strength from the day of its establishment.

Part I, 27–28; O. A. Brownson, "The Present State of Society," *Democratic Review*, XIII, 34 (July, 1843); see also O. A. Brownson, *Address on Social Reform*, 5–6.

[17] Benton in the Senate, March 22, 1834, *Register of Debates*, 23 Congress 1 Session, 1092–1093; Cambreleng to Van Buren, November 2, 1835, Van Buren Papers. Cf. Gouge, *Paper Money*, Part I, 53: "The regulation of the currency is one of the most important prerogatives of sovereignty. This prerogative is now, in point of fact, surrendered to the Banks."

The question between it and the people has become one of power." Biddle's conduct, in 1834, in refusing to allow a House committee to investigate the Bank records or examine the Bank officers, was simply the climax of his oft-expressed theory of the Bank's independence. "This powerful corporation, and those who defend it," as Taney said, without much exaggeration, "seem to regard it as an independent sovereignty, and to have forgotten that it owes any duties to the People, or is bound by any laws but its own will." [18]

But Biddle was simply exhibiting on a larger scale habits long established in banking experience. William Graham Sumner concisely summed up the pretensions of the banks: —

> The bankers had methods of doing things which were customary and conventional, but . . . contrary both to ordinary morality and to law as applied to similar matters outside of banks. . . . The banks also disregarded law so habitually that it became a commonplace that law could not bind them. . . . We search almost in vain through the law reports for any decisions on the rights or authority of the State over banks or the duties of banks to the State. It may be said that no attempts were made to test or enforce the right of the State against banks, and that, as a matter of practice, it had none. The banks were almost irresponsible. Such decisions as bear at all on the authority of the State over banks proceed from the attempts of the banks to resist the exercise of any authority whatever.

Such a situation obviously could not be long borne. As Theophilus Fisk put it, "Either the State is sovereign, or the Banks are." [19]

5

The social argument — the battle against domination by "the rich and powerful" — represented the culmination of the hard-money doctrine. The economic and political arguments, though capable of standing by themselves, were ultimately directed at conditions preliminary to the question: who shall rule in the state? The recurrent economic crises were evil, not only in themselves, but because they facilitated a redistribution of wealth that built up the moneyed aristocracy. The irresponsible political sovereignties were evil, not

---

[18] Jackson's first draft of the "Paper Read to the Cabinet," Jackson, *Correspondence*, V, 194; *Washington Globe*, October 1, 1834.
[19] Sumner, *History of Banking in the United States*, 351–352; Fisk, *Banking Bubble Burst*, 72.

only in themselves, but because they provided the aristocracy with instruments of power and places of refuge.

The Bank War compelled people to speculate once again about the conflict of classes. "There are but two parties," exclaimed Thomas Hart Benton, giving the period its keynote; "there never has been but two parties . . . founded in the radical question, whether PEOPLE, or PROPERTY, shall govern? Democracy implies a government by the people. . . . Aristocracy implies a government of the rich. . . . and in these words are contained the sum of party distinction." [20]

The paper banking system was considered to play a leading role in this everlasting struggle. Men living by the issue and circulation of paper money produced nothing; they added nothing to the national income; yet, they flourished and grew wealthy. Their prosperity, it was argued, must be stolen from the proceeds of productive labor — in other words, from the honest but defenseless "humble members of society"; and Gouge extensively annotated the modes of plunder.

The system was further important in the strategy of the warfare. Taney described the big Bank as "the centre, and the citadel of the moneyed power." "A national bank," declared the Massachusetts Democratic convention of 1837, "is the bulwark of the aristocracy; its outpost, and its rallying point. It is the bond of union for those who hold that Government should rest on property." [21] To a lesser degree all banks acted as strongholds of conservatism. They provided the funds and often the initiative for combat. Their lawyers, lobbyists and newspapers were eternally active. Politicians would gather in their board rooms and consult their presidents and accept gifts of stock. More than any other kind of corporate enterprise, banks boldly intervened in politics when they felt their interests menaced.

The hard-money policy attacked both the techniques of plunder and the general strategy of warfare. By doing away with paper money, it proposed to restrict the steady transfer of wealth from the farmer and laborer to the business community. By limiting banks to commercial credit and denying them control over the currency, it proposed to lessen their influence and power. By reducing the proportion of paper money, it proposed to moderate the business cycle, and order the economy to the advantage of the worker rather than the speculator. It was a coherent policy, based on the best economic thought of the day, and formulated on a higher intellectual level than the alternatives of the opposition.

[20] *Niles' Register*, August 29, 1835.
[21] *Washington Globe*, August 25, 1834, October 27, 1837.

By origin and interest, it was a policy which appealed mainly to the submerged classes of the East and to the farmers of the South rather than to the frontier. Historians have too long been misled by the tableau of Jackson, the wild backwoodsman, erupting into the White House. In fact, the hard-money doctrine, which was not at all a frontier doctrine, was the controlling policy of the administration from the winter of 1833 on; and for some time it had been the secret goal of a small group, led by Jackson, Taney, Benton and Kendall, and passively encouraged by Van Buren. From the removal of the deposits to the end of Van Buren's presidency in 1840 this clique of radical Democrats sought to carry out the policy in its full implications. As soon as the hard-money program was divorced from the glamour of the Hero of New Orleans and had to rest on its inherent appeal, it did very badly in the West.

Andrew Jackson ably summed up its broad aims. "The planter, the farmer, the mechanic, and the laborer," he wrote, "all know that their success depends upon their own industry and economy, and that they must not expect to become suddenly rich by the fruits of their toil." These classes "form the great body of the people of the United States; they are the bone and sinew of the country." Yet "they are in constant danger of losing their fair influence in the Government." Why? "The mischief springs from the power which the moneyed interest derives from a paper currency, which they are able to control, from the multitude of corporations with exclusive privileges which they have succeeded in obtaining in the different States." His warning to his people was solemn. "Unless you become more watchful . . . you will in the end find that the most important powers of Government have been given or bartered away, and the control over your dearest interests has passed into the hands of these corporations." [22]

6

Taney and Benton worked out the details of the immediate hard-money measures. They proposed to increase the metallic basis of the currency in two directions: by the restoration of gold to circulation, and by the suppression of small notes. The first measure had been for many years close to Benton's heart. Gold had long been undervalued, at the ratio of 15 to 1, with the result that no gold eagles and only a scattering of other gold coins had been minted since 1805, and most of these rapidly left the country. Benton argued that, if the gold were not thus expelled, the amount of specie derivable from

[22] Richardson, comp., *Messages and Papers*, III, 305–306.

foreign commerce, added to the amount obtained from American mines, could supply all financial needs without recourse to small notes or "shinplasters." [23] In June, 1834, his bill to revise the valuation to 16 to 1 passed Congress. As an expression of the strictly economic intentions of the hard-money policy, it made a broad appeal to all men of good will, winning the support of John Quincy Adams, Webster and Calhoun. Only diehards like Clay and Horace Binney opposed it.

The change in the coinage ratio was one of Benton's greatest triumphs. He exulted in the new flow of gold to the government mints. "This is the money the Constitution provides," he would say, "and I will not have anything to do with any other kind." Or, in another mood, "What! Do you want a coroner's jury to sit and say, 'Old Bullion died of shinplasters?' " [24] Old Bullion was the name his hard-money fixation had won him, among his friends, at least; his enemies called him sarcastically the Gold Humbug. For a time, foes of the hard-money policy sought to ridicule Benton's reform out of existence. Gilt counters were circulated, with grotesque figures and caustic inscriptions — the "whole hog" and the "better currency." But no one dared argue directly that this infusion of specie would not improve the health of the economy.

The effects of revaluation were immediate. Levi Woodbury reported in December, 1836, that more gold had been coined in the twelve months preceding than in the first sixteen years of the mint's existence, and more in the two and a half years since revaluation than in the thirty-one before. In October, 1833, there had been only thirty million dollars of specie in the country, of which twenty-six million was in banks. In December, 1836, there was seventy-three million dollars, of which only forty-five million was in banks. [25]

Yet the revival of gold would hardly be enough without measures to suppress small notes. This proposal had the sanction, not only of the theory of Adam Smith (and of Nicholas Biddle), but of the

[23] See Benton's great speech on the gold currency, in the Senate, March 21–22, 1834, *Register of Debates*, 23 Congress 1 Session, especially 1073–1084; Benton, *Thirty Years' View*, I, 436–457.

[24] Meigs, *Benton*, 263.

[25] Levi Woodbury, "Report from the Secretary of the Treasury," December 6, 1836, *Register of Debates*, 24 Congress 2 Session, Appendix, 79. It is hard to assess the hard-money claim that specie could have altogether displaced small notes. Gouge calculated in 1841 that "barely by detaining in the country such amounts of gold and silver as come to us in the present course of trade, we should, in ten or twelve years, have a perfectly sound circulating medium." *Journal of Banking*, December 22, 1841. Whether or not one-hundred-per-cent displacement was possible, or desirable, an increase in the proportion of specie was badly needed.

example of Great Britain, which had established a £5 minimum in 1829. Most economically literate conservatives acknowledged the theoretical advantages of suppression; [26] and Congress and the Treasury, drawing on their authority to define the kind of money receivable in federal payments, could exert real, if limited, influence on the issues of state banks. A joint resolution of 1816 had made all notes from specie-paying banks acceptable in tax payments. In a Treasury circular of April, 1835, all notes under $5 were banned, and banks holding govern-ment deposits were forbidden to issue such notes. In February, 1836, a similar circular banned notes under $10, and a congressional act of April, 1836, prohibited notes under $20 after March 3, 1837, and required immediate convertibility for all notes. The conditions imposed on the deposit banks controlled their stock transactions, as well as their note issue, calling for weekly statements and ordering that they should always be open for examination. Declared Secretary Wood-bury, "All mystery on the subject of banking should cease." [27]

But these regulations had little effect on the general banking situa-tion. Only by deliberately rousing public opinion within the states could the administration hope to abolish small notes. In some states tattered shinplasters circulated with face values of 12½ or even 6¼ cents. In December, 1834, Jackson appealed to the states to follow the national example. Pennsylvania, Maryland and Virginia already had legislation against small bills. In 1835 Maine, Connecticut and New York outlawed notes below $5, while North Carolina, Georgia, Ala-bama, Ohio, Indiana and Missouri also passed restrictive measures. [28]

7

But the administration's campaign came too late. The wise coun-sels of the hard-money advocates were drowned out by the roar of the nation's greatest boom in years. The Bank of the United States alone enlarged its loans an average of two and a half million dollars a month and its paper circulation by a total of ten million dollars between December, 1834, and July, 1835. [29] Smaller banks rushed to follow,

[26] Some conservatives would argue of shinplasters, however, like a Massachusetts committee in 1840, "They float as free as the snow flakes, and every hand is held out to catch as much as it can of the beneficial shower. If they were found to be unsafe or inconvenient, they would instantly be rejected." Massachusetts *House Document*, no. 66 (1840), 5.

[27] Levi Woodbury, "Report on the Present System of Keeping and Disbursing the Public Money," December 12, 1834, *Register of Debates*, 23 Congress 2 Session, Appendix, 105.

[28] D. R. Dewey, *State Banking before the Civil War*, 68–71.

[29] *Washington Globe*, June 10, 1835, May 12, 1836.

increasing the amount of paper money from eighty-two million dollars on January 1, 1835, to one hundred and eight million, a year later, and one hundred and twenty million by December 1, 1836.[30]

Wages climbed, opportunity seemed limitless and riches appeared to lie everywhere. A popular tract of 1836 — *The Book of Wealth; in Which It Is Proved from the Bible, that It Is the Duty of Every Man to Become Rich* — suggests the temper of the day. Designed to allay any religious misgivings about joining at the trough, the book earnestly declared one thing to be certain: "no man can be obedient to God's will as revealed in the Bible, without, as the general result, becoming wealthy." [31]

The administration watched the speculative mania with profound alarm. In the *Globe* Frank Blair repeatedly voiced the deep anxieties of the hard-money circle. "We have again and again warned the community," he wrote in the spring of 1835, "of the infatuation which had seized them since the panic, to embark in every species of extravagant speculation." A month later: "this state of things cannot last. . . . A reaction is as certain to take place as the sun is to continue its diurnal course." After a year of similar remarks: "The only remedy is to be found in banking less and trading less." [32]

Jackson, in the early months of 1836, lifted his voice in conversation against "the mad career" in which the nation was rushing to ruin. Benton declared angrily in the Senate: "I did not join in putting down the Bank of the United States, to put up a wilderness of local banks. I did not join in putting down the paper currency of a national bank, to put up a national paper currency of a thousand local banks. I did not strike Caesar," he concluded in magnificent wrath, "to make Anthony master of Rome. . . . The present bloat in the paper system cannot continue. . . . The revulsion will come, as surely as it did in 1819–'20." When Secretary Woodbury made his report in December, 1836, he had to predict that the inflation would "produce much distress, embarrassment, and ruin, before this specie can be duly equalized, the excesses of paper sufficiently curtailed, and the exorbitant discounts gradually lessened." [33]

A basic cause of the inflation was land speculation, and the ad-

---

[30] Levi Woodbury, "Report from the Secretary of the Treasury," December 6, 1836, *Register of Debates*, 24 Congress 2 Session, Appendix, 80.

[31] Thomas P. Hunt, *The Book of Wealth*, 5, 22, 24.

[32] *Washington Globe*, May 23, June 10, 1835, May 31, 1836.

[33] Jackson's conversation reported by "A Yeoman," *Washington Globe*, August 11, 1837; Benton in the Senate, January 27, 1837, *Register of Debates*, 24 Congress 2 Session, 610; Levi Woodbury, "Report from the Secretary of the Treasury," December 6, 1836, *Register of Debates*, 24 Congress 2 Session, Appendix, 80.

ministration had already moved to plug up this great hole in the national economy. The receivability of bank notes in payment for the public lands had practically converted the national domain into a fund for the redemption of the notes, providing in effect a capital for seven or eight hundred institutions to bank on, and filling the Treasury with more or less worthless paper. Benton had pointed out in detail how land sales passed on to the government the job of underwriting the whole banking system. Speculators would borrow five, ten, twenty, fifty thousand dollars in paper from banks on the condition of using it on the frontier. They would then pay the notes to government land offices in exchange for land, which served as security for additional loans; meanwhile, the notes circulated freely as land-office money, some never returning to the original bank for redemption, the rest only after a long interval. This racket not only subsidized the banking interest — land sales had risen from four million dollars a year to five million a quarter — but it also, in Benton's words, irretrievably entangled "the federal Government with the ups and downs of the whole paper system, and all the fluctuations, convulsions, and disasters, to which it was subject." [34]

Benton introduced a resolution requiring that the public lands be paid for in specie. Webster, with his usual policy of supporting sound money except when concrete measures were proposed which might secure it, led the attack on this measure, and a combination of Whigs and conservative Democrats killed it in the Senate. But after adjournment Jackson had Benton draw up an executive order embodying his idea, and the famous "Specie Circular" was issued.

The business community grew furious over this latest evidence of executive despotism. When Congress reassembled in December, the Whigs demanded the repeal of the Circular and the reopening of the land offices to wildcat money, and the Democrats split wide under the pressure. One wing, led by William Cabell Rives of Virginia and N. P. Tallmadge of New York, emerged as defenders of the state banks. Benton vainly urged the imminence of a financial explosion which would leave the Treasury holding the bag; but his efforts won him little more than denunciation as "that most miserable Jacobin of the woods of Missouri, who, with an impudence and insolence unparalleled, has attempted to overthrow the commercial and financial relations and institutions of this country." [35] The final vote disclosed a tiny group of five men, led by Benton and Silas Wright, upholding

[34] Benton in the Senate, April 23, 1836, *Register of Debates*, 24 Congress 1 Session, 1255–1257. See also *Washington Globe*, July 12, 1836.
[35] *Boston Commercial Gazette*, February 27, 1837.

the hard-money position. The bill passed the House and went to the President on the day before adjournment. Firm to the end, the old General returned it with his veto.

Jackson thus had to overrule Congress to sustain the hard-money policy. But the Specie Circular furnished the only tense financial issue in the last years of his administration. After the panic session the great scenes of battle began to shift to the states. Here, in places inaccessible to the long arm and grim energy of General Jackson, little bands of devoted Jacksonians fought to stem the rush for bank and corporate charters, unfolding the potentialities of the Jacksonian program, enriching the techniques and amplifying the intellectual resources.

Above all, these local battles called forth the common people in cities, towns and country — the poor day laborer, the industrious mechanic, the hard-handed farmer — the "humble members of society" everywhere. They listened for hours on hot summer days to dry expositions of financial policy. They crowded in bare and unheated halls on cold winter nights to hear about the evils of banking. They read, and thumbed, and passed along tracts and speeches attacking the paper system. They saw the dizzy climb of prices, wages lagging behind, raged silently at discounted bank notes, and wondered at the behavior of Democratic politicians pledged against voting for incorporations. They talked among themselves, with shrewdness and good sense and alarm. . . . Their discontent was real and widespread. It found its leaders, and the experience of these years prepared them for one great final drive on the national scene.

XI CREDO OF THE WORKINGMEN

DURING the eighteen-twenties, the new industrial order had stirred deep currents of discontent through the laboring classes of the North and East. The tensions of adjustment to new modes of employment and production created pervasive anxieties, and evidence of actual suffering under the new system led humble working people to fear for their very self-respect and status in society. An inexorable destiny seemed to be pressing them into a separate estate as the dis-possessed of the nation, and they were struggling frantically to escape.

1

Some beneficiaries of the new order sought to explain away industrial poverty by proclaiming its inevitability, when they did not proclaim its nonexistence. Such men as Mathew Carey supplied a valuable corrective. Carey was no radical — rather, a rich Philadelphia businessman of conservative political views; but the lower classes seemed to him no more naturally depraved than any other class, and he proposed that the main cause of their discontent was wages too low for subsistence.

Carey set forth this view in indignant pamphlets, fortified by statistics and by the reports of competent observers, detailing the plight of those who supported themselves by their hands. Seamstresses and other female workers, laborers on canals and turnpikes, construction workers and hod carriers, day laborers of all kinds in cities through the land — Carey estimated there to be eight or nine million of them, and sought to tell their story.

He carefully pointed out to the men of Chestnut Street that there was another part of Philadelphia, where they could find *"fifty-five families, containing two hundred and fifty-three individuals huddled together in thirty tenements,* WITHOUT THE CONVENIENCE OF A PRIVY!!!!"* All very regrettable, Chestnut Street might answer, yet what can we do? Are not wages automatically set by laws of supply and demand? "But I contend for it," said Carey, "that every principle .of honour, justice, and generosity, forbids the employer to take advantage of the distress and wretchedness of those he employs, and cut down their wages below the minimum necessary to procure a sufficiency." His list of "erroneous opinions" about the poor is an apt comment on the folklore of the possessing classes to this day.

1. That every man, woman, and grown child able and willing to work may find employment.
2. That the poor, by industry, prudence, and economy, may at all times support themselves comfortably, without depending on eleemosynary aid — and, as a corollary from these positions.
3. That their sufferings and distresses chiefly, if not wholly, arise from their idleness, their dissipation, and their extravagance.
4. That taxes for the support of the poor, and aid afforded them by charitable individuals, or benevolent societies, are pernicious, as by encouraging the poor to depend on them, they foster their idleness and improvidence, and thus produce, or at least increase, the poverty and distress they are intended to relieve.

The remedy? Carey despaired of finding any, so long as the supply of labor exceeded the demand, and suggested only palliatives, chiefly charity and self-restraint.[1]

Though mechanics and small shopkeepers in the towns and men on the farms did not themselves ordinarily experience this direct physical distress, such reports as those of Carey produced among them a grim determination to resist the extension of this misery. Active opposition thus first arose among these still fairly prosperous groups, not yet injured by the new industrialism, but frightened by the desolation it spread elsewhere.

Their demands accordingly had little to do with specific economic grievances. For them the central concern was, in the words of a Workingmen's leader from western Massachusetts, "that the laboring classes in our country, in consequence of the inroads and usurpations of the wealthy and powerful, have for years been gradually sinking in the scale of public estimation." The main source of this growing sense of inequality, as another Workingmen's orator put it, lay in the "continued prevalence of irrational, anti-republican and unchristian opinions in relation to the worth and respectability of *manual labor*." [2]

[1] Mathew Carey, *Appeal to the Wealthy of the Land* (3rd edition), 3–5, 33; Mathew Carey, *Letters on the Condition of the Poor* (2nd edition), 16–17. For the opposite view, see, for example, the article signed by "M." in the *National Intelligencer*, March 23, 1829, attacking charity as encouraging idleness and intemperance.
[2] John B. Eldredge in the *New England Artisan*, October 18, 1832; Samuel Whitcomb, Jr., *Address before the Working-Men's Society of Dedham, Delivered . . . September 7, 1831,* 6.

The first necessity in combating this assault on the dignity of labor was the unity of the working classes; and after this came a series of special demands, intended to improve labor morale rather than its economic position. These made regular appearances, with slight variations, on the mastheads of nearly all the Workingmen's papers: —

Equal Universal Education.

Abolition of Imprisonment for Debt.

Abolition of all Licensed Monopolies.

An entire Revision, or Abolition of the present Militia System.

A Less Expensive Law System.

Equal Taxation on Property.

An Effective Lien Law for Laborers.

All Officers to be Elected by the People.

No Legislation on Religion.[3]

2

The most important of the planks were the demands for education and for the abolition of imprisonment for debt. Education would diffuse knowledge, and knowledge, the early labor leaders believed, was power. In these United States, said Dr. Charles Douglas, an ardent New England radical, "knowledge and union will always insure reform." Labor agitation played an important part in the rise of education in these years.[4]

But the main specific grievance came to be the question of imprisonment for debt. In 1830 five sixths of the persons in the jails of New England and the Middle states were debtors, most of them owing less than twenty dollars.[5] The law was thus, in effect, a class law, applying chiefly to the poor. It was an irrational law, for, by withdrawing debtors from the economic world, it prevented their saving up and paying off. It was, moreover, insulting, for in last analysis it assumed that debtors would never meet their obligations unless

[3] This version is from the *Working-Man's Gazette* (Woodstock, Vermont), quoted in D. M. Ludlum, *Social Ferment in Vermont, 1791–1850*, 204; for other versions, see, e.g., *Working Man's Advocate* (New York), *Boston Reformer, Greenfield Gazette and Franklin Herald*, etc.; also J. R. Commons and associates, *History of Labour in the United States*, I, 217–218.

[4] *New England Artisan*, November 15, 1832. For the influence of the Workingmen's movement on education, see F. T. Carlton, *Economic Influences upon Educational Progress in the United States, 1820–1850*.

[5] D. R. Fox, *Decline of Aristocracy in the Politics of New York*, 353.

prompted by terror of punishment. General fears about loss of status thus began to focus on imprisonment for debt as a peculiarly cruel and wanton agency of degradation.[6]

The first bill calling for a complete repeal of the system, except in instances of fraud, was introduced in the New York Senate in 1817 by Martin Van Buren, who had sponsored a bill for the relief of small debtors as early as 1813. Colonel Richard M. Johnson, a debtor himself in 1819 and many other years, soon began a similar campaign, in Kentucky. In December, 1822, Johnson proposed a bill in the United States Senate abolishing imprisonment as a punishment for complaints of debt in federal courts. Van Buren and others supported him, but for some years it failed of passage. Punctually Johnson would reintroduce it each session, delivering a new speech crammed with fresh and horrifying examples and ending with a stirring appeal to democratic principles. His object was less to achieve a concrete reform, for the number of people imprisoned on federal writs was negligible, than to give the whole movement national significance. His orations, widely reprinted and circulated, spread the agitation through the land.[7]

The chief opposition came from the business community with its vague but deep conviction that imprisonment for debt was bound up with sanctity of contracts. "I shall surely get no thanks from any one," wrote John Quincy Adams testily in 1831, contemplating a letter on this question, "for pointing to the consequences . . . upon the security of property and upon fidelity to contracts, as well as upon credit." Van Buren reported meeting the greatest hostility among merchants and lawyers. Actually, even on the narrowest commercial grounds, the objections of the business community were ill-advised. Years later Thurlow Weed discovered certain prominent businessmen of Albany incredulous at the idea they could have fought the reform until he showed them antiabolition petitions headed by their own names.[8]

When Jackson became President, he added his prestige to Johnson's

---

[6] This was more true in the city than in the country. Agricultural debtors, confronted with the surrender of their land as the normal alternative to imprisonment, were consequently less enthusiastic about the reform, preferring to suffer imprisonment themselves while leaving their families to run the farm. For an admirable account and analysis of the agitation, see G. P. Bauer, "The Movement against Imprisonment for Debt in the United States," unpublished doctoral thesis, Harvard University.

[7] Bauer, "Movement against Imprisonment for Debt," 179–186, 225–232; L. W. Meyer, *Life and Times of Colonel Richard M. Johnson of Kentucky*, 282–288.

[8] Adams, *Memoirs*, VIII, 427–428; Van Buren, *Autobiography*, 212–213; Thurlow Weed, *Autobiography*, Harriet A. Weed, ed., 380.

perseverance ("it should be the care of a republic not to exert a grinding power over misfortune and poverty"),[9] and finally, in 1832, the bill passed both Houses and became a law. In another decade the penalty had disappeared from the statute books of nearly all the states.

3

Colonel Johnson's tireless work on behalf of the poor debtors gave him the special confidence of the working class. His role in another controversy was now to establish him more than ever as their faithful champion.

Social radicalism in America had long been tinged with anticlericalism. The old alliances of church establishments with local aristocracies, and the widespread assumption of the clergy that God was a disciple of Alexander Hamilton, had antagonized men of liberal inclination; and European deism obligingly provided plausible arguments from history and philosophy for detesting the clergy and spurning revealed religion. The French Revolution sharpened the issue when its antireligious excesses provoked preachers through the country to warn against too much democracy. The writings of Ethan Allen, Joel Barlow and Elihu Palmer, and the free-thinking societies which dotted the young nation in the seventeen-nineties, were notable expressions of this republican anticlericalism.[10]

In the election of 1800 Federalist ministers loudly bewailed from their pulpits the fate of all religion and morality should the "atheist" Jefferson become President. But Jefferson's failure to live up to their dismal expectations, and the steady abolition of church establishments in the states, tended soon to remove the question from politics. Yet if anticlericalism was no longer a real issue by the War of 1812, it remained latent in the Jeffersonian tradition, ready to appear like Barbarossa from the hills should the clergy once again assault the citadel of democracy. In 1815, when Lyman Beecher, emerging as a Presbyterian leader, proposed that a qualified religious instructor be set up for every thousand persons, Jefferson himself launched into a violent diatribe which showed the basic strength of the anticlerical sentiment.[11]

[9] Richardson, comp., *Messages and Papers*, II, 454.
[10] G. Adolf Koch, *Republican Religion*.
[11] "You judge truly that I am not afraid of priests. They have tried upon me all their various batteries, of pious whining, hypocritical canting, lying & slandering, without being able to give me one moment of pain. I have contemplated their order from the Magi of the East to the Saints of the West and I have found no

Beecher's suggestion came to nothing, but the evangelicals continued in a quiet, expert way to stimulate missionary activity, found societies like the American Bible Society and the American Tract Society and build up Sunday-school associations. This activity convinced many excited Jeffersonians of the existence of a plan to organize religion as a political bloc and work for the union of Church and State. In 1824 Robert Owen, the latest exponent of the rationalist tradition of Paine and Godwin, brought a new infusion of anticlericalism to America. Owen's case against the priesthood, expounded in the *New Harmony Gazette*, along with the eloquent warnings of Frances Wright on her lecture tours, and the independent agitation of George Houston and the Free Press Association in New York, helped solidify the old Jeffersonian prejudices.[12]

This revival of anticlericalism answered oddly well to certain perplexities of the working classes. The discontent stirred up by industrial change needed intensely an object on which it could release its aggressions, and it settled upon this alleged conspiracy to reunite Church and State.

The final event, which came as a striking confirmation of Jeffersonian suspicions and Owenite predictions, was a Fourth of July sermon delivered in Philadelphia in 1827 by the Reverend Ezra Stiles Ely of the Presbyterian church. Ely was an old friend of Jackson's, and his address was actually a concealed attack on Adams as a Unitarian. Yet it contained passages which seemed to disclose the most secret intentions of the evangelical sects. "I propose, fellow-citizens," said Ely, "a new sort of union, or, if you please, *a Christian party in politics*." If the Presbyterians, Baptists, Methodists, Congregationalists and Episcopalians would only unite on voting day, Ely declared, they "could govern every public election in our country."[13]

4

A Christian party in politics: the phrase rang ominously in the ears of the leaders of the workingmen. Then, in the next May, a convention of ministers and laymen met in New York to form the

difference of character, but of more or less caution, in proportion to their information or ignorance of those on whom their interested duperies were to be plaid off," etc. Jefferson to H. G. Spafford, January 10, 1816, Jefferson, *Writings*, P. L. Ford, ed., X, 12–13.

[12] R. W. Leopold, *Robert Dale Owen*, 56–59.

[13] Ezra Stiles Ely, *The Duty of Christian Freemen to Elect Christian Rulers*, 8, 11. In 1829 Ely complicated matters further by taking a leading part in the attack on the reputation of Mrs. Eaton.

General Union for Promoting the Observance of the Christian Sabbath.

The chief danger to the purity of the Sabbath, according to the General Union, lay in the transportation of mail on that day. In 1810 postmasters had been ordered to keep their offices open for one hour on Sundays after the arrival of mail. Remonstrances against this practice drifted into Congress during the next few years but to no effect. In 1825 post offices which received mail on Sunday were required to be kept open all day. It was this deed of profanation which the Sabbatarians now determined to undo.

Most of the leaders in the campaign were conservative businessmen, disturbed by the rumblings of the people and longing for the restoration of moral authority. Merchants like Peter C. Brooks, Abbott Lawrence, Arthur Tappan; judges like Ambrose Spencer, Isaac Parker, Peter Oxenbridge Thacher; old Federalists like Theodore Dwight, Noah Webster, Josiah Quincy: such names as these stared out of the petitions and memorials which began to flood Congress in 1829. John Quincy Adams was an ardent Sabbatarian, even presiding in 1844 over a Lord's Day convention in Baltimore. Another prominent political Sabbatarian was Theodore Frelinghuysen, the Senator from New Jersey, whose pastel of Mr. Biddle, "calm as a summer's morning," was to delight the nation.[14]

But what was all this agitation but the Reverend Mr. Ely's "Christian party in politics"? The workingmen and their press, in some alarm, began a hard-hitting opposition. Frances Wright declared in October, 1829, in the *Free Enquirer*, as she had renamed the *New Harmony Gazette* after moving it to New York, that the mail question "betrayed the whole soul of priestcraft. . . . A standard is reared under which all the party-colored ranks of orthodoxy may rally into one phalanx."[15] Robert Dale Owen carried on the attack in the *Daily Sentinel*. George H. Evans denounced the "Church and State" party in the *Working Man's Advocate*.[16] Orestes A. Brownson, the stalwart

[14] *Memorials to Congress Respecting Sabbath Mails*, 25–27; *National Intelligencer*, January 17, 1829. See also *Address of the General Union for Promoting the Observance of the Christian Sabbath*.

[15] *Free Enquirer*, October 31, 1829. Cf. her later judgment of the Sabbatarian movement as an attempt "to effect a union of Church and State, and with it, a lasting union of Bank and State; and thus effectually prostrate the independence of the people, and the institutions of the country." Frances Wright, *Biography, Notes, and Political Letters of Frances Wright D'Arusmont*, 34.

[16] Evans believed that the Anti-Masonic party was the Christian party in disguise, pointing out the duplication of personnel and financial support in the two groups in New York. "Ay! these very men who join the Anti-Masonic standard and cry down all secret Societies, *are themselves members of the most dangerous*

Universalist minister of Auburn, already slipping into unbelief, lashed at the Presbyterians in the columns of the *Free Enquirer* and the *Sentinel* as well as in upstate papers of his own. Another Universalist preacher, the vociferous Theophilus Fisk, charged in his semimonthly *Priestcraft Unmasked* that there existed "among the leaders of a proud and aspiring priesthood, a determination to establish an *Ecclesiastical Hierarchy*, and to reduce us to a worse than Egyptian bondage." [17]

The flow of petitions to Congress was meanwhile diverted to a Senate committee headed by Colonel Johnson, which rejected them with a resounding statement of religious liberty. A House report the next year, also sponsored by Johnson, who had been returned as a Representative in 1829, reiterated the sentiments. "It is not the legitimate province of the Legislature to determine what religion is true, or what false," Johnson declared in his first report. "Our Government is a civil, and not a religious institution." [18]

These views infuriated the evangelical sects, who promised dire penalties on behalf of Providence. The *Spirit of the Pilgrims*, the organ of Lyman Beecher, observed menacingly, "Whoever contended with his

---

Secret Society that ever existed in this Republic." *Working Man's Advocate*, October 30, 1833.

In 1835 C. C. Cambreleng charged that the Christian party had now turned to the abolition of slavery; Cambreleng to R. H. Baptist, September 16, 1835, *Washington Globe*, February 13, 1836. Though neither of these remarks is strictly accurate, there are interesting continuities among the three parties in New York, especially in the role played in all of them by the Tappan brothers.

[17] *Priestcraft Unmasked*, January 1, 1830.

[18] R. M. Johnson, *Report on the Transportation of the Mail on Sunday*, 5–6. Johnson's second report, when reprinted in London in 1853, was declared to be "probably the ablest state document on record on the non-interference of government with the observance of the Sabbath, and the noblest political plea for the rights of conscience produced in modern times." *The Parliamentary Observance of the Sabbath an Infringement of Public Right and Liberty of Conscience*, 3.

The actual authorship of the report is a matter of some question. It was produced in the home of the Reverend O. B. Brown, for some years the center of the Kentucky influence in Washington. Johnson boarded there, Amos Kendall put up there when he first came to Washington, and Brown himself was chief clerk of the Post Office Department under William T. Barry on week days, in addition to being a Baptist preacher on Sundays. The reports are written in a loose rhetorical style, at which Johnson, Barry, Brown and Kendall were all adept. Probably Brown did most of the actual writing, in consultation with Johnson. Kendall later revised the report. Johnson took the responsibility and never refused the credit. Brown later came to grief when a Senate committee accused him of using his position to borrow from mail contractors and invest in mail contracts. See Meyer, *Johnson*, 256–263; Kendall, *Autobiography*, 288, 307; *Washington Globe*, February 10, 1835; Ben: Perley Poore, *Reminiscences*, I, 96, 218. The report was also attributed, without any perceptible reason, to Calhoun; A. Mazyck to R. K. Crallé, September 13, 1854 [1844], F. W. Moore, ed., "Calhoun by His Political Friends," *Publications of Southern History Association*, VII, 420.

Maker and prospered? Does He not hold at his disposal all the sources of national prosperity, and all the engines of national chastisement?" But the ungodly ignored the warning, and so did the people in general. With its simple and strong appeal to sentiments held dear by all Americans, the report made a roaring hit. Widely republished, widely read, it was eventually printed on satin and framed in parlors, stage offices and barrooms over the land. Richard M. Johnson, the opponent of imprisonment for debt, now became in addition the great champion of religious liberty.[19]

5

George H. Evans expressed the gratitude of labor by raising the standard of Johnson for President in the *Working Man's Advocate*. Robert Dale Owen wrote enthusiastically in the *Free Enquirer*, "I know of no man whom I believe more likely to unite the votes of the Mechanics than Col. Johnson." Theophilus Fisk endorsed this "author of the second declaration of American independence" as his candidate. When the Clayton Committee visited Philadelphia in 1832 to investigate the Bank, an observer commented, "Col. Johnson receives all the popular honours & is invited to the theatres &c. being announced in the placards & Newspapers." An obscure citizen of Charlestown, Massachusetts, reported to Frank Blair: "There is no individual in the U. S. that has a greater popularity than Richᵈ M. Johnson, in this quarter with all descriptions of people." While Andrew Jackson was still a vague figure in the minds of the urban working classes, Richard Mentor Johnson was a hero.[20]

Colonel Johnson was fifty years old in 1830. First elected to Congress at the age of twenty-five, he had been a staunch supporter of Jefferson and a War Hawk before 1812. When war came, he raised a regiment of Kentucky cavalry and took a distinguished part in the fighting in the West, expanding the tactics of frontier war by his brilliant use of mounted men. His greatest success came at the Battle of the Thames, where a cavalry charge, at the critical moment, undertaken on his own responsibility and under his own leadership, reversed the tide of battle. Johnson, at the head of his men, astride his

[19] "Review of Mr. Johnson's Report on Sabbath Mails," *Spirit of the Pilgrims*, II, 156 (March, 1829). See also "Dangerous Combinations," *ibid.*, II, 352–359 (July, 1829).

[20] *Working Man's Advocate*, April 3, 1830; *Free Enquirer*, March 6, 1830; *New York Daily Sentinel*, February 20, 1830; *Priestcraft Unmasked*, March 1, 1830; H. D. Gilpin to Edward Livingston, April 9, 1832, Gilpin Letterbooks; A. W. Austin to Blair, May 20, 1832, Blair-Rives Papers.

white horse, rode unperturbed through a hail of bullets, hacked his way into the midst of the enemy lines and there killed an important Indian chief, later supposed to have been Tecumseh, the great Shawnee leader. Twenty-five balls struck his horse, his clothes and his body, five wounding him severely, leaving him scarred, one hand mutilated, and his constitution broken for the rest of his life.

He was a burly, genial, very good-looking man, with a jovial face and wandering curly light-auburn hair, turning to silver-gray; in public he was conspicuous in a flaming-scarlet waistcoat. He was, above all, a man of the utmost sweetness of nature, "the most tender hearted, mild, affectionate and benevolent of men" — the source of his weakness and his strength.[21] His home in Kentucky was open to everyone, and he treated all, including children and servants, with instinctive courtesy. He established the Choctaw Academy for Indians and fought for it in Congress. For many years he carried on a liaison with a Negro girl, educated their children and tried even to bring them into society. His pervading kindliness gave him, as Van Buren admitted, "much real delicacy of feeling," which equipped him admirably for composing human differences.[22] He thus appeared often as a conciliator, as in the Eaton affair, or between Calhoun and Frank Blair, or between Jackson and John Quincy Adams.

But this very good will won him unworthy friends, whose requests he could not resist, and who systematically imposed on his loyalty. He could never stay out of debt himself for very long, and this sometimes colored his motives. "Johnson's politics are too deeply involved with his private interests," wrote John Quincy Adams, adding that he was "warm and honest-hearted, but plunged irrevocably into private bank, land, and money speculations, till he has lost the thread of his morals."[23] He could not even resist the temptation to make a little money on the side out of the Choctaw Academy.

Yet, during the eighteen-twenties, Johnson stood out as the one Senator who consistently advocated the rights of the common man, from his attack on the Supreme Court to his defense of the Sunday mails, from his attack on debtors' prisons to his defense of settlers' rights in the public land. Moreover, as the supposed slayer of Tecumseh, he figured as something of a national hero. Among all the public men of the day, he seemed the one most likely to play a prominent role in an upsurge of democratic reform. But when the upsurge came, Johnson dwindled into genial inconsequence.

[21] Margaret B. Smith, *First Forty Years of Washington Society*, 128.
[22] Van Buren, *Autobiography*, 323.
[23] Adams, *Memoirs*, V, 328.

Johnson's failure in the thirties throws light on the departure of Jacksonian policy from the creed of the frontier. The question was changing from political liberty to economic liberty, and Johnson, for all his spontaneous popular sympathies, could not cope with the new situation. A good party man, he accepted the Maysville veto while disapproving it; he wheeled into line on the tariff and the Bank; but he was finished as a creative politician. This new quest for economic democracy meant little to men of the West, however deeply they cared about political and civil freedoms. The Jacksonian program, overriding most of Johnson's old positions on economic issues, left him stranded on the wayside.

By now, his chief motive for party fidelity was ambition. He was naïvely eager for the vice-presidential nomination in 1832, and it took the best efforts of W. B. Lewis to persuade him to withdraw. A kind of brain trust gathered to advance his aspirations, led by William Emmons, a Boston printer and veteran foe of debt imprisonment, and Dr. Richard Emmons of Great Crossing, Kentucky, author of that interminable epic of the War of 1812, *The Fredoniad*, in which Johnson cut a heroic swath. He was useful now as a vote-getter, a figurehead and a front man, but no longer as a fighter for democracy.[24]

6

Johnson had struck fire with the working classes because his embodiment of political democracy in the Western manner coincided in good part with the Eastern workingmen's fears of loss of status: this natural classlessness of the frontier was precisely what they felt was vanishing from their lives. But the Bank War raised new questions. How much, in fact, had the standard Workingmen's program to do with the causes of labor discontent?

Measured in terms of the antagonisms which Jackson was beginning to uncover, their platform seemed increasingly irrelevant. It was, in fact, a humanitarian program, formulated out of a sympathy for distress rather than out of the experience of exploitation, thus appealing to almost anyone of humane and generous disposition. Most conservatives were actually as much in favor of education as the laboring classes, if

[24] The campaign biographies of Johnson by William Emmons (1833) and Asahel Langworthy (1843) contain useful information; there is a careful modern biography by L. W. Meyer (1932). See also Bernard Mayo, "The Man Who Killed Tecumseh," *American Mercury*, XIX, 446–453 (April, 1930); John Catron to Jackson, March 21, 1835, Jackson, *Correspondence*, V, 331; Ben: P. Poore, *Perley's Reminiscences*, I, 71, 153, 164; Martineau, *Retrospect of Western Travel*, I, 257; Gustave Koerner, *Memoirs . . . 1809–1896*. T. J. McCormack, ed., I, 451.

only because it seemed the way to make the best of universal suffrage. Many conservatives were as much opposed to imprisonment for debt.[25] Many conservatives favored Sunday mails;[26] and few people in any case took the question very seriously. In fact, the whole Sunday-mail controversy evaporated with great rapidity. There was not a shred of evidence for the great Church and State conspiracy, and in the second year of its existence the General Union for Promoting the Observance of the Christian Sabbath had only twenty-six local chapters and less than $230 in its treasury.[27] The main Workingmen's issues thus hardly touched the economic grounds of their dilemma.

The Jacksonian movement brought the decisive reminder that this dilemma was a problem, not of clericalism or of education, but of wealth. Politicians and middle-class intellectuals, enlightened by Jeffersonian insights into the economic basis of democracy, began to bring the working classes nearer the actual causes of their discontent. During the Bank War, laboring men began slowly to turn to Jackson as their leader, and his party as their party. Their own parties, engaged in kindhearted activity on the periphery of the problem, disappeared.

This conversion of the working classes to the hard-money policy injected new strength and determination into the hard-money party. It took place mainly in the states, mainly in terms of local issues, mainly out of local experiences. From it would come the impetus to carry through the second stage in the national struggles of Jacksonian democracy.

[25] In New York J. C. Spencer, Millard Fillmore, Thurlow Weed, in Massachusetts, Edward and Alexander Everett, Harrison Gray Otis and the *North American Review* favored abolition of imprisonment for debt; even Webster supported it for debts less than $30. Bauer, "Movement against Imprisonment for Debt," 252; Webster to Louis Dwight, May 2, 1830, Webster, *Works*, VI, 533–535.

[26] See, for example, *National Intelligencer*, January 15, 1829.

[27] *Missionary Herald*, XXVI, 263 (August, 1830).

XII STIRRINGS IN THE
BAY STATE

IF THE IMPACT of the Industrial Revolution was responsible for the particular direction which the Jacksonians gave to the philosophy of Jefferson, then the most serious discussion of Jacksonian issues was to be looked for in the states most dominated by the new industrialism. These states were Massachusetts and New York. In them, the banking system was firmly entrenched. Manufacturing had gained a strong foothold. Financial, industrial and commercial groups were active in politics. The working classes were becoming conscious of a common plight which required unity for defense. When the Jacksonian effort shifted in the middle thirties to the states, it was thus in Massachusetts and New York that the crucial problems of Jacksonian democracy received most urgent attention.

1

Massachusetts succumbed to the Industrial Revolution in the first three decades of the nineteenth century. Slowly mills, factories and banks displaced shipbuilding and seafaring as the focus of business activity. The curve of this change could be traced in the permutations of Daniel Webster's views on the tariff, as his thunderous briefs for the merchant and free trade began to hesitate and quaver, till they gave way to equally thunderous briefs for the mill owner and protection.

Massachusetts leaders like John Quincy Adams, Justice Story, Governor Levi Lincoln and Alexander H. Everett, editor of the *North American Review*, had already assisted at the transformation of right-wing Jeffersonianism into the National Republican party; and most of the former Federalists, like Webster, eventually joined them there in defense of the American System. A few, however, like Theodore Lyman, declined to have any truck with the apostate Adams, or, like Henry Lee, with the protective tariff, even accepting the consequences of their position sufficiently to work hard for Jackson in 1828.

But the Bank War encouraged them to resume the natural alliance with their class, even at the cost of a high tariff; and the defeat of Henry Lee, the free trader, by Nathan Appleton, the protectionist, in the Boston congressional election of 1830 pretty well ended the split in the governing group. Though such men as Lee and Judge Lemuel Shaw of the state Supreme Court persisted in their free-trade convictions, they recognized the danger of dividing the ranks and tapered off their agitation.

With Webster, Adams and Lincoln at their head, the National Republicans ran the state politically. Among the younger group, the most promising in 1830 was perhaps Edward Everett, that pale, courteous and polished man, tall and erect, with his handsome, conventional face and his fatal flow of rhetoric, who was nearly smothered by the adulation which surrounded him. Barely turned twenty, he had been a brilliant minister whose sermons moved John Quincy Adams to tears. Soon he left the pulpit for a chair at Harvard where his golden periods re-created Greece for Ralph Waldo Emerson. Now he shone in politics, a leading member of the House and the white hope of the clubs of Boston. In John Davis of Worcester, the conservatives had a good lawyer, reliable legislator and enormously successful vote-getter; he was known as "Honest John Davis," which is supposed to have provoked Henry Clay to exclaim, *"Honest John Davis, I say, Cunning John Fox!"* [1] From the bar conservatism recruited such talented younger men as Rufus Choate and Caleb Cushing, and from the business community itself came the independent and conscientious Nathan Appleton and able Abbott Lawrence.

Alexander H. Everett, Edward's older brother, helped organize Culture for political purposes in his dual role as National Republican member of the legislature and editor of the *North American Review*. He had been a protégé of John Quincy Adams, a professional diplomat and an amateur literary man and economist. Like his brother, he was learned, facile and restless. His literary abilities gained him prominence in Massachusetts politics as an author of protectionist and National Republican manifestoes; but he never established himself with the party or the people. His sister-in-law, Edward's wife, pronounced him "changeable and visionary," and Emerson's crisp comment summed up the general view — "very accomplished, but inspires no confidence." [2]

---

[1] *Reminiscences of the Rev. George Allen of Worcester*, F. P. Rice, ed., 54.
[2] Charlotte B. Everett to Edward Everett, January 6, 1833, Everett Papers; Emerson, *Journals*, III, 375. Emerson had regarded Everett's early book *Europe* as (in 1823) "the most considerable American book that has been published."

The sanction of Culture was reinforced by the immutable prescriptions of Justice and Law, as interpreted by such judges as Peter Oxenbridge Thacher and such lawyers as Jeremiah Mason. The clergy
hastened to add Religion. Some preachers, like James Walker and
Hubbard Winslow, openly advocated conservatism, while others, like
William Ellery Channing, accomplished much the same end by urging
reform, but only in ways in which it could not practically be achieved.
The work of Channing in sabotaging the liberal impulses of his day
by his theory of "internal" reform, with its indifference to external
social change, has never been properly appreciated.

Thus on all fronts the "natural aristocracy" of Massachusetts
wheeled into action. Richard Hildreth, associate editor of the furious
Whig sheet, the *Boston Atlas*, frankly described the result: —

> The truth is, that so stern, severe, active and influential was the
> authority which the allied hierarchy exercised, that few men who
> had property, standing, character, friends, to lose, cared to risk
> the consequences of those bulls of excommunication which were
> fulminated from the pulpit and the press, and those torrents of
> calumny, denunciation, and abuse, poured forth by a thousand
> fluent tongues, against whomsoever deserted the ark of the cove-
> nant, and allied himself to the uncircumcised Philistines.[3]

2

And what of the Philistines? "This day assemble in State convention the Jackson party," the librarian of the American Antiquarian
Society noted in his diary on September 1, 1831. ". . . It is rather a
miserable concern and is composed of such as want office and the
disaffected of all parties." [4]

Who else would be a Democrat? In 1828 two factions had supported Jackson: the diehard Federalists, led by Theodore Lyman,
and a group of small businessmen and politicians, refused social and

---

Emerson to J. B. Hill, March 12, 1823, Emerson, *Letters*, R. L. Rusk, ed., I, 107.
For an interesting and pathetic evidence of Everett's intoxication with reverie, see
his poem "Enigma," *Democratic Review*, I, 81 (October, 1837).

[3] Richard Hildreth, *Despotism in America*, 13–14.

[4] C. C. Baldwin, *Diary*, 139. Cf. Hildreth's account of the Democrats: "The
mass of the party seemed made up like the band of David, when he rose in rebellion against the Lord's anointed; — all who were in debt, all who were in distress, all who were discontented, enlisted beneath this banner; and to believe the
account of their opponents, not the tatterdemalions of Falstaff's enlistment were
more idle, vicious, dishonest and dangerous." *Despotism in America*, 13.

political acceptance by the governing class, led by David Henshaw. Jackson's victory made Henshaw collector of the Port of Boston, with control over the federal patronage, and thus boss of the party in the state. Gruff, candid and confident, Henshaw aimed straight at his objectives and accomplished them with a minimum of moral scruple. His health was bad, and in later years the gout ruined an already unstable temper.

Henshaw had made a fortune in the wholesale drug business. His administrative talents, now applied to politics, built up a smooth-running machine, generally known as the "Custom House" party. His leading aides were Andrew Dunlap, Attorney General of the state, an able lawyer who commanded even Justice Story's respect; John K. Simpson, a soft-spoken and wily businessman; and Nathaniel Greene, editor of the Henshaw organ, the *Statesman*, and later postmaster of Boston. Henshaw, who had sunk about thirty thousand dollars into the *Statesman*, procured Greene's appointment in part to insure repayment. The paper, replaced in 1831 by the *Boston Post*, passed on to the effervescent Charles Gordon Greene, Nathaniel's younger brother. His bright editing soon made it one of the country's leading Democratic sheets.[5]

Though a wealthy man, Henshaw had many of the prejudices of his humble origin. His personal rancor toward the aristocracy which had snubbed him was not unlike that of his good friend Isaac Hill. He took a forthright progressive stand on issues like imprisonment for debt and ballot reform; and he led the fight for a free bridge across the Charles River, a project bitterly opposed by conservatives because it threatened the profits of a neighboring toll-bridge, owned by Harvard and by prominent Bostonians.

But liberal Whigs like Alexander H. Everett also took these positions, and economic issues quickly exposed the limits of Henshaw's audacity. He was as much in favor of the banking system as Daniel Webster. His pamphlet of 1831 against Biddle's Bank contained, for example, no objections to banking and note issue in general, none to state banks nor to the social or economic implications of paper money. His hostility to the Bank was based chiefly on a desire to replace it by a larger and more powerful bank in which he, John K. Simpson, An-

---

[5] The standard work on Massachusetts politics for this period is A. B. Darling, *Political Changes in Massachusetts, 1824–1848*. For Henshaw, see also A. H. Ward, "David Henshaw," *Memorial Biographies of the New England Historic Genealogical Society*, I, 483–499; Bancroft to Van Buren, July 18, 1843, Van Buren Papers; Edward Everett, Diary, September 25, 1829, Everett Papers; P. M. Wetmore to W. L. Marcy, September 7, 1843, Marcy Papers.

drew Dunlap, Nathaniel Greene, Theodore Lyman, Henry Lee and other deserving characters of Democratic inclination should exercise control.[6]

3

For many years Massachusetts had required little more than these minor differences between a Henshaw and a Webster. But industrialism was stirring up new political demands which a straight line drawn between Webster and Henshaw failed to hold in check. The factory system, appearing at a time when both farmers and independent journeymen found the going increasingly hard, seemed to prefigure the gloomy end to which the laboring class was descending. The mill owners inadvertently intensified these anxieties by insisting on reprinting grim tales of English factory conditions as part of their campaign for a protective tariff.

Actual conditions in the factories, particularly at Lowell, were probably not bad. If they were not the "schools for virtuous industry" which Hezekiah Niles thought them, they were certainly not in these early days the "abode of wretchedness, disease and misery" that they seemed to overwrought men like Charles Douglas.[7] Yet their rise imposed on Massachusetts a sad and oppressive sense of its destiny. "It cannot be denied, or disguised," declared a House committee in 1836, "that the employments, and consequently the condition, of large classes of the population of New England, and especially of Massachusetts, are changed and are rapidly changing." The barren soil, the inexhaustible water power, the relatively dense population, the mechanical ingenuity of the people — all present the "sons and daughters of New England . . . with the alternative of becoming essentially a manufacturing people, or of bidding adieu to their native hills . . . and following the rising glories of the west." [8]

The first mutterings of the inevitable protest came in western

---

[6] One radical opponent, not unfairly, charged Henshaw with seeing "a wonderful difference between Democratic banks and corporations, and those of the Federal stamp; and it has been a favorite doctrine with him, to fight the latter with the former." *Bay State Democrat* (Boston), March 23, 1843. For Henshaw's petition for a $50,000,000 bank, see *Boston Post*, October 9, 1834; see also [David Henshaw], *Remarks upon the Bank of the United States.*

[7] *Niles' Register*, July 31, 1830; Commons, ed., *Documentary History*, VI, 217. When Lord Morpeth visited Lowell, he was reminded chiefly of "Mr. Owen's establishment at Lanark, without its conceits and drawbacks." Diary, manuscript transcript, 26.

[8] Massachusetts *House Document*, no. 49 (1836), 6–7.

Massachusetts. Farming and sheep-raising had at best been marginal activities, and the rising prices with the loss of labor to the mills were liquidating the margin, extending the reign of mortgages in a way reminiscent of the time of Shays' Rebellion. The result was the spontaneous formation of "Workingmen's" groups, with platforms revolving around the characteristic issues of status, free from class appeals or explicit economic arguments. "Our object is not to excite jealousy in one class of society towards another. We proscribe none; we are no levellers, our object is the public good." Thus their leaders were generally persons of unimpeachable conservatism, entirely orthodox on national issues. Henry Shaw, for example, was the Workingmen's candidate for Governor and at the same time the National Republican candidate for State Senator.[9]

During 1830, in the towns of eastern Massachusetts, small mechanics and workers, similarly apprehensive over their role in an industrialized future, began to form urban chapters of the Workingmen's party. The movement spread. A meeting at Boston, in February, 1832, was followed in September by a general convention of what was now called the "New England Association of Farmers, Mechanics and other Workingmen." Dr. Charles Douglas presided, and the delegates included Workingmen leaders like John B. Eldredge, Samuel Whitcomb, Jr., and Seth Luther; William Foster, a Boston merchant and intellectual, active in the free-trade movement; J. G. Harris, an able New Bedford newspaperman; and representatives of Berkshire discontent like William W. Thompson and W. S. Wait.[10]

Douglas, originally from New London, Connecticut, helped found in 1831 the *New England Artisan*, a weekly labor paper, published first at Pawtucket and then at Providence in Rhode Island. By the summer of 1832 it claimed a thousand subscribers, and through it Douglas sought to provide the movement with intellectual guidance. But a more colorful champion of the New England Association was the *Artisan*'s "Travelling Agent," Seth Luther. In 1832 Luther was nearly forty, tall and lanky, tending toward baldness, with a cud of tobacco generally in his mouth, and cherishing a bitter passion for the working classes.[11] He had knocked a good deal around the country,

[9] *Greenfield Gazette and Franklin Herald*, March 22, 1831. See also *ibid.*, November 30, December 7, 1830, March 15, 26, 1831.
[10] *New England Artisan*, October 11, 1832; *Boston Post*, September 7, October 9, 1832. For an earlier Boston meeting, see *Working Man's Advocate* (New York), August 28, 1830.
[11] Louis Hartz, "Seth Luther: Working Class Rebel," *New England Quarterly*, XIII, 401–403; *Columbian Centinel* (Boston), July 1, 1837.

East and West, town and frontier, even taking long trips through the wilderness.

When he returned to New England about 1830, he found the independent Yankee yeoman confronted by the menace of the new industrialism. His ready sympathies seized on the situation, spurred on by the writings of Douglas and of Theophilus Fisk (who had now left *Priestcraft Unmasked* to make a hard-hitting radical sheet out of the *New Haven Examiner*). In 1832 Luther, conspicuous in his famous green jacket, traveled through the mill towns, haranguing the operatives, checking on conditions and agitating for the New England Association, though few of its members were themselves factory workers. The intense interest excited by his reports of mill life reflected the deep concern with which the submerged classes were contemplating their future.

Luther shared the general range of Workingmen notions. His actual program was routine and rather harmless, and his special diagnosis of little interest. Social inequality, he argued, was "produced and sustained by *Avarice*" and was to be cured by education, especially by the establishment of manual-labor schools.[12] But his tone and manner were inflammatory, stirring emotions which might someday demand more basic solutions. No pamphleteer of the day surpassed him in real power of compassionate and horrifying description. There would rise up in his writing passages of crude but genuine feeling, condensing in imperative images the anxieties which were eating away at the security of the New England workingmen: bitter sketches of children whipped from bed at four in the morning, wakened by a plunge in cold water and sent off to work; of managers turning clocks backward or forward to cheat the workers of vital minutes of rest; of a dead gray life, crushed by want and oppression.

He was the master of a certain lurid rhetoric, grim, sarcastic and highly colored. His picture of Henry Clay visiting a factory is characteristic: —

> He sees the rosy face of *Houries* inhabiting this place of beauty. He is in ecstasy. He is almost *dumbfounded*. — He enjoys the enchanting scene with the most intense delight. For an hour more he seems to be in the regions described in Oriental song. His feelings are overpowered, and he retires almost unconscious of the cheers which follow his steps. . . .

[12] Seth Luther, *An Address to the Working-Men of New England*, 6. See also *An Address on the Right of Free Suffrage* and *An Address on the Origin and Progress of Avarice, and Its Deleterious Effects on Human Happiness*.

And the facts? Luther could never forget

> The widow's grief, the orphan's nakedness,
> The poor man's woe,
> These they *can never* see;
> And their dull ear
> Can never catch the wailing wretchedness
> Wrung from the lowly lived.
> The bitter tears that sickness or misfortune
> Cause to flow, ne'er warmed the *ice*
> Of their *obdurate* hearts.[13]

Yet these facts were not to be allayed by manual-labor schools, nor by the abolition of imprisonment for debt. Douglas, Luther, the *Artisan*, the New England Association volubly acknowledged the insecurities, but their remedies were feeble. Douglas, in particular, had little use for politics which he regarded as the domain of "the aristocracy, who now control all the political parties of the day." Following his lead, the New England Association, meeting shortly after the Bank veto, carefully avoided endorsements in the impending election, and a writer could declare in the *Artisan* on the very eve of voting, "The Bank of the United States, suitably constituted, is *the best bank the people can have*." [14]

4

In 1829 Samuel Clesson Allen made the last long trip home from Washington, leaving behind the House of Representatives, where he had served so faithfully for a decade, and returning to his beloved Northfield. He had come there, thirty-seven years before, a young man of twenty, first as a teacher, then as pastor of the village church. A stalwart man, of strong, logical mind, Allen proved too harshly Calvinistic for the kindly village. In 1798 he was discharged from the pulpit, at his own request, and turned to the law. He entered politics, served in the state legislature, was a delegate to the Hartford Convention and in 1819 was sent to Congress. The sabotage of Adams's administration by the aimlessly hostile Congress finally disgusted him. "A more corrupt body — (between you and me) not excepting Cromwell's Rump Parl^t. or the French Convention — was perhaps never assembled. . . . I hope we shall strive to keep the State gov^{ts}. pure and vigorous. They are our best hope and only sure refuge." [15]

---

[13] *Washington Globe*, May 14, 1832; Luther, *Address to the Working-Men*, 16.
[14] *New England Artisan*, October 11, 25, 1832.
[15] Allen to Samuel Lathrop, May 14, 1828, February 20, 1829, Miscellaneous

The ambitions of Jackson, that "man covered with crimes," darkened his thoughts of the future.

But when he returned to Northfield, living steadily in the village the whole year round, chatting with farmers down the road, mulling over the talk of the countryside, Allen found that the temper of the quiet village had changed, the old serene confidence was ebbing away. Perhaps Allen himself possessed misgivings, subdued up to now by the clatter of politics and the iron rule of party discipline. The unaccustomed leisure gave him the opportunity to play freely with his doubts, hunches and insights; and the spread of mortgages on every side provided ample material for worried analysis. What could be more dangerous to liberty than transferring the greater part of the landed property of the commonwealth to moneyed capitalists, turning the independent yeomanry into a helpless and degraded tenantry?

Allen proposed to set forth the dilemma of the Berkshire farmer in an address, in the fall of 1830, to the Hampshire, Franklin and Hampden Agricultural Society. But, as he worked out the principles of this dilemma, he discovered that they applied "not only to farmers, but to all other producers of the materials of wealth." The basic factors, he decided, were "the laws which govern the economical interests of men"; these "contribute more than government, more than morals, more than religion, to make society what it is in every country." And the basic distinction was not, say, between farmers and city dwellers, but between the productive and unproductive classes, between those whose labor increased the national wealth and those whose labor did not.[16]

In the primitive stages of society, Allen argued, every man had enjoyed the fruits of his own industry. The advances of technology and the increasing division of labor had "brought a great accession to the power of production, and seemed to be a remedy for the then existing evils of society." But the enormous gain in productive power had on the whole injured the lot of the worker. "What a state of things does society in Europe present! — an overstocked market and laborers without employment; provisions musting and tainting in the store-houses, and men perishing with hunger by the side of them; and yet there is no remedy." Nor was America likely to be immune from this destiny. "Is not the march of society in this country

Papers, Pennsylvania Historical Society. See also Herbert C. Parsons, *A Puritan Outpost*, especially 494-495; S. C. Allen, *An Oration, Delivered at Petersham, July 4, 1806.*

[16] S. C. Allen, *An Address Delivered . . . before the Hampshire, Franklin & Hampden Agricultural Society, October 27, 1830*, 5-6.

the same it has been there? . . . The unsettled lands in the West may retard its celerity here, and there may be several generations before it will reach the goal, but this is an accidental circumstance, and does not affect the certainty of the results." This condition of poverty and plenty arose, not, of course, from any lack of productive capacity, but from "an artificial state of things" which stood in the way of full production. "The natural limit of production," he pointed out, "is the wants of the consumers. Till these are supplied there is no reason why production should stop." Yet production obviously did stop far short of supplying these wants.

> There may be wool enough in the hands of the grower, and unemployed laborers ready to do the work, and yet the cloth for this man's coat cannot be made. . . . There exist the power and material of production and the want of the product, and yet the work of production cannot go forward.[17]

The trouble, Allen declared, lay in the fact that the colossal productivity had created a new class, which amassed wealth without creating it. "Trade gave rise to a currency, and credit, and the interest of money, and *these*, though they produced none of the objects of wealth, of themselves, became . . . mighty instruments of accumulation." In what did great fortunes now consist? "In stocks and bonds and notes and mortgages — in claims upon the future products of the land, and upon the future earnings of the industrious." The expense of a paper currency, for example, fell "on the productive class, and not on the capitalist." This was the pattern of society.

> However complicated the economical relations of men may become in an artificial state of society, the great truth cannot be concealed, that he who does not raise his own bread, eats the fruits of another man's labor.

This "race of non-producers, who render no equivalent to society for what they consume," their power founded on capital, not on land, without permanence, nationality or sense of moral obligation, constituted "a new sort of aristocracy, of a more uncompromising character than the feudal, or any landed aristocracy, ever can be." [18] The capitalist class had captured the state, and the workingman languished in oppression under its sway. "All wealth is the product of labor and belongs of right to him who produces it, and yet how small a part of the products of its labor falls to the laboring class!" [19]

[17] *Ibid.*, 7, 9, 10, 13. [18] *Ibid.*, 19, 11, 20, 30, 28.
[19] Allen to O. A. Brownson, August 18, 1834, H. F. Brownson, *Orestes A. Brownson's Early Life*, 116.

This political ascendancy of the financial aristocracy was the nub of the problem. "What have governments been, and what are they now, but the combinations of the rich and powerful to increase their riches and extend their power? . . . what have the laboring class to expect from their justice or their charity? What from a government in their control?" [20]

And the solution? "If you would renovate society you must begin with its economical relations." [21] He did not flinch from the political implications of such a program. "The rod of the oppressor must be broken," he said, "he will not throw it away. Thanks to our free political forms, the people can now do it without violence or wrong." In the administration of Andrew Jackson, Samuel Clesson Allen began to see the first essential steps toward reform.[22]

In near-by Stockbridge Theodore Sedgwick proceeded with similar directness from the agricultural grievances of western Massachusetts to a general theory of class oppression. Like Allen, Sedgwick came from a Federalist background. His father, the honest and hot-tempered Judge Sedgwick, considered Thomas Jefferson "the greatest rascal and traitor in the United States." [23] Theodore himself remained of Federalist disposition till after the War of 1812, when reading and reflection began to betray him. He became a friend of Van Buren's, studied Adam Smith, Say and Ricardo, followed the great Huskisson debate in Parliament in 1820 and emerged a convinced champion of free trade. His sympathy for the laboring classes grew increasingly marked. He read and pondered Byllesby, an Owenite pamphleteer, and undoubtedly Owen too, and his thoughts returned constantly to the means of improving the position of the wage earner.[24]

Jackson and the Bank War renewed his interest, as it had Allen's, in politics. For once, partisan battles seemed to Sedgwick to be based "on those fundamental distinctions . . . between the reformers and the Antireformers . . . and by Reform, I mean *Economical Reform* — the war for fair Play, on the part of the *poor*, & the *Labourers* will not end in my day." For Sedgwick, a radical free trader, the main end

[20] *Ibid.*, 115, 116.

[21] Allen, *Address*, 30.

[22] Brownson, *Brownson's Early Life*, 117, 118.

[23] Sarah Cabot Sedgwick and Christina Sedgwick Marquand, *Stockbridge, 1739–1939, A Chronicle*, 172; Mary E. Dewey, *Life and Letters of Catharine M. Sedgwick*, 34–35.

[24] Parke Godwin, *Bryant*, I, 184; W. C. Bryant, "Theodore Sedgwick," *The Biographical Annual, Containing Memoirs of Eminent Persons, Recently Deceased*, R. W. Griswold, ed., 19–21. Sedgwick's copy of L. Byllesby, *Observations on the Sources and Effects of Unequal Wealth*, is now in the Harvard College Library.

of reform was the destruction of monopolies; "and what is Monopoly," he declared, "other than one class getting all they can." [25]

A kindly nature made him shy off from some of the realities of party warfare. But, though he disliked some of Jackson's methods, he approved Jackson's ends so stoutly that by 1833 his old friend Daniel Webster was pompously cutting him in the street.[26] In *Public and Private Economy*, an amiable, rambling and didactic work, published in three volumes from 1836 to 1839, Sedgwick sketched his hopes for the future, based on his observations of British and American industrialism. The hatred of monopoly and sympathy for the common man which animated the treatise made it an appealing expression of the reasons which a humane and cultivated gentleman found to battle for Jacksonian democracy.

5

For all its background of Massachusetts Federalism, the diagnosis of Allen and Sedgwick resembled strikingly that of John Taylor of Caroline. The plight of the farmer in the shadow of capitalism drove them all to general speculations about industrial society. They agreed on the superior virtue of agriculture.[27] They named paper money and the rising financial aristocracy as the chief menace to liberty; and Allen's distinction between the producing and nonproducing classes was simply a restatement of Taylor's between "natural" and "artificial" property. Taylor carried his analysis to much greater detail than Allen, at least in any surviving work, and he adorned it with a brilliance of style, a prolixity and a perversity which are wanting from the steady, straightforward, almost elliptic writings of Allen. Yet the drift of their ideas was remarkably similar, not because the two men shared the same intellectual influences, but because they passed through the same experiences.

Allen was prepared to follow his premises to their conclusions. If the men along the Connecticut and in the Berkshires were growing increasingly helpless, in the grip of the new speculative order, they should break the ancient alliance with the Boston aristocracy and join Jackson in his fight against the Bank. Sedgwick similarly responded with enthusiasm to the hard-money program. But other Workingmen

---

[25] Sedgwick to Theodore Sedgwick, Jr., March 21, 1833, Sedgwick Papers.
[26] The same, October 30, 1833, Sedgwick Papers.
[27] "Every state has its chief interest in its soil. It is this, which constitutes it, a state." Allen, *Address*, 28. "Of all property, *land* is the most important." Sedgwick, *Public and Private Economy*, I, 41.

of western Massachusetts, who shared the original discontent, but failed to stiffen it into a doctrine, scurried back to the old alliance in face of the new challenge, ignoring their economic interests in favor of the more powerful commands of tradition, habit and the need for security.[28]

Yet in the meantime mechanics and operatives in the towns were waking to the paper-money issue. Having suffered less from the banking system of Massachusetts than from its mills and factories, they enlisted less quickly than the wage-earners of New York and Philadelphia in the campaign against the Bank, and their mentors, especially Douglas, Luther and the *Artisan*, were slow to detect any significance in Jackson's policy. "The first measure which served to rouse the people on this subject," as Frederick Robinson, the fiery radical from Marblehead, wrote in 1837, "was the President's veto." [29]

The excitement of the election was followed by Amos Kendall's speech to the Central Hickory Club in December, 1832, part of which seemed directly addressed to the dilemma of New England labor. Kendall concisely analyzed the effects of "Manufacturing Monopolies" upon the states in which they were located. "They cut up the farming interest; they break down the independent mechanic interest; they make large masses of people the dependents of a few capitalists, laboring for little else than a bare subsistence; already we have heard of their male operatives carted to the polls to vote for the will of their masters, and of their females subjected to worse than slavish labor and most brutal punishment." The speaker, who still made regular visits to his family at Dunstable, could talk with knowledge and conviction. "In fine, they make the people of the North *slaves to a few capitalists*, while the South and the West escape with being only *tributaries*." [30]

Such intimations from Washington, Jackson's triumphant tour of New England and the example of the New York Workingmen helped break down labor neutrality. Late in 1833 Samuel Clesson Allen rejected overtures to become the National Republican nominee for Governor with an able statement of his grounds for backing Jackson:

There are two great classes in the community founded in the relation they respectively bear to the subject of its *wealth*. The one is

[28] I am indebted to Malcolm Stearns, Jr., now Lieutenant (j.g.), U.S.N.R., for a clarification of the character of the Workingmen's movement; the completion of his researches will much enrich our knowledge of the Workingmen's agitation, a movement never adequately studied.

[29] *Boston Reformer*, July 28, 1837.

[30] *Washington Globe*, December 13, 1832.

the *producer*, and the other the *accumulator*. The whole products are divided between them. Has not one an interest to retain as much as it can, and the other an interest to *get* as much as it can? . . .

The administration of every government, whether it is seen or not, will be guided and controled by one or the other of these interests. . . .

It is in the nature of things that government will always adapt its policy, be the theory of its constitution what it may, to the interests and aims of the predominating class. . . .

I ask if labor has ever had a predominating influence in any government? . . .

I should be glad to see an experiment of *one* administration, of which the interests of this class should be the guiding star. . . .

I am encouraged in my hopes of an economical reform by the course which the President has taken in regard to the United States Bank. . . .

What government in these days has been able to stand against the power of *associated wealth?* It is the *real dynasty* of modern states.

The New England Association promptly endorsed Allen's letter, and a few days later a committee of Charlestown Workingmen invited him to be their candidate for Governor.[31]

Even Douglas was now overcoming his inhibitions sufficiently to call attention to the money question;[32] and the second Workingmen's party, which ran Allen for Governor in 1833 and 1834 and Sedgwick for the House in 1834, was much more urban, radical, specific and determined than the Workingmen's party of 1830–1831. "We predicted a month since, from indications then apparent," observed a Whig paper in 1834, "that Working-Menism and Jacksonism would turn out to be identical. Every day's development goes to confirm this belief. . . . the large majority of the prominent Working Men, are avowed Jackson men."[33]

Allen meanwhile lived on at Northfield. "I have engaged myself in my favorite studies," he told Van Buren; and in 1833 he delivered a

[31] Allen to the editor of the *Courier*, September 28, 1833, *Boston Courier*, October 1, 1833. For the National Republican overtures, see *ibid.*, January 26, September 16, 1833; for the convention and Allen's letter of acceptance, see *ibid.*, October 30, 1833, *Boston Post*. September 30, 1833, *New England Artisan*, October 2, 10, 1833.
[32] *New England Artisan*, January 10, August 8, 1833, etc.
[33] *Franklin Mercury*, November 1, 1834. Cf. *Northampton Courier*, October 29, 1834, "The Jackson party . . . are now playing a new and deadly game. They assume great humility and bite the dust and cry out we are the suffering people, the oppressed Working Men."

course of lectures on political economy at Amherst.[34] The panic session confirmed his worst fears about the capitalist aristocracy. "The question now at issue," he wrote vehemently to James K. Polk, "is whether we are to have a moneyed Dynasty, no a Bank Bill Dynasty in this country instead of a government by the people. . . . It is a question of *power*, yes of *sovereignty* and there can be no compromise." [35]

He repeated his stern warnings a month later in a public letter the Democratic press spread across the land.[36] To Orestes A. Brownson, now a Unitarian preacher at Canton, Allen wrote that, while ordinarily the working classes had little stake in party politics, "there are sometimes conflicts in the government which divide the public opinion in which their welfare is deeply involved. . . . The people ought to rally round Gen. Jackson in support of his measures. . . . This is a question between labor and the associated wealth of the country." [37] Under Allen's leadership the Workingmen's party in Massachusetts began to get wholeheartedly behind the hard-money policy and Andrew Jackson.

[34] Allen to Van Buren, May 13, 1833, Van Buren Papers; *Boston Reformer*, November 3, 1834.
[35] Allen to Polk, January 20, 1834, Polk Papers.
[36] *Washington Globe*, March 4, 1834, etc.
[37] Allen to Brownson, August 8, 1834, Brownson, *Brownson's Early Life*, 118.

XIII GEORGE BANCROFT AND RADICALISM IN MASSACHUSETTS

IN 1834 a third leader emerged in western Massachusetts, younger and more aggressive than Allen or Sedgwick. George Bancroft of Northampton, like the others, sharply repudiated his past in assuming his new role. He was the son of the Reverend Aaron Bancroft of Worcester, president of the American Unitarian Association and a staunch conservative. He was the son-in-law of Jonathan Dwight, a wealthy capitalist of Springfield. He was, moreover, the brother-in-law of Honest John Davis, soon to succeed Levi Lincoln as Governor, and Edward Everett had been one of his closest friends since Harvard days. He was a constant contributor to the *North American Review*, and till 1831 was co-proprietor of the Round Hill School at Northampton, which drew its students from some of the richest families in the country. All Bancroft's normal allegiances, in short, were with the "natural aristocracy."

1

Yet Bancroft was too clever and too skeptical to accept the values of Boston with the piety of an Everett, or to tailor his talents according to specifications laid down by Harvard and State Street. He went to Europe after finishing college in 1817; and when he returned the Athens of America seemed flat and disappointing. He appeared in a few pulpits, tutored a little at Harvard, published a book of poems and finally in 1823 helped establish a progressive school at Northampton. Though the Round Hill School flourished in the twenties, Bancroft was no great teacher, and Northampton too restricted a stage. More and more his writings won him attention as a rising young literary man.

Politics, too, vaguely attracted him. In 1826, in a Fourth of July speech at Northampton, he declared bravely in favor of "a democracy, a determined, uncompromising democracy," at a time when the word still sounded in some Massachusetts ears with the horrors of the French Revolution.[1] But when actually elected to the state legislature in 1830 by the Workingmen's party, he declined to serve. In the fall of 1830 he ignored the plea of the Jackson paper in Springfield that he stand for Congress. Early in 1831 he declined the nomination of the Workingmen for the state Senate. A few months later he even incorporated in an essay for the *North American Review* a passage discouraging young men of talent and education from entering politics.[2]

In the meantime, however, he wrote, also for the *North American*, an article on the United States Bank so unfriendly as to shock the Everetts and delight Martin Van Buren. Warning the Everetts that they might find his remarks on the McDuffie report "a little heretical," Bancroft still allowed them to believe that he ultimately favored recharter. Edward Everett confessed himself "embarrassed" over what should be done with the somewhat irreverent manuscript, and A. H. Everett tried to fix it up by tacking on a final sentence which explicitly advocated recharter. "I thought it on the whole more politic in the interest of the Review that this point should be quite clear," he explained to Bancroft in words which perhaps lend color to the charge that the *North American* was in the pay of the Bank. But Everett's conclusion hardly followed from Bancroft's argument. "There is very little reason to doubt," Bancroft had blandly declared, "that the sun would still rise and set, and the day be spent in its usual business, and merchandise be bought and sold, and bills of exchange be negotiated, even without . . . the Bank of the United States." This was more than a "little heretical," and Everett found a follow-up article "so decidedly hostile" to the Bank that he saw no choice but to refuse it.[3]

Bancroft, who knew what he was about, took care that Van Buren should see the *North American* piece, confiding to him that he con-

---

[1] George Bancroft, *An Oration Delivered on the Fourth of July, 1826, at Northampton, Mass.*, 19.

[2] A. H. Everett to Bancroft, May 21, 1830, Bancroft Papers; *Greenfield Gazette and Franklin Herald*, October 26, 1830; George Ticknor to Bancroft, March 19, 1831, A. H. Everett to Bancroft, March 26, July 6, 1831, Bancroft Papers.

[3] For the letters about Bancroft's article, see Bancroft to E. Everett, June 22, 1830, A. H. Everett to Bancroft, December 15, 1831, July 31, 1831, Bancroft Papers; E. Everett to A. H. Everett, August 6, 1830, Everett Papers; A. H. Everett to Jared Sparks, April 10, 1831, Sparks Papers. The long quotation is from Bancroft, "The Bank of the United States," *North American Review*, XXXII, 23 (January, 1831).

The charge that the *North American* was in the Bank's pay was made in 1837 by Richard Hildreth, high in the inner councils of the Whig party in this period; having apparently received no denial, he repeated it in 1840. [Richard Hildreth], *The History of Banks*, 82; Hildreth, *Banks, Banking, and Paper Currencies*, 86.

sidered the Bank contrary to the principles of equal rights. Actually, his case in the article rested much more on state-banking prejudices than on broad principle. "The undoubted merits of the National Bank are urged too exclusively," he suavely observed, "as though other sound establishments of the country were not just as wisely, moderately, and efficiently conducted." [4] The display of technical knowledge suggests that he consulted with Jonathan Dwight, his father-in-law and a heavy investor in state banks.

Bancroft was still not ready to make the break. When he attended a presidential reception in 1831, he was still the supercilious Harvardian, conceding Jackson's good manners and warm heart, "but touching his qualifications for President, avast there — Sparta hath many a wiser son than he." The next year at the National Republican State Convention at Worcester he served, along with Edward Everett, Abbott Lawrence and others, on the committee which issued a ringing anti-Jackson address to the people.[5]

Yet, sometime after the election of 1832, he decided to abandon his class and cast his lot with the despised Democrats and Workingmen. Political apostasy is too complex a problem to be ascribed simply to ambition or treachery. Bancroft's whole life had been a series of minor revolts against the "natural aristocracy," and occasional outbursts like his speech of 1826 betrayed a profound sympathy with the idea of democracy. But his whole upbringing proscribed these liberal impulses. Thus a precarious balance of loyalties developed, producing a vacillation which was by no means evidence of insincerity.

What precipitated the final decision? Bancroft had already begun work on his great history of the United States, the first volume of which would come out in 1834. This determination to devote his life to such a history, which he conceived as the story of the invincible progress of human liberty, undoubtedly released his democratic prepossessions in full flood. The Bank War was contributing to his political education. Perhaps disappointment over his slow advancement in the National Republican party was making him restless. Earnest conversations with men like Samuel C. Allen in near-by Northfield, and Judge Marcus Morton, perennial Democratic nominee for Governor, who came occasionally to Northampton on his circuit, allowed him to explore the implications of democracy.

[4] Bancroft to Van Buren, January 10, 1831, *Proceedings of the Massachusetts Historical Society*, XLII, 382; Bancroft, "The Bank of the United States," *North American Review*, XXXII, 23 (January, 1831).

[5] Bancroft to Sarah Dwight Bancroft, December 25, 27, 1831, M. A. DeWolfe Howe, *Life and Letters of George Bancroft*, I, 192–196; *Journal of the Proceedings of the National Republican Convention, Held at Worcester, October 11, 1832,* 6.

He finally took the step, not as an item in political opportunism, but as an act of faith. Though he often in later life ignored his views of 1834, he never recanted them. And, in expressing them in 1834, joining a minority group in a solidly conservative state, he clearly had little to gain. "I have never made disclaimers or apologies," he said rather sadly a decade later. "To advocate Democracy in Massachusetts, is no holiday pastime. . . . Our course is not too often enlivened by success; we are wounded sometimes even by our friends. We tread a thorny path, but it leads upwards to the home of freedom, of justice, of truth." [6]

Much in the career of this brilliant and devious man is open to question. Ambition repeatedly led him to insincere flattery and insincere condemnation, to betraying his friends and aiding his enemies. But these defects of character operated after 1834 within the limits of the democratic creed. That, at least, was authentic, deeply felt and irrevocable, and the evidence for its honesty was the patient and conscientious devotion with which George Bancroft, laboring through the years, wrote his *History*. There was an integrity about the masterpiece which overwhelmed all the petty duplicities of the man.

2

Bancroft announced his conversion in two remarkable letters published in October, 1834. The first, addressed to "the Workingmen of Northampton," dealt mainly with the Bank question. He now rested his case on thoroughgoing hard-money arguments, stated with great power and eloquence. The economic effect of paper money was bad, the political power of the Bank too great ("no man or body of men ought ever to be invested with such exorbitant powers that, in case of misdemeanor, the guilty cannot be arraigned without plunging the country in distress"); "but the great objection in my mind to the continuance of the present United States Bank," he declared, "lies in its tendency to promote extreme inequalities in point of fortune."

With a wealth of historical illustration, he set forth the fate of political liberty when not founded on economic equality. "Where the people possess no authority, their rights obtain no respect." Economic oligarchy led to despotism. "Show me one instance where popular institutions have violated the rights of property, and I will show you a hundred, nay a thousand instances, where the people have been pillaged by the greedy cupidity of a privileged class. There is more danger from monopolies than from combinations of workmen. There is

---

[6] *Bay State Democrat*, December 5, 1843.

more danger that capital will swallow up the profits of labor, than that labor will confiscate capital." On every side, he cried, the business community was exerting its power, and social conflict was irrepressible. "The feud between the capitalist and the laborer, the house of Have and the house of Want, is as old as social union, and can never be entirely quieted." [7]

His second letter sought to show how the influence of the few had blocked government by the people. Capital controlled the press and the schools. Through corporations it was extending its rule over industry, and through mortgages it was despoiling agriculture of its profits. And these obstacles to the free exercise of the people's power might turn into threats to its very existence. The great menace to liberty, Bancroft said, "lies in the increasing, unequal distribution of wealth." He returned again to the urgent issue of the day. "It is in reference to the inequalities of condition, that the question respecting the United States Bank becomes important." [8]

The felicity of phrase and luster of style brought the letters state-wide attention. The response of Bancroft's old friends was rapid and venomous. In Northampton the respectable people whispered that he had deserted the Whig party out of disappointment at not being nominated for Congress in 1834. "We despise him," declared the local paper, "for his political inconstancy, arising from causes *we know* to be wholly mercenary." [9] The dinner tables at Springfield buzzed with gossip over Bancroft's political vagaries. When someone asked Edmund Dwight, a brother-in-law, whether Bancroft possessed a moral sense, the reply was prompt: "Certainly not." The *American Monthly Magazine* took it upon itself to deny at elaborate length that Bancroft was insane or, conversely, an atheist. The conservative *Boston Atlas* added that the wage earners of Boston, "from the halls of infidelity and atheism; from the dram shops and dram cellars . . . are loud in the praises of their new leader and co-worker." [10]

The storm raged furiously, and the sharp-eyed ex-schoolmaster was

[7] Bancroft to the Workingmen of Northampton, October 1, 1834, *Boston Courier*, October 22, 1834.

[8] Bancroft to the public, October 22, 1834, *Northampton Courier*, October 29, 1834.

[9] Quoted in the *Boston Centinel and Gazette*, August 26, 1836. A variation on this canard appeared in a series of articles published in the *Baltimore Patriot* in 1846, under the signature of "Northampton," and later gathered in a pamphlet entitled *To George Bancroft, Secretary of the Navy, the Traducer and Eulogist of General Andrew Jackson.*

[10] Edmund Dwight to Bancroft, February 20, 1843, Bancroft Papers; "Bancroft's Oration," *American Monthly Magazine*, II, 305 (September, 1836); *Boston Atlas*, quoted in the *Boston Post*, November 7, 1834.

chilled by its blasts. "I have been attacked with unmeasured severity," he reported to Van Buren; and to Edward Everett he declared that, though he was indifferent to "unmerited censure, . . . I shall probably remove to Philadelphia; and make my abiding place within the quiet of that city." [11]

But there were compensations. For a moment, Bancroft became the conscience of the Democratic party in Massachusetts, crystallizing the impulses of reform so long ignored by the Custom House. Judge Morton snatched a minute from a capital trial in Cambridge to scrawl his enthusiasm. Orestes A. Brownson exclaimed to a friend, "We may now take hope, the cause of the people is safe." Samuel C. Allen approved, and Workingmen leaders pledged their support.[12] Outside the state, Bancroft won new fame. Van Buren and James K. Paulding consoled him for the conservative recriminations, and liberal papers, like the *New York Evening Post*, republished the letters.[13]

In February, 1835, Bancroft, who soon abandoned all thought of Philadelphia, advanced his interpretation of Democratic principle another step. In a brilliant discourse at Deerfield on Washington's Birthday, he distinguished among the three theories of government: the Tory, which taught that rulers govern by divine right; the Whig, which made political liberties a matter of contract between rulers and ruled; and the Democratic, which declared that the right of government comes from the people, resides in them, and is theirs and theirs alone.

The great threat to democratic freedom, he declared, came from the supremacy of the Whig moneyed aristocracy, which had overthrown Tory feudalism in Britain and "with a few exceptions" had ruled the United States "ever since the adoption of the Constitution." This aristocracy had three branches: commerce, corporations and slaveholders. Manufacturing corporations gained his special condemnation for dividing society "into two great classes of employers and operatives," but the slaveholding aristocracy seemed to him "the most selfish, the most united, and the most overbearing of all." [14]

It was a bold speech — "a fearless and earnest declaration," said the

[11] Bancroft to Van Buren, November 17, 1834, *Proceedings of the Massachusetts Historical Society*, XLII, 383; Bancroft to Everett, December 29, 1834, Bancroft Papers.

[12] Morton to Bancroft, December 18, 1834, Morton Letterbooks; Brownson to Bancroft, September 24, 1836, W. S. Wait to Bancroft, October 15, 1834, J. B. Eldredge to Bancroft, September 20, 1834, Bancroft Papers.

[13] Paulding to Bancroft, November 21, 1834, Bancroft Papers; *New York Evening Post*, November 20, 1834.

[14] *Franklin Mercury*, February 24, March 3, 1835.

Hampshire Republican, "of the principles, which, for a short time
past, have been known by the name of the principles of the Workingmen"[15] — and the confident affirmation of the democratic creed appealed strongly to men restless under the perfunctory leadership of
David Henshaw. By 1835 Bancroft's influence was so great that Henshaw had to invite him to write the address of the party at its annual
convention.

The young schoolmaster had his defects for the new role of politician. An insignificant, scholarly-looking man, his manners abrupt,
disconcerting and peculiar, many found him irritating. In conversation he was nervous, incisive, sparkling and extremely intelligent. As
one observer reported, "He is full charged; and gives it off like an
electric jar."[16] As a speaker he had few advantages of person or voice;
but his well-stocked mind, his persuasive flow of ornate language and
his earnestness of bearing carried over to his audience. His political
judgment was penetrating, and his temperament inclined him toward
the offensive. The political future lay open for those prepared to
grasp it.

3

David Henshaw was learning that it was dangerous to try to
ride out a revolution in which you only half believe. Even in the city of
Boston, beneath the very doors of the Custom House, there were stirrings of revolt. The convention of the New England Association in
1833 had charged its members to consult together "with a view to
the establishment of *trades unions*," and in January, 1834, a Workingmen's committee, led by Charles Douglas and Seth Luther, resolved
to set up a General Trades Union in Boston. By July 4 the Union
held a large celebration. Its parade was acknowledged by Charles
Gordon Greene's *Boston Post* to be "the most splendid" of the day.[17]

The rise of the Union provoked the bitter opposition of conservatism. Twenty-two religious societies denied the Union the use of their
halls for the Fourth of July.[18] Law added its disapproval. Judge Peter
Oxenbridge Thacher of the Municipal Court, stockholder in the
Bank of the United States, opponent of the Sunday mails, was ac-

[15] *Hampshire Republican*, March 11, 1835.
[16] Lucian Minor, "A Virginian in New England Thirty-five Years Ago," *Atlantic Monthly*, XXVII, 682 (June, 1871).
[17] *Niles' Register*, October 26, 1833; *Boston Post*, July 7, 1834. For the formation
of the Union, see *Post*, March 6, 15, 1834, and Frederick Robinson, *An Oration
Delivered before the Trades Union of Boston*, Appendix.
[18] *Boston Post*, July 7, 1834.

customed to incorporate his prejudices into charges to the Suffolk County Grand Jury with which, as Charles Greene put it, "the public for several years past, have been periodically bored." [19] In 1832 Thacher had declared that the doctrine of criminal conspiracy applied to "combinations, amongst journeymen mechanics and laborers, to raise their wages, and regulate the hours of work," even if nothing was done to carry this intention into effect. In 1834 the Judge returned to his fears, denouncing those who "attempt to excite the employed against the employers, and borrowers against lenders, and thus to lead the poor to wage a civil war against the rich." [20]

Respectable society seconded these opinions. Samuel Gridley Howe, who had fought for the independence of Greece, was considered an expert on revolutions, and his words were ominous. "Ten years ago," he wrote in 1834, "and who would have foretold so early a division among the people, and the existence of a feeling of hostility between the rich and the poor? But is not this dreadful state at hand?" Two months later the *New-England Magazine* assailed the "ultra-radicals" who, "by establishing newspaper organs, feeing lecturers, proposing strikes for wages, . . . have endeavored to keep themselves in a party distinct from all others." No one could doubt the origin of this subversive spirit. "Jacksonism and Radicalism amount, however, to about the same thing; it is only in the names, that there is any difference." Theophilus Parsons delivered a terrified address on the duties of educated men in a republic to the Phi Beta Kappa Society of Harvard College in 1835, pleading with the young gentlemen to save society by teaching the masses "the clear and simple truths, on which the rights of property rest." [21]

But the Union continued to prosper. Rising prices and the growing demand for labor during 1835 so emboldened the workingmen that in the spring the building trades launched a campaign for a ten-hour day. The master stonecutters agreed to accede if the other employers would. At a heated meeting of the stonecutters in April, the general sentiment favored striking anyway and taking the consequences. "I am for arraying the poor against the *principles* that keep them poor," declared A. H. Wood, a union leader, "and if this be

[19] *Boston Post,* December 24, 1834.
[20] P. O. Thacher, *Charge to the Grand Jury of the County of Suffolk,* (1832), 7, (1834), 16. For Greene's acid comments, see *Boston Post,* December 6, 1832, December 24, 26, 1834.
[21] S. G. Howe, "Atheism in New-England," *New-England Magazine,* VII, 500 (December, 1834); "Radicalism," *ibid.,* VIII, 143 (February, 1835); Theophilus Parsons, *An Address Delivered before the Phi Beta Kappa Society of Harvard University, 27 August, 1835,* 16.

arraying the poor against the rich, then I say go on with tenfold fury." The desire for the shorter day was nearly unanimous. "By the old system," as one speaker bitterly put it, "we have no time for mental cultivation — and that is the policy of the big bugs — they endeavor to keep people ignorant by keeping them always at work." [22] Strikes followed, but apparently only the plasterers were successful, and the organization began to break up. By October it was reported that no one was left in the Union but the president. [23]

A main cause of the decay of the Union was the enthusiasm with which the workingmen were turning to politics. The *Post* had always treated them (on behalf of Mr. Henshaw), not as enemies to society, but as fellow workers in the same vineyard, and Charles Greene had defended with vigor their right to organize. [24] When the currency question emphasized the identity of interest, the mutual sympathy was transformed into co-operation. In March, 1834, while friends of the Bank deluged Washington with complaints and pleas, a meeting gathered at Faneuil Hall to oppose the restoration of the deposits. The speakers included, not only Henshaw's crew of ward bosses, but Seth Luther and Charles Douglas; and after a series of prepared resolutions had attacked the Bank along the Henshaw line, Douglas rose, his face hard and serious, to offer a final resolution assailing the whole paper system as tending "to subject the honest productive laborers to the control of the non-producers, and thereby to place undue power in the hands of the monied aristocracy." These were new premises, more familiar to General Jackson than to David Henshaw, but he had no choice but to accept. [25]

4

At the Union celebration on July 4, Frederick Robinson, Democratic member of the legislature, made a special bid for labor support.

[22] *Boston Post*, April 17, 1835. In May, Wood and Seth Luther drew up a circular on the ten-hour day. "The work in which we are now engaged," the statement declared, "is neither more nor less than a contest between *Money* and LABOR: *Capital* which can only be made productive by *labor* is endeavoring to crush *labor* the only source of all wealth." *Post*, May 6, 7, 1835; *Boston Investigator*, May 15, 1835; Commons, ed., *Documentary History*, VI, 73 ff.

[23] *Boston Post*, October 6, 1835.

[24] "If the plan of forming a Trades Union proves as successful as present appearances give us reason to anticipate, it will tend more to elevate the character and increase the . . . influence of the Workingmen, than anything which has heretofore been attempted." *Boston Post*, April 5, 1834. This paper is a much neglected source for labor history.

[25] *Boston Post*, March 12, 13, 15, 17, 1834.

A leader of the Democratic left wing and a good friend of Charles Douglas's, Robinson was thirty-five years old, a shrewd parliamentarian and an effective speaker, if somewhat given to ranting. He had fought his bill abolishing imprisonment for debt through the legislature, and his career was based on a clear conviction of the class basis of politics. "There always exists, in every community, two great interest[s]," he once declared: —

> — that of the producer, whose interest it is to secure to himself, as much as he can of the fruit of the labor, of his own hands; and that of the capitalist, whose interest it is to take from the producer as much as he possibly can of the productions of his industry. A contest between these two classes is always going on in every country, where the capitalist has not completely reduced the producer to a state of slavery. . . . In whatever way the wealth of the community can be absorbed into few hands, the end must always be the same; it must be slavery for the masses.

Robinson foresaw a dismal future for the people, "obliged to labor on, from generation to generation, the servile tenants of haughty landlords . . . or in the monotonous, never-ceasing labor of the mills — devoting whole lives, perhaps, to the daily toil of watching the progress of a single thread in the looms . . . while the whole surplus of the fruit of their labor" supports a powerful aristocracy. What could the people do against their oppressors? "All the fountains of information are in their hands." Schools and colleges, pulpit, bar and press were all under their patronage. The only hope for the working-men, he told the General Trades Union, was "by union among ourselves, and by acting in concert with the democracy of the country." [26]

The wage earners saw the point, and their growing absorption in practical politics was bringing new leaders to the fore. Douglas, too much a doctrinaire, became increasingly unhappy and in 1836 returned to New London. Seth Luther, with as little liking for politics, now resumed his travels, continuing labor agitation in New York, Cincinnati and elsewhere. In their place A. H. Wood was emerging

[26] Theophilus Fisk (quoting Robinson), *Banking Bubble Burst*, 49; *Boston Post*, March 10, 1835; Robinson, *Oration Delivered before the Trades Union*, 6. On the same July 4, William Emmons, the friend of Colonel Johnson, speaking on Boston Common, promised the working classes, "The time is fast approaching when they are to control the destiny of this nation." Emmons, *An Oration . . . Delivered Fourth of July, 1834, on Boston Common*, 10–11. For Charles Douglas on Robinson, see his letter to A. H. Wood, March 17, 1837, *Boston Reformer*, March 24, 1837.

as the main representative of the trade-union movement, but he did not inspire much zeal, and the actual reins of leadership fell rather to men outside the working classes.

William Foster, candidate for Congress from Boston in 1834 on both Workingmen and Democratic tickets, was an elderly Boston merchant. As a youth he had participated with enthusiasm in the French Revolution, and in later years he used to contribute essays, under the pseudonym of "Franklin," to newspapers up and down the Atlantic coast, generally attacking the protective tariff. He supported Henry Lee for Congress, in 1830, but when the Bank War drove most Boston free traders back into National Republican ranks, Foster, accepting the logic of his principles, opposed the Bank. For him, as for Theodore Sedgwick, free trade meant unqualified enmity to monopoly, and he added the same sympathy for the underprivileged. "We are accused of exciting the evil passions of the poor, against the rich," he once declared. ". . . I would destroy those evil passions . . . by destroying *poverty* itself. To admit that the poor exist *in sufficient numbers, in this country*, in a degree to cause alarm to the rich, is the severest censure that could be passed on all our boasted institutions." [27]

Theophilus Fisk, another new Workingmen leader, had begun to attract attention in Boston at the series of Trades Union lectures in the winter of 1834–1835. Thirty-three years old in 1834, he was a graduate of Norwich Academy who had abandoned a promising career in the Universalist pulpit for *Priestcraft Unmasked* and the *New Haven Examiner*. At New Haven his passionate anticlericalism began to merge into an equally passionate anticapitalism. Fisk's style was bold, vivid and declamatory, abounding in figures of speech, often destroying its effect by its very vehemence and trailing into bombast.[28]

His political thinking owed a great deal to friendships with Samuel Clesson Allen, Foster, Robinson and A. H. Everett, as well as to studies of the writings of W. M. Gouge and William Leggett. But, with his facility of pen and intensity of feeling, he sometimes put radical ideas more strikingly, or developed them more implacably, than their originators. His address to the mechanics of Boston at Julien Hall in May, 1835, entitled "Capital against Labor," was a brilliant

[27] *Boston Post*, March 18, 1834. See also Frederick C. Pierce, *Foster Genealogy*, 954–956; Foster to Van Buren, June 30, 1833, to Silas Wright, January 3, 1835, to Van Buren, January 27, 1838, Van Buren Papers.

[28] John Fairfield to his wife, December 5, 1835, Fairfield, *Letters*, 37; *Washington Globe*, December 28, 1835; *New York New Era*, July 4, 1840; W. A. Ellis, ed., *Norwich University, 1819–1911*, II, 110.

and fervent summary of the radical position.[29] Again and again in his writings he returned to his basic theme: "This artificial and unequal distribution of property, is at the foundation, is the fruitful source, of all the evils and vice of which society complains."[30]

Early in 1835 he became co-editor of the *Boston Reformer*, as the *New England Artisan* had been rechristened when moved to Boston in 1834. Charles Douglas, his predecessor, lacked journalistic sense, and Fisk, along with L. S. Everett, another ex-Universalist preacher, brought new liveliness to the sheet. After a time they were succeeded by A. H. Wood. In the spring of 1836 Fisk went south to Charleston. The *Reformer* remained the organ of the radical Democrats until the summer of 1836. Then it fell into the hands of Orestes A. Brownson, who tried to steer it through a heated presidential campaign on a non-political tack till angry readers forced his dismissal.[31] While the *Reformer* never really challenged the *Post*, mainly because the *Post* was a much better newspaper, it represented a volume of feeling which might someday embarrass David Henshaw.

5

Marcus Morton of the state Supreme Court was Henshaw's perennial candidate for Governor. At the start, they worked well together. Morton accepted the necessity of strict party organization, and his own political views were unobtrusive. His particular friend in Washington was Calhoun, with whom he had gone to law school at Litchfield, and his instinct was to oppose the campaign against the Bank and even a second term for Jackson. Yet he also was deeply persuaded that democracy's main foe was the "powerful monied aristocracy," and he kept warning Henshaw, "All societies are neces-

[29] Theophilus Fisk, "Capital against Labor," *Working Man's Advocate*, July 25, 1835; *New York Evening Post*, August 6, 1835.

[30] Fisk, *Labor the Only True Source of Wealth*, 3–4.

[31] The first issue came out on November 3, 1834, under the title of the *Daily Reformer*, with Douglas billed as editor. By February, 1835, the title was the *Chronicle and Reformer*, with Everett and Fisk as "Editors and Proprietors." In July it was called the *Independent Chronicle, and Boston Daily Evening Reformer*, published "By ʌn Association of Mechanics," with no editor named. By June, 1836, it had become, under the title of the *Boston Reformer*, a triweekly paper published by A. H. Wood. In July Brownson became its editor, Wood staying as publisher, but by November Brownson was out, Wood was editor and publisher, and the paper, now a weekly, was called the *Boston Weekly Reformer, or Herald of Union & Progress*. Brownson returned for a good part of 1837. The paper was still alive as a weekly in 1838, under the name of the *Boston Reformer and Anti-Monopolist*, with Wood as editor.

sarily divided into two parts. . . . It ought, in some way, to be made apparent to the people, that we rally upon this division." [32]

The struggle over recharter provided further political education. Morton learned that radical emotions required radical policies, and he gradually accepted the full implications of the hard-money program.

> My opinion [he explained to Calhoun in 1834] is that the danger most to be feared and guarded against is encroachment by the powerful upon the weak — and by the rich upon the poor — and not the reverse. My constant apprehension is that the weaker members of the community will be divested of, or restricted in their rights. The greatest vigilance is needed to protect the common mass of the community — the industrious, quiet, producing classes of Society against the overbearing influence of the rich and the powerful. . . . If I am not always found on the side of the weak against the strong, whether in reference to Governments, corporations or people, it will be because I err in finding which that side is.

That simple, heartfelt statement expressed unyielding conviction. As Morton wrote years later, "I was born, have lived, and shall die a *radical* Democrat. I can no more abandon my faith in Democracy than in Christianity." [33]

The accession of the Workingmen — whom Henshaw a few years before had declared to be as alien to the Democratic party as the Federalists [34] — put new emphasis on the question of political objectives, and the boom of 1834–1835 made the hard-money program a crucial issue. Henshaw and his group, with their heavy investments in bank and corporation stock, had no intention of sticking by the hard-money policy. Early in 1835 the radicals and the *Reformer* accordingly began a bitter fight on the issues of state banking, small notes and the overissue of paper money. [35]

As the fall elections drew near, Henshaw, his hand forced by the rising radical sentiment, had to concede George Bancroft's appointment to draft the party platform. Bancroft now meditated his position: how far could he go in committing the party? Morton gave him a blank check early in September: "I have no fear that any one will represent *too strongly* my radical democracy, my hostility to monopolies and everything approaching or resembling them." A week

[32] Morton to Calhoun, December 8, 1828, to Henshaw, February 11, 1830, Morton Letterbooks.

[33] Morton to Calhoun, February 13, 1834, to F. A. Hildreth, May 11, 1849, Morton Letterbooks.

[34] J. B. Derby, *Political Reminiscences*, 112.

[35] *Boston Post*, March 26, 30, September 5, 1835; *Franklin Mercury*, April 7, 1835; *New York Evening Post*, March 11, 1835; *Niles' Register*, May 30, 1835.

later Henshaw transmitted through Charles Gordon Greene the wistful hope that there would be "no wild, thoughtless, and extravagant doctrines introduced." [36]

But Bancroft's mind was made up, and his address proved to be a ringing affirmation of "the mission of America" as "the culture and the happiness of the masses." [37] When Henshaw made no move to pick up the gauntlet, party unity seemed assured. But shortly before election day antagonisms flared up again in Boston, where the radicals were most intransigent and most suspicious, and the *Reformer* finally bolted the whole organization in favor of a ticket of its own, headed by George Bancroft for Governor. [38] Notice was served on the Democratic party that it must cleave to the Jackson line if it wanted the labor vote.

6

The ratio of paper money to specie in the state was increasing alarmingly. In 1828 it had been a little more than 3 to 1; by 1833 it was over 8½ to 1. The capitalization of banks had risen from nineteen million dollars to twenty-eight, and the notes in circulation had more than doubled, while the amount of specie in the state had actually declined. [39] In the legislature, the first line of defense, a few Democrats tried to check the drive for more incorporations and increased capitalization. Frederick Robinson and, from 1837, Samuel Clesson Allen, Jr., took the floor repeatedly against banking and corporation bills.

But the most effective Democrat in the legislature was Robert Rantoul, Jr., of Gloucester. Only thirty years old in 1835, he had gone to Andover and then to Harvard (where he had helped make life miserable for George Bancroft, the young tutor, just returned from Europe). Slender and quick, talking rapidly and nervously, his head thrown back, his pale face and sallow cheeks glowing with excitement, Rantoul would deliver his slashing speeches, witty, earnest, savage, indignant, by turn, till half a dozen opponents would spring to their feet in desperate effort to reconstruct their shattered cases. [40]

[36] Morton to Bancroft, September 9, 1835, Greene to Bancroft, September 16, 1835, Bancroft Papers.

[37] *Boston Post*, October 16, 1835.

[38] *Boston Post*, November 24, 1835. William Lloyd Garrison was on this ticket as candidate for Congress.

[39] *Abstract Exhibiting the Condition of the Banks in Massachusetts on the First Saturday of August, 1843*, prepared by J. A. Bolles, 18–19.

[40] See the vivid description, probably by Whittier, in the *New York Evening Post*, November 21, 1835; Luther Hamilton, *Rantoul*, 312, 847; *Madisonian* (Washington), August 7, 1840; Eben Stone, "Address Delivered before the Essex Bar,"

His insight into economic problems was unexcelled among Massachusetts politicians. Among the first to grasp the technical implications of the hard-money policy, he inveighed repeatedly and acutely against the unrestrained issue of paper money. His description of the relationship of banking inflation and the business cycle was detailed, and in part original. He stated most clearly the radical criteria for new corporate proposals.[41] Yet, for all his ability, Rantoul was not always to be relied upon. Deeply ambitious for political advancement, he made one deal after another with the conservative Democrats, instead of standing by his natural alliance with Bancroft and Morton. Never courageous enough to line up wholeheartedly with the radicals, never cynical enough to go over completely to the Custom House, he never shared unconditionally in either side's triumph.

The sudden devotion in 1836 of Benjamin F. Hallett to the anti-monopoly cause brought forward, however, a far more unprincipled careerist. Hallett's brief political past had already revealed his main characteristic: an unswerving loyalty to any party so long as it promised personal advantage. His own reputation was established in the Anti-Masonic movement. When Anti-Masonry began to founder, Hallett dallied with Garrison and the abolitionists, toward whom he had been friendly when the press was almost unanimously hostile; with the anti-Catholic movement, which he assisted by writing an introduction to *Six Months in a Convent;* and with Edward Everett and the Whigs, with whom he was intriguing in 1835, at the same time denouncing strikes and the ten-hour day. But in 1836 he finally made up his mind and sprang forth, full-panoplied, into the ranks of the radical Democrats.[42]

An energetic and thick-skinned politician, Hallett could be no more ignored than trusted. Charles G. Greene christened him the "soldier of fortune," who had "fought for, and betrayed, every party and faction that has arisen since his entrance into political life," and the

---

Historical Collections of the Essex Institute, XXVI, 34–35; Merle E. Curti, "Robert Rantoul, Jr., the Reformer in Politics," *New England Quarterly,* V, 264–280.

[41] "To grant no charters, unless a strong case could be made out by the applicants *for* a charter; unless the objects for which they prayed a charter were likely to be beneficial to the Commonwealth, — also, that they had the capital they named, — and that such capital was actually put into the concern. Restrictions, too, should be imposed upon them, so as to prevent their departing from the purposes they professed to pursue. The burden of proof was on the applicants." Hamilton, *Rantoul,* 313.

[42] W. P. and F. J. Garrison, *William Lloyd Garrison, 1805–1879,* I, 482, II, 32, 43; *Boston Post,* March 21, 27, 1835; Edward Everett, Journal, March 18, 1835, Everett Papers; *Boston Press, and Semi-Weekly Advocate,* September 1, 1835.

nickname stuck.[43] Marcus Morton reported in 1845 that "all the Whigs and three quarters of the democrats" thought him dishonest, Edward Everett shuddered at his "blackness of heart," and Daniel Webster summed up the general feeling with the contemptuous observation, "He is a pretty vile fellow." [44] There could be no more solid tribute to the popular appeal of radical democracy than that Ben Hallett considered it wise to pose as a radical Democrat.

In a similar way, the attachment of men like Amasa Walker to the party was testimony to the honesty of its radicalism. Walker, a philanthropist overflowing with a desire to improve mankind, differed from the sentimental do-gooders of his day chiefly in not fearing that politics would contaminate him. Thirty-six years old in 1835 and a successful merchant, he had been the first secretary of the Boston Lyceum, an antislavery and temperance man, an Anti-Mason, a pacifist. His business experience and the reading of Gouge convinced him that the Bank was "a great central despotism, dangerous to the liberties and injurious to the pecuniary interests of the people," and against the disapproval of his friends he joined the Jackson party.[45]

The rise of the radical wing, ornamented by names like Bancroft, Allen, Sedgwick, Walker, gave the Democratic party new intellectual prestige. Late in 1835 it made the further acquisition of Alexander H. Everett, former editor of the *North American,* whose brother was now Whig Governor. Balked in his own political ambitions, Everett had embarked on an increasingly liberal course in the legislature, first favoring free bridges and the abolition of imprisonment for debt and by 1835 standing up with Robinson and Rantoul in defense of the hard-money policy. With his wife breaking into tears when she spoke of her husband's prospects, Everett left his party and in the fall of 1835 headed the Democratic ticket for the state Senate.[46]

[43] In a more jovial mood, Greene would ask, "Why is the Editor of the Advocate [Hallett's paper] a good bedfellow? Ans. Because he *lies, still.*" *Boston Post,* April 20, 25, 1837. In later years Greene would have abundant practice in going to bed politically with Hallett; it was always a question as to which was seducer and which seduced.

[44] Morton to Bancroft, February 28, 1845, Bancroft Papers; Edward Everett to A. H. Everett, June 10, 1836, Webster to Edward Everett, June 6, 1836, Everett Papers.

[45] Walker's recollections, quoted by J. P. Munroe, *Life of Francis Amasa Walker,* 12. See also F. A. Walker, "Amasa Walker," *New England Historical and Genealogical Register,* XLII, 133–141 (April, 1888).

[46] A. H. Everett to Bancroft, October 16, 1834, Bancroft Papers; Charlotte B. Everett to Edward Everett, January 18, 1835, Edward Everett to A. H. Everett, April 22, 1835, Everett Papers; *Boston Post,* May 26, June 6, November 4, 1835; *Bunker-Hill Aurora and Boston Mirror,* October 3, 1835; *Boston Atlas,* November 12, 1835.

He was consoled by a friend who himself had once deserted the Boston aristocracy. "Their treachery to you sits heavily on their Souls," wrote John Quincy Adams; "and as usual they are labouring to transform it into your treachery to them." But in the privacy of his journal Adams was less generous, commenting sourly that Everett had "passed from one extreme of party devotion to another extreme of the opposite party, and his character is between the upper and the nether millstone." Though his literary skills made Everett useful, the Democrats never thoroughly accepted him. Amos Lawrence expressed a suspicion not confined to Whigs when he observed, "Everett is *hungry*, & wants office to supply himself with food." In 1836 and 1837, when not dunning the administration for jobs, Everett was busy trying to borrow money from friends.[47]

7

National backing for the radical policy made the Bancroft-Morton wing confident and determined. Late in 1835, at Cincinnati, Benton set the keynote. The war with the Bank, he declared, was just the beginning; "the States abound with other monopolies, just as much at war with the Rights of the People as that great one was. . . . Chartered companies, with exclusive and extraordinary privileges, are the legislative evil and opprobrium of the age in which we live." [48] But how would David Henshaw regard such doctrine?

Weakened by gout and perhaps by disappointment, Henshaw fell ill and proposed to resign the collectorship. Morton, fearing for the already precarious party harmony, induced Henshaw to hold on till after the presidential election. In the meantime, the administration made its own decision about the succession. Hard-money men in Washington knew that the victory of their policy depended on having hard-money men in power in the states. In May the collectorship was offered secretly to Morton, and when he declined he was given to understand that he would have its disposal.[49]

On July 4 the Collector made a last attempt to win his party back

[47] Adams to Everett, December 1, 1835, *American Historical Review*, XI, 349; Adams, *Memoirs*, IX, 361; Lawrence to A. A. Lawrence, November 15, 1836, Lawrence Papers. See also Everett to Jared Sparks, December 21, 1836, Sparks Papers; Morton to Van Buren, April 8, 1837, Morton Letterbooks.
[48] *Washington Globe*, November 21, 1835.
[49] The Henshaw group favored John K. Simpson, the radicals Frederick Robinson. See Rantoul to Van Buren, October 10, 1837, William Foster to Van Buren, January 27, 1838, Van Buren Papers; Blair to Bancroft, January 9, 1837[8], Morton to Bancroft, September 7, 1841. Bancroft Papers; *Boston Atlas*, June 10, 1836.

to the ways of the conservative Democrats, defending corporations from the charge of monopoly, attacking trade-unions and adding that the "possession of wealth" was "presumptive proof of industry and frugality and honesty." [50] But on the same day George Bancroft was again setting forth the radical dream, before a rapt crowd at Springfield, and Henshaw's injunctions of prudence were impressive only to holders of bank stocks. Hallett, anxious to establish himself as an uncompromising radical, led the assault. Henshaw's star was falling.

Bancroft provoked, of course, the expected measure of abuse from old friends. The *Northampton Courier* regarded his Springfield oration "with feelings of unutterable disgust," and a Boston paper observed that "a more thoroughgoing demagogue or profligate politician is not to be found in the State." [51] But Martin Van Buren read the address aloud to some Southern gentlemen who called upon him at Saratoga Springs, and wrote its author, "I think it better than any thing I have ever before seen upon the subject." Even such doctrinaire radicals as Charles Douglas and Orestes A. Brownson sent Bancroft their warm approval. [52]

The congressional ticket for 1836 showed the strength of the radicals. The list was headed by Bancroft, Samuel Clesson Allen, Theodore Sedgwick, Alexander H. Everett and Amasa Walker. William Foster was now the nominee for Lieutenant Governor. The platform was unequivocally radical. As one paper remarked, the Workingmen's measures had now been "adopted in all the addresses and at all the conventions of the Democratic party, and are, in fact, part and parcel of their cause." [53]

The transformation from the philosophy of David Henshaw to the philosophy of Andrew Jackson was nearly complete. It paid both in men and in votes. The Democrats presented strong candidates in 1836 for a party which had been a despised minority a few years before; and, though the Whigs still carried the state, Morton's vote reached a new high of nearly thirty-six thousand, an increase of almost eleven thousand over 1835 and of thirty-one and a half thousand over 1828.

[50] David Henshaw, *An Address Delivered . . . Boston, July 4, 1836,* 27–28.
[51] *Northampton Courier,* quoted by *Boston Centinel and Gazette,* August 26, 1836; *Boston Commercial Gazette,* November 21, 1836.
[52] Douglas to Bancroft, September 29, 1836, Brownson to Bancroft, September 24, 1836, Bancroft Papers.
[53] *New Bedford Gazette,* quoted by the *Boston Press, and Semi-Weekly Advocate,* November 8, 1836.

XIV RADICALISM IN
NEW YORK

IN NEW YORK, the old Jeffersonian party was dominant
rather than the party of the business community, and the crucial Jacksonian struggles thus began within the Democratic organization. The
powerful commercial groups which had inevitably clustered round
the governing party fought grimly with the men of labor and the
radical democrats, each faction vying with the other in bringing pressure on the people who controlled the party machine — above all, on
Martin Van Buren and the Albany Regency.

1

Van Buren's power within the state rested in great part on
this informal organization. The Regency directed policy, distributed
offices, ran campaigns and made the important party decisions. Its
political unity was cemented by close personal relations. The members
dined and drank together, talked, joked and argued till late in the
night. Their families were friendly, and their wives kissed when they
met. They took care that no one who served the Regency should
suffer as a consequence, and young men of talent and Jeffersonian
principle were certain of rapid promotion. Their ideal of public
service was high. Thurlow Weed, who grew to know the Regency
through years of fighting them, later observed, "They were men of
great ability, great industry, indomitable courage, and strict personal
integrity." [1]

Van Buren dominated the group. All agreed that his advancement
to the presidency had priority over other political considerations.

[1] Weed, *Autobiography*, 103. Cf. the judgment of Gideon Welles: "an association of politicians and statesmen of wonderful mental capacity, whose integrity
is unquestioned and who, while maintaining ascendancy, exerted themselves to administer the government for the good of all." Welles, *Diary*, J. T. Morse, Jr., ed.,
III, 225. For some personal details, see James Gordon Bennett, Diary, July 28,
1831, New York Public Library: J. D. Hammond, *History of Political Parties in
the State of New-York*, II, 225.

Silas Wright, though the youngest of the inner circle, was next on the escalator. No member of the Regency, save perhaps Van Buren, so commanded the confidence both of his associates and of the people.

Third in importance was William L. Marcy, who rose steadily in rank, becoming Comptroller, Judge of the state Supreme Court, Senator in 1831, and Governor in 1833. A heavy man, sluggish in his movements, with a bold forehead and a shaggy brow masking observant eyes, Marcy gave an impression of power. He was an indefatigable worker, sitting long hours at his desk in his dressing gown, occasionally reaching for a pinch of snuff and sneezing into the old red handkerchief which lay on the table before him. His gruff voice was well adapted to the pragmatism of mind which provoked his most famous remark, "that to the victors belong the spoils of the enemy." [2]

But Marcy was not the political hack which this realistic observation seems to have forever stamped him. He was an educated man, an able administrator and the most cultivated member of the Regency. He had, indeed, a genuine passion for literature, especially for the books of the seventeenth century — George Herbert and Sir William Temple were favorites — and he was enthusiastic about Coleridge at a time when admiration was confined to advanced young clergymen, like Mr. Emerson of Concord.[3] Marcy was honestly reconciled to Silas Wright's precedence for higher office. "Certainly the great man of the Senate," he once said of Wright in his confidential correspondence; "but for *one* thing (and there is much less of that than is imagined) he would be our best candidate for Pres^t." [4]

Next to Marcy stood Azariah C. Flagg, Comptroller of the state during much of the Regency rule. A small man, with the air of a clerk, dressed in blue stockings and a shabby coat, Flagg was a relentless Jeffersonian. To fire and conviction, he added first-class administrative ability and a strict sense of party discipline. Without Flagg the Regency would have altogether lost its reform drive after Van Buren and Wright left Albany to devote themselves to national affairs.[5]

These were the leaders of the Regency. Around them were lesser

[2] Marcy in the Senate, January 24–25, 1832, *Register of Debates*, 22 Congress 1 Session, 1325. See also Ben: Perley Poore, *Perley's Reminiscences*, I, 333; Welles, *Diary*, III, 225–226.

[3] See especially Marcy to P. M. Wetmore, July 3, 1838, Marcy Papers. Marcy's long correspondence with Wetmore, a second-rate versifier and third-rate politician of New York City, displays his unexpected side.

[4] Marcy to Wetmore, April 13, 1842, Marcy Papers.

[5] Pierson, *Tocqueville and Beaumont in America*, 176; H. D. A. Donovan, *The Barnburners*, 20; Welles, *Diary*, III, 226.

figures: Edwin Croswell, suave editor of the *Albany Argus*, the Regency organ; the gentle and attractive John A. Dix, protégé of Silas Wright; Colonel Samuel Young, a stalwart and aggressive radical; the reckless and witty Michael Hoffman; and a group of promising younger men — John Worth Edmonds, a vigorous lawyer who argued for trade-unions, Preston King, the fat, sunny and clever representative from St. Lawrence County, and a wizened, nervous, very intelligent youth named Samuel J. Tilden.

C. C. Cambreleng, while not strictly of the Regency, was attached to it by personal intimacy with Van Buren. Benjamin F. Butler, Van Buren's old law partner, had a similar informal connection. Forty years old in 1835, Butler was an unusual man to show up in the rough and tumble of New York politics. With his unworldly face, small, pale and refined, his tremulous lips, quick, black eyes and white fingers, he looked out of place among the hearty, red-faced politicians of Albany, their pockets stuffed with strong cigars. Butler was a religious man, with piety so fervent that he was troubled by the godlessness of Jefferson, in every other respect his hero. Alone among the radical Jacksonians, he was conspicuous in the temperance movement, and he even signed petitions against the Sunday mail. His real interests lay not in politics but in public service. He helped, for example, to prepare the *Revised Statutes* of the State of New York, an early experiment in codification, and in 1838 he headed the law department of the newly founded University of the City of New York.

But his friendship for Van Buren constantly drew him into party affairs. In 1833 Van Buren even wanted to send Butler to the Senate in preference to Nathaniel P. Tallmadge, a protectionist and close in the councils of New York banking interests. Butler declined as usual, but later in the year he felt conscience-bound to accept the Attorney Generalship when Taney became Secretary of the Treasury in the midst of the struggle over the deposits. So remote and gentle a spirit was for a long time uncomfortable in politics. "He is really too amiable a man," observed Marcy, "to be a very great one." But there was strength in simple honesty, and the future would disclose emotions burning within Benjamin F. Butler which the mild lawyer hardly suggested in 1833.[6]

Other things being equal, the Regency favored reform. Van Buren,

[6] Marcy to Wetmore, June 21, 1839, Marcy Papers. See also W. A. Butler, *A Retrospect of Forty Years, 1825–1865*, Harriet A. Butler, ed., *passim;* B. F. Butler to H. S. Randall, November 12, 1850, Miscellaneous Letters, Library of Congress; Martineau, *Retrospect of Western Travel*, I, 276; *Proceedings and Addresses on . . . the Death of Benjamin F. Butler, of New York*, especially 11–12.

a veteran of bitter fights against imprisonment for debt and for the extension of the suffrage, pushed through the safety-fund act of 1829, which, for all its weaknesses, at least forced the banks to yield for the first time to conditions prescribed by the legislature.[7] Butler, Wright, Flagg and Dix were also in the progressive wing. But Marcy, whose father-in-law was heavily involved in state banks, and Croswell, an incurable speculator, as well as the many careerists who attached themselves to the Regency, were reformers only when politically expedient. After Van Buren went to Washington in 1829, the conservative wing went into the ascendancy at Albany.

2

In the meantime deeper urgencies were at work among the laboring classes. New York was affected no less than Massachusetts by sudden fears of dispossession sweeping among the wage earners like chill ocean winds. But the New York movement was much more an urban affair because of the comparative prosperity of the farmers upstate. The struggles over debt imprisonment and the Sunday mails were intense, especially in New York City, and through the decade of the twenties there was an insistent demand for action on most of the items in the familiar platform of Workingmen's grievances.[8]

The most ambitious attempt to provide a new platform for labor unrest had been made by Robert Owen, the Scotch philanthropist, in the middle twenties. Though many of his remarks on property and some on religion appealed to the wage earners, his general solution — a co-operative commonwealth along the lines of New Harmony — was essentially unreal, both for people whose habits and obligations bound them to existing society, and for an economy whose greatest potentialities, for production and for profit, lay in the direction of increased industrialization.

In 1826 a certain L. Byllesby published a book in New York entitled *Observations on the Sources and Effects of Unequal Wealth*, an attempt to restate Owenism without the antireligious bias or the emphasis on the establishment of new communities. Though labor was the source of wealth, Byllesby declared, "the products of labour belong to almost any other than the producer, who generally obtains from the application of his powers, no more than a bare subsistence." Labor-saving machinery only increased the inequities. The salvation

[7] Abijah Mann to Flagg, February 6, 1868, A. C. Flagg, *Banks and Banking in the State of New York*, 39.
[8] Fox, *Decline of Aristocracy*, 352–356.

for the workingmen, urged Byllesby, was to labor co-operatively, not competitively, and to abolish the credit system. Co-operation would release new productive powers until "an application of labour not exceeding four or five hours per day, would surround every one with an abundance of all things that the most voluptuous now enjoy." [9] Much of the book was interestingly argued, but it appeared before public sentiment was prepared for it, and it lacked orientation toward immediate and practical reforms.

The Owenite theories had a greater impact through the influence of Frances Wright. A young Scotswoman, who had come to America in 1818 and again with Lafayette in 1824, she had undertaken in 1826 the famous Nashoba experiment in an attempt to mitigate the slavery problem. Failure at Nashoba settled her conviction that the basic obstacle to reform was the corruption of the American people by a false system of education maintained by the clergy. Her belief in the omnipotence of the environment in forming character, as well as her anticlericalism, inclined her to a sympathy with Owen. On visits to New Harmony, she won an enthusiastic follower in Robert Dale Owen. In 1828 she became co-editor of the *New Harmony Gazette* with young Owen, and in 1829 they moved the journal to New York, renaming it the *Free Enquirer*.

Thirty-five years old in 1830, Fanny Wright had an attractive, unclouded face, with chestnut hair falling in natural curls, large blue eyes, clear and serious, and a tall, slender, graceful figure. She spoke in a rich, musical voice, disarming the most bitter by her radiant enthusiasm. Her mind was courageous, logical and independent, and she wrote militant and vivid prose. Her followers adored her. Hard-handed mechanics and workers crowded the halls when she lectured, and pored over copies of the *Free Enquirer* in flickering light late into the evening.

A carpenter named Walter Whitman, staunch radical Democrat and admirer of Tom Paine, listened raptly to Miss Wright and subscribed to the *Free Enquirer*. He named one son after Thomas Jefferson and another after Andrew Jackson; a third, whom he called simply Walter, after himself, used to muse in later years on lovely Fanny Wright. "She has always been to me one of the sweetest of sweet memories," he said: "we all loved her: fell down before her: her very appearance seemed to enthrall us . . . graceful, deer-like. . . . she was beautiful in bodily shape and gifts of soul." Old Walt Whitman was deep in recollection. "I never felt so glowingly towards

[9] Byllesby, *Observations*, 42, 68, 115–116. The copy in the Harvard University Library was owned by Theodore Sedgwick.

any other woman," he finally said. ". . . she possessed herself of my body and soul." [10]

This was Fanny Wright — this was "the great Red Harlot of Infidelity." [11] Around her gathered the live spirits of the Workingmen's movement. Robert Dale Owen, her closest associate, was six years younger, a short, blue-eyed, sandy-haired man. His clumsy gestures and rasping voice made him a less effective speaker than Fanny Wright, but he was clever, deeply persuaded of the imminent perfectibility of man, and dead in earnest. To him fell more and more the editorial responsibilities of the *Free Enquirer*.[12]

They discovered a useful ally in George H. Evans, an English printer who had come to America some years before. Like the others, Evans was an agnostic and an anticlerical. Late in 1829 he founded the *Working Man's Advocate*, perhaps the most influential of the labor papers. Working tirelessly in his murky office on Thames Street, this indefatigable editor, compiler, writer, printer finally destroyed his own health in the cause.[13] Honest John Windt, to whom Miss Wright always liked to confide her manuscripts, was another agnostic journeyman printer who would figure in virtually all the reform agitations in New York for thirty years.[14]

On the outskirts of the group, more interested in the anticlerical than the anticapitalist side of the *Free Enquirer*, was another Englishman, Dr. Gilbert Vale, who had come to New York in 1823. A man of some learning in the sciences, especially astronomy and navigation, he edited a free-thinking journal called *The Beacon* and wrote a biography of Tom Paine. " 'A valuable rare old man to know,' " Walt Whitman thought. " 'Take a man: take all sentiment, poetry, philosophy out of him: that is Vaill.' Yet 'Vaill was a hard nut' — that is to say, 'was a character not to be trifled, ridiculed away.' " [15] In November, 1829, Orestes A. Brownson, then a minister upstate, became a corresponding editor of the *Free Enquirer*, and Nicholas P. Trist,

[10] Horace Traubel, *With Walt Whitman in Camden*, II, 205, 445, 499, 500. See also O. A. Brownson, "The Convert," *Works of Orestes A. Brownson*, H. F. Brownson, ed., V, 58; R. D. Owen, "My Experience of Community Life," *Atlantic Monthly*, XXXII, 347–348 (September, 1873).

[11] *New York Courier and Enquirer*, quoted in the *Free Enquirer*, June 19, 1830.

[12] There is an excellent biography by Richard W. Leopold, *Robert Dale Owen;* see especially 109, 157.

[13] Fitzwilliam Byrdsall, *History of the Loco-Foco or Equal Rights Party*, 14; Lewis Masquerier, *Sociology: or, the Reconstruction of Society, Government, and Property*, 99, 103.

[14] Masquerier, *Sociology*, 107.

[15] Traubel, *Whitman in Camden*, III, 140. See also Masquerier, *Sociology*, 105; Adams, *Memoirs*, XI, 408–409; *Brooklyn Eagle*, October 22, 1904.

General Jackson's private secretary, was also an occasional though anonymous contributor.

3

But Fanny Wright dominated the group. Her thrilling perceptions of the social crisis inflamed everyone dissatisfied with the existing order. "The most dull can perceive that a moral excitement, new in its nature and rapid in its progress, pervades the world," she would say in her fine contralto voice. ". . . The priest trembles for his craft, the rich man for his hoard, the politician for his influence. . . . From the people — ay! from the people, arise the hum and stir of awakening intelligence, enquiry, and preparation."

What were the causes of the crisis? First, the stimulus given to business enterprise by technological improvements, and even more by competition, which would continue "until it results in the ruin of small capitalists, and in the oppression of the whole laboring class of the community"; second, the banking system and paper money, "one of the deepest sources of industrial oppression and national demoralization"; third, the "professional aristocracy" of priests, lawyers and politicians, using their power to cheat the people; and fourth and most fundamental, "a false system of education, stolen from aristocratic Europe."

This was the crisis, and it was to be distinguished by the fact that it was "evidently, openly and acknowledgedly, *a war of class*, and that this war is universal. . . . it is now every where the oppressed millions who are making common cause against oppression; it is the ridden people of the earth who are struggling to throw from their backs the 'booted and spurred' riders."

The crisis might terminate, she said, in three possible ways. It might end in total enslavement of the people by "a crafty priesthood, and a monied aristocracy" — but this destiny was unlikely for America. It might end in violent revolution on the part of a people goaded too long by oppression. But, if "the industrious classes, and all honest men of all classes, unite for a gradual, but radical reform," they could avoid these dreadful fates, and Fanny Wright's scheme for salvation was the state-guardianship system of education. This plan contemplated the education of all children by the state in boarding schools under conditions of the most rigid equality, thereby eliminating class prejudices at the source. For Owen, Wright and Evans it became the vital reform, demanding precedence over everything else.[16]

[16] *Free Enquirer*, July 24, 31, November 27, 1830.

Fanny Wright's vivid sense of impending revolution infected much of the Workingmen's movement. But not everyone favored state guardianship. A competing panacea was a form of agrarianism, expounded by Thomas Skidmore and Alexander Ming, Sr., which would cure society by redistributing the land. Skidmore set forth his plan in a verbose book, *The Rights of Man to Property!*, published in New York, in 1829, and he used to urge it in speeches, tearing off coat and neckcloth and arguing in a violent manner. But Skidmore was even more of a fanatic than the champions of "EQUAL, NATIONAL, REPUBLICAN EDUCATION," and the Workingmen's movement was soon purged of his erratic influence.[17]

Apart from state guardianship, the Owen-Evans wing was at first far from radical. Like all Workingmen's parties before the Bank War, it eschewed the fight against economic exploitation: "*We desire to form no exclusive party;* not even of the producers against the nonproducers."[18] But, as the administration began to put its weight behind hard money, there were signs of awakening to the economic issue. Fanny Wright began soon to call for two "indispensable" reforms, of which the second was "AN IMPROVED CIRCULATING MEDIUM," and the labor daily declared apologetically but firmly of paper money, "dry or not, this is a subject which the Workingmen must take up and examine." ("We have hitherto abstained from canvassing this matter at all," it went on to explain, "because we thought the subject of Public Education much more important.")[19]

The Democrats in the state legislature, in the meantime, abolished imprisonment for debt and reformed the militia system, and the Democratic City Council passed a mechanics' lien law. Such friendly gestures led the Workingmen, already weakened by the inroads of a pseudo-Workingmen's organization under National Republican sponsorship, to return after 1831 to Tammany Hall, a union hastened by the Bank War. "Get the Workies to be up and doing on the U. S. B. question," wrote Cambreleng to Tammany early in 1832, adding accurately, "They are democrats in principle."[20]

---

[17] Thomas Skidmore, *The Rights of Man to Property!*, *passim; Free Enquirer*, October 31, 1829, January 9, 1830; R. D. Owen to the Editor, February 6, 1838, *Madisonian* (Washington), February 13, 1838.

[18] *Working Man's Advocate*, September 4, 1830. The Workingmen's candidate for Governor in 1830, Ezekiel Williams, was a leather manufacturer who favored internal improvements, and Isaac S. Smith, the nominee for Lieutenant Governor, was a merchant. The Workingmen's hero in national politics was, of course, Colonel Richard M. Johnson.

[19] *Free Enquirer*, September 25, 1830; *Daily Sentinel*, quoted in *Free Enquirer*, May 22, 1830.

[20] Cambreleng to Jesse Hoyt, February 6, 1832, W. L. MacKenzie, *Lives and*

William H. Hale's *Useful Knowledge for the Producers of Wealth*, published by Evans in 1833, signalized the conversion. It carried excerpts from Amos Kendall's Hickory Club speech on the cover, argued vigorously for hard money, and put it up to the laboring classes "to say, while they have the power, whether this republic shall, by banks, monopolies, and irresponsible legislation, become a nation of princes and paupers." "In a little while," he concluded ominously, "it will be beyond their power to decide this question by any other means than force of arms." [21]

By 1834, when the *Dedham Patriot* denounced Evans for being too Jacksonian, he replied with scorn, "Will the Dedham Patriot be kind enough to inform us how we could be 'devoted to the cause of the Working Men' *without* being 'tinctured with the spirit of Jacksonism,' so long as *Jackson* is so strongly tinctured with the spirit of *workeyism?*" The alliance was complete. "Mechanics, Carters, Laborers," the ex-Workingmen sang: —

> Must form a close connection
> And show the rich Aristocrats
> Their powers, at this election. . . .
> Yankee Doodle, smoke 'em out,
> The proud, the banking faction.
> None but such as Hartford Feds
> Oppose the poor and Jackson.[22]

4

The *New York Evening Post* had come far for a paper founded by Alexander Hamilton. When William Coleman, the original editor, died in 1829, it passed into the hands of William Cullen Bryant, a literary man from Massachusetts. As a child Bryant had delighted his Federalist father by writing a poetical satire against Jefferson; but Theodore Sedgwick, a friend of the family, assisted in his political emancipation, and he came to New York in 1826 already a confirmed free trader. There he met James Fenimore Cooper, G. C. Verplanck and Benjamin F. Butler, all ardent Democrats. In the election of 1828

Opinions of Benj'n Franklin Butler and Jesse Hoyt, 100. For a contemporary discussion of the relationship between the Workingmen and the Democratic parties, see Hobart Berrian, *A Brief Sketch of the Origin and Rise of the Workingmen's Party in the City of New York*.

[21] W. H. Hale, *Useful Knowledge*, 31.

[22] *Working Man's Advocate*, September 13, 1834; *Man* (New York), March 25, 1834; Fox, *Decline of Aristocracy*, 386.

he contributed a vote and an ode to Jackson's victory. By 1830 Edward Everett had to report him regretfully as "poisoned with the gall of Jacksonism." [23]

A man of middle height, thirty-six years old in 1830, Bryant had a large, sallow face, piercing gray eyes and heavy eyebrows which gave him an almost saturnine cast of countenance, too often verified by his coldness of manner, though intimates sometimes found him chatty and even gay. He worked painfully at a small space, cleared by main force, on a desk piled two feet high with books, pamphlets, political documents, opened letters and forgotten manuscripts, scrawling his editorials on the back of pieces of waste paper and objecting to all proposals for improvement.[24]

Though his free-trade convictions first inclined him toward Jackson, they were not the cause of his continued support. When other free traders, like J. G. King and Verplanck, turned against the administration because of the Bank War, Bryant stoutly backed the old General, to the horror of the business community which the *Evening Post* primarily served. Like Sedgwick and Foster, Bryant was genuinely a humanitarian radical. And, for all his austerity, he was capable of direct action. When he got into a quarrel in 1831, with Colonel William L. Stone, editor of the conservative *Commercial Advertiser*, he tried to horsewhip Stone on the streets of New York. Stone in response splintered a bamboo cane on Bryant's arm, revealing a dagger inside. For a moment the atmosphere was charged; then spectators swept in and separated them.[25]

Early in 1829 Bryant hired a literary man-about-town named William Leggett as his assistant. Leggett had been court-martialed out of the navy in 1825 for a number of offenses, among them insulting his commanding officer by quoting abusive verses of Byron. As John Quincy Adams mildly observed of Leggett's conduct at his trial, "The tone and character of his defense, so called . . . consisting of a continual invective upon his commander, ought not to have passed without reprehension and rebuke." [26] Such talents had greater uses in literary criticism. Returning to New York, Leggett founded a clever but unsuccessful literary magazine, and then joined the *Post*.

[23] Edward Everett to A. H. Everett, March 4, 1830, Everett Papers. See also Bryant, "Reminiscences of Miss Sedgwick," Mary E. Dewey, *Life and Letters of Catharine M. Sedgwick*, 440–442; Parke Godwin, *Bryant*, I, 243.

[24] Godwin, *Bryant*, I, 334–335; Bungay, *Off-hand Takings*, 314–315; John Bigelow, *William Cullen Bryant*, 73, 109–111.

[25] Philip Hone, *Diary*, I, 40; Walt Whitman, *New York Dissected*, Emory Holloway and Ralph Adimari, eds., 235–236.

[26] "Naval Court Martial. Trial of Midshipman William Leggett," *New York Evening Post*, July 8, 24, 1835.

The Bank War led him to define his economic ideas, and he quickly advanced, through sheer passion for logic, to extreme radical positions. He was most interested, as he constantly reiterated, in general principles of government. His body of editorials constituted an education in political philosophy for the New York Democrats. From the axioms of equal rights, which he enunciated with shining eloquence, he would deploy to assail specific evils: here his style, lucid, supple and picturesque, his powers of exposition, irony and bloodcurdling invective, would come most fully into play. His work had a penetration, a courage and, at the same time, a good humor and gusto, which make it memorable in American political journalism.[27]

Like Bryant, Leggett was ready to prove his determination in the cause by assaulting a fellow editor. Leggett chose James Watson Webb of the *Courier and Enquirer*, who had reversed his stand on the Bank after receiving large loans from Nicholas Biddle. In the midst of an angry newspaper feud in 1833, Leggett met Webb on Wall Street, and, announcing, "Colonel Webb, you are a coward and a scoundrel, and I spit upon you," proceeded to do so. The subsequent brawl attracted a distinguished audience, headed by Albert Gallatin, and the contestants argued for days in their papers over which was the victor.[28]

While accepting Leggett's general position and submitting to his audacity, Bryant was less excited about the philosophy of government, preferring to examine concrete examples of failure or transgression; and where Leggett wrote as if his pen were a cutlass, Bryant was cool and circumstantial. But he spoke no less sternly, and his masterly indictments may have converted as many people as Leggett's inspired gasconade.

In 1835 they were joined by Theodore Sedgwick, Jr., the bright twenty-four-year-old son of Bryant's old friend in Stockbridge. Young Sedgwick had gone to George Bancroft's school at Round Hill, from which he was expelled for infractions of discipline, and then to Columbia. After graduation he went abroad for a year to Paris, where he dined with Lafayette and drank with Alexis de Tocqueville, visited with Edward Livingston and James Fenimore Cooper, and completed the more urbane phases of his education.

Early in 1834, his curiosity about the Old World satisfied, he yearned to live again, as he wrote to his father's friend, Mr. Van Buren, "under

[27] Oddly enough, the writer today whose work most resembles Leggett's, both in its merits and its defects, is Samuel Grafton, who is carrying on Leggett's tradition (if with somewhat less humor and somewhat more petulance) in Leggett's own paper, the *New York Post*.

[28] *New York Evening Post*, April 10, 1833; *Boston Post*, April 13, 1833; *Boston Courier*, April 15, 1833; *Niles' Register*, April 20, 1833.

those institutions which make us all if not Agrarians or Owenites — at least — Workies." When he went to New York to work in his uncle's law office, he found Leggett, short-handed with Bryant away in Europe, pleased to accept contributions on this theme in the *Post*. The occasional pithy articles signed by "Veto" became a valuable addition to the *Post*'s influence. Sedgwick was an attractive young man. Fanny Kemble was fond of him, and Charles Sumner declared him in 1841 to be "the cleverest and most gentlemanly person I have seen in New York," even if a Democrat. But he inherited his father's distaste for violence, refraining, for example, from performing assault and battery on editors with whom he disagreed.[29]

5

The Bank War stimulated the brethren of the *Post* to launch into the questions of currency and incorporation. Leggett had an edition of Gouge's *Paper Money* stereotyped at his own expense,[30] and Sedgwick set forth the position on monopoly in a series of articles, beginning in the *Post* late in 1834, afterwards expanded into a responsible and reasoned pamphlet entitled *What Is a Monopoly?*

His main object of attack was the system of special charters, which made, as he said, each act of incorporation "a grant of exclusive privilege, and every grant of exclusive privilege," he went on, "strictly speaking, creates a monopoly." That is, every such grant carried on its face that the corporators had received special advantages from which the mass of the people were excluded. "This is the very substance of monopoly. . . . Every corporate grant is directly in the teeth of the doctrine of equal rights." Since our nation had been founded on that doctrine, exceptions to it should be permitted only when the objects attained were of "paramount public necessity," and obtainable no other way. Was this the case with corporations? Sedgwick thought not, and proposed to show that the commercial advantages could be more equitably secured under another system.

What should be done? "Enact a general law," Sedgwick answered, under which any group of individuals might form a corporation without application to the legislature. Let all businesses, and banking among them, be thrown open to universal competition (except for railroads and turnpikes, where the object could not be attained without

[29] Sedgwick to Van Buren, February 1, 1834, Letterbook, Sedgwick Papers; Sumner to G. S. Hillard, January 24, 1841, E. L. Pierce, *Memoir and Letters of Charles Sumner*, II, 172. See also Sedgwick to Leggett, August 24, 1834, Letterbook, Sedgwick Papers.
[30] *Journal of Banking*, July 7, 1841.

monopoly rights, but here the charters should have reservations of revocability). The antimonopoly party must smash the system of special charters, with its by-products of graft, log-rolling, lobbying and political dishonesty, and open the field to genuine free enterprise.[31]

Sedgwick's unimpassioned manner, the force of his documentation and the good sense of his solution aroused wide attention; and when these arguments were transmuted by Leggett's flaming pen into editorials for the *Evening Post*, they caused a sensation. Bryant, Leggett and Sedgwick were saved from traveling the conservative path of most free traders by their vivid sense of class conflict. Basic to their use of the laissez-faire arsenal was a perception of what Sedgwick called "the social division of parties" — a division which, he pointed out, had run through our history. The upper classes, distinguished socially by exclusiveness, economically by wealth, and politically by mistrust of the people, had always grasped after all the power in the state. Jackson had revived the democratic tradition, and "the *'upper classes'* are now perhaps more universally arrayed against us than they have ever yet been." Leggett characteristically rejoiced in the situation. "It may be said that this open and direct array of one class of the community against the other, is dangerous to the future peace and happiness of our city. . . . Well, so it is. But who has drawn the line? Who has beat the alarm?" "We venture to predict," said Bryant, "that so long as our legislative bodies continue to deal out with unsparing hand, bank charters . . . this feeling of the poor towards the rich will become every day more aggravated." [32]

[31] Sedgwick, *What Is a Monopoly?*, 12, 13, 29, 18, 19, 34. For an interesting criticism from the viewpoint of a conservative businessman, see Peter C. Brooks to Edward Everett, February 6, 1836, Everett Papers.

[32] "The Social Division of Parties," by "Veto," *New York Evening Post*, September 16, 1834; editorials by Leggett and Bryant, *ibid.*, March 10, 1834, May 26, 1836.

XV RISE OF THE LOCOFOCOS

THE BEGINNINGS of inflation in 1834 sharpened the interest with which the common people of New York and their mentors watched the banking situation. Early in August, Leggett declared that the *Post* would support only those candidates committed unequivocally against bills under $5 and against further bank charters. Following his lead, the Workingmen's party secured pledges from the Democratic nominees in exchange for labor endorsement. When the Democrats swept the fall elections, Leggett continued his pressure on Governor Marcy and the new legislature. ("Marcy, as usual, got so frightened whilst the Post was at him," John Van Buren wrote to his father, "that before the Message came out, he was a pretty thorough radical.") [1] With the opening of the session, the issue was posed. Would the New York Democrats oppose all irresponsible paper money, or only paper put out by Whig banks?

1

A few days supplied the answer. The conservative Democrats, developing a theory of "judicious" opposition to monopoly (i.e., opposition to Whig monopoly), proceeded to churn out bank charters for deserving Democrats. When Leggett lashed out at the betrayers of the pledges, the state organization responded by instituting a smear campaign against the *Post*. As James K. Paulding wrote angrily to Van Buren, "That Paper is denounced as an apostate from the Democratic party, for advocating democratic principles. . . . I feel confoundedly puzzled." [2]

Leggett kept up the fight, but in a short time he stumbled into a new quarrel which temporarily ended his usefulness to the anti-monopoly cause. Amos Kendall, as Postmaster General, had acceded to the censorship of abolitionist literature in the mails by Southern postmasters. Leggett now tore into Kendall, hitherto one of his favorites. But abolitionism was the great untouchable issue for Demo-

---

[1] John Van Buren to Martin Van Buren, January 14, 1835, Van Buren Papers.
[2] Paulding to Van Buren, January 19, 1835, Van Buren Papers.

crats, and Frank Blair's rebuke in the *Washington Globe* was so severe that Leggett accepted it as an excommunication. . . . He was nearing physical breakdown, and his editorial course was fatal for a paper so dependent for subscriptions and advertising on the business community. In October he finally fell dangerously ill. A few friends, including Sedgwick, pitched in to keep the *Post* alive. When Bryant returned the next February, he found the paper's income about a quarter of what it had been two years before. Leggett had to sell his third of the paper in payments of debts. Bryant would not promise him freedom in the future to write as he pleased, and they accordingly parted, but without ill feeling. Leggett's later ventures had the *Post's* warmest support.[8]

Leggett's collapse came just as the movement he inspired was getting under way. In October, 1835, the radicals gave a dinner for Colonel Johnson, where C. C. Cambreleng spoke meaningfully on the obligation of pledges, and John Windt, Moses Jaques, and Theophilus Fisk, down from Boston, gave ringing radical toasts. Near the end of the month the Democrats of the city, now aroused, met at Tammany Hall to pass on the nominations for the impending election. Preliminary mutterings indicated that the proceedings would be less perfunctory than usual. By six-thirty, a throng of determined men had gathered outside the hall, and when the doors were opened, they rushed in, taking the seats nearest the platform. The atmosphere grew quickly tense, with the conservative Democrats alarmed about their slate, and the radicals waiting impatiently to bring their own list forward.

The organization ticket was finally announced to a chorus of hisses, hoots and catcalls. In the midst of the tumult the committee declared their nominations carried and hastily retired. The crowd roared that Joel Curtis, a veteran of the early Workingmen's party, be made chairman, raised banners with radical mottoes and booed the Bank Democrats. Alexander Ming, Jr., son of the agrarian of a few years back, a printer and officeholder, climbed up on a table and motioned for silence. The hubbub quieted down; but, before he could speak, the gas lights went out, throwing the hall into darkness — an ancient and honorable formula for quelling mutiny at Tammany. This time the insurgents were prepared. Taking from their pockets the new friction matches, popularly known as "locofocos," they lined the platform with fifty lighted candles. The people said, "let there be light," as one orator put it, and there was light. The meeting then named its

---

[8] Allan Nevins, *The Evening Post: a Century of Journalism*, 152, 153, 166; Bigelow, *Bryant*, 85, 89, 332.

own candidates and eventually dissolved into a boisterous torchlight procession.[4]

The conservative Democrats stuck to their candidate, Gideon Lee, who won, probably with Whig support. But Charles G. Ferris, the radical nominee, polled over 3500 votes, and the Locofocos, as they were called, first sarcastically by their enemies, then proudly by themselves, took heart for the future. If Tammany Hall would not heed them, they could always strike out for the balance of power.

2

Labor was also beginning to organize in the economic field. Rising prices encouraged united action, and a successful carpenters' strike in the spring of 1833 led progressively to the formation of a General Trades Union. By the end of the year, twenty-one societies and four thousand workers were marching in a Union parade.[5]

Ely Moore of the Typographical Association, first president of the Union, was the outstanding leader. A sallow, restless man, with keen, nervous eyes and long black hair brushed back from his forehead, well dressed, often carrying a heavy ivory-headed cane, he enjoyed a tremendous reputation for eloquence. He first appeared as an enemy of the "Christian Party," declaring that Colonel Johnson had done more for *"pure and unadulterated democracy*, than any man in our country — by arresting the schemes of an ambitious, *irreligious* priesthood."[6] But by 1833, like other labor leaders, he was beginning to decide that democracy was facing graver perils.

The imminent danger, "which threatens the stability of our government, and the liberty of the people," he told the General Trades' Union, "is an undue accumulation and distribution of wealth." How could this be checked? Only "by unity of purpose, and concert of action, on the part of the *producing classes*." If such unity could secure to the laboring men "a fair, certain, and equitable compensation for their toil and skill, we insure a more just and equal distribution of wealth than can ever be effected by statutory law." Trade-unions, by promoting a more healthful distribution of property, thus helped

[4] For several accounts from the New York press, see *Niles' Register*, November 7, 1835; also Byrdsall, *Loco-Foco Party*, 23–27.

[5] Commons *et al.*, eds., *Documentary History of American Industrial Society*, V, 203–205, 212 ff.

[6] [William Emmons], *Authentic Biography of Col. Richard M. Johnson, of Kentucky*, 89. See also *New York Evening Post*, February 3, 1834; *New York Independent Press*, October 16, 1835; Ben: Perley Poore, *Perley's Reminiscences*, I, 156.

preserve the economic foundations of democracy. The situation, Moore insisted, was growing urgent. "As the line of distinction between the employer and employed is *widened*, the condition of the latter inevitably verges toward a state of vassalage . . . hostile to the best interests of the community, as well as to the spirit and genius of our government." [7]

In 1834 the General Trades' Union, encouraged by the flurry of labor organization through the East, issued a call for a national convention. Through five hot August days, thirty earnest men were gathered in New York to found the National Trades' Union. This first nation-wide labor association was a loose organization, without control over local unions, but its meetings brought labor leaders together for a valuable exchange of ideas and co-ordination of effort. Charles Douglas came down from Boston. John Ferral, William English and Thomas Hogan headed the Philadelphia delegation. Moore was chosen president, and it was decided to hold annual conventions. The National Trades' Union met again in New York in 1835 (with Seth Luther and Theophilus Fisk among those present), and in Philadelphia in 1836. It would disappear in the depression of 1837.[8]

The union movement soon began to split, as the Workingmen's party had before it, between the friends and enemies of collaboration with the Jacksonians.[9] Ely Moore himself swung to the Jacksonian view, and in 1834 Tammany sent him to Congress, where he became the first labor leader to sit in the House of Representatives. But the movement as a whole stuck to the old question of social status. "Our object in the formation of Trades' Unions," the union organ declared in 1836, ". . . was not to create a feeling of enmity against the non-producers; . . . [but] to raise in the estimation of themselves and others, those who are the producers of the necessaries and luxuries of life." [10] When the problem of politics was brought up at the first meeting of the National Trades' Union, Charles Douglas expressed the general sentiment in his remark that the workingmen "belonged

[7] Ely Moore, *Address Delivered before the General Trades' Union*, 7, 9, 10.

[8] Commons, ed., *Documentary History*, V, 22–23, VI, 191–193, 196 ff.; *Boston Post*, September 1, 1834; *Working Man's Advocate*, October 10, 1835.

[9] It is interesting to note that few of the leaders of the old Workingmen's party were much interested in unionism. George H. Evans, for example, was not even a union member; Owen and Fanny Wright had left New York, but they never displayed much interest in unions; and, though John Windt was president of the Typographical Association, his main enthusiasm remained politics. For all their sympathy with the unionists, they thought, as the Locofoco paper observed on the establishment of the union organ, "the evils complained of, having been produced by legislation, will also have to be cured by legislation, and therefore a 'political party' seems absolutely necessary." *New York Democrat*, March 9, 1836.

[10] *The Union* (New York), April 21, 1836.

to no party; they were neither disciples of Jacksonism nor Clayism, Van Burenism nor Websterism, nor any other *ism* but *workeyism*." [11]

But workeyism, even without Jacksonism, was quite bad enough for respectable opinion.[12] The immigrant Francis Lieber, assembling the battery of German scholarship, sought to demonstrate that unions formed "a most oppressive and flagrant, and unrighteous aristocracy." [13] "The rights of *employers* are invaded by these associations," moaned the *New-York Review* with a bathos kept laboriously alive by the National Association of Manufacturers a century later. "They are not permitted to negotiate with their workmen on terms of equality." If this article was not written by Alonzo Potter, soon to be a bishop of the Protestant Episcopal Church, then he stole portions of it for his book on *Political Economy*, going on to point out that union leaders were generally atheists and foreigners, and that labor had no just grounds for discontent.[14]

The courts viewed these emotions with deference, and a judicial campaign in 1835 and 1836 checked the union movement. The first case occurred at Geneva, in Ontario County. The journeymen shoemakers of Geneva agreed not to work for any master shoemaker who declined to abide by union rules. When one employer proceeded to hire a journeyman at a wage below union rates, the other journeymen in the shop quit work till the nonunion shoemaker was discharged. The strikers were then indicted for criminal conspiracy, their alleged offense lying not in coercion or violence, but simply in refusing to work. When the case reached the state Supreme Court, Chief Justice Savage's decision completely backed the employer. "If journeymen boot makers," he said, "by extravagant demands for wages, so enhance the price of boots made in *Geneva*, for instance, that boots made elsewhere, in *Auburn*, for example, can be sold cheaper, is not such an act injurious to trade? . . . It is important to the best interests of society that the price of labor be left to regulate itself. . . . Competition is the life of trade." [15]

Meanwhile a new dispute was brewing in New York City. In the fall of 1835 the Society of Journeymen Tailors increased its rates,

---

[11] Commons, ed., *Documentary History*, VI, 213.

[12] As James Fenimore Cooper learned, when passages in the first volume of his *Sketches of Switzerland* were interpreted as favoring unions; see Cooper, *Sketches of Switzerland, Part Second*, I, iv–v.

[13] Francis Lieber, *Manual of Political Ethics*, II, 348. Lieber apparently never troubled to discover what a union actually was, to judge from his description in his *Essays on Property and Labour*, 180.

[14] "Trades' Unions," *New-York Review*, II, 29 (January, 1838). Cf. Alonzo Potter, *Political Economy: Its Objects, Uses, and Principles*, 233–302.

[15] 14 Wendell 13, 18.

winning recognition of the increase after a brief strike. In January, 1836, their employers combined to roll back the rates to the original level. The tailors promptly struck again. Each side employed its weapons of picketing and black list, and fights between the strikers and the "dungs," as scabs were then called, led to considerable bitterness. When Savage rendered decision in the Geneva case, the employers took the hint and had twenty of the leading tailors arrested for criminal conspiracy. The strike alone constituted the offense in accordance with the Geneva doctrine; incidental violence was irrelevant to the indictment. Judge Edwards modeled his charge to the jury on Savage, and the tailors were convicted.

William Cullen Bryant, now back in active control of the *Post*, led the attack on Judge Edwards. "According to his position, a combination to take a settled price and no less, for any thing to be sold, is a conspiracy injurious to trade and commerce, and is punishable." Apply this, Bryant dryly proposed, to bankers, to owners of packet ships, to butchers, insurance directors and newspapers with their uniform rates for advertising and subscriptions. "Or will it be allowed that the law would be unjust and oppressive if enforced against the opulent and prosperous, while it is contended that it is just and equitable, when those who depend only on the labour of their hands are made its victims?" [16]

The workingmen, at least, did not think so, and they paraded the streets holding aloft banners: "No SURRENDER, BY THE ETERNAL!" A handbill circulated, with a coffin crudely printed on top and the bitter title, "THE RICH AGAINST THE POOR!" Sentence will be pronounced on Monday, it declared: "Go! Go! . . . Let the courtroom, the City Hall, yea! the whole park be filled with *mourners*. But remember, offer no violence to Judge Edwards. Bend meekly, and receive the chain wherewith you are to be bound! Keep the peace! Above all things, keep the peace!" [17]

On the day of sentence Edwards denounced the unions as "of foreign origin, and . . . mainly upheld by foreigners," and fined the defendants a total of $1150. As the tailors advanced to pay the fines, one of the officers of the court said he had been employed for three weeks at ten shillings a day and wanted to give it all to the men. Even the *New York Times*, exasperated by Edwards's reckless accusations, threw back the canard that only aliens were in the Union. "It is a low calculation when we estimate that two-thirds of the working men

[16] *New York Evening Post*, June 2, 1836.
[17] *Niles' Register*, April 23, 1836; Hone, *Diary*, I, 211; Commons and associates, *History of Labour*, I, 408–409.

in this city, numbering several thousand, belong to it." Cold with indignation, William Cullen Bryant inscribed in memorable words the case's epitaph: —

> They were condemned because they had determined not to work for the wages that were offered them! Can any thing be imagined more abhorrent. . . . If this is not SLAVERY, we have forgotten its definition. Strike the right of associating for the sale of labour from the privileges of a freeman, and you may as well at once bind him to a master. . . . If it be not in the colour of his skin, and in the poor franchise of naming his own terms in a contract for work, what advantage has the labourer of the north over the bondman of the south? [18]

On the evening of June 13 twenty-five thousand people crowded into the Park to protest the sentence. Few could recall so large a public meeting.[19]

The campaign against labor began to have national reverberations. Waddy Thompson, of South Carolina, smugly flung back to Northern conservatives the ancient taunt of the prospect of a servile rebellion, warning the "property-holders of the North" of "this army of day laborers" which was organizing in their bosom. "Let gentlemen look to it: they are in quite as much danger of insurrection as we are." [20]

Ely Moore rose from a sickbed to make labor's reply. Leaning on his ivory-headed cane, visibly trying to bring the wavering House into focus, steadying himself by fixing on the calm gaze of Mr. Polk in the black morocco Speaker's chair, Moore declared in loud, clear tones that the workingmen had been "denounced as agrarians, levellers, and anarchists, and their union as unlawful and mischievous. . . . I regret the attack has been made." But it serves to establish "more distinctly, and more permanently" the division between the two great parties of the country, the democracy and the aristocracy. "Sir, I fear that those attacks upon the people — the democracy — which have become so common of late, are a prelude to a premeditated assault upon popular freedom."

Whenever the aristocracy moved to increase its own power, Moore warned, it first charged the people with revolutionary designs. "Sir, can it be seriously and honestly believed," he asked, his voice ringing through the chamber, ". . . that the interest and safety of the State will be plotted against by three fourths of the people composing the

[18] *New York Evening Post*, June 13, 1836.
[19] *Ibid.*, June 14, 1836; *Union* (New York), June 14, 15, 1836.
[20] Thompson in the House, March 2, 1836, *Register of Debates*, 24 Congress 1 Session, 2678.

State?" The real danger lay in the other direction. "Where there is one instance where the rights of property have been violated by the people, or popular institutions, there are five thousand instances where the people have been plundered and beggared by the heartless cupidity of the privileged few. Sir, there is much greater danger that capital will unjustly appropriate to itself the avails of labor, than that labor will unlawfully seize on capital."

And what of unionism? "Why, it has been asked with alarm and indignation, why this commotion among the laboring classes? Why this banding together and forming of unions throughout the country? Sir, these associations are intended as counterpoises against capital, whenever it shall attempt to exert an unlawful, or undue influence. They are a measure of self defence." . . . The hall was listening with grim attention. One Southern Congressman murmured that the high priest of revolution was singing his war song. Moore continued, growing paler than ever till suddenly his face became dead white, his hands clawed the air, he tottered and fell insensible. From the gallery there sounded the scream of his terrified wife.[21]

Moore's oration went through four editions in less than two months.[22] It helped produce, with the aid of the case of the journeymen tailors, a growing feeling that the antilabor drive had gone too far. A few weeks after the tailors' case, eight poor shoemakers were haled into court at Hudson, New York, on the familiar charge. Members of the local Society of Journeymen Cordwainers, they had walked out when their employers tried to cut their pay below union rates. Their lawyer was John Worth Edmonds, a rising young Democratic politician of radical leanings, in the confidence of the Regency, a tall, shaggy man, with bushy brows and uncontrollable hair. He curtly set forth the consequences for wage earners of the Geneva doctrine. "You place them at the mercy of their employers — you forbid to them that union which alone can enable them to resist the oppressions of avarice — you condemn them to constant labor for such a pittance as others may choose." In short, the rate of wages was committed to those "whose interest it is to reduce it."

The judge's charge differed sharply; but, even though the Hudson case had closed-shop implications absent from the other cases, the jury was sufficiently moved by Edmonds's eloquence and by the general public exasperation to vote for acquittal. Bryant, in welcoming this

---

[21] Moore in the House, April 28, 1836, *Register of Debates*, 24 Congress 1 Session, 3428–3439. See also "Glances at Congress," *Democratic Review*, I, 75–76 (October, 1837).

[22] *Washington Globe*, June 27, 1836.

result, pointed the moral. "What but a general revolt of all the labouring classes is to be gained," he asked, "by these wanton and unprovoked
attacks upon their rights?" [23]

3

The Military and Civic Hotel was a dingy, yellow frame building, not quite two stories high, on the corner of Broome Street and
the Bowery. Many nights in 1836 and 1837 groups of men would
descend the two or three steps from the street, pass the bar to the
shabby staircase, faintly lit by a dark japanned lamp, and climb the
half story to the meeting room. There, under the low ceiling, the walls
smoked up by candle black, with a platform barely large enough for
a small table and three or four chairs, the Locofocos gathered. The
bold eloquence of Alexander Ming, Jr., or the honest brogue of John
Commerford, or the rant of Levi D. Slamm would echo through the
room, and the applause roar back till the window sashes rattled in
their shrunken casements. It was a modest home for a group which
proposed to bring the Democratic party back to first principles, but
these men cared little for backdrops. "The Founder of Christianity was
born in a manger," said the historian of the party; "and it is perfectly
in character that the principles of christian democracy should be
proclaimed in such humble places as the Military and Civic Hotel." [24]

Some who climbed the well-worn stairs — John Windt, Gilbert Vale,
Joel Curtis, George H. Evans (in poor health and soon to retire to a
New Jersey farm) — had been Workingmen in the days of Fanny
Wright. Others, like Alexander Ming, Jr., were steadfast Democrats
fed up with Tammany dictatorship. Still others were ordinary men
turning to politics because they felt the issues reached down to themselves. The Hecker brothers, hard-working German bakers, set up a
hand press in the garret of their shop and printed hard-money sentiments on the back of paper currency they received from their cus-
tomers. [25]

And still others were vagrant intellectuals, to whom the Jackson
administration had given a sense of the urgency of politics — Clinton
Roosevelt, for example, a man of great good will and ingenuity, equally

[23] *Union* (New York), July 1, 1836; *New York Evening Post*, July 2, 1836. See
also Commons, ed., *Documentary History*, IV, 303; Carl Carmer, "How Eight Poor
Shoemakers of Hudson, N.Y., Won Union Labor's First Victory 105 Years Ago,"
PM, June 1, 1941.

[24] Byrdsall, *Loco-Foco Party*, 45; W. C. Gover, *The Tammany Hall Democracy
of the City of New York*, 12–13.

[25] V. F. Holden, *Early Years of Isaac Thomas Hecker (1819–1844)*, 38.

adept at inventing machines or systems of government, whose early pamphlet, *The Mode of Protecting Domestic Industries*, had assailed the high tariff and paper money, and broached a new currency plan guaranteed to solve the problems of the day. Roosevelt's own nostrum attracted no following, but he caught on with the Locofocos, out of his benevolent desire for human betterment, though in a few years he would be a forcible critic of the laissez-faire philosophy they espoused.[26]

From the trade-union movement the Locofocos gained three leaders: John Commerford of the Chair-makers and Gilders, an honest and outspoken radical; the redheaded, ambitious and unreliable Levi D. Slamm of the Journeymen Locksmiths; and Robert Townsend, Jr., of the House Carpenters.[27] Thus when the courts struck down the unions early in 1836, the Locofocos stood ready to redirect labor energy into political channels and become the receivers of the union movement.

They had already set up an independent organization, which had run Ming for Mayor in the spring elections of 1836, and they had a paper, the *Democrat*, printed by John Windt and edited by Clinton Roosevelt. The great meeting in the Park to protest the conviction of the tailors took up the Locofoco call for a state convention. In September ninety-three delegates met at Utica, nominating Isaac S. Smith, a veteran of the old Workingmen's party, for Governor, and Moses Jaques for Lieutenant Governor. The city organization filled out the ticket, combining with the Whigs on several nominations.[28]

The elections showed that the Locofocos had the balance of power. Cambreleng and Ely Moore, the only successful Tammany congressional candidates, both had Locofoco support. Townsend and Roosevelt were sent to the assembly in the deal with the Whigs, and in exchange the Locofocos helped elect one Whig to Congress and another to the state Senate, both of whom promptly forgot the antimonopoly pledges they had signed before election. The Democratic organization thus suffered deep inroads, because it refused to follow the policy of the national administration.

[26] Byrdsall, *Loco-Foco Party*, 92; Fox, *Decline of Aristocracy*, 395; *New York Evening Post*, January 6, 1838, October 17, 1839.

[27] Marcy once observed that he preferred Clinton Roosevelt to Townsend "because I prefer a combination of folly and craziness to downright knavery." Marcy to P. M. Wetmore, October 25, 1837. See also Byrdsall, *Loco-Foco Party*, 75–77, 134.

[28] The decision of the Locofocos to affiliate with the Whigs proved neither their naïveté nor the Whigs' liberalism. It proceeded from the same motives which one hundred years later prompted the American Labor party in New York City to fuse with the Republicans in local elections against the Tammany Democrats.

4

The national administration in the meantime had been watching the New York Democratic organization with a disgust hardly less than that of the Locofocos. As early as February, 1835, Cambreleng had set forth what many believed to be Van Buren's views in a plain-spoken speech in the House. The period of reform, he said, had begun, and the most vital field for action lay outside the power of Washington. "Our State Governments, some at least, if not all, have outstripped even this Government in a rapid career of vicious and corrupt legislation." Corporations have multiplied, speculation flourishes, but "the greatest and most alarming abuse now existing in this country is the incorporation of near 600 banks of circulation." [29] Such sentiments hardly raised the roof in Albany.

Dissatisfaction grew among the radical wing of the Regency as the conservative Democrats succumbed comfortably to the temptations of boom. "I have long since ceased to watch the proceedings of our Legislature," Silas Wright exclaimed bitterly, "for any other purpose than to see when they would adjourn." For the first time in his political life he stopped reading the *Albany Argus,* which Edwin Croswell had transformed into the mouthpiece of the state-banking Democrats. "If we cannot get a different class of men into the legislature," John A. Dix told Van Buren, "the sooner we go into a minority the better. . . . We must have less strength or more virtue if we would administer the affairs of the State either for our own honor or the public good." [30]

The split in New York State reflected the split in the New York delegation at Washington, first over the distribution of the surplus revenue, then over the specie circular, with Silas Wright heading one group and N. P. Tallmadge the other. In June, 1836, Tallmadge made a bid for national recognition as leader of the conservative Democrats by defending the inflation against the slurs of "political economists," who were "frightened at this prosperity" and blind to "the cause which makes us, above all others, a happy, great, and prosperous people." What could that be? "Sir, it is contained in two words: it is our CREDIT SYSTEM." [31] The lines within the party were drawing tight.

[29] Cambreleng in the House, February 11, 1835, *Register of Debates,* 23 Congress 2 Session, 1308–1311.
[30] Wright to Flagg, May 25, 1836, Flagg Papers; Dix to Van Buren, June 7, 1836, Van Buren Papers.
[31] Tallmadge in the Senate, June 17, 1836, *Register of Debates,* 24 Congress 1 Session, 1828–1829.

XVI THE PATTERN OF LOCOFOCOISM

Pennsylvania had to orient its political conflicts about the problems of industrialism nearly to the same extent as Massachusetts and New York. Philadelphia, the home of Nicholas Biddle and the United States Bank, was also the home of America's first city central labor union, in 1827, and of the first Workingmen's party the next year. The contrast between the Greek temple on Chestnut Street and the slums which so appalled Mathew Carey provided a background against which the Bank War raged with unusual intensity.

1

But the Bank was resourceful and had many ways of circumventing opposition. The leading spokesman of the Philadelphia Workingmen's party of 1828–1831 was Stephen Simpson, a political careerist in his early forties, formerly a cashier in Stephen Girard's bank and for many years a journalist. An "original" Jackson man as early as 1822, he failed of his expected reward in 1829 and turned against the administration, emerging in the fall of 1830 as nominee for Congress on the Federal ticket.[1] (Federalism still lingered in Philadelphia, even then a main backwater of American politics.) He also obtained the Workingmen's endorsement. He was beaten; but his political intuitions were aroused, as when a pointer lifts his nose at the whiff of game, and he turned to writing a book which would insinuate himself into the confidence of the growing labor movement.

The result was a curious volume, published in Philadelphia in 1831, entitled *The Working Man's Manual*. Simpson was not without ability, and he developed some of the leading motifs of the Workingmen's

[1] Henry Simpson, *Lives of Eminent Philadelphians*, 893–895; Jackson to Simpson, May 23, 1825, June 27, 1829, Jackson, *Correspondence*, III, 297, IV, 48; statement of A. J. Donelson, *ibid.*, IV, 202–203. Cf. J. N. Barker to Van Buren, April 9, 1837, Van Buren Papers: "Mr. Stephen Simpson declares that his brother is a great scoundrel; his brother Henry returns the compliment; and the community is not disposed to question the veracity, in this point at least, of either."

agitation more ably than their own writers had yet succeeded in doing. The book appealed powerfully to the fears of social degradation, declaring that the "children of toil" had been depressed to a point where they were "as much shunned in society, as if they were leprous convicts just emerged from loathsome cells." It dealt effectively with the economic foundations of inequality and set forth the case against the paper credit system along good hard-money lines.

But midway through the book Simpson suddenly began to reach astonishing conclusions, coming out for internal improvements, for the protective tariff, indeed for the entire American System ("what can be more noble, laudable, and virtuous?"), and arguing vigorously in an appendix for the United States Bank.[2] This abrupt change of heart was probably not unrelated to the acceptance by Simpson, early in 1831, of the editorship of the conservative *Pennsylvania Whig*. In July he joined with other "original Jackson men" in renouncing the administration at a public ceremony for its hostility to the American System.[3] He completed his expiation in 1832 by writing a laudatory biography of the banker Girard. The wind had changed, and the smell of game was coming from another direction.

Those whom the Bank could not seduce, it sought to annihilate. When Roberts Vaux, philanthropist and prison reformer, one of Philadelphia's best-loved citizens, declared against the Bank, "an edict of social extermination," as an observer described it, "was forthwith registered against him." Friends abandoned him, and attempts were even made to expel him from various literary and philanthropic societies, some of which he had helped found.[4] When Charles Jared Ingersoll, another foe of the Bank, proposed a friend for the American Philosophical Society, the candidate was vengefully blackballed; and Richard Rush, Secretary of the Treasury under John Quincy Adams, son of Benjamin Rush and himself a distinguished lawyer, was blackballed by the Philosophical Society in the autumn of 1833 for the acknowledged reason that he approved General Jackson's paper on the removal of the deposits. A few years later, when Rush returned from settling the Smithsonian bequest in London, he found that old friends still shunned him, and in his own family only one brother maintained close relations with him.[5]

[2] Simpson, *The Working Man's Manual: a New Theory of Political Economy, on the Principle of Production the Source of Wealth*, 27, 133.

[3] P. S. Klein, *Pennsylvania Politics, 1817–1832*, 345; Commons and associates, *History of Labour*, I, 211 n.

[4] Henry Wikoff, *Reminiscences of an Idler*, 65–66.

[5] "Charles Jared Ingersoll," *Democratic Review*, VI, 349 (October, 1839); Rush to Van Buren, August 6, 1840, Van Buren Papers. It is conceivable that Rush was

Philadelphia forgave slowly. In 1839 when a Philadelphia firm published Walter Savage Landor's *Pericles and Aspasia*, it carefully omitted the dedicatory ode with which the author began the second volume, "To General Andrew Jackson. President of the United States."

> . . . How rare the sight, how grand!
> Behold the golden scales of Justice stand
> Self-balanced in a mailed hand. . . .[6]

2

Yet the pressure of General Jackson was as much a natural fact as the pressure of Philadelphia, and, in some respects, more effective. Biddle had cagily relied as much as possible on Pennsylvania Democrats in the campaign for recharter. Senator G. M. Dallas was scheduled to manage the fight in the upper house; and Charles Jared Ingersoll represented the Bank in some of its negotiations with the government. But the veto made them think a second time, and when the smoke of battle cleared both had hurried over to the Jackson camp. Dallas was little more than a party wheelhorse, but the brilliant, erratic and charming Ingersoll, with his quizzical smile, his close-cropped brown hair, his elastic step, provided after 1833 consistent leadership in the fight against corporations and paper money. Unfortunately his judgment was not equal to his abilities, and he never quite commanded the influence which his talent and experience should have given him.[7]

Henry D. Gilpin was another intellectual converted to the Jacksonian cause. A slender man, wearing gold-rimmed spectacles, thirty-two years old in 1833, he was a good lawyer with a cultivated background and literary inclinations. For six years he edited the *Atlantic Souvenir*, an annual, and he was later to become president of the Pennsylvania Academy of Fine Arts. As government director of the Bank, he learned its character at first hand, becoming profoundly convinced that corporations were the "great question of the time in morals as much as politics." Along with Ingersoll, Rush and a few others, he braved the displeasure of his class to associate with radicals, trade-unionists, Democratic politicians and other disreputable characters. An intimate friend of Van Buren and of George Bancroft, he

---

the man proposed by Ingersoll, and only one man was blackballed by the Philosophical Society for the Jacksonian heresy.

[6] W. S. Landor, *Pericles and Aspasia* (London, 1836), II, v–vii. The Philadelphia firm was E. L. Carey and A. Hart.

[7] Sarah M. Maury, *The Statesmen of America in 1846*, 155–160; Gideon Welles, "Political History of the Forties," 22, Welles Papers.

kept them informed of the progress of radical democracy in Pennsylvania.[8]

Late in 1833 the Philadelphia labor movement began to revive, and by 1836 the Trades' Union of the City and Council of Philadelphia claimed about fifty societies and more than ten thousand members. Its leaders were John Ferral, a hand-loom weaver, for many years a tireless champion of labor interests, and William English, an ambitious and unreliable journeyman shoemaker.[9] English's impassioned oratory gave the movement a radical and intransigent tone. "The war waged by capital against labour is co-existent with capital itself," he declared at the Union celebration on July 4, 1835.

> In all ages, in all countries, capital has been used as a never-failing means of obtaining power, and the oppression and impoverishment of the productive classes are the certain consequences of such a combination.
>
> The history of the world is but a history of the wrongs practised by privileged wealth upon oppressed poverty. Even in this country, this boasted land of liberty, has the omnipotence of wealth . . . rendered the condition of the labourer little better than that of the slave.[10]

In a lively sheet called *The Radical Reformer and Working Man's Advocate*, Thomas Brothers, an English radical and disciple of Cobbett, come to examine the experiment of democracy, sought to rally labor behind the cause of hard money.

From the first the Union was active in politics. The Bank War mobilized labor, and the *Pennsylvanian* of Philadelphia, organ of the progressive Democrats, acknowledged the alliance by defending the right to organize and even supporting strikes for a ten-hour day. H. D. Gilpin was in correspondence with English and Ferral, as well as Ely Moore; and Charles Jared Ingersoll, as counsel for the Philadelphia plasterers in 1836, won their acquittal in one of the cases which helped

---

[8] Gilpin to T. Butler, December 16, 1837, Gilpin Letterbooks. See also Wikoff, *Reminiscences*, 60.

[9] English had been a leader in the Workingmen's party of 1829–1831 and a participant in the hard-money meeting of 1829. Later, in the Pennsylvania state Senate, he helped the Bank get its state charter and opposed the attempt to repeal this charter. Thomas Brothers observed of him that he "had not an idea becoming a man except what he borrowed or stole from others." Brothers, *The United States of North America as They Are; Not as They Are Generally Described: Being a Cure for Radicalism*, 224–225, 227; *Niles' Register*, April 1, 1837. For unionism in Philadelphia, Commons, ed., *Documentary History*, V, 94, 325–327.

[10] *Radical Reformer and Working Man's Advocate* (Philadelphia), August 1, 1835.

end the application of the doctrine of criminal conspiracy to labor organizations.[11]

The boom of 1834–1835 caused the same split in the Pennsylvania Democratic party as in New York and Massachusetts. The progressive wing favored Henry A. Muhlenberg, the leading radical in the Pennsylvania delegation in Congress, over George Wolf, the conservative Democratic Governor, and finally ran him on a separate ticket.[12] In their view, the state-banking system had to be reformed along hard-money lines or "the great object to be attained in putting down the Bank of the United States . . . will not be accomplished." [13] In Philadelphia the Muhlenberg ticket, supported by the *Pennsylvanian* and by the labor leaders, included William English as nominee for the state Senate, and Thomas Hogan, another union man, for the Assembly. The conservative candidate, Ritner, romped in because of the split Democratic vote; but the schism plainly showed the determination of the radical wing. As in New York and Massachusetts, the progressives were fighting to force their views on the whole state party.

3

This was the pattern of Locofocoism.[14] In every state, the reckless expansion of banking facilities provoked widespread popular disgust; and Locofocoism, the expression of that disgust, accordingly was strongest in the states where issues of currency and incorporation were most vital. It was thus an *Eastern* movement, designed to meet *Eastern* economic difficulties, preoccupied with fears to which the West was largely indifferent. As Locofocoism began more and more to shape the policy of the administration, that policy departed increasingly from the desires of the West.

[11] Commons, ed., *Documentary History*, IV, 335–341.

[12] Muhlenberg, the son of the great Lutheran pastor and himself a minister at Reading, had gone to Congress after retiring from the pulpit in 1827 at the age of forty-five because of ill health. The firmness of his stand in the House against the Bank prompted Jackson to nickname him *General* Muhlenberg. When Buchanan once protested that Muhlenberg was no general, the President replied, "No matter, he ought to have been." "Biographical Memoir of the Late Henry A. Muhlenberg," *Democratic Review*, XVI, 73–75 (January, 1845).

[13] Jesse Miller to the committee for the Democratic celebration of July 4, 1835, *Radical Reformer*, July 18, 1835.

[14] In Connecticut, to take another example, radical Democrats waged a similar fight, under the leadership of John Milton Niles, the bent, wrinkled, red-haired Senator. As editor of the *Hartford Times* and as Senator. Niles operated on a simple creed: "In all legislation affecting the great interests of the country, whether in Congress or the State Legislatures, there has been a tendency to favor capital rather than labor." See John Fairfield to his wife, February 2, 1845, Fairfield,

Jackson's original Western support, it has been pointed out, sprang from the glowing enthusiasm for the Hero of New Orleans and was largely uninformed by ideas, beyond a vague impression that the General was a friend of the American System. His first administration then produced a series of decisions, almost every one of which was basically unpopular on the frontier, even if none could harm Jackson's invincible personal position. The Maysville veto weakened the administration through most of the West. In Michigan and Illinois, indeed, the Democrats ignored its message and far exceeded the Whigs in their passion for internal improvements; in general, the Western Democrats favored a spendthrift policy no less than the Whigs.[15] The tariff was not an urgent question in the thirties, except in connection with nullification, but the Western Democrats resisted the free-trade tendencies of radical Democrats in the East and South (and of Jackson). As for the Bank, Jackson had to allow his hard-money aims to be misunderstood in the West, where the important anti-Bank sentiment came from the desire to liberate credit and paper money from Eastern control; in other words, he was largely supported by people who regarded the veto as an inflationary rather than a deflationary action.[16] None of these decisions was demanded by the West, and none, save the misinterpreted war against the Bank, won its zealous backing.

The unveiling of the hard-money program during the second term brought the conflict into the open. Caring much more for self-determination and home rule than for economic democracy, most of the Western politicians found it hard to go along with the President

---

Letters, 359; Niles in the Senate, February 24, 1837, *Register of Debates*, 24 Congress 2 Session, 957; Gideon Welles to Van Buren, April 29, June 13, 1843, Van Buren Papers.

Gideon Welles, Niles's successor both on the *Times* and in Connecticut politics, made an influential report to the state legislature in 1835 on incorporation. "A system of partial and exclusive legislation, calculated to make the rich richer and the poor poorer, has been fostered," he declared. ". . . Its inevitable tendency is to create inequalities of fortune, by exalting capital at the expense of labor." He recommended that the system of special incorporation be replaced by a general law of incorporation, a proposal repeated by Henry Edwards, the Democratic Governor, in 1836, and embodied in the Hinsdale Act of 1837, the first modern corporation law. Welles's report was reprinted in the *Radical Reformer*, June 13, 1835, and elsewhere. See also J. M. Morse, *A Neglected Period of Connecticut's History*, 297, 302.

[15] F. B. Streeter, *Political Parties in Michigan, 1837–60*, 9; T. C. Pease, *The Frontier State, 1818–1848*, Centennial History of Illinois, 219; F. P. Weisenburger, *The Passing of the Frontier, 1825–1850*, 229–230, 242, 244, 254, 272.

[16] In actual fact, there seems to have been little interest in the Bank before the veto through much of the West — Ohio, for example — except where, as in Kentucky, politics had systematically played upon the issue. See Weisenburger, *Passing of the Frontier*, 261, 277; also chapter vii above.

on the currency question. Either they left the party, like White, Bell and Eaton, or gave the hard-money policy halfhearted support nationally while ignoring the question within their states, like Lewis Cass and Richard M. Johnson.

When Western Democrats did advocate Locofoco positions, they did so in many cases for motives which the great social fluidity of the West rendered highly temporary and accidental. The case of Franklin Plummer of Mississippi, who gave probably the most radical speech delivered by a Westerner in Congress during Jackson's presidency, is in this respect instructive.

Rising in the House near the end of the panic session, Plummer launched into a harangue on the Workingmen's party. He set forth the familiar platform — "the leading measures advocated by that despised party of which I have the honor of being an humble member" — and went on to assail at great length "this American banking system, this rag-money system, this system of legalized monopolies, which makes the rich richer and the poor poorer." Jackson he admired, and he would stick with the administration: "I will not go against the party until the party goes against the principles of the working-men." But he denounced the Democratic organization and stated ingeniously the Workingmen's case against politics in general.

There were two classes in society, he said, one subsisting by labor, the other by law. The second, and smaller, class, by its control of the government, systematically deprived the larger class of the products of its labor. But the smaller class, the aristocracy, was itself separated into two groups, "the ins and the outs." The outs always appeal to the voters by attacking the misdeeds of those in power; but when the people respond by raising them to power, they "laugh at their credulity, and continue, and even increase, those abuses which they have been elected to correct. . . . The gamblers alternately win, while the great mass of the people, who pay the fiddler and other expenses of carrying on the operation, have not even a solitary chance in the game." The Bank issue, Plummer declared, was the only issue disputed by the aristocracy in which the masses had any real interest.[17]

Plummer was a New Englander who had emigrated to Mississippi. A glib man, with an entertaining flow of language and the shrewdness of a Yankee peddler, he became a first-class jury lawyer and a great political favorite. A contemporary reported that he was "as a cross-road and stump orator unequalled — as a bush-whacker and log-cabin electioneerer unrivalled." On one campaign Plummer, canvass-

[17] Plummer in the House, May 26, 1834, *Register of Debates*, 23 Congress 1 Session, 4830–4832.

ing the district with his competitor, stopped at a farm for noon dinner. His rival took the occasion to commend himself to the farmer's wife by kissing her little girl and praising her beauty; "but she was completely carried away when she saw Plummer pick up her wee toddling boy, lay it gently across his lap, turn over its little petticoat, and go to *hunting red bugs!* 'They are powerful bad,' said Plummer, 'and mighty hard on babies.' She was enchanted, and never forgot that tender hearted Congressman." [18]

The small farmers of the pine woods of eastern Mississippi sent Plummer to Congress in 1828. In 1832 he was opposed by the nominal Jackson organization but won anyway; hence his lofty attitude toward established parties. But Plummer was too good a vote getter to be wasted on the Workingmen. In 1835 the bankers of Natchez invited him to town, gave him banquets, loaned him twenty-five thousand dollars and encouraged him to run for Senator. Plummer bought a barouche, hired a servant in livery and started out on a campaign. He had betrayed himself, of course, and failing in the election he somehow lost his nerve, sinking out of politics and dying an obscure drunkard in Jackson in 1847.

The rise and fall of Plummer showed the temptations which surrounded radicalism on the frontier. An unstable society, with extremes of poverty and wealth, but with easy access to riches and a quick turnover in the composition of the aristocracy, might produce a brief, frenetic and opportunistic radicalism; but it was not likely to produce radicalism which was serious, unbribable and consistent. Such men as Plummer would denounce riches loudly enough, but were always ready to change their tune should the next speculation prove successful.

There were certainly leaders in the West dedicated to the principles of democracy — men like Moses Dawson, Thomas Morris, Benjamin Tappan and William Allen in Ohio, Robert Dale Owen now serving as a Democrat in the legislature of Indiana, Kingsley Bingham in Michigan, Polk and William Carroll in Tennessee, Benton in Missouri — but even their ideas and solutions were largely borrowed from the East. In the thirties this radical group was strongest in Ohio, which most approximated the economic conditions of the East and actually underwent its own version of the Locofoco schism in 1836.[19] In the

---

[18] J. F. H. Claiborne, *Mississippi, as a Province, Territory and State,* 411–412, 423–427.

[19] Weisenburger, *Passing of the Frontier,* 308–311. See also Streeter, *Political Parties in Michigan,* 31–32; McClure, *Opposition in Missouri to Thomas Hart Benton,* 12–2²

forties, as the dominion of the new finance crept westward, the radical Democrats grew stronger, and Locofoco ideas played a vital and sometimes dominating role in the state constitutional conventions of that and the next decade.

But the East remained the source of the effective expression of Jacksonian radicalism, and Eastern ideas rose to supremacy in Washington as Jacksonianism changed from an agitation into a program. (The test of this would come when Jacksonian measures were presented to the West without the magic of Andrew Jackson.) The East simply had the consistent and bitter experience which alone could serve as a crucible of radicalism.

The great illusion of historians of the frontier has been that social equality produces economic equalitarianism. In fact, the demand for economic equality is generally born out of conditions of social inequality, and becomes the more passionate, deeply felt and specific as the inequality becomes more rigid. The actual existence of equal opportunities is likely to diminish the vigilance with which they are guarded, and to stimulate the race for power and privilege. The fur capitalists of St. Louis and the land speculators of Mississippi were as characteristic of the West as Andrew Jackson.

XVII THE THIRD TERM

HENRY CLAY had described the revolution as "hitherto bloodless," but how long would the qualification hold true? Calhoun opened 1835 with premonitions of catastrophe; the government was so corrupt, he said, that "the time had arrived when reformation or revolution must go on." Many agreed, and for a time feeling ran so high that Van Buren took to wearing a brace of pistols, even when presiding over the Senate.[1]

Hezekiah Niles meanwhile kept conscientious account of the upsurge of popular violence. "The time predicted seems rapidly approaching when the mob shall rule." In the first week of September alone, he clipped over five hundred items from the press of the country. "*Society seems everywhere unhinged,*" he said, "and the demon of 'blood and slaughter' has been let loose upon us." What had happened? "The character of our countrymen seems suddenly changed." Niles grew increasingly melancholy and ended with a quotation from Gouverneur Morris.[2]

Disorder afflicted foreign travelers with misgivings, even some who had come to admire the great democratic experiment. The Saint-Simonian Michel Chevalier, deciding that the reign of terror had begun, devoted a chapter in his book on America to "Symptomes de Révolution." Thomas Brothers, the Philadelphia radical, shocked altogether out of his passion for change, snarled his farewell to Utopia in *The United States of North America as They Are; Not as They Are Generally Described: Being a Cure for Radicalism*, devoting a neat appendix to "Miscellaneous Murders, Riots, and other Outrages, in 1834, 1835, 1836, 1837, and 1838."

1

But the impending election gave stability a fresh chance to reassert itself. Unable to unite on a candidate, the Whigs decided to run popular local favorites, in the hope of throwing the election to

---

[1] Calhoun in the Senate, January 28, February 2, 1835, *Register of Debates*, 23 Congress 2 Session, 268, 276; Van Buren, *Autobiography*, 761.
[2] *Niles' Register*, August 8, September 5, 1835.

the House. They made their major challenge in the Southwest, where they bid for the conservative Democratic vote by backing an old friend of Jackson's, Hugh Lawson White, Senator from Tennessee. Just over sixty, White was a lean, sinewy man, with a long, emaciated face and flowing gray hair, thrown back from his forehead and curling on his shoulders. His plain manners, firm conscience and sturdy sense of honor had won him wide respect.[3]

As one of Jackson's first supporters, White had watched the dwindling of Western influence and the rise of Van Buren and Locofocoism with alarm. White himself had been for many years president of the State Bank of Tennessee, and Samuel Jaudon, the cashier of the United States Bank and an influential figure in Bank activities, was his son-in-law.[4] The open adoption of the hard-money policy thus increased his anxiety. When Jackson consulted him in the summer of 1833 about removing the deposits, White strongly opposed the idea, though party fidelity led him to defend it in the Senate.[5]

Meanwhile he had married a divorcée who kept the Washington boardinghouse in which he had lived for twelve years. Her ambitions for him, and his own misgivings and disappointments, made him particularly receptive to suggestions for 1836. John Bell took the lead in persuading White, and Daniel Webster used his massive presence to inflame the hopes of Mrs. White. *"Judge White is on the track,"* a Kentucky Whig soon wrote back to a friend, *"running gayly, and won't come off; and if he would, his wife won't let him."* [6]

For the Northwest, the Whigs dug up the Clerk of the Court of Common Pleas in Cincinnati, a genial antiquity still vaguely remembered as the hero of the battle of Tippecanoe almost a quarter of a century before. Nicholas Biddle delivered in memorable language the instructions for William Henry Harrison's campaign: —

Let him say not one single word about his principles, or his creed — let him say nothing — promise nothing. Let no Committee, no convention — no town meeting ever extract from him a single word, about what he thinks now, or what he will do hereafter. Let the use of pen and ink be wholly forbidden as if he were a mad poet in Bedlam.[7]

[3] S. G. Heiskell, *Andrew Jackson and Early Tennessee History*, I, 643; Nancy N. Scott, *Memoir of Hugh Lawson White*, 240, 243; Wise, *Seven Decades of the Union*, 162.
[4] *New York Evening Post*, April 22, 1835; *Washington Globe*, February 8, 1836.
[5] Scott, *White*, 143.
[6] Benton, *Thirty Years' View*, II, 185. See also Van Buren, *Autobiography*, 226 n.
[7] Biddle to Herman Cope, August 11, 1835, Biddle, *Correspondence*, 256.

In the Northeast, Webster would stand where General Harrison did not; and in the Southeast, John C. Calhoun could be relied upon to regard the election with an indifference which would not benefit Van Buren.

2

For the Democrats the first problem was to dispose of Colonel Johnson. Both his own ambition and his popularity among the workingmen were as strong as ever. As early as January, 1833, George H. Evans had put forward Johnson's name for 1836, and in August of that year flaming handbills to the same effect, supposedly issued by the Workingmen of Boston, were posted on grocery doors in the remotest backwoods towns of Indiana.[8]

The Johnson campaign was under way. Soon William Emmons contributed a biography, someone else turned out a ballad entitled "The Warrior Sage, a National Song," and Richard Emmons was delivered of *Tecumseh; or, the Battle of the Thames, a National Drama, in Five Acts.* This last opened in Baltimore in January, 1834, under the direction of a good press agent, who endowed the cast with the *"identical dress"* worn by Tecumseh at his death and the *"same pistols* with which the hero slew his savage foe." The Secretary of War also co-operated by allowing the actual British standard captured by Johnson to be displayed in the course of the evening.[9] When the play came to Washington, the warrior sage himself sat in a box and acknowledged the salutes of the audience.

Van Buren's managers, impressed by Johnson's activity, decided to silence him by offering the vice-presidency. Sentiment was not, however, unanimous. John Catron, an old friend of Jackson's from Tennessee, soon to be elevated to the Supreme Court, rejected the view that "a lucky random shot, even if it did hit Tecumseh, qualifies a man for Vice President."[10] The South in general opposed Johnson because of his domestic arrangements. He had two daughters by his housekeeper, a mulatto named Julia Chinn. The girls were well educated and attractive, eventually marrying white men and inheriting part of their father's estate. After Julia's death Johnson took up with another high-yellow girl, who ran off with an Indian in 1835. When he recaptured the fugitives, gossip whispered, he sold the girl

[8] *Free Enquirer*, February 9, 1833; John Law to Van Buren, August 20, 1833, Van Buren Papers.
[9] *Niles' Register*, February 1, 1834.
[10] Catron to Jackson, March 21, 1835, Jackson, *Correspondence*, V, 331–332.

down the river and moved on to her sister. The facts themselves could hardly have been shocking to a plantation society, but Johnson's failure to conceal them was, and the South did not propose to reward such misplaced candor by the vice-presidency. In the convention, Johnson finally won out with Van Buren's support over William Cabell Rives of Virginia, but the Virginia delegation broke into hisses and refused to support the Kentuckian at the election.[11]

Van Buren himself, overcoming the fears which undid him during the removal of the deposits, had decided to advance the revolution. "The ground, that this is in truth a question between Aristocracy and Democracy," he declared in 1834, "cannot be too often or too forcibly impressed upon the minds of the people." In 1835 there appeared Professor William M. Holland's semi-authorized campaign biography, written by a former contributor to the *Free Enquirer* with the endorsement of Benjamin F. Butler, and inspired by the author's belief, as he put it, "in the most ultra democratic doctrines, and his partiality towards the subject of this narrative as the champion of those doctrines." [12]

Except for the Locofoco party in New York, nearly all the radicals were rallying around Van Buren: Bancroft and Allen in Massachusetts, Robert Dale Owen in Indiana, Ely Moore and William Leggett in New York. Fanny Wright began a long lecture tour in May, 1836, to explain the urgency of the election. In New York she tried to end the Locofoco schism, feeling that the menace of Whiggery left no time for petulance over doctrine. In Boston, attended by Abner Kneeland of the local Society of Free Enquirers, she spoke to an audience of two hundred, including thirty-two women. Her interests, reporters noted, seemed now exclusively political; her speech "did not contain a single allusion, direct or indirect, to any theological topic." [13]

3

But the Whigs were equally active, concentrating their energies on a brilliant smear campaign from which Van Buren's reputation has never quite recovered. It had long been a favorite tactic to denounce the administration by fixing on sinister advisers in the back-

---

[11] Meyer, *Johnson*, 317–321, 341, 418–419; *Niles' Register*, May 30, June 6, 1835.
[12] Van Buren to Jackson, July 22, 1834, Jackson, *Correspondence*, V, 274; W. M. Holland, *Life and Political Opinions of Martin Van Buren*, 363.
[13] *Boston Post*, October 29, 1836. See also A. J. G. Perkins and T. Wolfson, *Frances Wright: Free Enquirer*, 329, 332.

ground rather than affronting directly the national enthusiasm for the Hero of New Orleans. Amos Kendall was a leading nominee for scapegoat-in-chief. "For the last eight years," cried a Whig politician in 1837, "Amos Kendall (who before he was driven from Kentucky by public indignation, had reduced this state to almost utter ruin), has been emphatically the president of the United States. . . . he has for eight years, through an infatuated and imbecile old man, ruled and ruined this nation." [14]

On the whole, however, Van Buren nosed out Kendall for this distinction. In the words of William H. Seward, the rising young Whig leader in New York, Van Buren was "a crawling reptile, whose only claim was that he had inveigled the confidence of a credulous, blind, dotard, old man." [15] Webster and Calhoun had developed this theme in thundering denunciations in the Senate. Davy Crockett, the ex-frontier hero, lent his name to a so-called biography of Van Buren which reproduced the pattern in its crudest form.[16] Another version was to be found in the most famous series of Jack Downing papers, written by Charles A. Davis, a director of the New York branch of the United States Bank and close friend of Nicholas Biddle's. Beverley Tucker's novel, *The Partisan Leader*, published by Duff Green in 1836, set forth the Van Buren stereotype in somewhat more literate terms and from the point of view of an admirer of Calhoun. A thousand Whig jokes and cartoons and broadsides depicted the smooth and sly Van Buren manipulating his foolish chief for diabolical ends.

Colonel Johnson, denounced in the North as a slaveholder and in the South as an "amalgamationist," came off no better. Whig minstrels were as much stimulated by his misadventures as Democrats were by his status as Warrior Sage. "Johnson's Wife of Old Kentucky" burlesqued a popular ballad: —

> The wave that heaves by Congo's shore,
> Heaves not so high nor darkly wide
> As Sukey in her midnight snore,
> Close by Tecumseh Johnson's side.[17]

[14] Robert Wickliffe, quoted in *Niles' Register*, June 17, 1837.

[15] *New York Evening Post*, November 2, 1836.

[16] See, for example, the famous description of Van Buren: "When he enters the senate-chamber in the morning, he struts and swaggers like a crow in a gutter. He is laced up in corsets, such as women in a town wear, and, if possible, tighter than the best of them. It would be difficult to say, from his personal appearance, whether he was man or woman, but for his large *red* and *gray* whiskers." Crockett, *Life of Martin Van Buren*, 80–81.

[17] Bernard Mayo, "The Man Who Killed Tecumseh." *American Mercury*, XIX, 450.

Yet all the caterwauling could not compete against the confidence in Jackson in the West, and the solid respect with which Van Buren was regarded in the East by people who knew him other than by reputation. White ran as a "true" Jacksonian, and not insincerely; he certainly stood for what a good deal of the West thought Jackson had stood for in 1828 and 1832. To Jackson's disgust, he carried Tennessee, and young Westerners like Andrew Johnson and Abraham Lincoln voted for him. Webster won only Massachusetts, and barely polled 55 per cent of the votes there. The surprise was Harrison's strong showing — seven states in his pocket and good results wherever he was on the ticket. But Van Buren ran far too well, amassing 170 electoral votes to the aggregate 124 of his opponents. The Jacksonian revolution was going into its third term.

4

Parting gifts flooded the White House as the old General labored with Roger B. Taney on his Farewell Address and preparations began for the final removal. March 4, 1837, was clear and tranquil. Jackson, pale, composed and happy, rode by Van Buren's side to the Capitol. At noon the two men appeared on the eastern portico. Chief Justice Taney, rejected by the Senate for the offices of Secretary of the Treasury and Associate Justice of the Supreme Court, now administered the oath to Martin Van Buren, rejected as Minister to England, and Jackson, plain and contented as a private citizen, watched with deep satisfaction.

The crowd which packed the East Lawn, their faces upturned in the noon sun, were profoundly silent. After the inaugural address the old General started slowly down the broad steps toward the carriage below. As he descended the people yielded to their feelings; the pent-up flood of cheers and shouts broke forth; and they paid their long, last, irresistible tribute to the man they loved. . . . Thomas Hart Benton, watching from a side window, felt himself stirred as never before. In later years he would recall many inaugurations, but compared to this they all seemed as pageants, "empty and soulless, brief to the view, unreal to the touch, and soon to vanish." [18] This was reality, the living relation between a man and his people, distilled for a pause in the rhythm of events, rising for a moment of wild and soaring enthusiasm, then dying away into the chambers of memory.

Philip Hone scribbled a vengeful farewell to the "terrible old man." "This is the end of Gen. Jackson's administration — the most disastrous

[18] Benton, *Thirty Years' View*, I, 735.

in the annals of the country." But who was Philip Hone to speak for the people? "This day," wrote William Leggett, "completes a period that will shine in American history with more inherent and undying lustre, than any other which the chronicler has yet recorded, or which perhaps will ever form a portion of our country's annals."

"This day," wrote a patriarchal New England preacher, "closes the administration of Andrew Jackson, who has spent the greater part of his life in public services. . . . I know of nothing, that a people may reasonably expect from good government, but that the United States have enjoyed under his administration." [19]

[19] Hone, *Diary*, I, 242, 244; Leggett in the *Plaindealer*, March 4, 1837; L. F. Greene, *Writings of the Late Elder John Leland*, 740–741.

XVIII PANIC

THE MONEY boom roared on through 1836, to the increasing alarm of hard-money men. "When will the bubble burst?" asked William Cullen Bryant in the spring. "When will the great catastrophe which the banks have been preparing for us actually come?" Robert Rantoul predicted collapse within a year, and in the fall John A. Dix wrote glumly, "We are on the eve of one of the severest reactions in business of almost every description with which we have been visited for years. . . . Do not set me down for a croaker." [1]

1

But who would not set him down for a croaker? Even nominal hard-money men were not convinced by exercises in extrapolation. Some months after the first rumblings, in February, 1837, Benton, beckoning the President-elect into the finance committee room of the Senate, told him that the nation was on the verge of a financial explosion. Van Buren smilingly chaffed Old Bullion: "Your friends think you a little exalted in the head on that subject"; and Benton, stopping short in his economic exposition, only muttered to himself, *"You will soon feel the thunderbolt."* ("I should not mention this," Benton said in the Senate three years later, "if it was not that the President himself well remembers it, and often mentions it.") [2]

Croakers soon had their evidence. The proportion of paper to specie lengthened, gambling in banks, internal improvements and public lands grew more frenzied, and the economic structure became increasingly speculative and unsound. Crop failures in 1835 toppled the first domino. Farmers could not pay merchants and speculators, who in turn could not pay banks; and the decline of agricultural exports, making the international balance of trade unusually heavy against the United States, caused an unexpected demand abroad for

---

[1] *New York Evening Post*, April 7, 1836; Luther Hamilton, *Rantoul*, 341; Dix to ?, November 28, 1836, Morgan Dix, *Memoirs of John Adams Dix*, I, 148–149.
[2] Benton in the Senate, January 16, 1840, *Congressional Globe*, 26 Congress 1 Session, Appendix, 121; Benton, *Thirty Years' View*, II, 10–11.

payment in specie. Meanwhile, the Specie Circular called the bluff of banks issuing their notes on the public land.

Then Henry Clay's Distribution Act, vigorously opposed by Benton, Silas Wright and the hard-money men, went into operation on January 1, 1837; it provided for the distribution of the federal surplus among the states, which meant a withdrawal of public funds from deposit banks, and a general contraction of the money market. Late in 1836 important British business houses failed, throwing their American securities on the market. Credit tightened, specie fled the country, and in its wake the shades of depression fell fast across the land.

In destroying the Bank, Jackson had removed a valuable brake on credit expansion; and in sponsoring the system of deposit in state banks, he had accelerated the tendencies toward inflation. Yet the hard-money Democrats at least understood the danger and tried vainly, by the example of the federal government and by pressure within the states, to halt the dizzy pyramiding of paper credits. The business community, however, fascinated by the illusion of quick returns, fought the hard-money program all along the line.[3] Now they were reaping the whirlwind.

2

The crash brought suffering and distress. Prices of essential foods shot out of the reach of the poor. Flour, which had sold at $5.62 a barrel in March, 1835, rose to $7.75 in March, 1836, and $12 in March, 1837. Pork climbed from $10 in March, 1835, to $16.25 a year later and to $18.25 in March, 1837. The wholesale price of coal mounted from $6 a ton in January, 1835, to $10.50 in January, 1837, and rents increased proportionately.[4]

In the cities during the winter of 1836–1837 mutterings of dis-

---

[3] Even so determined a conservative as Philip Hone could not avoid occasional inadvertent expressions of disgust. "This is another evidence of the reckless manner in which business has been conducted," he allowed himself to say of one failure — though he quickly caught himself and returned to the party line, "or rather, to speak more charitably, of the straits to which men have been driven by the wicked interference of the government with the currency of the country." Hone, *Diary*, I, 248–249.

[4] The flour and pork prices are taken from the speech in the House by Henry Williams, June 4, 1840, *Congressional Globe*, 26 Congress 1 Session, Appendix, 528. They agree fairly well with other contemporary tables, e.g., *The Rough-Hewer*, April 30, 1840, and with A. H. Cole, *Wholesale Commodity Prices in the United States, 1700–1861*, from which the figures for coal are taken, Statistical Supplement, 246 ff.

satisfaction turned into growls. One day in February New York awoke to find the city placarded with angry posters.

BREAD, MEAT, RENT, AND FUEL!
Their prices must come down!

The VOICE OF THE PEOPLE shall be heard and will prevail! The people will meet in the Park, rain or shine, at 4 o'clock, P.M., on Monday afternoon. . . . All friends of humanity determined to resist monopolists and extortioners are invited to attend.

It was signed by Moses Jaques, Alexander Ming, Jr., John Windt and other Locofocos.

Four or five thousand persons huddled in the Park on a bitter cold day to hear Ming and Windt, under the motto "As the currency expands, the loaf contracts," attack the paper system for bringing on the collapse. The excited crowd gradually began to break up into small, angry groups. On the outskirts furious speakers started to denounce the flour dealers. The Locofocos tried to quiet the newcomers and adjourn the meeting, but it was too late. Someone cried out, "Hart's Flour Store," the word was taken up, and a mob of nearly a thousand people flocked up Washington Street and stormed the store of Eli Hart and Company. When Mayor Cornelius Lawrence tried to send the rioters back, he was forced to retreat in a shower of sticks, stones and barrel staves. The throng swept into the store, trampled flour and wheat over the floor, and surged on to other warehouses, till they were finally stopped by the police.[5]

The flour riots struck terror in the hearts of the conservatives. Mobs clamoring for bread had started the French Revolution, it was recalled, and no less formidable an objective seemed to be in the minds of those "Jackson-jacobins," Jaques and Ming.[6] Even William Leggett declared, "There never was a riot, in any place, on any previous occasion, for which there existed less pretence. There is no circumstance to extenuate it."[7] Hezekiah Niles placed the events on record,

---

[5] Byrdsall, *Loco-Foco Party*, 100–105.

[6] See, for example, *New York Commercial Advertiser*, February 14, 1837.

[7] Leggett's position rested on his deep faith in *laissez-faire*. The dealers in any commodity, he said, have "a perfect natural right to fix their own price," just as laborers had to combine in unions; the flour was "absolutely their property, to do what they pleased with it." Leggett was promptly rebuked by a scorching article in Richard Adams Locke's *New Era* ("Causeless! Heaven knows there was cause enough for an outrage a thousand times more violent and unsparing, however unlawful it might have been"). See *Plaindealer*, February 18, 25, 1837. Businessmen were no doubt impressed by the ferocity of this new radicalism, which made even William Leggett a conservative.

as he said with gloomy satisfaction, "to enable the future historian to trace the downward course of this republic." [8]

Yet it was plain that the Locofocos did not intend the riot, nor did their speakers incite it. None of the fifty-three rioters arrested was a Locofoco. When blamed for calling together so many angry people under conditions which might burst into violence, the Locofocos logically retorted that the best way to prevent riots was to remove their causes. Some observers, indeed, lodged ultimate responsibility with the dealers themselves, charging that they had claimed a nonexistent scarcity as an excuse for keeping prices up. According to Richard Adams Locke's outspoken new daily, the *New Era*, foreign grain arriving at the port was instantly snatched up by merchants whose warehouses were already jammed to bursting with native flour; Eli Hart and Company itself was reported to have just obtained a loan from the new State Bank (of which Mayor Lawrence was president) in order to corner foreign wheat and prevent independent operators from entering the market. [9]

Though the outburst was not repeated, suffering continued into the spring. In May, the *New Era* declared of New York, "At no period of its history has there been as great a degree of general distress as there is at this day." (But some, in the manner which so irritated Mathew Carey, were not impressed; Alonzo Potter, the young minister, for example, would soon observe, "Scarcely any thing is required for happiness, improvement, or usefulness, which is not attainable by the labouring population.") At least ten thousand mechanics and workingmen were unemployed, the *New Era* continued, their wives and families would make another ten thousand, and over two thousand clerks had been dismissed. ("Could the factious and discontented be induced to reflect dispassionately on their condition," mused Alonzo Potter, "they could not but feel, that if with such advantages they are not happy and enlightened, and virtuous too, the fault must be their own.") Of seamstresses, bookbinders, bonnetmakers and other working women, at least three thousand were in pining destitution; and the *New Era* reporter noted sadly the "wan and squalid appearance" of the women and children in the poorer parts of the city. ("If with the wages which they receive now, they are rest-

[8] *Niles' Register*, February 18, 25, 1837.
[9] The *New Era* indictment was specific, naming six stores as leaders in the "odious and avaricious combination," all of which had quantities of monopolized wheat that they had combined to sell at a price "which they well knew the necessity of this city . . . would be compelled to pay." Reprinted in the *Plaindealer*, February 25, 1837.

less and dissatisfied, yet higher wages would only tempt them to idleness and prodigality.") "Men who would feel happy to toil," concluded the *New Era*, ". . . cannot now obtain the privilege of doing so. This is really an awful fact, in a free and equal country like this." ("The highest welfare of the labouring classes depends, after all, upon themselves," concluded Alonzo Potter; ". . . without virtuous principles and habits, no increase of compensation can either enrich or elevate them.")[10]

3

Silas Wright, on his way to Washington for the last session of the Twenty-fourth Congress, found N. P. Tallmadge, his conservative Democratic colleague, and Senator Hubbard, Democrat, of New Hampshire, among his boat-mates. As Wright was sitting peaceably in the crowded cabin before breakfast, an upstate Congressman, greatly agitated, called him to the after part of the ship. There, he found Hubbard in the midst of an animated speech, surrounded by Tallmadge, Matthew L. Davis, the political columnist who wrote under the name "The Spy in Washington," several Congressmen and several businessmen.

Hubbard paused, shook hands with Wright, then said boldly: "I will repeat what I was saying, that I have been unable to learn, nor do I believe there are, but three men in the Union who approved of the Specie order." He stopped, then went on. "I will now name the men. I mean *old* Jackson, Kendall and Blair, and I would thank any man to show me another man who approves that d——d order."

A loud laugh followed, led by Hubbard and chorused by the audience. Silas Wright observed coldly that he had always tried to avoid the name of a stagecoach or steamboat politician. "I will only, therefore, do myself the pleasure to show you, Sir, and any others, if there be any others here to whom such a sight would be a curiosity, a fourth person . . . who approves that d——d order." The group became still, with Tallmadge looking pale and very nervous; then they broke up. ("I was a little too fast," Hubbard told Wright, "but you was d——d clever.") [11]

The crash was giving new courage to the conservative Democrats, now emerging as a distinct faction under the leadership of Tallmadge

---

[10] *New Era*, May 25, 1837; [Alonzo Potter]: "Trades' Unions," *New York Review*, II, 27–28 (January, 1838).

[11] Wright to Flagg, January 9, 1837, Flagg Papers.

and W. C. Rives. They proposed to control Van Buren as they never dared try to control his predecessor, and their immediate plans centered on repealing the Specie Circular as the first step in dismantling the whole hard-money program.

The new President pondered their hot arguments for repeal, and then turned to a memorandum, drawn up by Gouge, on the "Probable Consequences" of such an action. The weakness of the Specie Circular, the memorandum urged, was "not that it is too powerful, but that it is not powerful enough." "The disease under which the country is at this moment suffering," Gouge declared, "is overtrading, produced by over-banking. The true remedy . . . is to bank less and trade less. The Treasury Order has in no way contributed to the disease. On the contrary, it has checked it." [12] This seemed good sense, as well as good hard-money doctrine, and Van Buren quietly endorsed a list of questions he had thought to put to his cabinet: "Not submitted as I decided to take the entire responsibility and had moreover reason to believe that the Cabinet would be divided upon the subject. *MVB*." [13] The example of Jackson had not been wasted, and the circular was for the moment preserved.

But so small a setback only increased the pressure. Nicholas Biddle, complete with delusions of grandeur, now presented himself at the White House. (Biddle's hold on actuality had long since disappeared. "As to mere power," he boasted, "I have been for years in the daily exercise of more personal authority than any President habitually enjoys." When old Thomas Cooper, of South Carolina, a man of no political consequence, proposed the White House to him, Biddle answered modestly that he stood ready for the country's service. Ever confident that the Bank was about to be restored, he kept writing letters to Forsyth or J. K. Poinsett of Van Buren's cabinet offering compromises.) [14] When Van Buren received him with imperturbable good manners but asked no advice about public affairs, Biddle had a hurt paragraph inserted in the papers animadverting on the President's unaccountable failure to take advantage of his opportunity. [15]

In April a Committee of Fifty, chosen by New York merchants to "remonstrate" with the President, brought a somewhat more serious expression of business sentiment. One merchant had refused to serve, saying bitterly that he would "never consent, under any circumstances,

[12] [W. M. Gouge], "Probable Consequences of the Repeal of the Treasury Circular," March 19, 1837, Van Buren Papers.

[13] Undated memorandum [1837], Van Buren Papers.

[14] Biddle to Cooper, May 8, 1837, Biddle, *Correspondence*, 278.

[15] Benton, *Thirty Years' View*, II, 219.

to 'remonstrate' with Martin Van Buren. . . . When some *other* and more summary course is proposed, and the pursuing it placed in the hands of a committee of *ten thousand*, I, for one, hold myself ready to discharge my duty to my country." [16]

Others were found, however, and Van Buren received the delegation with his usual politeness. But he gave no satisfaction; the Committee reported itself compelled to surrender all hope that "either the justice of our claims or the severity of our sufferings, will induce the Executive to abandon or relax the policy which has produced such desolating effects." The meeting which convened to hear the report was more violent than the original one, even after Philip Hone succeeded in softening some of the resolutions. Van Buren was declared to have "uniformly acted, and uniformly succeeded," on the principle that "the poor naturally hate the rich." "In a great majority of cases," it was comfortably asserted, "the possession of property is the proof of merit." While forgoing rebellion, the assembled merchants allowed that "the pages of history record, and the opinions of mankind justify, numerous instances of popular insurrection, the provocation to which was less severe than the evils of which we complain." [17]

4

This last observation contained a threat often sounded in these days of tension (and coming perhaps with ill grace from men who disapproved of flour riots). In May, for example, a group of Boston businessmen, meeting at Faneuil Hall to protest against a law requiring the payment of specie at the post offices, considered a resolution urging that the law be resisted, " 'peaceably' if it were possible, 'forcibly' if it were necessary — at any rate it should be AT ALL HAZARDS RESISTED." Abbott Lawrence, the cotton magnate, who had himself voted for the law when Congress enacted it a year before, now assured the meeting that "men with the feelings of men" could not repress their indignation: "THERE IS NO PEOPLE ON THE FACE OF GOD'S EARTH THAT IS SO ABUSED, CHEATED, PLUNDERED AND TRAMPLED BY THEIR RULERS, AS ARE THE PEOPLE OF THE UNITED STATES." [18] From a fairly responsible source this was quite an indictment.

[16] The merchant was Edward S. Gould. *Washington Globe*, April 29, 1837; *Plaindealer*, April 29, 1837.

[17] *Plaindealer*, May 13, 1837. See also Hone, *Diary*, I, 255–256; Benton, *Thirty Years' View*, II, 15–20.

[18] *Boston Atlas*, May 18, 1837. The *Atlas* commented editorially, "As surely as there is a sun in heaven, resistance, FORCIBLE RESISTANCE, WILL FOLLOW, if the Government undertake the enforcement of their ABOMINABLE EDICTS." See also *Boston*

The Faneuil Hall outburst was no isolated episode. Such menaces and denunciations became the staple of the Whig press. "It is our right and our *duty* to resist oppression," declared a New York paper. ". . . never was our country in a position when it was absolutely necessary that this right should be exercised as at this moment." The word *revolution* had "no peculiar horror" for those who felt that it now meant "the preservation of our constitution and the protection of our lives and property. . . . Our fathers exercised it, and their descendants may and will resort to it, when necessary." (The Locofoco leaders might well blush at their diffidence in the Park in February.) "We unhesitatingly say," a Whig editor observed of the Specie Circular, "that it is a more high-handed measure of *tyranny* than that which cost *Charles* the 1st his crown and his head . . . one which calls more loudly for resistance than any act of Great Britain which led to the Declaration of Independence." [19]

Philip Hone, with the conservative weakness for classical analogy, noted that Jackson, Van Buren and Benton formed a triumvirate more fatal to the prosperity of America than Caesar, Pompey and Crassus were to the liberties of Rome. "Where will it end?" he asked. " — In ruin, revolution, perhaps civil war." Robert Mayo published his *Chapter of Sketches on Finance*, the outpourings of a disappointed brain truster, and confirmed the worst suspicions of the merchants. "The conclusion is inevitable," wrote Mayo, "that *revolution is already more than half accomplished!*" The convictions were strong enough in his own mind, he added, to place Amos Kendall's head on the scaffold.[20]. . . Everywhere government was charged with conspiring to destroy business, and always in the background were the ominous threats of direct action.

On May 10, in this atmosphere of gathering crisis, the banks of New York City suspended specie payments, refusing any longer to redeem their paper bank notes in hard money. Within a few days all the banks in the country had followed New York's example.

The nationwide suspension brought events to a head. The business community rushed to defend it as a natural and necessary step, some of its hangers-on even extolling it as an act of virtue. "From a sense of duty to the public," cried the Reverend Andrew Preston Peabody

---

Commercial Gazette, May 18, *Boston Post*, May 22, 1837. For the original version of the Lawrence remark, so often quoted in one form or another by the Democratic press, I am indebted to Mr. Robert L. Edwards, whose forthcoming biography of Abbott Lawrence will cast light upon the period.

[19] See quotations in the *Washington Globe*, April 24, 25, 1837.

[20] Hone, *Diary*, I, 260, 255; Robert Mayo, *Chapter of Sketches on Finance*, 101.

in a sermon of May 14 on the banks, "they spare their creditors, and themselves ask to be spared. . . . Let institutions, that have never yet betrayed the public confidence, still be a rallying point for those hopes, that pierce the cloud and dissipate the gloom." [21]

But not even all the conservatives could agree that the action of the banks exhibited a high sense of public duty.[22] Nathan Appleton in 1841 was to define suspension as "the gentle name applied to the failure or refusal to perform the promise contained on the face of a bank note." When one bank suspends, he said, it is stigmatized as bankrupt, but let a number suspend, "all the others follow, and the public submit, not only without a murmur, but give it their commendation." [23] Albert Gallatin was equally caustic, and other businessmen shared their misgivings, especially as the political exploitation of the crisis became more and more blatant.

In midsummer William Foster asked John Quincy Adams for his opinion. The testy old man replied that the only difference he could see between the officers of a suspended bank and the forger of bank notes was that the criminal gave evidence of superior skill and superior modesty. "It requires more talent to sign another man's name than one's own, and the counterfeiter does at least his work in the dark, while the suspenders of specie payments brazen it in the face of day, and laugh at the victims and dupes who have put faith in their promises." [24]

Yet, for all the qualms of responsible Whigs and opposition of radical Democrats, state legislatures enacted laws exempting banks from the penalties of suspension just about as the business community specified. The time seemed ripe for an all-out attack on the hard-money system. The Whig press grew increasingly violent and peremptory. Daniel Webster was ordered on a great speaking tour through the nation. Van Buren and Benton were sent hundreds of parody bank-notes, inscribed *This is what you have brought the country to*" or

[21] A. P. Peabody, *Views of Duty Adapted to the Times. Sermon Preached . . . May 14, 1837*, 8, 11.

[22] Some felt perhaps the justice of Frank Blair's dry reminders that the classes which had been loudest in condemning the relief laws of Kentucky were now loudest in demanding that such laws be invoked in their own interest, and that the very people who denounced workingmen for combining in trade-unions were now combining themselves "for the purpose of sustaining each other in setting the laws at defiance, and refusing to pay their debts." *Washington Globe*, May 22, 27, 1837.

[23] Nathan Appleton, *Remarks on Currency and Banking*, 14.

[24] Adams to Foster, July 1, 1837, *Washington Globe*, August 1, 1837. The Whigs in general turned to rend Adams for his "poor, base, slanderous" letter, accusing him of dabbling in the "dirty waters" of Locofocoism, and adding that it was difficult to decide whether he most deserved pity or contempt. *Boston Centinel & Gazette*, August 9, 1837.

"*The gold humbug exploded*" or "*Behold the effects of tampering with the currency*" or sentiments less printable.[25]

Intimidation would have been wasted on General Jackson. But a wily politician, a magician, a red fox, like Martin Van Buren — could he hold out against an aroused people?

Or, did the business leaders, as so often, miscalculate? "They will, with their accustomed wisdom, mistake the opinion of stock holders and speculators for public sentiment," predicted C. C. Cambreleng, "and think that they are going to carry every thing before them. They forgot that [while] Wall St. may be converted into a Bedlam nations seldom run mad except in war or revolution." [26]

[25] Benton, *Thirty Years' View*, II, 26.
[26] Cambreleng to Van Buren, April 8, 1837, Van Buren Papers.

XIX DIVORCE OF BANK
AND STATE

V AN BUREN now faced three possibilities. He could struggle on with the state-bank system. He could retreat gracefully, strike the Jacksonian flag and restore the big Bank. Or, he could head into the gale, fight the hard-money policy one step further and urge the separation of the fiscal affairs of the government from all banks. Each form of government cohabitation with banks had been tried twice, and twice was considered to have failed; but the business community as a whole was grimly convinced that one or the other relation was necessary. The third system — divorce of bank and state — was untried. It found its only backing among intellectuals and radicals.

1

Jefferson and John Randolph had mentioned the idea of total separation vaguely in private letters; but the first serious statement of an independent treasury or "subtreasury" plan came in 1833 in William M. Gouge's *History of Paper Money*. The public funds, Gouge argued, should be kept in public custody and not be deposited in private banks.[1] In Washington he continued to warn of the deposit system based on state banks, and in the summer of 1836 he set down the details of his scheme in a special memorandum for the White House.

In the meantime a somewhat different version had reached the floors of Congress. In 1834 Condy Raguet, the lank, frosty and balding Philadelphia economist, friend and admirer of Gouge, sought to persuade several political leaders of the necessity for separation. After making little impression on Hugh L. White, Calhoun or William Preston, he found an eager listener in William F. Gordon of Virginia. Originally a Democrat, who had fought for the extension of the suffrage at the Virginia constitutional convention of 1829, Gordon had followed Calhoun out of the party and, by 1834, was opposing the administration on the grounds of "executive despotism." But he had misgivings over alliance with the Whigs and was casting about

[1] Gouge, *Paper Money*, especially Part I, 111–113, Part II, 218. See also *Journal of Banking*, December 8, 1841.

for some way to unite those who opposed the United States Bank as well as the nullification proclamation.

Raguet's plan seemed the perfect answer. On June 20, 1834, Gordon proposed the divorce of Bank and state in the House, and on January 2, 1835, Roger L. Gamble of Georgia introduced a similar resolution, with A. S. Clayton of Georgia making a speech in its favor the next day. On February 10 Gordon made a final appeal. But the plan interested only the small group of Southerners hostile alike to Jackson and to Biddle, and in addition a few Whigs who wanted to embarrass the administration. Secretary Woodbury officially dismissed the idea as practicable, but not at the moment advisable.[2]

Still the efforts of Gouge and Gordon put the plan in circulation. In various forms it began to be discussed among the hard-money men. In February, 1834, John Windt proposed a version at a New York meeting (and Moses Jaques was supposed to have suggested a similar system to Cambreleng as early as 1832).[3] By July, 1836, the *Evening Post* had enthusiastically adopted the general idea, Bryant urging the Democrats "to demand in plain and imperative language, the absolute and unconditional SEPARATION OF BANK AND STATE." [4]

The next step in the formulation of the plan came in April, 1836. The abandonment of banks as physical depositories would achieve only partial separation so long as bank paper was still itself receivable in federal payments. Benton, pointing out that the process of disentanglement from the banks thus involved two stages, "the disuse of their paper, and the disuse of their vaults," proposed to take care of the first by a "specie clause," which would gradually exclude paper bills from government payments.[5]

Benton had been familiar with the independent-treasury idea since 1829, when Randolph had outlined it to him, and he used later to insist that he and Jackson never intended the state-bank system as anything more than a means of getting the aid of the state banks against Biddle — a "half-way house" to be deserted as soon as the hard-money

[2] Raguet to White, March 28, 1834, Scott, *White*, 144; *Niles' Register*, September 29, 1838; A. C. Gordon, *William Fitzhugh Gordon*, 198, 211, 231–236; Gordon in the House, June 20, 1834, *Register of Debates*, 23 Congress 1 Session, 4640–4641.

[3] *Working Man's Advocate*, February 15, 1834; Byrdsall, *Loco-Foco Party*, 144.

[4] *New York Evening Post*, July 19, 1836. See also Leggett to Bryant, December 4, 1838, Bryant Papers.

[5] Benton in the Senate, April 23, 1836, *Register of Debates*, 24 Congress 1 Session, 1255. See also speech of June 7, *ibid.*, 1718–1719; Benton to Gouge, September 22, 1836, read by Benton in the Senate, January 16, 1840, *Congressional Globe*, 26 Congress 1 Session, Appendix. 121.

men felt like taking on the whole banking interest.[6] Jackson had certainly told a delegation of New York businessmen, in 1834, that "if the [state-bank] experiment failed, some scheme might be devised of collecting and depositing the revenue, without the intervention of any moneyed institution," and the subtreasury scheme was certainly the next logical extension of the hard-money policy.[7] Yet the administration was much less Machiavellian than pragmatic, simply holding the more extreme plan in reserve against the failure of the first.

The panic of 1837 signalized that failure. Gouge, in his notes for Van Buren on the question of repealing the Specie Circular, concluded with the emphatic declaration that, though no adequate remedy was available for the present evils, "it is in our power to prevent their recurrence by dissolving the connection between the Banks and the Government." In June, his *Inquiry into the Expediency of Dispensing with Bank Agency and Bank Paper in the Fiscal Concerns of the United States* developed this argument. It was a characteristic Gouge production, written in his terse, hard-hitting style, more polemic in tone than the *Paper Money*, but with the same virtues of plain talk, good sense, concrete detail and readability. "For the welfare of the country," he declared, "it is absolutely essential that the fiscal operations of the United States be placed on such a basis that they may be embarrassed as little as possible by the doings of banks and speculators." [8]

2

A few days after the Philadelphia banks suspended specie payments, Independence Square was filled with the largest crowd ever to assemble in the city, eventually totaling twenty thousand persons, called together by John Ferral, Thomas Hogan and other union leaders. Henry D. Gilpin moved among the throng. "It was temperate and orderly . . . but the feeling was very strong. . . . I have never seen the working classes more deeply agitated and roused." Speakers de-

[6] Benton, *Thirty Years' View*, I, 158; Gordon, *Gordon*, 236; Benton in the Senate, January 16, 1840, *Congressional Globe*, 26 Congress 1 Session, Appendix, 118–120.
[7] *New York Evening Post*, February 12, 1834.
[8] Gouge, "Probable Consequences of the Repeal of the Treasury Circular," March 19, 1837, Van Buren Papers; Gouge, *Inquiry*, 39. See also Gouge to Jackson, August 1, 1836, Jackson Papers; [Gouge] to Leggett, April, 1837, *Plaindealer*, April 22, 1837; Gouge to Benton, January 9, 1840, read by Benton in the Senate, January 16, 1840, *Congressional Globe*, 26 Congress 1 Session, Appendix, 121; Roberts Vaux to Gouge, January 24, 1835, Gouge to Van Buren, July 17, 1840, Van Buren Papers.

nounced the paper system, and a committee was appointed to discuss resumption with the local banks. It was, as Gilpin wrote privately to the President, a spontaneous outburst of labor discontent, "projected and carried on *entirely* by the working classes." [9]

Nicholas Biddle, still calm as a summer's morning, tried to induce the committee to recommend that the United States Bank be made a deposit bank, so that he and the government could once again be friends. "If *I* can forgive them," he said magnanimously, "they may forgive me." But the committee was unimpressed, and its report provoked the reconvened meeting to speak its mind. One resolution, noting the threats of violence from the business community, proposed the formation of a "volunteer legion of *ten thousand men,* to be as shortly as possible fully armed and equipped" and to hold itself ready, day and night, to "fly to the rescue of the public peace." Another simply demanded that the government sever its financial connections with the banks. [10]

Feeling was running high. Fanny Wright, reported to be the author of these resolutions, was rumored to be about to receive a government appointment, but instead she set up a new journal in Philadelphia, the *Manual of American Principles,* to uphold the hard-money policy and the administration. [11] Early in June Charles Jared Ingersoll followed Gouge and came out for the independent treasury. [12] Even Philadelphia seemed drenched in Jacksonian shame. . . . By the fall a despondent Philadelphia publisher began a series of *Agrarian Stories* to illustrate the "miserable consequences" of the "immoral and disorganizing principles that of late years have been so industriously spread among the more ignorant classes." [13]

The pattern was repeating itself up and down the coast. Suspension set Theophilus Fisk's pen scratching in burning excitement in Charleston, till, early in June, he finished a pamphlet violently entitled *The Banking Bubble Burst; or the Mammoth Corruptions of the Paper Money System Relieved by Bleeding.* Drawing volubly on Gouge, Leggett, William Foster and Frederick Robinson, Fisk assembled the popular hard-money arguments into a mass of hot-tempered prose. Would the present administration stand firm? Fisk declared his con-

[9] Gilpin to Van Buren, May 15, 21, 1837, Van Buren Papers; *Washington Globe,* May 17, 18, 1837.

[10] Gilpin to Van Buren, May 22, 1837, Van Buren Papers; *National Laborer* extra (Philadelphia), May 22, 1837.

[11] *New Era* (New York), May 25, 1837; A. J. G. Perkins and T. Wolfson, *Fanny Wright,* 332.

[12] *Washington Globe,* June 16, 1837.

[13] *New-York Review,* I, 446 (October, 1837).

fidence in Woodbury, in Kendall, in Colonel Johnson; but he had little faith in Van Buren.[14]

On July 4 he struck again, in an oration, *Labor the Only True Source of Wealth*, another brisk summary of the radical position. Our constitution, he said, may have forbidden a dynasty of hereditary rank, but "it has not proved a safeguard against a dynasty of associated wealth." Since labor alone could produce wealth, this dynasty must exist on proceeds stolen from labor; and the chief instruments of this plunder were "*Incorporated companies;* and the worst of all incorporated companies are *banks.*" [15]

The solid citizens of Charleston had apparently heard enough. They packed the hall when Fisk was billed to address a meeting on the financial situation on July 8, howled him down, and, when he would not leave the platform, some of the more valiant spirits slugged him. The Mayor sat silently by, evidently in quiet approval.[16]. . . The businessmen of Charleston could show the Locofocos a thing or two about breaking up meetings.

In Massachusetts and New York the banking crisis precipitated the final struggles between the conservative and radical wings of the Democratic party. Marcus Morton, George Bancroft and their following had increased steadily in strength, and suspension came as a crushing corroboration of their case against the Custom House group, most of whom were presidents, directors or at the very least stockholders of deposit banks. David Henshaw sought to stem the Locofoco tide by publishing a tract on corporations which sharply dissented from the Supreme Court decision in the Dartmouth College Case (of 1819) and urged the continuing authority of legislatures over charters as the crucial issue. "Sure I am," he said, "that the evils incident to corporate perpetuities may be remedied by legislative enactment if this decision be reversed." There was no need, in other words, to rush off in a crusade against the whole system of special charters. But the people ignored this red herring: they were hungry for stronger meat. When Henshaw made a final try for reinstatement by sending a belatedly radical letter to a Fourth of July celebration, the *Reformer* commented coldly, "We shall demand years of penance from him, before we will own him for even a sutler to the Loco Foco camp." [17]

[14] Fisk, *Banking Bubble Burst*, especially 75–77.
[15] Fisk, *Labor the Only True Source*, "Monopolies," front and back covers.
[16] *Boston Reformer*, August 4, 1837; *New York Evening Post*, August 16, 1837.
[17] Henshaw, *Remarks upon the Rights and Powers of Corporations*, 31; *Boston Reformer*, July 21, 1837.

3

The gap widened with even greater speed in the President's own state. The banking crisis gave the progressives the issue for which they had been waiting. The *Evening Post*, which had noted with pleasure early in 1836 the spreading conviction that the real issue lay "not between the people and the Bank of the United States, but between the people and all incorporated institutions," now renewed the appeal for complete divorce.[18]

Bryant had meanwhile gained some colleagues in the field. In December, 1836, William Leggett founded the *Plaindealer*, a weekly backed by Edwin Forrest, the actor, and modeled on the *London Examiner*. By February, 1837, its circulation was eleven hundred, with a newsstand sale of two to four hundred more.[19] Leggett's increasingly erratic course, however, was progressively alienating every group disposed to support him. His scorn for corporate monopoly had long since antagonized the Whigs and conservative Democrats; his attack on the flour riots as well as on their separate organization angered the Locofocos; and in March a bitter assault on Van Buren for anti-abolitionist sentiments in his inaugural disturbed the liberal Democrats. When he swung at the abolitionists in April, his isolation was complete. Yet he was still a powerful and flashing writer. Gideon Welles, dissatisfied in June with what seemed to him the faltering course of the *Globe*, urged Van Buren to replace Blair by Leggett, "the ablest editor in the Union." [20]

A new popular daily also entered the field in Richard Adams Locke's *New Era*. In 1835 Locke, a bright young English newspaperman who had come to New York a few years before, wrote for the *Sun* the famous "Moon Hoax," a story which set forth in sober detail observations of life on the moon supposedly made by Sir John Herschel, the astronomer.[21] A struggling young author named Edgar Allan Poe, whose own fantasy, "Hans Pfaal," was undercut by the moon hoax, later called Locke "one of the few men of *unquestionable genius* whom the country possesses," adding graciously, "I am acquainted with no person possessing so fine a forehead." Short, with pock-marked face,

---

[18] *New York Evening Post*, February 20, 1836.
[19] W. R. Alger, *Life of Edwin Forrest*, I, 373; Buckingham, *America*, I, 67; *Plaindealer*, February 25, 1837.
[20] Welles to Van Buren, June 9, 1837, Van Buren Papers.
[21] The *Sun* was the first successful penny paper; and Locke's exploit gave its prospectus a double meaning in its boast of "supplying the public with the news of the day at so cheap a rate as to lie within the means of all."

veering abruptly from coolness to excitement, Locke made the *New Era* an enterprising and lively sheet, which upheld trade-unions and strikes, attacked paper money and monopolies, and even corresponded with Chartist journals in England. After Locke left the paper, his successors, Theron Rudd, and then Levi D. Slamm of the Locofoco party, more or less preserved the *New Era's* truculence.[22]

The conservative Democrats in the meantime were rallying behind the stalwart figure of Senator N. P. Tallmadge. Short, corpulent, swarthy and affable, Tallmadge gave the appearance of a strong leader.[23] Elected Senator over Van Buren's opposition, he had rubber-stamped for the administration until 1836. Then, he fought for distribution and against the Specie Circular and delivered himself of the celebrated eulogy on the credit system. A few weeks after the banking suspension, he spoke out again for paper money in a public letter spread enthusiastically across the columns of the *Albany Argus*, and his views were endorsed a month later by over seven hundred Democrats of New York City, including Gideon Lee, Samuel Swartwout, the corrupt Collector of the Port, and Marcy's chum Prosper M. Wetmore. About the same time the Albany general committee repudiated the hard-money men in a party manifesto. By August a right-wing Democrat like Gideon Lee could write to Van Buren that "nothing short of a great moneyed power, ever will or ever can restore us to prosperity." If the scheme of "Mr. Gouge's pamphlet" was adopted, Lee continued fearfully, it was the opinion "of every practical man" that it must prove a failure.[24]

What of the Regency? Old friendships, drawn taut by the divergence on the economic issues, were beginning to snap. A. C. Flagg and John A. Dix made clear their disavowal of the Albany manifesto. Starting June 20, a series of articles appeared in the *St. Lawrence Republican* in which everyone recognized the sturdy and considered style of Silas Wright. They advocated the total separation of the national government from the banks and the thorough reform of the state-banking system; any other course might be fatal to the republic. "If the time shall ever come when a political party shall rise up and be successful in our country, whose principles shall be found in a bank charter, or in the charter of any other corporate money power,

---

[22] W. N. Griggs, *The Celebrated "Moon Story," Its Origin and Incidents*, 41–44; Edgar Allan Poe, *Works*, VII, 138, 139, 145–146, IX, 258. See also Locke's correspondence with Seth Luther, *New Era*, March 22, 24, 25, 1837; for Chartism, see, e.g., *ibid.*, August 17, 1840.

[23] W. H. Seward to his wife, February 16, 1831, F. W. Seward, *Autobiography of William H. Seward . . . with a Memoir of His Life*, 182.

[24] Lee to Van Buren, August 14, 1837, Van Buren Papers.

then may we class our government with the most dangerous aristocracies upon the earth." Some of the younger men were giving up altogether on the state organization. "It is this Equal Rights party that
can alone save the democracy," Theodore Sedgwick, Jr., wrote in
June; for all its "crude ideas," at least it held fast to Democratic
principle.[25]

And the Governor? Marcy approved the Albany manifesto, was
worried by the *Globe* and the *Evening Post;* his father-in-law, moreover, was seriously involved in bank speculations. When the legislature obediently complied with the banking demand that the safety-
fund act be set aside during the suspension, he signed the law without
hesitation.[26] He came increasingly to feel that there was "not a sound
state of things at Washington." Jackson's public letters troubled him.
"According to the laws of drama the hero in a tragedy should die
in the last act if not before. I fear our old hero will live too long
for his fame." He confessed to "fearful forebodings" about Van
Buren. Was Amos Kendall gaining too much influence in the administration? The Governor looked uneasily into the shadowed future.[27]

4

It was a spring and summer of decision in Washington. From
the first, Van Buren had apparently recognized that divorce was the
only measure which would not mean surrender. Gouge's arguments
impressed him, and he was also struck by the plan of a Virginia banker
named Dr. John Brockenbrough, a friend of Randolph and Gordon,
which provided for a system of federal depositories but did not insist on the "specie clause" — a right-wing version of the independent
treasury.[28] The President quietly meditated the possibilities, roughed
out a preliminary scheme in May and submitted it to his advisers.

Cambreleng and Butler had already announced for separation. Silas
Wright had doubts about the political risks, but made up his mind by
June. Thomas Hart Benton, James K. Paulding and James Buchanan,
A. C. Flagg and Robert Rantoul, Jr., gave additional support.[29] Above
all, resolutions poured in from meetings across the country, Bunker

[25] R. H. Gillet, *Silas Wright,* I, 564; Sedgwick in the *Plaindealer,* July 22, 1837.
[26] When Cambreleng opposed this measure in a private letter, he was publicly
warned not to appear in Wall Street.
[27] See Marcy's letters to P. M. Wetmore, especially July 20 and August 18, 1837,
Marcy Papers.
[28] Brockenbrough to W. C. Rives, May 20, 1837, Van Buren Papers.
[29] R. B. Taney, oddly enough, opposed the plan, recommending instead a hard-
money version of the existing system, in which government funds would be kept

Hill and Tammany Hall and Independence Square, large towns and small, demanding the divorce of bank and state.

In retirement at the stately Hermitage, Andrew Jackson watched the progress of politics with a hawklike eye and regularly scrawled in his large indignant hand long letters of advice and encouragement to Blair, to Kendall, to the President. His instinct about his people was still unerring, and, as storms raged around the White House, the Hermitage counseled Van Buren to hold firm. "The people are everywhere becoming more aroused against the proceedings of the Banks and will sustain the Executive Government in any course that will coerce them to specie payments; and in any plan that will hereafter secure them from . . . the corrupt paper credit system." [30] When Amos Kendall visited the Hermitage in 1838, driving up on a bitter-cold day, he found the venerable chief at his gate, a quarter of a mile from the house, without an overcoat, waiting for the mail carrier and the newspapers. "He looks as well as he usually did at Washington," Kendall reported, "but does not move with the same elasticity." [31] Bones must stiffen, but the eyes still flashed with fire.

On July 7 the *Washington Globe* came out for divorce and printed the first installment of Gouge's pamphlet. The conservative Democrats retorted by setting up a paper in Washington, the *Madisonian*, devoted to Democratic principles "as delineated by Mr. Madison" (rather than by Mr. Jefferson or General Jackson?). From the start the *Madisonian* assailed "visionary theories, and an unwise adherence to the plan for an *exclusive metallic* currency," attacked Gouge and his "spirit of Jacobinism and anarchy," and expounded with feeling the beauties of the state bank system.[32]

In the early days of a still hot September Congressmen streamed back to Washington for the special session, and on September 4 came the long-awaited presidential message. After a trenchant analysis of the panic, Van Buren decisively rejected the system of deposit in banks, whether one large or many small, and declared for an independent treasury. Locofocoism now bore the *imprimatur* of the White House.[33]

---

and disbursed by selected banks, but the banks would be forbidden the use of the money for commercial purposes, and the specie clause would obtain in collecting the revenue. See letters from Cambreleng, Wright, Buchanan, Niles, Flagg, Rantoul, Paulding, Taney in Van Buren Papers. Apparently, Van Buren first asked for comments on Brockenbrough's scheme; then, around June 21, another set of questions was drafted by Gouge, to which a second group of letters respond.
[30] Jackson to Kendall, June 23, 1837, Jackson, *Correspondence*, V, 489–490.
[31] Kendall to Van Buren, October 20, 1838, Van Buren Papers.
[32] *Madisonian*, August 16, 1837, *et seq.*
[33] From July 7, when the *Globe* took its stand, there could have been no real

5

"Tell me frankly," Van Buren wrote in his sprawling script on a copy of the message intended for Theodore Sedgwick, "how near this comes to what you think it ought to be." The President need have had no doubts. A thrill of exultation burst through the ranks of the hard-money men. Frank Blair called it "the boldest and highest stand ever taken by a Chief Magistrate in defence of the rights of the people. . . . a second declaration of independence." Bryant and Leggett rejoiced, and the Locofocos promptly gathered for a special meeting to commend Van Buren. A. H. Wood of Boston expressed the general sentiment: "Like his predecessor he now stands at the head of radical democracy." Letters of congratulation poured into the White House: from Gideon Welles, from J. K. Paulding, from N. P. Trist, from Moses Dawson of Ohio, from Theodore Sedgwick, from a hundred others.[34] And through the country humble men, drawing a precarious existence from some hillside farm, or supporting a family on the meager returns of bootmaking, or working long gray hours in a factory, felt a surge of renewing confidence in their government. It was still their country and not Nicholas Biddle's.

The horror of the business community was about as single-minded as the enthusiasm of the working people.

The message is a heartless, cold-blooded attack upon our most valuable and most cherished classes of citizens. (*New York Gazette*)

The people, the country, the business men have nothing to hope from the message, Mr. Van Buren, or any of his clan. (*New York Express*)

It is the incarnation of the Bentonian-Jacksonism — a sophistical sermon of the favorite text of "Perish commerce — perish credit," and an ungenerous appeal to the irrational passions of the worst party in the country. (*Philadelphia National Gazette*)

He has identified himself wholly with the loco-focos — come forth

---

doubt about Van Buren's decision. Yet conservative Democrats and Whigs continued up to the end to indulge in orgies of wishful thinking. As late as August 28, for example, "Leonardo," Washington correspondent of the *Columbian Centinel* of Boston, reported it as "the general opinion that Mr. Van Buren has entirely repudiated Loco Focoism." *Columbian Centinel*, August 30, 1837. The incorrigible Biddle told Abbott Lawrence (who was not impressed) that the government had already decided to return to the Bank of the United States. Adams, *Memoirs*, IX, 363. They were mainly dupes of their own legend, which made Van Buren an opportunistic and time-serving politician.

[34] *Washington Globe*, September 5, 1837; *Boston Reformer*, September 15, 1837. For letters, see Van Buren Papers.

a champion of the most destructive species of ultraism — and aimed at the vital interests of the country a blow, which if it do not recoil upon the aggressor, must be productive to the country of lasting mischief, perhaps of irretrievable anarchy. (*Boston Atlas*)

He has gone full length with the Plaindealer, the Evening Post, the Washington Globe, Blair, Kendall, and General Jackson. (*New York Courier and Enquirer*) [35]

Philip Hone, who admitted a grudging liking for Van Buren, observed sadly, "It is a long document, written with ability, but the most mischievous in its tendency that has ever been presented to the American people." [36] A young New York journalist, named Horace Greeley, declared savagely that its doctrines differed "little or nothing from those which the country had been accustomed to sneer at as preposterous when promulgated by a ragged regiment in New-York city, who were known as Loco-Focos." [37] The *Madisonian* traced the independent treasury back to the Workingmen's party. [38] Conservatives everywhere, Whigs or Democrats, were distraught and angry. [39]

In New York Governor Marcy read the message with amazement. Immediately afterward Benjamin F. Butler called on him, and for

[35] For round-ups of Whig opinion, *New York Evening Post*, September 7, *Plaindealer*, September 9, *Washington Globe*, September 12, 1837.

[36] Hone, *Diary*, I, 282.

[37] *Jeffersonian*, July 21, 1838. Cf. *Log Cabin*, September 5, 1840.

[38] *Madisonian*, January 30, 1838. This impression endured for the generation which remembered the bitterness over the subtreasury. E.g., *American Whig Review* in 1845 on Van Buren: "He had taken to his embrace all the ultra-radicals of the country and listened to their counsels. There was not a vagary so wild, nor a theory so impracticable, that it could not find protection and friendship under the robe of the new Democracy." "The Position of Parties," I, 17 (January, 1845).

[39] In this connection the ambiguous and typically erratic course of John Quincy Adams on the subtreasury should be noted. In his letter to Foster of July 1, 1837, Adams declared that the only "practicable" remedy was to "wipe out all old scores and begin again. This is the hard money system, and so far as I can judge, it is the essential system of the present administration — it is to detach the government from all banking, and deal in nothing but the precious metals. If Mr. Van Buren is made of stuff to go through with this operation, I wish him well out of it; but he will want . . . other advisers than presidents or directors of broken banks, or land-jobbers upon loans from deposite banks." *Washington Globe*, August 1, 1837. Yet, when Van Buren followed this program, he got no support from Adams who was saying by November, "As to the sub-treasury — Bedlam seems to me the only place where it could have originated. . . . A Divorce of Bank and State! Why a divorce of Trade and Shipping would be as wise," etc. Adams to A. H. Everett, November 7, 1837, *American Historical Review*, XI, 354. As late as March, 1838, George Bancroft was trying to win Adams over to the Democrats, appealing to him as fundamentally a hard-money man; see Bancroft to Adams (draft), March 26, 1838. Bancroft Papers; Adams, *Memoirs*, IX, 518.

over two hours the old friends hotly discussed the new plan, Butler
speaking with subdued passion, his face pale and earnest, Marcy becoming increasingly blunt and increasingly exasperated. "I uttered
more and more imprudent things. . . . I suppose I am regarded as
one that has bolted from the course or willing to seek occasion to do
so." Edwin Croswell of the *Albany Argus* was also present and uncon-
vinced; the *Argus*, the ancient organ of the Regency, did not endorse
the plan until Van Buren after several weeks put the heat on from
Washington.

In his first furious reaction Marcy apparently encouraged Tallmadge to break with the administration, but after a fortnight prudence
intervened and he swallowed his own resentment. "You were doubtless prepared for some diversity of opinion," he wrote the President
in gingerly acknowledgment of a franked copy of the message.
". . . I sincerely hope it will not be greater than you have anticipated."
In private he still fumed at "the insolence of the locofocos who pre-
tend they have (and for aught that appears they certainly have) a
full endorsement of all their doctrines by the President." As late as
December he was still warning Van Buren: "You may rely upon it—
that *all interests* in the country are alarmed at the tendency of what is
supposed to be the doctrines entertained at Washington." But in the
end Marcy reluctantly got into line.[40]

Not many of the conservative Democrats proved so amenable.
Tallmadge's energetic leadership nerved them to reject the President's
"Locofoco, Fanny Wright, and Tom Paine doctrines" and strike out on
their own.[41] A good many of these Conservatives, as they were now
known, were men with state-banking connections, who had blithely
supported Jackson in his war on Biddle's bank but objected to the
extension of the logic to their own institutions. But others, like Washington Irving, for example, an intimate of the President's and a devoted admirer of Jackson, were honestly alarmed over the rise of

---

[40] See letters from Marcy to Van Buren, P. M. Wetmore, Albert Gallup, September–December, 1837, Marcy Papers and Van Buren Papers. For his relations to
Tallmadge, see Marcy to Wetmore, October 26, 1838, Marcy Papers.

[41] J. W. Crockett to his constituents, July 20, 1838, *Jeffersonian*, September 8,
1838. See also the address of the Conservative state convention, a proceeding dominated by Gideon Lee: "One class of citizens . . . responded to the recommendation of the Sub-Treasury with fellow-feeling and sympathising affection. They
were the band of Agrarians and Radicals, who, under the instructions of Fanny
Wright and other teachers of her school, had long been aiming at the overthrow of all existing institutions and all laws for the protection of property. The
ravings of these atheists in religion and fanatics in politics, were viewed as harmless . . . until a portion of their policy was adopted as the leading measure of the
present Administration, and as the only touchstone of Republican principles."
Jeffersonian, October 20, 1838.

radicalism in Washington. He had no liking, Irving explained, for doctrinaires (in a letter written from the country home of John Jacob Astor, no doctrinaire he). "I have, therefore, felt a strong distaste for some of those loco-foco luminaries who of late have been urging strong and sweeping measures, subversive of the interests of great classes of the community." He deplored the pressure on "the great trading and financial classes," and concluded that he could no longer go on with so violent an administration.[42]

6

Another century finds a strange disproportion between the uproar over the independent treasury and the plan itself, which, after all, simply proposed that the government take care of its own funds and require payment in legal tender. Why should the radical Democrats look on this innocent scheme as a second Declaration of Independence, and conservatives denounce it as wild, subversive and dangerous, deserving resistance almost on the barricades?

The plan was certainly vulnerable on economic grounds. It enforced a decentralization of the banking system which in the end would prove so cumbersome that the policy was reversed with the establishment of the Federal Reserve System. But this was not the cause of the outcry against it. Indeed, the economic objections were barely mentioned, and they would not become urgent till after the Civil War. Instead, the independent treasury was denounced for political and social reasons — as a movement toward despotism, and a conspiracy against private property.

The divorce of bank and state represented primarily — both for friends and foes — a further extension of the hard-money policy. That policy, it will be remembered, had three ends: the diminution of periodic economic crises; the destruction of irresponsible sovereignties within the political state; and the prevention of a moneyed aristocracy. The independent treasury served the policy in each respect. By removing the public funds from the banks, it reduced the amount of specie on which paper could be issued and thus had a sobering tendency on the economy. By rejecting bank notes in payment of the revenue, it considerably restricted the power of banks over the currency. By confining banks to the needs of the commercial community, it held them to "legitimate" economic operations and limited their capacity for redistributing wealth in favor of a single class.

[42] Irving to Gouverneur Kemble, January 10, 1838, P. M. Irving, *Irving*, III, 120–121.

Thus, the business community fought the project as the culmination of the whole hard-money campaign. The scheme "could only be founded," wrote one Whig pamphleteer, "upon the supposition, that the banks, and the currency which they supply, are of too unsafe a character to be employed by the government. If unsafe for the government, they must also be unsafe for the people." "What then, sir, is the policy of the administration?" asked a Whig orator. ". . . For myself, I believe it to be . . . a war of extermination on commerce and the currency." "Disguise it as you may," cried N. P. Tallmadge in the Senate, "it is no more nor less than a war upon the whole banking system." [43]

But more yet was involved than simply hard money and the banking system. "Those who regard it in no higher aspect than a mere financial arrangement," as John M. Niles declared, ". . . cannot appreciate the motive of those who consider it as the first important step in the reform of our wretched paper money system, on the one hand, and of our political institutions on the other." Its object, he said, was "the entire separation and exclusion of the organized moneyed power from our political institutions." [44]

For those who believed, with Hamilton, that the business class had a proprietary right to government favor, the bill thus seemed an assault on the very fabric of society. "Its leading feature," exclaimed Philip Hone in horror, "seems to be the total preclusion of the merchants, whose enterprise supports the government, from any participation in the use of money collected through their means." William M. Gouge made the repudiation of Hamilton inescapable. "If there ever should be a surplus of public funds," he wrote, "we know not what particular merit there is in the banking and speculating interests, that they should lay claim to its exclusive use. . . . If any classes of the community deserve the favor of the government, in any country, they are the farmers, mechanics, and other hard-working men." [45]

[43] Richard Hildreth, *Banks, Banking, and Paper Currencies*, 98; D. D. Barnard, *Speeches and Reports on the Assembly of New-York, at the Annual Session of 1838*, 46, 95; Tallmadge in the Senate, September 22, 1837, *Register of Debates*, 25 Congress 1 Session, 171. Gouge and Biddle appropriately agreed on the importance of the struggle. "The war between specie and paper money," said Gouge, "is now fairly begun. . . . The result will determine the destinies of the country." "One or other must fall," answered Biddle. "There can be no other issue. It is not a question of correcting errors or reforming abuses, but of absolute destruction; not which shall conquer but which shall survive." Gouge, *Inquiry*, 7; Biddle to J. Q. Adams, April 5, 1838, *Financial Register*, April 25, 1838.
[44] Niles in the Senate, January 5, 1839, *Congressional Globe*, 25 Congress 3 Session, Appendix, 85.
[45] Hone, *Diary*, I, 299; Gouge, *Inquiry*, 27–28. Gouge's statement voiced a theme incessantly repeated. The people, observed Van Buren himself, can see no reason

The philosophy of Federalism was thus at stake. Said the *Madisonian*, "The contest now waging, we regard as a battle between civilization and barbarism." "We have reached that point of national existence," declared a respectable magazine, "when a much longer toleration of misrule . . . is impossible. Either revolution — a revolution of violence, and perhaps of blood — or renovation, must soon change the aspect of affairs." [46]

Democrats answered in kind. Frank Blair declared the scheme put the axe "to the root of that complicated system of measures by which HAMILTON and his party sought to destroy the spirit, while maintaining the forms of the Constitution." Fanny Wright grew ecstatic. "It is the national independence realized. It is the effective, definitive annulment of this country's vassalage. It is the first practical, efficient, decisive realization of the Declaration of '76." [47]

Depression drew the lines tight. In 1837 and 1838, American businessmen were as much united against their government as they ever have been. The ultimate question was whether, in the last resort, the government dared overrule this unanimity — and this was the obverse of the other question: who was to make the decisions for the nation, the business community or the government?

For a Jeffersonian there could be but one answer. The vital decisions must in the last resort be made by men responsible to the people, and not by irresponsible private groups. In last analysis, said Martin Van Buren by his refusal to yield on the subtreasury, the democratically elected government *must* have control over the business community, for this may be the only way to safeguard the life, liberty and property of the humble members of society. [48]

"why the stockholders and debtors of banks should have an exclusive privilege to make themselves rich out of the use of the public money. . . . They see that its effect is to build up a rich privileged order at their expense to control the Government and destroy all equality among the people." Van Buren to J. M. McCalla, *et al.*, July 4, 1840, *New York Evening Post*, July 27, 1840.

[46] *Madisonian*, November 7, 1837; "Political Regeneration," *American Monthly Magazine*, V, 297–298 (April, 1838).

[47] *Washington Globe*, July 1, 1840; Frances Wright, *What Is the Matter?*, 15–16.

[48] The judgment of the historian of the frontier on the significance of this measure, with which the frontier had small sympathy, throws an interesting sidelight on the question of the frontier and democracy. "The project of an independent treasury," wrote Frederick Jackson Turner, "constituted an important turning point in the relations between the capitalist and the government. Thereafter, until our own time, the so-called 'money power' had to operate more or less *sub rosa* instead of being an integral part of the government." *The United States, 1830–1850*, 464 n.

XX THE SOUTHERN DILEMMA

JOHN C. CALHOUN was facing a major decision. As he rode north from Pendleton in the Indian summer of 1837, his lips compressed, his face drawn with concentration, his manner absent and taciturn, he weighed his future course with infinite exactness. Before him lay the special session of Congress and the battle over the independent treasury. On his decision — on every decision till the insoluble question was solved — might tremble the future of the South.

1

Calhoun was no longer merely the aspiring politician who had feuded with Jackson in 1830. Personal ambition was now increasingly submerged in a cold monomania for South Carolina and slavery. Many, like Harriet Martineau, found they could no longer communicate with him. He felt so deeply that he rarely heard argument, so passionately that he never forgot his responsibility. "There is no *relaxation* with him," cried his devoted friend Dixon H. Lewis of Alabama (who weighed three hundred and fifty pounds, and spoke with feeling). "On the contrary, when I seek relaxation in him, he screws me only the higher in some sort of excitement." He appeared to subsist in an unimaginable intellectual solitude, his mind committed to his interminable obligation, focusing forever on a single shining point, which for him was the center of the universe. He was becoming "the cast-iron man," as Miss Martineau saw him, "who looks as if he had never been born, and never could be extinguished." [1]

But he became a startling figure when he rose to speak in the Senate, eyes burning like live coals in his pale face, hair bristling and erect, skin loose over his prominent bones, words pouring out in an abrupt, condensed, closely reasoned flow. His voice was metallic and harsh, his gestures monotonous, and his ventriloquist's tones came from nowhere and sounded equally in all corners of the chamber. Yet the commanding eye, the grim earnestness of manner, the utter integrity of sentiment held the galleries in anxious attention. Standing in the

[1] Lewis to R. K. Crallé, March 20, 1840, F. W. Moore, ed., "Calhoun by His Political Friends," *Publications of the Southern History Association*, VII, 355; Harriet Martineau, *Retrospect*, I, 243–244.

narrow aisle of the Senate, bracing himself on the desks beside him, he averaged perhaps one hundred and eighty words a minute of terse and unconquerable argument.[2]

His was the supreme intelligence among the statesmen of the day. Where Clay relied on a richness and audacity of feeling, Webster on a certain massiveness of rhetoric, Benton on the sheer weight of facts, and all indulged in orgies of shameless verbiage, Calhoun's speeches were stripped bare, arguing the facts with an iron logic drawn to the highest pitch of tension. Nourished on Aristotle, Machiavelli and Burke, he possessed an uncanny ability to cut through to the substance of problems.[3] His processes of thought were intricate, merciless and unsentimental in a day when none of these qualities was in demand.

More than any of the others, he understood that he was living in one of the critical periods of history. It was, for him, a revolutionary age — "a period of transition, which must always necessarily be one of uncertainty, confusion, error, and wild and fierce fanaticism" — and he looked with anxiety on what was plainly a "great approaching change in the political and social condition of the country." "Modern society," he exclaimed, almost with horror, "seems to be rushing to some new and untried condition." The "great question" of the future would be that of "the distribution of wealth — a question least explored, and the most important of any in the whole range of political economy." [4]

The emerging outlines of industrial society filled him with foreboding. The new economy, he felt, was enriching a small group of capitalists at the expense of the great mass of the people. The "tendency of Capital to destroy and absorb the property of society and produce a collision between itself and operatives" was a source of deep alarm. "In the North you are running into anarchy," he told Albert Brisbane. ". . . The capitalist owns the instruments of labor, and he seeks to draw out of labor all of the profits, leaving the laborer to shift for himself in age and disease. This can only engender antagonism; the result will be hostility and conflict, ending in civil war, and the North may fall into a state of social dissolution." Both the growing power of

[2] For sketches of Calhoun in action, see *New York Evening Post*, February 19, 1838; *Boston Post*, December 16, 1833; Milburn, *Ten Years of Preacher-Life*, 152–153; Willis, *Hurry-Graphs: or, Sketches of Scenery, Celebrities and Society*, 180–181; Ingersoll, *Historical Sketch*, II, 258.

[3] Meigs, *Calhoun*, II, 100; Calhoun to A. D. Wallace, December 17, 1840, Calhoun, *Correspondence*, J. F. Jameson, ed., 468–469.

[4] Calhoun, "A Disquisition on Government," *Works*, I, 90; Calhoun to J. H. Hammond, February 18, 1837, *Correspondence*, 367; Calhoun in the Senate, January 13, 1834, *Register of Debates*, 23 Congress 1 Session, 218.

the capitalists and the growing frustration of the masses seemed to threaten the fabric of society.[5]

And the consequences for the South? The business party placed a premium on conservatism and stability; yet no group was more concerned to expand the power of the central government and whittle away the rights of the states. If, as Calhoun believed, the union of bank and state would "inevitably draw all the powers of the system into the vortex of the general government," what safeguards would remain for the South? [6] And a second danger lay in the inescapable economic clash between Northern finance and Southern cotton. As Francis W. Pickens candidly stated the hard facts which underwrote Calhoun's logic, the South must decide "whether cotton shall control exchanges and importations, or whether the banks and the stock interests shall do it. . . . Break down the swindling of bankers, . . . and cotton will do the exchanges of the commercial world." [7]

On the other hand, the party which opposed the business class contained in itself ominous threats to Southern security. Equalitarian and radical, thriving on agitation and forever fomenting new projects of reform, it must prove an ever-flowing fount of libertarian dogma. Yet, for all its excesses, it was primarily interested in limiting the power of the business community, and in so doing it was employing the State-rights doctrine so vital to the South.

The Southern dilemma was this: which was the greater menace to the plantation system — radical democracy or finance capital? Should the ruling class of the South ally itself to the upper class of the North, and thus to broad construction, capitalism and conservatism, or to the lower classes of the North, and thus to State rights, agrarianism and reform? Should the South join the Whigs in their fight against radicalism, or should it join the Democrats in their fight against business rule?

2

Many Southerners had already made their choice. Thomas Cooper voiced a profound planting conviction when he observed, in

[5] Memorandum of a conversation with Calhoun, December 4, 1831, Calhoun, *Correspondence*, 305; Redelia Brisbane, *Albert Brisbane: a Mental Biography*, 222.
[6] Calhoun to R. H. Goodwyn, *et al.*, September 1, 1838, *Niles' Register*, September 29, 1838.
[7] Pickens to J. H. Hammond, July 13, 1837, R. C. McGrane, *Panic of 1837*, 159. See also Calhoun to J. E. Calhoun, September 7, 1837, *Correspondence*, 377; Calhoun in the Senate, October 3, 1837, *Register of Debates*, 25 Congress 1 Session, 475–476; Calhoun to Calvin Graves, *et al.*, September 6, 1838, *Washington Globe*, October 13, 1838.

1830, that universal suffrage was the root of political evil. Political power must fall thereby "into the hands of the operatives, mechanics and labouring classes, the men of no property." The consequence? "We say, without hesitation, the wealth of the wealthy is in danger."[8] This was clearly no sectional problem, and Cooper himself by 1837 was turning to Nicholas Biddle, the very embodiment of finance capital, as the best hope for the South.

George McDuffie similarly managed to be a champion both of nullification and the United States Bank. In 1834 he declared that "the wealth and intelligence of the northern and middle States" provided the South its best security against abolitionism as it would emerge from "unbalanced democracy."[9] Northern Whigs responded to such sentiments with feeling. We shall "appeal to our brethren of the south for their generous coöperation," said one group rather explicitly, "and promise them that those who believe that the possession of property is an evidence of merit, will be the last to interfere with the rights of property of any kind."[10] The Southern support for White in 1836 showed the strength of the belief in an alliance with Northern conservatism. In Virginia even strict State-rights men backed the Whig ticket, and John Tyler, who had cast the single vote against the force bill in nullification days, now stood as Whig candidate for Vice-President.[11]

Yet Calhoun knew that the business community would in the end exact a price for its protection, and the price would be Southern acquiescence in the American System and broad construction. Could the South afford to pay it? Calhoun was skeptical. If the South surrendered its economic and constitutional bastions, it would exist only on the sufferance of the North.

And the alternative? In 1836 Calhoun could not bring himself to support the Democrats any more than the Whigs. But the panic of 1837 transformed the situation. If Van Buren remained faithful to the hard-money policy, he must come out for the divorce of bank and state. Should not the South seize this opportunity to strengthen its economic position, fortify its constitutional bulwarks and check Northern capitalism, even at the cost of giving more power to Northern radicals?

[8] [Thomas Cooper], "Agrarian and Education Systems," *Southern Review*, VI, 29–30, 31 (August, 1830).

[9] McDuffie's inaugural address as Governor of South Carolina, *Washington Globe*, December 25, 1834.

[10] Report of the Committee of Fifty, *Plaindealer*, May 13, 1837.

[11] H. H. Simms, *Rise of the Whigs in Virginia, 1824–1840*, 67–81; O. P. Chitwood. *John Tyler: Champion of the Old South*, 115, 155.

John Taylor had already endorsed the alliance with radicalism as the best strategy against finance capital. "The question is," he had written, "whether the landed interest . . . had not better unite with the other popular interests, to strangle in its cradle any infant visibly resembling this terrible giant." [12] In the end, Calhoun could not but see the struggle in Jeffersonian terms, between landed capital and business capital — not, as the Southern Whigs saw it, in Federalist terms, between property, whether in land or business, and the propertyless. His decision showed how profoundly he inherited the Jeffersonian tradition.

Van Buren's message sealed his intention. "We have now a fair opportunity to break the last of our commercial Shackles," Calhoun declared with delight.[13] With a sense of vast relief, now restored to a position "much more congenial to my feelings," he broke his partnership with the Whigs, throwing his influence to what he had called not many months before the "more filthy" portion of the Democratic party, "under Benton, Kendal, Blair and Johnson," and backing the personal measure of his ancient enemy, Martin Van Buren.[14] But he was a man of principle, and he would follow where principle led.

3

The issues between Calhoun and the Southern Whigs were clearly expressed in a straggling but bitter debate in the House in September and October. A few weeks after the message Caleb Cushing, the fluent Whig Congressman from Massachusetts, made an able bid for Southern support. The attack on the state banks, he said, was first an attack on State rights, and then an attack on property in general. "By destroying the banks, then, you will revolutionize the property of the country. . . . you revolutionize society." With dramatic emphasis Cushing appealed to the South. "Will not the same desperado spirit, which strikes at one form of property strike at another? If it ravages the North, will it spare the South? Can law, order, property, be torn down at one end of the country, and stand untouched and unshaken at the other? Will not anarchy in half be anarchy in the whole? It seems to me," he concluded, "to become every part

[12] John Taylor, *Inquiry*, 551–552; see also *Tyranny Unmasked*, 197–199.
[13] Calhoun to J. E. Calhoun, September 7, 1837, Calhoun, *Correspondence*, 377. See also Calhoun to J. Bauskett, *et al.*, November 3, 1837, *Niles' Register*, December 2, 1837.
[14] Calhoun to Anna Marie Calhoun, September 8, 1837, to J. H. Hammond, February 18, 1837, Calhoun, *Correspondence*, 379, 367.

of the country, North as well [as] South, and not least of all, the South, to guard well the conservative elements in the social organization of these United States." [15]

This powerful statement impressed many planters. But Calhoun thought differently, and Francis W. Pickens, his spokesman in the House, delivered the South Carolina retort. It might be to the advantage of Northern capital to rob labor of its full product, Pickens observed, but it was to the advantage of the South that labor receive its full product, for in the South labor and capital were identical. "When we contend for the undivided profits and proceeds of our labor," he cried, "do you not see that we stand precisely in the same situation as the laborer of the North? We are, to all intents and purposes, in the place of laborers. We are the only class of capitalists, as far as pecuniary interest is concerned, which, as a class, are identified with the laborers of the country." We must therefore join with Northern labor in its resistance to Northern capital.[16] . . . When, later in the debate, Ely Moore rose to denounce some Northern Whigs who had lashed into Pickens, the alliance appeared complete.[17]

The axis between Moore and Pickens, between Martin Van Buren and John C. Calhoun, was firm, but brittle. Agreement was perfect up to a point, and thereafter disagreement was infinite. "I am an aristocrat," John Randolph once remarked in a brilliant summary of the Southern position; "I love liberty, I hate equality." [18] Calhoun's political line was the median between love of liberty and hatred of equality. Indeed, his fear of radical democracy, with its equalitarian and majoritarian tendencies, remained second only to his fear of capitalism itself. He flinched even from the name. "The word democrat better applies to the north than the South," he said in 1838, "and as usually

[15] Cushing in the House, September 25, 1837, *Register of Debates*, 25 Congress 1 Session, 885–887.

[16] Pickens in the House, October 10, 1837, *Register of Debates*, 25 Congress 1 Session, 1393–1395. John Quincy Adams was infuriated by Pickens, "a coarse sample of the South Carolina school of orator statesmen — pompous, flashy, and shallow," and by his speech, "delivered with an air of authority and a tone of dogmatism as if he was speaking to his slaves." Adams, *Memoirs*, IX, 399.

[17] After half an hour of thunder, Moore broke down as he had before and was carried home to be bled. His collapse came rather to the relief of Adams, who had been impressed by his "prepossessing countenance, a rather courteous deportment, . . . a good command of language," and appalled by his "whole system of insurrection against the rich." "If his strength were equal to his will," Adams decided, "he would be a very dangerous man. As it is, he is a very unsafe one." *Memoirs*, IX, 405–406. For Moore in the House, October 13, 1837, see *Register of Debates*, 25 Congress 1 Session, 1470, 1588.

[18] Bruce, *Randolph*, II, 203.

understood means those who are in favour of the government of the absolute numerical majority to which I am utterly opposed and the prevalence of . which would destroy our system and destroy the South." [19] In leisure moments, he worked out an elaborate system of minority rule which promised to come into sharp conflict with the majoritarianism of his Northern allies.[20]

The reasoning which justified this alliance with radicalism was indeed too subtle for most planters. Calhoun carried his own circle of bright young men — Pickens, J. H. Hammond, Dixon H. Lewis, R. B. Rhett — and a select group of politicians, including W. F. Gordon of Virginia, and William P. Taylor, the son of John Taylor of Caroline. But he failed to move the planting class as a whole, neither the Virginia school, with its real if less radical concern for State rights, nor the Southern Whigs, with their scorn for "abstractions." The Virginians dissented sharply on the subtreasury, and in 1840 Abel P. Upshur published *A Brief Enquiry into the True Nature and Character of Our Federal Government*, the classic attempt to reconcile the State-rights position with Whiggery — and thereby to rationalize the Harrisburg convention, which had just nominated William Henry Harrison and John Tyler.

But the illusion of Tyler, Upshur, Henry A. Wise and their associates that they could be Whigs for Jeffersonian reasons was quickly dispelled after 1840. Calhoun had observed correctly that the North would demand its price; and, when Clay unveiled the Whig economic program, the Virginia school, led by Tyler, woke to realities and left the party. Their confession of error was signalized when, after Upshur's death, Calhoun, a better logician, succeeded him as Secretary of State.

Even after the Tyler defection, however, the wealthy planters remained predominantly Whig. Two thirds to three quarters of the slaves were in Whig hands. And, as Calhoun had foreseen, those who threw themselves on the protection of Northern conservatism were steadily obliged to accept the Whig economic program. They had re-

[19] Calhoun to R. B. Rhett, September 13, 1838, Calhoun, *Correspondence*, 399. Cf. J. H. Hammond's remark: "Circumstances had placed us in alliance (connection rather) with the Democratic party of the country, tho' we professed at the same time to be of a higher school of democracy, one of fixed principles and incompatible faith." Hammond to Calhoun, May 4, 1840, *Correspondence Addressed to John C. Calhoun, 1837–1849*, C. S. Boucher and R. P. Brooks, eds., 823.

[20] The administration was equally aware of the underlying differences. Frank Blair laid down the terms of the alliance in a series of editorials in the *Washington Globe*, September 7, 8, 10, 11, 1838. Taking as much care as Calhoun himself not to call the Southerners "democrats," Blair emphasized that this union between "the Democracy of the North and the planters of the South" was for mutual safety against a common enemy.

jected Calhoun as a "metaphysician" and Tyler as an "abstractionist," and, being practical men, they bartered away their economic and constitutional advantages for the uncertain patronage of Northern business. They came, in the fifties, to decide that Calhoun had been right. But it was too late, the game was lost.[21]

[21] A. C. Cole, *The Whig Party in the South;* U. B. Phillips, "The Southern Whigs, 1834–1854," *Turner Essays in American History;* Simms, *Rise of the Whigs in Virginia.*

XXI RADICALISM AT HIGH WATER

THE REVEREND THEOPHILUS FISK preached the first sermon in the Capitol after the independent-treasury message, but was defeated in the contest for the chaplaincy of the House — an omen for the special session. Silas Wright then introduced the subtreasury bill, Calhoun added the "specie clause," and angry debate began. The opposition was suitably horrified, but the country demanded action and the measure soon passed the Senate, complete with Calhoun's amendment. In the House, Henry A. Wise of Virginia, who, as the *New York Evening Post* observed, was seldom silent "except when forced to be so by organic disease," led a furious counterattack with a flow of invective unequaled since the days of Randolph. Flinging epithets about with riotous abandon — "Honest Iago" Kendall and "Big Bully Bottom" Benton were typical — Wise rallied the Whig and right-wing Democratic forces against what he called "the proposition . . . to destroy all banking institutions." [1] The House responded, and the independent treasury was tabled.

1

The administration was depressed but not defeated. Silas Wright remarked, with his peculiar combination of resolution and gloom, that the war against the banks might go on for years, and reintroduced the bill at the regular session. [2] The new burst of debate added little to anyone's knowledge of the issues. Henry Clay declared his "full and solemn conviction that all the calamities of war with the most potent power on earth would be a blessing compared with the consequences of this measure," and N. P. Tallmadge charged the administration with planning "THE DESTRUCTION OF THE WHOLE BANKING SYSTEM OF THE COUNTRY, THE REPEAL OF CHARTERS, AND THE ABROGATION OF VESTED RIGHTS." [3] But the measure passed the Senate

---

[1] Wise in the House, October 13, 1837, *Register of Debates*, 25 Congress 1 Session, 1633, 1651, 1654; for the *Evening Post*'s remark, see *New York Evening Post*, March 31, 1840.

[2] E. T. Throop to Van Buren, November 23, 1837, Van Buren Papers.

[3] Clay in the Senate, January 31, 1838, Tallmadge, February 8, 1838, *Congressional Globe*, 25 Congress 2 Session, 151, Appendix, 620.

again, though this time Whigs and Conservatives (anti-subtreasury Democrats) succeeded, with the help of Western Democrats, in striking out the specie clause. Calhoun consequently turned against the measure, and the faithful Pickens spoke with contempt in the House of this "emasculated bill . . . having the form of a man with the spirit of a eunuch." (Sergeant of Pennsylvania remarked that he would support the bill if he really thought it was a eunuch, which, after all, was the "sort of thing that, in some parts of the world, was entrusted with the care of a treasury.") [4] But the independent treasury failed again in the House, and the men of finance sighed in relief.

In the meantime the business community was being whipped into a frenzy against Van Buren's proposal. In Philadelphia, distraught merchants told George Combe, the visiting British phrenologist, that they would rather have a military despotism than the present administration; "others, more moderate, inform me, that they would prefer a government like that of the British in Canada to their own democracy." [5] Wall Street boggled at the triumph of Locofoco principles at the White House. By the spring of 1838 the Governor of Connecticut could declare in his address to the legislature: "Our business is disappearing like the melting snow under the meridian sun. . . . The manufacturers of New England are baffled, crippled and desponding and beyond endurance." [6]

From the nation's capital the *Madisonian* directed the propaganda campaign, sending forth an inexhaustible stream of anti-administration material, circulating the speeches of Wise, Tallmadge and Clay, and outdoing even the Democratic press in the fertility of its abuse. On Van Buren, for example: —

Aye, as well might the Fathers of the Church be contrasted with Robert Dale Owen and his infidel adherents, or the chastest matrons of the land with the followers of Fanny Wright, as Henry Clay with Martin Van Buren.

On Ely Moore: —

We will not say that he is a debauchee of the grossest character — nor that he is accustomed to the grog-shop and the brothel, nor that he is incapable of appreciating a moral obligation. . . . This is not necessary to be said, nor would it be in good taste.

[4] Pickens and Sergeant in the House, March 27, 1838, *Congressional Globe*, 25 Congress 2 Session, 266.
[5] Combe, *Notes on the United States of North America*, I, 194.
[6] *New York Evening Post*, May 15, 1838.

On the general situation (as of March 6, 1838): —

> THIS REPUBLIC WAS NEVER IN GREATER DANGER THAN AT THIS
> MOMENT! . . . The sway of Caesar and the tyranny of Nero fol-
> low! [etc., etc.] [7]

The charges of the *Madisonian*, incessantly repeated, had their effect.
By the middle of 1839 even the *Washington Globe* was complaining
of "the uniform and bitter hostility of the mass of the merchants to
the Democratic administration," and the *New York Evening Post* felt
obliged to deny that the administration and its supporters were "the
enemies and oppressors of the commercial class," that they had "a
project on foot for breaking all the banks," that they contemplated
"a general repartition of property . . . sharing it equally among the
various members of the community," or that they proposed to attack
religion and turn "churches into lecture rooms for infidel philoso-
phers." [8]

Yet the continued suspension of the banks was in the meantime
seriously threatening the unity of the business community. Responsible
bankers felt an obligation to resume specie payments as quickly as
possible. As early as August, 1837, a committee headed by Albert Gallatin sent circulars to the banks of the nation on behalf of the banks
of New York, pointing out the "paramount and most sacred duty"
to resume and proposing a general convention to decide on means.[9]
Most cities replied favorably, but Boston was evasive and Philadelphia
and Baltimore flatly denied any duty to act.

The actual convention in November disclosed the issues more clearly.
For men like Gallatin, Nathan Appleton of Boston (who was carefully excluded from the Boston delegation because of his support of
resumption),[10] and Samuel Ward of Prime, Ward & King, New York's
leading private banker, the decision was purely economic. As soon
as financially feasible, the banks must resume. But for others the decision was chiefly political. The banks, in other words, should use
suspension as a form of blackmail to defeat the independent treasury
and compel the restoration of the big Bank. This school was led by
Nicholas Biddle, the bloody but unbowed champion of a similar

---

[7] *Madisonian*, August 14, June 29, 1839, March 6, 1838.

[8] *Washington Globe*, July 1, 1839; *New York Evening Post*, July 18, 1839. The
reappearance of somewhat the same indictment a century later suggests that
hysteria in the face of change is likely to express itself in a distressingly unoriginal series of fantasies.

[9] Gallatin, *et al.*, Circular to the Banks, August 18, 1837, Flagg Papers.

[10] Appleton, "Sketches of Autobiography," *Proceedings of the Massachusetts
Historical Society*, V, 289.

strategy of pressure in 1834, and it included the Philadelphia and Boston delegations. Together they successfully prevented united action.

Defeated nationally, Gallatin and Ward pushed through plans for their own state. "The position of our Banks is one of extraordinary strength," wrote Ward in February, 1838, "but . . . the fear of Mr. Biddle, — of the sub treasury scheme — of the Bill holders, depositors &c. &c. have been working in the brains of our many headed monster, until like a frightened school boy they have become afraid of a shadow." [11] Some bankers even sought from the legislature an extension of the period in which suspension was possible without forfeiture of charter, but Gallatin thwarted this move. (Later both he and Appleton declared that this punitive state law alone compelled resumption.) [12]

On April 5, as New York was perfecting its plans, Biddle issued a public letter boldly defending suspension as a political measure and indicating that no resumption should take place until his Bank was restored. Gallatin regarded this manifesto as a declaration of war against the other banks and the government, and Charles King of the *New York American*, one of the most conservative editors of the day, pronounced it the "most arrogant and audacious document" he ever saw.[13]

There can be little doubt that Biddle planned raiding the New York money market and forcing the New York banks to close their doors again; but Samuel Ward in the nick of time negotiated a loan of five million dollars in gold bars from the Bank of England, and Biddle was frustrated. But still undiscouraged: late in June he announced that the defeat of the independent treasury was "exclusively" the result of the Bank's policy (in contrast to the ignominious "surrender" of the New York banks).[14] By July, however, public opinion, stirred up by the example of New York, forced the rest of the country, including Biddle's own bank, to return to specie payments. Actually, the government, by using specie as much as possible in its own operations and resisting all efforts to reinstate bank notes, started a flow of it through the economy which played a great part in making resumption possible.[15]

[11] Ward to Appleton, February 7, 1838, Appleton Papers. Ward was the grandfather of Julia Ward Howe and F. Marion Crawford.

[12] Gallatin to R. M. T. Hunter, July 12, 1841, Gallatin, *Writings*, II, 554; Appleton, *Remarks on Currency and Banking*, 30.

[13] T. W. Olcott to A. C. Flagg, April 10, 1838, Flagg Papers.

[14] Biddle to S. Jaudon, June 29, 1838, Biddle, *Correspondence*, 315.

[15] Woodbury to Appleton, March 18, 1838, Appleton Papers; David Kinley, *The Independent Treasury of the United States*, 209–210.

2

In the meantime the independent-treasury issue had pretty well solved the conflicts within the Democratic party by driving most of the conservatives into open opposition. In Massachusetts its promulgation was followed shortly by the clear triumph of the radical wing. J. K. Simpson, Henshaw's candidate for the collectorship of Boston, had unwisely remarked during the summer that the subtreasury would ruin the party; his death in the fall of 1837 simply ratified his political demise.[16] In January 1838, after Marcus Morton turned down the collectorship again, it was offered to George Bancroft, who became thereby the new Democratic boss of Massachusetts.

The honor completed Bancroft's social downfall. "A more odious appointment, for Collector, could not be made," commented one respectable Boston paper politely.[17] Old acquaintances grew even chillier. Only a few, like his fellow historian Prescott and the brilliant young lawyer Charles Sumner, kept up their friendships, and both were discounted for their eccentricities. But there were compensations. With Henshaw out and Morton sympathetic, Bancroft was free to build up the party along truly advanced lines. The new Collector set to work with immense enthusiasm.

One of the first recruits he brought into Democratic councils was the minister Orestes A. Brownson. Now thirty-four years old, Brownson bore the scars of a varied and picturesque intellectual experience. He had been successively a Presbyterian, a Universalist and an agnostic before coming to a temporary rest in the comfortable compromise of Unitarianism. Politically, he had worked with Frances Wright in the New York Workingmen's party, then entered an antipolitical phase when religion came to seem the only means of social salvation. A Fourth of July address in 1834, after he had moved to Massachusetts, won the notice of Samuel C. Allen who decisively pointed out to Brownson the weakness of his position: his indifference to economic reform.

In 1836 he moved to Chelsea on the outskirts of Boston, where he founded his Society for Christian Union and Progress, an attempt to elevate the laboring class by exhortation. He was now a commanding figure on the rostrum, two inches over six feet, his dark hair brushed straight back from his forehead, his deepset gray eyes flashing black with feeling, the tails of his broadcloth coat flapping behind him as

---

[16] *Washington Globe*, January 20, 1838; *Boston Post*, January 27, 1838.
[17] *Columbian Centinel* (Boston), January 10, 1838.

he strode vigorously back and forth. In June he became editor of the *Boston Reformer* which under his guidance seemed to Harriet Martineau to come nearer the "principles of exact justice" than any similar publication she had ever seen.[18]

Still convinced that reform could only come from within, he measured the existing parties by standards of purity which politics could never satisfy. "General Jackson went into office with unbounded popularity," he would write, ". . . and full resolution to be a Reformer, but of all the reforms he specified in his Inaugural Address, not one has been effected."[19] But Brownson's readers believed that General Jackson had accomplished certain things, even if he had left some problems unsolved, and they began to protest against Brownson for betraying their cause. Eventually he was forced to resign the editorship.

The crisis soon showed the inadequacy of the moralistic approach. As the depression deepened, Brownson's theories began to fade before desperate facts of suffering and starvation. The suspension of the banks completed his education. Their "wickedness" in refusing to pay their debts and the "moral obtuseness" of the community which condoned their conduct made him suddenly fear that the nation was falling under the control of associated wealth.[20]

On May 28, two weeks after suspension, he preached a bitter sermon on the text "Babylon is falling." "The contest is now between the privileged and the underprivileged," he cried, "and a terrible one it is. . . . The *people* rise in stern and awful majesty, and demand in strange tones their ever despised and hitherto denied rights." Meanwhile, he resumed the editorship of the *Reformer* and put it on a strong Locofoco tack. "The contest is now between Capital or Money and Labor," he would declare grimly. "They may disguise the matter as they will, the laboring class comes up and demands its turn in the government of the world and its turn it will have."[21]

Bancroft had long had his eye on the vehement young minister. He now encouraged Brownson in his plan of starting a new review, and soon contributed a subsidy out of the federal patronage by making Brownson steward of the naval hospital at Chelsea. The able pens of Brownson, Bancroft and Alexander H. Everett quickly made the *Boston Quarterly Review* the organ of the Democratic intellectuals,

[18] Harriet Martineau, *Society in America*, I, 153; for her comment on the Society for Christian Union and Progress, II, 358.
[19] *Boston Reformer*, August 6, 1836.
[20] O. A. Brownson, *Works*, H. F. Brownson, ed., XV, 285. See also Arthur M. Schlesinger, Jr., *Orestes A. Brownson: a Pilgrim's Progress*, chap. iii.
[21] Brownson, *Babylon Is Falling*, 20–21; *Boston Reformer*, August 4, 1837.

where keen and detailed defenses of the administration would alternate with recondite essays on theology, metaphysics and political theory. Brownson also rose rapidly in practical politics. His literary skill put him in demand as author of party manifestoes and resolutions, and he proved a good, slashing stump speaker, whose biting phrases could raise roars from the crowd.[22]

Conservatism watched Bancroft's ascendancy with alarm. "Our Loco Focos here at home are even more outrageous and destructive . . . than the Loco Focos at Washington," snarled the *Boston Atlas*. Since the party has fallen "under the control of such men as Bancroft, Brownson and Hallett, they have introduced . . . certain metaphysical and mystical dogmas, borrowed apparently from the most violent Jacobins of the French Revolution, according to which, if they can get the power, they propose to reconstruct the existing order of society." Bancroft, the particular target of Whig invective, was charged with using his authority "to vex, harrass and to incommode the whole mercantile community" and with fully supporting the government in its "remorseless and unappeasable hatred of the mercantile classes." [23] No wonder the doors of Winthrop Square were closing before the historian, and Harvard was regarding him as a traitor to his class.

In this increasingly charged atmosphere the campaign of 1839 was particularly hard-fought. The modest six thousand votes Marcus Morton had received eleven years before had grown nearly seven times in the decade, and the Democrats were further encouraged by the enactment under Whig auspices of a law forbidding the sale of liquor in quantities less than fifteen gallons, an obvious piece of class legislation. Bancroft, Brownson and Hallett dominated the state convention, and the party went into the canvass with more than usual hope.[24]

The race for Governor was the closest in Massachusetts history. For days, through the wintry month of December, the result hung in doubt. The total number of votes cast was 102,066, of which 51,034 constituted the majority necessary for election. After due weighing of

[22] *Boston Post*, March 23, November 2, 1838; Charles T. Congdon, *Reminiscences of a Journalist*, 61–62.

[23] *Boston Atlas*, October 26, July 17, 1839.

[24] Tragedy marred the last days of the campaign. Theodore Sedgwick, who in 1838 had succeeded William Foster as Democratic candidate for Lieutenant Governor, was too sick to run again in 1839; but he came out of retirement a few days before election to address a Democratic meeting. After finishing his speech, he suddenly staggered and fell, seized by an apoplectic stroke which paralyzed the left side of his body. In a few hours he was dead, to the sorrow of Democrats across the country. He was fifty-eight years old. A Federalist minister in Connecticut was moved to comment in his diary: "Theodore Sedgwick, of Stockbridge, has died suddenly, as by a stroke from God." *Diary of Thomas Robbins, D.D., 1796–1854* (Boston, 1886–1887), Increase N. Tarbox, ed., II, 550.

doubtful ballots, Morton was adjudged to have precisely 51,034, Everett 50,725, with 307 votes scattering.

The Democratic administration was ushered in by Morton's inaugural address, which proved to be a cogent summary of Locofoco views on state government. Bancroft remarked cheerily that it would cause a yell in State Street which would be heard beyond the Berkshires, and he was pretty nearly right. Ex-Governor Everett, noting "very long and very radical" in his diary, told Daniel Webster that he hoped Massachusetts would realize that it had been better off under King Log than it would be under King Stork. Webster replied, "I did not expect him to be quite so radical," and classed Morton with Benton: "they are apt Scholars in the School of Fanny Wright." [25]

Webster and Everett need not have worried. The Whig majority in the legislature hamstrung Morton's program and made King Stork as ineffective as King Log. But the Democratic party was only confirmed in its purposes. "To defend the rights of labor is the glory of the age," declared the convention of Democratic members of the legislature. "The democracy demands, as the test of its measures, their tendency to elevate the laboring classes." [26]

3

In New York, also, the Democratic party experienced a distinct leftward drift. The fugitives from the independent treasury were even more numerous than in Massachusetts because the state-banking interest bulked larger among the New York Democrats, and because N. P. Tallmadge with his "Conservative" movement gave more direction to the dissidents. The exodus of Tallmadge and his followers from the party established state politics more firmly than ever on class lines.[27]

[25] Everett, Journal, January 22, 1840, Everett to Webster, February 11, 1840, Webster to Everett, February 16, 1840, Everett Papers. For Bancroft's remark, see R. C. Winthrop to Everett, n.d. [January, 1840], Everett Papers.

[26] Boston Post, April 15, 1840.

[27] "There is scarcely a movement in history more susceptible of the economic interpretation, than that of the Conservatives." Fox, Decline of Aristocracy in the Politics of New York, 401 n. Fox's statistical analyses in chapter xiv of this work establish beyond any doubt the class character of the vote. The method here employed is often more profitable, I think, for an understanding of the politics of this period than the Turner thesis, the indiscriminate application of which mars such otherwise excellent state political histories as A. B. Darling's Political Changes in Massachusetts. For the Conservatives, see also Hammond, History of Political Parties in New-York, II, 478; [Joseph Scoville], The Old Merchants of New York City, I, 81: "The mass of large and little merchants have like a flock of sheep gathered either into the Federal, Whig, Clay, or Republican folds. The Democratic merchants could have easily been stowed away in a large Eighth avenue railroad car."

It also weakened the party politically, and the Whigs made striking gains in the election of 1837.

The Conservative schism placed Governor Marcy in an increasingly equivocal position. His first rage at the independent treasury cooled as winter drew on; and he set about composing his own annual message to the legislature, in language so admirably vague that, on the one hand, it conciliated the radicals, and, on the other, its ambiguities permitted his friends to deny that he really approved of Van Buren's scheme.[28] After a few more months Marcy even came to accept the independent treasury.[29] But he still opposed the spirit of radicalism at work in the party. "I am not surprised," he said, "at the alarm which pervaded not only the monied aristocracy but the mass of men engaged in such kinds of business as required the use of considerable sums of money." [30] It was this Locofoco extremism, Marcy believed, which caused the Democratic setback in the fall election.

But the radicals tended to blame the Whig victory on Marcy's own temporizing and the vacillations of the Albany group. "What in hell is the difference between democratic principles this year and last year?" exclaimed Preston King, the able representative from St. Lawrence County, where Democratic lines held firm in protest against the strategy of appeasement. ". . . What has democracy to do with compromise, with conciliation? . . . I say damn the idea of compromise." The danger was not too little deference to business but too much. "Van Buren's message is a banner in the sky — Stand to its doctrines and the democracy will rally and sustain them. . . . I am afraid I shall become *ultra* — I begin to feel the marrow moving in my bones." [31]

Many Democrats were beginning to feel the marrow moving in their bones. Through 1838 the radicals solidified their influence. A meeting at Tammany Hall resolved that the party felt "no more disturbed at the present day, on being called 'Agrarians,' 'Loco Focos,' or 'Radicals,' than it did in the brightest days of the illustrious Jefferson, at being called 'Democrats and Jacobins.' " [32] The remnants of the old Workingmen's party, with John Commerford in a prominent role, pledged their support.[33] Fanny Wright was enabled, through the

---

[28] Marcy to P. M. Wetmore, January 22, 1838, Marcy Papers; *New York Times,* October 19, 20, 1838.

[29] Marcy to Wetmore, June 29, 1838, Marcy Papers.

[30] Marcy to Wetmore, December 11, 1838, Marcy Papers.

[31] King to A. C. Flagg, November 22, 1837, Flagg Papers.

[32] *A Voice from Old Tammany! Meeting of the People!*, 10.

[33] *New York Evening Post,* February 7, 1838.

intervention of a Tammany alderman, to hire Masonic Hall for a series of lectures in defense of the administration.[34] On the Fourth of July Edwin Forrest, the actor, delivered a radical address at the crowded Tabernacle, so eloquent that William Leggett had to deny having written it.[35] In October, when Forrest declined the Tammany nomination for Congress, a strong Leggett movement failed chiefly because he refused to modify his passionate views on slavery.

But the election of 1838 resulted in another Whig sweep, with William H. Seward now defeating Marcy as Governor. The argument which followed the reverses of the year before was promptly reopened in sharper form. Marcy again put the blame on the Locofocos, while the *Democratic Review*, newly established in Washington under the patronage of Benjamin F. Butler, strongly backed the radical case. The ex-Governor was thrown into a rage by this *"decree"* from Washington, as he called it, presuming that Van Buren and Wright shared its views.[36] Van Buren, for his part, made no particular attempt to mend the breach. When he visited New York in the summer of 1839, he attended the Bowery Theater with Mr. and Mrs. Alexander Ming; everywhere he went, according to Philip Hone, he was surrounded by the "Loco-foco rabble." [37]

With such encouragement the Democrats of New York City became increasingly bold. When their outspoken resolutions were used by the Whigs against the party in the conservative farming counties, they displayed no particular embarrassment, an attitude shocking to a professional like Marcy. William Cullen Bryant and Richard Adams Locke would acknowledge that this candor might have a "temporary adverse influence upon the politics of the interior," but argued cheerfully that the ultimate effect would be to expel those whose only interest in the party was the spoils of victory, and thus could not be relied on anyway.[38] When the *Democratic Review* echoed this line in its December issue, Marcy in fury canceled his subscription and complained to Wright and Van Buren.[39] With the Conservatives out of the party and Marcy disaffected, the old days of easy Democratic triumphs were coming to an end.

[34] One Whig paper denounced her as a "She-Benton." Perkins and Wolfson, *Frances Wright*, 333–334.
[35] *Boston Post*, July 7, 9, 1838.
[36] Marcy to Albert Gallup, February 11, 1839, Marcy Papers.
[37] Hone, *Diary*, I, 404.
[38] *New York Evening Post*, November 8, 1839; quotations from *New York New Era, Bay State Democrat* (Boston), November 22, 29, 1839.
[39] Marcy to Wetmore, January 27, 1840, Wright to Marcy, February 4, 1840, Marcy Papers.

In the meantime the radicals had lost a champion but gained a martyr. William Leggett was already a sick man in 1837. His eloquence was lapsing into nervous shrillness, and he was lashing out, with reckless promiscuity, at everything which displeased him. The failure of the *Plaindealer* later in the year plunged him into despondency. Now, without a paper, without former friends, for his course had estranged many of his earlier admirers, he was a tired, wasted man, overwhelmed with debts and contemplating suicide. At this point Edwin Forrest, who had already lost about fifteen thousand dollars in Leggett's editorial ventures, stepped in again, paid some of his debts and set him up in a house at New Rochelle at some six thousand dollars more.[40]

But it was late. The fire was burning low. Leggett's sharp refusal to compromise on slavery kept him off the Democratic congressional ticket in 1838. Then Van Buren, hearing of Leggett's plight and with no thought of Leggett's bitter attack of two years before, offered him early in 1839 the post of Consul to Guatemala. There under the shining tropical skies he saw a chance to regain health. But his energies were ebbing fast, and in May he died in New Rochelle.

In death Leggett suddenly received the tributes he never had in life. His gallant spirit caught the imagination of the party as no one had since Jackson himself. He became the hero of poems and orations; he was the point of a thousand allusions and the toast of a thousand banquets; his memory was revered, and his example became an inspiration. Tammany Hall in October ordered expunged from the records the resolution of 1835 excommunicating Leggett for his attack on Amos Kendall's post-office order, and in the November *Democratic Review* William Cullen Bryant poured out his feelings in fine and moving verse: —

> For when the death-frost came to lie,
>   Upon that warm and mighty heart,
> And quench that bold and friendly eye,
>   His spirit did not all depart.

> The words of fire, that from his pen
>   Were flung upon the lucid page,
> Still move, still shake the hearts of men,
>   Amid a cold and coward age.

[40] Alger, *Forrest*, I, 373. Forrest, a loyal and generous friend, had to fight a lawsuit later over the house in New Rochelle (see 7 Hill 463); and after Leggett's death he made provision for his widow by buying his library for seven thousand dollars. *Niles' Register*, October 12, 1839.

His love of Truth, too warm, too strong,
  For hope or fear to chain or chill,
His hate of tyranny and wrong,
  Burn in the breasts he kindled still.[41]

4

Through the East the battle over the independent treasury precipitated the latent radicalism in the Jacksonian party. Orations, party
addresses, convention resolutions voiced increasingly an open appeal
to the humble members of society to arrest the might of the rich
and powerful. The very name — Locofoco — hitherto confined to the
little band in New York City, was soon applied by universal consent
to the whole party.

Nearly all the radicals of the early thirties supported Van Buren,
and many of them were appointed to office. Fanny Wright, Robert
Dale Owen, Samuel Clesson Allen, George Bancroft, Orestes A.
Brownson, John Commerford, Theodore Sedgwick, William Leggett
were all Democrats now. Dr. Charles Douglas was a clerk in the patent
office at Washington; [42] Frederick Robinson was weigher and gauger at
the Boston Custom House; Ely Moore, after his defeat for Congress in
1839, became surveyor of the New York port; Moses Jaques in 1840
was chairman of the Democratic state convention in New Jersey:

[41] Bryant, "William Leggett," *Democratic Review*, VI, 430 (November, 1839).
In 1841 a bust of Leggett was gravely placed in the very room in Tammany where
he had been denounced a few years before. The ironies stirred John Greenleaf
Whittier to eloquent derision: —

Yes, pile the marbles o'er him! It is well
  That ye who mocked him in his long stern strife,
  And planted in the pathway of his life
The ploughshares of your hatred hot from hell,
  Who clamored down the bold reformer when
  He pleaded for his captive fellow-men,
Who spurned him in the market-place, and sought
  Within thy walls, St. Tammany, to bind
In party chains the free and honest thought,
  The angel utterance of an upright mind,
Well is it now that o'er his grave ye raise
The stony tribute of your tardy praise,
For not alone that pile shall tell to Fame
Of the brave heart beneath, but of the builders' shame.

Whittier, *Works* (1888), IV, 22.

[42] St. George L. Sioussat, ed., "Diaries of S. H. Laughlin of Tennessee, 1840,
1843," *Tennessee Historical Magazine*, II, 53. For Douglas's attempts to get a South
American appointment, see S. C. Allen to Bancroft, January 29, 1838, Bancroft
Papers, J. M. Niles to Van Buren, October 27, 1839, Van Buren Papers.

everywhere radicals were taken to the bosom of the party.[43] The organization politicians, the Ben Halletts and Fernando Woods, bowed to the inevitable and acquired a protective coloration of progressivism.[44]

In the East the independent treasury thus rallied the common man to the side of the administration. In the West it produced quite a different effect, and the difference throws light on the vexed problem of Western influences on Jacksonian democracy. The frontier had watched the unfolding of the hard-money policy with increasing coolness. When, for example, Congress early in 1837 considered repealing Jackson's Specie Circular, a basic part of the hard-money program, the West voted 13 to 3 in the Senate and 43 to 10 in the House in favor of repeal.[45]

The independent treasury itself fared little better. In the special session Western Senators backed Calhoun's specie clause 12 to 8, but Western Representatives voted 47 to 18 in favor of tabling the measure. In 1838 at the regular session Western Senators divided 11 to 11 on the specie clause, voted 17 to 4 in favor of the repeal of the Specie Circular and 15 to 7 in favor of the bill. Westerners in the House voted 46 to 19 against a third reading. When the bill finally passed in 1840, Western Senators supported it 11 to 9 and Western Representatives opposed it 33 to 32. A House resolution of 1838, declaring substantially that the government should underwrite suspended banks by accepting their worthless notes, was supported 43 to 13 by the West.

[43] *Boston Post*, April 28, 1838, May 28, 1840; *Longworth's American Almanac, New-York Register, and City Directory* (New York, 1840), *passim*. John Ferral was an applicant for a job in the Post Office Department, with what success I do not know. See H. D. Gilpin to J. Farrell [sic], July 31, 1840, Gilpin Letterbooks.

[44] Observe Hallett's frantic oration on July 4, 1839: "*Labor is the only source of wealth;* and when we look with this view at the tendencies of legislation and institutions in government, we are surprised to find *how small a portion of this wealth, in all civilized countries, even the best governed, is left in the hands that create it.* This is the great political lesson . . . to impress on the public mind." Etc., etc. Hallett, *Oration . . . at Millbury, July 4, 1839,* 33. Fernando Wood helped lead the movement within Tammany to canonize William Leggett.

[45] Though the distribution plan was perhaps not strictly a hard-money issue, the division on it split along hard-money–paper-money lines. The West supported it by a vote of 12 to 5 in the Senate and 53 to 3 in the House.

For the purpose of this analysis, I have given the broadest possible interpretation to "West": it includes Alabama, Louisiana, Mississippi, Tennessee, Kentucky, Missouri, Ohio, Indiana, Illinois, and, for the later sessions, Arkansas and Michigan. If the Southern states were omitted, the votes against the hard-money program would be considerably heavier. My computation varies slightly from that of R. G. Wellington, *The Political and Sectional Influence of the Public Lands, 1828–1842,* 54, 67–68, but by a vote or two and without affecting at all the conclusions.

The dismay of Western states at the divorce proposal fills out the picture. The legislatures of Kentucky and Tennessee, for example, passed resolutions against the scheme. A Tennessee Democrat told Polk in August, 1837, that nearly everyone was in favor of some kind of federal bank, and that the sponsorship of the independent treasury would lose Tennessee for the Democracy. The measure split the Democrats in Illinois.[46]

So pronounced, indeed, was Western opposition that William Foster advanced the theory, which won the support of the *New York Evening Post*, that the independent treasury was really a sectional issue, with the East playing the liberal role and the West the conservative. Though a case can be made for Foster's thesis by an analysis of votes in Congress, Henry D. Gilpin answered it in language as conclusive for Foster's theory of Jacksonian democracy as for the frontier theory. It was not a "question between Atlantic and Western States," Gilpin declared, " — but between trade and productive labour . . . not a question of locality." [47] It seems clear now that more can be understood about Jacksonian democracy if it is regarded as a problem not of sections but of classes. In 1837 Van Buren received what support he got from the West, apart from that of a few men like Benton and Polk, chiefly because of his control over the party organization.

5

As President, Van Buren was weak in the very respect in which he might have been expected to excel — as a politician. For a man who in the past had been so skillful in party management, he showed himself negligent and maladroit during his own administration. His appointments failed to strengthen him. It was sheer indulgence, for example, to make James K. Paulding Secretary of the Navy, and it was worse to consider Washington Irving for the post (as Van Buren did) after Irving had come out against the independent treasury. For three years, he left his secretaries to act pretty much on their own responsibility. Not until the fourth year did he display some executive energy, making himself really the head of the government,

[46] E. I. McCormac, *James K. Polk*, 660–661; Pease, *The Frontier State, 1818–1848*, 246. T. P. Abernethy describes hard-money ideas as "very unpopular" in Tennessee. "The Origin of the Whig Party in Tennessee," *Mississippi Valley Historical Review*, XII, 515. According to Wellington, the independent treasury with the specie clause "was not acceptable to the West as a whole." *Political Influence of the Public Lands*, 67.

[47] *New York Evening Post*, July 20, 1838; Gilpin to Foster, July 20, 1838, Gilpin Letterbooks.

and that was the most successful year of his presidency. The *Globe* for a good part of this period exhibited more spirit than the White House. "I feel myself to be a sort of Representative of the Mechanical Classes, the working people of all sorts who support the administration," Frank Blair remarked to the President, and he acted this role with unflagging vigor.[48]

Nor did Van Buren show particular skill in dealing with disunity in the party. He allowed the Tallmadge split to grow almost into a rebellion, while similar splits under Jackson never became more than individual desertions. He coped badly with the slavery question, gaining an undeserved pro-Southern reputation in the North while failing to win the confidence of the South. This unexpected political ineptness weakened his administration and delayed until 1840 the passage of the independent treasury.[49]

He had to face the final struggle with Nicholas Biddle before his policy achieved victory. The national resumption of specie payments in 1838 found Biddle's bank in an increasingly unstable position. "There is scarcely anything vicious and unsound in banking," wrote William Graham Sumner of Biddle's policy in these last years, "which the great bank did not illustrate." [50] Biddle himself left the sinking ship in March, 1839, but his policy lingered on. For a time the Bank hoped to conceal its own condition by tricky financial operations which would cause the New York banks to suspend first. When this scheme failed, it closed its doors on October 9, carrying down with it most of the banks of the country except those of New York and New England. As late as October 23 it was still trying to organize runs on the New York banks; but Albert Gallatin and Samuel Ward held them firm. Ward, who rose from a sickbed for the fight, suffered a relapse and died shortly after.[51]

The second suspension produced Gallatin's mature judgment of the Bank. It was the judgment of a man who in 1832 had supported re-charter, and few businessmen of the day would have contradicted it.

That bank, subsequent to the first general suspension of May, 1837, has been the principal, if not the sole, cause of the delay in resuming and of the subsequent suspensions. In every respect it has been a public nuisance. The original error consisted in the ambitious attempt to control and direct the commerce of the coun-

[48] Francis P. Blair to Van Buren, August 26, 1838, Van Buren Papers.
[49] For able technical criticism of Van Buren's political management during these years, see Hammond, *History of Political Parties in New-York*, II, 530–531; also George Bancroft to U. S. Grant, March 5, 1869, Howe, *Bancroft*, II, 225.
[50] Sumner, *Jackson*, 340.
[51] Sumner, *History of Banking in the United States*, 305.

try; in the arrogant assumption of a pretended right to decide on the expediency of performing that which was an absolute duty; and in the manifest and deliberate deviation from the acknowledged principles of sound and legitimate banking. . . . The mismanagement and gross neglect, which could in a few years devour two-thirds of a capital of thirty-five millions, are incomprehensible, and have no parallel in the history of banks. . . . It is due to the moral feeling of this country, not less than to the security of its financial concerns, that this disgraced and dangerous corporation should not be permitted any longer to exist.[52]

The elder statesman of American finance had delivered his verdict. In the end it agreed strangely with that of General Jackson.

The second suspension heightened the public sentiment in favor of divorce. A new Congress was elected with the subtreasury as an issue. The plan, tirelessly reintroduced by Silas Wright, went steadily through Senate and House, complete with a specie clause scheduled to go into full effect in 1843. On July 4, 1840, Van Buren finally signed what Blair had called the second Declaration of Independence. The evening before, loyal Democrats crowded Tammany Hall for a celebration. The speakers, raising cheer after cheer from the excited audience, represented exactly a union of the forces which had triumphed: Benjamin F. Butler, the middle-class liberal; Seth Luther, the champion of labor; and Theophilus Fisk, well on his way to becoming a pure Calhoun anticapitalist.[53]

In the meantime Van Buren performed by executive order the second great service of his administration. On March 31 he declared that no person should labor more than ten hours a day on federal public works, and that this should go into effect without a reduction of wages.[54] This measure was an unmistakable declaration that the people's government would act on behalf of the people as freely as in the past the capitalists' government had acted on behalf of the capitalists. The Whigs promptly cried that Van Buren was infringing on the right to work and demanded that pay be reduced correspondingly.

[52] Gallatin, "Suggestions on the Banks and Currency" (1841), *Writings*, III, 406. But many businessmen (and some historians) clung to the myth. Henry C. Carey, for example, a respected conservative economist as well as a man with "practical" business experience, wrote letter after letter to Nathan Appleton in 1840 begging him to desist from attacks on the Bank. See Appleton Papers.

[53] *New York New Era*, July 4; *New York Evening Post*, July 6, 1840.

[54] Richardson, *Messages and Papers*, III, 602. A ten-hour day already existed in the navy yards at New York and Philadelphia, but the hours were sunrise to sunset at Portsmouth, Boston, Norfolk, Washington and Pensacola. "Statement of the Working Hours at the Different Navy Yards," March 27, 1840, Van Buren Papers.

Said Horace Greeley, the great alleged friend of labor: "We do not regard this measure as promising any great benefit." The length of a day's labor should be left to "mutual agreement. . . . What have Governments and Presidents to do with it?" [55]

But Van Buren might have felt repaid for all the uproar if he could have read the words which Michael Shiner, the free Negro who worked in the Washington Navy Yard, wrote painfully years later: "the Working Class of people of the United States Machanic and laboures ought to never forget the Hon ex president Van Buren for the ten hour sistom. . . . May the lord Bless Mr Van Buren it seimes like they have forgot Mr Van Buren his name ought to be Recorded in evry Working Man heart." [56]

The calm, smiling little President might have had a worse epitaph. He governed during years of strain and anxiety, burdened with stern decisions, cluttered by the wreck of friendships and the clash of loyalties. For those on the firing lines the years cast themselves inevitably in the image of a battlefield. In a poem in the *Democratic Review*, William Cullen Bryant expressed for all the fighters the sorrows, the misgivings, the terrible loneliness, and the ultimate hope: —

> A friendless warfare! lingering long
> Through weary day and weary year;
> A wild and many-weaponed throng
> Hang on thy front and flank and rear.
>
> Yet nerve thy spirit to the proof,
> And blench not at thy chosen lot;
> The timid good may stand aloof,
> The sage may frown — yet faint thou not!
>
> *   *   *
>
> Truth, crushed to earth, shall rise again!
> The eternal years of God are her's;
> But Error, wounded, writhes with pain
> And dies among his worshippers. [57]

[55] *Log Cabin*, May 30, 1840. For other conservative comment, see, for example, *Boston Advertiser*, April 13 *et seq.*, 1840; *Greenfield Gazette*, quoted in the *Boston Post*, May 4, 1840.

[56] Michael Shiner, manuscript diary, Library of Congress, p. 77. The omitted sentences read: "for when they youster have to work in the Hot Broiling sun from sun to sun when they wher Building the treasure office Befor he gave the time from six to 6 the laboures youster have to go ther and get the Bricks and Mortar up on the scaffold Befor the Masons came until the president ishued a proclamation that all the Mechanics and labourours that wher employed By the day By the federal government Should Work the ten hour Sistom."

[57] Bryant, "The Battlefield," *Democratic Review*, i, 16 (October, 1837).

XXII THE WHIG COUNTER-REFORMATION

T HE PRESIDENCY of Jackson accomplished a revolution in political values. It destroyed neo-Federalism as a public social philosophy and restated fundamentally the presuppositions of American political life. No one ever again could talk with hope of success in the language of Fisher Ames, of Chancellor Kent, of Jeremiah Mason.

1

To those accustomed to regard the vocabulary of Federalism as absolutely descriptive of society, its disappearance meant the end of a world. Old-school conservatives exchanged lamentations, looked darkly into the future and sank into ever blacker gloom. "I think that our experiment of self government approaches to a total failure," observed William Sullivan of Massachusetts. "My opinion is," said Chancellor Kent, "that the admission of universal suffrage and a licentious press are incompatible with government and security to property, and that the government and character of this country are going to ruin." In 1837 Kent, drinking the waters of Saratoga in company with gentlemen of like mind, reported that all the talk was on the "sad hopes of self-governing democracies." "We are going to destruction," he summed it up with a kind of mournful relish, "— all checks and balances and institutions in this country are threatened with destruction from the ascendancy of the democracy of numbers and radicalism and the horrible doctrine and influence of Jacksonism." [1]

The same year the aged conservative publicist Noah Webster set forth a plan to halt the disintegration and reconstruct society according to Federalist principles. While the American people, he said, were not divided into orders, like the nobility and commoners of Britain, "the distinction of rich and poor does exist, and must always exist; no human power or device can prevent it." Would it not be

---

[1] Sullivan to Nathan Appleton, February 29, 1832, Appleton Papers; Kent to Moss Kent, April 3, 1835, William Kent, *Memoirs and Letters of James Kent, LL.D.*, 218; J. T. Horton, *James Kent. A Study in Conservatism*, 318 n.

sensible, then, to recognize this distinction in the structure of government? After all, "the man who has half a million of dollars in property . . . has a much higher interest in government, than the man who has little or no property." Let us therefore end the popular election of Presidents, for the "great mass of people are and always must be very incompetent judges." Let us destroy the theory that the rich exploit the poor, and that corporations are "aristocratic in their tendency"; these are among the "most pernicious doctrines that ever cursed a nation." Let us divide the electorate into two classes, "the qualifications of one of which shall be superior age, and the possession of a certain amount of property," and let each class choose one house of Congress. Thus the supremacy of property may be assured, and America yet saved from democracy.[2]

This proposal was the last gasp of Federalism. The mere act of stating such a program, after eight years of General Jackson, showed how unreal Federalism had become. No politician could espouse such ideas. No populace would submit to them. Not only were they dead, but the corpses were fatal to the touch.

Their death was not, however, as cataclysmic for everyone as it was for the Websters and Kents. Conservatism was a political party as well as a social faith; and, while the guardians of the faith were cherishing it in all its purity, the leaders of the party were quietly making a series of minor practical adjustments, entered into piecemeal and prescribed by the technical necessity of getting votes. Success rather than doctrinal soundness was their test: if the hallowed principles of Federalism did not work, they would have to go. Many conservatives, moreover, were themselves in part infected by the ideals of Jackson and hoped sincerely to reconcile these ideals with the continued rule of the business classes.

The result was the emergence of a new temper for conservatism — a temper whose characteristics paid tribute to both the political and moral strength of Jackson. It influenced first the neighborhood politicians, then the state organizations, and reached the heads of the party almost last, because the Websters and Clays were farthest from the people and most committed to the ancient dogmas. But it reached them too, and they modified, remolded and extemporized in conformity to the new moods they dimly felt. In this way, fresh elements made their way into conservative thought and almost transformed it before anyone knew what was happening.

[2] [Noah Webster], *Letter to the Hon. Daniel Webster, on the Political Affairs of the United States*, 15, 17, 19, 22, 16.

2

First to go was the basic Hamiltonian theory of the relationship of power and property within the state. Daniel Webster had set forth that theory with great cogency in 1820. "There is not a more dangerous experiment," he said, "than to place property in the hands of one class, and political power in those of another. . . . If property cannot retain the political power, the political power will draw after it the property." The supporters of universal suffrage must thus expect "that property should be as equally divided as political power." [3] What then was to happen when political power was, in fact, passed on to the relatively propertyless by the broadening of the suffrage?

John Taylor of Caroline had already given the answer in meeting a similar argument of John Adams. "It is true, as Mr. Adams asserts, . . . 'that wealth, is the great machine for governing the world.' Hence wealth, like suffrage, must be considerably distributed, to sustain a democratick republick." [4] Was not Webster now committed by his own premises to promoting such widespread distribution? Had he not himself written that there was no more dangerous experiment than to "place property in the hands of one class, and political power in those of another"?

Webster and his fellows were not disposed to sacrifice their loyalties and interests to their logic. Accordingly they quietly abandoned the theory which had been the keystone of Federalism and prepared to justify the very situation which Webster had earlier described as the "dangerous experiment."

Freed from the theory of the relations of power and property, conservatism was now in a position to dispense with certain of its corollaries, especially with the increasingly embarrassing views of social classes held by the early Federalists. The problem of government, Justice Story had once said, was "how the property-holding part of the community may be sustained against the inroads of poverty and vice." [5] But now that "poverty and vice" had been granted the vote, it was essential to discover some less insulting way of talking about them. The radicals, moreover, were beginning to turn Federalist axioms against the Federalists with great political effect. The Hamiltonian demonstrations of the innate hostility of numbers to wealth,

[3] Webster, "The Law of Creditor and Debtor," *North American Review*, XI, 206–207 (July, 1820).

[4] Taylor, *Inquiry*, 274–275.

[5] *Journal of Debates and Proceedings in the Convention . . . to Revise the Constitution of Massachusetts*, 286.

for example, now appeared powerful proof of the innate hostility of wealth to numbers. The result in votes lost of this restatement of their own argument impelled the conservatives to work out more affectionate theories of the relationship between the "rich and well-born" and the masses.

In place of the class-conflict doctrines of Federalism, conservatism began to dwell on various theories of the identity of class interests. "Never was an error more pernicious," exclaimed Dr. Robert Hare, the eminent Philadelphia scientist, "than that of supposing that any separation could be practicable between the interests of the rich and the working classes. However selfish may be the disposition of the wealthy, they cannot benefit themselves without serving the labourer." (The moral was plain enough: "If the labouring classes are desirous of having the prosperity of the country restored, they must sanction all measures tending to reinstate our commercial credit, without which the wealthy will be impoverished.")[6]

Not only were the interests of the classes identical, but there were, come to think of it, no classes at all in America. Daniel Webster became the chief champion of this view, as he had been the champion of the opposing view two decades before. In Europe, he would admit, there was a "clear and well defined line, between capital and labor," but "we have no such visible and broad distinction."[7] "These phrases, *higher orders*, and *lower orders*, are of European origin, and have no place in our Yankee dialect," a conservative critic of Seth Luther could observe five years before Noah Webster made a final attempt to erect a Federalist republic upon them.[8]

If there were no class distinctions, then there were two possibilities: everyone might be a workingman, or everyone might be a capitalist. The conservatives adopted both theories. Edward Everett unabashedly told a hard-handed audience from Charlestown in 1830 that he was a workingman as well as they; and the *New-England Magazine* exploded angrily at those who got up the cry of workeyism, "as if, forsooth, every man in New-England did not work."[9]

But the other view was in the long run more popular. As Edward Everett remarked in 1838, the paths of wealth are open to all; "the

---

[6] Robert Hare, *Suggestions Respecting the Reformation of the Banking System*, 28–29.

[7] Webster in the Senate, March 12, 1838, *Congressional Globe*, 25 Congress 2 Session, Appendix, 633.

[8] Josiah Bigelow, *Review of Seth Luther's Address to the Working Men of New England*, 23.

[9] Edward Everett, *Lecture on the Working Men's Party*; "Radicalism," *New-England Magazine*, VIII, 143 (February, 1835).

wheel of fortune is in constant operation, and the poor in one generation furnish the rich of the next." "Every American laborer," wrote
Calvin Colton, "can stand up proudly, and say, I AM THE AMERICAN
CAPITALIST, which is not a metaphor but literal truth." And the conclusion? "The blow aimed at the moneyed capitalist strikes over on
the head of the laborer, and is sure to hurt the latter more than the
former." [10]

The theory of mutual dependence found its best expression in a
political issue in the wages argument for the protective tariff. The
people who in the eighteen-twenties had complained that high wages
hindered the development of manufacturing, and even favored closing
the frontier to keep wages down, now suddenly advanced as the main
argument for a high tariff that it would keep wages up and preserve the
American workingman from competition with pauper labor abroad.
(The advocates of this argument, however, rarely hesitated to import
pauper labor and carry on the competition at home.) In this manner,
protection was transformed into a workingmen's measure and thrust
forward as evidence of the identity of class interests. [11]

3

As an associated strategy, the business community worked out
a kind of pastoral mythology about the laboring classes, describing
the beauty of the relations between capital and labor, and hinting,
sometimes not too subtly, that the workingman was far happier than
the wealthy capitalist. The propertyless classes, once a menace to
social stability, now became the sturdy core of the nation. Manufacturing was portrayed with almost lyric delight. Lowell, for example,
was transfigured from an early factory town into an idyl. "Nothing,"
observed Edward Everett flatly, "can exceed the comfort & elegance
of the recently constructed mills." [12] The employment of women was
simply another charming feature of the scene, reminiscent almost of
Marie Antoinette in the forests of Versailles. "Does not the spectacle
present, in a delightful aspect, the operation and effect of our truly
republican institutions?" asked a Boston paper. [13] The *Boston Courier*

[10] Everett, *Address Delivered before the Mercantile Library Association,* 13;
[Calvin Colton], "Junius," *Labor and Capital,* 11, 14.
[11] G. B. Mangold, *The Labor Argument in the American Protective Tariff Discussion.* For an excellent critical examination of this argument, see W. F. Stolper
and P. A. Samuelson, "Protection and Real Wages," *Review of Economic Studies,*
IX, 58–73.
[12] Everett to Henry Holland, July 25, 1848, Everett Papers.
[13] *Boston Courier,* quoted in *Niles' Register,* July 6, 1833. Cf. the *Register,*

gave the essence of Whig pastoralism when it ran the "Song of the
Manchester Factory Girl": —

> O sing me a song of the Factory Girl
>   So merry and glad and free —
> The bloom on her cheeks, of health it speaks! —
>   O a happy creature is she!
>
> She tends the loom, she watches the spindle,
>   And cheerfully talketh away;
> Mid the din of wheels, how her bright eyes kindle!
>   And her bosom is ever gay.
>
> * * *
>
> O sing me a song of the Factory Girl!
>   Link not her name with the SLAVES. —
> She is brave and free as the old elm tree,
>   That over her homestead waves.[14]

This pastoral literature depicted the lot of the wealthy as weary and
harassed, a grim contrast to the carefree life of the workers. The
title of Catharine M. Sedgwick's didactic novel *The Poor Rich Man,
and the Rich Poor Man* made the point concisely. The poor man, in
other words, must not envy the rich man, because wealth brings
cares, and poverty permits one to make of his own life something
finer than gold. According to William Ellery Channing, the famous
Unitarian preacher, the hardships of the working classes were greatly
exaggerated; "it may be doubted whether they have not the easiest
lot," compared to the struggles and disappointments of lawyers, doc-
tors and merchants. "That some of the indigent among us die of
scanty food is undoubtedly true," Channing conceded; "but vastly
more in this community die from eating too much than from eating
too little." Doubtless some of the poor may shiver from want of
clothing, but it is much less than the suffering among the rich "from
absurd and criminal modes of dress which fashion has sanctioned."
The poor perhaps are sometimes overworked; but "how many of our
daughters are victims of *ennui*, a misery unknown to the poor, and
more intolerable than the weariness of excessive toil!" [15]

As a final strategy, to take care of those whom pastoralism did not

---

April 30, 1836: "The 'employment of females' is one of the secrets of the wealth
of New England — and the girls are much the better for it."

[14] By John H. Warland, who also wrote many Whig campaign songs. J. T.
Buckingham, *Personal Memoirs and Recollections of Editorial Life*, II, 207–209.

[15] Channing to Elizabeth P. Peabody, September, 1840, E. P. Peabody, *Reminiscences of Rev. Wm. Ellery Channing*, 415; *Niles' Register*, August 8, 1835.

altogether convince, there developed the doctrine of internal reform. The main point of this theory was to dissuade humanitarian energies from seeking economic change. Channing's conception of the "elevation of the labouring classes" defined the field of reform. 'It is not an outward change of condition. It is not release from labour. It is not struggling for another rank. It is not political power. I understand something deeper. I know but one elevation of a human being, and that is Elevation of Soul." [16] Political and economic action, in other words, was useless and should be discouraged. As Channing told some English miners in 1841, "Your true strength lies in growing intelligence, uprightness, self-respect, trust in God, and trust in one another. These cannot fail to secure to you your just share of social privileges." [17]

Channing's doctrine enabled men of good will to indulge an honest compassion for the working classes without facing the economic implications of the problem. One reformer of this persuasion, for example, ended an address on pauperism by asking what could be done about low wages. "Legislation can do nothing; combinations among the working classes could probably effect no permanent remedy. It must be left to the justice and mercy of the employer." [18] The labors of the social worker Joseph Tuckerman, in Boston, showed how far the doctrine of internal reform sanctioned private attempts to atone for the imperfections of the "justice and mercy of the employer," but the employer himself was to be left sacrosanct. It is not recorded whether laboring men were much consoled by this doctrine. It is certain, however, that Channing's theory was most successful in relieving the conscience of the upper middle class.

This complex of attitudes — the identity of interests between the classes, the unimportance of class, the nonexistence of class, the superior happiness of the laborer, the necessity for internal reform — satisfied the feeling of the business community in all the shades of ambivalence, from the compulsions toward power to the lurking intuitions of guilt. It represented a vigorous and versatile strategy, finding enormous support in the hopes of American life and a certain support in its realities. The Democrats were never quite able to meet it.

[16] Channing, *Lectures on the Elevation of the Labouring Portion of the Community*, 15.

[17] Channing to the Mechanic Institute of Slaithwaite, England, March 1, 1841, W. H. Channing, *Memoir of William Ellery Channing*, III, 57. When a Cornish laborer quoted a fellow artisan as having said that Channing's writings had "reconciled him to being a working man," Channing broke into tears of joy. Frances A. Kemble, *Records of Later Life*, 355.

[18] R. C. Waterston, *Address on Pauperism, Its Extent, Causes, and the Best Means of Prevention*, 35.

They often tried to defeat the argument of mutual interests on a logical level. "Let no man deceive himself by the plausible and beautiful theory that all classes in the body politic have a mutual dependence," warned Francis Pickens. ". . . Let no man suppose that that which adds power and profit to a specie of capital necessarily has a corresponding effect upon labor. I utterly deny the ingenious doctrine . . . that there is no such thing in this country as capital and labor; that all are capitalists and all are laborers." "There is but one state of society in the world," added Barnwell Rhett — and here he gave the conclusive answer to the Whig doctrine — "where labor and capital are identical in interest; and that is where domestic slavery exists. . . . In such a form of society, there is no collision between capital and labor." [19]

Orestes A. Brownson provided a more caustic refutation: —

The lamb is necessary to the wolf; for without the lamb the wolf might want a dinner; and the wolf is necessary to the lamb, for without the wolf the lamb might fail to be eaten. "Therefore," says the benevolent wolf to the lamb, "do not be hostile to us, nor excite your brother lambs against us; for you see we wolves and you lambs are mutually necessary to each other. We are dependent on you for something to eat, as you are on us to be eaten." "But I don't want to be eaten," exclaims the lamb in great trepidation. "Not want to be eaten!" replies the wolf. "Now that's odd. You and I are very far from thinking alike, and I must needs consider you very unreasonable, and radical in your mode of thinking." [20]

The radicals similarly sought to counteract pastoralism by exposing the supposed horrors of mill life. Where the Whigs sang of the merry factory maiden, the Democrats presented a more melancholy picture: —

'Twas on a winter's morning,
 The weather was wet and wild,
Three hours before the dawning,
 The father roused his child;
Her daily morsel bringing,
 The darksome room he paced,
And cried, "The bell is ringing,
 My hapless darling, haste."

[19] Pickens in the House, June 19, 1838, Rhett in the House, June 25, 1838, *Congressional Globe*, 25 Congress 2 Session, Appendix, 429–430, 506.
[20] "Conversations with a Radical," *Boston Quarterly Review*, IV, 35–36 (January, 1841). For an earlier version, *Boston Reformer*, July 21, 1837.

"Father, I'm up, but weary,
   I scarce can reach the door,
And long the way and dreary —
   O, carry me once more!
To help us we've no mother,
   And you have no employ;
They killed my little brother, —
   Like him I'll work and die!"

Her wasted form seemed nothing,
   The load was at his heart,
The sufferer he kept soothing,
   Till at the mill they part.
The overlooker met her,
   As to her frame she crept,
And with his thong he beat her,
   And cursed her as she wept.[21]

They struggled against the creed of internal reform. Brownson, again, brilliantly set forth its futility. "The plain English of it is, perfect the individual before you undertake to perfect society; make your men perfect, before you seek to make your institutions perfect." But does not this make perfection of institutions the end, and perfection of individuals the means? "Perfect all your men, and no doubt, you could then perfect easily and safely your institutions. But when all your men are perfect, what need of perfecting your institutions? And wherein are those institutions, under which all individuals may attain to the full perfection admitted by human nature, imperfect?"[22] But logic was a frail weapon against a cluster of belief which filled such urgent inner needs.

4

Conservatism was not content simply with pressing conciliatory alternatives to Democratic theories of class conflict. It went on the offensive itself, and when the radicals charged that conservatives favored the rule of an aristocracy, the conservatives began to answer that the Democrats favored the rule of a despot. The issue, they said, was not class tyranny but executive tyranny. The basic conflict was not between exploiters and exploited, but between the governors and the governed. The main threat to liberty came, not from a propertied

---

[21] *Bay State Democrat*, February 22, 1840.
[22] *Boston Quarterly Review*, I, 127 (January, 1838).

class, but from a bureaucratic class. The people should rise and rebuke the pretensions, not of wealth, but of government.

While Webster had planted the seed of this argument at the time of the Bank veto, and the followers of Calhoun nurtured it in the struggle over nullification, it did not reach full flower till the removal of the deposits. Then "executive despotism" provided a platform with room for all the enemies of Jackson, pro-Bank or anti-Bank, broad-construction or State-rights, North or South; and it allowed the Bank to substitute for recharter the "fresher and far more popular issue" of redressing a great wrong committed by an arbitrary and unconstitutional exercise of executive authority.[23]

Webster, Clay and Calhoun submerged their rivalries in a formidable agreement that the encroachments of the White House threatened the very existence of freedom. Who would have believed, exclaimed the *New York American*, that "in this land of liberty, *all* the powers of our national government would be usurped by a single man, possessing no one qualification for any single trust, and who, like a maniac, or a driveller, should make it his daily pastime to tear our constitutional charter into rags and tatters, and trample the rights of the people under his feet?" "OUR LIBERTIES ARE IN DANGER," roared the New York Whig convention of 1834. "At this moment, if by your votes you concede the powers that are claimed, your *president* has become your MONARCH." The independent treasury — "a measure," according to Joseph Story, "designed to concentrate in the executive department the whole power over the currency of the country" — came in 1837 as further evidence of Democratic intentions.[24]

How real were these apprehensions? Jackson certainly made the presidency more powerful than it had ever been before. He used the veto power, for example, more than all his predecessors put together. The fear of executive despotism, moreover, is no fancy, as the experience of the one-party states of the twentieth century clearly shows. Yet it seems unlikely that many raised this cry against Jackson who would not have fought him anyway. The charge of tyrant has been made against every strong democratic President by those whose interests he threatens.

[23] For Van Buren's keen analysis, *Autobiography*, 658–659.

[24] *New York American*, October 4, 1833; *Niles' Register*, October 4, 1834; Story to Harriet Martineau, January 19, 1839, Story, *Life and Letters*, II, 308. Some of the Whig statements are very sweeping. "The legislative power, as established by the constitution, has been mastered, bound, enslaved," said the *American Monthly Magazine* in 1837; ". . . all its essential functions have been assumed by, and absorbed in, the executive alone." This pundit warned that "our condition will shortly be little better than that of the miserable Russian serfs" — which suggests that even the horrible example of Russia is not an invention of the twentieth century. "The Times," *American Monthly Magazine*, IV, 215–216 (September, 1837).

From Federalist days, furthermore, the traditional conservative position had been to distrust the legislative and aggrandize the executive. Alexander Hamilton had favored a President chosen for life; it was John Taylor of Caroline who set forth the arguments against executive despotism. But the actualities of the eighteen-thirties were simply that the Democrats possessed the executive; and it looked very much as if the greatest potentialities for democratic action might continue to reside in the executive rather than in the legislative. Accordingly conservatism abandoned its historic position and emerged as the champion of congressional prerogative — a role it has tended to play ever since.

5

Before conservatism was streamlined for the post-Jacksonian world, it had to rid itself of the social exclusiveness so characteristic of Federalism. The Federalists had dressed differently, talked differently, behaved differently, and were exceedingly proud of the difference. Gentlemen, in their view, should enjoy a monopoly of government, and the lower orders must accept their place. "A farmer never looks so well as when he has a hand upon the plough," observed a Boston paper as late as 1834; "with his huge paw upon the statutes what can he do? It is as proper for a blacksmith to attempt to repair watches, as a farmer, in general, to legislate." [25]

Such expressions of aristocratic superiority, once the badges of gentlemanhood, were becoming more and more invitations to the abuse of the rising and irreverent democracy. Distinctions in dress began to disappear. Politicians found they must assume increasingly the manner and language of the common man.

Early in the Bank War, it became clear that the most effective opponents of General Jackson were the cracker-box pundits, drawling to the people in their own accent, countering the fighting democracy of the Jacksonians with the homely conservatism and complacent wisdom of the village sage. Major Jack Downing, as depicted by Charles A. Davis, friend of Nicholas Biddle and director of the New York branch of the Bank, was a better advocate than all the Websters and Clays of the Senate. Jackson, in the Downing papers, was a vain, pettish old man, played upon by those wily villains, Van Buren and Amos "Kindle," while the character of kindly Squire Biddle gave an artless picture of the benevolence of the Bank. "There is one kind of *monied aristocracy* I am plaguy afeard of," Major Jack would say, promoting the new emphasis on the dangers of bureaucracy, "— and that is when politicians manage to git hold of the money of the people,

[25] *Boston Courier*, June 28, 1834.

and keep turnin it to their own account." "It ain't in the natur of things, for people who have got money to lend, to do any thing agin the gineral prosperity of the country. . . . Whenever they take a hand in politics, it is to prevent politicians gettings things wrong eend first." And so on; only the cynical could resist this rustic sagacity.[26]

Conservatism was definitely in the market for homespun. Its first great showpiece was Colonel Davy Crockett of Tennessee. The tough, lanky frontiersman, black-haired and dressed in buckskin, with his honest drawl and miraculous tall talk, was authentically of the people. Elected to Congress from the shakes of Tennessee, he had burst upon Washington first in 1827. "I'm David Crockett," he had told them, according to the familiar story, "fresh from the backwoods, half horse, half alligator, a little touched with snapping turtle. I can wade the Mississippi, leap the Ohio, ride a streak of lightning, slip without a scratch down a honey locust, whip my weight in wildcats, hug a bear too close for comfort and eat any man opposed to Jackson!" [27]

But Crockett broke with the administration over some land bills and was defeated in 1831. Re-elected in 1833, he returned to Washington as homely evidence of the revolt of the common man against the despotic government. The Whigs took him up, invented anecdotes in his name and in the spring of 1834 sent him on a tour of the Northeast. He attended banquets, inspected factories, defended the Bank and dutifully blamed the depression on Jackson. Visiting Lowell under supervision of Abbott Lawrence, he faithfully added his own testimony to the idyllic picture of mill life in Massachusetts. Corrupted by the flattery of the best citizens, Crockett had lost some of the flavor of 1827. "I was very genteel and quiet," he remarked of himself, "and so I suppose I disappointed some . . . who expected to see a half horse half alligator sort of fellow." [28]

The victory of the administration in the fight over the deposits embittered him. In 1835, an increasingly disappointed man, he lent his

[26] [C. A. Davis], *Letters of J. Downing, Major*, 227. The character was actually invented by Seba Smith of the *Portland Courier* in 1830, though Davis's series was brighter and probably more widely read. See James, *Jackson: Portrait of a President*, 604; *Boston Post*, February 28, 1834. The competition for the character was heated. Even the workingmen employed it, and the *New England Artisan* printed letters from Downingville saying, "I see by reading your truly republikin paper, that the Mechanicks up there in Boston have bin formin a Trades' Union. . . . i think it is time for the workinmen to *begin* to do sumthin for themselves, and no longer be under the influence of monoperlists and lawyers." Etc. *Working Man's Advocate*, June 21, 1834.

[27] Constance Rourke, *Davy Crockett*, 128–129.

[28] Crockett, *Life of Col. David Crockett, Written by Himself*, 218. The actual authorship of this work is doubtful. See also Walter Blair, "Six Davy Crocketts," *Southwest Review*, XXV, 443–462.

name to a savage *Life of Martin Van Buren*, written by A. S. Clayton of Georgia in the interests of the White campaign.[29] Defeated soon for re-election, he resentfully left Tennessee for Texas. "Before I will submit to his Government," Crockett once said of Van Buren, "I will go to the wildes of Texas." [30] But, when Van Buren became President, Crockett was silent forever. True in the end to his best nature, he had fallen heroically at the Alamo before the guns and knives of Santa Anna.

General William Henry Harrison was the first beneficiary in presidential politics of the literary triumphs of Major Downing and Colonel Crockett. A military hero, a Westerner, living modestly in Ohio, without pretensions, even without personality, he became the spontaneous choice of those who did not care for the Jacksonian policy but yet were partially seduced by the Jacksonian emotions. Harrison's popular vote in 1836 astounded the professionals.

6

The metamorphosis of conservatism revived it politically but ruined it intellectually. The Federalists had thought about society in an intelligent and hard-boiled way. Their ideas had considerable relevance to the conflicts and tensions of the life around them. But the Whigs, in scuttling Federalism, replaced it by a social philosophy founded, not on ideas, but on subterfuges and sentimentalities. As Henry Adams observed, "Of all the parties that have existed in the United States, the famous Whig party was the most feeble in ideas." [31]

Federalism and Whiggery represented the same interests in society, the same aspirations for power, the same essential economic policies; but Federalism spoke of these interests, aspirations and policies in a tone of candor, Whiggery, of evasion. The vocabulary of Federalism had something to do with actualities; it was useful as a scheme of analysis; it aided one's understanding of society. The vocabulary of Whiggery had nothing to do with actualities; it was useful mainly as a disguise; its object was to promote confusion rather than comprehension. Both intended to serve the business classes, but the revolution in political values forced the Whigs to talk as if they intended primarily to serve the common man.[32]

[29] J. D. Wade, "The Authorship of David Crockett's 'Autobiography,' " *Georgia Historical Quarterly*, VI, 265–268.

[30] Crockett to Charles Shultz, December 25, 1834, *Magazine of History*, XXV, 75–76.

[31] Adams, *Gallatin*, 635.

[32] "Whatever we may think generally of the older Hamiltonians, we must con-

The greatest intellectual casualty of the new Whig line was Daniel Webster. A man of powerful intelligence, with a taste for' general ideas and a concern for broad social questions, he had been trained in the Federalist school and thus equipped with many cogent and honest notions about government. His speeches and articles in 1820 represent perhaps the classic formulations of Federalism. But the theory of power and property he expressed so ably permitted only two, lines of development: he could work openly either for the monopoly of property and power by one class, or for the diffusion of property and power among all classes. Webster rejected both the logical alternatives. The first was impossible politically, the second impossible personally. He replaced his Federalism by another set of ideas which, however helpful in concealing Whig purposes, were worse than useless for the understanding of society.

The substitution crippled his thought: a mind divided against itself cannot produce searching social theory. There was no more talk in terms of property and power. Instead, Webster served up huge gobs of senatorial rhetoric. In 1840 his statement of "Whig Principles and Purposes" announced the Whig devotion to free speech and press, free discussion, popular education, the "widest dissemination of knowledge and of truth," public liberty, the Constitution and the Union.[33] The omission of God, home and mother was no doubt accidental. Webster grew increasingly maudlin through the years till he could be heard pleasantly only in the manner recommended by Emerson: "abstracting myself from his sense merely for the luxury of such noble explosions of sound." [34] His massive intelligence, forbidden realistic inquiry into society, wasted itself in rhetoric increasingly overwrought and constitutional argument increasingly scholastic. While Calhoun's social thought, for example, matured and developed, nourished by his severe and unrelenting attention to actualities, Webster's philosophy dwindled into a set of Jeffersonian platitudes, uttered without conviction.

The dilemma of those who tried to maintain their private convictions and live an intellectual double life was exhibited in the case of Calvin Colton. The close friend and official biographer of Henry Clay, a Whig pamphleteer and general party handy man, Colton was a Yale graduate who left a successful career in the ministry for an even more

---

cede them an honorable distinction: they did not claim to be Jeffersonians." F. W. Coker, "American Traditions Concerning Property and Liberty," *American Political Science Review*, XXX, 5. This article is a very able analysis of this same problem in relation to contemporary Republican ideas.

[33] Webster, *Works*, II, 41–52.
[34] Emerson, *Journals*, VI, 341–342.

successful career as editor and propagandist. The series of political tracts he wrote under the name of Junius present the most complete and forceful statement of all the new Whig positions — pastoralism, class harmony, the struggle against executive despotism, the essential democracy of the Whig party. Yet, they were very far from expressing Colton's secret views. Evidently unable to rest in silence, but unwilling to jeopardize his party, he published anonymously in London in 1839 a book called *A Voice from America to England* and signed *By an American Gentleman.*

A Voice from America was a frank, thoughtful and intelligent book. American society, Colton argued, had manifested two opposite tendencies, "one towards the lowest level of democracy, and the other towards a spiritual supremacy." The Constitution was "framed by men who foresaw the tendency of the public mind towards democracy, and who purposely constructed this instrument to arrest the downward progress." Since 1788 "the great struggle in America, and that on which the fate of the Republic is suspended, is between the Constitution and the Democracy." On one side is a conservative party which desires "a return of the people to the good sense which characterized the framers," on the other a radical party "which threatens a dissolution and overthrow of the republic." The advantage in this struggle lay with the radicals because of their resort to opportunistic and demagogic tactics.

The result, Colton pointed out with some care, had been to make *democracy* "a word of deep meaning and great potency in America. No political party can dispense with it there. Whatever their principles, radical or conservative, their best passport is democracy." The present leaders of the conservative party, he said, were "perfectly aware of the apostasy from these [constitutional] principles in the actual Government of the country"; they were perfectly aware of the menace of radicalism; but, he continued significantly, "the delicate position of the most elevated statesmen, on whom devolves the greatest responsibility, may suggest caution, and impose silence on their lips, not allowing them to utter all that they fear." [35]

Colton's own delicate position eventually imposed the same silence on his lips, and that silence became imperative for any conservative with serious political ambitions. The result was the breakdown of Whig thought. A whole flock of neo-Jeffersonians appeared, led by Horace Greeley and Daniel D. Barnard of New York, to stage a boarding party against Democratic principles and rally the business community under the stolen banners. Barnard would trace his party

[35] [Calvin Colton], *A Voice from America*, vii, 45, 57, 220, 3, 220.

back to the "republican doctrines" of 1798. The policy of other governments, he said, has been to perpetuate property in a few hands,
while our policy is "to distribute and equalize it, as far as may be
without interfering with individual right, and the due encouragement
of individual exertion." (He went on to explain that he knew "no
instrumentality more efficient for both objects, than that of our
private corporations.") [36]

But in the midst of Barnard's letter-perfect Jeffersonianism the old
Hamiltonian emotions constantly reappeared. He would discourse on
the people, for example, their inalienable rights, their perfect equality,
and yet they are "credulous; easily imposed on; apt to be deceived;
susceptible of flattery; vain; trusting to appearances where there is no
reality; and dazzled and captivated with any shows got up to astonish
or amuse." [37]

The widening chasm between private belief and public profession
took all seriousness out of Whiggery as a social philosophy, turning it
into a miscellaneous collection of stock political appeals, consistent
only in a steady but muted enmity to change. It may be argued, of
course, that the intellectual collapse of conservatism was unimportant,
since the first criterion of a political creed is its success and not its
profundity. Yet it may be speculated whether the repeated failure of
conservatism in this country to govern effectively may not be related
to the increasing flabbiness of conservative thought. Individuals might
continue thinking in Federalist terms, reserving the Whig phrases for
public consumption; but such a thoroughly Machiavellian position is
difficult to sustain. When a party starts out by deceiving the people,
it is likely to finish by deceiving itself.

In the end, as Whiggism became the dominant language, all conservatives more or less had to talk in it, and ultimately most came to
believe it. Politicians so systematically misled as to the character of
society were not likely to provide effective government, unless, like
Mark Hanna, they were Machiavellians, or, like William Howard
Taft, they were possessed of an executive instinct which could triumph
over all illusions.

[36] Barnard, *Speeches and Reports*, 48, 77.
[37] Barnard, *Address Delivered before the Philoclean and Peithessophian Societies
of Rutgers College*, 26.

XXIII 1840

THE ASSIMILATION by conservatism of the new democratic moods came first in the West, where orthodox Federalism had never discovered a social basis. This democratization was, however, mainly an unconscious process. Western leaders like Clay and Harrison, however much they maintained the Hamiltonian policies, could feel no compulsion to repudiate a Hamiltonian social philosophy they had never really possessed. In the East, where class distinctions had kept the Federalist philosophy alive, assimilation of the new values was hardly possible without deliberate rejection of the old, an intellectual exercise not required on the frontier. Among the Whigs of the eighteen-thirties, as among the Democrats, the conscious assertion of radicalism came in the main from the seaboard, not from the forest.

1

The task of conservatism, if it were to succeed in post-Jacksonian America, was to purge itself of the discredited past — manners, principles, issues — and to set the case of the business community on fresh and unspoiled grounds. The conservatives of New York, kept from power for a quarter of a century by the dead hand of Federalism, saw with special clarity the need for a new departure, and two politicians of remarkable ability arose during the thirties to show the way.

William H. Seward and Thurlow Weed represented accurately the double impulse behind the new conservatism. Seward, a man of passion and principle, had a genuine if qualified belief in Jacksonian ideals. Weed, a personal reactionary, had a cynical recognition that Jacksonian professions were necessary for political success. Where, for example, Seward thought New York's constitution of 1821, if anything too conservative, Weed strongly but privately disapproved of it as dangerously radical. Where Seward was a great believer in popular rule and frequent elections, Weed feared, to the end of his life, that universal suffrage would "occasion universal political demoralization, and ultimately overthrow our government" — though this fear never deterred him from encouraging this demoralization when it paid him to do so.[1]

[1] Weed, *Autobiography*, 89–90; F. W. Seward, *Seward*, 50, 76.

New types for New York conservatism, both showed the change from the aloof distinction of a Rufus King. Seward was a small, blue-eyed man, slender and slouching, with wiry red hair, grizzly eyebrows and a big beaked nose. His voice was hoarse, his talk free and colloquial, and he would sprawl about comfortably in disordered clothes, snorting and coughing and puffing huge clouds of smoke from his eternal cigar.[2] Weed, tall, dark, soft-spoken, was the great manipulator, passing out cigars in the lobbies at Albany, stretching long legs in smoke-filled party councils, chatting with mild, ruthless realism on political strategy. (In fifty-four years, according to his own computation, he smoked or gave away at least 80,000 cigars.) For him sincerity was an inessential, when not a handicap. A form of self-delusion from which he was immune, he tended to suspect it in others.[3]

Yet Seward and Weed collaborated in perfect harmony. Each regarded the other's field with a benign approval which resulted in Weed's tolerant association with Seward's crusades, and Seward's with Weed's schemes for public plunder. Though their convictions often differed, their diagnoses and aims converged. The Anti-Masonic movement, that invaluable school for demagoguery, had instilled in both a contempt for the tactics of silk-stocking Federalism. If conservatism were to be profitable in the thirties, they saw that it must capitalize on the prevailing liberalism, not resist it.

"Our party as at present organized," Weed wrote in 1834, "is doomed to fight merely to be beaten. . . . The longer we fight Jacksonianism with our present weapons, *the more it won't die!*" The poor are almost all against us, and continued support of the Bank "will make them unanimously so." Seward was equally emphatic. "It is utterly impossible, I am convinced, to defeat Van Buren," he wrote Weed in 1835. "The people are for him. Not so much for him as for the principle they suppose he represents. That principle is Democracy. . . . It is with them, the poor against the rich; and it is not to be disguised, that, since the last election, the array of parties has very strongly taken that character." What was to be done but for the Whigs themselves to become more democratic than the Democrats? Thus, both favored repudiation of the Bank and adoption of more progressive policies, Seward because he more or less believed in these steps, Weed (who

---

[2] Seward, *Seward*, 238, 481; Henry Adams to C. F. Adams, Jr., December 9, 1860, *Letters of Henry Adams (1858–1891)*, 62; Henry Adams, *Education of Henry Adams* (Modern Library), 104.

[3] Weed, *Autobiography*, 44; Horace Greeley, *Recollections of a Busy Life*, 312; Adams, *Education*, 146-147.

privately thought the Bank "necessary" to the country) because he believed them indispensable for success.[4]

The new tendencies were reinforced, after N. P. Tallmadge's revolution fizzled out in 1838, by the accession of right-wing Democrats bringing with them slightly faded Jeffersonian principles.[5] Weed, meanwhile, in a quest for a man to run a cheap popular weekly setting forth the new ideas, looked up the editor of the *New Yorker*, a literary journal which had occasionally defended the boom, the credit system, speculation and other Whig specialties. He discovered a tall, clumsy man of twenty-six, coat off and sleeves rolled up, standing at the printer's case, peering nearsightedly as he was about to insert another stick of type.[6] This was Horace Greeley, a New Englander, an ardent Whig and a worshiper of Henry Clay. Under Weed's encouragement Greeley founded the *Jeffersonian*, a periodical whose title, tone and language appalled conservatives of an older school. An impulsive warmhearted man, deeply devoted to the people, Greeley could expound the new policy with a fire, wit and conviction of which Weed himself was incapable, perhaps because of his private reservations.

2

The basic Seward strategy was to turn the popular democratic unrest to Whig ends. His accents were often Jacksonian in their vigor. Social inequality, he would say, is the cause of "the ignorance, the crime, and the suffering of the people. Let it excite no wonder when I say that this inequality exists among us." What should be done? "We should be degenerate descendants of our heroic forefathers did we not assail this aristocracy, remove the barriers between the rich and the poor, break the control of the few over the many, extend the largest liberty to the greatest number, and strengthen in every way the democratic principles of our constitution."

Such sentiments might appear inflammatory — but Seward was quick

[4] Weed to Francis Granger, November 23, 1834, E. M. Carroll, *Origins of the Whig Party*, 219–220; Seward to Weed, April 12, 1835, Seward, *Seward*, 257–258. See also Weed, *Autobiography*, 371–372, 424, 431; Fox, *Decline of Aristocracy*, 366 n.

[5] Tallmadge, who could no more compete with Seward and Weed than with Van Buren and Wright, spent his declining years a spiritualist in heated conversations with the ghosts of Webster and Clay; on one occasion he was serenaded by the spirit of John C. Calhoun performing on a guitar. See J. W. Edmonds and George T. Dexter, *Spiritualism*, with an appendix by N. P. Tallmadge (New York, 1853), 393–442. Conservatives had no monopoly on spirit conversations; the bulk of this book is devoted to the spiritualist adventures of John Worth Edmonds of the Regency.

[6] Weed, *Autobiography*, 466.

to remove the sting. "What is the secret of aristocracy?" he would go on to ask. "It is, that knowledge is power. . . . What makes *this* man a common laborer, and the *other* a usurer — *this* man a slave and the *other* a tyrant? Knowledge. . . ." And he would wind up with a plea for more education — excellent enough, but clearly innocuous from the point of view of the business community.[7] "Seward is for *equality*," observed the sardonic Michael Hoffman, " — he wants every man woman child bank city state to owe as deeply as he does."[8] Yet Seward was talking about things and in terms which had no place in the previous conservative scheme. By giving conservative arguments a neo-Jeffersonian coloration, he was helping restore the conservative contact with the masses.

The liberal Whigs in their legislative strategy sought similarly to forestall the Democrats by advocating necessary reforms themselves, proposing thereby to control changes which were in any case inevitable, and thus to insure that reform would come in the shape least distasteful to the business community. The success of this strategy was displayed in the affair of the New York general banking law of 1838. The repeal of the system of special charters, especially for banking, was one of the oldest and most honorable radical demands. Early in 1837 the long campaign carried on in the *Evening Post* and the *Working Man's Advocate*, by Leggett, Bryant and Evans, by A. C. Flagg, Colonel Samuel Young and Preston King, resulted in the repeal of the restraining law upon private banks of discount and deposit. Suspension stimulated the radicals to press for a law which would establish free competition among banks of issue as well. In his message of January 2, 1838, Governor Marcy endorsed this movement.

Conservatism protested by reflex action; but the liberal Whigs suddenly began to see that a general banking law could interfere with business only if it imposed severe restrictions on the issue of paper money, and it would impose such restrictions only if Democrats were allowed to write it. Accordingly, they seized the initiative and in 1838 passed a general law with such slight restrictions that most Democrats felt obliged to vote against it. The Whigs thus captured the credit and minimized the danger of banking reform in a single stroke.[9]

[7] Seward, *Works*, G. E. Baker, ed., III, 209–210.
[8] Hoffman to A. C. Flagg, n.d. (1842?), Flagg Papers.
[9] This law embarrassed hard-money Democrats. Most, like Cambreleng in the House and the *Evening Post*, hailed it as a step in the right direction, while clearly resenting the fact that it had been captured and deformed by Whigs. For Democratic comment, see Cambreleng in the House, May 11, 1838, *Congressional Globe*, 25 Congress 2 Session, 364; *New York Evening Post*, April 18, 20, 1838, March 7,

The lesson was plain. It showed that the formulas of radicalism were not necessarily fatal, and that conservatism, if it had the enterprise to appropriate them, could turn them to its own purposes while winning the reputation for progressivism so essential to success.

But this lesson was not easily learned. Men like Chancellor Kent, Charles King, James Watson Webb were angered at the repudiation of the Bank. They felt that the Seward wing was altogether too equalitarian in tone, too favorably disposed toward foreigners and Negroes, too tolerant of abolitionism. In seeking to imitate Jackson it had surrendered to him. When Philip Hone was told in 1839 not to try for office — "no gentleman can succeed" — he thought bitterly, "If they are right in what they say, the party is not worth sustaining; better it would be that everything should go back to the dunghill of Democracy." "The Whigs are at this day more democratic in their devices and principles than the Democrats were in the days of Jefferson," wrote Horace Binney of Philadelphia with obvious disapproval.[10]

The old guard had its own notion of what kind of appeal to make. It was stated, most explicitly, in the report of the Committee of Merchants in May, 1837. "Omit all those appeals to popular prejudice in which demagogues have found their strength." "Avow your belief that in a great majority of cases the possession of property is the proof of merit." Convince the people that their happiness rests with business, and "that the security and prosperity of merchants cannot be sustained without the aid of a national bank." [11]

This theory, point by point opposed to that of Seward and Weed, exhibited conclusively the main characteristic of the old guard: its utter inability to learn. "I find from the Experience of 40 Years in Politics," Chancellor Kent had written in 1832, "that the more levelling, violent, democratic & unprincipled side of the electoral Contest for Power, is generally successful." [12] When Thurlow Weed made the same observation, he proceeded to act upon it.

But all Seward's eloquence and Weed's cunning could not win over the reactionaries, who remained a steady drag on the new policy. "My principles are too liberal, too philanthropic, if it be not vain to say so, for my party," exclaimed Seward in a moment of weariness in 1841.

December 16, 1839, January 22, 1841; "Free Banking," *Democratic Review*, V, 238 (February, 1839); "The General Banking Law of the State of New York," *ibid.*, V, 427–438 (May, 1839); *Journal of Banking*, January 19, June 8, 1842.

[10] Hone, *Diary*, I, 427; C. C. Binney, *Binney*, 451. See also Weed, *Autobiography*, 372; Seward, *Seward*, 757–758; J. D. Hammond, *Life and Times of Silas Wright*, 290, 482.

[11] *Plaindealer*, May 13, 1837.

[12] Kent to Edward Everett, September 17, 1832, Everett Papers.

"The promulgation of them offends many; the operation of them injures many; and their sincerity is questioned by all." [13]

3

In Massachusetts the Whigs, as a majority party, felt less external pressure to change their tactics than they had in New York. Nevertheless the currents toward democratization were running strong. John Quincy Adams, in his erratic way, encouraged various liberal agitations, and the clear if diffident intelligence of Edward Everett perceived plainly that the old Federalism was dead. Under the influence of the Anti-Masonic movement, with which they both flirted, Adams and Everett led a brief revolt against Daniel Webster and the old guard. Adams assailed Webster without mercy in the House, and Everett, remarking that George Bancroft's radicalism was based on a "good principle viz'. that the ultra Whig policy would injure the State," sought as Governor to steer a relatively liberal course.[14] But in last analysis Adams was too unstable and Everett too timid to provide effective leadership. After gestures of defiance Adams went his lonely way and Everett crept back under Webster's wing.

The advocacy of liberalism among Massachusetts Whigs now fell to the political managers. Their motives were unashamed. "Those may sneer who choose at appeals to popular sympathies," observed the *Boston Atlas*, ". . . but it is only by means like these, that masses of men, whether great or small, are ever brought to act together." Since we live in a democracy, "in the long run those will always have the ascendancy in it, who take the most pains to secure the favor and good will, and to gain the ear of the people. Those who would have votes must descend into the forum and take the voters by the hand." [15]

The editor of the *Atlas* was Richard Haughton, a shrewd political strategist, and the chief editorial writer was the incisive Richard Hildreth, who, like Greeley, supported the new program out of his own humanitarian fervor (which in a few years would drive him from the party altogether). Announcing itself to be in agreement with "the abstract ideas of government advanced by the Globe, the Advo-

---

[13] Seward to Christopher Morgan [1841], Seward, *Seward*, 547. See also Hammond, *Wright*, 565–566, 680–681.

[14] Everett to Jared Sparks, November 10, 1834, Sparks Papers. Everett's gubernatorial message of 1836 prompted one New York Democrat to exclaim: "It breathes more of the spirit of democracy than any thing I have seen from that quarter. It is a part of the same plan which no doubt J. Q. Adams is engaged in bringing about; — the destruction of the present dinasty in Mass." R. Wardwell to A. C. Flagg, January 23, 1836, Flagg Papers.

[15] *Boston Atlas*, quoted in *New York Evening Post*, September 20, 1838.

cate and the Bay State Democrat," the *Atlas* led the movement to capture those ideas for conservatism.[16] The contrast between Boston's "respectable daily," the *Advertiser*, austere, scholarly and suffused with reverence for Daniel Webster, and the brawling and thoroughly irreverent *Atlas* displayed eloquently the difference between the old conservatism and the new.

Similarly in Pennsylvania, under the leadership of such former Anti-Masons as Thaddeus Stevens and Joseph Ritner, the Whig party moved to take up the banner of the common man. Through the North, conservatism was tending to split into liberal and diehard wings, the strength of each often depending on the relative importance of ex-Anti-Masons, or of ex-National Republicans (or ex-Federalists) in the party organization.

Eighteen-forty forced the party to the concrete choice. Should the campaign be fought once more with the issues and leaders with which the Whigs had repeatedly gone down to defeat? Or should the past be forgotten, and the party enter the canvass unencumbered by its former issues and leaders?

For the liberals the decision was clear. Early in Van Buren's administration they set out to knife the "aristocratic" possibilities and clear the field for a "democratic" candidate. The first victim was Daniel Webster. Webster's great opportunity had come in 1837 when the business community in its crisis had instinctively turned to him as the most formidable intellect among the Whigs. When he could provide no solution more stirring than a return to the Bank, he lost his chance. In 1838 the *Atlas* led the wolf-pack against him, declaring in a series of editorials that his nomination would ruin the party.[17] Webster went unhappily to England in 1839 knowing that revolt in his home state had destroyed his availability. As for Henry Clay, Thurlow Weed personally conducted the campaign of elimination, imperturbably passing the word to the convention delegates that the people would have no more of him. Their own candidate had been settled by the popular vote in 1836.[18] A Westerner, a military hero,

---

[16] *Boston Atlas*, quoted in *Boston Press and Advocate*, Dec. 11, 1838. Charles Gordon Greene of the *Post* once described the *Atlas* as "a print which we quote as 'a leading Whig paper,' when we wish to disgrace that party the most." *Boston Post*, August 6, 1835. Brownson called it "the leading whig paper in New England. It is conducted with more ability, has more life and freshness and exerts greater influence than any other whig paper." *Boston Quarterly Review*, III, 242 (April, 1840).

[17] Richard Hildreth, *My Connection with the Atlas Newspaper*; Congdon, *Reminiscences*, 67; Hudson, *Journalism in the United States*, 393.

[18] Caleb Cushing's succession of opinions shows how the new school reversed itself on Harrison. In 1835, according to Cushing, Harrison was "sheer naught.

and a plain man of the people, innocent of the Jacksonian controversies, who could be a better nominee than William Henry Harrison?

Henry Clay anxiously awaited news from Harrisburg and the convention in a Washington hotel, repeatedly filling his glass from the well-loaded sideboard to pass away the moments of suspense. As he drank, he cursed the intriguers against him in a wild and profane soliloquy. Suddenly stopping, he wheeled on two appalled strangers, dressed in black and come to meet their hero. "Gentlemen, for aught I know, from your cloth you may be *parsons*, and shocked at my words," said Clay. "Let us take a glass of wine." The visitors retired in disillusion. "That man," said one sadly, "can never be my political idol again."

Clay drank on; and, when the news of Harrison's nomination arrived, a black cloud of fury passed over the unforgettable face, and he broke into a rage of oaths and accusations. Fiercely pacing the floor, he cried in despair, "My friends are not worth the powder and shot it would take to kill them! . . . I am the most unfortunate man in the history of parties: always run by my friends when sure to be defeated, and now betrayed for a nomination when I, or any one, would be sure of an election." [19]

4

Successful in their candidate, the new-school Whigs entered the campaign with energy and enthusiasm. Almost immediately the Democrats played into their hands. A Baltimore paper observed loftily that Harrison would be entirely happy on his backwoods farm if he had a pension, a log cabin and a barrel of hard cider. Over some excellent madeira at Thomas Elder's fine mansion on the Susquehanna, Elder, a bank president, and Richard S. Elliott, a Whig editor from Harrisburg, considered how they could turn this squib to political uses.[20]

. . . Neither his intellectual character nor his general habits can give him vogue at the North." Cushing to Edward Everett, December 17, 1835, Everett Papers. In 1840 Cushing emerged as the proud author of a glowing biography, *Outline of the Life and Public Service, Civil and Military, of General Harrison.*

[19] Wise, *Seven Decades of the Union*, 170–172. General Winfield Scott, the other leading candidate for the Whig nomination, observed similarly, when taking leave of guests one night, "I could have been elected as easy as I could walk down these stairs." Hilliard, *Politics and Pen Pictures*, 12–13. A good deal of sentimental emotion has been expended on the failure of the Whig party to nominate Clay or Webster in 1840. There were other views. Almost a quarter of a century later, Seward and Lincoln agreed in calling Clay and Webster "hard and selfish leaders, whose private personal ambition had contributed to the ruin of their party." Welles, *Diary*, I, 5C7.

[20] R. S. Elliott. *Notes Taken in Sixty Years*, 122.

Hard cider and a log cabin? . . . Yes, the answer soon rang across the land, the Whig party *is* the party of hard cider and log cabins, and it will defend them to the end against all the sneers of the Democrats.

With tireless industry and bewildering resources Whigs everywhere rushed to doff their broadcloth and flaunt their homespun. Every speech, song and slogan held up the rustic and plebeian as closest to the Whig soul. The staid meetings of their past gave way to barbecues, clambakes, excursions and noisy processions. Raucous campaign songs echoed in the streets, as the Whigs marched by in disorder, shouting and staggering in the yellow light of torches: —

> Farewell, dear Van,
> You're not our man;
> To guide the ship,
> We'll try old Tip.

Log cabins were everywhere — hung to watch chains and earrings, in parlor pictures and shop windows, mounted on wheels, decorated with coonskins and hauled in magnificent parades. Large ones were set up in the principal cities, surrounded by barrels of cider, with the latchstring dangling out in welcome for all comers. Enthusiastic Whig clubs rolled huge balls in derisive reference to Benton's boast when the Senate expunged its records of the censure against Jackson: "Solitary and alone, I set this ball in motion." From Cleveland a huge tin ball, twelve feet in diameter, was pushed to Berea, thence to Wellington, Medina and finally Columbus, where it met another ball, fifteen feet in diameter, covered with cowhide and drawn from Muskingum County by twenty-four milk-white oxen: —

> With heart and soul
> This ball we roll;
> May times improve
> As on we move.

> This Democratic ball
> Set rolling first by Benton,
> Is on another track
> From that it first was sent on.

Wood engravers and lithographers were kept perpetually busy turning out pictures: Harrison, the Hero of Tippecanoe, astride a monumental horse; Harrison as Cincinnatus at the plow; Harrison greeting his comrades at arms at the door of his log cabin, with a long latchstring hanging down; Harrison as an Indian chief, paddling furiously toward the White House from which Van Buren ("the Flying Dutch-man") was fleeing; Harrison as a boxer administering a thrashing to Van Buren, with Old Hickory, as Van Buren's trainer, looking on in gloom. Brass and copper medals were struck off, with a log cabin, a flag, a barrel and a cup on one side, Harrison on the other: "*He leaves the plough to save his country.*" And always the din of songs, the blare of drum and fife, the hoarse voices of orators, the immense crowds, the endless processions, the barrel on barrel of cider, the torches smoking and flaring in the night.[21]

> As rolls the ball,
> Van's reign does fall,
> And he may look
> To Kinderhook.

Harrison himself, born a Virginia aristocrat, watched without pro-test his transmutation into a plain man of the people, while his spacious house in Ohio was reshaped into a humble log cabin. Nicholas Biddle's advice of 1836 was not forgotten: pen and ink were as wholly for-bidden as if he were indeed a mad poet in Bedlam. A committee, adept at ambiguities, answered all his correspondence. (The *Washington Globe* called them "the keepers of General Harrison's conscience.") [22] His public appearances were infrequent, vague and highly effective. The weatherbeaten old soldier, exchanging his tall silk hat for a broad-brimmed rustic model, speaking with great earnestness to little effect, delighted crowds already exhilarated by Whig hard cider. "I believe and I say it is true Democratic feeling," Harrison would say, "that all the measures of the Government are directed to the purpose of mak-ing the rich richer and the poor poorer," and the people would roar in response.[23] Occasionally, came a significant admission. "Methinks," he said at Dayton, "I hear a soft voice asking, Are you in favor of paper money? I am." [24] But on most major issues Harrison's views were carefully concealed, doubtless even from himself.

A host of cracker-box orators appeared to verify the Whigs' new-found democracy: John W. Baer, the Buckeye Blacksmith, Tom Corwin, the Wagon Boy, Henry Wilson, the Natick Cobbler, Honest

[21] Elliott, *Notes*, 126; Seward, *Seward*, 498–499; Benton, *Thirty Years' View*, II, 205; Nathan Sargent, *Public Men and Events*, II, 108–109; C. I. Bushnell, *Bushnell's American Tokens, passim*; G. W. Julian, *Political Recollections 1840 to 1872*, 11–21; A. B. Norton, *The Great Revolution of 1840*; Freeman Cleaves, *Old Tippecanoe*, ch. 24; T. A. Knight, *Tippecanoe*.

[22] *Washington Globe*, April 13, 1840.

[23] Certified copy by James Riley of a speech delivered by Harrison, October 1, 1840, Van Buren Papers.

[24] Shepard. *Van Buren*, 327.

Abe Lincoln, the Railsplitter. Everyone's opinion became important, down to those of Chang and Eng, the Siamese twins, who, Whig papers proudly announced, were going to vote for Harrison.[25]

No leader, however eminent, was exempt. Henry Clay, swallowing his disappointment, solemnly proclaimed the struggle to be between the log cabins and the palaces, between hard cider and champagne. Daniel Webster, back from London, where his magnificent head produced a sensation even if he was generally understood to be the author of the dictionary, exhibited himself in profound lamentation for his own failure to be born in a log cabin, though he could say with pride that his elder brother and sisters had been more fortunate. "The man that says that I am an aristocrat," Webster would shout, " — Is a Liar!" A person who makes this charge "and then will not come within the reach of my arm, is not only a liar but a coward." [26]

The Whigs overlooked no opportunity to appear as the champions of labor. Their spellbinders would denounce the independent treasury as "a measure of conspiracy against the working classes," thereby completely reversing their line of 1837.[27] The cornerstone of the campaign was provided on April 14, 1840, when Charles Ogle of Pennsylvania moved that appropriations of $3665 be denied the President for the repair of the White House. In ringing tones Ogle accused Van Buren of *"spending the public money of the People with a lavish hand, and, at the same time, saving his own with sordid parsimony."* The White House, Ogle cried, is a "Palace *as splendid as that of the Caesars, and as richly adorned as the proudest Asiatic mansion."* "What, sir, will the honest locofoco say to Mr. Van Buren for spending the People's cash in Foreign Fanny Kemble Green Finger Cups, in which to wash his pretty, tapering, soft, white lily-fingers, after dining on fricandeau de veau and omelette soufflé?" [28]

Ogle's speech was a combination of irrelevancies and falsehoods. James Silk Buckingham, who visited the White House in 1838, described it as "greatly inferior in size and splendour to the country residences of most of our nobility." The furniture, "though sufficiently commodious and appropriate, is far from being elegant or costly," and the whole air is one of "unostentatious comfort, without parade or display." [29] When another Congressman tried out an earlier version

[25] *Boston Atlas,* November 26, 1840.
[26] *New York Evening Post,* September 24, 1840; Norton, *Great Revolution,* 233, 323. For Webster in London, see Harvey, *Reminiscences of Webster,* 388; N. P. Willis, "Jottings Down in London," *Boston Post,* August 22, 1839.
[27] Norton, *Great Revolution,* 346.
[28] Ogle, *The Royal Splendor of the President's Palace,* 1, 6, 20.
[29] Buckingham, *America,* I, 286.

of Ogle's diatribe, Levi Lincoln, who had left the governorship of Massachusetts for the House, delivered an exasperated rebuke: —

> With reference to the President's Mansion, about the costliness of which the gentleman had complained so much, it was a disgrace to the country; and in many of the rooms the gentleman would not lodge his negro, if he kept one. Mr. L. had not a constituent who voted for him whose rooms were not better furnished than those in which the President received company of both sexes. The roof and wings of the building leaked, and yet the gentleman from New Jersey would withhold the appropriation to put it in repair, to stop the leaks.[30]

Lincoln, indeed, though strongly opposed to Van Buren's re-election, actually answered Ogle in a speech to which the Democrats gave wide circulation, but all in vain. Replies on an intellectual level in 1840 were as fruitless as rejoinders addressed to a thunderstorm. Ogle's fantasies produced the best-seller of the Whig campaign.

5

The most effective Whig paper was the *Log Cabin*, edited by the protégé of Thurlow Weed. The campaign of 1840 displayed Horace Greeley's gifts for the first time on a large scale, both in their weakness and their strength. Greeley's feeling for the people was certainly sincere. His compassion had been stirred by the harsh winter of 1837, and no one surpassed him in defending the Whig program in terms of its benefits for the workingman. He was an enthusiastic pastoralist, reprinting Channing's "Essay on the Laboring Classes" with approval, while denouncing Amos Kendall's somewhat less narcotic "Address to the People of the United States" as the "raving and froth of this desperate demagogue." The *Log Cabin* was fond of poems which contained such sentiments as

> What paupers are th' ambitious rich! —
> How wealthy the contented poor! [31]

These democratic flourishes were all very well, but they hardly explain the myth of Greeley the reformer.[32] Of course, he looked the

---

[30] Lincoln in the House, March 21, 1838, *Congressional Globe*, 25 Congress 2 Session, 249.

[31] *Log Cabin*, May 9, June 13, August 1, 1840.

[32] The historical foundations of this myth are supplied compactly in J. R. Commons, "Horace Greeley and the Working Class Origins of the Republican Party," *Political Science Quarterly*, XXIV, 468–488. This essay abounds in such statements as "Horace Greeley was to the social revolution of the forties what Thomas

part, this vague, benign man, with his large, nervous head, bald in
front, with a brush of benevolent white hair behind, an old white hat
stuck precariously on its back, his shirt open at the collar, a vest which
seemed (said one observer) "as though it had been put on with a
pitch-fork," his pockets overflowing with papers, trousers with one
leg in the boot and the other out.[33]

But his appearance was hardly enough to justify his reputation.
Greeley was, in fact, completely sold on the Whig economic program. His great idol was Henry Clay, and the high tariff, internal
improvements and the Bank seemed to him the most vital practical
steps toward social salvation. Indeed, an early cause of friction with
Thurlow Weed was Greeley's insistence on supporting the United
States Bank as late as 1842, when even Daniel Webster had abandoned
it as an "obsolete idea." [34] He was persuaded to found the *Tribune*
by Whig friends, anxious for a penny daily which would reach the
laboring class. At no time did Greeley oppose the party on an important economic issue.

He looked on the hard-boiled radicalism of the Democrats as
"Jacobinic clamor." [35] Van Buren, he charged, had betrayed democracy
in 1837 for "Fanny Wright Loco-Focoism," and the attacks on the
banking system and protective tariff seemed to him to be endanger-
ing the great conservative interests of society.

> Teach the poor man to believe the rich are his natural enemies —
> that they rob him of his just earnings, and drive him from his
> proper place in society, and you teach him not merely to be
> averse to labor, envious, discontented and malignant, but you
> instigate him also to *reclaim* what has been unjustly wrested from
> him. . . . Teach him that the Rich have engrossed unequal and
> unjust privileges and monopolies which grind him to the earth,
> and you bid him, if he has the spirit of a man, to rise and assert
> his rights — if need be, by the sabre and bayonet.[36]

Greeley's reputation (apart from his strong if belated stand on
slavery) rests mainly on his feverish advocacy of sideshow reforms.

Jefferson was to the political revolution of 1800." My own view is more in accord
with Norman Ware's admirable treatment of Greeley, *The Industrial Worker*,
21–22, 167. For an attack on Greeley from the point of view of a contemporary
radical, see Thomas A. Devyr, *The Odd Book of the Nineteenth Century*, 96–107.
    [33] Bungay, *Crayon Sketches*, 30–32; T. L. Nichols, *Forty Years of American Life*,
II, 193–195.
    [34] Greeley, *Recollections*, 166; Greeley to Weed, September 10, 1842, T. W.
Barnes, *Memoir of Thurlow Weed*, 97.
    [35] Greeley, *Hints toward Reforms* (second edition), 366.
    [36] *Log Cabin*, August 1, 1840.

He was eminently a "safe" radical. When he devotedly fought for the American System, what did it matter if he allowed Albert Brisbane to pay him $150 a week for printing a column on Fourierism? [37] Brisbane was in any case a cheap price for a progressive reputation. It was much better to print his harmless visions — which at worst would only encourage romantic humanitarians to isolate themselves in communities when they might otherwise be unsettling society — than to print, say, Amos Kendall on the banking system. While it might annoy the old guard, it would relieve many twinges of guilt by giving countless Whigs the illusion of participating in movements toward reform. The reforms involved no direct conflict with any existing interests, and they cast a genial glow over the operations of the new Whig party. As Greeley wrote to Weed, "Hitherto all the devotees of social reform . . . all the social discontent of the country has been regularly repelled from the Whig party and attracted to its opposite. . . . It strikes me that it is unwise to persist in this course, unless we are ambitious to be considered the enemies of improvement and the bulwarks of an outgrown aristocracy." [38]

Greeley's friends accounted his social enthusiasms — whether Fourier or land reform — as personal quirks, on the same level as his hatred of tobacco and liquor. "His peculiarities in this respect," said Thurlow Weed, speaking of his social views, "never turned him away from or impaired his consistent and hearty efforts in the Whig cause." [39] When the two men finally quarreled, it was not over issues of policy, but over Greeley's belief that he had been done out of an office he thought his services to the party deserved.

6

Colonel Johnson provided the Democrats with their first embarrassment. His affabilities had worn badly in the vice-presidential chair, and his honest liberalism had disappeared before a rather vulgar obsession for office. One observer, noting him presiding over the Senate in 1838, described him as "shabbily dressed, and to the last degree clumsy." [40] Odd rumors began to float back from Kentucky. When Amos Kendall went there in the fall of 1838, he heard that the Vice-President had spent the summer running an inn, superintending everything personally down to the purchase of eggs and the

[37] Oliver Carlson, *Brisbane; a Candid Biography*, 48.
[38] Greeley to Weed, February 19, 1841, Barnes, *Weed*, 93. (This letter is obviously misdated.)
[39] Weed, *Autobiography*, 468.
[40] H. B. Stanton, *Random Recollections* (second edition), 36.

sale of watermelons, and showing conspicuous devotion to his third consort, the sister of the girl he had sold for infidelity. "She is some eighteen or nineteen years of age and quite handsome," wrote one Kentuckian, "— plays on the piano, calls him my *dear Colonel*, and is called *my dear* in return, and is said to be very *loving*. . . . How can he expect friends to countenance and sustain him, when he . . . shamelessly lives in adultery with a buxom young *negro wench?*" [41]

The Whigs were quick to exploit the Colonel's foibles. Halstead of New Jersey attacked the administration in 1838 in a speech filled with complicated puns directed at Dickie Johnson, saying meaningfully that "the Democrats had turned dandies," and that "the dandies had a great liking for *dickies*," and that "the *dickies* had a close affinity to *darkies* or *blackies*." [42] Whispers had been handicap enough in 1836, and Kendall felt that Johnson's behavior released the party from any further obligation. General Jackson was also against Johnson, preferring James K. Polk, who had left the House to become Governor of Tennessee. Eventually the Democrats left Van Buren without a running mate, proposing that each state vote for its favorite. Johnson, however, put on a vigorous speaking campaign, boasting that he had been born in a canebrake and cradled in a sap trough, tearing open his shirt to show his scars of war and delivering rambling and incoherent addresses.[43] In the end, he was about the only Democratic orator to operate on the intellectual level of the year.

For the most part, Democrats conducted their canvass along well-worn lines. "Years ago the democracy of Massachusetts published its faith on this point," declared the convention of the Democratic members of the legislature; "and from that faith it will never swerve. We repeat it: To Assert the Rights of Labor, Is the Mission of the Age." [44] In almost every respect the Democratic line consisted of such repetitions from the past, reaffirming the old ideals and discussing the old issues.[45] A broadside summed it up: "The Producer's Election Hymn, or an Address to Poor Men": —

[41] Kendall to Van Buren, August 22, 1839, and enclosures, Van Buren Papers.
[42] Halstead's speech was not recorded. Quotation from Jesse A. Bynum in the House, March 13, 1838, *Congressional Globe*, 25 Congress 2 Session, Appendix, 280. See also Ratliff Boon in the House, March 22, 1838, *Congressional Globe*, 25 Congress 2 Session, 251.
[43] Meyer, *Johnson*, 290, 433–449.
[44] *Boston Post*, April 15, 1840.
[45] Even the old New York Workingmen's party was celebrated. Hobart Berrian of the Office of the Fourth Auditor of the Treasury, editor of the *Working Man's Advocate* of Washington and local agent for the New York *New Era*, wrote a glowing pamphlet (*Brief Sketch of the Origin and Rise of the Workingmen's Party in the City of New York*) describing that party as the fountain of the ideas so splendidly carried out in Van Buren's administration.

> Arise! Arise! Sustain your rights,
> Ye sons of labor rise!

* * *

> *The Paper Plague* afflicts us all,
>   Its pains are past enduring;
> Still, we have hope in Jackson's robe,
>   Whilst it wraps around VAN BUREN.
>   Then let the working class,
>   As a congregated man,
>   Behold an insidious enemy:
>   For each *Banker* is a foe,
>   And his aim is for our woe —
> He's the *canker-worm of liberty!*

* * *

> *Then to the polls like victors go!*
> *Rushing like a river's flow,*
> *Urged by wastes of melting snow:*
> *Mark a Whig, and lo, a foe!*
> *That would enslave you, work your woe!*
> *Therefore support Van Buren!* [46]

There were occasional flashes of ingenuity. In New York, for example, the *New Era* enriched the language with the phrase O.K. — "Old Kinderhook." By April, Democratic ward meetings were resolving, "We will say to Martin Van Buren, O.K., you can remain at the white house for another four years." [47] But Democrats on the whole had lost their capacity for improvisation in face of the hurricane tactics of the Whigs. They were baffled by the songs and parades and bonfires. "The question is not whether Harrison drinks hard cider," said William Cullen Bryant plaintively. ". . . The question is what he and his party will do if they obtain the power." [48] But the crowds roared back: "Tippecanoe and Tyler Too." "Are the Whigs contending for the privilege of living in log cabins?" asked one bitter Democrat. "Is there any despot in the land who prevents them from pulling down their mansions of bricks, of granite, and of marble, and putting up log cabins in their place?" [49] The crowds replied: "Van, Van is a Used-up Man. . . ." It was futile to argue against the elements.

[46] Broadside, Van Buren Papers.
[47] *New Era*, April 11, 1840. See Allen Walker Read's probably conclusive article, "The Evidence on 'O.K.,'" *Saturday Review of Literature*, July 19, 1941.
[48] *New York Evening Post*, March 10, 1840.
[49] [Anon.], *The Great Contest. What the Two Political Parties Are Struggling For*, 1.

By main force the Whigs were making themselves a party of the people. "They have at last learned from defeat the very act of victory!" cried the *Democratic Review.* "We have taught them how to conquer us!" [50]

7

The campaign of 1840 produced one of the most remarkable of the documents of Jacksonian democracy. Orestes A. Brownson, pondering the workings of industrial society, reached in the spring of 1840 certain conclusions which, as was his nature, he felt he must instantly impart to the world. In the July issue of the *Boston Quarterly Review* he set them forth in a brilliant and perverse article entitled "The Laboring Classes."

Everywhere, Brownson began in familiar vein, the actual producer of wealth is shut out from the main benefits of society. "All over the world this fact stares us in the face, the workingman is poor and depressed, while a large portion of the non-workingmen . . . are wealthy." How much longer would the laboring classes submit to this unequal distribution of the fruits of their own labor? Already Brownson saw intimations of "that most dreaded of all wars, the war of the poor against the rich, a war which, however long it may be delayed, will come, and come with all its horrors."

There were two existing labor systems, he pointed out, slave and free. Of the two, the system of free labor deprived the workingman of the proceeds of labor most efficiently. "Wages," said Brownson, "is a cunning device of the devil, for the benefit of tender consciences, who would retain all the advantages of the slave system, without the expense, trouble, and odium of being slave-holders. . . . If there must always be a laboring population distinct from proprietors and employers, we regard the slave system as decidedly preferable to the system at wages." But free labor will everywhere win out, because it sounds better and costs less.

What then does the future hold for the "actual laborers, who are laborers and not proprietors, owners of none of the funds of production, neither houses, nor shops, nor lands, nor implements of labor, being therefore solely dependent on their hands"? There was no reasonable chance, Brownson answered, that many of them could ever become owners of enough capital to secure their independence. Indeed, their condition could only become worse; "the wilderness has receded,

[50] "The War of the Five Campaigns," *Democratic Review,* VII, 486 (June, 1840).

and already the new lands are beyond the reach of the mere laborer, and the employer has him at his mercy." This age must recognize its responsibility. "Our business is to emancipate the proletaries, as the past has emancipated the slaves."

How was this to be done? Internal reform was not enough. "We look not for the regeneration of the race from priests and pedagogues." They "seek to reform without disturbing the social arrangements which render reform necessary. . . . Self-culture is a good thing, but it cannot abolish inequality." So much for pastoralism and Dr. Channing: the price of salvation was not so cheap.

The first step, declared Brownson, must be the destruction of the priesthood and the revival of the Christianity of Christ. When the gospel of Jesus had quickened, in all souls, the capacity for reform, we must then resort to government, first repealing all laws bearing against the laboring classes and enacting the laws necessary to enable them to attain equality; next divorcing the government altogether from the banking system, which represents "the interests of the business in opposition to the laboring community"; then the grand and indispensable measure — abolition of the hereditary descent of property.

Brownson was not optimistic about this program. "The rich, the business community, will never voluntarily consent to it. . . . It will come, if it ever come at all, only at the conclusion of war, the like of which the world as yet has never witnessed, and from which, however inevitable it may seem to the eye of philosophy, the heart of Humanity recoils with horror." [51]

How did Brownson envisage his new society? The article was obscure on this issue, saying, at one point, that the system of wages "must" be replaced, at another contemplating modifications which would guarantee the industrious operative enough "to be an independent laborer on his own capital, — on his own farm or in his own shop." A second article in October was slightly more precise. The great evil, Brownson declared, "is the separation of the capitalist from the laborer." Politics held out no hope of solving the growing inequalities. "Universal suffrage is little better than a mockery," when not founded on a wide distribution of property. "No matter what party you support, no matter what men you elect, property is always the basis of your governmental action." The only solution was thus to "combine labor and capital in the same individual. What we object

---

[51] Brownson, "The Laboring Classes," *Boston Quarterly Review*, III, 358–395 (July, 1840). For a more detailed analysis, A. M. Schlesinger, Jr., *Brownson*, 89–100.

to, is the division of society into two classes, of which one class owns the capital, and the other performs the labor." [52]

Brownson saw the main obstacle to his program in the Hamiltonian policy, which, as he said in a Fourth of July address at Worcester, regarded government as "mainly for the protection of capital, and especially of business capital." Who, after all, led the Whigs? "The chiefs of this party we all know are the chiefs of the business community, as distinguished from the agricultural and labouring community." Their aim? "To lock up the whole capital of the country in close corporations, to give up to these corporations the monopoly of every branch of industry," and thereby to establish the laboring classes in a condition of virtual servitude. The war for the independent treasury thus became vital "to keep the government free from the special control of a particular class of the community, and open to the whole people." [53]

Brownson's essay was based squarely on the Jacksonian analysis — the standard theories of banking, of monopoly, of the unequal distribution of the fruits of labor, of class conflict — but his implacable logic would not halt short of the most ruthless conclusions. He drew a sharper line between the propertyless workers and the middle class. He set forth a more ferocious vision of class war. He seemed to propose (though his discussion abounds in ambiguities) a much more drastic attack on the whole system of wages. In general, he stated the implications of the radical democratic doctrines in their most extreme form.

His own concrete suggestions were of small importance. When they departed from the Democratic platform, they became impracticable, like the scheme he borrowed from Saint-Simon for the abolition of inheritance.[54] But thrown into the middle of a roaring political campaign, they were taken as the pronouncement of a leading Democrat on immediate issues. The attack on the priesthood and the inheritance

[52] Brownson, "The Laboring Classes" (second article), *Boston Quarterly Review*, III, 420–512 (October, 1840).

[53] Brownson, *Oration before the Democracy of Worcester and Vicinity*, 20, 22, 35, 36.

[54] The essay actually falls into two parts, the second of which (377–391, 393–395) is much the less substantial. In a perplexed state of religious belief himself, Brownson poured into this part all his disgust with the business of organized religion, his scorn for the timidity of the clergy, his revulsion from theological subtleties, and yielded to his anguished desire to surrender to the simplicities of Christ. These emotions, shaped by quotations from Tom Paine, echoes of the *Free Enquirer*, recollections of Fanny Wright and the Sunday-mail controversy, and dogmas from the *Nouveau Christianisme* of Saint-Simon, led to an assault on the "priesthood," which reflected Brownson's own dilemmas much more than it did those of society.

proposal, both misrepresented and torn from context, became objects of partisan fury. The Whigs claimed them as conclusive proof of what they had always said about the Democrats: that their doctrines led inevitably to assaults on religion and property. The *Madisonian,* quoting William Cullen Bryant and Francis Pickens to the effect that the independent treasury was but the first in a series of reforms, seized on Brownson's article as a confession of ultimate Democratic intentions. The shocking program was now revealed:

I.   The destruction of the system of free labor and wages.
II. The overthrow of the Church in all its forms and sects.
III. The abolition of the laws relating to the descent of property.

"These abominable purposes . . . these atrocious doctrines . . . ," sputtered the *Madisonian.*[55] Horace Greeley agreed that Brownson's outburst proved that Locofocoism was "utterly subversive of all Rights of Property whatever." [56]

The Whig *New-York Review* regretted in succession that he could not be handled by the treadmill, the penitentiary, the pillory and the whipping-post.[57] Daniel Webster thundered at him in a speech on Bunker Hill. Henry A. Wise and William Cabell Rives explained to Virginia how Brownson had disclosed the full iniquity of Van Buren's plans. In Georgia John M. Berrien, once Attorney General under Jackson, denounced the views of the *Boston Quarterly* as "agrarian, Jacobinical, and anti-religious." [58] A pamphleteer accused Van Buren of the "settled purpose of revolution," declaring that his policy was based on the tenets of "Tom Paine, Fanny Wright, Robert Dale Owen, Orestes A. Brownson, and Wm. M. Holland, cemented by the promise of sub-Treasury spoils." [59] Calvin Colton devoted two of his Junius tracts to Brownson. If, he wrote, "the project of subduing the American people, by physical force, to the chains of such a dynasty of lust and blood, is so far matured as to be openly announced through an accredited public organ, subsisting on the bounty of the Government," then must the people rise and act.[60] "CHRISTIANS! PATRIOTS!

---

[55] *Madisonian,* August 4, 1840.

[56] *Log Cabin,* August 1, 1840.

[57] "Brownson on the Laboring Classes," *New-York Review,* VII, 515–522 (October, 1840). For other comments, see *Christian Review,* V, 419–442 (September, 1840); *Methodist Quarterly Review,* XXIII, 92–122 (January, 1841); *Boston Atlas,* July 21, 24, 29, 1840; etc.

[58] W. Hall McAllister to Bancroft, August 6, 1840, Thomas Ritchie to Levi Woodbury, October 9, 1840, Bancroft Papers.

[59] [Anon.], *A Word in Season . . . By a Harrison Democrat,* 6, 7.

[60] [Calvin Colton], *American Jacobinism,* 2; see also *Sequel to the Crisis of the Country.*

FATHERS!" cried Thurlow Weed's paper. "READ AND REFLECT." [61] The
Boston Harrison Club improved the tale: —

> *It has been boastingly uttered that the blood of the Whigs would
> soon flow down our streets; AND A DISTINGUISHED
> LEADER OF THE PARTY, AND AN OFFICER IN THE
> BOSTON CUSTOM HOUSE, HAS RECENTLY STATED
> THAT THE WHIGS SHOULD SOON HAVE A CHANCE
> TO EXPERIENCE THE PHYSICAL FORCE OF THE LOCO-
> FOCOS; THAT HE WOULD BRING ONE HUNDRED MEN
> IN THIS CITY WHO WOULD FLOG ANY THOUSAND
> WHIGS . . . AND THAT WHILE THIS BATTLE WAS
> GOING ON HE WOULD GO UP TO BEACON STREET
> AND SET FIRE TO THE WHIG HOUSES.[62]*

Brownson's own party looked on his doctrines with something less
than enthusiasm; but the romantic picture Brownson gave, in his
autobiography, of "one universal scream of horror" was considerably
exaggerated.[63] In fact, the first Democratic reaction, after the disavow-
ing of the inheritance proposal, was to praise the article for what the
New York Evening Post described as "the same spirit of free thought
and bold expression" which had always marked the *Boston Quarterly*.[64]
But the uproar continued till by October Levi Woodbury was
writing from Washington to George Bancroft, who had refused to fire
Brownson from his government job, "Everybody is loud in their
denunciation of him. Why is he kept there? Why?" [65] Conservative
Democratic journals, like the *Albany Argus*, took pleasure in abusing
Brownson. Yet even the *Boston Post*, for example, continued to be
much more violent against the Whigs for misusing the article than
against Brownson for writing it. "Judge Taney, we believe, is a
Catholic; are all democrats, therefore, Roman Catholics?" [66] The
Evening Post, yielding not an inch, published a number of editorials
defending Brownson's right to his opinions.[67] The essay did not seriously affect either Brownson's usefulness or his popularity in the

[61] *Loco-Focoism; as Displayed in the Boston Magazine against Schools and Ministers, and in Favor of Robbing Children of the Property of their Parents*, [1].
[62] *Conspiracy of the Office Holders Unmasked*, 3; *Boston Atlas*, October 27,
1840.
[63] Brownson, "The Convert," *Works*, V, 103.
[64] *New York Evening Post*, July 17, 1840. For similar articles, see *Boston Post*,
July 7; *Bay State Democrat*, July 28; *Salem Advertiser*, quoted in the *Bay State
Democrat*, July 25.
[65] Endorsement by Woodbury on Ritchie to Woodbury, October 9, 1840,
Bancroft Papers.
[66] *Boston Post*, July 28, 1840.
[67] *New York Evening Post*, August 8, October 2, 7, 1840.

Massachusetts Democratic party, and he was in constant demand all over the state in the tense closing days of the campaign.[68]

8

And so the canvass continued in its rollicking way, with music and invective drowning out argument, and issues dwindling in the glare of huge bonfires. The Maine elections in September, sending Whig hopes to new ecstasies of enthusiasm, produced the hit song of the year: —

> And have you heard the news from Maine,
>   And what old Maine can do?
> She went hell-bent for Governor Kent,
>   And Tippecanoe and Tyler too,
>   And Tippecanoe and Tyler too.

Through the fall the parades marched, and the torches flared, and the hard cider flowed, and Whig orators stumped the country. One by one the states went to the polls. One by one the returns came in. The result was decisive: Harrison, 234 votes, Van Buren, 60. The President, sitting silently in the White House through November gloom, heard the inevitable refrain in the streets outside. "Van, Van, is a used-up man. . . ."

Yet the majority was not as great as the electoral result indicated. Van Buren's 1,129,102 votes were an increase of 366,424 over the vote which had elected him in 1836; it was indeed a much larger total than any victorious President had polled before 1840. Out of nearly two and a half million votes cast, Harrison's margin was 145,914. A shift of a little over eight thousand votes, properly distributed, would have given Van Buren the election.[69]

The achievement of Whig hullabaloo lay, not in changing Democratic votes, but in bringing out people who had never been to the polls before. Few of the million new voters had much idea what all the shouting was about. "So far as ideas entered into my support of the Whig candidate," recollected one veteran of the campaign, "I simply regarded him as a poor man, whose home was in a log cabin, and who would in some way help the people . . . while I was fully persuaded that Van Buren was not only a graceless aristocrat and a

---

[68] *Boston Post*, September 30, October 6, 12, 22, 23, 31, 1840.
[69] Van Buren lost New York, Pennsylvania, Maine and New Jersey by narrow margins. With a properly allocated shift of 8184 votes, he could have carried these states and won in the electoral college, 150–144. H. R. Fraser, *Democracy in the Making*, has similar, though somewhat inaccurate, calculations.

dandy, but a cunning conspirator, seeking the overthrow of this country's liberties." "As to what the 'Sub-Treasury' really was," confessed another, "I had not the remotest idea; but this I knew; — that it was the most wicked outrage ever committed by a remorseless tyrant upon a long-suffering people." [70] But the revelry and fun, and incessant repetition of the charges against Matty Van, were irresistible.

> Farewell, dear Van,
> You're not our man;
> To guide the ship,
> We'll try old Tip.

The defeat threw many Democrats into deep dejection. They could not understand how their people could have forsaken them. But, though a long view is perhaps inadequately comforting in the short run, the election of 1840, if a setback for the Democrats, was not necessarily a setback for democracy. In a sense, it was the most conclusive evidence of the triumph of Jackson. Conservatism had carried the election, but it had to assume the manner of the popular party in order to do it. The champions of inequality were forced to take over the slogans of the new dispensation.

Jackson's success was not to mean the end of all conflict. Democracy cannot exist without conflict, and it becomes meaningless when one party can suppress all opposition. But the Jacksonian triumph did mean that the struggle would be renewed on Jackson's terms, and not on those of Daniel Webster or Nicholas Biddle.

[70] Julian, *Political Recollections*, 11–12; Andrew D. White, *Autobiography* (New York, 1905), I, 52.

XXIV JACKSONIAN DEMOCRACY AS AN INTELLECTUAL MOVEMENT

THE JACKSONIAN revolution rested on premises which the struggles of the thirties hammered together into a kind of practical social philosophy. The outline of this way of thinking about society was clear. It was stated and restated, as we have seen, on every level of political discourse from presidential messages to stump speeches, from newspaper editorials to private letters. It provided the intellectual background without which the party battles of the day cannot be understood.

1

The Jacksonians believed that there was a deep-rooted conflict in society between the "producing" and "non-producing" classes — the farmers and laborers, on the one hand, and the business community on the other. The business community was considered to hold high cards in this conflict through its network of banks and corporations, its control of education and the press, above all, its power over the state: it was therefore able to strip the working classes of the fruits of their labor. "Those who produce all wealth," said Amos Kendall, "are themselves left poor. They see principalities extending and palaces built around them, without being aware that the entire expense is a tax upon themselves." [1]

If they wished to preserve their liberty, the producing classes would have to unite against the movement "to make the rich richer and the potent more powerful." Constitutional prescriptions and political promises afforded no sure protection. "We have heretofore been too disregardful of the fact," observed William M. Gouge, "that social order is quite as dependent on the laws which regulate the distribution of wealth, as on political organization." The program now was to resist every attempt to concentrate wealth and power further in a single class. Since free elections do not annihilate the opposition, the fight would be unceasing. "The struggle for power," said C. C.

[1] *Washington Globe*, November 7, 1834.

Cambreleng, "is as eternal as the division of society. A defeat cannot destroy the boundary which perpetually separates the democracy from the aristocracy." [2]

The specific problem was to control the power of the capitalistic groups, mainly Eastern, for the benefit of the noncapitalist groups, farmers and laboring men, East, West and South. The basic Jacksonian ideas came naturally enough from the East, which best understood the nature of business power and reacted most sharply against it. The legend that Jacksonian democracy was the explosion of the frontier, lifting into the government some violent men filled with rustic prejudices against big business, does not explain the facts, which were somewhat more complex. Jacksonian democracy was rather a second American phase of that enduring struggle between the business community and the rest of society which is the guarantee of freedom in a liberal capitalist state. [3]

Like any social philosophy, Jacksonian democracy drew on several intellectual traditions. Basically, it was a revival of Jeffersonianism, but the Jeffersonian inheritance was strengthened by the infusion of fresh influences; notably the antimonopolistic tradition, formulated

[2] Gouge, *Paper Money*, Part II, 235; Cambreleng to Van Buren, November 15, 1837, Van Buren Papers.

[3] It may be well to observe contemporary apprehensions long enough to discuss the relationship of the Jacksonian analysis to Marxism. Clarification would be useful, both for conservatives who declare that any talk of class conflict is Communistic, and for Communists who claim promiscuously any kind of economic insight as the exclusive result of their infallible method. In truth, the Jacksonian analysis, far from being Marxist, is the very core of our radical democratic tradition. The fact that the *Communist Manifesto* was not written until 1848 would seem conclusive on this point; and Marx and Lenin, unlike their disciples, made no irresponsible pretense to the invention of the theory of class conflict. Marx wrote to Weydemeyer, March 5, 1852: "As far as I am concerned, the honour does not belong to me for having discovered the existence either of classes in modern society or of the struggle between the classes. Bourgeois historians a long time before me expounded the historical development of this class struggle, and bourgeois economists, the economic anatomy of classes. What was new on my part, was to prove the following: (1) that the existence of classes is connected only with certain historical struggles which arise out of the development of production; (2) that class struggle necessarily leads to the dictatorship of the proletariat; (3) that this dictatorship is itself only a transition to the abolition of all classes and to a classless society."

Lenin is, if possible, more explicit. "The theory of the class struggle was *not* created by Marx, but by the bourgeoisie *before* Marx and is, generally speaking, *acceptable* to the bourgeoisie. He who recognizes *only* the class struggle is not yet a Marxist; he may be found not to have gone beyond the boundaries of bourgeois reasoning and politics. To limit Marxism to the teaching of the class struggle means to curtail Marxism — to distort it, to reduce it to something which is acceptable to the bourgeoisie. A Marxist is one who *extends* the acceptance of the class struggle to the acceptance of the *dictatorship of the proletariat*." V. I. Lenin, *State and Revolution* (New York, 1932), 29, 30.

primarily by Adam Smith and expounded in America by Gouge, Leggett, Sedgwick, Cambreleng; and the pro-labor tradition, formulated primarily by William Cobbett and expounded by G. H. Evans, Ely Moore, John Ferral.[4]

2

The inspiration of Jeffersonianism was so all-pervading and fundamental for its every aspect that Jacksonian democracy can be properly regarded as a somewhat more hard-headed and determined version of Jeffersonian democracy. But it is easy to understate the differences. Jefferson himself, though widely revered and quoted, had no personal influence on any of the leading Jacksonians save perhaps Van Buren. Madison and Monroe were accorded still more vague and perfunctory homage. The radical Jeffersonians, Taylor, Randolph and Macon, who had regarded the reign of Virginia as almost an era of betrayal, were much more vivid in the minds of the Jacksonians.

Yet even Taylor's contributions to the later period have been exaggerated. His great work, the *Inquiry into the Principles and Policy of the Government of the United States*, published in 1814 just before the Madisonian surrender, had no significant contemporary vogue except among the faithful; and its difficult style, baffling organization and interminable length prevented it ever from gaining wide currency. By Jackson's presidency it was long out of print. In 1835 it was reported unobtainable in New York and to be procured only "with great difficulty" in Virginia.[5] There is little trace of its peculiar terminology in the Jacksonian literature.[6]

While the *Inquiry* properly endured as the most brilliant discussion

[4] The experience of Samuel Clesson Allen, reaching Jacksonian conclusions along paths altogether independent of the main Jacksonian influences, is an important reminder that the vital origins of an effective social philosophy are the concrete needs of the day.

[5] *New York Evening Post*, June 24, 1835. Leggett in a highly interesting editorial says of Taylor: "He is such a reasoner as a country produces but once in the course of ages, and we cannot but think it a great misfortune, that most of our leading statesmen seem scarcely aware that he ever existed. . . . He stands, in our opinion, at the head of all champions of free institutions as applicable to this country. His dissection of the nature, origin, and consequences of aristocracy . . . is profound. . . . Mr. Taylor is the author of two works, well known in Virginia, and almost unknown every where else."

[6] His constitutional tracts, *Construction Construed* and *New Views of the Constitution*, providing a Jeffersonian commentary to counter the heresies of Marshall and Kent, were much more influential. Benton mentions *Construction Construed* and *The Arator*, his politico-agricultural essays, as Taylor's principal contributions, saying nothing about the *Inquiry*. *Thirty Years' View*, I, 45–46. To this list should be added his early pamphlet *Definition of Parties, or the Political Effects of the*

of the foundations of democracy, many of its details were in fact obsolete by 1830. It was oriented to an important degree around the use of the national debt as the mechanism of aristocracy; in Jackson's day the debt had been extinguished but the aristocracy remained. Moreover, Taylor's arguments against executive power, against the party system and for a revivified militia had lost their point for the Jacksonians. George Bancroft voiced a widely felt need when he called, in 1834, for a general work on American society. "Where doubts arise upon any point relating to the business of government," one radical wrote in response, "no dependence can be placed upon any treatise that has yet appeared which professes to discuss this subject. You must draw upon your own resources, you must think, — and think alone." [7]

The obsolescence of Taylor was caused by the enormous change in the face of America. The period of conservative supremacy from 1816 to 1828 had irrevocably destroyed the agricultural paradise, and the Jacksonians were accommodating the insights of Jefferson to the new concrete situations. This process of readjustment involved a moderately thorough overhauling of favorite Jeffersonian doctrines.

The central Jefferson hope had been a nation of small freeholders, each acquiring thereby so much moral probity, economic security and political independence as to render unnecessary any invasion of the rights or liberties of others. The basis of such a society, as Jefferson clearly recognized, was agriculture and handicraft. What was the status of the Jeffersonian hope now that it was clear that, at best, agriculture must share the future with industry and finance?

Orestes A. Brownson exhausted one possibility in his essay on "The Laboring Classes." He reaffirmed the Jeffersonian demand: "we ask that every man become an independent proprietor, possessing enough of the goods of this world, to be able by his own moderate industry to provide for the wants of his body." But what, in practice, would this mean? As Brownson acknowledged years later, his plan would have "broken up the whole modern commercial system, prostrated the great industries, . . . and thrown the mass of the people back on the land to get their living by agricultural and mechanical pursuits." [8] Merely to state its consequences was to prove its futility. The dominion of the small freeholder was at an end.

Paper System Considered, of which the *Washington Globe* remarked (February 11, 1839), "Of all the productions of this extraordinary man, we consider the pamphlet before us the most remarkable."

[7] W. S. Wait to Bancroft, October 15, 1834, Bancroft Papers.

[8] Brownson, "Our Future Policy," *Boston Quarterly Review*, IV, 81 (January, 1841); Brownson, "The Convert," *Works*, V, 117.

The new industrialism had to be accepted: banks, mills, factories, industrial capital, industrial labor. These were all distasteful realities for orthodox Jeffersonians, and, not least, the propertyless workers. "The mobs of great cities," Jefferson had said, "add just so much to the support of pure government, as sores do to the strength of the human body." The very ferocity of his images expressed the violence of his feelings. "When we get piled upon one another in large cities, as in Europe," he told Madison, "we shall become corrupt as in Europe, and go to eating one another as they do there." [9] It was a universal sentiment among his followers. "No man should live," Nathaniel Macon used to say, "where he can hear his neighbour's dog bark." [10]

Yet the plain political necessity of winning the labor vote obliged a change of mood. Slowly, with some embarrassment, the Jeffersonian preferences for the common man were enlarged to take in the city workers.[11] In 1833 the New York Evening Post, declaring that, if anywhere, a large city of mixed population would display the evils of universal suffrage, asked if this had been the case in New York and answered: No. Amasa Walker set out the same year to prove that "great cities are not necessarily, as the proverb says, 'great sores,'" and looked forward cheerily to the day when they would be "great fountains of healthful moral influence, sending forth streams that shall fertilize and bless the land." The elder Theodore Sedgwick added that the cause of the bad reputation of cities was economic: "it is the sleeping in garrets and cellars; the living in holes and dens; in dirty, unpaved, unlighted streets, without the accommodations of wells, cisterns, baths, and other means of cleanliness and health" — clear up this situation, and cities will be all right.[12]

Jackson himself never betrayed any of Jefferson's revulsion to industrialism. He was, for example, deeply interested by the mills of

[9] Jefferson, "Notes on Virginia," Writings (Memorial Edition), II, 230; Jefferson to Madison, December 20, 1787, ibid., VI, 392–393. For similar comments, see Charles A. Beard, Economic Origins of Jeffersonian Democracy, 247, 421–426; W. A. Robinson, Jeffersonian Democracy in New England, 102.

[10] Ingersoll, Historical Sketch of the Second War between the United States of America and Great Britain, I, 212–213.

[11] The situation in New York, where the country regularly voted Whig and the city Democratic, very much worried the Democratic Review, a fairly pious organ of Jeffersonianism. "As a general rule," the Review observed in some perplexity, "we are free to confess that we prefer the suffrages of the country to those of the city. . . . The farmer is naturally a Democrat — the citizen may be so, but it is in spite of many obstacles." "New York City vs. New York State," Democratic Review, VI, 500 (December, 1839).

[12] New York Evening Post, July 5, 1833; Amasa Walker, Address Delivered . . . on the Fiftyseventh Anniversary of American Independence, 12–13; Theodore Sedgwick, Public and Private Economy, III, 121, 138, 143.

Lowell in 1833, and his inquiries respecting hours, wages and production showed, observers reported, "that the subject of domestic
manufactures had previously engaged his attentive observation." [13] His
presidential allusions to the "producing classes" always included the
workingmen of the cities.

3

The acceptance of the propertyless laboring classes involved
a retreat from one of the strongest Jeffersonian positions. John Taylor's
distinction between "natural" and "artificial" property had enabled the
Jeffersonians to enlist the moral and emotional resources contained in
the notion of property. They could claim to be the protectors of
property rights, while the business community, by despoiling the producers of the fruits of their labor, were the enemies of property. Yet,
this distinction, if it were to have other than a metaphorical existence,
had to rest on the dominance of agriculture and small handicraft. The
proceeds of the labor of a farmer, or a blacksmith, could be measured
with some exactness; but who could say what the "just" fruits of labor
were for a girl whose labor consisted in one small operation in the
total process of manufacturing cotton cloth? In what sense could
propertyless people be deprived of their property?

Taylor had repeatedly warned that "fictitious" property would seek
to win over "real" property by posing as the champion of all property
against the mob. Now that the Democrats were the party, not only
of small holders, but of propertyless workers, the conservative pose
seemed more plausible. The Whigs diligently set forth to make every
attack on "fictitious" capital an attack on all property rights. "The
philosophy that denounces accumulation," said Edward Everett, "is
the philosophy of barbarism." [14] The outcry over monopoly, added
Henry Clay, is "but a new form of attacking the rights of property. A
man may not use his property in what form he pleases, even if
sanctioned by the laws of the community in which he lives, without
being denounced as a monopolist." [15]

The Whigs slowly won the battle. The discovery of the courts that
a corporation was really a person completed their victory. By 1843

[13] *Boston Atlas,* quoted in *Niles' Register,* July 6, 1833. See also Josiah Quincy,
Figures of the Past, 374.

[14] Everett, *Address, Delivered before the Mercantile Library Association,* 10.

[15] Clay in the Senate, February 14, 1840, *Congressional Globe,* 26 Congress 1
Session, Appendix, 178. Benton made the Jeffersonian reply, declaring himself
"sorry to hear the monarchical cry against attacks on property. It was an old cry,
beginning with the origin of monopolies, and continued down to the present
day. There were but two parties in politics, and never had been, and never would

William S. Wait could strike the Jeffersonian flag: " 'Security to property' no longer means security to the citizen in the possession of his moderate competency, but security to him who monopolizes thousands — security to a few, who may live in luxury and ease upon the blood and sweat of many." [16]

Jacksonians now tended to exalt human rights as a counterweight to property rights. The Whigs, charged Frank Blair, were seeking such an extension of "the rights of property as to swallow up and annihilate those of persons"; the Democratic party would "do all in its power to preserve and defend them." "We believe property should be held subordinate to man, and not man to property," said Orestes A. Brownson; "and therefore that it is always lawful to make such modifications of its constitution as the good of Humanity requires." [17] The early decisions of Roger B. Taney's court helped establish the priority of the public welfare. But the Democrats had surrendered an important ideological bastion. The right to property provided a sturdy foundation for liberalism, while talk of human rights too often might end up in sentimentality or blood.

In several respects, then, the Jacksonians revised the Jeffersonian faith for America. They moderated that side of Jeffersonianism which talked of agricultural virtue, independent proprietors, "natural" property, abolition of industrialism, and expanded immensely that side which talked of economic equality, the laboring classes, human rights and the control of industrialism. This readjustment enabled the Jacksonians to attack economic problems which had baffled and defeated the Jeffersonians. It made for a greater realism, and was accompanied by a general toughening of the basic Jeffersonian conceptions. While the loss of "property" was serious, both symbolically and intellectually, this notion had been for most Jeffersonians somewhat submerged next to the romantic image of the free and virtuous cultivator; and the Jacksonians grew much more insistent about theories of capitalist alienation. Where, for the Jeffersonians, the tensions of class conflict tended to dissolve in vague generalizations about the democracy and the aristocracy, many Jacksonians would have agreed with A. H. Wood's remark, "It is in vain to talk of Aristocracy and Democracy — these terms are too variable and indeterminate to convey adequate

---

be [but two]. . . . One of these parties, after getting undue advantages, formerly by force, now by corporations and monopolies, always raise the cry of attacks on property when any of their undue acquisitions were in danger. . . . Far from attacking property, it was monopoly which was attacked." *Ibid.*, 179.

[16] *Springfield* (Illinois) *Gazette*, August 25, 1843.

[17] *Washington Globe*, June 12, 1839; Brownson, "The Laboring Classes" (second article), *Boston Quarterly Review*, III, 481 (October, 1840).

ideas of the present opposing interests; the division is between the rich and the poor — the warfare is between them." [18]

This greater realism was due, in the main, to the passage of time. The fears of Jefferson were now actualities. One handled fears by exorcism, but actualities by adjustment. For the Jeffersonians mistrust of banks and corporations was chiefly a matter of theory; for the Jacksonians it was a matter of experience. The contrast between the scintillating metaphors of John Taylor and the sober detail of William M. Gouge expressed the difference. Jefferson rejected the Industrial Revolution and sought to perpetuate the smiling society which preceded it (at least, so the philosopher; facts compelled the President toward a different policy), while Jackson, accepting industrialism as an ineradicable and even useful part of the economic landscape, sought rather to control it. Jeffersonian democracy looked wistfully back toward a past slipping further every minute into the mists of memory, while Jacksonian democracy came straightforwardly to grips with a rough and unlovely present.

The interlude saw also the gradual unfolding of certain consequences of the democratic dogma which had not been so clear to the previous generation. Though theoretically aware of the relation between political and economic power, the Jeffersonians had been occupied, chiefly, with establishing political equality. This was their mission, and they had little time to grapple with the economic questions.

But the very assertion of political equality raised inevitably the whole range of problems involved in property and class conflict. How could political equality mean anything without relative economic equality among the classes of the country? This question engaged the Jacksonians. As Orestes A. Brownson said, "A Loco-foco is a Jeffersonian Democrat, who having realized political equality, passed through one phase of the revolution, now passes on to another, and attempts the realization of social equality, so that the actual condition of men in society shall be in harmony with their acknowledged rights as citizens." [19] This gap between Jeffersonian and Jacksonian democracy enabled men like John Quincy Adams, Henry Clay, Joseph Story and many others, who had been honest Jeffersonians, to balk at the economic extremities to which Jackson proposed to lead them.

The Jacksonians thus opened irrevocably the economic question,

[18] In a speech at a meeting of the Stonecutters' Union, *Boston Post*, April 17, 1835.

[19] Brownson, "Address to the Workingmen," *Boston Quarterly Review*, IV, 117 (January, 1841).

which the Jeffersonians had only touched halfheartedly. Yet, while they clarified these economic implications of democracy, the Jacksonians were no more successful than their predecessors in resolving certain political ambiguities. Of these, two were outstanding — the problem of the virtue of majorities, and the problem of the evil of government. Since the Jacksonians made useful explorations of these issues after 1840, they will be reserved for later discussion.

4

A second source of inspiration for the Jacksonians was the libertarian economic thought stirred up by Adam Smith and *The Wealth of Nations*. Believers in the myth of Adam Smith, as expounded by present-day publicists both of the right and of the left, may find this singular; but the real Adam Smith was rich in ammunition for the Jacksonians, as for any foe of business manipulation of the state.[20]

The Wealth of Nations quietly, precisely and implacably attacked the alliance of government and business, showing how monopoly retarded the economic growth of nations and promoted the exploitation of the people. It was, in effect, a criticism of the kind of mercantilist policy which, in modified form, Hamilton had instituted in the Federalist program of the seventeen-nineties. Smith's classic argument against monopoly appealed strongly to the Jacksonians, and his distinction between productive and unproductive labor converged with the Jacksonian distinction between the producers and the nonproducers. They adopted his labor theory of value, in preference to the physiocratic doctrine which argued that value originated exclusively in land, and toward which Jefferson leaned. Smith's currency views were on the moderate hard-money line, favoring the suppression of notes under five pounds. And, contrary to the Adam Smith of folklore, the real Smith had no objection to government intervention which would protect, not exploit, the nation. "Those exertions of the natural liberty of a few individuals," he wrote, discussing the question of banking control, "which might endanger the security of the whole society, are, and ought to be, restrained by the laws of all governments; of the most free, as well as of the most despotical." [21] His advocacy of education and his general hope for the well-being of the farming and laboring classes further recommended him to the Jacksonians.

[20] For a corrective of the distortions of Adam Smith, see the essays by John M. Clark and Jacob Viner in *Adam Smith, 1776–1926*, and Eli Ginzberg, *The House of Adam Smith*.

[21] Adam Smith, *Wealth of Nations*, book ii, chapter 2.

In many respects, Adam Smith formulated on the economic level the same sentiments which Jefferson put into glowing moral and political language. Jefferson himself thought *The Wealth of Nations* "the best book extant" on economic questions.[22] The translation of J. B. Say's popularization of Smith increased the currency of laissez-faire doctrine. The little village of Stockbridge in Massachusetts was a particular center of free-trade thought. When Theodore Sedgwick observed of Adam Smith in 1838, "His voice has been ringing in the world's ears for sixty years, but it is only now in the United States that he is listened to, reverenced, and followed," the credit for this awakening went in great part to himself.[23] His missionary efforts converted William Cullen Bryant, David Dudley Field and Theodore Sedgwick, Jr., and it was doubtless from Bryant that the previously nonpolitical Leggett got his introduction to *The Wealth of Nations*.

Leggett's brand of radicalism consisted almost entirely in a vigorous and unsparing effort to apply the doctrine of Adam Smith to the emerging corporate society.[24] "If we analyze the nature and essence of free governments," Leggett wrote, "we shall find that they are more or less free in proportion to the absence of *monopolies*." [25] From this central conviction stemmed his denunciation of the Bank, of the paper system and of the exclusive character of corporate grants. The *Evening Post* remained under Bryant's editorship the most consistently able organ of free-trade opinion. The radical wing of New York Democrats were the special advocates of *laissez faire*. C. C. Cambreleng, defending the Jacksonian program from the charge of agrarianism, once exclaimed indignantly in the House, "Were Franklin and Jefferson agrarians, sir? Was Adam Smith an agrarian?" [26] Colonel Samuel Young was a student of Smith and Say, as well as of Bentham, and the original Locofocos were free traders of the most doctrinaire sort.[27]

[22] Jefferson to Thomas Mann Randolph, May 30, 1790, Jefferson, *Writings* (Memorial Edition), VIII, 31. Cf. Jefferson to John Norvell, June 11, 1807, *ibid.*, XI, 223.

[23] Sedgwick, *Public and Private Economy*, II, 119.

[24] In 1834 George H. Evans suggested that the series on banking in the *Working Man's Advocate* in 1831 had first called Leggett's attention to the subject. Leggett replied that he could not recall ever having read the articles; "our sentiments on the subject of banking are the result of reflections occasioned by the perusal of political economists," and the "earliest notions" came from Adam Smith. *New York Evening Post*, September 18, 1834.

[25] *New York Evening Post*, March 20, 1834.

[26] Cambreleng in the House, February 11, 1835, *Register of Debates*, 23 Congress 2 Session, 1316.

[27] Some Democrats would have nothing to do with Smith. Thomas Hart Benton repudiated him, John Ferral, the Philadelphia labor leader, was highly suspicious, and John Commerford of New York felt that his theories had been destroyed by

The basic economic conception, which Adam Smith shared with Jefferson, was of a "natural order of things," that, once cleared of monopolistic clogs, would function to the greatest good of the greatest number. This conception, for all its apparent clarity, soon turned out to be packed with ambiguities. Free enterprise might mean, as with Leggett, a fighting belief in the virtue of competition, or it might mean, as with present-day conservatives, a fighting belief in the evil of government intervention. The battles of the Jackson era showed how these two interpretations of *laissez faire* were to come into increasing conflict.

The Jacksonians, vigorously in the first camp, had no hesitation in advocating government intervention in order to restore competition. In any case, their conception of the "natural order" — the region in which government was obligated not to interfere — included the right of the workingman to the full proceeds of his labor. Government, said Van Buren, should always be administered so as to insure to the laboring classes "a full enjoyment of the fruits of their industry."

> Left to itself, and free from the blighting influence of partial legislation, monopolies, congregated wealth, and interested combinations, the compensation of labor will always preserve this salutary relation. It is only when the natural order of society is disturbed by one or other of these causes, that the wages of labor become inadequate.[28]

The prescription of free enterprise thus became government action to destroy the "blighting influence of partial legislation, monopolies, congregated wealth, and interested combinations" in the interests of the "natural order of society."

But the language of Adam Smith, as a result of its origin in a critique of mercantilism as government policy, lent itself also to attacks on government intervention. The presidency of Jackson had begun to reduce the conservative enthusiasm, in the manner of Hamilton, for state interference, and the business community commenced now to pur-

---

the development of machinery. Benton in the Senate, January 27, 1837, *Register of Debates*, 24 Congress 2 Session, 589–590; Ferral in the *Radical Reformer*, July 18, 1835; Commerford in the *Working Man's Advocate*, March 30, 1844.

Smith was, at this time, much disapproved of in conservative circles. *The Wealth of Nations* sets forth crushing arguments against the claims of business to special favors from the state; and Henry C. Carey evolved the theory that free trade was a low British plot to prevent the development of manufacturing in America.

[28] Van Buren to Isaac Lippincott, *et al.*, September 14, 1840, *Bay State Democrat*, September 26, 1840.

loin the phrases of *laissez faire*. By 1888 E. M. Shepard, a Grover Cleveland Democrat, could dedicate a biography of Van Buren to the thesis that Van Buren was a thoroughgoing foe of government intervention — a thesis which required the total omission of such measures as the order establishing the ten-hour day.[29]

In the end, business altogether captured the phrases of *laissez faire* and used them more or less ruthlessly in defense of monopoly, even coupling them with arguments for the protective tariff, a juxtaposition which would at least have given earlier conservatives a decent sense of embarrassment. Adam Smith himself doubted whether large businessmen really believed in free competition. The sequel confirmed his doubts. The irony was that the slogans of free trade, which he developed in order to destroy monopoly, should end up as its bulwark.

5

A third important stimulus to the Jacksonians was the foaming tide of social revolt in Britain, reaching them primarily through the writings of William Cobbett. As the "Peter Porcupine" of Federalist journalism, Cobbett had been an early object of Jeffersonian wrath. But, on returning to Britain after some years in America, Cobbett discovered that the conservative values he had been so stalwartly defending were rapidly disappearing before the smoky ravages of industrialism. He gave splendid and angry expression to the hatred of independent workingmen for the impending degradation, and his fluent, robust, abusive prose created a new political consciousness among the common people of Britain.

A vehement advocate of the rights of workers to the full fruits of their industry, and a savage enemy of the new financial aristocracy, he found a rapt audience in America, especially in the labor movement. *Paper against Gold*, reprinted in New York in 1834, helped the hard-money campaign. William H. Hale of New York, the author of *Useful Knowledge for the Producers of Wealth*, and Thomas Brothers, the editor of the *Radical Reformer* of Philadelphia, were perhaps his leading disciples, but his unquenchable vitality inspired the whole radical wing.[30]

Cobbett on his part watched events across the Atlantic with immense enthusiasm. Jackson's fight against the Bank stirred him to the inordinate conclusion that Jackson was "the bravest and greatest man

[29] In other respects the Shepard biography is an excellent piece of work, still perhaps the best life of Van Buren.

[30] For Cobbett's influence, see *New York Evening Post*, September 7, 1835.

now living in this world, or that ever has lived in this world, as far as my knowledge extends." He wrote a life of Jackson (or rather interpolated characteristic comments into a reprint of Eaton's book), and even issued an abridged version of Gouge's *Paper Money*, under the title of *The Curse of Paper-Money and Banking*. He addressed superb open letters to the American President, and his admiration for "the greatest soldier and the greatest statesman whose name has ever yet appeared upon the records of valour and of wisdom" never faltered.[31]

Yet, with all his passion for social justice, Cobbett talked very little about democracy. He seemed almost to feel — and his American followers had similar overtones — that, if the speculators, rag barons and capitalists were thrown out, and the lower classes instituted in power, the main problems of society would be solved. His gusty idealization of the British yeoman, redolent of beef and beer, led him away from theories of class balance into implications of class infallibility, almost at times leaning from democracy toward socialism. These were but shadings, and in his American disciples shades of shadings. Yet George H. Evans, John Commerford, John Ferral and the early labor leaders seemed to regard democracy as more protective doctrine than good in itself. In power they might have acted little differently — if toward different ends — from Daniel Webster and Nicholas Biddle.

6

The radical democrats had a definite conception of their relation to history. From the Jeffersonian analysis, fortified by the insights of Adam Smith and Cobbett, they sketched out an interpretation of modern times which gave meaning and status to the Jacksonian struggles.

Power, said the Jacksonians, goes with property. In the Middle Ages the feudal nobility held power in society through its monopoly of land under feudal tenure. The overthrow of feudalism, with the rise of new forms of property, marked the first step in the long march toward freedom. The struggle was carried on by the rising business community — "commercial, or business capital, against landed capital; merchants, traders, manufacturers, artizans, against the owners of the soil, the great landed nobility." [32] It lasted from the close of the twelfth century to the Whig Revolution of 1688 in Britain.

The aristocracy of capital thus destroyed the aristocracy of land.

---

[31] Cobbett, *Life of Andrew Jackson*, iii, iv. See also *Cobbett's Political Register*, September 15, 1832, April 5, 1834, February 14, 1835; *Niles' Register*, September 6, 1834.

[32] Brownson, *Oration before the Democracy of Worcester and Vicinity*. 14.

The business classes here performed their vital role in the drama of liberty. The victory over feudalism, as the *Democratic Review* put it, "opened the way for the entrance of the democratic principle into the Government." [33] But the business community gained from this exploit an undeserved reputation as the champion of liberty. Its real motive had been to establish itself in power, not to free mankind; to found government on property, not on the equal rights of the people. "I know perfectly well what I am saying," cried George Bancroft, "and I assert expressly, and challenge contradiction, that in all the history of the world there is not to be found an instance of a commercial community establishing rules for self-government upon democratic principles." [34] "It is a mistake to suppose commerce favorable to liberty," added Fenimore Cooper. "Its tendency is to a monied aristocracy." [35] "Instead of setting man free," said Amos Kendall, it has "only increased the number of his masters." [36]

The next great blow for liberty was the American Revolution, "effected not in favor of men in classes; . . . but in favor of men." [37] But the work of Hamilton halted the march of democracy. "He established the money power," wrote Van Buren, "upon precisely the same foundations upon which it had been raised in England." [38] The subsequent history of the United States was the struggle to overthrow the Hamiltonian policy and fulfill the ideals of the Revolution.

What of the future? The Jacksonians were sublimely confident: history was on their side. "It is now for the yeomanry and the mechanics to march at the head of civilization," said Bancroft. "The merchants and the lawyers, that is, the moneyed interest broke up feudalism. The day for the multitude has now dawned." "All classes, each in turn, have possessed the government," exclaimed Brownson; "and the time has come for all predominance of class to end; for Man, the People to rule." [39]

[33] "European Views of American Democracy. — No. II," *Democratic Review*, II, 343 (July, 1838).
[34] *Franklin Mercury*, March 3, 1835. Cf. Bancroft, *Oration Delivered before the Democracy of Springfield*, 6–9.
[35] Cooper, *The American Democrat*, H. L. Mencken, ed., 160. Cf. Cooper, *Gleanings in Europe*, R. E. Spiller, ed., II, 177: "Commerce detests popular rights. It is, in itself, an aristocracy of wealth."
[36] *Washington Globe*, September 24, 1840.
[37] Brownson, "Tendency of Modern Civilization," *Boston Quarterly Review*, I, 236 (April, 1838).
[38] Van Buren, *Political Parties*, 166.
[39] Bancroft to Brownson, September 21, 1836, H. F. Brownson, *Brownson's Early Life*, 180–181; Brownson, "Tendency of Modern Civilization," *loc. cit.*, 237. The sentiment was widespread. Richard Hildreth, formerly editor of the *Boston Atlas*, could write: "The clergy, the nobles, the king, the burghers have all had

This was not simply a national movement. It was a movement of all people, everywhere, against their masters, and the Jacksonians watched with keen interest the stirrings of revolt abroad. Jackson and his cabinet joined in the celebrations in Washington which followed the Revolution of 1830 in France; and Van Buren, as Secretary of State, ordered the new government informed that the American people were "universally and enthusiastically in favor of that change, and of the principle upon which it was effected." (The Whigs, on the other hand, in spite of Clay's support of national revolutions in Greece and South America, remained significantly lukewarm.) [40] Lamennais, the eloquent voice of French popular aspirations, was read in Jacksonian circles. The *Paroles d'un Croyant* influenced Orestes A. Brownson, and in 1839 *Le Livre du Peuple* was published in Boston under the title of *The People's Own Book*, translated by Nathaniel Greene, postmaster of Boston, brother of Charles Gordon Greene of the *Post* and intimate of David Henshaw.

Democrats followed with similar enthusiasm the progress of the Reform Bill in England, while the Whigs sympathized with the Tories. The Chartist uprisings at the end of the decade were greeted with delight by the Democratic press. British reformers returned this interest. Not only Cobbett and Savage Landor but the veteran radical Jeremy Bentham observed Jackson's administration with approval. Bentham, a friend of John Quincy Adams, had been disappointed at the triumph in 1828 of this military hero; but early in 1830, as he huddled by his hissing steam radiator, he heard read aloud Jackson's first message to Congress. The old man was highly pleased to discover greater agreement with the new President than with the old. Later he wrote that lengthy and cryptic memorandum entitled *Anti-Senatica*, intended to aid Jackson in the problems of his administration.[41]

Jacksonians everywhere had this faith in the international significance of their fight. For this reason, as well as from a desire to capture their votes, Democratic leaders made special appeals to newly naturalized citizens.[42] Where many Whigs tended to oppose immigration and de-

---

their turn. Is there never to be an *Age of the People* — of the working classes?" *Theory of Politics*, 267.

[40] E. N. Curtis, "American Opinion of the French Nineteenth Century Revolutions," *American Historical Review*, XXIX, 249–270; E. N. Curtis, "La Révolution de 1830 et l'Opinion Publique en Amérique," *La Révolution de 1848*, XVIII, 64–73, 81–118.

[41] Bentham to Jackson, April 26, 1830, Bentham, *Works*, XI, 40; Bentham, *Anti-Senatica*, C. W. Everett, ed., especially 209–210.

[42] See, for example, Henry E. Riell, *An Appeal to the Voluntary Citizens of the United States*.

mand sanctions against it, Democrats welcomed the newcomers with open arms and attacked the nativist agitation. The United States must remain a refuge from tyranny. "The capitalist class," said Samuel J. Tilden, "has banded together all over the world and organized the *modern dynasty of associated wealth*, which maintains an unquestioned ascendency over most of the civilized portions of our race." America was the proving-ground of democracy, and it was the mission of American Democrats to exhibit to the world the glories of government by the people. They were on the spearhead of history. They would not be denied. "With the friends of freedom throughout the world," declared Theophilus Fisk, "let us be co-workers." "The People of the World," cried Fanny Wright, "have but one Cause." [43]

[43] John Bigelow, *Life of Samuel J. Tilden*, I, 39; Fisk, "Capital against Labor," *Working Man's Advocate*, July 25, 1835; Frances Wright in the *Free Enquirer*, October 9, 1830.

XXV JACKSONIAN DEMOCRACY AND THE LAW

DEFEATED in the open field by Jefferson, Federalism had retreated to prepared defenses. Under the resourceful leadership of John Marshall it entrenched itself in the courts of law and sought to make them unshakable bulwarks against change. Like every great democratic movement in American history, Jacksonian democracy eventually collided with the courts, running up sharply against their inclination to devise new guarantees for property and throw up new obstacles to popular control. The ensuing conflict had two main aspects: the struggle to change the personnel of the courts, and the struggle to simplify and reform the law itself.

1

The battle of the Supreme Court presented this conflict in its most compact and dramatic form. The long and superb series of decisions written by Marshall, or under his influence, had pretty well established the Constitution as a document which forbade government interference with private property, even on the ground of the public welfare. The jurists of many of the states were cast more or less crudely in Marshall's image. All agreed in repeating his prejudices, though rarely with his profundity, and all, operating as a kind of high priesthood of the law, agreed in detesting Jacksonian democracy. Chief Justice Spencer of New York would speak of "that barbarian Jackson," while Chancellor Kent called him "a detestable, ignorant, reckless, vain & malignant tyrant," and Chief Justice Daggett of Connecticut confessed in 1832 that he had never felt such forebodings: "The nation is too young, though corrupt enough, for destruction. May Heaven defend us!" [1]

But the Supreme Court remained the fortress of conservatism; and Joseph Story, next to Marshall its main pillar, freely expressed the prevalent fears. Six years of Andrew Jackson had convinced Story that

[1] Ambrose Spencer to Kent, September 21, 1832, Kent, *Kent*, 213; Kent to Story, April 11, 1834, *Proceedings of the Massachusetts Historical Society*, Second Series, XIV, 418; David Daggett to Kent, October 29, 1832, Kent, *Kent*, 217.

the country was "sinking down into despotism, under the disguise of a democratic government," and the Whig party supplied the only hope for the future.[2] "I am a Whig," he declared proudly to Henry Clay, and he could actually say to Nicholas Biddle, as late as 1838, that, if he had attained "a little to your approbation by my labor as a public magistrate," he would be much consoled, for he knew little "which ought to gratify one more, than to have a place in the respect of the wise, the good, and the honored of our times."[3] A man of somewhat more learning than wisdom, Story at times grew so insistent about the failure of democratic institutions that foreigners considered his remarks almost treasonable.[4]

The death of Marshall in the summer of 1835 perfected the conservative despair. The last bulwark of their cause, or, as they preferred to describe it, their country's liberties, had fallen. With his next appointment Jackson would have not only the Chief Justice but a majority of the Court. William Leggett candidly observed for the Democrats that Marshall's power on the Court had always been "an occasion of lively regret. That he is at length removed from that station is a source of satisfaction."[5]

Some Whigs began to torment themselves with the thought of Benton as Marshall's successor, but the Missouri colossus himself exploded at the idea. "These fellows are no more able to comprehend me," he wrote, ". . . than a rabbit, which breeds twelve times a year, could comprehend the gestation of an elephant, which carries two years. So of these fellows and me. Dying for small offices themselves, they cannot understand that I can refuse all. . . . Taney is my favorite for that place."[6] Taney was also Jackson's favorite, and in every respect the logical choice. Marshall himself had favored him for an earlier appointment as Associate Justice, for which he had been rejected by the Senate, and the conservatives could hardly have expected a better selection. But they remained angry and unforgiving.

[2] Charles Warren, *The Supreme Court in United States History* (revised edition), I, 796.

[3] Story to Clay, August 3, 1842, Story to Biddle, March 22, 1838, Swisher, *Taney,* 430, 202.

[4] Lord Morpeth, Diary, manuscript transcript, December 11, 1841, on a dinner at Story's; Jeremiah Mason, Josiah Quincy and George Ticknor were also present. "The judge our host talked with incessant but pleasant and kindly flow; the conversation approached very near to treason against their own constitution; they pronounce it an utter failure, especially with respect to the election of fit men for the office of President; . . . they talk much as Lord Grey would talk of the present proceedings of the Reform Parliament."

[5] *New York Evening Post,* July 8, 1835.

[6] Benton to Van Buren, June 7, 1835, Van Buren Papers.

"The pure ermine of the Supreme Court," observed the *New York American* after Taney's confirmation, "is sullied by the appointment of that political hack."[7]

2

The new Chief Justice wore trousers instead of the traditional knee breeches, and he showed in other ways that he was prepared to ignore the past. Two important issues in his first term gave him the chance to start breaking new trails. One involved the question whether corporate charters should be construed in favor of the corporation or in favor of the community. The second involved questions of the power of states to enforce laws affecting interstate commerce. Taney's answers, formulated with the same realism and lucidity, the same powerful appeal to principles rather than to precedents, the same classic finality as Marshall's, revealed the drift of the Court in the direction of narrowing the immunities of corporations and enlarging the scope of social legislation.[8]

The crucial case in the retreat from Federalism was the fight, so long a staple of Massachusetts politics, between the Charles River Bridge and the Warren Bridge. The question was whether the legislature of Massachusetts, by authorizing the construction of a free bridge over the Charles River at a point where it would interfere with the profits of a privately owned toll bridge, had impaired the contract of the toll-bridge corporation. The case had been argued before the Supreme Court in 1831, but no decision was handed down. It was reargued in 1837, with Daniel Webster as one of the counsels for the bridge company. The fact that Harvard College, as well as many leading citizens of Boston, held stock in the Charles River Bridge increased the general tension.

The issue brought the Federalist and Jeffersonian views of the place of corporations in society into sharp collision. "I consider the interference of the legislature in the management of our private affairs, whether those affairs are committed to a company or remain under individual direction," John Marshall had written, "as equally dangerous and unwise."[9] His decision in the Dartmouth College case that a charter was a contract which a state could not impair was de-

---

[7] *New York American*, March 17, 1836; Warren, *Supreme Court*, II, 16.

[8] My account owes a great deal to Swisher's analysis in his excellent life of Taney. See also the relevant chapters in Warren, *Supreme Court*, Boudin, *Government by Judiciary*, and C. W. Smith, Jr., *Roger B. Taney: Jacksonian Jurist*.

[9] Marshall to Greenhow, October 17, 1809, A. J. Beveridge, *Life of John Marshall*, IV, 479–480.

signed to put corporations safely out of reach of state intervention.

Taney, on the other hand, had made clear as Attorney General that in his mind an act of incorporation — particularly in the case of corporations which perform essential public services, such as constructing roads and bridges — could "never be considered as having been granted for the exclusive benefit of the corporators. Certain privileges are given to them, in order to obtain a public convenience; and the interest of the public must, I presume, always be regarded as the main object of every charter for a toll-bridge or a turnpike road." [10]

He had furthermore informed Jackson privately that, with regard to other than strictly public-utility corporations: —

> It would be against the spirit of our free institutions, by which equal rights are intended to be secured to all, to grant peculiar franchises and privileges to a body of individuals merely for the purpose of enabling them more conveniently and effectually to advance their own private interests. . . . The consideration upon which alone, such peculiar privileges can be granted is the expectation and prospect of promoting thereby some public interest.[11]

An advanced radical Democrat, Taney, like Marshall for the quarter century preceding, set out to read his "economic predilections" into the Constitution.

The Supreme Court handed down the bridge decision on February 14, 1837, with Taney holding in the majority opinion that no rights were granted in a corporate charter except those explicitly conferred by the words of the charter. Charters of incorporation, in other words, could not be construed inferentially against the community. "The object and end of all government," Taney declared in words central to an understanding of Jacksonian democracy, "is to promote the happiness and prosperity of the community by which it is established; and it can never be assumed, that the government intended to diminish its power of accomplishing the end for which it was created. . . . The continued existence of a government would be of no great value, if by implications and presumptions, it was disarmed of the powers necessary to accomplish the ends of its creation; and the functions it was designed to perform, transferred to the hands of privileged corporations." But what of the rights of property? "While the rights of private property are sacredly guarded," rejoined Taney,

---

[10] Taney, "The Norfolk Drawbridge Co. and the United States," May 16, 1832, *Official Opinions of the Attorneys General of the United States*, B. F. Hall, comp., II, 514.

[11] Taney memorandum in Jackson Papers, Swisher, *Taney*, 366–367.

"we must not forget that the community also have rights, and that the happiness and well being of every citizen depends on their faithful preservation." [12]

He argued, in effect, that the absolute protection of property rights did not infallibly secure the general welfare — a repudiation of the tacit major premise of Federalism. Only Justice Story differed, in a long and tedious opinion — crammed with citation of precedent — opaque next to Taney's luminous argument. Now and then Story's apprehensions burst through his logic. "The very agitation of a question of this sort," he exclaimed, "is sufficient to alarm every stockholder in every public enterprise of this sort, throughout the whole country." Privately he declared that "a case of grosser injustice, or more oppressive legislation, never existed." [13]

The second critical case was the *City of New York v. Miln*. The question was whether in the absence of congressional legislation a state could require ship captains to report certain information about passengers from other states. Philip P. Barbour of Virginia, author of the majority opinion (Story alone dissenting), justified the New York port regulation as an exercise of police power. A state has "undeniable and unlimited jurisdiction over all persons and things within its territorial limits," Barbour declared, except as restrained by the Constitution. The powers of internal police are not thus restrained. What, then, constitute police measures? "We should say that every law came within this description which concerned the welfare of the whole people of a State, or any individual within it." [14] Later decisions showed that Taney considered the New York law constitutional as a commerce measure as well; he ruled, in other words, that states could pass laws regulating interstate commerce so long as they did not clash with federal legislation on the same subject. This enlargement of police power and limitation of the "dormant" commerce clause greatly increased the freedom of the states in economic legislation. [15]

A third case in the same term, *Briscoe v. The Bank of the Commonwealth of Kentucky*, further widened the realm of state legislation on social questions. Where Marshall had called a halt to the attempts of a state to restrain property on behalf of the community, Taney, by restricting the interpretation of contracts and expanding the com-

[12] 11 Peters 547, 548.
[13] 11 Peters 608; Story to Sarah W. Story, February 14, 1837, Story, *Story*, II, 268.
[14] 11 Peters 139.
[15] Felix Frankfurter, *The Commerce Clause under Marshall, Taney and Waite*, 50.

merce clause and the doctrine of police power, greatly increased the capacity of the states to act for the public welfare. Story remained in lonely dissent.

3

These new constitutional readings, cast in the teeth of embattled Federalism, excited wild alarm. Story returned to Massachusetts in utter dejection, contemplating resignation and overflowing with predictions of disaster. "I am the last of the old race of Judges," he lamented. "I stand their solitary representative, with a pained heart, and a subdued confidence. Do you remember the story of the last dinner of a club, who dined once a year? I am in the predicament of the last survivor." [16]

When Chancellor Kent first looked into Taney's opinion, he "dropped the pamphlet in disgust and read no more." Two months later he steeled himself to try again "and with increased disgust. . . . I have lost my confidence and hopes in the constitutional guardianship and protection of the Supreme Court." [17] What, then, was left? A few months later Kent poured out his melancholy at length. The Charles River Bridge decision, he said, "undermines the foundations of morality, confidence, and truth." The doctrine of strict construction of corporate charters was appalling: "what destruction of rights under a contract can be more complete?" The old man was beyond consolation. "When we consider the revolution in opinion, in policy, and in numbers that has recently changed the character of the Supreme Court, we can scarcely avoid being reduced nearly to a state of despair of the commonwealth." [18]

Conservatism was everywhere deep in gloom. Daniel Webster had been sure a year before that the Court was "*gone* . . . and almost everything is gone, or seem rapidly going." [19] After the bridge decision the Washington correspondent of a Boston paper warned darkly that investors in corporations "will do well to remember that this kind of property is no longer under the protection of law, but is held at the good pleasure of the legislature." [20] The *North American Review* observed sadly that the Court, "the last quarter to which we should have looked for any cause of concern," was in the hands of

[16] Story to Harriet Martineau, April 7, 1837, Story, *Story*, II, 277.
[17] Kent to Story, April 18, 1837, June 23, 1837, Story, *Story*, II, 237, 270.
[18] [James Kent], "Supreme Court of the United States," *New-York Review*, II, 387, 389, 402 (April, 1838).
[19] Webster to Caroline Webster, January 10, 1836, Webster, *Letters*, 198.
[20] *Independent Chronicle and Boston Patriot*, February 22, 1837.

the enemy. "We have fallen under a new dispensation in respect to the judiciary." [21]

4

The next year, Justice McKinley, riding federal circuit in Alabama, contributed a new doctrine to horrify the Whigs. The Bank of Augusta, Georgia, sought to sue certain Alabama debtors for refusing to pay bills of exchange. The question was whether a corporation could make an enforceable contract in commonwealths other than the one which created it. McKinley dismissed the suit on the ground that corporations could not make contracts in other states; in other words, that banks could not employ their banking powers outside the states which had directly chartered them. The implications of this decision for all interstate trade by corporations were staggering. "What then has dictated the unwarrantable and destructive innovation of Judge McKinley?" asked the furious *Madisonian*. "— The party spirit of Loco Focoism, which, being repudiated by the people, seeks the accomplishment of its diabolical purposes, by summary process!" [22]

Bank of Augusta v. Earle, with a cluster of similar cases, was quickly appealed to the Supreme Court. Daniel Webster and John Sergeant argued for the Bank of Augusta, and Charles J. Ingersoll upheld the McKinley ruling. In a passionate plea Ingersoll declared that the Court, if it licensed the activities of foreign corporations, would, in effect, create them in places where the people had not seen fit to do so. Webster, with equal vehemence, took the opposite position: that corporations were guaranteed privileges and immunities in all states by the constitutional provision entitling citizens of each state to the privileges of citizens of the several states. This argument would have made corporations almost impregnable.

Taney, writing the majority opinion, steered brilliantly between the alternatives. Recognizing the usefulness of corporations, he declined to destroy them; recognizing their danger, he declined to sanctify them. He therefore conceded the power of corporations to make contracts in other states through agents by virtue of comity; but he conceded also the right of states to exclude such corporations by express action. In the absence of specific prohibition, however, the

---

[21] [C. S. Davies], "Constitutional Law," *North American Review*, XLVI, 128, 153 (January, 1838). See also "Political Regeneration," *American Monthly Magazine*, V, 299 (April, 1838).

[22] *Madisonian*, June 16, 1838.

right to transact business was to be presumed. The actual decision thus favored the Bank of Augusta, but the grounds supplied the states with new resources of regulatory power. By affirming the right of the state to repudiate the principle of comity, Taney provided a formula for later legislation on out-of-state corporations; and by rejecting Webster's theory that corporations were protected by the privileges and immunities of the Constitution, he staved off the notion that a corporation was a citizen.[23]

But characteristically the Court failed to live up to either the hopes of the radicals or the fears of the conservatives. The uproar of 1837 soon subsided, the profligate judges settled into respectability, and the Court began to recover its former reputation. The most determined critic of judicial usurpation is likely to succumb, once on the Court, to a loyalty to the institution and a faith in its power when used on the right side. Moreover, however ingenious the judge, conservatism is inherent in the very process of *stare decisis;* and in the case of Taney and the Southern judges, a certain indifference to the sanctity of corporate property was balanced by a mounting solicitude for slave property. Justice Daniel of Virginia continued a lonely opposition to any appeasement of corporations, but the Court as a whole advanced very little from the positions it took in its first term.[24]

Some progressives continued to urge Supreme Court reform. Van Buren, like Jefferson before him, favored an elective judiciary, and men like John Wentworth of Illinois would occasionally propose that terms on the Court be limited, but the comparative self-denial of the Taney Court stilled the bitter complaints aroused by the judicial imperialism of Marshall.[25]

5

A leading source of the power of judges and lawyers, the Jacksonians felt, lay in the ambiguities of the law. The existing chaos of statutes and common law was held to hand over great discretionary power to the courts as well as to make a mystery out of justice which rendered the bar indispensable, thereby creating a legal and judicial aristocracy. Radical Democrats accordingly began to initiate movements toward legal reform — toward simplifying the laws and pro-

---

[23] For an excellent analysis, see G. C. Henderson, *Position of Foreign Corporations in American Constitutional Law.*
[24] B. F. Wright, Jr., *Contract Clause of the Constitution*, 62.
[25] Van Buren, *Autobiography*, 184–185; B. F. Perry, *Reminiscences of Public Men, Second Series*, 184; Wentworth to George Barstow, *et al.*, February 22, 1840, *Boston Post*, May 9, 1840.

cedure, toward making courts more accessible to public opinion, and toward codification, especially of the common law.

The neo-Federalists, keenly aware of the importance of preserving control over the courts, resisted such proposals. Men like Story regarded "the wholesome principles of the common law" as "the bulwark of our public liberties, and the protecting shield of our private property." [26] In their pastoral moods Whigs would sing of the common law as "emphatically the law of the people. . . . they carry it about with them unconsciously: it waits like an invisible spirit on their secret thoughts: the monitor of the breast speaks to them in its language. . . . Statutes are further off from the people: they are formal things." [27] This was very touching, perhaps, but the people themselves were developing a low suspicion that the monitor of the breast was too often speaking the bidding of their masters.

As Robert Rantoul pointed out, the common law, "indefinitely and vaguely settled, and its exact limits unknown," gave far too much scope to the discretion of judges. Theophilus Fisk added harshly that the common law, "based upon deception, extortion, villainy and fraud," was "one of the most potent of all engines in the hand of an air bubble aristocracy, to rob the many to benefit the few." Even a Whig like Richard Hildreth, much influenced by Bentham, was moved to describe it as "directly hostile to the spirit of democracy." It should not so much be regarded as a system for the administration of justice, he said, "as a contrivance for setting aside the laws, and defeating the intentions of the legislative body, whenever those laws and those intentions fail to meet the approbation of the judges." "Under an enlightened democratical government," he concluded, "it is entirely out of place — becoming, in fact, a contrivance to enable the few to defeat the wishes of the many." [28]

The spreading dissatisfaction bred a movement toward codification, both of the common law and of the statutes, led by Edward Livingston of Louisiana. A friend of Bentham's, a careful student of jurisprudence and an able lawyer, Livingston made proposals for codification in Louisiana which attracted national attention. His close friendship with Jackson and his place in the cabinet helped the doctrines of legal reform to penetrate the Democratic party.

Bentham himself was favorably known to the Jacksonians. A toast at a Democratic July Fourth celebration at Boston in 1835 pronounced

[26] 11 Peters 639.
[27] [Theodore Frelinghuysen?], *An Inquiry into the Moral and Religious Character of the American Government*, 91–92.
[28] Rantoul, "Oration at Scituate, July 4, 1836," Hamilton, *Rantoul*, 278; Fisk, *Labor the Only True Source of Wealth*, 16; Hildreth, *Theory of Politics*, 264.

him "the modern apostle of liberty and reform. . . . may every democrat and workingman remember that he has most happily combined the essence of their principles in one short line — 'The greatest good of the greatest number.' " [29] Hildreth, the leading American Benthamite, was a Whig, but his translation of Dumont's redaction of Bentham's *Theory of Legislation* was welcomed in Democratic journals. The *Democratic Review*, while skeptical of utility as the ultimate ethical standard, was enthusiastic about it as the test for legislation and paid warm tribute to "the father of law reform, the founder of legislative science, the powerful advocate of political emancipation, and a distinguished friend of the moral advancement of the human race." [30]

The fight for codification took place against strong conservative opposition. As Chancellor Kent observed to Livingston, "I have spent the best years of my life in administering the old common law . . . *with all its imperfections on its head*." [31] Why change it? But the pressure for change was too strong. In 1827 Benjamin F. Butler took a leading part in the preparation of the *Revised Statutes of the State of New York*, the first successful attempt to put together in a systematic code the common law and the existing colonial and state laws. Pennsylvania followed suit in the early eighteen-thirties; in 1833–1834 Salmon P. Chase produced the *Revision of the Statutes of Ohio;* and, in 1836, Robert Rantoul's tireless agitation in Massachusetts resulted in the appointment of a committee on the expediency of codifying the common law, though Justice Story, as chairman, was able to keep it from doing very much. "We have not yet become votaries to the notions of Jeremy Bentham," Story said privately. "But the present state of popular opinion here makes it necessary to do something on the subject." [32] Where the Jacksonian attack did not achieve immediate consolidation of the statutes, it often succeeded in simplifying procedure and particularly in reforming the baffling systems of special pleading and practice. The constitutions of the new Western states also showed the mark of the Jacksonian reforms.

[29] Gorham A. Parks of Maine, *Boston Post*, July 7, 1835.

[30] "Jeremy Bentham," *Democratic Review*, VIII, 252 (September, 1840). For similar comments, see, e.g., *Boston Post*, May 16, 1840, *New York Evening Post*, June 11, 1840.

[31] Kent to Livingston, n.d., *American Jurist*, XVI, 320; Horton, *Kent*, 271 n.

[32] Story to J. J. Wilkinson, December 26, 1836, *Proceedings of the Massachusetts Historical Society*, second series, XV, 221. See also Hamilton, *Rantoul*, 48. The campaign against the common law centered particularly on the common-law doctrine of criminal libel. The *Boston Post* several times came to the defense of political opponents when their freedom of expression appeared to be threatened by the courts: e.g., George B. Cheever in 1835 and Richard Hildreth in 1837. For a general account, see Charles Warren, *History of the American Bar*, 508–531.

6

Stockbridge was again a particular center of reform enthusiasm. The elder Theodore Sedgwick had long advocated changes in practice, particularly the abolition of costs, and he inspired his son with a concern for reform which produced several pamphlets and treatises.

But the outstanding figure among the law reformers was David Dudley Field. Born in Connecticut in 1805, he grew up in Stockbridge and became one of the most striking products of that remarkable village. In the end the Fields were an even more distinguished family than the Sedgwicks. Of David Dudley's brothers, Cyrus laid the transatlantic cable, Stephen had fifty-four years of useful service on the Supreme Court, and Henry married Henriette Desportes, the charming governess who figured so enigmatically in the murder of the Duchesse de Praslin.

An energetic youth, David Dudley entered the law office of Robert and Henry D. Sedgwick in New York and ultimately rose to partnership. He became a fervent champion of free trade and aligned himself politically with Martin Van Buren. He was too arrogant for political success, but his hard brilliance made him a good trial lawyer, and his industry and persistence equipped him for his tireless battle for law reform. Early struck by the gratuitous complexity of the statute book, Field grew increasingly concerned with the need for codification. Livingston's *Report on a Code for Louisiana,* and the encouragement of the Sedgwicks, finally made him an active advocate.

Field's pamphlets and speeches helped stir up the sentiment which resulted in inserting into the New York constitution of 1846 two provisions aiming at a general code and reform of the practice of the courts. Appointed a commissioner in 1847 under these provisions, Field labored day and night on reconstructing the codes of procedure. By 1850 complete revisions of criminal and civil procedure were submitted to the legislature. In 1857 he secured the passage of an act ordering the codification of the whole body of law.

New York actually was very slow in adopting the codes drawn up under this act, and some were never adopted; but, as usual with reform in American history, the new states were less suspicious and proceeded to put into operation reforms worked out in the old. With Field's aid and advice, and in spite of harsh criticism in certain circles, his codes were enacted and imitated all over the country. Twenty-seven states and territories adopted his work as a whole or in part.

Field, who later was attorney for Boss Tweed and close friend of Jay Gould and Jim Fisk, was in many respects an unusual reformer. But he was passionately interested in improving the administration of justice, and, with all his vagaries, he represented the culmination of the Jacksonian demand for legal reform.[33] In the work of Roger B. Taney and David Dudley Field, history records most conveniently the impact of Jacksonian democracy on the law.

[33] H. M. Field, *Life of David Dudley Field;* Sedgwick and Marquand, *Stockbridge, 1739–1939,* 196–198; Theodore Sedgwick to Theodore Sedgwick, Jr., November 20, 1826, Sedgwick Papers.

XXVI JACKSONIAN DEMOCRACY
AND INDUSTRIALISM

FROM THE START of the century, first in banking and insurance, then in transportation, canals, bridges, turnpikes, then in manufacturing, the corporation was gradually becoming the dominant form of economic organization. The generation of Jackson was the first to face large-scale adjustment to this new economic mechanism. For owners and large investors, the adjustment presented no particular problem. But those on the outside had a feeling of deep misgiving which was less an economic or political than a moral protest: it was basically a sense of shock.

1

Economic life before the corporation, at least according to the prevalent conceptions, was more or less controlled by a feeling of mutual responsibility among the persons concerned. Economic relationships were generally personal — between master and workman laboring together in the same shop, between buyer and seller living together in the same village. The very character of this relation produced some restraints upon the tendency of the master to exploit the workman, or of the seller to cheat the buyer. Reciprocal confidence was necessarily the keynote of a system so much dominated by personal relations. Business and private affairs were governed by much the same ethical code.

But industrialism brought the growing depersonalization of economic life. With the increase in size of the labor force, the master was further and further removed from his workmen, till the head of a factory could have only the most tenuous community of feeling with his men. With the development of manufacturing and improved means of distribution, the seller lost all contact with the buyer, and feelings of responsibility to the consumer inevitably diminished. The expansion of investment tended to bring on absentee ownership, with the divorce of ownership and management; and the rise of cities enfeebled the paternal sentiments with which many capitalists had regarded their workers in towns and villages. Slowly the vital economic relationships were becoming impersonal, passing out of the control of a personal moral code. Slowly private morality and business morality grew apart. Slowly the commercial community developed a collection of devices and ceremonials which enabled businessmen to set aside the ethic which ruled their private life and personal relations.

Of these devices the most dramatic and generally intelligible was the corporation. For a people still yearning for an economy dominated by individual responsibility, still under the spell of the Jeffersonian dream, the corporation had one outstanding characteristic: its moral irresponsibility. "Corporations have neither bodies to be kicked, nor souls to be damned," went a favorite aphorism. Beyond good and evil, insensible to argument or appeal, they symbolized the mounting independence of the new economy from the restraints and scruples of personal life.

"As directors of a company," wrote William M. Gouge, "men will sanction actions of which they would scorn to be guilty in their private capacity. A crime which would press heavily on the conscience of one man, becomes quite endurable when divided among many." Even businessmen could not deny the accusation. "Corporations will do what individuals would not dare to do," exclaimed Peter C. Brooks, the wealthiest man in Boston. " — Where the dishonesty is the work of *all* the Members, every *one* can say with Macbeth in the murder of Banquo 'thou canst not say *I* did it.' " It is difficult to exaggerate the frequency with which the corporation was condemned as a technique for the stilling of conscience. "These artificial creatures," said a committee of the Massachusetts legislature, ". . . unlike individual employers, are not chastened and restrained in their dealings with the laborers, by human sympathy and direct personal responsibility to conscience and to the bar of public opinion." [1]

In 1840 Amos Kendall urged the inculcation of the belief that "there is but one code of morals for private and public affairs." [2] His very concern was a confession that two codes existed. The new economy had burst the bonds of the old personal morality, and the consequences were fundamental for the whole Jeffersonian tradition.

As long as individual responsibility existed in the economic system, as long as a single code more or less governed business and personal life, the Jeffersonians were right, and that government was best which governed least. But these were the moral characteristics of a society of small freeholds, as Jefferson well understood. When the economy be-

<hr>

[1] Gouge, *Paper Money*, Part I, 43; Brooks to Edward Everett, July 15, 1845, Everett Papers; Massachusetts *House Document*, no. 153 (1850), 24.
[2] *Bay State Democrat*, May 29, 1840.

came too complex to admit of much personal responsibility, when ownership became attenuated and liability limited and diffused, when impersonality began to dominate the system and produce irresponsibility, when, in short, economic life began to throw off the control of personal scruple, then government had to extend its function in order to preserve the ties which hold society together. The history of government intervention is thus a history of the growing ineffectiveness of private conscience as a means of social control. With private conscience powerless, the only alternative to tyranny or anarchy was the growth of the public conscience, and the natural expression of the public conscience was the democratic government.

2

In spite of Jeffersonian inhibitions, then, the Jacksonians were forced to intervene in the affairs of business. Their ultimate aim was to safeguard the equitable distribution of property which they felt alone could sustain democracy, but this effort inevitably required a battle against the concentration of wealth and power in a single class.

The most conspicuous form of corporation was the bank, and, according to Jacksonian economic theory, no institution played a more important role in transferring wealth from the producing class to the accumulators. The hard-money policy was, of course, primarily designed to reduce the power and increase the stability of the paper system. Within the states, Jacksonians developed various types of structural control: periodic supervision, compulsory publicity, requirements of a broad specie basis for circulation and discounts. These proposals, however innocent in appearance, often provoked bitter resistance. In Massachusetts in 1840 a Whig committee rebuked a proposal that banks be required to keep ten per cent of their capital in specie as a measure which would "palpably 'violate the contract' made by the Legislature with the banks, and essentially 'alter and impair their rights.' "[3] But in the end most such reforms won reluctant acceptance.

The main Jacksonian proposal, however, was to attack the monopoly character of banking by enacting general laws of incorporation; and this reform was quickly adapted for the whole corporate system. Incorporation by special charter had little to recommend it, except for people who already had their own charters and wanted to keep out competitors. It was a prolific source of legislative corruption as well

[3] Massachusetts *Senate Document*, no. 41 (1840), 8.

as a system of special privilege hardly consistent with democracy; and it created banks and corporations in response to political pressure rather than to economic need. The radical Democrats thus advocated free banking, at least for the functions of discount and deposit (along with sharp limitation and prospective abolition of the power of note issue), instead of the uneconomic and undemocratic banking monopoly. Similarly, they favored general laws of incorporation which would extend corporate exemption to all business groups satisfying certain requirements, instead of limiting it, on a basis of legal "monopoly," to those able to cajole, bully or bribe state legislatures.

The movement toward general laws was assisted by the development, from the experience of the early land companies, of the private business association, an organization midway between the corporation and the simple partnership. In some aspects, the general laws were a recognition of the power and usefulness of the business association, giving it status before the courts and bestowing on it the few legal privileges of corporations which it had not yet gained.[4]

In 1836 Henry Edwards, the Democratic Governor of Connecticut, called for a general law of incorporation, and in 1837 the legislature passed the Hinsdale Act, the first modern corporation law.[5] In the next few years other states passed limited general laws. The question was agitated by the radicals in the legislatures, brought up at state constitutional conventions, blared out in crowded halls at election time and set forth with homely illustrations on the hustings. After the Civil War general laws became customary, and today they are so universal that it is hard to conceive of any other system. They constitute a direct legacy from Jacksonian democracy.[6]

3

The fate of the Jacksonian economic legislation was that common historical irony: it on the whole promoted the very ends it was intended to defeat. The general laws sprinkled holy water on corporations, cleansing them of the legal status of monopoly and sending them forth as the benevolent agencies of free competition. A series of court decisions, arising out of the New York general banking law of 1838, concluded that pre–general-law corporations were legally the

---

[4] This viewpoint is emphasized in Shaw Livermore, *Early American Land Companies: Their Influence in Corporate Development*.

[5] J. M. Morse, *A Neglected Period of Connecticut's History, 1818–1850*, 297, 302.

[6] E. M. Dodd, Jr., and R. J. Baker, *Cases on Business Associations*, 19–20; A. A. Berle, Jr., and G. C. Means, *The Modern Corporation and Private Property*, 136.

same as those created under the new dispensation.[7] Even the one-time "monopoly" was thereby transmuted into a laissez-faire corporation and endowed with new prestige and virtue. Capitalism, in the end, gained a new moral force from the incorporation laws.

Yet the fact that the Jacksonian program was eventually beneficial to economic enterprise does not mean that the business world was astute enough to recognize this in advance. In fact, businessmen fought the Jacksonian program bitterly, step by step, and indulged in interminable wails of calamity and disaster. Taney's opinion in the Charles River Bridge case, for example, was clearly more responsive to the necessities of capitalistic expansion than Story's, which would have held back the development of transportation for years. Yet businessmen of the day agreed with Story and denounced Taney as a radical.

One inference from this episode is perhaps that the mass of businessmen did not really want free competition. They might accept it in principle, but in practice they were likely to be seduced by the fatal allure of monopoly. Many in Jackson's day were excluded from the immediate benefits of the system of special charters. Some had been themselves thwarted in getting a charter by the efforts of richer and more influential persons, already in the business, to preserve their monopoly. Some even tried to beat the system by forming private business associations. Yet they thought always in terms of the special charter and its special advantages, fascinated perhaps by the lurking expectation that someday they could employ those advantages to frustrate potential competitors. Rather than abandon this dream, they steadfastly opposed the antimonopoly policy of Jackson, just as in other times they have resented attempts by rival capitalists or by government action to restore competition in some field from which it has been driven. While the business community finally succeeded in capturing the symbols of free enterprise and used them as incantations against government interference, it largely disregarded them as principles of its own behavior.

The fact that the Jacksonian policy benefited business enterprise does not mean that, even in its own terms, it was a failure. No legislative program could have been enacted which would not eventually have been mastered by the overpowering energies of the new capitalism. Moreover, the Jacksonians had no intention of restricting honest enterprise. They had too strong a conviction of the relation between economic diversity and political freedom: their aim was rather to pre-

[7] Bray Hammond, "Free Banks and Corporations: the New York Free Banking Act of 1838," *Journal of Political Economy*, XLIV, 184–209.

serve capitalism and keep the government out of the hands of the capitalists. "Commerce is entitled to a complete and efficient protection in all its legal rights," as Fenimore Cooper put it, "but the moment it presumes to control . . . it should be frowned on, and rebuked." This sentiment was universal among the Jacksonians. "We must protect these merchants," exclaimed George Bancroft, "but not be governed by them." "We do not assail property," declared Samuel J. Tilden, "we merely deny it political power." [8] For a time, the Jacksonian economic policy, by broadening the field of competitive enterprise, admirably served these purposes.

4

The frontal attack on capitalist domination had to be supported by the full mobilization of the noncapitalist groups. The Jeffersonian tradition had already rallied the farmers and the artisans. But the Jeffersonians, no less than the Federalists, looked on industrial labor as an element, fortunately small, to be regarded with mistrust and abhorrence. Without property the working classes of great cities must be without independence, factious and corrupt, the prey of demagogues and tyrants. This analysis may not have been altogether inaccurate, but neither the Jeffersonians nor especially the Federalists accompanied it by serious attempts to prevent the new industrialism from spawning the class whose influence they so much feared.

The class thus grew, for all the disapproval of the old parties, and eventually its power commanded recognition. Jacksonian democracy acted on this new political fact. Class consciousness was much greater a century ago than people imagine who believe it was invented in the Great Depression. Jacksonian speeches roused it, much Jacksonian legislation was based on it, the Jacksonian press appealed to it. Democratic papers opened their columns to the defense of trade-unionism, printed reports of union meetings and assailed the enemies of labor organization. Such Democratic politicians as Charles Jared Ingersoll and John Worth Edmonds defended unions in the courts against charges of criminal conspiracy. Robert Rantoul, Jr., the brilliant and ambitious Massachusetts Democrat, won labor's greatest legal victory by his argument in the famous case of *Commonwealth v. Hunt.*

In October, 1840, Hunt and others, members of the Boston Bootmakers' Society, were on trial in the Boston municipal court for combining to compel master bootmakers to employ only union men.

---

[8] Cooper, *The American Democrat*, 161; Bancroft to Jared Sparks, August 22, 1834, Sparks Papers; Tilden, *Writings and Speeches*, John Bigelow, ed., I, 85.

The testimony, including that of master bootmakers, disclosed that the union had improved the quality and efficiency of the work, and Rantoul sought to show that the English common law under which the men were indicted had no status in a Massachusetts court. Judge Peter Oxenbridge Thacher conceded in his charge to the jury that it was lawful for the defendants to refuse individually to work for a master who employed nonunion workmen; but "if they combined together to control, by force of numbers, the employment of other persons, . . . I consider that both the means and the object were violations of law." If unions were allowed to continue, "all industry and enterprise would be suspended, and all property would become insecure. . . . A frightful despotism would soon be erected on the ruins of this free and happy commonwealth." [9] Judge Thacher's juries were not in the habit of defying him, and this one returned a verdict of guilty in two hours and ten minutes.[10]

The case was promptly appealed to the state Supreme Court, where in the March term, 1842, Rantoul assailed the indictment as defective "because each of the defendants had a right to do that which is charged against them jointly." [11] The decision was handed down by Lemuel Shaw, Chief Justice of the court. While also a former Federalist, Shaw was not, like Thacher, blinded by party preferences to the facts of life. He had no particular sympathy for democracy, but he had a very real sense of the imperatives of change. "The strength of that great judge," observed Justice Oliver Wendell Holmes, "lay in an accurate appreciation of the requirements of the community whose officer he was. . . . few have lived who were his equals in their understanding of the grounds of public policy to which all laws must ultimately be referred." [12]

Shaw pointed out that two different questions were involved: the legality of the combination, and the legality of its methods. On the first point he accepted Rantoul's argument: a combination could not be criminal unless the actual object of that combination were criminal. On the second point Shaw, noting that the means proposed was the refusal to work for a master employing nonunion labor, declared, "We cannot perceive, that it is criminal for men to agree together to exercise their own acknowledged rights, in such a manner as best to subserve their own interests." [13]

Shaw's decision aroused considerable protest. "Startling and not

[9] *Thacher's Criminal Cases*, 613, 645, 653, 654.
[10] *Boston Post*, October 21, 23, 1840.
[11] 4 Metcalf 119.
[12] O. W. Holmes, Jr., *The Common Law* (Boston, 1881), 106.
[13] 4 Metcalf 130.

sound," exclaimed Francis Lieber, adding that in the case of trade-unions "we know to what insufferable social tyranny, to what evil habits and fearful crimes they lead." [14] But, though Shaw's justification of strikes for the closed shop did not gain much acceptance, the basic legality of unions *per se* was thereafter substantially established. The death knell was sounded for indictments of unions as criminal conspiracies.[15]

5

The debate over unionism exhibited another aspect of the struggle for *laissez faire*. From the first, conservatism had rested part of its case on the ground that unions interrupted the freedom of trade. As early as 1832 Judge Thacher had declared that the law must protect "in full extent, the principle of equal and fair competition. If individuals may combine together, to gain an unfair advantage over others, it would violate this principle." Chief Justice Savage of New York, in his decision in the case of the Geneva bootmakers, indulged in similar invocations of free trade. "It is important to the best interests of society that the price of labor be left to regulate itself," he said. ". . . Competition is the life of trade." [16]

Yet these doctrines immediately caused contradictions if they were applied only to unions and not to corporations. What, for example, of the policy of Hamilton? What of the United States Bank? For men like Thacher and Savage, who rejected the broad application, free competition was obviously an exorcism, not a faith.

In any case, the very principles could yield arguments quite as cogent on the other side. As that ardent apostle of *laissez faire*, William Leggett, put it, "We are for leaving trade free; and the right to combine is an indispensable attribute of its freedom." [17] (Unlike some Jacksonians, Leggett was willing to extend this right to business as well as to labor.) John Worth Edmonds's argument in the case of the Hudson shoemakers rested on a thoroughgoing free-trade position.

[14] Lieber to G. S. Hillard, August 24, 1842, Perry, *Lieber*, 172.

[15] Walter Nelles, "Commonwealth v. Hunt," *Columbia Law Review*, XXXII, 1128–1169.

[16] Thacher, *Charge to the Grand Jury of the County of Suffolk* (1832), 9; Savage in 14 Wendell 18, 19. *Niles' Register*, commenting in 1837 on a strike in Rochester where the laborers refused to work or allow others to work fifteen hours a day for $4.50 a week, asked in similar vein: "What becomes of individual liberty, and the right of every man to exchange his own labor against whatever he may choose to accept as an equivalent?" The *New York American* added, by way of rebuke to the strikers, "Now we know of instances in this vicinity, where laborers gratefully accept $5 per month, with board and lodging, and work hard too." *Niles' Register*, July 8, 1837.

[17] *Plaindealer*, February 18, 1837.

And Judge Lemuel Shaw, who had not deserted the free-trade convictions of his trading forebears, supposed his defense of unions to come as inevitably from his principles as Thacher doubtless supposed the reverse. "It is through . . . competition," he said, "that the best interests of trade and industry are promoted" — almost the same words as Chief Justice Savage's, and leading to almost exactly opposite conclusions.[18]

It was becoming clear that people could prove anything from the maxims of free trade, including even (what would have most shocked Adam Smith) the transcendent virtue of monopoly.

6

The Democrats also supported the workingmen's struggle for a shorter day. The average length of the working day in Lowell in 1845 varied from eleven hours and twenty-four minutes in December and January to thirteen hours and thirty-one minutes in April — ordinarily from sunrise to sunset.[19] In the eighteen-thirties labor organizations raised the cry for reduction, and radical Democrats took it up with enthusiasm. An ardent young Jacksonian named Ben Butler carried on the agitation in the very shadow of the mills, where workers hardly dared attend protest meetings for fear of discharge and the black list, which would prevent their employment by other large corporations.[20]

Van Buren's executive order of 1840 gave the movement official blessing. In Massachusetts in the next fifteen years Democrats several times presented ten-hour laws to the legislature. But the proposals were killed by Whig committees, like the one which visited Lowell in 1845 and returned "fully satisfied, that the order, decorum, and general appearance of things in and about the mills, could not be improved by any suggestion of theirs, or by any act of the Legislature." [21] This was a mild expression of conservative disapproval. In

---

[18] 4 Metcalf 134. For Shaw as free trader, see S. S. Shaw, et al., *Lemuel Shaw*, 20; F. H. Chase, *Lemuel Shaw*, 311.

[19] Massachusetts *House Document*, no. 50 (1845), 9.

[20] Benjamin F. Butler, *Butler's Book*, 91.

[21] Massachusetts *House Document*, no. 50 (1845), 8. The chairman of the committee was William Schouler, father of the historian and editor of the principal paper in Lowell. The report exploited the tricks of pastoralism to a high degree. "Labor is on an equality with capital," it said, "and indeed controls it, and so it ever will be while free education and free constitutions exist. . . . Labor is intelligent enough to make its own bargains, and look out for its own interests without any interference from us." The evidence for the abuses was impressive, and the committee concluded: "We acknowledge all this, but we say, the remedy is not

other moods Whigs denounced the ten-hour movement as "one of the worst deformities in their deformed code. To work only ten hours in summer and eight hours in winter is to waste life." [22] But the ten-hour campaign flourished during the forties and fifties, to the cordial applause of the radical Democrats.[23]

Another part of the Jacksonian effort sought to guarantee the political rights of labor. Having gained the ballot, the workingman now faced the problem of making sure he voted as he pleased. Employers not seldom threatened to discharge those who dared vote the radical ticket, and Fenimore Cooper reported that he had heard this practice openly defended.[24] As late as 1850 in Massachusetts the chairman of the Whig state central committee sent a circular to prominent Whigs, asking them to use their influence over their employees in the coming election. The superintendent of the Boott Mills in Lowell obligingly replied that he would fire every man who voted the ten-hour ticket.[25]

The fight to make the labor vote effective took several forms. In Massachusetts, where the state Senate was based on property rather than population, the Democrats tried sporadically to revise the method of apportionment. They were unsuccessful till 1853. They also urged ballot reform. David Henshaw in 1829 fought through to the state Supreme Court a suit which resulted in securing legal recognition for the printed ballot, the first step toward uniform ballots, and from 1849 Amasa Walker led a campaign for the adoption of the secret ballot. The secret-ballot law eventually enacted by a liberal legislature was repealed by the Whigs in 1853 on the ground that it "insulted the manliness and independence of the laboring men." [26] The Democratic movement to reduce the poll tax similarly produced the ingenious Whig theory that the lower classes would consider them-

---

with us. We look for it in the progressive improvement in art and science, in a higher appreciation of man's destiny, in a less love for money, and a more ardent love for social happiness and intellectual superiority." *Ibid.*, 16. This last passage might almost have come from the writings of Dr. William Ellery Channing.

[22] *New York Journal of Commerce,* quoted by the *Cincinnati Gazette,* May 23, 1837; McGrane, *Panic of 1837,* 134.

[23] See, e.g., *Bay State Democrat,* November 2, 1843, for a striking picture of the relationship between the labor movement and the Democratic party.

[24] Cooper, *A Letter to His Countrymen,* 91. Edward L. Pierce, the friend and biographer of Charles Sumner, declared in the *Dedham Gazette,* July 30, 1853: "In Massachusetts and the manufacturing States intimidation is constantly practised. . . . Many . . . boldly avow their right to discharge those who vote against their peculiar interests." Amasa Walker, *The Test of Experience,* 4. See also *Boston Post,* December 26, 1834, April 30, 1840.

[25] Walker, *Test of Experience,* 5.

[26] Quoted in Darling, *Political Changes in Massachusetts,* 171.

selves degraded by such an action.[27] The Democrats sought further
to repeal the sunset law, which made it hard for a workingman to vote
by closing the polls at sunset. As a party they remained constantly receptive to projects for improving and protecting the suffrage.

Yet the radical Democrats never committed the fallacy of resting
everything on political mechanisms. The pervading insight of the
Jacksonians into the relation of democracy and a wide distribution
of property kept them from tumbling into excessive optimism over
minor reforms. Security of the vote would help the laboring class,
but their vital need was economic independence, and the best way
of elevating labor was to enact the economic program of the radical
Democracy.

7

The problem of labor for the Jacksonians, then, consisted in
mobilizing the votes of the workingmen to support a policy which
would increase their share in the national income. In their attempt to
preserve the economic base of labor action they had a potent ally —
the public domain in the West. The broad expanse across green forests
and illimitable prairies and fertile plains offered inviting refuge to the
discontented and underprivileged of the East; and the greater the number drawn to the frontier from the settled states, the higher the
wages and the easier the life for those who stayed behind.

Both new states and old thus benefited from the migration to the
cheap lands beyond the Alleghenies. "The West, the Paradise of the
Poor," a writer called it in the *Democratic Review*. "It forms a practical corrective of the evils caused by the tendency of property to
accumulate in large masses." "If some of our cities are not like Bir-
mingham and Manchester," said George Bancroft, "it is owing not
to our legislation, but to the happy accident of our possessing the
West." The popular conception of the value of the frontier was
summed up in a single famous phrase: "It is sometimes said, that the
abundance of vacant land operates as the safety valve of our system." [28]

Yet the safety-valve theory was already beginning to crack at the

[27] "Does his Excellency think that the agricultural laborers, young mechanics,
and professional men of the State, will consider it a boon to be made in the eye
of the law, *paupers?*" *Address of the Whig Members of the Senate and House of
Representatives of Massachusetts* (1843), 9.
[28] W. Kirkland, "The West, the Paradise of the Poor," *Democratic Review*, XV,
189 (August, 1844); Bancroft to the Public, October 22, 1834, *Northampton
Courier*, October 29, 1834; "Reform," *New-England Magazine*, II, 71 (January,
1832).

seams. Anticipating the historians' controversy of a century later, journalists were busily engaged in pointing out how much of it was already illusion. Orestes A. Brownson was not alone in emphasizing the increasing unreality of the escape. The population of a manufacturing town, the *Boston Post* noted as early as 1834, was "physically and morally indisposed for the hardy life of a western agriculturist." [29] Few wage earners had laid enough by to get the more fertile land, few perhaps could even afford to move home and family a thousand weary miles to the West. A New England reformer put the case forcibly in 1847: —

One hundred and sixty acres of land even may be yours in Iowa or Wisconsin, if you will settle upon it, and yet this offer may be of no advantage to you. You may not have the ability to go there, or be able to make a settlement, when arrived. Barren, unimproved acres do not present a very inviting aspect to a destitute man. Or you may not wish to go there. You may not wish to exile yourself from your early and long cherished home. You may not wish to withdraw from civilization to the wilderness. You may not wish to give up the social institutions of New England, her Sabbath and her churches, her schools and her widely diffused intelligence; the social intercourse of friends and of a comparatively dense population for the far West, where all these are wanting. . . . Besides, you are not cultivators; you are mechanics, artizans, clerks, laborers of every variety. . . . This is not a corrective of the evil; it is only a fleeing of it. And woe is left for them who cannot escape.[30]

Whatever broad effects the frontier had on the price level, the labor supply, the incentives toward capital investment or the general economic atmosphere, it had ceased even by the time of Jackson to serve as a real alternative for the workers of the Eastern states.[31]

In the future, moreover, hung the awful possibility of its disappearance. In time, the last free acres would be foreclosed, and the safety valve would choke up. When? No one could say. In 1840 Orestes A. Brownson guessed fifty years.[32] Others might have named

[29] *Boston Post*, October 28, 1834.
[30] [Anon.], *The Condition of Labor. An Address to the Members of the Labor Reform League of New England*, 19–20.
[31] For able modern discussions of this problem, see Fred A. Shannon, "The Homestead Act and the Labor Surplus," *American Historical Review*, XLI, 637–651; Carter Goodrich and Sol Davison, "The Wage-Earner in the Westward Movement," *Political Science Quarterly*, L, 161–185, LI, 61–116.
[32] Brownson, "The Laboring Classes" (second article), *Boston Quarterly Review*, III, 473–474.

longer periods, but all agreed that the free institutions of America would in the end have to face their bitterest test. "It is the accident of our situation alone," declared R. B. Rhett in 1838, "having a continent to people, which has enabled us so long to maintain them. But the time will come, — is rapidly approaching, when the way to the West will be blocked up." [33]

What then? "Decree that when her workpeople feel the iron hand of competition pressing too harshly, they shall not be allowed to escape to the free woods and rich lands of the Far West," said Robert Dale Owen. "And what assurance should we have that in Lowell, and Lynn, and Salem, the same scenes would not soon be re-produced that now win our sympathy for the oppressed laborer of Britain?" [34]

8

The Jacksonians thus regarded the keeping open of the public domain as a democratic imperative. It was not for them a sectional question alone. The poorer people of the West demanded easy access and cheap lands for their own direct benefit. The poorer people of the East similarly required a liberal land policy, to provide for some a refuge, and to relieve the pressure on the great majority by draining off rural population which might otherwise flock to town and swell the labor surplus.[35] All agreed in advocating every preference for the

[33] Rhett in the House, June 25, 1838, *Congressional Globe*, 25 Congress 2 Session, Appendix, 506.

[34] Owen, "One of the Problems of the Age," *Democratic Review*, XIV, 167 (February, 1844).

[35] The *New York Evening Post* ran, on February 3, 1837, an eloquent defense of the pre-emption law, probably written by William Cullen Bryant at a time when he was himself contemplating moving to the West. "We have seen them [the squatters] amid the broad prairies where they raise their harvests, and beside the noble woods where they hunt their game, and we have shared the hospitality of their cabins. . . . No man who has once visited the west, scruples, if his convenience should lead him, to seat himself upon the unoccupied territory belonging to the government, the sale of which is not yet permitted. Here he builds his log cabin, in the edge of a grove, splits the tall trees into rails, fences in a portion of the wide and rich prairies, turns up the virgin soil . . . and pastures his herd on the vast, uninclosed, flowery champaign before his dwelling. . . . We all have a general interest in this matter. We know not who may die in the course of this present year, and we know not who may remove to the west. Men will go from Broadway and the Bowery, from Pearl street and Chatham street, from the villages and farms along the Sound and the Hudson, who perhaps are now little thinking of such an adventure. They will find the best of the lands which have been brought into the market, already in the hands of speculators, and they will be compelled to seek for desirable situations in those tracts which have not yet been offered for sale. We ourselves are now penning an article for the Evening Post, but in two years from this time we may be winging a wood pigeon on the banks

actual settler in order to prevent the seizure of large areas of fertile land by speculators.

For the Eastern conservatives the land problem assumed the same significance. Westward migration, as John Quincy Adams's Secretary of the Treasury explained in candid detail in 1827, was against the interests of manufacturing capital.[36] It was clearly to their advantage to have a large labor supply driving wages down by competition among themselves.

The conflict of interests bred two opposing theories about the public lands. John Quincy Adams and Henry Clay wanted to sell land high, using the domain primarily as a fund to finance internal improvements and hoping to hold back colonization. In 1830 Senator Foot of Connecticut even offered a resolution inquiring into the expediency of limiting the further sale of public lands. Benton's massive attack on this proposal laid the preliminaries for the celebrated (if comparatively unimportant) debate between Webster and Hayne. As Benton charged in 1832, "It is well known that the manufacturers are opposed to any relaxation in the sale or disposition of the public lands; because they want to confine the poor people to the old States, to work in the factories." [37]

Against this "revenue" theory of the national domain, the Jacksonians, for whom Benton was the chief spokesman on land policy, advanced the "settlement" theory, proposing to lower land prices and thus to encourage migration. Though the political revolution of the thirties compelled the Whigs to disguise their attitude under various specious theories, and eventually to support certain forms of homestead provision, the initiative toward actual settlement continued to come from the Democrats.

Jackson and Van Buren both called in their annual messages for a liberalization of the land laws. Their proposals generally recommended themselves to the West without delay; but the job of awakening the East to the land issue fell to that small group of radicals around the *Working Man's Advocate,* of which George H. Evans was the leading spirit. As early as 1834 Evans was beginning to dwell on the stake of Eastern workingmen in the national domain. During his years on his New Jersey farm he slowly built up an elaborate scheme

---

of the Iowa or the Charlton, where lands were never yet conveyed by the formality of signing and sealing, and the only title which the settler has to shew, is the marks scored with his ax on the trees of the forest, and the stakes he has set in the tall grass of the prairie."

[36] *Register of Debates,* 20 Congress 1 Session, Appendix, 2831–2833.

[37] Benton in the Senate, March 20, 1832, *Register of Debates,* 22 Congress 1 Session, 666.

of land reform. In 1841 he began to expound his views in a monthly called *The Radical*, urging the opening up of the land to actual set. tlers, the limitation of the holdings of any single person, and the exemption of the homestead from suits for debt.[38] His program was decorated by a complex theory of natural right in land which explained all the deformities of society as the consequences of improper aliena- tion.

Gradually his plan gripped him with a kind of fanatic intensity. No substantial improvement, he felt, was possible until the land monopoly was destroyed; then all problems were solved. In February, 1844, he returned to New York and called some of his old friends together for a meeting in John Windt's print shop. Here he set forth his scheme with persuasive eloquence, and in the next month he began a new series of the *Working Man's Advocate*, soon to be rechristened *Young America*. His enthusiasm infected many of the New York radicals. Windt, John Commerford and for a time the ebullient Mike Walsh espoused the cause.

The group organized itself into a corps of speakers, assembling in parks and on street corners, passing broadsides out to workmen as they went home at sunset, and holding vociferous evening meetings at Croton Hall, on the corner of Division Street and the Bowery. Their motto — *Vote yourself a farm* — passed quickly into circulation, and Horace Greeley, always on the lookout for safe reforms, flirted with them ardently in the columns of the *Tribune*. For five hard years Evans kept his paper going, in the expectation that one day his plan would sweep the country. In 1849, worn out and penniless, he sadly went back to New Jersey where he died seven years later. The Na- tional Reform Association, as he called his group, broke up and scat- tered away.[39]

Yet his work was not in vain. The seed was planted, and the com- pulsions of geography would bring it to maturity. Whatever the ob- jections of Eastern capitalists or Southern planters or Western specu- lators, the West had to be opened up; the common man everywhere demanded it; no one could check the course of empire. From 1846 on, a morose, ambitious and extremely able young Jacksonian from Tennessee named Andrew Johnson kept up a persistent agitation for a homestead bill. In May, 1852, he went to New York and spoke at a mass meeting arranged by friends of Evans.[40] In the meantime Horace

[38] Helene S. Zahler, *Eastern Workingmen and National Land Policy, 1829–1862*, 21–39.

[39] Masquerier, *Sociology*, 94–99.

[40] St. G. L. Sioussat, "Andrew Johnson and the Early Phases of the Homestead Bill," *Mississippi Valley Historical Review*, V, 283.

Greeley, serving a term in Congress, introduced another homestead bill in 1849, and after 1850 the forces of land reform were strengthened by the addition of Galusha A. Grow, a Pennsylvania Democrat, intimate friend and disciple of Benton. Their efforts finally triumphed with the passage of the Homestead Act of 1862.

Though the national domain may have been in the narrow sense a Western problem, the needs and energies which shaped the national policy toward it were by no means exclusively Western. The opening up of the public lands was nearly as vital for Eastern workingmen and farmers as for the people of the West. The importance of the land question is evidence less of the Western character of Jacksonianism than of its overmastering desire to preserve everywhere the economic democracy which alone could give political democracy meaning.

XXVII JACKSONIAN DEMOCRACY AND RELIGION

FEDERALISM had valued the clergy, as well as the judiciary, as a great stabilizing influence in society, hoping thus to identify the malcontent as the foe both of God and the law. Hamilton's curious project, in 1802, of a "Christian Constitutional Society" disclosed the fervor with which conservatism, when defeated at the polls, was turning to religion and law for salvation. In the next quarter-century conservatism, in collaboration with the pulpit, worked out a systematic view of America as essentially and legally a religious nation in which the church should assist the state in preserving the existing social order. Jacksonian democracy ran sharply up against these conceptions both of religion and of government.

1

The Sabbatarian controversy of the late eighteen-twenties revived the religious community as a national political-pressure group; and the very defeat of the campaign against the Sunday mails only strengthened the conviction that religious-minded persons must unite to save the country from infidelity and radicalism. Two issues in Jackson's first term confirmed the clerical groups in a hostility already stirred up by their predominantly conservative reaction to his economic measures.

The first was the case of the Georgia missionaries. Eleven missionaries to the Cherokee Indians were arrested for violating a Georgia law forbidding whites to dwell among the Indians without state licenses. Two of the group fought the case through to the Supreme Court, which decided in their favor; but the state defied the Court, Jackson refused to intercede, and the missionaries remained in prison for over a year. Henry Clay raised the second question, a few months before the election of 1832, by offering a resolution requesting the President to reconsider his refusal to declare a national day of fasting and prayer in order to avert the cholera epidemic. The two incidents provided the conservative party, already impressed with the urgency of mobilizing all their resources, the means of making a powerful appeal to the church vote.

Even people with the most nominal religious interests were beginning to regard the breakdown of Christian ties as a major cause of radicalism. In the words of a Whig report to the Massachusetts state Senate on the competency of nonbelievers as witnesses, atheism was not only hostile to religion, "but to all decency and regularity, to the peace of all communities, and the safety of all governments. . . . Atheism is a levelling system. In religion and in politics, it labors to overthrow all ancient customs — all established institutions."[1]

The Jackson administration appeared to some writers as the culmination of organized irreligion. "Incorporating itself with national politics, in order to acquire favor among the populace, it [atheism] marches under the banners of political reform," charged the *American Monthly Magazine*. ". . . It declares a war of extermination upon the established institutions of religion and government. It denominates all religion priestcraft, all property a monopoly, and all jurisprudence an organized fraud upon the liberties of mankind."[2]

The best cure for this contagion of political radicalism seemed clearly to lie in the re-establishment of the belief in the religious character of the state and, thus, in the supremacy of religious interests. The leading advocate of this view in secular politics was Theodore Frelinghuysen, for many years Senator from New Jersey. A staunch conservative, he defended the United States Bank (his was the picture of Biddle "calm as a summer's morning"), supported the Whig economic program and even was said to have volunteered to act as counsel against the journeymen shoemakers of Newark when they dared to go out on strike.[3] He was also a man of the most persevering religiosity, prominent on the American Board of Commissioners for Foreign Missions, the American Bible Society, the American Tract Society, the American Sunday School Union and the American Temperance Union. His ardor in the fight against the Sunday mail, for the Georgia missionaries and for the national fast day, on top of his diligence in organizing congressional prayer meetings, made him the special champion of religion in politics. Nothing, however, seemed to shake his faith in the moral excellences of Henry Clay and Daniel Webster.

---

[1] Massachusetts *Senate Document*, no. 22 (1838), 53–54.

[2] The goal of this "Atheistical system," according to the author, was to "abolish all property. Every thing is to be embodied in one common stock, to which each is to contribute by his daily labor, and from which all are to receive their stated rations of food and clothing." James H. Lanman, "Social Disorganization," *American Monthly Magazine*, II, 577–578, 582 (December, 1836).

[3] *The Campaign*, November 2, 1844.

In 1838 a work appeared in New York entitled *An Inquiry into the Moral and Religious Character of the American Government*, which was quickly and widely ascribed to Frelinghuysen.[4] Whether or not he actually wrote it, the argument certainly accorded with his known views. The book was designed to combat the separation of religion and politics. The author gloomily traced the progress of "*political irreligion*" from Jefferson's refusal to recommend a day of humiliation and prayer in 1807 through the episode of the Sunday mails to Jackson's refusal to declare a fast day in 1832. "The evil is spreading. . . . The whole land is infected." Religion "is everywhere *politically set at nought*."

The solution was to place the government on a religious basis; and, in a long legal and historical argument, the work sought to establish the constitutional primacy of Christianity. The rights of conscience, it argued, applied only to believers, for conscience could exist only with respect to belief in God. ("Is liberty of conscience to be confounded with the license that acts against conscience?") Christianity thus was a constituent part of the common law, the structure of the republic was "radically Christian" and the administration of the government must expect to meet Christian tests. "Are christian institutions to be administered by unchristian agents?" Only by placing religious persons in high office could the nation be saved from the ravages of radicalism. "Without religion, law ceases to be law, for it has no bond, and cannot hold society together."[5]

2

This work provided the most comprehensive statement of a prevailing Whig view that, as Daniel D. Barnard put it, America had "a national religion, as well as a national government." Small attempt was made to hide the political function of this view. "The principle of obedience would sit lightly on the people," in Barnard's words, "unless it were enforced by a common sense of religious obligation. . . . Our only safety consists in having a popular religious sense to fall back upon." Even slaves, Barnard pointed out, could be more easily governed when "brought under the influence of a common religious faith."[6] Later he went farther. "The great economical and social questions between Capital and Labor" must be solved by re-

[4] It is also ascribed to Henry Whitings Warner.
[5] *Inquiry into the Moral and Religious Character of the American Government*. 14, 18, 19, 89, 92, 109, 206, 133.
[6] Barnard, *Plea for Social and Popular Repose*, 8.

ligion. "I am not preaching a sermon," he declared. ". . . I am endeavoring to state and insist on an economical truth." [7]

Professor Tayler Lewis even maintained in the *American Whig Review* that "religion — revealed religion, Christianity — should regulate legislation," and added a defense in principle of persecution for religious heresy, though he judiciously allowed that it might be impracticable in America.[8] Daniel Webster gave typical rhetorical variations on the Whig theme in his argument in the Girard Will case, and Calvin Colton made perhaps the ablest formulation in terms of Tocqueville's apothegm: "How is it possible that society should escape destruction, if the moral tie be not strengthened in proportion as the political tie is relaxed?" Colton went on to attack the separation of church and state as the great evil, urging that Churches thereafter be supported by taxation.[9]

The clergy loyally carried out its side of the alliance. Most of the leading ministers voted the Whig ticket, and many argued for conservatism from the pulpit. One New York preacher, for example, roundly condemned the men who broached "the pompous doctrine that 'all men are born both free and equal' " in the teeth "of all the providence of God, in whose unsearchable wisdom, one is born in a manger and another on a throne." "The axiom of 'equal rights,' " this gentleman continued, "is infidel, not christian, and strikes at all that is beautiful in civil, or sacred in divine institutions." [10]

In every election the Jackson party had to face the charge of being antireligious. "The community was made to believe, that there was danger the bible would be taken out of their hands," said George Bancroft bitterly after a typical canvass in the Connecticut valley. "Democracy was said to be a branch of atheism. . . . A perfect fever was got up." It is no wonder that the usually equable Van Buren was driven to the sour description of the religious community as "a

---

[7] Barnard, *The Social System*, 28.

[8] Tayler Lewis, "Has the State a Religion?" *American Whig Review*, III, 273, 286 (March, 1846). Lewis began his article by saying that, merely by asking the question, he expected to be "set down at once as the enemy of free institutions, of the rights of man" by those on the "extreme left of democracy."

[9] Webster, *Writings and Speeches*, XI, 133–184; Colton, *Voice from America to England*, 60, 87, 151–200.

[10] Flavel S. Mines, *The Church the Pillar and Ground of the Truth*, 11, 12. Cf. Cooper's satiric account in *The Monikins*, when his hero tells what he has learned from the minister Dr. Etherington: "I heard principles which went to show that society was of necessity divided into orders; that it was not only impolitic but wicked to weaken the barriers by which they were separated; that Heaven had its seraphs and cherubs, its archangels and angels, its saints and its merely happy, and that, by obvious induction, this world ought to have its kings, lords, and commons." *The Monikins*, 51–52. Like much of the novel, this is as much reporting as parody.

class among us easily instigated to meddle in public affairs and seldom free, on such occasions, from a uniform political bias." [11]

3

Against the Whig theory of the "national religion" the Democrats set up a theory of religious nonintervention. "Our Constitution recognises in every person," said Richard M. Johnson's Sunday-mail report, the main Jacksonian document on the side of religious liberty, "the right to choose his own religion, and to enjoy it freely, without molestation." [12] The state, in other words, was a secular institution, whose single obligation to religion was the guarantee of equal rights to all faiths; it had no title to intervene in the private beliefs of individuals. "If a man entertain heretical sentiments," as Johnson observed in 1840, "who shall be his judge? Our creator has not delegated this power to man. He is himself the only competent judge; and it concerns him much more than it does us, to define the crime and inflict the penalty." [13]

Total separation of church and state was considered the best safeguard for the health of each. As Jackson explained, in refusing to name a fast day, he feared to "disturb the security which religion now enjoys in this country, in its complete separation from the political concerns of the General Government." [14]

This principle did not enjoin an exclusively defensive policy. Church and state were not, in fact, completely separated; and a part of the Jacksonian program became not only to guard against new clerical interference, as in the case of the Sunday mails, but to eradicate the lingering traces of theocracy. In Connecticut in 1828, for example, Judge David Daggett, former Federalist candidate for Governor, ruled as head of the state Supreme Court that disbelievers in accountability to God or in an afterlife were not competent witnesses, whereupon he threw out testimony given in a lower court by a Universalist. The *Hartford Times*, John M. Niles's paper, attacked the decision; but Gideon Welles's proposal in the legislature that religious belief should not be the qualification for testimony was defeated, and the conservatives even pushed a bill through the lower house making Daggett's

[11] Bancroft to Edward Everett, November 17, 1834, Bancroft Papers; Van Buren, *Autobiography*, 284.
[12] Johnson, *Report on the Transportation of the Mail on Sunday*, 5.
[13] Johnson to Barnabas Bates, *et al.*, March 14, 1840, *New York Evening Post*, April 1, 1840.
[14] Jackson to the General Synod of the Dutch Reformed Church, June 12, 1832, Charles Warren, *Odd Byways in American History*, 228.

decision law. In 1830 a compromise bill permitted Universalists to testify but drew the line at unbelievers.[15]

In New York Thomas Herttell, a radical Democrat, led a similar fight, and the Democrats backed movements to end remuneration to chaplains of the legislature and to exclude clergymen from the public schools.[16] Wherever religious tests survived, they were under fire from Democrats, while Whigs, in general, sought to sustain the authority of religion.

The Democratic theory of the relations of church and state did not necessarily imply a weaker personal faith. Some who insisted most strongly on separation, like O. B. Brown and Elder John Leland, were ministers themselves. The evangelical sects in many states were predominantly Democratic, and many of the leading Jacksonians were deeply religious. Benjamin F. Butler was celebrated for his piety, Jackson himself was a regular churchgoer though not a communicant till 1839, and James K. Polk was faithful in his Sunday observance. But they all firmly opposed the political aspirations of religion. Polk, infuriated by a Presbyterian minister who came to see him as President, told him "that, thank God, under our constitution there was no connection between Church and State, and that in my action as President of the U.S. I recognized no distinction of creeds in my appointments to office." He had met no one in these first two years of his administration, Polk later wrote, who so disgusted him. "I have a great veneration and regard for Religion & sincere piety, but a hypocrite or a bigotted fanatic without reason I cannot bear." [17]

Yet the Whig charges that the Democratic party was the party of irreligion were not without basis. The unrelenting conservatism of so many of the clergy had poisoned not a few liberals. "The clergy, as a class," Samuel Clesson Allen put it, "have always been ready to come in for a share in the advantages of the privileged classes, and in return for the ease and convenience accorded to them by these classes, to spread their broad mantle over them." [18] Occasionally Democratic politicians launched into bitter vituperation of the clergy on the floors of Congress: —

In the earlier stages of society [declared Jesse A. Bynum of North Carolina], priestcraft was the universal method resorted to by the

[15] Morse, *Neglected Period of Connecticut's History*, 101–105.

[16] Fox, *Decline of Aristocracy*, 389–390; Albert Post, *Popular Free-thought in America, 1825–1850*, 129–130, 214–215.

[17] James K. Polk, *Diary . . . during his Presidency*, M. M. Quaife, ed., II, 187–191.

[18] Allen to Brownson, August 18, 1834, Brownson, *Brownson's Early Life*, 114.

sons of luxury and idleness to filch the pocket of industry and labor . . . and perhaps no system ever was, or ever will again be, devised . . . more effectually to retain in bondage the human intellect, and steep in ignorance, debasement, and degradation, the great mass of mankind. . . . I contend that Christ himself was betrayed . . . by priestcraft.[19]

Tom Paine, whom the Whigs were already busy turning into a filthy little atheist, was still a Democratic hero, admired by Jackson, toasted at party celebrations and defended from conservative smears.[20]

Most of the professional agnostics and atheists of the day, moreover, were active Jacksonians. Robert Dale Owen and Fanny Wright of the *Free Enquirer*, Gilbert Vale of the *Beacon*, Abner Kneeland of the *Boston Investigator*, the leading trade journals of free thought, were all strong Democrats. N. P. Trist, Jackson's private secretary, contributed to the *Free Enquirer*, and many other Democratic politicians — such as Senator Benjamin Tappan of Ohio, Ely Moore, John Ferral, George H. Evans, Thomas Herttell — had skeptical leanings. The infamous infidel and birth-control champion Dr. Charles Knowlton was prominent in local Democratic politics. Deists and nonbelievers even held weekly services in New York at Tammany Hall.

4

The Whig and Democratic views of the proper role of religion in the state came into the most spectacular conflict in the case of Abner Kneeland in Boston. Kneeland was a kindly old gentleman, white-haired, ruddy and sixty, who had happened to become a preacher of infidelity. Expelled from the Universalist fellowship in 1829, he had shortly after founded in Boston the First Society of Free Enquirers and in 1831 the *Boston Investigator*, a weekly journal of skepticism. This magazine carried on a cheerful assault on the churches and on Calvinist theology, and also opposed the Whigs in state elections, looked on Jackson and Johnson with veneration, and printed such enthusiastic political toasts (given on the birthday of Tom Paine) as "Andrew Jackson and Abner Kneeland, Friends of the people but

[19] Bynum in the House, June, 1838, *Congressional Globe*, 25 Congress 2 Session, Appendix, 423.
[20] Jackson to Herttell, quoted by Dixon Wecter, "The Hero in Reverse," *Virginia Quarterly Review*, XVIII, 253 (Spring, 1942). For specimens of Democratic eulogy, see, e.g., *New York Evening Post*, April 23, 1835, *Boston Post*, January 28, 1842; of Whig outrage, see *Boston Atlas*, July 7, 1836.

the dread of aristocracy and priestcraft." [21] Nineteen twentieths of Kneeland's followers were reputed to be Democrats.[22]

Conservatism watched his growing audiences with alarm; and early in 1834 he was indicted for publishing in the *Investigator* of December 20, 1833, a "scandalous, impious, obscene, blasphemous and profane libel of and concerning God." [23] Three articles had been found offensive. The first quoted Voltaire's epigram on the Immaculate Conception — a remark held too crude to be repeated in public court, though it could be found in any Boston bookshop which carried the *Philosophical Dictionary*. The second article was considered to hold the Christian doctrine of prayer up to ridicule by comparing the Deity to General Jackson snowed under by various and conflicting petitions. The third, which alone was actually written by Kneeland, stated his disbelief in Christ, in miracles, in immortality, and concluded ambiguously, "Universalists believe in a god which I do not" — a declaration variously interpreted by prosecution and defense, according to whether the comma was supposed to have been left out by accident or design.[24]

Most conservatives were delighted by the indictment. Samuel Gridley Howe would soon write his violent attack on Kneeland for the *New-England Magazine,* and John Quincy Adams's only regret about the case was that, in spite of it, Kneeland continued to meet his flock on Federal Street.[25] Pamphlets were circulated, reprinting the prosecutor's denunciation of the old man for allegedly encouraging birth control, holding "cheap dances" and carrying on similar sinister ac-

---

[21] *Boston Investigator*, February 6, 1835. The mood of this publication is well illustrated in this typical doggerel of February 26, 1836: —

> Religion is falling and can't long remain,
>   Its dark sable face is unmasked by A. K.;
> It had its death blow by the arrow of Paine —
>   The monster is dying and fading away.

> Huzza! we are free — there's now no defence,
>   The cloud of religion is driven away;
> The sky has been clear'd by pure Common Sense,
>   Huzza! for the world and this thrice happy day!

[22] "If any person will procure the Boston Anti-Bank Memorial, he shall find among its subscribers nearly every man who attends the Infidel orgies at the Federal-street Theatre. I have no doubt that the Infidel party constitutes at least one-third of the Jackson party of the City at this moment. . . . The Van Buren party throughout the Union, embraces in its ranks the Infidels and sceptics of all the States." Derby, *Political Reminiscences*, 143.

[23] 20 Pickering 206.

[24] The best account is by Henry S. Commager, "The Blasphemy of Abner Kneeland," *New England Quarterly*, VIII, 29–41.

[25] Howe, "Atheism in New-England," *New-England Magazine*, VII, 500–509, VIII, 53–62 (December, 1834, January, 1835); Adams, *Memoirs*, IX, 186.

tivity, all intended to "root up the foundations of society, & make all property common, & all women common as brutes." [26]

The first trial, held before Judge Peter Oxenbridge Thacher in the Boston Municipal Court, had political implications from the start. Andrew Dunlap, rabid Democrat and close friend of David Henshaw, defended Kneeland, and Thacher clearly disclosed the fears which underlay the indictment in his long and worried charge to the jury. Kneeland's magazine, he observed, circulated "among thousands of the poor and laboring classes of this community." Then he cited Erskine's remarks in the trial of Thomas Williams for publishing Paine's *Age of Reason:* "the poor stand most in need of the consolations of religion, and the country has the deepest stake in their enjoying it . . . *because no man can be expected to be faithful to the authority of man, who revolts against the government of God."* [27] The jury took the hint and found Kneeland guilty.

Kneeland promptly appealed and was tried before the Superior Court in the May term of 1834. This time the jury disagreed, voting 11–1 for conviction. The hold-out was, by some mysterious coincidence, Charles Gordon Greene of the *Boston Post.*[28] A third trial also resulted in a hung jury. Finally a fourth trial, in the November term of 1835, produced a conviction, and Kneeland was sentenced to sixty days in the common jail. The old man, now conducting his own case, appealed to the Supreme Court of the state. The political angles had meanwhile grown more pronounced than ever. After one of his trials Kneeland published a letter of congratulation (accompanied by a gift of money), with introductory remarks applicable, said one observer, "to no other person but Col. Johnson." [29] Henshaw wrote articles for the *Post* and even a pamphlet in Kneeland's defense, Dunlap's speeches were widely distributed, and Greene ran a series of editorials against the case.

The Supreme Court did not announce its decision till April, 1838, with Chief Justice Lemuel Shaw delivering the majority opinion, which sustained the lower court, and Judge Marcus Morton dissenting. As Kneeland began to serve his time, Greene called the sentence a "disgrace to the age, the country, and the community we live in," and Democratic papers through the land extended sympathy.[30] The case was beginning to appall others than Democrats. A petition for

[26] S. D. Parker, *et al., Arguments of the Attorney of the Commonwealth in the Trials of Abner Kneeland, for Blasphemy,* 81.
[27] *Thacher's Criminal Cases,* 386–387.
[28] *Boston Post,* May 26, 1834.
[29] Derby, *Political Reminiscences,* 144.
[30] *Boston Post,* May 12, June 19, 25, 1838.

pardon now circulated among liberal Unitarians, winning the signatures of Dr. Channing, George Ripley, Theodore Parker, Ralph Waldo Emerson and others. But S. K. Lothrop, pastor of the conservative Brattle Street Church, of which Thacher was deacon, defended the conviction from his pulpit and started a petition of his own, which gained considerable respectable support.

In the end Kneeland served his sixty days. Fanny Wright had meantime joined him in editing the *Investigator*. On his release Kneeland's thoughts turned away from Boston. He was old, but never too old for change. In the spring of 1839 he left for Van Buren County in the distant territory of Iowa. In 1840 he was Democratic candidate for the upper house of the territorial legislature and in 1842 chairman of the county Democratic convention. His neighbors must have wondered that this silver-haired, patriarchal man could have been considered so dangerous to society by the Commonwealth of Massachusetts. In 1844 he died, seventy years old.[31]

He had lost his personal battle, but his principles had been established in his defeat. Not since Abner Kneeland has a man been convicted in Massachusetts on the charge of blasphemy. Not for a century after was the state employed as the secular arm of the church.[32] The Whig view of the relation of church and state, while successfully condemning Abner Kneeland to the common jail, at the same time condemned itself to extinction.

5

For some Democrats, however, Christianity, far from being the partner of privilege, was, potentially, the most radical of all faiths. Realization of the typically conservative role of the clergy made them advocate the separation of church and state; but true Christianity, in their minds, could alone release the energies of reform in all their strength. Infidelity, said one Workingmen's leader, is a "singular charge when the great object of the workingmen is to place the business of society on the basis of the moral righteousness of Christianity." [33]

George Bancroft and Orestes A. Brownson, for whom religion was not the rigid Calvinism of the century before but the more radiant faith suggested in the first awakening of Transcendentalism, were particularly confident of the support which religion eventually would

[31] Mary R. Whitcomb, "Abner Kneeland: His Relations to Early Iowa History," *Annals of Iowa*, Third Series, VI, 340–363.

[32] Zechariah Chafee, Jr., *The Inquiring Mind* (N. Y., 1928), 111.

[33] George Dickinson to Bancroft, January 27, 1835, Bancroft Papers.

give to popular rights. "The cause of democracy," as Bancroft put
it, "is the cause of pure religion not less than of justice; it is the cause
of practical christianity." [34] Indeed, those passages in Brownson's
essay on "The Laboring Classes" most generally accounted irreligious
were actually his most passionate assertions of his faith in religion. He
wished to destroy the priesthood, but "we cannot proceed a single
step, with the least safety, in the great work of elevating the laboring
classes, without the exaltation of sentiment, the generous sympathy
and the moral courage which Christianity alone is fitted to produce." [35]
John L. O'Sullivan in the *Democratic Review* protested repeatedly the
fundamentally Christian character of the Democratic movement.

In this view, the mission of Jesus had been betrayed by his clergy.
If I should repeat the words of Jesus in the marketplace, Brownson
had cried in 1836, "You would call me a 'radical,' an 'agrarian,' a
'trades-unionist,' a 'leveller.' " [36] The problem, as he put it a few years
later, was to teach Christianity in a way which would not permit men
to feel that they were good Christians, "although rich and with eyes
standing out with fatness, while the great mass of their brethren are
suffering from iniquitous laws, from mischievous social arrangements,
and pining away from the want of . . . the necessaries of life." [37]

Yet this radical faith in Christianity was always a faith in its quick-
ening power in the individual soul, not a belief in the infallibility of
church or priesthood. Bancroft and Brownson were pointing out the
realm in which religion could safely maintain authority. Their record
of political failure in its opposition to Jackson had damaged the
prestige of the clergy. By asserting their dominion in personal affairs,
the radical Democrats were enabling them to retire gracefully from
their vulnerable position as public arbiters.

Jacksonianism thus assisted the growing secularization of society.
Its substantial effect was to divert the church toward what many in
this century believe its true function: to lead the individual soul to
salvation, not to interfere in politics. Religion, the Jacksonians felt,
could best serve itself by ending its entangling alliances with political
reaction.

[34] Bancroft to Sylvester Judd, *et al.*, October 1, 1834, *Boston Courier*, October
22, 1834.
[35] Brownson, "The Laboring Classes," *Boston Quarterly Review*, III, 389–39
(July, 1840).
[36] Harriet Martineau, *Society in America*, II, 412.
[37] Brownson, "The Laboring Classes," *loc. cit.*, 389.

XXVIII JACKSONIAN DEMOCRACY AND UTOPIA

THE DECADE of the eighteen-forties was marked by outbursts of Utopian enthusiasm. Literary men, appalled by the drabness of life around them, sought refuge in social orders of their own fabrication. Some fled physically, as well as intellectually, retiring to model communities where the contemplation of their own principles would protect them from the challenges of the new industrialism. Literary men of later generations, perhaps equipped by their own timidities to sympathize with this earlier retreat from responsibility, have since glorified this movement until the impression has passed into the tradition that these fugitives had almost a monopoly of the reform impulse. It is pertinent to inquire into the relations of Jacksonian democracy and the passion for Utopia.

1

The most popular of the Utopian faiths in America was the gospel of Fourier, of which the prophet was Albert Brisbane. A tall, slim, round-shouldered man, with jutting chin and deep-set eyes, he had gone to Europe in the late eighteen-twenties, spurred on by "an irresistible desire to solve the mystery of man's destiny." When he returned a few years later, man's destiny had become an open book. The book was written by Fourier. Brisbane took over the main core of Fourierism, purged it of its more obviously fantastic details (the fornication of the planets, and the ocean turned to soda water) and set forth the residue in a work entitled *The Social Destiny of Man*, published in Philadelphia in 1840.[1]

As a diagnosis of industrial society, Fourierism was filled with many keen insights. It insisted at bottom that man must be accepted as a whole, with all his needs, passions and instincts. No society, it emphasized, which regularly ignored, stifled or thwarted the basic drives of man could be stable or happy. Brisbane was at his best in his account of the ways in which the capitalist order baffled and frustrated the industrial man. The evidence lay on every hand. "In society as

[1] Redelia Brisbane, *Albert Brisbane. A Mental Biography*, 54–195.

it is now constituted," he cried, "monotony, uniformity, intellectual inaction and torpor reign: distrust, isolation, separation, conflict and antagonism are almost universal: very little expansion of the generous affections and feelings obtain. . . . Society is spiritually a desert." [2]

The Fourierites projected a reconstruction of society based on a realistic acceptance of human instinct: they desired a social organization which would respect the fundamental passions of mankind and convert them to useful social purposes. Insecurity and anxiety would then disappear, coherence and harmony would blossom, and the full creative energies of humanity would be released to build a glorious future.

But the cure fell several levels below the diagnosis. God, Brisbane reported, had not created the passions of man at random, but had calculated their action and interplay "with mathematical precision." "If they are at present condemned as depraved and vicious, it is because science has not discovered the social order intended for them." [3] But the mathematics of Fourierism were more than equal to the problem. An intricate psychological analysis produced the conclusion that the "phalanstery" was the ideal form of social organization. Laborious computation proved it to be capable of satisfying all the impulses of man with the maximum of efficiency. Each phalanstery would consist of 1620 persons, selected according to the master scheme of passions. Remodeled into a federation of phalanxes, society could expect a future of illimitable brotherhood.

2

Brisbane was in important respects a highly typical Fourierite. An epileptic, of delicate physical frame, he had considerable verbal facility, an active dislike for actuality and a neurotic hatred of disorder. His description of his life at the Sorbonne summed up his whole intellectual outlook: "So much was I interested in general and abstract questions, I paid but little attention to the physical sciences. . . . In my absorbing desire to comprehend universal problems I left those that appeared concrete and practical aside." His wife reported that "his very mental constitution rendered it impossible for him ever to attain to a commonplace, common-sense appreciation of the matter-of-fact world; and he never dealt successfully with either men or matter." [4] Forever wrapped in syllogisms, he was shielded from the

[2] *Bay State Democrat*, January 15, 1844.
[3] Brisbane, *Social Destiny of Man*, 256.
[4] Brisbane, *Brisbane*, 72, 7.

wildness of experience. He became so intent on reorganizing society to suit individual needs that he quickly forgot about the individual. "Somehow or other," remarked Walt Whitman, "he always looks as if he were attempting to think out some problem a little too hard for him." [5]

But other sensitive men of the day, feeling the same repugnance at the senseless confusion and moral anarchy of the new industrialism, delighted in Brisbane's confident solution. The blueprints for Utopia especially attracted those whose high logical fluency and low practical experience would lead them, in admiration of the ingenuity, to overlook such minor omissions as industrialism, technology and political power. "Associationism," as Brisbane christened Fourierism for American consumption, appeased their consciences without committing them to any very drastic action. It bestowed on them a gratifying sense of being bold reformers and daring social thinkers, without demanding of them much more than, perhaps, living in rural surroundings with a few fellow spirits and engaging in a little manual labor.

Most of them came from Whig backgrounds, moreover, and found little in the basic Fourierite presuppositions to repel them. Associationism had little in common with the Jeffersonian tradition. It rarely talked about democracy, exhibited no interest in equality and attached small value to political liberty. Far from claiming the right of the workingman to the full proceeds of labor, it guaranteed the earnings of capital, proposing to stabilize the distribution of income among capital, labor and skill in the ratio of 4:5:3. Fortunes, said Brisbane, should be "proportional to classes." [6]

"According to the notions of the Fourierites," observed a sardonic German refugee, "the working man in their Phalanx would do from inclination what, in his present work, he does to keep himself from hunger. It would become in a sense his religion to make the capitalist rich. For that end, everything should be so arranged that the working man would be well fed, well housed, well dressed, perhaps even better than the slave in the south." [7] Fourierism in a way was a scheme to perpetuate capitalism by incorporating feudal satisfactions in work and status into the new processes of production.

This attempt was accompanied by an earnest belief in the necessity of social harmony, even for the imperfect society of 1840, and vigorous disavowal of class conflict. According to Parke Godwin, next to Brisbane the leading American spokesman, Fourierism assured the

[5] Whitman, *New York Dissected*, 129.
[6] Brisbane, *Social Destiny*, 58, 155 n., 354.
[7] Herman Kriege in the New York *Volks Tribun*, September 26, 1846, Commons, *Documentary History*, VII, 230.

"higher classes that their possessions and their advantages are all theirs, and that it has no design of infringing them in the slightest respect." "He, who proposes a fundamental change in society," declared Brisbane, "should propose a plan for accomplishing it, which would conflict with the interests and prejudices of no part of the community." "My object," said L. W. Ryckman of Brook Farm, "is not to array one class against another, but, by a glorious unity of interests, make all harmony and ensure universal intelligence, elevation and happiness." [8]

With its keynotes of class harmony and pastoralism, its promise to curb radical discontent without surrendering the privileges of capital, Fourierism naturally appealed to humanitarian Whigs. ("How escape the impending Social Revolution?" asked an Associationist journal. "By ORGANIZING INDUSTRY. This is the *only* answer." [9]) Horace Greeley inevitably became its champion — "just damned fool enough to believe such nonsense," said Park Benjamin [10] — but he gave the cause less publicity after Henry J. Raymond of the *Times* engaged him in a heated newspaper debate.

The Associationists, in fact, staked out an ideal position. They could piously ignore or oppose all practical reform for its "degrading littleness and insufficiency" without sacrificing for a moment the pleasant illusion that they were reformers. They could denounce the ten-hour day or strikes or attacks on the banking system with as hearty good will as their conservative friends, while placating their consciences by advocating a social reorganization so unlikely that it was perfectly safe. They were, of course, not seriously interested in changing society. They were concerned with expressing their own fantasies and appeasing their own feelings of guilt. They secretly dreaded responsibility and preferred to luxuriate in gaudy visions of the future. [11]

3

The background of this sideshow speculation in the Jacksonian struggles is clear enough. Democratic editors and politicians had spent a decade in raising the question of the distribution of property, in calling attention to the inadequacies of capitalism, in demanding so-

[8] Godwin, *Popular View of the Doctrines of Charles Fourier*, 111; Brisbane, *Social Destiny*, 105; Ryckman quoted in Ware, *Industrial Worker*, 210.

[9] *Spirit of the Age*, November 17, 1849.

[10] Brisbane, *Brisbane*, 204.

[11] For good general analyses of Fourierism, see C. Bouglé, *Socialismes Français*, 111–138; Ware, *Industrial Worker*, 168–174.

cial reform. Their incessant agitation was finally penetrating the studies and parlors of secluded intellectuals, who recognized the justice of the outcry, but were temperamentally debarred from the rough-and-tumble of politics and thus leaned toward the easier path of theoretical brotherhood.

For their part, the Democrats were glad to promote the efforts of Brisbane, Godwin, Ryckman and others in whipping up feeling about the evils of society. Brisbane himself contributed to the *Democratic Review* and the *Boston Quarterly Review,* as well as to such Democratic papers as the *Bay State Democrat* in Boston and the *Plebeian,* the successor to the *New Era,* in New York. But Fourierism had little to contribute to the Jacksonian analysis, and, at least from the viewpoint of tough-minded politicians, nothing to contribute to the Jacksonian solution. When Brisbane called on Thomas Hart Benton in 1842 and made clear the nature of his interests, Benton "took no pains to conceal his more than indifference, not failing to improve the first opportunity to turn away from me." [12]

The Associationists, on the other hand, tended to regard Democrats with positive disapproval. On practical issues they ordinarily managed, for ingenious reasons of their own, to end up on the Whig side. Brisbane, for example, attacked the hard-money policy, not presumably because he really favored the Whig system, but because he had some crank greenback theory of his own: yet the effect was to support the Whig program.[13] Similarly Parke Godwin denounced the Locofoco attack on monopolies with as much gusto as the Whigs, even if allegedly for different reasons.[14] The Associationist press was voluble in criticism of strikes and of agitation for the ten-hour day.[15]

More basically, they resented the whole Jacksonian assumption of class conflict. Writing the *Social Destiny of Man* in the midst of the campaign of 1840, Brisbane took care to dissociate himself from Locofoco radicalism. "We wish to excite, not a war of the poor against the rich — as a certain political party is accused of doing — but the just indignation, of all those who suffer" — and in Brisbane's reckoning everyone, rich and poor, suffered from the existing system. Brisbane told Emerson that the Democracy did not wish to

[12] Brisbane speaks of "his clear insight into a certain range of questions." Brisbane, *Brisbane,* 226. Benton was one of the few men active in politics to whom the Fourierites accorded much respect. See, e.g., Godwin, "Constructive and Pacific Democracy," *Present,* I, 190 (December 15, 1843).

[13] Brisbane, *Brisbane,* 198 ff.

[14] Godwin, "Constructive and Pacific Democracy," *loc. cit.,* 190.

[15] *Phalanx,* November 4, 1843, May 18, 1844, Commons, *Documentary History,* VII, 231–233; Ware, *Industrial Worker,* 210.

build, "only to tear down, God and the Bank, and everything else they could see." [16]

At the bottom of the Fourierite attitude was a fundamental indifference to politics. They regarded it, in Godwin's words, as "utterly inane and useless . . . fit only, like the bull-baitings and carnivals of older nations, to amuse the coarser tastes of the populace." It was capable, added Brisbane, of bringing about only "mere negations and denunciations, or very superficial reforms." "Little or nothing," declared Godwin, "is to be done by any form of political action." [17] This rejection of politics was, to a degree, a rejection of democracy. The Utopians, fearing the hard-boiled give-and-take of party contests, dreamed of a golden day when all change would come by spontaneous agreement and all men would be brothers.

The issues between the Democrat and the Utopian were well set forth in a dialogue in the *Spirit of the Age*. For a full comprehension of the Utopian mentality, it should be understood that the "Socialist" is supposed to be scoring heavily on the benighted "Radical."

> *Radical.* This Age is one of War of Principles, war to the knife; and only by making a clearing through old abuses, can the road be opened for a peaceful progress of mankind.
> *Socialist.* The spirit from which you speak is certainly rife enough; but it belongs to the *last* age, not to THIS. There are Nimrods abroad, great and small, slaying the savage beasts of oppression; but man longs rather to see an Orpheus taming them by music. . . .
> *Radical.* Your whole tone of thought is mystical, transcendental, abstract; you do not know the people, their sorrows and wants, their indignation and impatience. The true way to talk now, is in the sphere of immediate interest; tell men how to make two dollars for one, how to overturn the whole gambling system of trade, how to do away with interest on money, how to set labor free from its chains, in a word, how to tumble into the dust that Old Man of the Mountain, Capital. . . . Call things by their right names; let the blood-suckers, who by banking, brokerage and all modes of spunging, are draining the vitals of the productive classes, know that they shall be choked off. . . .
> *Socialist.* The *ends* you have in view are for the most part right. . . . But your summary *measures* will be found to be of much less sure and speedy efficacy than words of peace and deeds of co-operation. . . . Demand universal amnesty, universal disarming,

[16] Brisbane, *Social Destiny*, 4; Emerson, *Journals*, VI, 355.
[17] Godwin, "Constructive and Pacific Democracy," *loc. cit.*, 194; Brisbane, "Reform Movements Originating among the Producing Classes," *Harbinger*, January 24. 1846. See also Brisbane, *Social Destiny*, viii–ix.

universal fraternity. Let the privileged be told cordially, that there is not the remotest thought of spoiling them of their means of culture, honor, enjoyment, but that proposed plans of reform will benefit them as well as the poor.

Radical. You think soft words and kindly sentiments will tame these wolves into fellowship with the flocks they worry. It is — with due respect to your feelings — the sheerest nonsense. . . . What is wanted is a certain divine vengeance, swift as the whirlwind and earth-quake shock, an upheaval of the people lifting oppressions and oppressors, and tossing them aside forever. . . .

Socialist. The last age tried thoroughly retributive force; let this age try more thoroughly redeeming forgiveness. . . . This sounds to you like visionary rant; well, you will live to learn; seeming folly ridiculed to-day, proves to be wisdom to-morrow.[18]

4

Tomorrow has come . . . but Fourierism failed to go very deep even for its own generation. It was the hobbyhorse of a decade rather than the passion of a lifetime, distracting the conscience but not transforming the will. It prepared its followers to grapple effectively with none of the big problems of American life. History thus provided it with no nourishment, demonstrating neither its truth nor even its falsity, but what was much more fatal, its irrelevance. As Emerson said, it skipped no fact but life.

Even in its own day, it was essentially a posture of romantic despair, assumed in terror before a few economic complexities, self-exposed at every crisis. Horace Greeley invariably forgot socialism in favor of Whig economics when the chips were down. Parke Godwin outlived the audacities of youth to become one of the most pompous conservative journalists of a day when competition was stiff. Albert Brisbane admiringly pronounced Ulysses S. Grant to be the first statesman since Calhoun to express an original idea. Charles A. Dana turned into the cynical and conservative editor of the *New York Sun.* W. H. Channing, one of the most ardent Fourierites, wrote of James A. Garfield, "His picture still shines down upon me with Washington and 'Uncle Abe,' with Michael Angelo and the infant Samuel. . . . it is as clear as noontide to me that he was our Ideal President!"[19] Oh, the last lingering visions of Utopia, fading, vanishing, in the dazzling sunshine of this glorious day! . . . Fourier provided no defense against

[18] *Spirit of the Age,* July 28, 1849.
[19] Brisbane, *Brisbane,* 225; O. B. Frothingham, *Memoir of William Henry Channing,* 409–410.

the industrial empire. He diverted early qualms and smoothed the way for eventual acceptance.

Literary fashion has been a distorter of history. Much more important for the national democratic tradition than this intellectual dalliance with pseudo-reform was the tainted, corrupt, unsatisfactory work performed by the Locofoco politicians. The emotions of Utopia have been admired long enough. It is time to pass along from the sideshows into the main arena and watch the men who were actually fighting the battles of reform in the place where they had to be fought. All the prose about brotherhood and the pretty experiments in group living made no conservative sleep less easily at night. The politicians might have sold their souls to Party, but at least they had something to show for it.

Yet, let no one forget the generous and humane aspirations which animated the Utopian faith. Some people must dream broadly and guilelessly, if only to balance those who never dream at all.

XXIX JACKSONIAN DEMOCRACY AND LITERATURE

Historians of revolution describe a phenomenon they have named the "desertion of the intellectuals." This is the stage in society when the artists, the writers, the intellectuals in general, no longer find enough sustenance in the established order to feel much loyalty to it. They are filled with a pervading sense at once of alienation and of longing, which, one way or another, controls their work, directly if they are political writers, obliquely and at many removes if they are poets. The age of Jackson was such a period. One world was passing away, while another struggled to be born, and the political battles of the Jacksonians helped set in motion a whole train of changes in other spheres. "The strife has been of a character to call forth all the resources of the popular intelligence," Theodore Sedgwick, Jr., wrote in 1835. ". . . It has urged forward the whole American mind."[1]

1

Not all writers were politically active, not even all those possessed by visions of a new world. Some, like Emerson and Thoreau, preoccupied most profoundly with the questions raised up by the change, spent years quietly ignoring politics. But, even with such important exceptions, it is yet remarkable how many of the leading authors and artists publicly aligned themselves with the Jacksonian party. Nathaniel Hawthorne, William Cullen Bryant, Walt Whitman, James Fenimore Cooper, George Bancroft, Washington Irving (until the pressure became too great), James K. Paulding, Orestes A. Brownson, William Leggett, John L. O'Sullivan, John L. Stephens, Horatio Greenough, Hiram Powers, Edwin Forrest, Frances Wright, Robert Dale Owen, for example, were all Jacksonians. As Harriet Martineau observed, the Democratic party included the underprivileged classes, the careerists,

[1] Sedgwick, *What Is a Monopoly?*, 7. It would require another and a different book to show how the literature of the day tried to resolve on the moral and artistic level some of the problems faced by Jacksonian democracy in politics and economics. Much of this ground has been acutely covered by F. O. Matthiessen in *American Renaissance*. My purpose here is simply to indicate some of the direct responses of writers to politics.

the humanitarians and "an accession small in number, but inestimable in power, — the men of genius." [2]

The Democrats were exceedingly proud of their intellectuals. "It is a fact well known," boasted the *Boston Post*, "that with few exceptions, our first literary men belong to the democratic party. Almost every man of note in letters, — historians, poets, and indeed nearly all who have acquired fame as writers and authors are, as might be expected, favorable to democracy." [3] Van Buren himself offered government jobs to Bancroft, Hawthorne, Irving, Paulding, Brownson and Leggett. Even Whigs complained that the word "Locofoco" ought to be used as the "synonyme of ignorance; and yet that party certainly numbers amongst its leaders some celebrated literary characters." [4] For many this fact was cause for indignation. "Why in this fearful struggle which we are obliged to sustain," cried Edward Everett of Hawthorne, "is he on the side of barbarism & vandalism against order, law, & constitutional liberty?" [5]

Many of the authors regarded a position of political liberalism as an artistic imperative. They felt that the Whigs cared only to preserve the tame, reliable and derivative culture of which men like Everett and Longfellow were faithful representatives. The only future for a powerful native literature, dealing fearlessly in truth and reality, seemed to lie in a bold exploration of the possibilities of democracy. "The vital principle of an American national literature," declared the *Democratic Review*, "must be democracy." [6] "The man of letters," as George Bancroft told Everett, "should be the man of the people," and his own monumental *History* revealed how a living faith in the people could quicken, unify and transmute into art a narrative which had heretofore been but dry chronicles.[7] Orestes A. Brownson was even more specific. The question of capital and labor seemed to him

[2] Martineau, *Society in America*, I, 13–14. Cf. George Combe, *Notes on the United States of North America*, II, 216: "The Whig party in America claims the wealth of the Union on their side, and the Democrats claim the genius."

[3] *Boston Post*, October 11, 1838. See also *New York Evening Post*, August 14, 1838.

[4] Francis Baylies, *Speech . . . before the Whigs of Taunton*, 3.

[5] Everett to G. S. Hillard, June 21, 1849, Everett Papers. Henry Wadsworth Longfellow charged darkly in 1839 that the Locofocos were organizing a "new politico-literary system." Longfellow to G. W. Greene, July 23, 1839, Hawthorne, *The American Notebooks*, Randall Stewart, ed., 288.

[6] "Introduction," *Democratic Review*, I, 14 (October, 1837).

[7] Bancroft to Everett, February 7, 1835, Bancroft Papers. Cf. Bancroft to Jared Sparks, August 22, 1834, Sparks Papers: "A vein of public feeling, of democratic independence, of popular liberty, ought to be infused into our literature. Let Mammon rule in the marts; but not on the holy mountain of letters. The rich ought not to be flattered; let truth, let humanity speak through the public journals and through American literature."

supreme: "In the struggle of these two elements, true American literature will be born." [8]

2

A first requisite for a literature is a medium for publication.
The respectable magazines — the *North American,* the *American
Quarterly,* the *New-England Magazine,* and so on — were in Whig
hands, and during the eighteen-thirties the need for a monthly journal
of liberal sympathies became increasingly pronounced. At this junc-
ture a bright young man named John L. O'Sullivan, who had been
running a small newspaper in Washington, appeared with the project
of a Democratic review.

O'Sullivan was descended from a long line of picaresque Irishmen
whose actual careers remain buried under family legend. His father
had lived an obscure life, sometimes as American Consul in such places
as Mogador and Teneriffe, more often as master, supercargo or owner
of ships engaged in the South American trade. A cloud of mystery
hangs over many of his transactions, and he was several times charged
with bribery and extortion and even suspected of piracy. One aunt
paid a call on ex-President Madison in 1827, dressed as a man and
followed by four children, and told a fantastic tale of adventures in
Europe and America.[9]

Young O'Sullivan graduated from Columbia in 1831 and began a
life of free-lance journalism. He was a charming, gay and rather
indolent man, with a sanguine temperament, often disappointed but
rarely depressed. Nathaniel Hawthorne, while feeling him to be superficial, very much enjoyed his company, and a sterner nature like
Thoreau thought him "puny-looking" and overtalkative but still one
of the "not-bad." O'Sullivan's sister (handsome enough to provoke
even Emerson to enthusiastic comment) had married another young
writer named S. D. Langtree, and together in 1837 the two approached
Benjamin F. Butler with the proposal of a Democratic literary magazine.[10]

[8] Brownson, "American Literature," *Boston Quarterly Review,* III, 76 (January,
1840).
[9] J. W. Pratt, "John L. O'Sullivan and Manifest Destiny," *New York History,*
XXXI, 214–217.
[10] Poe thought him an ass, and Longfellow, a humbug — both judgments occasionally having their foundation. Julia Ward Howe, meeting Yeats, in 1903, and
noting his fiery temperament, his slight figure, his blue eyes and dark hair, was
irresistibly reminded of O'Sullivan. Julian Hawthorne, *Nathaniel Hawthorne and
His Wife,* I, 160; Nathaniel Hawthorne, *Love Letters,* Roswell Field, ed., II, 242;
Rose H. Lathrop, *Memories of Hawthorne,* 77; Thoreau to Emerson, January 24,

Butler, who was given to cultural dabbling and even wrote verse for publication, took fire at the idea, subscribed five hundred dollars himself and urged other Democratic politicians to aid in financing the *Democratic Review*. Henry D. Gilpin also took an active part in the search for backing. Jackson, who had long hoped for such a journal, encouraged the project and became the first subscriber. During the summer the editors approached writers the country over, and in October a preliminary number appeared, with contributions by Bryant, Hawthorne, Whittier and others. (When Langtree applied to John Quincy Adams, the old man testily replied that literature by its nature would always be aristocratic, and that the idea of a Democratic literary magazine was self-contradictory.) [11]

Whatever O'Sullivan's failings, he was an excellent editor. He was assiduous in seeking out new talent, and he quickly made the *Democratic Review* by far the liveliest journal of the day. His authors included Bryant, Hawthorne, Thoreau, Whittier, Walt Whitman, Poe, Longfellow, Lowell, Paulding, William Gilmore Simms, Bancroft, Brownson, A. H. Everett and many more. Politically the magazine aligned itself vigorously with the radical wing of the party. The *Madisonian* described it as "a sort of political hygroscope, indicating the state of the air breathed in the party councils of the ruling dynasty," and even men like Marcy regarded it as an "organ of the administration." [12] There is no evidence, however, that Van Buren used the

---

1843, F. B. Sanborn, *Hawthorne and His Friends*, 30; G. E. Woodberry, *Life of Edgar Allan Poe*, I, 353; Hawthorne, *The American Notebooks*, 288–289; Laura E. Richards and Maud Howe Elliott, *Julia Ward Howe, 1819–1910*, II, 319; Emerson to Margaret Fuller, February 24, 1843, Emerson, *Letters*, III, 149.

[11] O'Sullivan to Rufus Griswold, September 8, 1842, *Passages from the Correspondence of Rufus W. Griswold*, William Griswold, ed., 213; Butler to Bancroft, May 1, 1838, Bancroft Papers; Butler to Gilpin, April 24, 1838, Gilpin Papers; Jackson to Langtree and O'Sullivan, March 6, 1837, *Washington Globe*, March 13, 1837; Adams, *Memoirs*, IX, 416; Frank L. Mott, *History of American Magazines*, I, 677–684.

[12] This reputation discredited the *Democratic Review* in conservative circles. "Will you believe," wrote George Sumner, from Europe, to a friend in Boston, "that because that article on Greece appeared in the *Democratic Review*, the only review we have which goes to foreign capitals, the review which champions in a moderate way those principles upon which our Government is founded, . . . the review which Advaros (Min. of Pub. Ins. in Russ.) hailed as a publication which gave a tone to America abroad, and enabled her to appear with a review not a poor repetition of the poor matter of the English reviews — because that article appeared in the *Democratic Review*, it is trodden under foot, and I am denounced as 'an Administration man.' " His brother Charles had written him that Nathan Hale refused to reprint the article in the *Boston Advertiser;* George Ticknor was "sorry to see it in such company"; Justice Story was "much troubled," but "of course did not speak of it out of delicacy to me"; Professor Greenleaf of

Democratic Review for trial balloons, and in the end the magazine left Washington when Blair's jealousy denied it a share of the government printing.[13] It resumed publication in New York and remained under O'Sullivan's control till 1846. Its circulation in 1843 was 3500.[14]

In the meantime Orestes Brownson had provided the liberals with another organ in his *Boston Quarterly Review*. The concurrence of motives behind this journal showed the wide front of the cultural revolt. His object, Brownson said, was to support the new movement in all its manifestations, "whether it be effecting a reform in the Church, giving us a purer and more rational theology; in philosophy seeking something profounder and more inspiriting than the heartless Sensualism of the last century; or whether in society demanding the elevation of labor with the Loco foco, or the freedom of the slave with the Abolitionist." [15]

The *Boston Quarterly* thus became a compendium of the desertion of the intellectuals, defending in detail the repudiation of the old order in religion, philosophy and politics. Not only Bancroft and A. H. Everett but George Ripley and Theodore Parker, Bronson Alcott and Margaret Fuller were essential in Brownson's broad purpose. To him the fight was all one, though later the political motive grew more dominant, and it almost seemed, as Brownson told Van Buren, that the review was established "for the purpose of enlisting Literature, Religion, and Philosophy on the side of Democracy." [16]

Less bright and varied than the *Democratic Review*, the *Boston Quarterly* was more learned, serious and penetrating. Brownson's personality pervaded the journal — he became increasingly the exclusive author — and he endowed it with a vigor and cogency which commanded wide attention. John C. Calhoun, for example, was a faithful reader, and even the impassive Levi Woodbury, Secretary of the Treasury, was moved to exclaim of one issue, "What an excellent number was Mr. Brownson's last! Exhort him from me to give us

---

the Harvard Law School was "grieved" and reported that it had been "lamented by many people who were prepared to be your friends." "Seriously, my dear George," Charles Sumner wrote, "think of abandoning your leaky craft." George Sumner's response was violent: "God *damn* them *all!!* . . . I cannot but laugh, roars of horrid laughter, on thinking of all these things. . . . How the demon of party feeling must have crazed the minds and feelings of men whose characters one would suppose firm and high." George Sumner to G. W. Greene, November [?], 1842, *Proceedings of the Massachusetts Historical Society*, XLVI, 359–360.
[13] Mott, *History of American Magazines*, I, 679–680.
[14] O'Sullivan to Charles Sumner, April 12, 1843, Sumner Papers.
[15] "Introductory Remarks," *Boston Quarterly Review*, I, 6 (January, 1838).
[16] Brownson to Van Buren, April 2, 1838, Van Buren Papers.

more." [17] (When Brownson began a few months later to give them more, Woodbury became markedly less enthusiastic.)

In 1842 the *Democratic Review* and the *Boston Quarterly* merged, but not before each had left a distinct mark on the development of American letters. Each journal, on its own level, was the best of its day, and both gained much of their energy, courage and free vigor from their immersion in the political ideals of Jacksonian democracy.

3

A surprising number of writers were themselves active in politics or the government service. George Bancroft, driven ahead by an unstable combination of democratic idealism and personal ambition, became party boss of Massachusetts and later Polk's Secretary of the Navy. Brownson held office under Van Buren and ran for Congress during the Civil War. Washington Irving and Alexander H. Everett were in the diplomatic service.

James K. Paulding spent many years on government pay rolls, first as Naval Agent of New York, later as Van Buren's Secretary of the Navy. This bluff, amusing Dutchman was a stout Jacksonian, if by a roundabout road. A man of obstinate good sense, he disliked the cant of radicalism, but disliked the cant of conservatism even more. His famous satire *The Merry Tales of the Three Wise Men of Gotham* (1826) poked fun impartially at the common law, on the one hand, and the dreams of Robert Owen, on the other. Many brief political essays, bearing the stamp of his gruff irony and hearty common sense, appeared in the *Washington Globe* and the *New York Evening Post*.[18]

Nathaniel Hawthorne was another Democratic pensioner, holding office under three administrations. Unlike Paulding, he was not much of a party journalist, though there was once a possibility of his joining the *Globe* under Frank Blair, and in 1852 he wrote a campaign life of Franklin Pierce.[19] Yet he was not as perfunctory a Democrat as some biographers have insisted. His quiet sense of sin and his hatred of human pride immunized him against the claims of Whig conservatism to moral or political superiority. He was not much impressed by Utopianism either. The current of his sympathies, as expressed in his notebook jottings, ran clear and strong with the plain, solid, common life of the people. *The House of the Seven Gables* em-

[17] Woodbury to Bancroft, November 21, 1839, Bancroft Papers.

[18] See Paulding's letters to Van Buren and to A. C. Flagg in the respective collections.

[19] For Hawthorne and the *Globe*, see Franklin Pierce to Hawthorne, March 5, 1836, Julian Hawthorne, *Hawthorne and His Wife*, I, 134–135.

bodied massively his conviction of the fatal isolation worked by property and privilege, and his fascination with the rude energies of change and reform.[20] The "Locofoco Surveyor," as he described himself in the preface to *The Scarlet Letter*, was permanently marked by that day in 1833 when he walked through the falling shadows of a Salem dusk to catch a glimpse of General Andrew Jackson.

4

Of all the literary men of the day, however, James Fenimore Cooper has probably suffered the most inquiry into his politics. Because these examinations have generally been carried on without detailed knowledge of the concrete party background, it may be illuminating to reopen his case more squarely in terms of the actual issues of the day.[21]

Cooper was basically an upstate New York squire whose politics were determined ultimately by his sense of the security of landed property. His father had been a prominent Federalist; but Cooper early found Jefferson's views on agricultural virtue and popular rule more congenial. By the eighteen-thirties he was ready to believe that Federalist leaders had actually contemplated revolution and monarchy; and in *The Monikins* (1835) he set forth his famous lampoon of Federalism as the "social stake system." [22]

For Cooper, "the heart and strength of the nation" was "its rural population," and the agricultural foundations of the republic seemed to him, as to most Jeffersonians, to be menaced by the commercial community.[23] He was convinced that the "natural antipathy between trade and democracy" was causing businessmen to plot a financial oligarchy. "Most of all," he wrote, "commerce detests popular rights." [24] The history of Britain, fortified by his own experience in France in the early eighteen-thirties, proved the inevitable tendency of business rule toward a moneyed aristocracy. "No government that is

[20] See the discussion in Matthiessen, *American Renaissance*, 316–337.

[21] Dorothy Waples's valuable *Whig Myth of James Fenimore Cooper* has done much to place Cooper's reputation in proper perspective, by showing how he was systematically vilified by the Whig press for his political views. Robert E. Spiller's *Fenimore Cooper: Critic of His Times* develops the general implications of his social criticism. Ethel R. Outland's *The "Effingham" Libels on Cooper* supplies basic information about Cooper's feud with the press. All these books suffer, however, from an imperfect appreciation of the radical extent to which Cooper's views changed from 1834 to 1850.

[22] Cooper, *Sketches of Switzerland* [Part First], II, 158; *Monikins*, 74, 82.

[23] For the quotation, see *Sketches of Switzerland*, Part Second, II, 181.

[24] Cooper, *Gleanings in Europe*, II, 177.

essentially influenced by commerce," he concluded, "has ever been otherwise than exclusive, or aristocrat." [25] To his political fears he added the contempt of the landed gentleman for the *parvenu* business-man. "Of all the sources of human pride," he would write, "mere wealth is the basest and most vulgar minded. Real gentlemen are almost invariably above this low feeling." [26]

These prepossessions, deeply grounded in Cooper's experience, controlled his creative impulses as well as his arguments. The sketches of the Effingham cousins in *Homeward Bound* suggest as vividly as any of his explicit statements Cooper's feelings about the respective effects of owning property in land and in trade. Edward Effingham was "winning in appearance," John "if not positively forbidding, at least distant and repulsive. . . . The noble outline of face in Edward Effingham had got to be cold severity in that of John; the aquiline nose of the latter, seeming to possess an eaglelike and hostile curvature, — his compressed lip, sarcastic and cold expression, . . . a haughty scorn that caused strangers usually to avoid him." What accounted for this differentiation? "Edward Effingham possessed a large hereditary property, that brought a good income, and which attached him to this world of ours by kindly feelings toward its land and water; while John, much the wealthier of the two, having inherited a large commercial fortune, did not own ground enough to bury him. As he sometimes deridingly said, he 'kept his gold in corporations, that were as soulless as himself.' " [27]

Cooper's faith in the land and hatred for the financial aristocracy naturally led him, on his return to America in 1833, to become an enthusiastic supporter of the Jackson administration. He adopted the most radical Democratic positions on all questions but the tariff, and was in particular a staunch advocate of the hard-money policy. [28] The rule of property, he said in 1836, is "the most corrupt, narrow and vicious form of polity that has ever been devised." [29] While he had no faith in the infallibility of the whole people, he had even less faith in that of any part of the people. "Though majorities often decide wrong, it is believed that they are less liable to do so than minorities." [30]

In *A Letter to His Countrymen* (1834) he denounced the whole Whig position as an attempt to pervert the American form of government by construing it falsely on British analogies in the hope of end-

[25] Cooper, *Monikins*, 408; see also *Letter to His Countrymen*, 65–67.
[26] Cooper, *American Democrat*, 131–132; see also *Excursions in Italy*, 184–185.
[27] Cooper, *Homeward Bound*, 12–13.
[28] See especially *American Democrat*, 163–165.
[29] *Sketches of Switzerland*, Part Second, I, 36.
[30] *American Democrat*, 46.

ing up with a commercial oligarchy on the British model. *The Moni-kins* (1835) was a lengthy satirical allegory, at times brilliant, at times tedious, intended to show in more detail in what danger America stood from imitating the business politics of Britain. In both volumes, in the series of travel books he was turning out and in articles for the *New York Evening Post* he attacked the Whig arguments against Jackson's alleged constitutional excesses. In *The American Democrat* (1838) he even defended Jackson's theory of the right of independent adjudication of constitutionality, as developed in the Bank veto.

In his writings throughout the decade, however, there appears beside the approval of Jacksonianism a mounting irritation with the "tyranny of opinion" in America, which, by *The American Democrat* and his novels of 1837 and 1838, *Homeward Bound* and *Home as Found*, was becoming a major theme. Literary historians have interpreted this complaint as evidence of his discomfort under the pressure toward uniformity supposedly exerted by "Jacksonian democracy."

Before accepting this conclusion, it is essential to understand *whose* opinion Cooper was denouncing as tyrannous. In *Sketches of Switzerland* (1836) he declared, "I have never yet been in a country in which what are called the lower orders have not clearer and sounder views than their betters of the great principles which ought to predominate in the control of human affairs." A few pages later, after setting forth a number of routine Democratic arguments in defense of Jackson's use of the presidential power, he commented that current reasoning on these questions "among what are called the enlightened classes" showed how far opinion had lagged behind facts.[31]

There were, in fact, these *two* public opinions for Cooper — that of "what are called the lower orders," which he respected, and that of "what are called the enlightened classes," which he disliked. Yet Cooper was a careless writer, and he could say, immediately after attacks on the "enlightened classes," "I am aware that these are bold opinions to utter in a country where the mass has become so consolidated that it has no longer any integral parts; where the individual is fast losing his individuality in the common identity." [32] In view of the fact that his opinions were "bold" only among "what are called the enlightened classes," it is clear that in this context Cooper's attack on the "tyranny of opinion" is actually an attack on tyranny of opinion *in his class*.

This is, in fact, the key to his assaults on "tyranny of opinion" in the eighteen-thirties (though not in the eighteen-forties). He would

[31] *Sketches of Switzerland* [Part First], I, 177, 212.
[32] *Ibid.*, 212.

say that if certain progressive opinions were laid before "that portion of the American public which comprises the reading classes," they would have no effect on these classes "on account of their hatred of the rights of the mass"; and in the next sentence he would assert flatly, "I know no country that has retrograded in opinion, so much as our own, within the last five years" — when again he clearly meant, not the whole country, but the "reading classes." [33] "After having passed years in foreign countries, I affirm that I know no state of society in which liberal sentiments are so little relished as in our own, among the upper classes," he would write.[34] But when he began laying about with invective, he tended to forget the qualifications and to accuse the entire nation.

An incident in 1837 intensified Cooper's fears of the "tyranny of opinion." He owned some land on Otsego Lake known as Three Mile Point, which the Coopers had always opened to the village of Cooperstown as a picnic place. In time the villagers began to regard Three Mile Point as public property, and Cooper's attempt to reassert his ownership provoked violent newspaper attacks. Yet it is again hardly just to ascribe these attacks to "Jacksonian democracy." The campaign against Cooper was conducted by the New York Whig press, led by Thurlow Weed, James Watson Webb, William L. Stone and Horace Greeley, most of whom Cooper later chastised by libel suits, while the Jacksonian press, especially the *New York Evening Post* and the *Albany Argus*, rushed to his defense. "It appears that he is ordained to be hunted down," observed the *New Era*. "The British Whig aristocracy here cry havoc, and their creatures throughout the land echo the cry." [35]

Cooper was, in fact, reacting against a pressure toward uniformity, but it was the pressure, not of mass opinion, but of class opinion. It becomes nonsense to say that Cooper revolted against Jacksonian democracy because of its tyranny over opinion, when actually such tyranny over opinion as he experienced in the eighteen-thirties was provoked in great part by his expression of views favorable to Jacksonian democracy.

Cooper's bitter reaction was reflected in the detailed indictment of public opinion he drew up in *The American Democrat* (1838). But the very points at which he chose to attack public opinion as tyrannous were precisely the points where, as he considered, Whig editors

---

[33] *Sketches of Switzerland*, Part Second, II, 189–190.
[34] Cooper to Bedford Brown, March 24, 1838, *Historical Papers Published by the Historical Society of Trinity College*, VIII, 2.
[35] *New Era*, June 4, 1840.

had improperly meddled in his private affairs, and on every current issue discussed he resolutely took the Democratic side. His novels of this period set forth these same emotions. *Home as Found*, though artistically less expert than *Homeward Bound*, was particularly revealing. Like *The American Democrat*, it had two pervading revulsions: on the one hand, the self-constituted aristocracy of the American Whigs, with their pretensions and snobberies, their servility toward the British, their hatred of "that monster" General Jackson and their scorn for the lower classes; on the other, the menace of the democratic demagogue.[36]

But the fear of the democratic demagogue did not shake his allegiance to the Democratic party. In New York, in any case, as the Seward-Weed policy gained adherents, the most objectionable demagogues mouthing democratic professions were on the Whig side. "The present political struggle, in this country," he wrote in 1838, "appears to be a contest between men and dollars."[37] The Whig victory of 1840 seemed to him, in his pessimistic later years, "little more than the proof of the power of money and leisure" to make the masses "the instruments of their own subjection."[38] In the campaign of 1844, he attended his first political meeting in twenty-five years, "and if anything could bring me on the stump," he declared vigorously, "it would be to help put down the bold and factious party that is now striving to place Mr. Clay in the chair of state." He denounced the Whig party as "much the falsest and most dangerous association of the sort that has appeared in the country in my day."[39]

Yet Cooper's radicalism was soon to disappear. It was founded, we have seen, in the opposition of landed capital to business capital, the traditional dislike of the *rentier* for the speculator. But in the middle forties Cooper was suddenly asked to decide whether landed property was not in more peril from radicalism than from business. This question was raised sharply by the antirenters, a group of farmers seeking a revision of the semifeudal seigneurial relations between patroons and tenants in the huge estates along the Hudson. As a champion of the land, Cooper had rejoiced at the Jacksonian attacks on business; but now demagogues were extending the attack, under the same rallying cries, to the land itself. Would not their victory destroy the foundations of property the nation over? "The existence of true lib-

---

[36] For the Jackson reference, *Home as Found*, 123.
[37] Cooper to Bedford Brown, March 24, 1838, *loc. cit.*
[38] Cooper, *The Redskins*, vi.
[39] Cooper to C. A. Secor, *et al.*, September 8, 1844, *The Campaign*, September 21, 1844.

erty among us, the perpetuity of the institutions, and the safety of public morals, are all dependent on putting down, wholly, absolutely, and unqualifiedly, the false and dishonest theories and statements that have been boldly advanced." [40] From a minor fault of democracy the "demagogue" was becoming a major threat, and the vicious agitators of the antirent trilogy showed Cooper's abhorrence of the class. The trilogy itself, emerging splendidly out of deeply felt and concrete emotions, demonstrated how profoundly Cooper's outlook was rooted in the existing land relationships. His obstinately personal attitude quickly changed any menace to these sacred arrangements into a national calamity.

The antirent troubles did more than shake his belief in popular rule. They destroyed his Jeffersonian faith in the moral infallibility of life on the land. "We do not believe any more," he said, "in the superior innocence and virtue of a rural population." [41] His pessimism deepened. *The Lake Gun* (1850) set forth his fears for the Union, excited inevitably by demagogues; this time he clearly had Seward in mind. Despondency welled up most freely in his last work, *The Towns of Manhattan*. The book itself was destroyed by fire, but the introduction indicates the general temper. If property continued to be assailed, Cooper argued, it would take measures to protect itself. The result might well be fatal to popular liberties, but it would also be the just result of the abuse of popular liberties. There seemed but three possible solutions — military dictatorship, a return to original principles, or "the sway of money." [42] Of the three, the financial aristocracy seemed to him most likely. His old hatred of the commercial oligarchy had weakened, and he recognized it as the only bulwark of property. But his confidence in it was not strong, nor were his hopes for the future bright. This irresolute and baffled conclusion, all the more significant in a man of Cooper's ordinary certainty, suggests the depths of his despair. A year later he was dead.

5

The transcendentalists of Massachusetts constituted the one important literary group never much impressed by Jacksonian democracy. This immunity was all the more singular because for two occasional members, George Bancroft and Orestes A. Brownson, the relations between transcendentalism and democracy seemed close and

[40] Cooper, *Satanstoe*, vii.
[41] Cooper, *New York*, 56.
[42] *New York*, 51.

vital. The Jacksonians, in the minds of Bancroft and Brownson, were carrying on the same revolt against the dead hand of John Locke in politics which the transcendentalists were carrying on in religion. Both Democrat and transcendentalist agreed in asserting the rights of the free mind against the pretensions of precedents or institutions. Both shared a living faith in the integrity and perfectibility of man. Both proclaimed self-reliance. Both detested special groups claiming authority to mediate between the common man and the truth. Both aimed to plant the individual squarely on his instincts, responsible only to himself and to God. "The soul must and will assert its rightful ascendancy," exclaimed the *Bay State Democrat*, "over all those arbitrary and conventional forms which a false state of things has riveted upon society." "Democracy," cried Bancroft, "has given to conscience absolute liberty." [43]

But transcendentalism in its Concord form was infinitely individualistic, providing no means for reconciling the diverse intuitions of different men and deciding which was better and which worse. This did not worry most transcendentalists, who would allow Nicholas Biddle the authority of his inner voice and asked only to be allowed equally the authority of their own. The obligations of politics were not so flexible. Bancroft's great modification of transcendentalism was to add that the collective sense of the people provided the indispensable check on the anarchy of individual intuitions. "If reason is a universal faculty, the decision of the common mind is the nearest criterion of truth." Democracy thus perfected the insights of transcendentalism. "Individuals make proclamation of their own fancies; the spirit of God breathes through the combined intelligence of the people. . . . It is, when the multitude give council, that right purposes find safety; theirs is the fixedness that cannot be shaken; theirs is the understanding which exceeds in wisdom." [44]

For Bancroft and Brownson the battle against the past was indivisible, involving politics as much as philosophy. In his brilliant chapter on the Quakers in the second volume of his *History* (1837), Bancroft set forth in luminous prose his conception of the relations between the liberation of the soul of man and of his body. For Brownson conservatism in religion and in society were so nearly identical that he could observe of Victor Cousin, the French philosopher, "His

[43] *Bay State Democrat*, May 3, 1839; Bancroft, "Address to the Democratic Electors of Massachusetts," *Boston Post*, October 16, 1835.

[44] Bancroft, "On the Progress of Civilization, or Reasons Why the Natural Association of Men of Letters Is with the Democracy," *Boston Quarterly Review*, I, 395 (October, 1838); Bancroft, "Address to the Democratic Electors of Massachusetts," *Boston Post*, October 16, 1835.

works have made many young men among us Democrats." To Cousin himself he proudly declared, "We are combining philosophy with politics," adding that the Democratic party would soon adopt the views of the new school.[45] When Bancroft reviewed George Ripley's *Philosophical Miscellanies*, an anthology of French and German metaphysics, for the *Washington Globe,* he called it "a sort of manifesto of philosophical Democracy," and described how the glory of Jefferson had found new witnesses in the work of Cousin, Jouffroy and Constant.[46] An anonymous essayist in a Democratic paper even admonished the young men, in oddly Emersonian phrases, to "TRUST TO YOURSELF" and hymned the virtues of *"self-dependence."* [47]

Yet, for all the inspiration some Democrats found in transcendentalism, the transcendentalists remained singularly unmoved by the exertions of the Democrats. From their book-lined studies or their shady walks in cool Concord woods, they found the hullabaloo of party politics unedifying and vulgar. The rebuke of Nature was crushing: "So hot? my little Sir." Life was short, and much better to contemplate verities and vibrate to that iron spring than to make commitments to practicality. A political party, like society itself, was a joint-stock company, in which the members agreed, for the better securing of bread to each shareholder, to surrender the liberty and culture of the eater. "The virtue in most request is conformity. Self-reliance is its aversion."

But for the typical transcendentalist the flinching from politics perhaps expressed a failure they were seeking to erect into a virtue. The exigencies of responsibility were exhausting: much better to demand perfection and indignantly reject the half loaf, than wear out body and spirit in vain grapplings with overmastering reality. The headlong escape into perfection left responsibility far behind for a magic domain where mystic sentiment and gnomic utterance exorcised the rude intrusions of the world. But it was easier to rule the state from Concord than from Washington. And the state had to be ruled, it was the implacable vacuum: if Bronson Alcott preferred Fruitlands, he was not to complain when James K. Polk preferred the White House.

Yet these were the worst, the pure transcendentalists, incapable of effective human relations, terrified of responsibility, given to transforming evasion into a moral triumph. The tougher-minded men on the transcendental margin recognized that certain obligations could

---

[45] Brownson to Bancroft, September 24, 1836, Bancroft Papers; Brownson to Cousin, June 23, 1838, Brownson Papers.
[46] *Washington Globe*, March 9, 1838.
[47] "To the Young Men," by "H. P.," *Bay State Democrat*, August 16, 1839.

not be shaken. The existence of society depended on a mutuality of confidence, the maintenance of which required that the demands of hunger, want and insecurity be met, lest desperation shatter the social chain. These basic agonies were not to be dissolved in the maternal embrace of the oversoul. George Ripley, unlike Bronson Alcott, did not despise those who held the ordinary affairs of life to be important. Whiggery in politics persuaded him as little as Whiggery in religion, and the energy of his friends Bancroft and Brownson stimulated him to work with transcendental insights on the ills of society. "He has fairly philosophized himself into Democracy," wrote Brownson in 1836. Ripley himself bravely declared to Bancroft a year later that "almost to a man, those who shew any marks of genius or intellectual enterprise are philosophical democrats." (The date was September 20, but he had no observations on the independent treasury.) The intellectual ferment of Boston was heady. "There is a great feeding on the mulberry leaves, and it will be hard if silken robes are not woven for the shining ones. . . . I almost hope to see the time, when religion, philosophy and politics will be united in a holy Trinity, for the redemption and blessedness of our social institutions." [48]

But Ripley's gestures toward the Democratic party were those of a pure young man engaged in audacious coquetry with an experienced woman of shady reputation. He smiled, inclined, almost yielded, then snatched away with an air of indignation, his head flushed with the pleasing excitement and his virtue intact. When Bancroft allowed some of Ripley's remarks to fill an anonymous paragraph in the *Boston Post*, Ripley wrote with alarm, "I insist on the distinction between the philosophical principles of democracy, and the democratic party in this country." (His timid advances were being taken with undue seriousness; almost he was invited to meet the family.) ". . . So it is with my young men. They have little faith in parties, but a great zeal for principles. They love nothing about the Whigs but the personal worth which they possess; but they are inclined to doubt whether the opponents of the Whigs are after all true democrats. It is certain, I must confess, that some of the warmest advocates of democratical principles, some who cherish the loftiest faith in the progress of humanity, are found in the Whig ranks." [49] The notes were revealing, for Ripley was not the most innocent of the transcendentalists. Yet he seemed to have no conception at all of, say, the role of measures and policies in underwriting "democratical principles." The diet of mul-

[48] Brownson to Bancroft, September 24, 1836, Ripley to Bancroft, September 20, 1837, Bancroft Papers.
[49] Ripley to Bancroft, November 6, 1837, Bancroft Papers.

berry leaves might weave robes for the shining ones, but it gave small nourishment to a realistic view of society.

Ripley had escaped, but his conscience continued peremptory. Then, in 1840, a fairer and more chaste maiden appeared in the vision of Brook Farm, and he was saved from the worldly life of Politics. For him, and for the other transcendentalists who shared his inability to explain away suffering, Brook Farm appeared as a serious solution of the conditions which had driven Bancroft and Brownson into the arms of Party. Their faith was a variant of Utopianism, and Brook Farm appropriately ended up as a Fourierite phalanx.

6

The Oversoul thus comforted the tender transcendentalists, while the tough mowed the hay and raked the dirt at Brook Farm. But beyond the transcendentalists, accepting their inspiration but safe from their illusions, was Emerson, the wisest man of the day. He was too concretely aware of the complexities of experience to be altogether consoled by vagueness and reverie. The doctrine of compensation had its limits, and he was not deceived by Ripley's community. "At Education Farm, the noblest theory of life sat on the noblest figures of young men and maidens, quite powerless and melancholy. It would not rake or pitch a ton of hay; it would not rub down a horse; and the men and maidens it left pale and hungry." [50] Yet politics represent his greatest failure. He would not succumb to verbal panaceas, neither would he make the ultimate moral effort of Thoreau and cast off all obligation to society. Instead he lingered indecisively, accepting without enthusiasm certain relations to government but never confronting directly the implications of acceptance.

He acknowledged the claims of the Democratic party expounded so ardently by Bancroft and Brownson. "The philosopher, the poet, or the religious man, will, of course, wish to cast his vote with the democrat, for free-trade, for wide suffrage, for the abolition of legal cruelties in the penal code, and for facilitating in every manner the access of the young and the poor to the sources of wealth and power." [51] He recognized, too, the inevitable drift of transcendentalism toward the democratic position. The first lecture of his series in 1839 on the "Present Age" was reported by Theodore Parker as "*Democratic-locofoco* throughout, and very much in the spirit of Brownson's article on Democracy and Reform in the last *Quarterly*." Bancroft

[50] Emerson, *Essays* (World's Classics), 300.
[51] *Essays*, 407–408.

left "in ecstasies . . . rapt beyond vision at the *locofocoism*," and one Boston conservative could only growl that Emerson must be angling for a place in the Custom House.[52]

Yet Emerson would go no farther. "Of the two great parties, which, at this hour, almost share the nation between them," he would lamely conclude, "I should say, that one has the best cause, and the other contains the best men." [53] This would have provided no excuse for inaction, even if it were true, for a man of Emersonian principle should follow his principle; but it was not even true.

Fear of institutions kept him cautious. A party seemed a form of church, and Emerson, a burnt child, shunned the fire. "Bancroft and Bryant," he said, "are historical democrats who are interested in dead or organized, but not in organizing, liberty." [54] He liked the *Washington Globe*'s motto — "The world is governed too much" — though it appalled him that so many people read the paper. But in an imperfect world, should he not settle for "historical democrats" and *Washington Globes*, or at least remark on the alternative? Emerson was well aware of the discipline of choice. Yet here he failed himself, and ignored the responsibilities of his own moral position.

Fundamentally he did not care, and thus he was betrayed, almost without struggle, into the clichés of conservatism which had surrounded him from birth. In a flash of insight he could see that "banks and tariffs, the newspaper and caucus" were "flat and dull to dull people, but rest on the same foundations of wonder as the town of Troy, and the temple of Delphos." [55] Yet, in life at Concord, day in, day out, banks and tariffs were flat and dull to him. As he glanced at party contests, he was most impressed by "the meanness of our politics." [56]

He had little idea of the significance of the struggles of the eighteen-thirties. His ejaculation to Carlyle in 1834 — "a most unfit man in the Presidency has been doing the worst things" — about exhausted his conception of the Jackson administration.[57] His reluctance to break with the Whigs was increased by his invention of a statesman named Daniel Webster to whom he gave profound devotion and whom he carelessly confused with the popular Whig politician of the same

[52] Parker to Convers Francis, December 6, 1839, J. E. Cabot, *Memoir of Ralph Waldo Emerson*, 400–401.

[53] *Essays*, 407.

[54] *Journals*, VI, 315.

[55] *Essays*, 285.

[56] *Essays*, 185.

[57] Emerson to Carlyle, May 14, 1834, *Correspondence of Thomas Carlyle and Ralph Waldo Emerson, 1834–1872*, C. E. Norton, ed., I, 16.

name. "That great forehead which I followed about all my young
days, from court-house to senate chamber, from caucus to street" cast
a hypnotic spell over a man otherwise hard to fool.[58] His comments,
scattered over two decades of loyalty, show a literary fascination with
the massiveness of personality, the stately rhetoric, the marble brow
and face black as thunder; but little concern for his views on practical
policy. This Webster was a mirage peculiar to Emerson. For Bryant,
Bancroft, Cooper, Whitman and Hawthorne, Webster was the most
vulnerable celebrity of the day.[59] But for Emerson he remained a great
statesman — until Webster finally ran up against an issue which really
excited Emerson's imagination and commanded his full attention, and
the speech on the Compromise of 1850 disclosed to Emerson what he
should have known for years. The steady wisdom of the sage of
Concord faltered, in this one field, into sentimentality.

7

Of all the New England group who shunned political choice.
Thoreau alone lived at a degree of moral tension which imposed responsibilities equivalent to those borne by men who sought to govern.
He could not delude himself with fantasies of easy salvation, like
Alcott or Ripley, nor could he accept the status of citizenship, like
Emerson, and dally with its obligations. For him the moral life admitted but one possibility: the complete assumption of all responsibility
by the individual. The highest good, said Thoreau, was the living
unity of the ethical consciousness and its direct, solid expression in
art and life.

In practice he achieved the goal best by a deliberate reduction of
life to its essentials — a cabin by blue Walden, blackberries in the
summer, the indomitable woodchuck, the wild sweet song of the evening robin, the geese flying low over the woods, the last blaze of sun in

[58] Emerson to Carlyle, August 8, 1839, *ibid.*, I, 255.
[59] Webster was the butt of the Democratic literary men, as his peculiar combination of cynicism and external moral grandeur made inevitable. Hawthorne's
sketch of Webster as "Old Stony Phiz" in "The Great Stone Face" is well-known
and penetrating, presenting him as "a man of mighty faculties and little aims, whose
life, with all its high performances, was vague and empty, because no high purpose had endowed it with reality." Hawthorne, *Writings*, III, 51. For Bancroft's
ribald running comment on Webster, see his correspondence with Van Buren.
Bryant's famous editorial on Webster's humor in the *New York Evening Post* of
November 20, 1837, is to be found in Bryant, *Prose Writings*, Parke Godwin, ed.,
II, 383–385. A typical Cooper reference is in *The Monikins*, 414. Whitman summed
them all up with his brief remark that Webster was "overrated more than any other
public man ever prominent in America." *Brooklyn Eagle*, April 11, 1846, *Gathering of the Forces*, II, 182.

the west. But he could not dwell forever at Walden; he had other lives to live; and he returned to society, now fulfilling his singleness of feeling by fusing his superb style till the words, as he said, fell like boulders across the page. Back in the world again, he was face to face with the enemies of the moral life: the new industrialism, which would deform the moral self, and the state, which would corrupt it. In society people lived in quiet desperation, sick at heart, their integrity menaced, clouded and compromised. The only man worth having, thought Thoreau, was the man of principle, and he was worth any expense to the state.

The state, he said, had no moral status. Its rule was expediency, its method, force. It had no right to act on its subjects in terms of obligation and duty. Individuals could have no moral relation to it: the soul was indefeasible, and its burdens could not be assumed by the state. Men should tolerate the state in its milder moments, but, when it seeks to violate their integrity by immoral actions of its own, they must shake themselves free of all complicity. "The only government that I recognize — and it matters not how few are at the head of it, or how small its army — is that power that establishes justice in the land, never that which establishes injustice." Was not the presumption always against the state, that "semihuman tiger or ox, stalking over the earth, with its heart taken out and the top of its brain shot away"? "Is it not possible," he cried, "that an individual may be right and a government wrong?" Man must achieve his moral unity, if necessary at the cost of civil disobedience. This was the sublimest heroism; "for once we are lifted out of the trivialness and dust of politics into the region of truth and manhood." Only a succession of *men*, carrying out such defiances, could tame the semihuman tiger till the state should recognize the individual "as a higher and independent power, from which all its own power and authority are derived, and treats him accordingly." [60]

Thoreau's case was consistent and irrevocable. It was his by bitter conquest, and into holding it he poured the energies of his life. No position could be more exhausting and more pitiless. The relentless pressure of everlasting responsibility beat down on the frail individual, deprived of the possibility of diffusing his guilt among society, alone against the universe, armed only with his own inner righteousness.

Few men could stand the unimaginable strain: for most it leads to hypocrisy or collapse. "Man is neither angel nor brute," observed Pascal, "and the unfortunate thing is that he who would act the

[60] Thoreau, "Plea for Captain John Brown," *Works*, IV, 430, 429, 437; "Civil Disobedience," *Works*, IV, 387.

angel acts the brute." It is for this reason that society has proscribed those evaders who claim the prerogatives of a Thoreau without un- dergoing his intense moral ordeal. Civil disobedience is justified only by the sternest private obedience, and angels are all too likely to turn into brutes. Thoreau earned his beliefs and his immunities. Little men, covering cowardice with a veil of self-righteousness, lay claim to the exemptions of a Thoreau with the most intolerable pretense. The camp followers of a war which he fought, they are presently the camp fol- lowers of a war fought by the rest of society, accepting the protec- tion of the state but disclaiming any obligations. Their performance should not compromise his case. The writings and life of Thoreau presented democracy with a profound moral challenge.

8

Thoreau said Nay to the claims of democracy, but Walt Whit- man sent back the thunderous affirmation, echoing off the roof-tops of the world. Twenty-one in the year of Tippecanoe, Whitman was already up to his neck in radical Democratic politics. In a year, he would be speaking at a huge party mass meeting and contributing to the *Democratic Review*. In 1844 he would join the movement to draft Silas Wright for Governor and elect James K. Polk. In 1846 he would become editor of the *Brooklyn Daily Eagle,* and while in Brooklyn serve on the Democratic General Committee and the Fourth of July Celebration Committee.

Brooklyn knew him as Walter Whitman, an amiable and relaxed young man, with a ruddy pleasant face and a short beard, wandering indolently through the bustling streets with an easy word for every- one, from merchant to cartman. After his stint for the *Eagle* he would go down to Gray's Swimming Bath at the foot of Fulton Street and lounge for twenty minutes in the water. Then the office boy would give him a shower, and he would take the evening ferry back to New York through the dying sunset.[61] ("Flood-tide below me! I see you face to face! Clouds of the west — sun there half an hour high — I see you also face to face.")

These were days of quiet immersion in the flood of experience which would later sweep aside the conventions of verse to achieve their own expression, poignant, tender, gusty, barbaric, incoherent and magnificent. He drank in not just the sea gulls, floating high in the air on motionless wings, their bodies lit up glistening yellow by the setting sun, not just the men and women on the street, "the blab of

---

[61] Whitman, *Gathering of the Forces,* I, xix–xxiii.

the pave, tires of carts, sluff of boot-soles, talk of the promenaders."
He drank in the feelings of the people themselves, their anxieties, hopes,
aspirations.

For Whitman none of the doubts of Thoreau. For him only a
vigorous acceptance and mastery of the democratic opportunity. "To
attack the turbulence and destructiveness of the Democratic spirit," he
said, "is an old story. . . . Why, all that is good and grand in any
political organization in the world, is the result of this turbulence and
destructiveness; and controlled by the intelligence and common sense
of such a people as the Americans, it never has brought harm, and
never can."

Politics a noisy show, unworthy of the attention of serious men?
"It is the fashion of a certain set to assume to despise 'politics' . . .
they look at the fierce struggle, and at the battle of principles and
candidates, and their weak nerves retreat dismayed from the neighborhood of such scenes of convulsion. But to our view, the spectacle
is always a grand one — full of the most august and sublime attri-
butes."

The enthusiasm of democracy an evil? "All the noisy tempestuous
scenes of politics witnessed in this country — all the excitement and
strife, even — are *good* to behold. They evince that the *people act;*
they are the discipline of the young giant, getting his maturer strength."

Is democracy then perfect? Let no one be distracted by detail. "We
know, well enough, that the workings of Democracy are not always
justifiable, in every trivial point. But the great winds that purify the
air, without which nature would flag into ruin — are they to be
condemned because a tree is prostrated here and there, in their
course?" [62]

Through the blast of Whitman's prose sounded the answer to
Thoreau. Man, he affirmed, could have a relation of moral significance
to the state, so long as the state was truly the expression of the popular
will and the best in man. Perfection? No, for the state, like the people
which created it, had failings and flaws. (Whitman, unlike Thoreau,
had a certain sympathy for imperfections.) Belief in the people should
not be discouraged by trivialities or weakened by petty disappointments. In the greatness of his faith in the people Whitman could not
but declare his faith in the possibilities of democratic government.

In 1856 Henry Thoreau and Walt Whitman, meeting for the first
time, had a stiff conversation in Whitman's attic study in New York.
Thoreau felt that he did not get very far. "Among the few things

[62] Whitman, "American Democracy," *Brooklyn Eagle*, April 20, 1847, *Gathering of the Forces*, I, 3–6.

which I chanced to say, I remember that one was . . . that I did not think much of America or of politics, and so on, which may have been somewhat of a damper to him." No doubt it was, and Whitman carried away a vivid impression of Thoreau's "disdain for men (for Tom, Dick, and Harry): inability to appreciate the average life — even the exceptional life: it seemed to me a want of imagination. He couldn't put his life into any other life — realize why one man was so and another man was not so: was impatient with other people on the street and so forth." They had, as Whitman recalled it, rather a hot discussion. "It was a bitter difference: it was rather a surprise to me to meet in Thoreau such a very aggravated case of superciliousness." [63]

Thoreau himself contemplated no social reconstruction. He simply wanted to live his own life under standards higher than men like Whitman, who could put off some of their own guilt on the rest of society. But the mass of men must live in society, or in their visions of a new society; and while there is room for superciliousness in a democracy, it provides an inadequate basis for a political philosophy. The impulse of Whitman was healthier for the social state. His life was spent in an exultation in the potentialities, and a scourging of the failures, of democracy. If the state was not to be a semihuman tiger, with its heart taken out and the top of its brain shot away, it would probably be due more to the Whitmans than to the Thoreaus. As Whitman himself declared, "There is no week nor day nor hour when tyranny may not enter upon this country, if the people lose their supreme confidence in themselves, — and lose their roughness and spirit of defiance — Tyranny may always enter — there is no charm no bar against it — the only bar against it is a large resolute breed of men." [64]

[63] Thoreau to Harrison Blake, December 7, 1856, *Works*, XI, 347; Traubel, *With Whitman in Camden*, I, 212. See also H. S. Canby, *Thoreau*, 412–417.
[64] "Notes for Lectures on Democracy and 'Adhesiveness,'" C. J. Furness, *Walt Whitman's Workshop*, 58.

XXX TYLER TOO

AMERICAN history has been marked by recurrent swings of conservatism and of liberalism. During the periods of inaction, unsolved social problems pile up till the demand for reform becomes overwhelming. Then a liberal government comes to power, the dam breaks and a flood of change sweeps away a great deal in a short time. After fifteen or twenty years the liberal impulse is exhausted, the day of "consolidation" and inaction arrives, and conservatism, once again, expresses the mood of the country, but generally on the terms of the liberalism it displaces.[1] So with Jacksonian democracy. In time it satisfied the popular desire for change. As it developed vested party interests of its own, and its internal paths to power became choked up, able younger men — the Sewards, Lincolns, Thaddeus Stevenses — began to go into the opposition. Partly because of this infusion of fresh blood, and partly because of the lessons of defeat, the Whigs soft-pedaled their diehard aims and began to borrow the Jacksonian phrases. They prepared for the popular reaction. Their reward was victory in 1840.

1

Defeat was a terrific blow to Democratic morale. Not since 1796, nearly half a century before, had a conservative candidate gained the presidency. (Even John Quincy Adams was elected as a Jeffersonian Republican.) Moreover, the people had not only chosen a conservative, but they had chosen a conservative masquerading, as it seemed to the Jacksonians, clumsily and cynically as a democrat.

The administration was plunged in dejection. The French Minister, calling on Poinsett, the Secretary of War, and Paulding, the Secretary of the Navy, in late November, 1840, found them both depressed, saying bitterly that the world had become ungovernable and republicanism furnished no solution.[2] "Labor has carried the election against itself!" cried Benjamin F. Hallett of Massachusetts. ". . . It has deserted the first President who ever . . . braved the power of associated

[1] See Arthur M. Schlesinger, "Tides of American Politics," *Yale Review*, XXIX, 217–230 (December, 1939).
[2] De Bacourt, *Souvenirs d'un Diplomate*, 211.

wealth in the inflexible support of the only measures that, in the distribution of wealth resulting from the union of capital and labor, can secure to the latter a just share." [3] "I confess I never had such gloomy forebodings in my life as haunt me at present," wrote an Ohio politician to Van Buren. "Can this people govern themselves?" [4]

The President himself, quiet and urbane in the White House, took refuge in what became the official explanation: that he had lost because of fraud and corruption — the only theory which accounted for the defeat without impugning the party faith in the masses. "The sober, second thought of the people," he had said some years before, "is never wrong, and always efficient." [5] Democrats now retired from office to await the fruits of this consoling maxim.

Men who have worked together in prosperity often fall to quarrels and recriminations in the darker days. No Democrat remained in Washington in 1841 who could impose unity on the party with the authority of a Van Buren or a Jackson. Benton had the personal force, but not the prestige; Silas Wright, the prestige, but not the personal force. The usual arguments divided the party over whether defeat had been caused by too little radicalism or too much.[6] Various individual intrigues, aiming toward 1844, complicated the situation.

One aspect of the breakup was exhibited in the sad wrangling between Amos Kendall and Frank Blair. Kendall's postmaster-generalship had won him universal praise. He had reorganized the chaotic financial arrangements, improved the speed and coverage of the postal system, and put the post office on a paying basis.[7] It was a remarkable administrative achievement, but it exhausted an already weary man. After Van Buren's defeat Kendall wanted to recoup both health and money by starting a paper in New York. But a lawsuit arising out of

[3] Hallett, *Oration before the Democratic Citizens of Oxford, July 5, 1841,* 9–10.

[4] Thomas L. Hamer to Van Buren, November 18, 1840, Van Buren Papers.

[5] Van Buren used this phrase in a private letter of 1829. It was revived by B. F. Hallett in a speech at Barnstable in 1836 and again in a speech at Middleboro in 1838, from which it passed into general circulation. See *Washington Globe,* November 6, 1838; Hallett, *Oration before the Democratic Citizens of Worcester County . . . July 4, 1839,* 10–11 n.

[6] For the eternal Southern Democratic point of view, see *Appalachicola* (Florida) *Advertiser,* December 12, 1840: "The spirit which gave energy to the Democratic party was decidedly agrarian, and this agrarianism has destroyed its unanimity, and re-organisation, which shall exclude that spirit, will cause the representative of true Democratic Principles, be he who he may, to be again triumphant. . . . In the re-organisation, Messrs. Blair, Kendal, Benton, Wright, Hoyt, Butler, and their followers must be entirely omitted."

[7] See "The Progress and Present Condition of the General Post Office," *Democratic Review,* VI, especially 193–199 (September, 1839).

his post-office reforms involved him in a judgment of eleven thousand dollars' damages and confined him to the District of Columbia. (Later the Supreme Court decided in Kendall's favor, and Congress eventually paid all his costs in the case.)

With no other source of income available, he founded in Washington a fortnightly called *Kendall's Expositor*, intended to rouse the American freeman against measures designed to "deprive him of property or the power to acquire it, and make him the dependant of the idle and the rich, who, as a necessary consequence, will assume all the political powers of society." [8] Every two weeks, in the shabby, unfinished house at Kendall Green where he and his family lived a meager existence, Kendall, prematurely old, with drawn, gray face, scrawled out matter for his journal. Occasionally a telling phrase might suggest the great Amos Kendall, but most of the time he repeated without enthusiasm the staple arguments of the thirties. Tormented by conviction of failure, hardly able to meet the payments on his house or clothe his family, he soon even cashed in on his hero, General Jackson, by laboriously turning out a hack biography. [9]

Blair, always jealous of his control of the party press in Washington, had already driven out the *Democratic Review;* and he could hardly have looked with much pleasure on the competition, however indirect, of Amos Kendall. Yet he went to great lengths to help Kendall get financial backing and even proffered him editorial co-operation. But Kendall, urged on by his neurotic anxieties, began to denounce Blair to Van Buren and to work secretly for a share of the government printing. This ingratitude enraged Blair. In December, 1842, the two men had an angry correspondence, cold, circumstantial, even brutal, on the part of Blair and his partner John C. Rives, shrill and almost hysterical on the part of Kendall. Silas Wright managed to mediate some of the differences, restoring peace for a few months. By December, 1843, however, Blair and Kendall were again no longer on speaking terms. When in 1845 William Rufus Elliott, brother-in-law of John C. Rives, murdered William Kendall, Amos Kendall's son, the last chance of reconciliation probably disappeared. [10]

In the meantime Kendall had begun on a new career. The *Expositor* seemed plainly a failure when the eleven thousand who subscribed

[8] *Kendall's Expositor*, February 3, 1841.
[9] Kendall, *Autobiography*, 355–357.
[10] For the Blair-Rives-Kendall correspondence, 1842–1843, see Van Buren Papers; also Wright to Van Buren, December 23, 1842, Marcy to Van Buren, December 1, 1843, Van Buren Papers; Jackson to Blair, January 11, 1843, Blair to Jackson, December, 1843, Jackson, *Correspondence*, VI, 181, 250; W. E. Smith, *The Francis Preston Blair Family in Politics*, I, 159.

originally dwindled to sixteen hundred for the second year, and in 1844 he sold it to Theophilus Fisk. He now set himself up as professional lobbyist, an occupation for which his influence and connections well fitted him.

As Postmaster General he had probably seen a demonstration by Samuel F. B. Morse before Van Buren's cabinet in February, 1838, of a remarkable new invention called the telegraph. In any case, Kendall was reported in the *Democratic Review* of March, 1838, to have "long ago prophecied that electricity would ultimately be used, by means of wires confined in non-conducting tubes, to communicate intelligence . . . instantaneously . . . and he is now strongly of opinion that the project ought to be adopted and fostered by the Government." [11] Morse, still waiting in despair around Washington in the hope of getting government aid, now appointed Kendall his agent, and in 1845 made him business manager with full authority. Kendall proceeded to address his executive talents to the private exploitation of the telegraph. The great radical of the thirties was turning into one of the great capitalists of the fifties. The old political rancors slipped away, the old spiteful stories disappeared. When he retired in 1860 with a fortune, he was a patriarchal old man, with pure white hair and a kindly, upright face, living a mellow, contented life, famous for his piety and his charities.[12] . . . Those old days at the White House, with Jackson dictating under Rachel's picture, and the logs crackling in the fire, and Taney pacing the floor as he composed the Bank veto, were far, far behind.

2

William Henry Harrison had been elected as a figurehead, whom Clay and Webster and doubtless others had severally calculated on controlling. His early death installed John Tyler of the Virginia State-rights school in the White House. While Tyler's training had allowed him to join the Whigs in attacking executive despotism, it did not incline him to support the more arrantly Federalist items in the Whig program. He submitted to the repeal of the independent treasury; but, when Henry Clay pushed through a new Bank charter, Tyler returned it with a resolute veto.

By 1842 the Bank had lost most of its glamour for all but the most unreconstructed conservatives. Clay's project of resuscitation provoked

---

[11] "Amos Kendall," *Democratic Review*, I, 410–411 (March, 1838).
[12] James D. Reid, *The Telegraph in America* (New York, 1886), 99, 112–113; Kendall. *Autobiography*, 462, 526–555.

Nathan Appleton and Albert Gallatin to measured attacks on the revival of anything on the pattern of Biddle's enterprise. Webster (many years had passed since his retainer had been refreshed) observed coldly that a bank based on private subscription was an "obsolete idea." Even the *Christian Examiner*, the respectable religious magazine of Boston, printed an article austerely supporting the old Jacksonian charges.[13]

The fate of Biddle himself, standing wearily under criminal indictment in the dock in the city where once he had been toast and hero, was not encouraging to recharter. Lawyers obtained his release on a technicality, but he was a broken man. "The anti-Biddle feeling is very strong," reported Fenimore Cooper with delight, "and quite as ferocious as the pro-Biddle feeling was formerly."[14] The *Whig Almanac* of 1843 spoke of "Nick" Biddle as a rascal and declared that "his bank" was "corruptly managed." When Biddle died in 1844, William Cullen Bryant wrote that his end came "at his country seat, where he had passed the last of his days in elegant retirement, which, if justice had taken place, would have been spent in the penitentiary."[15]

While Clay and his followers still dallied with the Federalist dreams, Tyler went briskly ahead on the basis of his vetoes to make a palace guard out of such liberal Whigs as Caleb Cushing and Henry A. Wise, such conservative or complaisant Democrats as David Henshaw and Robert J. Walker, such men without parties as N. P. Tallmadge and William Cabell Rives. By directing his course about midway between the haughty conservatism of Clay and the Locofoco radicalism of Van Buren, Tyler hoped to create a strong middle-of-the-road party for himself. His power as President won him a small following, but his prestige as a political leader, none at all. Whigs, even liberal ones, tended to prefer Clay. Democrats, even conservative ones, tended to prefer Van Buren or Calhoun. Tyler lingered affably in the middle, a President with a policy but without a party.

[13] Webster, *Works*, II, 135; [Francis Wharton], "Banking and the Bank of the United States," *Christian Examiner*, XXXI, 1–38 (September, 1841). The article concluded "in the first place, that there was undue and dangerous power in the hands of the president of the bank; secondly, that there were distinct violations of its charter; thirdly, that there were considerable losses through the fraud and carelessness of its officers and agents; fourthly, that there was frequent interference, on its part, in the political affairs of the country; and fifthly, that there were constant fluctuations, through its agency, in the monetary system."

[14] Cooper to his wife, June 13, 1841, Cooper, *Correspondence*, II, 442.

[15] For the *Whig Almanac* quotes, see Sumner, *Jackson*, 342. Philip Hone quotes Bryant and adds, "How such a blackhearted misanthrope as Bryant should possess an imagination teeming with beautiful poetical images astonishes me; one would as soon expect to extract drops of honey from the fangs of a rattlesnake." Hone, *Diary*, II, 686–687.

Henry Clay, after the succession of vetoes convinced him that the administration was beyond redemption, delivered a farewell address to the Senate, resigned his seat and returned to Ashland where he awaited 1844, in the hope that it would make him both right and President. "I could not get rid of the impression," said Silas Wright after Clay's valedictory declarations of his indifference to personal advancement and his ardent wish for retirement, "that the heaviest weight upon his feelings at the moment was his heart felt fear that the Gods had determined to gratify him in that wish even if he should change his mind." [16]

3

The elms of Kinderhook rose gracefully toward the sky, and Martin Van Buren, a used-up man, placidly walked the wide lawns of his new home at Lindenwald. Peter Van Ness had built the great brick house in 1797 in a Hudson River adaptation of colonial Georgian. As a boy in Kinderhook Van Buren had doubtless looked with awe on the Van Ness mansion. Now he proceeded to improve it, according to random tastes picked up in Europe; and his revision of Lindenwald became an early item in the conspiracy of imported culture against the native architecture. The interior was remodeled on Gothic lines. Dormer windows in the attic broke up the sweep of the roof, and gingerbread adorned the eaves. A fondness for Italian added a four-story tower in the rear of the house and concealed the stately front door behind a heavy piazza.[17]

But the social atmosphere remained pleasant and unaffected. The ex-President rode in the mornings, played at farming, and carried on easy talk with friends during splendid dinners under the pictures of Jefferson and Jackson. In 1842 he took a long trip through the South, visiting Old Hickory at the Hermitage and renewing friendly rivalries with Henry Clay at Ashland. Occasional public letters kept his political opinions up to date, and nearly everyone expected him to be the Democratic candidate in 1844. (Everyone, that is, except John C. Calhoun, General Cass, Colonel Johnson, James Buchanan of Pennsylvania, their seconds and bottle-washers.)

As head of the party Van Buren had to hover in fine impartiality above the internecine struggles of the Democracy. Feuds between Locofoco and conservative, between those who wished to accept Tyler and those who wished to blackball him, between North and South, rum-

[16] Wright to Van Buren, April 2, 1842, Van Buren Papers.
[17] *New York Sun*, March 5, 1938.

bled on without his open interference. Yet in New York itself there were ominous intimations of a basic party split, and Van Buren could hardly long escape from indicating his preferences.

The first differences had arisen over state financial policy. The early profitability of De Witt Clinton's canal system encouraged the legislature in 1827 to dispense with direct taxation in the expectation of meeting state needs by the surplus revenue from canal tolls. But this policy soon began to deplete the general fund of the state; and in 1835 William L. Marcy, as Governor, and A. C. Flagg, as comptroller, declared that the state must either restore the direct tax or pile up a debt. They announced themselves as favoring the first. A second conflict arose from Silas Wright's attempt in 1827 to limit the extension of the system by setting up rigorous criteria for new canal projects.

The conservative wing tended more and more to the Whig policy of pledging the credit of the state to the extension of the system by entering into debt and digging new canals. Jacksonian fights over banking and incorporation increased rancor between the two groups. The conservative support of bills legalizing the suspension of 1837 and repealing the small-notes law drove the wedge even further. The independent-treasury proposal finally led many conservatives to abandon Van Buren for the leadership of N. P. Tallmadge.

In the meantime the Whigs had come into power in the state; and, with the aid of the conservative Democrats, Seward pushed through an ambitious program of canal expansion. By 1842 the debt had increased 225 per cent, the state credit had fallen alarmingly, and public opinion gathered behind the radical demand for retrenchment. Michael Hoffman introduced the "Stop and Tax" bill which would immediately suspend all canal construction not absolutely essential and impose a light direct tax. The measure passed after heated debate, but the Democratic state convention in October, 1842, was badly split on the issue. Eventually, the conservatives provided the nominees, the radicals the platform, and the combination produced a great Democratic victory.[18]

The conservatives were known as Hunkers because they were supposed to "hanker" after office. Their new Governor, William C. Bouck, was of small consequence, but they had able leaders, especially Edwin Croswell, still editing the *Albany Argus*, Daniel S. Dickinson and a rising young man named Horatio Seymour (whom Gideon Welles, striving for the *mot juste* many years later, observed to be

[18] The clearest account of these particular confusions of New York politics is in H. D. A. Donovan, *The Barnburners*, especially 14–24.

"of the Marcy school rather than of the Silas Wright school, — a distinction well understood in New York").[19] Marcy himself remained enigmatic behind shaggy eyebrows. His conduct with respect to the independent treasury had illustrated both his uneasiness over the radical policy and his unwillingness to desert the star of Van Buren.

The radical wing had its place in New York political nomenclature as the Barnburners, in allusion to the farmer who burned his barn to kill the rats. Their organs were the *Albany Atlas*, the *New York Evening Post*, and the *New York Plebeian*, the lively and erratic successor to the *New Era*, edited by the venal Levi D. Slamm, former trade-unionist and Locofoco, who, to judge from contemporary references, was about the most detested man of the day. The Barnburner leaders were in the main the radicals in the old Regency — Flagg, John Dix, Colonel Samuel Young, Preston King, Silas Wright, Benjamin F. Butler, Bryant, David Dudley Field. Michael Hoffman, their legislative leader, had served in Congress during the Bank War. Now past middle age, iron-gray hair falling on his shoulders, dressed usually in a mixed suit of plain clothes, with the air of a farmer, Hoffman was an effective speaker, ordinarily quiet and logical in the Regency manner, but capable of scathing wit (as when he remarked, after Clay's feud with Tyler had split the Whigs, "Sad misfortune when a man outlives his party. Clay gave his prussic acid when he ought to have taken it himself — a small mistake — like that of one of my clients who . . . cut his wife's throat instead [of] his own but repaired the error by hanging himself after conviction wherein Mr. Clay perhaps intends to immitate him").[20] He was a doctrinaire hard-money man; with fierce opinions torn from an increasingly pain-racked body, he argued, nagged, pleaded and drove his party to support his policy.[21]

But the shining hope of the Barnburners was young John Van Buren, the ex-President's brilliant son. Thirty-two years old in 1842, he possessed great promise, capacity and charm. A Yale graduate, he spent his college years in aristocratic dissipation. The reports which reached his father of a life in which, as Van Buren said, "eating, and drinking, and dressing appear to be the most important, not to say least exceptionable of your pursuits," induced worried hours.[22] But the elder Van Buren could no more resist his son than anyone else could, and John went to London with him as attaché at the ministry.

[19] Welles, *Diary*, I, 154.
[20] Hoffman to Flagg, October 17, 1843, Flagg Papers.
[21] N. S. Benton, *A History of Herkimer County*, 323–336; *New York Journal of Commerce*, September 28, 1848; Weed, *Autobiography*, 33–34; Stanton, *Random Recollections*, 173.
[22] Martin Van Buren to John Van Buren, September 3, 1830, Van Buren Papers.

His British exploits, including dances with Princess Victoria, won him the sarcastic title of "Prince John" in the Whig press. When he returned, his imperious bearing and sparkling wit gave him the title in earnest, among his Democratic followers.

He was a tall, spare man, his features clean-cut and winning, with a frank and almost reckless way about him, a twinkle in his blue eyes and a quip always on his tongue. He possessed great power of adapting himself to all people and occasions. He could fascinate the frigid spirits of Boston — "I am much attached to him personally," confessed Charles Sumner, and even the snobbish Richard Henry Dana admitted "something quite taking about him" — and then mingle easily with the rough crowd on the Bowery.[23] A glittering figure in high society, a hero in low-class New York barrooms, he everywhere preserved his identity.

Before a crowd he was cool and self-possessed, speaking in an off-hand style, with high-pitched and rather cultivated voice, rarely using gestures or growing excited. Though he was a cogent and tricky debater, his great power lay in his dry, careless wit. His caustic remarks fell with superb nonchalance and threw merciless ridicule on the opposition. Always unruffled and innocent himself, he moved the masses as he willed, to laughter, or, when the spirit was on him, to indignation. He was perhaps the best popular orator of the day.

And yet there was something lacking. "There never lived another man in this country," said one observer, "who wasted such opportunities and such talents." [24] In 1842 no one could foresee his destiny, but many felt a basic moral indolence. "He is so frank, so generous, and so gifted, he is the man the people will delight to honor," warned a contemporary; "but he must not, like Alcibiades, deface the images of the gods and expect to be pardoned on the score of eccentricity." [25] At first glance, he might seem Martin Van Buren with all flaws remedied; but he wanted a certain sturdiness of soul. "He only needs the graceful polish, the serene dignity of his father . . . to render him one of the most useful, honorable and distinguished men of the nineteenth century." [26] But that serenity came from a fundamental serious-

[23] Sumner to John Bigelow, October 24, 1851, Bigelow, *Retrospections of an Active Life*, I, 121; C. F. Adams, *Richard Henry Dana*, I, 172.

[24] M. B. Field, *Memories of Many Men*, 181.

[25] The appreciative and vivid sketch in Bungay, *Crayon Sketches*, 67. Alcibiades was the inevitable comparison. Cf. Bigelow, *Retrospections*, I, 87: "His birth, his accomplishments, his wit and his unbounded self-assurance made him unhappily the Alcibiades of his time." The *New York Tribune* preferred to call him, on his death, "the Beaumarchais of his time." *New York Tribune*, October 20, 1866.

[26] Bungay, *Crayon Sketches*, 68.

ness of intention. Prince John, in last analysis, had all the qualities of Prince Hal, except the capacity to become Henry V.[27]

Family loyalty, as well as political inclination, thus drew the ex-President toward the Barnburners; and in national politics also, while avoiding steps which might alienate the conservative wing, he maintained his most intimate private relations with Benton, Blair and Silas Wright. The group was bound to Van Buren, not only by their common Jacksonian experience, but by deep personal friendship. Blair regularly enlightened him about Washington in long, chatty and illegible letters, and Benton and Wright, both unusually selfless men, were eager to renominate Van Buren in 1844.

Through the states the old Locofocos were affiliated with the Benton-Blair-Barnburner front behind Van Buren for '44. In Massachusetts, for example, George Bancroft, Samuel C. Allen, Jr., and Marcus Morton led the Van Buren forces and tried to unfurl again the old antimonopoly flag. In Connecticut John M. Niles was incapacitated by a nervous breakdown which deepened into severe melancholia, but Gideon Welles kept the Van Buren spirit alive. Everywhere the real Locofocos, the hard-money men, the strongest Jacksonians, tended to demand Martin Van Buren as Democratic nominee in 1844.

[27] In addition to previous references, see *New York Tribune*, October 17, 1866; *New York Times*, October 17, 1866; Traubel, *With Whitman in Camden*, III, 228 ("I knew him well," said Whitman of John Van Buren: "a bright, manly fellow: full of life, vivacity: built like Tom Donaldson, with much of Tom's humor, animal spirits"); Charles H. Peck, "John Van Buren," *Magazine of American History*, XVII, 58–70, 202–213, 318–329.

XXXI MINORITIES AND MAJORITIES

LISTING "the essential principles of our Government" in his first inaugural, Thomas Jefferson made vigorous affirmation of what he called the "vital principle of republics" — "absolute acquiescence in the decisions of the majority." But what were the other "essential principles" of his enumeration but a bill of exceptions to this "vital principle"? They were, in fact, a catalogue of rights placed out of reach of the majority, for fear that the majority might destroy them. Elsewhere in the same address Jefferson even declared explicitly that, though the will of the majority was "in all cases" to prevail, that will "to be rightful must be reasonable." "The minority possess their equal rights . . . and to violate [them] would be oppression." [1]

If the will of the majority was entitled to "absolute acquiescence," if it was "in all cases" to prevail, what safeguard was there for the rights of minorities? Yet if minorities were indulged in their claims, how was the maintenance of their "equal rights" to be restrained from leading to minority rule? These questions from the start constituted a basic ambiguity in American democratic theory.

1

The politicians of the Democracy, equipped by experience for occasional setbacks, recovered from the defeat of 1840 without developing serious doubts about popular government. "The sober, second thought of the people is never wrong, and always efficient." But for many of the doctrinaire Democrats, 1840 was not simply defeat. It was catastrophe, and it went to the very roots of democratic theory. For Orestes A. Brownson, the most implacably logical of them all, it was the desertion by the people of their leaders for a song, a barrel of hard cider and a shabby military hero; and he could not but conclude that something had been radically wrong with his conception of democracy. "We must now fall back on first principles, and take a fresh

[1] Richardson, *Messages and Papers*, I, 322, 323.

start," he wrote early in December, "and when we come up, come up with something worth having." [2]

But what were the first principles of government? As he pondered the election, his mind turned irresistibly to the single terrible fact: the people had become the dupes of their worst enemies. If they could so easily fall victim to demagogues, how could they be the infallible depository of truth and justice? And if this fickleness were characteristic of the people, might not freedom and good government require stronger guarantees than free suffrage and popular virtue and intelligence?

Shaken to the foundations of his political thought, Brownson cast about for instruction. He read Aristotle on Politics for the first time, glanced through other systematic thinkers, and gave particular attention to his friend John C. Calhoun, the one philosophical statesman of the day. Clearly if the individual were naturally good, as the Jeffersonians and transcendentalists asserted, then that government was best which governed least; and when government became unavoidable, then the majority — as a majority of good beings — could be trusted to rule for all. But if the individual was imperfect, as Calhoun and Aristotle (not to mention Calvin) argued, then government became itself a positive good, necessary to restrain and guide the passions of men; and the majority, being merely a majority of imperfect beings, had claim only to superior force, not to superior wisdom. In fact, experience — the election of 1840 — suggested that, in the long run, the numerical majority would always be at the mercy of the most powerful economic group, which would use it to prostrate the weaker economic interests and establish its own supremacy.

Government founded on the principle of the sanctity of the numerical majority contained, moreover, inherent tendencies toward unlimited government, because the majority had the power to destroy all the rights of minorities and repeal all restrictions on its own authority. "The Government of the absolute majority," as Calhoun put it in 1833, "instead of the Government of the people, is but the Government of the strongest interests; and when not efficiently checked, is the most tyrannical and oppressive that can be devised. . . . Whatever interest obtains possession of the Government will, from the nature of things, be in favor of the powers, and against the limitations imposed by the constitution, and will resort to every device that can be imagined to remove those restraints." [3] The system of numerical

[2] Letter from Brownson, December 5, 1840, *New York Evening Post*, December 7, 1840.

[3] Calhoun in the Senate, February 15, 1833, *Register of Debates*, 22 Congress 2 Session, 547, 549.

majorities thus interposed no efficient check to the wholesale exploitation of the country by the dominant economic class.

How then to keep the majority from liquidating the constitutional limitations on its own power or, in other words, how to curb the power of the dominant economic interests over the weaker interests? "To maintain the ascendancy of the constitution over the law-making majority," Calhoun answered, "is the great and essential point." [4] But would not strict construction preserve this ascendancy? "Every body is for strict construction," Calhoun declared with scorn; it was only the construction which each minority in turn would try to enforce against the party in power. [5] "There is a remedy," however, "and but one": to organize society with reference, not to individuals, but to interests. This could be done only "by giving to each part the right of self-protection." [6]

The system of numerical majorities, Calhoun felt, was based on a misapprehension of the modern state. "In former days, the tendency of the organization of society, was for each man to stand alone in his individual and personal rights," declared Francis W. Pickens, in whom the principles of Calhoun sometimes stood out with brutal clarity. ". . . But the tendency in the modern organization of society, is the reverse of all this. It tends toward aggregation, under which whole classes and interests are brought to act together, with the vigor and unity of single individuals, and the great contest is between classes." [7] The working units were no longer individuals, but interests.

But what was the mechanism which would secure to each interest its "right of self-protection"? For Calhoun the states qualified as effective expressions of his economic interests, and his solutions were always in terms of state action. The first scheme was nullification; but, though it won its point, Jackson so managed the situation that, attempted again, nullification would surely be treated as rebellion. In a heated exchange with James Buchanan in 1837 Calhoun sketched out another possibility. Buchanan, as Calhoun affected to understand him, had countenanced the principle that "the will of a mere numerical majority is paramount to the authority of law and constitution . . . meaning, as I understood him, that a mere majority might at their pleasure subvert the constitution and Government of a State, which

[4] *Ibid.*, 549.

[5] Calhoun to Duff Green, September 20, 1834, Calhoun, *Correspondence*, 341.

[6] Calhoun in the Senate, February 15, 1833, *loc. cit.*, 547.

[7] Pickens added, "It is by combination, that every thing is effected, and personal rights are not so much the object of solicitude, as the rights of classes and separate communities." Pickens, *Address, on the Great Points of Difference between Ancient and Modern Civilization*, 3.

he seemed to think was the essence of democracy." In contrast to this doctrine, Calhoun declared that the South Carolina constitution respected "the great interests of the State, giving to each a separate and distinct voice in the management of its political affairs." "Let me tell the Senator," Calhoun added vehemently, "it is a far more popular Government than if it had been based on the simple principle of the numerical majority. . . . It represents all the interests of the State, and is in fact the Government of the people, in the true sense of the term, and not that of the mere majority, or the dominant interests." [8]

South Carolina should, as usual, be the model for the nation; but how to secure on a national scale the effective participation of all the leading interests in the major decisions of the federal government? To this problem he addressed his main intellectual energies, and his posthumous "Disquisition on Government" represented his final solution. "There is but one way in which this can possibly be done," was his answer; "and that is, by such an organism as will furnish the ruled with the means of resisting successfully this tendency on the part of the rulers to oppression and abuse. Power can only be resisted by power." And the organism? Let each state (that is, each interest) be given a concurrent voice in the making of laws, or a veto on their execution. The various interests in the community would thus be protected, because government could not act without the consent of all. The system of "concurrent majorities" would set up obstacles to the tendencies toward economic tyranny inherent in an absolute democracy. [9]

But the rule of the concurrent majority was far in the future. Till it could be established, the practical guarantee for constitutionalism lay in building up the power of the slaveholders as a bulwark against the propensities of majoritarian democracy, "which, if unabated, will always oppress the poor, the ignorant and low." [10] (So much did majority

---

[8] Calhoun in the Senate, January 5, 1837, *Register of Debates*, 24 Congress 2 Session, 303.

[9] Calhoun, "Disquisition on Government," *Works*, I, 12, 25. Calhoun denied that "concurrent majorities" meant minority rule: "I am equally opposed to the government of a minority. They are both the government of a part over a part. I am in favor of the government of the whole." Calhoun to R. L. Dorr, March 21, 1847, *Niles' Register*, May 8, 1847.

[10] From a conversation with Charles J. Ingersoll, in which Calhoun argued the "absolute necessity of slavery to balance democracy." W. M. Meigs, *Life of Charles Jared Ingersoll*, 267. "I advocate slavery in the South," Calhoun told Albert Brisbane, "because it is a guarantee of stability . . . a counterpoise." Brisbane, *Brisbane*, 221–222. "In this tendency to conflict in the North between labor and capital," Calhoun said, in 1838, ". . . the weight of the South has and ever will be . . . against the aggression of one or the other side, which ever may tend to disturb

democracy seem to Calhoun the instrument of capitalism that he sometimes used the terms interchangeably.) This became his incessant theme. "People do not understand liberty or majorities," he would complain. "The will of a majority is the will of a rabble. Progressive democracy is incompatible with liberty." [11] If freedom lay with the supremacy of the Constitution, the only group basically concerned with maintaining this supremacy were the planters of the South.

Now Calhoun's political theory, like all other significant political theory, was immediately designed to protect a special group. Out of apprehensions excited in South Carolina by the high tariff and abolitionism he had crystallized a set of general principles behind which slaveholders might crouch with safety. Yet the measure of his intellectual accomplishment was the superb clarity, honesty and realism with which he argued. In the end his theory was not a lawyer's brief, adroitly constructed to advance the pretensions of slavery, but a brilliant and penetrating study of modern society, whose insights remain vital for any minority.

Brownson had once considered himself the member of a popular majority devoted to the establishment of democratic principles. Eighteen-forty had disclosed to him the majority as unstable and irresponsible. "Experience proves," he remarked in 1842, "that the more extended the suffrage, the greater will be the influence and the more certain the triumph of wealth, or rather of the business classes." [12] Those genuinely interested in emancipating the workingmen appeared to constitute only a minority, and Calhoun's theory demonstrated that majoritarianism might be as fatal to them as to his own or any other minority. The working classes of the North thus seemed to share the same platform as the South in relation to the federal government. It was an alliance, Brownson recognized, "made up of democrats and anti-democrats," but that was beside the point. "One thing is certain, that the increase of the powers of the Federal Government is unfavorable to the growth of Democracy. The action of that government, the moment it steps beyond its constitutional limits, is to favor business at the expense of labor, and to benefit the capitalist instead of the operative. Hence, it follows that every democrat *ought* to be a constitutionalist." [13]

---

the equilibrium of our political system." Calhoun in the Senate, January 10, 1838, *Congressional Globe*, 25 Congress 2 Session, Appendix, 62.

[11] J. S. Jenkins, *Life of John Caldwell Calhoun*, 453.

[12] Brownson, "Brook Farm," *Democratic Review*, XI, 454 (November, 1842).

[13] Brownson, "Our Future Policy," *Boston Quarterly Review*, IV, 86, 89 (January, 1841).

As the Whigs adopted Democratic claims for the virtue of majorities in order to push through their own economic program, Brownson went further along the path of Calhoun. In October, 1841, in a review of a new volume of George Bancroft's *History*, he explicitly warned the majoritarian Democrats that "an absolute democracy, without check or balance, except the virtue and intelligence of the people," could only result in the supremacy of business. The establishment of a "rigid constitutional order" seemed more than ever the only security for labor.[14]

Calhoun watched Brownson's progress with approval. "There is scarcely a view taken or a sentiment expressed," he declared of the Bancroft article, "in which I do not fully concur." As for Brownson, he saw no inconsistency in working for the people while vigorously denying their virtue and intelligence. "Democracy, as I understand and accept it," he declared, "requires me to sacrifice myself *for* the masses, not *to* them. Who knows not, that if you would save the people, you must often oppose them?"[15]

2

The Democratic party, as the party of the laboring classes, was beginning to split into two wings. Some friends of labor, like Bancroft and Van Buren, felt that the "people," though misled in 1840, were fundamentally sound, and could be relied on most of the time to back a democratic policy. Their sober second thoughts, in other words, would atone for occasional transgressions. Others, however, like Brownson, commenced to regard the "people" as an inchoate mass which would probably follow the side with the loudest songs and biggest torchlight processions. The real proponents of democracy, they believed, were a small group who would often have to save the people in spite of themselves.

The majoritarian Democrats clustered around Van Buren as their candidate for 1844. The minoritarians, accepting the logic of the Southern alliance, turned to Calhoun. For the bulk of the party the issue of minorities and majorities was never very real in its abstract form, and later this little band of doctrinaires was joined by a number of anti-Van Buren politicians, such as Fernando Wood, B. F. Hallett and Isaac Hill, whose convictions, insofar as they allowed themselves

---

[14] Brownson, "Bancroft's *History*," *loc. cit.*, IV, 517 (October, 1841); "The Distribution Bill," *loc. cit.*, V, 90 (January, 1842).

[15] Calhoun to Brownson, October 31, 1841, Brownson, *Brownson's Early Life*, 302; Brownson, *An Oration on the Scholar's Mission*, 32.

to have any, were majoritarian. But the first impulse behind the Calhoun boom in the North in 1842 came from men acting as self-appointed champions of the bewildered masses.

This strange prolabor enterprise operated on a double paradox — that the security of the people required the limitation of their power, and that the salvation of labor depended on the triumph of slavery. The moving spirits were mostly veterans of the "Rump" of the old Locofoco party, which had opposed reunion with the Democrats even after the independent-treasury message. Never really reconciled to Van Buren, they felt no loyalty to him; and, apparently responding to 1840 much in the manner of Brownson, they began to look to the South as the bulwark against business supremacy. The Calhoun platform was admirably designed to win them over: *"Free Trade — Low Duties — No Debt — No connection with Banks — Economy — Retrenchment — and a strict adherence to the Constitution."* [16]

The leader of the Calhoun agitation was Fitzwilliam Byrdsall, historian and former secretary of the Locofoco party, who was to remain for years a zealous defender of the Southern cause. (By 1847 he could write: "Never was any social institution more unfairly vilified than that which is termed Southern slavery." [17]) In 1842 he founded a Free-trade Association as a cover for the Calhoun campaign. John Commerford, the labor leader, was president, and other original Locofocos, such as John Windt, John and Isaac Hecker and Stephen Hasbrouck, played prominent roles. When George H. Evans returned from Jersey, he added his support.[18] They were aided by Joseph A. Scoville, a New York merchant once suspected of engaging in the slave trade and later Calhoun's private secretary.[19] At one point Levi D. Slamm, another original Locofoco, even secretly pledged the *Plebeian* to Calhoun, but friends of Van Buren intervened with promises of financial aid, and Slamm hastily reversed himself.[20]

[16] Hammond, *Silas Wright*, 335. This platform, appearing originally in the preamble to the resolution of the South Carolina legislature nominating Calhoun for 1844, was reprinted with slight variations on the campaign literature; see, e.g., the cover of *The Calhoun Text Book* (New York, 1843).

[17] Byrdsall to Calhoun, February 22, 1847, *Correspondence Addressed to Calhoun*, 368.

[18] Byrdsall to Calhoun, November 6, 1842, Calhoun, *Correspondence*, 862; T. N. Carr to Van Buren, September 15, 1843, Van Buren Papers; *Madisonian*, September 15, 1843; *Subterranean and Working Man's Advocate*, November 9, 1844.

[19] "Walter Barrett" [Joseph A. Scoville], *Old Merchants of New York City*, I, 130–131.

[20] D. H. Lewis to R. K. Crallé, June, 1842, Moore, "Calhoun by His Political Friends," *Publications of the Southern History Association*, VII, 360; Scoville to R. M. T. Hunter, August 29, November 21, 1842, *Correspondence of Robert M. T. Hunter, 1826–1876*, C. H. Ambler, ed., 40, 52; Slamm statement, *ibid.*, 48; A. Van-

Friends of labor outside New York pitched in. Brownson during 1842 turned out newspaper editorials along lines suggested by the Calhoun board of strategy, wrote addresses for Calhoun mass meetings, and even considered for a time in late 1843 editing a Calhoun paper in New York.[21] Theophilus Fisk, now editor of a paper in Virginia, pushed the Calhoun candidacy with similar enthusiasm.[22] Thus a strong representation of the men particularly identified with the cause of labor in the eighteen-thirties were for Calhoun in 1844. But all this talent and enthusiasm resulted in the kind of campaign which uninformed talent and enthusiasm will always produce. The raid on Tammany attempted by the New York group might have been a crucial victory, but it was badly bungled, and only the flight of certain disgruntled politicians to Calhoun's side in 1843 saved his boom in the North from total extinction.

3

The most colorful of the left-wing Calhoun leaders was a tough Irish rabble-rouser named Mike Walsh. Twenty-five or thirty years old in 1842 (no one knew quite when he was born or where), he had fought his way up the political ladder by a wonderful and unique combination of oratory, organization, democratic enthusiasm and violence. Slangy, raucous and sarcastic, with brassy face and cool, undaunted manner, he would drawl out rambling speeches which convulsed his audiences with their wit and ridicule. He was, moreover, shrewd and sharp, with a keen instinct for the weaknesses of his opponents, and all his efforts were filled with an honest sympathy for the common people. But he was thoroughly irresponsible, often drunk, an inveterate practical joker, and a chronic political rebel. The particular hero of the "Bowery b'hoys" and a great pal of Tom Hyer, the boxer, Mike headed a rowdy assemblage known as the Spartan Band, which he used to good effect on election days and at political meetings. The gang was his great technical contribution to American politics.[23]

Mike had risen to prominence through his almost single-handed

derpoel to Van Buren, August 29, 1842, Van Buren Papers; H. P. Barber to Calhoun, December 29, 1843, *Correspondence Addressed to Calhoun*, 196.

[21] Brownson, *Brownson's Early Life*, 326–340; Holden, *Early Years of Hecker*, 180–183; Lemuel Williams to Calhoun, September 6, 1843, Calhoun, *Correspondence*, 876.

[22] *Chronicle and Old Dominion* (Norfolk and Portsmouth), April 13, 1842.

[23] *New York Times*, March 18, 1859; M. P. Breen, *Thirty Years of New York Politics Up-to-date*, 302–307; James O'Meara, *Broderick and Gwin*, 6–7; J. F. McLaughlin, *Life and Times of John Kelly*, 145–152.

battle to destroy Tammany control over the Democratic organization in New York. The crowds at Tammany meetings would shout his name until the chairman had to call him to the platform, and Mike would amble up, cock a knowing eye at his audience, thrust his jaw forward and set to with his casual impudence, interrupted only by adoring cries of "Go it; Mike!" "Go it, my hero!" "Give it to them." Workingmen don't want "milk and water men to represent them," Mike would shout, " — men who are a mere connecting link between the animal and vegetable kingdom . . . that won't whistle 'We won't go home till morning,' because they haven't wind enough; and that are not lascivious, because they have not got stamina enough in their composition to keep their back-bone [as the papers reported the word] straight." The machine had always betrayed the working classes, he would declare. "What have we gained by the numberless political victories we have achieved? Nothing but a change of masters!" But the aroused people could overthrow the machine. "I know that we, the Subterranean Democracy, possess the power, if we will but exercise it." [24]

In 1843 he established a weekly called the *Subterranean* to carry on his battle. Under the motto

> Through ages thou has slept in chains and night,
> Arise now MAN and vindicate thy right!

Walsh turned out a picturesque and brawling sheet, impatient as a terrier, tenacious as a bulldog, forever snapping at the heels of respectability, and given a character — even a certain charm — by the good humor and unconquerable high spirits of its editor. It was in part a noble crusading paper in the Jacksonian tradition, but it was also a reckless, libelous, gossip-mongering rag. Mike spent two terms on Blackwell's Island serving out convictions for libel, and George Wilkes, his assistant, passed on from the *Subterranean* to found the *Police Gazette*. An able, dissolute and ruthless scoundrel, a frequenter of brothels and publisher of obscene books, Wilkes was probably still in 1843 the fancy man of Kate Ridgeley who ran a bawdy house in Duane Street.[25] Appropriately enough, Wilkes ended up as one of the first American Communist fellow travelers.

But beneath Walsh's braggadocio there stirred a strong and even bitter sense of social oppression. "The great and fruitful source of crime and misery on earth," he would exclaim, "is the *inequality of*

---

[24] Walsh, *Sketches of the Speeches and Writings of Michael Walsh*, 11, 30, 18.
[25] O'Meara, *Broderick and Gwin*, 8; J. F. Chamberlin, *The Answer . . . to the Complaint of George Wilkes*.

society — the abject dependence of honest, willing industry upon idle and dishonest capitalists." "Demagogues tell you that you are freemen," he would lash out at political meetings. "They lie; you are slaves. . . . No man, devoid of all other means of support but that which his own labor affords him, can be a freeman, under the present state of society."[26] George H. Evans, with whose Land Reform movement Mike allied himself briefly in 1844, paid him sincere tribute: —

> One man only in this city, since 1835, has had the mind to see, the honesty to embrace, the nerve to advocate, and the self-devotion to print the great truths that are to redeem the down trodden masses, and that man is MIKE WALSH. Others have possessed some of these requisites, but he alone has possessed them all.[27]

For obscure reasons Mike detested the friends of Van Buren. Benjamin F. Butler he once called a "canting, hypocritical humbug" with a voice like "the hungry squealing of a half-starved bull, or the sound of a cracked wash-bowl."[28] From supporting Tyler, Walsh easily moved on to Calhoun, not from any convictions about the numerical majority, but because Tammany Hall was for Van Buren. Calhoun cultivated Mike's friendship and excited his intense admiration. Their alliance signalized compactly the South Carolinian's success in passing as the champion of Northern labor.[29]

4

Suddenly, in the spring of 1842, the problem of majorities and minorities ceased to be an academic question. Rhode Island had been the only state without fairly wide manhood suffrage. It was still operating in 1841 on the colonial charter of 1663, which disfranchised everyone who did not own $134 in land. Over half the adult male population could not vote, and the spread of manufacturing was rapidly decreasing the proportion of the elect. The apportionment of seats in the legislature, moreover, gravely penalized the growing industrial towns to the advantage of the older villages. The charter had no bill of rights and lacked the democratic guarantees held necessary for

---

[26] Walsh, *Speeches*, 30; *Subterranean*, September 13, 1845.
[27] *Subterranean and Working Man's Advocate*, October 12, 1844. Evans and Walsh merged their papers in October; in November, Mike went to prison for libel, and in December he dissolved the merger because Evans insisted on toning down the articles which Mike was scribbling fiercely at Blackwell's Island.
[28] *Subterranean*, June 28, 1845.
[29] *Niles' Register*, September 23, 1843; E. A. Alderman and A. C. Gordon, *J. L. M. Curry: a Biography*, 78.

popular government. This situation provoked mounting discontent, as nonvoters began with increasing vehemence to demand a new constitution in whose creation they would be allowed to participate. Unluckily the charter failed to provide a means of making a new constitution, and conservatism stood obstinately on its exclusive rights.

In the middle eighteen-thirties a young man of conservative antecedents named Thomas Wilson Dorr came onto the scene. A Whig, a graduate of Exeter and Harvard, but singularly high-principled and conscientious, he became interested in remedying the suffrage inequities. Finding no support in his own party, he joined the Democrats in 1837. When the reform movement had one of its periodic spurts in 1841, Dorr emerged as its natural leader.

The new agitation abandoned from the first all resort to the existing government, proposing instead to appeal to the original sovereign rights of the people which underlay all government. By July, 1841, this strategy produced two constitutional conventions: one called hastily by the legislature to appease the popular resentments, and the other called by extraconstitutional procedures finding their sanction in the basic "constituent power" of the people. Soon two constitutions were laid before the state. The legislative or Freemen's Constitution, a stubbornly reactionary document, held forth only the most grudging concessions. It liberalized the suffrage, for example, by recommending that the possession of $500 in taxable personal property be accepted as an alternative to $134 in land; and it failed to redress the gravely unjust rotten-borough system. The People's Constitution, on the other hand, was not only more liberal, but was drawn with much greater care and ability. The Dorrites proceeded to use their power to defeat the Freemen's Constitution, and then submitted their own to the whole people, who endorsed it triumphantly. Indeed, enough legal voters supported the People's Constitution for the Dorrites to claim that it was sustained by a majority, not only of the adult males, but of the freemen.

The result was two state administrations, one under the old charter, the other under the People's Constitution. During the early months of 1842 the state remained quiet but tense. Then, on May 3, Dorr, as the People's Governor, started to organize his government. The charter government, under a severe punitive measure known as the "Algerine" law, began to arrest Dorr leaders. Dorr left for Washington and New York to canvass the possibilities of outside aid. Washington was discouraging, but the New York Barnburners gave him a reception which nerved him to further action. The *Evening Post* and the *Plebeian* took up his cause, and a huge mass meeting in the Park celebrated the enthusiasm of New York for the democratic aspirations of Rhode Island. Cambreleng presided, and the names of William Cullen Bryant, Theodore Sedgwick, Jr., John L. O'Sullivan, Ely Moore, Samuel J. Tilden, John Worth Edmonds and others adorned the call. Levi D. Slamm declared grandiloquently that he had already chartered a steamboat to carry a thousand fighting men to Rhode Island, if the federal government should intervene. Alexander Ming, Jr., offered his military company as an armed escort for Dorr on his way back to Providence. ("Allow me to say," Dorr replied, "that the time may not be far distant, when I may be obliged to call upon you.") [30]

On the foggy night of May 17, Dorr at the head of 234 men stormed the Providence Arsenal. With him, as "organizational secretary," was Seth Luther, the veteran agitator. When the men in the arsenal refused to surrender, Dorr ordered his cannon to be fired. They flashed out twice through the black night, but without result. Soon the bells of Providence were ringing wildly, and the streets began to fill with bewildered people. As the gray dawn broke, Dorr's following started to go home. By sunrise he had only about fifty men, and at breakfast time he was told that his government had resigned. His friends advised him to leave. Before nine o'clock he was heading for the border.

Dorr did not give up the fight. "The rights of the case," as he said, "were not taken away by a failure of arms." He believed that the fiasco at the arsenal was due to temporary causes and overestimated his general backing, mistaking expressions of sympathy for promises of aid. On June 21 he left New York for Norwich, Connecticut, accompanied by Mike Walsh and about twenty of the Spartan Band. Other supporters joined the group at Chepachet, Rhode Island, but the forces again dispersed. Dorr, convinced that his followers were against the use of violence to sustain his government, abandoned the struggle.

With the rebellion safely over, the charter government, which had previously spent most of its time sending frightened letters to President Tyler, now began to act with great boldness. Suppressing the letter of Dorr dissolving his movement, the state officials declared martial law on June 26, and for six weeks ran the state as if military insurrection lurked around every corner. Hundreds of men were arrested, hundreds of houses entered and searched. On the night of June 28 troops fired into a crowd at Pawtucket, killing a bystander in Massachusetts. A price was put on Dorr's head, and requisitions for his arrest went to the neighboring states, where they were honored

[30] *Niles' Register*, May 21, 1842.

by Whig Governors and indignantly rejected by the Democrats.

In 1843 a new and somewhat more equitable constitution was adopted by the legal voters. Dorr now declared that he would return to the state after the fall elections. On October 31 he quietly stepped off the train at Providence and was shortly after arrested under indictment of high treason. Many of his followers had already spent some time in prison. Seth Luther, for example, served a miserable few months, which he had whiled away by writing a long poem and then by setting fire to the jail in an attempt to escape. Dorr's trial took place in Newport in March, 1844. Of the entire panel of 118 available jurors, only three were Democrats; and Dorr's own jury was exclusively Whig. He was speedily found guilty, sentenced to solitary confinement at hard labor for life and denied a new trial.

The summariness of the proceedings, the vindictiveness of the sentence and Dorr's own obvious high-mindedness soon caused a revulsion of feeling. "Liberation" became the dominant political issue, and in June, 1845, Dorr was released by the act of a Democratic legislature, elected for that purpose. In 1851 his civil and political rights were restored, and in 1854 the court judgment against him was annulled. But, in the words of the historian of the Dorr Rebellion, "No act of any legislature could redress the injury . . . done to Governor Dorr." Worn out in mind and body, without spirit or energy, old before his time, he dragged out his life, dying in 1855 at the age of 49, a sacrifice to his struggle for popular government.[31]

5

The Dorr Rebellion sharply confronted the political pragmatists of the country with those "metaphysical" questions which had so deeply exercised men like Calhoun and Brownson. Calhoun in 1837 had curtly attacked the doctrine "that a mere majority might at their pleasure subvert the constitution and Government of a State," which Buchanan seemed to think was "the essence of democracy." The question, then so abstract, was now inescapable and explosive. Was or was not the unconditional right of the majority to make its own government the essence of democracy?

No one in the controversy disputed the ultimate right of the people to change their government as a right of revolution. The problem was

[31] Arthur M. Mowry, *The Dorr War*, 259 and *passim*. Though written in 1901, this is still the best account, and I have followed it fairly closely. For Seth Luther's role, see Louis Hartz, "Seth Luther: Working Class Rebel," *New England Quarterly*, XIII. 406–409.

whether this right existed in the normal, peaceable order of society. Could the "people" by their own action and without the consent of the constituted authorities create legally a new frame of government, or was this right restricted to the "people" enfranchised by the existing constitution and to the methods prescribed by it?

From the first, this basic question commanded general attention. Francis Wayland, president of Brown University, personally in favor of extending the suffrage, declared a few days after the skirmish at the arsenal that, if the principles of Dorr prevailed, not a constitution in the land would be worth the parchment it was written on. "The only law that would be known, would soon be the law of force," for, in last resort, how else was there to choose between rival parties, each claiming a majority and each asserting the superiority of the majority to established law? Dorrism, moreover, threatened all constitutional guarantees. If a majority out of power could overturn the constitution at will, then a majority in power could plainly do so, "and thus, all constitutional right is merged in the will of the strongest." [32]

The opposing case was generally argued, as in the popular pamphlet written by John A. Bolles, a leading Massachusetts Democrat and brother-in-law of John A. Dix, in terms of "the sovereign right of the people, to create, change, abolish government, as they may deem their interest to require." [33] But the question was not to be left to popular debate. The arrests under martial law brought the issues into court, and the case of *Luther v. Borden* eventually reached the Supreme Court of the United States.

Martin Luther, a shoemaker, was moderator of the Warren town meeting under the People's Constitution. He also took part in the election of the Dorr government. These acts were crimes under the Algerine law. When martial law was declared, Luther fled the state. In his absence nine men, led by Luther Borden, broke into Luther's house. Failing to find him, they vented their anger on his mother, his employees and his furniture. Returning to Rhode Island in 1843, Luther was arrested, convicted and sentenced to a heavy fine and six months in prison. Meanwhile, he had brought suit against Borden in the United States Circuit Court. When Borden justified his action by the martial law, Luther denied the validity of the martial law on the ground that the charter government had expired when the Dorr government took over. Joseph Story, the Circuit Judge, refused this plea, and the case was appealed to the Supreme Court.

[32] Francis Wayland, *The Affairs of Rhode Island*, 4–5, 7, 28.
[33] J. A. Bolles, *Review of Dr. Wayland's Discourse on the Affairs of Rhode Island*, 7.

Benjamin F. Hallett, appearing for Luther, rested a rambling case on the familiar assertion of the capacity of the people to reassume the powers of government without thereby engaging in revolution. "It is the right of the people," he asserted, "to change, alter, or abolish their government, in such manner as they please; a right, not of force, but of sovereignty." [34] Daniel Webster, for Borden, emphasized the indispensability of there being "some authentic mode of ascertaining the will of the people, else all is anarchy. It resolves itself into the law of the strongest, or, what is the same thing, of the most numerous for the moment." [35]

But Taney for the majority sidestepped the question of the legality of the charter government on the ground that the federal courts must deal with the decisions of the *de facto* state governments and their courts. Levi Woodbury, whom Polk had added to the Court, accepted Taney's reasoning on the political issue, but dissented from the approval of the martial law because the circumstances in his mind utterly failed to justify so drastic a suspension of constitutional guarantees.[36] With this evasive result in 1848, the question lapsed. The constitution of 1843 had removed the grievances, Dorr's injuries had been made up for, as much as acts of the legislature could, and no one now felt impelled to push the issue to a conclusion.

The Dorr War was one of those cases where technical right lay on one side, substantive right on the other. There can be small doubt that a stubborn and obtuse minority was determined to keep the control of the government to itself, and that the reformers had fairly well exhausted the possibilities of legal change. Nonetheless, in carrying out the reform, Dorr, perhaps too loyal to his state to admit that revolt against it was the only course left, invoked a theory of sovereignty which was, in fact, the "right" of revolution thinly disguised, and not a "right" of society. If his principles were accepted as normal political procedure, it is impossible to see how the disastrous consequences sketched by Wayland and Webster could be avoided.

Yet it remains true that the Rhode Island dilemma could not have been solved within the law in 1842, and that, without the Dorr War, there would have been no constitution as useful as the one finally adopted in 1843.[37] This somewhat immoral result must be blamed on

[34] Mowry, *The Dorr War*, 83.
[35] John Whipple and Daniel Webster, *The Rhode Island Question*, 43.
[36] Mowry, *The Dorr War*, 231–236.
[37] Cf. Mowry's conclusion, from a rather conservative viewpoint: "It must be acknowledged that, almost entirely because of the agitation, the constitution which went into effect in May, 1843, was liberal and well adapted to the needs of the State." *The Dorr War*, 297–298.

the conservatives, who at no time showed any sense of responsibility about governing their state. For many years, they resolutely failed to acknowledge injustices apparent to nearly everyone else in the United States. When pressure forced their hand in 1842, their response was to make a few reluctant and silly concessions. During the crisis they were weak and timid, and afterwards unduly harsh. In a similar situation in Maryland in 1836, when a Democratic uprising was threatened in protest against vast inequities in legislative representation, the Whig Governor himself led the movement for constitutional reform, thereby avoiding violence and preserving his own power.[38] If the Rhode Island conservatives had shown equal governing intelligence, they would have recognized long before that they could not maintain forever a charter dating from 1663. Recognizing this, they would have long before introduced a new constitution, gained the credit for the reform, and made sure that it would not go too far. But instead by their stupidity they made the excesses of the Dorrites inevitable. The pressures of history will work outside the law when legal paths are blocked: that is the lesson of the Dorr War.

6

Through the country people divided over the Dorr War pretty generally on political lines. Even such a vociferous champion of human rights among the Whigs as Horace Greeley roundly condemned Dorr, while Democrats rallied around the cause of suffrage. Leading Democrats, however, though voluble in announcing their indignation at the treatment of Dorr and at the injustices worked by the old charter, were chary about committing themselves to his theories. As George Bancroft observed sagely to Van Buren of the Rhode Island rebels, "Their affairs there are in confusion, and offer no safe ground for practical statesmanship." [39] Dorr, indeed, received his most unqualified support from Mike Walsh, who as late as June, 1845, was threatening to take five hundred of his b'hoys from New York and make Providence "as level and desolate as ancient Jerusalem was make [sic] by the Romans." [40] The Land Reformers also were concerned about Dorr and promoted Dorr Liberation Societies through

---

[38] *Niles' Register*, September–October, 1836; James McSherry, *History of Maryland*, 348–356; M. P. Andrews, *History of Maryland: Province and State*, 462–465. Most Whigs reacted like the Whigs of Rhode Island, regarding the whole business as a minor French Revolution, but a sensible Whig leadership prevented the tension from flaring up.
[39] Bancroft to Van Buren [October, 1843]. Van Buren Papers.
[40] *Subterranean*, June 21, 1845.

the East. The support of Walsh and the Land Reformers was all the more surprising because Dorr's case so vitally menaced the rights of minorities which their special hero, John C. Calhoun, was so busy defending.

As for the champion of minorities, his own reaction was emphatic and predictable. Dixon H. Lewis reported in May, 1842, that Calhoun, while favoring the extension of the franchise, regarded Dorr's methods as leading to the principle that majorities were supreme over constitutions. A year later, Calhoun amplified his views in a brilliant and conclusive public letter. After an incisive survey of constitutional precedents he declared that it would be the "death-blow of constitutional democracy, to admit the right of the numerical majority, to alter or abolish constitutions at pleasure"; it would be to attribute to majorities the same divine right to govern which Filmer claimed for kings.[41] Calhoun's sharp break with the Barnburners over the Rhode Island question probably impressed on him vividly the potential dangers of an alliance with the majoritarian Democrats.

The Dorr War, by posing the issues so imperatively, led to an extended and illuminating debate on the whole murky problem of minorities and majorities. Orestes A. Brownson, who took the minoritarian side, found his position not without its ironies. After Dorr's assault on the arsenal, an old Providence lady was heard to mutter, "Brownson is at the bottom of all this movement — they are only carrying out his doctrines." Indeed, not only had Brownson written his inflammatory articles in 1840, but in 1841, at Dorr's invitation, he had addressed a suffrage association in Providence, and on Dorr's installation Brownson addressed him a letter of encouragement and approval.[42] But as broader implications emerged he changed his mind and in 1842 set forth his new views in the organ of Barnburner majoritarianism, the *Democratic Review*, which had absorbed the *Boston Quarterly*. In so doing, he entered into a debate with its editor, John L. O'Sullivan.

It is well first to understand what Brownson was attacking. Like most enemies of majority rule, he tended to misrepresent the majoritarian position. He obviously felt that 1840 had wrought a decisive change in his own politics; yet his earlier writings were filled with constant reminders that justice must be held superior even to majorities, and he might have assumed that most majoritarians made similar reservations.

[41] Calhoun to William Smith, July 3, 1843, Calhoun, *Works*, VI, 229, 230.
[42] Anne C. Lynch to Brownson, May 1, 1842, Brownson Papers; Brownson, *Brownson's Early Life*, 342–344.

O'Sullivan, indeed, had already defined his position on "the great question . . . of the relative rights of majorities and minorities" in the first number of the *Democratic Review*. While supporting the principle of the supremacy of the majority, he said, "we acknowledge, in general, a strong sympathy with minorities, and consider that their rights have a high moral claim on the respect and justice of majorities." The fact that these rights have not always been fairly recognized was a most vulnerable point in the democratic argument. "We shall always be willing to meet this question frankly and fairly."

O'Sullivan then expounded what he took to be the minoritarian argument. Conceding the "greatest good of the greatest number" as the object of government, he declared for minoritarianism that it by no means followed that the greatest number always rightly understood its greatest good. When the more wealthy and cultivated classes were on the side of the minority, the disinterested observer might indeed hesitate before deciding, in a difficult and complicated question, in favor of the mere numerical majority. While this was a somewhat vulgar statement of the minoritarian position, it represented well enough the condition of that position as a Whig argument before it was deepened by the flashing perceptions of Calhoun.

In response, O'Sullivan addressed three arguments which together constitute a strong criticism of minority rule. In the first place, he said, majorities were "*more likely*, at least, as a general rule" to understand the general good than minorities would be. Second, a minority was more likely to exploit a majority than a majority to oppress a minority. "This is abundantly proved by the history of all aristocratic interests that have existed." In any case, there had never existed the supposed "original superiority of a minority class above the great mass of a community," and intelligence and ability were more likely to win their proper place when there were no class impediments to their free operation.

But O'Sullivan recognized that these arguments applied only to minority rule. "The question is not yet satisfactorily answered, how the relation between majorities and minorities, in the frequent case of collision," was to be adjusted. Majority government certainly afforded no "perfect guarantee against the misuse of its numerical power over the weakness of the minority." O'Sullivan's pragmatic conclusion was that "this chance of misuse is, as a general rule, far less than in the opposite relation." [43]

[43] O'Sullivan, "Introduction," *Democratic Review*, I, 2–6 (October, 1837). Later he would define democracy as "the political ascendancy of the people" but "not the government of a people permitted, in the plenitude of their power, to

O'Sullivan's case seems temperate and reasonable enough. It made no claim to mystical infallibility, it appealed throughout to historical evidence, it presented a practical face to specific situations, and it appears quite wanting in the totalitarian implications so feared by Calhoun and against which Brownson was directing his blasts.

Yet Brownson did have an opponent, though it was not O'Sullivan. His real foe was George Bancroft, whose brand of social transcendentalism did lead to a theory of democracy which reposed, not on O'Sullivan's empirical data, but on that inner light "never erring in the masses." "If reason is a universal faculty," Bancroft had declared, "the decision of the common mind is the nearest criterion of truth." The dictate of the majority was for him much more than the rough and approximate statement of preference: it was the voice of the over-soul speaking through the collective conscience of mankind — it was, as he once put it, "eternal justice ruling through the people." [44] The absolutist character of this majoritarian faith meant that democracy "totally rejects . . . 'the Right of Revolution.' " "To assert 'the Right of Revolution,' " he cried, "is either to use words without reason, or to assert for the wealthy minority, a right to overthrow our Democratic institutions." [45] But even Bancroft's sentiments about the infallibility of majorities were purely theoretical. In practice, he always subordinated his faith in the majority to some conception of proper policy, and, in fact, it is a rare and dedicated majoritarian who does not. Few persons can really believe that *vox populi* is invariably *vox Dei* when *vox populi* runs athwart their most cherished interests.

When Brownson joined the *Democratic Review*, O'Sullivan had already committed it to support of the Dorr principle. For a few months Brownson contented himself with grumbling about constitutionalism and minorities. Then, in April, 1843, in an article called "Democracy and Liberty," he came out openly for minoritarianism, ridiculed any reliance on the people ("this virtue and intelligence of the people is [sic] all a humbug"), assailed the Dorr heresy and concluded that the prolabor party had split into two groups, "one the radical section, seeking progress by destruction; the other the conservative section, seeking progress through and in obedience to existing institutions." [46]

---

do as they please, regardless alike of the restraints of written law or individual right." "The Course of Civilization," *Democratic Review*, VI, 213 (September, 1839). (It is possible, however, that O'Sullivan did not write this article.)

[44] Quoted by Brownson, "The Convert," *Works*, V, 101.

[45] *Boston Post*, October 16, 1835.

[46] Brownson, "Democracy and Liberty," *Democratic Review*, XII, 375 (April, 1843).

O'Sullivan could not allow this outburst to go unchallenged. "What if the People did make a blunder in 1840?" he asked mildly. ". . . Democracy lays no claim to infallibility for the People." Collectively and individually, the people have gone wrong time after time. "And yet after all, in the long run, Democracy, with its Liberty and Equality of Rights and Chances, is a something far better than any of the other forms of government by which the Few have in all ages plundered and defrauded the Many." O'Sullivan returned repeatedly to the main point: "All these expressions of 'confidence' in the People are merely comparative and relative." As for Brownson, he added dryly, it looked as if he were in that familiar transition by which the young liberal, after passing the grand climacteric of life, became the old conservative.[47]

The old conservative returned to the fray the next month. He recited again his disillusion after 1840 and his new conviction that money would always carry a popular election. The only course, he declared, would be to establish "practical guaranties" which would make it impossible for any government to do anything, and thereby would prevent any class — no matter what class — from using the government to plunder other classes. The object of government was to "enable a constitutional minority — not to rule the majority, but — to hinder effectually the majority, when so disposed, from encroaching . . . on the rights of minorities." The means had been revealed to Calhoun in his doctrine of concurrent majorities. O'Sullivan in his editorial retort admitted freely "the sacredness of the rights of minorities" but pointed out that Calhoun's system would only perpetuate the existing inequities and thus insure minority rule. "A good deal of positive government may be yet wanted to undo the manifold mischiefs of past mis-government. . . . For this work we want the People, the Majority."[48]

O'Sullivan, the determined pragmatist, kept his eye on concrete political problems. Brownson, the doctrinaire, regarded ultimate logical implications as much more real than any present and passing reality. In a few months Brownson was deep in the bog of Catholic authoritarianism, denouncing the pernicious doctrine of equal rights and flirting with theories of the organic state. O'Sullivan merely noted that "it is perhaps scarcely necessary to remark" that he disagreed.[49] In 1844 Brownson departed, with much mutual relief, established

[47] O'Sullivan, "Note," *Democratic Review*, XII, 387, 390, 391 (April, 1843).

[48] Brownson, "Popular Government," *Democratic Review*, XII, 532, 534 (May, 1843); O'Sullivan, "Note," *ibid.*, 538.

[49] O'Sullivan, "Note," *Democratic Review*, XIII, 129 (August, 1843).

Brownson's Quarterly Review and, before the year was out, was safe in the bosom of Rome.

The debate reached no conclusion; yet it stirred some fundamental issues. It showed, for one thing, that any unequivocal decision in favor either of majority rule or of minority rights would probably be disastrous for popular government. Jefferson had accurately expressed the instinct of democracy in the double emphasis of his inaugural address. Democracy shuns codification. It suspends in solution logical antimonies which work out more or less harmoniously in practice. Thereby it gains in flexibility and expands the range of political possibilities, whatever it may lose (to the sorrow of the dogmatist) in philosophical chastity.

The Jeffersonian ambiguity thus may be in fact a source of strength and stability. The circumstances of politics and the sentiments of the people will always set more effective limits on the tyranny of majorities or the obstinacy of minorities than any parchment formula. Like most important problems, the question of majorities and minorities is insoluble. The common sense on it was well set forth by an old Virginia Jeffersonian after some exposure to the conversation of Calhoun in 1843. "There is no doubt," wrote William H. Roane, "that he entertains opinions heterodox, and far too *refined* for the American taste. . . . I cannot comprehend or assent to all this learned jargon about *minorities*. I have never thought that they had any other *Right* than that of freely, peaceably & *legally* converting *themselves* into a *majority* whenever they can." [50]

[50] Roane to Van Buren, September 11, 1843, Van Buren Papers. For a brilliant, but perverse, discussion of this question, see Edwin Mims, Jr., *The Majority of the People*.

XXXII CLOUD ON THE HORIZON

THE POLITICAL struggles of the eighteen-thirties had revolved around questions of banking and the currency. The Democrats had been, in the main, victorious. Jackson destroyed the Bank of the United States, Van Buren terminated the title of the banking system to the free use of government funds, and in many of the states Jacksonians tamed the political ambitions of the banks. While it was possible to repeal the independent treasury after 1840, it was not possible to charter a new Bank. The banking interest was temporarily checked, and banking questions receded as a new issue began to demand the center of the stage.

1

The tariff, when it had last been extensively debated in 1833, had aroused such violent emotions that Clay and Calhoun, leaders of the opposing parties, hastily collaborated on a negotiated peace. A virtual moratorium was imposed on tariff discussion by providing for an automatic reduction of duties till 1842. Early in Tyler's administration the truce was drawing to a close. The Eastern industrialists, mobilizing for a restoration of high duties, now succeeded the bankers as the chief patrons of the Whig party; Abbott Lawrence displaced Nicholas Biddle as its guiding genius. The Jacksonians, somewhat weary from their war with the banks, rallied their forces for the new battle with the manufacturers.

The Jacksonian analysis of industrial society was perfectly clear in its estimate of protection. John Taylor of Caroline had made the basic points in 1822; and by the eighteen-forties the Jeffersonian arguments, reinforced with the dicta of Adam Smith and the British free traders, provided the Jacksonians with heavy intellectual ammunition. Amos Kendall set the Democratic case in its broadest context. "The interests of man in every nation and clime, are in one respect alike," he said: "*It is in the full enjoyment of the fruits of his own labor.*" Yet everywhere the ruling classes contrived "to live in idleness and extract subsistence and wealth from the labor of their fellow men." America had no nobility or priesthood "to take from man the fruits of his labor" — "Capitalists are our Nobles and our Priests; by the authority of law, they collect rents and tithes, appropriating to their own use a large portion of the Farmer's produce, and of the earnings of the Mechanic and Laborer." [1]

The protective tariff, in Kendall's analysis, made "the whole population contribute to the wealth of the Factory owners," some by working in the factories, the rest by paying higher prices for manufactured goods. Was this just a Southern grievance? Kendall was emphatic in denial. The only difference on this point between North and South, he said, was that most manufacturers lived in the North; "it is, therefore, to some extent, the transfer of wealth from one section to another." But did not the Northern farmer or worker "see his income, in common with that of the Southern Planter, taken from him to build up an Aristocracy, of which he is practically to be made slave?" Indeed, the whole tendency of protection was "to throw the property of the North into the hands of a few, as that of the South now is," and convert the white workers into virtual slaves. At bottom, Kendall urged incessantly, the tariff was a class question, not a sectional question.[2]

Many Jacksonians in the past had temporized and straddled on the tariff out of deference to its supposed popularity. But the inner tendencies of their social thought were hard to resist. Jackson had, long since, abandoned his tolerance of 1824, and Van Buren, who as representative of an industrial state had been responsible for much of the skittishness, finally committed himself against protection in 1843. For the Democratic minority of 1842, aroused by the organized drive of the manufacturing interests, the tariff signified much more than an increase in duties and the consequent transfer of wealth to the industrialists: it signified a new test of power between the business community and the rest of the population. As Horace Greeley remarked, the free-trade spirit in the North was "impelled rather by jealousy or hatred of wealth than by dislike to Protection *per se*. . . . It is the everlasting class war of a portion of those who HAVE NOT against the mass of those who HAVE." [3]

Yet, even as lines were drawing taut on the tariff, a more imperative issue began to shoulder it aside. And the new issue, unlike the tariff, had no clear place in the Jacksonian social analysis.

---

[1] *Kendall's Expositor*, December 2, 1841.
[2] *Kendall's Expositor* Extra, March 1, 1843.
[3] Greeley, "The Tariff Question," *American Whig Review*, II, 114 (August, 1845).

2

At first, it was like a cloud on the horizon, as they said in later years, no bigger than a man's hand. Then it rose, black and threatening. Soon it would fill the sky. Who could escape the shadow it promised to cast across the Union? . . . But the wise had long known that America must sometime face its conscience. The promises of democracy might be slow to exert their force; but, if America was to justify the dream, those promises had to be redeemed. Negro bondage was a living challenge to the American ethic — it was, said John Quincy Adams in 1820, "the great and foul stain upon the North American Union." Eventually the moral feeling of the land must wash it away, or the nation would lose its soul. "The seeds of the Declaration of Independence are yet maturing," wrote Adams as he watched the swirl of fear and hatred around the question of the admission of Missouri as a slave state. "The harvest will be what West, the painter, calls the terrible sublime."

Slavery was the most accusing, the most tragic and the most dangerous of all questions. It was implacable, it could not be winked away by compromise, and, as Adams knew in 1820, no man ought ever to agitate it without being prepared for the dissolution of the Union, "and reconciled to it, because it must end in that."[4] The nation knew this, too, in its heart of hearts, and like a man banishing a dreaded image from consciousness, it turned and twisted desperately to suppress and deny and bury the terrible fact. For almost a quarter of a century after the Missouri crisis, slavery was blocked from gaining full embodiment as a specific political issue. The trauma of 1820 was too intense. Yet the question could not be exorcised by repression. It remained ever just out of sight, occasionally flaring up for a moment in an exchange on the floors of Congress (often around Adams, who knew his responsibility), like a wild dream, shaking the night with its burst of anxiety; then disclaimed and forgotten, as the morning came again, and people returned securely to debating the Bank or the tariff.

The Jacksonians in the thirties were bitterly critical of abolitionists. The outcry against slavery, they felt, distracted attention from the vital economic questions of Bank and currency, while at the same time it menaced the Southern alliance so necessary for the success of the reform program. A good deal of Jacksonian energy, indeed, was expended in showing how the abolition movement was a conservative

[4] Adams. *Memoirs,* IV, 531, 492–493, 502, 517.

plot. C. C. Cambreleng declared the abolitionists to be "almost exclusively, the old 'Church and State' faction," and Theophilus Fisk agreed. Ely Moore spoke for much of labor in his charge that the Whigs planned to destroy the power of the Northern working classes by freeing the Negro "to compete with the Northern white man in the labor market."[5]

The Jacksonians reminded the abolitionists that reform began at home. "We hear the philanthropist moaning over the fate of the Southern slave," said Seth Luther, "when there are *thousands* of children in this State as truly slaves as the blacks of the South." One workingman, rising in a union meeting, observed that he heard much talk about emancipating the blacks; "but equal rights ought to be established at home first, and emancipation of the white slaves be effected before we go abroad." Some Northerners wondered quite honestly whether the slave was not better off in view of the helplessness of the free laborer in face of sickness and old age. "The want of liberty is a great drawback on happiness," remarked William M. Gouge: "but the slave is free from care." From reformers like Fanny Wright and Albert Brisbane to party leaders like Jackson and Van Buren the liberal movement united in denouncing the abolitionists.[6]

A few even verged toward the proslavery position. James K. Paulding, for example, wrote a book in praise of slavery in 1836. Many of the original Locofocos, as we have seen, attached themselves after 1840 to the cause of John C. Calhoun. Orestes A. Brownson, after early remarks in defense of abolitionism, gradually shifted to the other camp. To free the slave, he declared, in 1837, would be but "to release him from a tyrant to place him under the control of what M. de La Mennais has . . . said, 'has no name out of hell,'" and by 1843 he discovered the relationship between master and slave to be "of a more generous and touching nature" than between employer and workingman.[7] After becoming a Catholic, of course, he encountered little difficulty in clothing slavery with plausible moral justification.

Theophilus Fisk was even more unconditional in his defense of the South. "The abolitionists of the North have mistaken the *color* of American Slaves," he would say; "all the real Slaves in the United

---

[5] Cambreleng to R. H. Baptist, September 16, 1835, *Washington Globe*, February 13, 1836; Fisk, *The Nation's Bulwark*, 12–20; Moore in the House, February 4, 1839, *Congressional Globe*, 25 Congress 3 Session, Appendix, 241.

[6] Luther in the *Washington Globe*, May 14, 1832; meeting of the Stone Cutters, *Boston Post*, April 17, 1835; Gouge, *Paper Money*, Part I, 98–99; Perkins and Wolfson, *Wright*, 256; Brisbane, *Social Destiny of Man*, 102–103.

[7] *Boston Reformer*, July 21, 1837; "The Present State of Society," *Democratic Review*, XIII, 27 (July, 1843).

States have *pale* faces." He repeatedly inveighed against antislavery agitation. "Will charity ever begin at home?" he asked with scorn. "Are there no slaves North of the Potomac? . . . I will venture to affirm that there are more slaves in Lowell and Nashua alone than can be found South of the Potomac." For Fisk, Southern slavery was a form of philanthropy in which the master wore himself out "to enable his negroes to live like nabobs in comparative indolence." "Emancipate the slave, and what then! He would fiddle, steal, and then starve." In any case, it was no business of the North. "There is not an abolitionist in America but would hold slaves tomorrow, if he could buy them with wooden nutmegs." Let them free the wage slaves: "then come to the South with clean hands, and we will listen to your appeal." [8] Fitzwilliam Byrdsall and John Commerford vied with Fisk in their loyalty to Calhoun's sacred institution.

But many Jacksonians could not subdue their private conviction that slavery was evil. "To say that I am utterly opposed to slavery in every form, civil, political, or domestic," declared Marcus Morton in 1837 in a typical outburst, "is saying very little; for how can any man under the influence of any moral or religious principle, or of any correct political notions, justify or excuse it? . . . I deem slavery to be the greatest curse and the most portentous evil which a righteous God ever inflicted upon a nation." [9] George Bancroft had somewhat these views in his early years, though ambition prevented him from going out in front on so unpopular a question. After the murder of Elijah P. Lovejoy, the abolitionist editor, by a proslavery mob, such men as B. F. Hallett and Amasa Walker participated in indignation meetings, and Hallett's paper stood almost alone in its cordiality to William Lloyd Garrison. (Oddly enough, Hallett would end up as one of Boston's stoutest champions of slavery, even serving as prosecutor under the Fugitive Slave Law.) Thomas Morris, a Van Buren Democrat from Ohio, emerged from the fight over abolition petitions as the first real antislavery Senator. An urbane Democratic lawyer named James G. Birney was speaking to earnest groups through the North about forming a Liberty party. The Democrat in whom social radicalism and antislavery feeling united most impressively was William Leggett. Amos Kendall's act in barring abolitionist propaganda from the Southern mails knocked Leggett off the party line in 1835, and his growing perception of the kinship between Negro slavery and other forms of class exploitation made him by 1838 an open antislavery

[8] Fisk, *Banking Bubble Burst*, 84-85; *The Nation's Bulwark*, 14, 15, 20; *Our Country; Its Dangers and Destiny*, 10; *Democratic Expositor*, July 25, 1860.
　[9] Morton's Letter of September 28, 1837, *Niles' Register*, December 1, 1838.

man.[10] Through the party men were finding themselves driven by the inherent tendencies of their democratic creed to positions near those of Leggett and Morris and Birney.

3

The seeds of the Declaration of Independence were yet maturing, the harvest was not to be long put off. The new generation of the forties could barely remember the anxious days of the Missouri Compromise, and the imperative spell of expansion was fixing their eyes in new directions. The land was on fire with its new vision — a democratic nation, rich and magnificent, stretching from sea to sea. John L. O'Sullivan had been among the first to set down the tenets of the new faith. "We are the nation of human progress," he cried, in 1839, "and who will, what can, set limits to our onward march?" The "mission" of America, he said, was to spread the four freedoms through the world — "freedom of conscience, freedom of person, freedom of trade and business pursuits, universality of freedom and equality." [11] In 1844 O'Sullivan and Samuel J. Tilden established the *Morning News* in New York as successor to the *Plebeian*, and on December 27, 1845, O'Sullivan condensed the new imperialism into a single phrase. America's strongest claim to Oregon, he said, was "by the right of our manifest destiny to overspread and to possess the whole of the continent which Providence has given us for the . . . great experiment of liberty." [12]

Manifest Destiny signified a glowing faith in democracy and a passionate desire that it rule the world. No doubt it served in part as a mask for speculation in land and Texas scrip; but in part too it expressed an honest idealism about the future of the world. The enthusiasm for Louis Kossuth was as much its product as the Ostend Manifesto. The Northern masses and many of the Democratic leaders were under its spell. Bancroft had declared in 1844 that it was "the manifest purpose of Providence, that the light of democratic

[10] For Leggett's antiabolitionist writings, see, e.g., *New York Evening Post*, July 11, 1834, February 10, 1835. He feared particularly the effects on the Northern working classes of competition with the cheap labor of the emancipated Negroes.

[11] "The Great Nation of Futurity," *Democratic Review*, VI, 427 (November, 1839). I follow J. W. Pratt in his "O'Sullivan and Manifest Destiny," *New York History*, XXXI, 321, in ascribing this article to O'Sullivan. He had, however, resigned from the *Democratic Review* some months before (see V, 520, May, 1839), not to rejoin it till 1841, and he may not have written this piece.

[12] Pratt, "O'Sullivan and Manifest Destiny," *loc. cit.*, 222, 224. O'Sullivan had actually used the phrase in July, 1845, but it was the December editorial which gave it general currency.

freedom should be borne from our fires to the domain beyond the
Rocky Mountains." [13] Such other close friends of Van Buren as Cambreleng, Flagg, Gideon Welles, Frank Blair, such strong Van Buren
Democrats as Robert Dale Owen and Walt Whitman were for the
annexation of Texas. Thomas Hart Benton, though against the proposed mode of acquiring Texas, was one of the most eloquent proponents of Manifest Destiny. The Northern prolabor disciples of
Calhoun — Brownson, Byrdsall, Commerford, Evans — were equally
ardent expansionists, and Mike Walsh claimed characteristically in
1845 to have been "the first man" to advocate the annexation of
Texas. [14] Old General Jackson himself, in his pain-stricken last years at
the Hermitage, hoped to see Texas in the Union before he died. The
instinct of the people was demanding the land from sea to sea. (Even
Henry Thoreau, though he disapproved of expansion as a national
policy, found that when he went on an idle walk he instinctively set
out toward the southwest.)

The democratic enthusiasm naturally provoked the hostility of
conservatism. The Northern Whigs stood against Texas in 1844 (as
they were to stand against Kossuth in 1851), and even the Southern
Whigs on the whole opposed annexation and the war. Robert Rantoul
charged in 1848 that Whig enmity to expansion was part of their old
scheme to keep wages down. "So long as cheap land continues to be
abundant," he pointed out, "so long you cannot drive the wages of
labor to the starvation point. . . . Here, then, is the way in which
a comprehensive democratic statesmanship would begin to protect
labor: by affording it ample room, scope sufficient to work out its
will upon the whole unoccupied North American continent." [15]

4

Yet there were others, not conservatives, who saw a series of
explosive questions, which might imperil the whole democratic future,
waiting ominously in the trail of annexation. How could Texas be admitted without raising the problem of slavery extension? What friend
of the Declaration of Independence would introduce slavery into
an area where, under Mexican law, it had not existed? What good
Jacksonian would deliver the nation's inheritance in the West into
the hands of the planting aristocracy? And with the increase of slave
territory and Southern political power, would not the South abrogate

[13] Bancroft's letter accepting the Democratic nomination for Governor, August
15, 1844, Bancroft Papers.
[14] *Subterranean*, October 4, 1845.
[15] Hamilton, *Rantoul*, 687.

the alliance with the Northern Democracy which had made the Jacksonian revolution possible? Would not expansion thus place the entire Jacksonian program in jeopardy?

For many years Theodore Sedgwick, Jr., of New York had been convinced that slavery was "the greatest question which agitates or can agitate the Republic." The question clearly shaped itself in relation to democracy in the North. "Give us the real issue," he had cried in 1840 — "*Is Slavery a good or an evil to the free citizens of these States?*" The problem of Texas, he now declared in the *Evening Post*, becomes for this reason "the most important that has in our day been submitted to the judgment of the people." A series of eloquent articles explained why, in his mind, its annexation threatened the future of democracy. "It must incalculably increase the slaveholding interest," he wrote. ". . . The northern man must be false to his education, and blind to his interests, who does not, inch by inch, and hand to hand, resist the extension of the slaveholding power." Where slavery has existed, "it has plunged the laboring class into degradation, and made labor itself dishonorable." Do not be deceived: the admission of Texas was no simple territorial question. It was but "another name for '*the perpetuity of slavery*,' and we who now enjoy the rights and hold the soil of the Union, must bid farewell for ever to the hope of relieving ourselves from the danger, the odium and the disgrace inseparable from this pernicious institution." [16]

Circulated in pamphlet form, Sedgwick's arguments exerted great influence among the Barnburner Democrats. William Cullen Bryant and David Dudley Field were in firm agreement. A younger associate, first making his mark in politics, added his energetic support. Samuel J. Tilden was a slender, sandy-haired man, fussy and hypochondriacal, with a quick gait and a nervous and evasive manner, very able intellectually, but without personal charm. His life, both public and private, was under the sway of inhibition. He never married, though in middle age he engaged in a series of audacious flirtations and left a New Orleans belle a huge sum in his will; but his library contained a large collection of pornography. In political contacts people were annoyed by his querulous combination of caution and cold self-esteem, and his associates were amused by his habit of portentous whispering when talking politics. But underneath they sensed a certain narrow integrity, and no one could doubt his real gifts for political manipulation. [17]

[16] Sedgwick to his parents, October 8, 1833, to Harmanus Bleecker, September 14, 1841, Sedgwick Papers; *New York Evening Post*, February 20, 1840; *Thoughts on the Proposed Annexation of Texas*, 34, 35.

[17] A. C. Flick, *Samuel J. Tilden*; Flick, "Samuel Jones Tilden," *New York History*, XXIX, 347–359; John Bigelow, *Life of Samuel J. Tilden*; Bigelow, *Retrospections of an Active Life*. I, 66.

In Washington too Texas filled the radical Democrats with alarm. Benton exclaimed that he regarded annexation as a presidential intrigue for some, "*on the part of others, a Texas scrip and land speculation.*" Silas Wright declared that annexation "put all other questions in the shade" and steadfastly opposed it.[18]

Wright's protégé Preston King, who had entered the House of Representatives in 1843, was one of the most effective exponents of the Barnburner position. Thirty-seven when he went to Washington, he was a graduate of Union College and then a law student in Wright's office. A radical Jacksonian in New York politics in the thirties, he suffered a severe breakdown in 1838 and was confined to an asylum. Now recovered, he went to Congress, where his equability, self-possession and great good sense were to make him one of the most useful men over the next two decades. "Unambitious as well as unassuming," observed Gideon Welles, "few gave him credit for all he accomplished," adding that to Preston King "more than to any other one man may be ascribed the merit of boldly meeting the arrogant and imperious slaveholding oligarchy and organizing the party which eventually overthrew them." [19] His peculiar gift lay in influencing and rallying others and, while deeply agitated himself, remaining outwardly calm and cheerful. As Wright said, he would talk freely to everyone and "use more effort, with less appearance, to bring all to one point and that a safe and sound one, than any man I know." [20] King's opposition to Texas hung, he said, on "the single point of slavery"; without slavery "I would take Texas to night." [21]

The antislavery bloc was strengthened by the Democratic Senator from New Hampshire, the effervescent and witty John P. Hale, a large, stout man, with shining red face and twinkling blue eyes, hearty in manner and easy-going in temperament. Lazy, rather shallow, given to financial laxities, especially in later life, he was yet utterly fearless, a masterful popular orator and a lively catch-as-catch-can debater whose repartee rose to every crisis. His friends wished he was more reliable (he was "too much an offhand man," complained Salmon P. Chase), but even Southerners warmed to his irresistible good fellowship. A vigorous opponent of annexation, Hale was already arranging to go into practice in New York with Theodore Sedgwick, Jr., in

[18] Benton, *Thirty Years' View*, II, 583; Wright to Van Buren, April 8, 1844, Van Buren Papers.

[19] Welles, "Political History of the Forties," 19–21, Welles Papers; *Diary*, II, 385. See also Flagg to Van Buren, April 15, 1843, Van Buren Papers; Dix to Flagg, November 9, 1846, Flagg Papers; Weed, *Autobiography*, 471–472.

[20] Wright to Van Buren, April 10, 1843, Van Buren Papers.

[21] King to Flagg, December 21, 1844, January 11, 1845, Flagg Papers.

expectation of defeat. But when he returned and stumped New Hampshire before the election, the people took up his fight and in 1846 returned him to the Senate.[22]

These men were the sentries of democratic opinion, alert to all threats to the faith, but Martin Van Buren, quiet at Lindenwald, was moving slowly toward the same conclusions. He had never been too happy about Texas, and during his own presidency had resisted all movements toward its acquisition. Now he felt more keenly than ever its fatal significance. Yet he hoped for the Democratic nomination in 1844, and expansion was, North and South, the popular issue.

Late in April, 1844, the delegates on their way to Baltimore for the Democratic convention read with amazement the result of Van Buren's meditations. In a public letter on the eve of the nominations the leading contender came out against the popular issue and opposed immediate annexation. While political caution kept him from resting his case as openly as he would later on his fears of the slave power, he still was courting violent Southern disapproval. The antislavery Democrats responded with enthusiasm. It was "more noble, more desirable, more important, more patriotic," wrote Silas Wright, "to take boldly the side of truth and principle, though it may be disastrous in a popular sense, than to temporize with a matter which may prove to be so vital to the perpetuity of our institutions." [23] . . . But the men of the South had marked their enemy.

As a whole, the people of the North, like Van Buren, were against the spread of slavery, but the first impulse of Manifest Destiny aimed toward Oregon, where there could be no problem of slavery, and men in the street tended to resist seeing any necessary relation between the two questions. Some who acknowledged the relation were consoled by the doctrine that the acquisition of Texas would "diffuse" slavery, not increase it. Many more still felt, like Van Buren himself in the thirties, that the slavery question was irrelevant. But, in the Barnburner view, Texas showed that the evil they had previously ignored was now growing into a grave threat to democracy. Neutrality, isolationism, were no longer an aid to reform, as they had been in the decade before, but a menace to it. Neutrality, in fact, was no longer possible, as the South was preparing to make clear in the impending Democratic convention: Northern Democrats must face

---

[22] J. L. Hayes, *A Reminiscence of the Free-Soil Movement in New-Hampshire, 1845*, 15, 42; G. B. Spalding, *A Discourse Commemorative of . . . Hon. John Parker Hale*; H. S. Foote, *Casket of Reminiscences*, 76; Oliver Dyer, *Great Senators*, 127; G. W. Bungay, *Crayon Sketches*, 13–16; Chase to Sumner, April 28, 1851, Chase, *Diary and Correspondence*, 235.

[23] Wright to Van Buren, April 8, 1844, Van Buren Papers.

the choice of appeasing the slave power, or resisting it. If the democratic road was to be kept clear, it was becoming imperative to challenge the pretensions of the South to the control of the Democratic party and its policies.

5

The rise of antislavery sentiment presents a complex problem of historical causation. At bottom, the antislavery impulse was a moral impulse. No cause can command the deepest loyalties and the greatest sacrifices of men till it is presented under a moral aspect. It has been pointed out, by historical materialists, that crusades succeed only when they fill economic needs; but it could as well be said that crusades succeed only when they fill moral needs. The two motives are inseparable, and the presence of one does not discredit the other, as the Marxists appear capable of acknowledging only when their own crusade is concerned. Every moral movement in history has required a certain configuration of social and economic conditions for success, but this does not make it any less a moral movement, nor need we regard the Northerners who fought the Civil War as fools, deluded idealists, or the agents of a predatory capitalism.

In essence, the emotion which moved the North finally to battle-field and bloodshed was moral disgust. So long as the slave power did not interfere with Northern aspirations, the disgust remained the property of "fanatics" — that is, of people so dominated by ethical motives that they were disinterestedly impelled to attack slavery. The religious community, as we have seen, was anti-Jacksonian. Many of the ardent abolitionists were also ardent champions of the Georgia missionaries, the national fast and the sanctity of the Sabbath — "the old 'Church and State' faction," as Cambreleng had put it. From this source came the first momentum against slavery.[24]

But when the claims of the South began to constitute a concrete threat to Northern political intentions, then moral repugnance spread wide among the great mass of the people, and antislavery sentiment appeared in new sections of the community. The political grounds of antislavery were as indispensable as the religious, and perhaps more potent in stirring up the common man.

If the antislavery crusade awaited for its full vigor the day when the slave power threatened to strike directly at Northern aspirations, the question becomes relevant: aspirations toward what? Since the

[24] See the admirable account in G. H. Barnes, *The Antislavery Impulse, 1830-1844.*

Marxist revelation has been extended to the New World, it has become fashionable to answer: aspirations toward the robber-baron industrialism which ruled the country after the Civil War. The South, the argument goes, was the only hindrance to an unbridled "capitalist" control of the government; hence, the "capitalists," with a cynical invocation of the moralities, ruthlessly destroyed their rival.

The syllogism exhibits a characteristic doctrinaire skill at confusing consequences with motives, as well as a characteristic doctrinaire preference for deductive logic over fact. The aspirations which were first felt to be menaced by the slave power were in actuality democratic aspirations, that part of the population increasingly indulgent of Southern pretensions was the business community of the North, and the group which took the lead on the political stage in combating the slave power were the radical Democrats in the straight Jacksonian tradition.

XXXIII GATHERING OF THE STORM

JOHN TYLER'S last important link with the Whig party had broken when Webster resigned in May, 1843. His remaining hope for re-election was to build a personal party out of the disgruntled politicians of the Democracy and aim for the Democratic nomination of 1844. This strategy soon led him into close relations with Calhoun. While each, in the long run, intended to use the other, the two could work together for the moment in harmony, on patronage as well as on policy. The conservative wing of the party, starved during the years of Van Buren's ascendancy, thus began in 1843 to receive again the nutriment of office. In Massachusetts, for example, Robert Rantoul became Collector of the Port, and David Henshaw went to Washington as Secretary of the Navy. These men, with B. F. Hallett, Charles Gordon Greene and Isaac Hill of New Hampshire, headed the Tyler-Calhoun party in New England, and they proceeded to revive the old Henshaw machine under the noses of Bancroft, Marcus Morton and the Van Buren group.[1] The appointment of Calhoun as Secretary of State in March, 1844, belatedly acknowledged the alliance.

1

But the advent of 1844 had shown little loosening in Van Buren's hold on the rank and file. In January Calhoun released a statement refusing to allow his name to go before the convention, and Tyler appeared to have little strength, except among the federal officeholders who went through the motions of nominating him at a convention in Baltimore in May. His last-minute attempts to win over leading contenders by appointments failed. Van Buren and Silas Wright turned down seats on the Supreme Court, and James K. Polk, the chief vice-presidential aspirant, rejected the Secretaryship of the Navy (which Tyler offered him through Theophilus Fisk).[2]

[1] *Bay State Democrat*, November, 1843, *passim; Boston Advertiser*, September 14, 1843; Blair to Jackson, September 26, 1843, Jackson, *Correspondence*, VI, 231; Darling, *Political Changes*, 301–307.
[2] Wright to Van Buren, January 2, March 6, 1844, Van Buren Papers; Polk to Fisk, March 30, 1844, L. G. Tyler, *Letters and Times of the Tylers*, III, 133.

In the meantime the opposition to Van Buren was centering, more and more, around Lewis Cass of Michigan. James Buchanan of Pennsylvania and Levi Woodbury of New Hampshire had small favorite-son booms. Colonel Johnson was still traveling around the country in desperate pursuit of any honor available. Many felt with W. L. Marcy that Johnson was "not now even what he formerly was. It may be there never was so much of him as many of us were led to suppose." But though acquaintances regarded him with contempt ("such a mass of stupidity, vulgarity and immorality," remarked a friend of Calhoun's), he still retained what Silas Wright called a "disgusting popularity" with the people.[3] Yet as the day of the convention approached, Van Buren's triumph seemed increasingly certain. Then, too late for their own use, Tyler and Calhoun discovered the popularity of Texas and proceeded to make it the crucial issue.

The delegates thronged Baltimore in the last days of May, and the atmosphere was filled with uncertainty and excitement. The bombshell of Van Buren's letter was still in everyone's ears. What had he meant by turning against Texas? *Texas — Texas — Texas:* the name rang through the heated talks in the barrooms of the city, and on the streets, and in smoky hotel rooms. (They talked too, in some incredulity, about the miracle of May 24. A group of men, they heard, had waited around a queer contraption in the Supreme Court chamber in Washington, forty miles away, while here in Baltimore other men had pushed a lever. Then the wires had quivered, the words flashed, and the machines stuttered back and forth. "WHAT HATH GOD WROUGHT!" . . . "HAVE YOU ANY NEWS?" "NO." . . . "SEPARATE YOUR WORDS MORE." "OIL YOUR CLOCK-WORK." "BUCHANAN STOCK SAID TO BE RISING." . . . "VAN BUREN CANNON IN FRONT, WITH A FOX-TAIL ON IT.")[4] Robert J. Walker, the shrewd little Senator from Mississippi, with his wheezing voice and dead-pan expression, passed quietly among the newcomers, dropping soft, but meaningful, phrases. Henry D. Gilpin, sharing a room with Benjamin F. Butler, scribbled to Van Buren of his premonitory depression at the "most reckless and desperate system of political intrigue that I have ever witnessed."[5] Butler himself was carrying a secret letter written by Van Buren on May 20 offering to withdraw in favor of Silas Wright.

But how to defeat a man to whom a majority of the delegates were already pledged? The Democratic convention had nominated Jack-

---

[3] Marcy to Van Buren, November 1, 1843, Wright to Van Buren, February 27, 1844, Van Buren Papers; J. H. Hammond to Calhoun, September 10, 1842, *Correspondence Addressed to Calhoun*, 850.
[4] S. I. Prime, *Life of Samuel F. B. Morse, LL.D.*, 496–497.
[5] Gilpin to Van Buren, May 26, 1844, Van Buren Papers.

son in 1832 by a two-thirds vote as evidence of party unanimity. The two-thirds rule was used again in 1835, but was abandoned in 1839. Walker now sponsored a movement for its revival. His fluent and clever speech roused cheers and some hisses in the hot and crowded hall. Then Butler, his handsome intellectual face white and grave, rose to fight the motion, but his argument seemed too long, and its tone suggested to observers that he felt he was laboring against the tide. Walker sat near by, busily taking notes. Marcus Morton spoke tersely and effectively against the rule, Rantoul for it, and Walker delivered a brilliant debating rejoinder to Butler. On the vote the delegates instructed for Van Buren, but secretly favoring another candidate or opposing Van Buren on Texas, rushed to support it. Its passage sealed Van Buren's fate.

On the first ballot Van Buren received a majority of twenty-six but failed of two thirds by thirty-two votes, the North backing him almost unanimously, the South opposing him almost unanimously. For seven ballots the fight continued, with Van Buren's total slowly declining, Cass's slowly rising, but without any real prospect of breaking the deadlock. After the seventh ballot an Ohio delegate moved Van Buren's selection on the ground that he had received a majority on the first trial. The chair ruled this motion out of order, and a bitter wrangle over parliamentary procedure followed. Someone increased the confusion by moving that Andrew Jackson be nominated. This provoked wild applause but was also declared out of order. Finally the convention angrily adjourned.

Through the tense evening the managers circulated among the delegates. It was known that Colonel Johnson had withdrawn, releasing his votes for Cass, and the Van Buren men feared a stampede to Cass in the morning. Butler, ascertaining that the Van Buren vote was breaking up, spent till midnight trying to hold it in line for Silas Wright. But Wright had already declined to have his name go before the convention in a letter held by a member of the New York delegation.

In the meantime George Bancroft, also aware of the danger of Cass, decided that a more radical step was necessary. In James K. Polk of Tennessee, whom the Van Buren forces had previously fixed upon as their vice-presidential preference, Bancroft suddenly perceived the only man on whom the convention could unite. Before midnight he had spoken with the key men in the leading Northern delegations on the importance of compromising on Polk. In the morning Polk received forty-four votes on the eighth ballot. Then, on the ninth, Butler delivered to Polk the Van Buren votes from New York. Delegation after delegation wheeled into line, and, in a pattern made familiar by later conventions, the dark horse raced through to victory.

How fortuitous was Polk's nomination? Before Texas altered the situation, Polk's aspirations were for the vice-presidential nomination under Van Buren. Then in May Jackson, convinced that Van Buren had committed political suicide, talked seriously to Polk about the presidency. Silas Wright in the meantime, also despairing of Van Buren's chances, remarked on May 7 to Cave Johnson, Polk's political intimate, that Polk was the only man acceptable to the Northern Democrats if Van Buren was set aside. For a man of Polk's clear intelligence the possibilities of Baltimore were plain. "In the confusion which will prevail," as he observed significantly to Johnson, ". . . there is no telling what may occur." [6] But he moved with typical care in order not to alienate the Van Buren support by conspiring for his defeat. If lightning struck James K. Polk, it was because the rods had been set some time before. . . . Benjamin F. Butler, loyal to the end, returned to his room, threw himself upon his bed and cried like a child.

As a sop to Van Buren, the convention nominated Silas Wright for Vice-President. The news flashed over the telegraph wires to Washington, and Wright's curt answer came back: —

WASHINGTON. IMPORTANT! MR. WRIGHT IS HERE, AND SAYS, SAY TO THE NEW YORK DELEGATION, THAT HE CAN NOT ACCEPT THE NOMINATION.

AGAIN: MR. WRIGHT IS HERE, AND WILL SUPPORT MR. POLK CHEERFULLY, BUT CAN NOT ACCEPT THE NOMINATION FOR VICE-PRESIDENT.

The message was read to a skeptical convention, which preferred to await confirmation by horseback. The honor then went to George M. Dallas of Pennsylvania.[7]

2

The radicals took their defeat with public good grace, and private chagrin. Men like Cambreleng and Michael Hoffman, who had

[6] Polk to Johnson, May 13, 1844, "Letters of James K. Polk to Cave Johnson, 1833–1848," *Tennessee Historical Magazine*, I, 240.

[7] For the convention, see the reports of B. F. Butler and J. L. O'Sullivan to Van Buren, Van Buren Papers; the correspondence among Polk, A. J. Donelson, Cave Johnson and Gideon Pillow, *Tennessee Historical Magazine*, I, 209–256, III, 51–73, *American Historical Review*, XI, 832–843; Bancroft to Polk, July 6, 1844, Bancroft Papers; *New York Herald*, June 4, 1844; Hudson, *Journalism in the United States*, 599; Adlai E. Stevenson, *Something of Men I Have Known*, 129; Forney, *Anecdotes*, I, 117–118, II, 79; Hammond, *Silas Wright*, 446–471; Swisher, *Taney*, 434.

served in the House with Polk, deeply respected him, and it was felt in general that, with Van Buren out, Polk was the next best choice. Van Buren serenely congratulated the party on its nomination, and Thomas Hart Benton told Silas Wright to say to the ex-President that the party need not despair, especially with three such men as Van Buren, Wright and A. C. Flagg. "Three such men," Benton declared, "are sufficient not merely to save a party, but an age, a generation, an era. Tell him so. Tell him so, Sir. Tell him that I say so. It does not require five, as it did to save Sodom. Three are enough." [8] But, among themselves, the Barnburners were consumed with bitterness. "I consider the nomination brought about by a rascally fraud," exploded Theodore Sedgwick, "one that would disgrace a well organized den of thieves. . . . a complete surrender of the Majority to a slaveholding Minority." [9]

Polk's managers, for their part, were deeply concerned over the possible loss of New York, on which the election might well hang. They thus sought to conciliate the Barnburners and backed a movement to strengthen the New York ticket by running Silas Wright for Governor. Many radicals responded with enthusiasm, among them Preston King, Clinton Roosevelt and Walt Whitman.[10] But Wright himself was singularly reluctant to leave the Senate and only surrendered to the strongest pressure. His candidacy brought the Barnburners into the canvass with more energy, but without abating very much their opposition to Texas. Indeed, in the midst of the campaign the Barnburners of New York City circulated among the Democrats of the state a confidential letter, endorsing Polk but repudiating the Baltimore plank on annexation as having "no relation to the principles of the party" and urging the defeat of annexationist Congressmen. The names of Bryant, Sedgwick, John Worth Edmonds and David Dudley Field headed the list of signers.[11]

The Whigs had meanwhile nominated Henry Clay, with Theodore Frelinghuysen, the hero of the American Sunday School Association, as his running mate. Clay had spoken out against annexation about the same time as Van Buren in a letter which George Bancroft disagreeably

---

[8] Wright to Flagg, June 8, 1844, Flagg Papers.

[9] Sedgwick to Sumner, June 9, 1844, Sumner Papers.

[10] Wright to Erastus Corning, September 11, 1844, Gillet, *Wright*, II, 1588; W. C. Bryant to Roosevelt, November 23, 1884, clipping pasted in Roosevelt, *The Mode of Protecting Domestic Industries*, New York Public Library: "The DEMOCRAT was, I believe, the first paper in the State which nominated SILAS WRIGHT. I recollect many people doubted the expediency of this at the time [1844], though I did not"; for Whitman, see *Brooklyn Eagle*, April 6, 1847, *Gathering of the Forces*, II, 6.

[11] Hammond, *Wright*, 499–500.

(but accurately) interpreted to mean: "let me humbug the Northern abolitionists and after that humor the South." The humoring of the South was accomplished by a series of statements later in the campaign which left his attitude toward annexation anyone's guess. James G. Birney ran again as the Liberty party's candidate for President, while also running for the Michigan legislature as a Democrat; Thomas Morris, the former Democratic Senator from Ohio, was his partner on the Liberty ticket. From Nauvoo, Illinois, the nation was urged to vote for Joseph Smith, "the smartest man in the United States," until a mob destroyed the Mormon leader's aspirations and him later in the year.[12]

It was a confusing campaign. The Democrats tossed back the lessons of 1840.

> The magic names of Tip and Ty,
>   To humbug folks won't do, sirs,
> The people know them and defy,
>   Which makes them look quite blue, sirs;
> Their coons are dead, their cabins down,
>   Hard cider grown quite stale, sirs,
> And at the people's with'ring frown,
>   Their leader grows quite pale, sirs.[13]

Clay was ruthlessly defamed everywhere. The South, in particular, was given to understand that he was an abolitionist, which prompted one Mississippi journalist to scribble: —

> De niggar vote am quite surprising,
> We's all for Clay and Frelinghuysing.[14]

The Whigs for their part went to work with surprising confidence. Their wits talked endlessly of the alleged obscurity of Polk, thereby creating another campaign myth, which, as in the cases of Jackson and Van Buren, the next generation of Republican historians would accept as fact. Tom Corwin of Ohio, a favorite Whig spellbinder, used to ask in his drawling way, "And *who* have they nominated? James K. Polk, of Tennessee?" Then, pausing and turning his head slowly from one side of the audience to the other, with an expression of complete astonishment, "*After that*, who is safe?" [15]

[12] T. C. Smith, *The Liberty and Free Soil Parties in the Northwest*, 76–77; I. W. Riley, *The Founder of Mormonism*, 327.

[13] John Hickey, *The Democratic Lute, and Minstrel*, 5.

[14] J. E. Walmsley, "The Presidential Campaign of 1844 in Mississippi," *Publications of the Mississippi Historical Society*, IX, 197.

[15] E. D. Mansfield, *Personal Memories*, 223.

In New York, Horace Greeley gave heart and soul to the canvass, creeping to his lodgings at two or three in the morning, exhausted from long hours of labor, and dousing himself with water in order to get to sleep. For six months afterward he was covered with boils, sometimes fifty or sixty at once, till he had to pass night after night in an easy chair.[16] In New England, where the conscience needed assistance before it could support a dueler and slaveholder like Clay, Whiggism enlisted the dialectical ingenuity of Nathaniel W. Taylor, the great Yale Calvinist. "If two devils are candidates for the office," declared Dr. Taylor, "and the election of one is inevitable, is it not one's duty to vote for the least, in order to secure the greater good?" A promising young divine named Horace Bushnell blasted this heresy, with its Hopkinsian implication that sin could be the necessary means of the greatest good, and declared for absolute righteousness.[17] But the lesser devil carried Connecticut.

In the end, for all Corwin's wit and Greeley's boils and Taylor's theology, James K. Polk managed to squeak through. With less than forty thousand votes' majority, he received 170 electoral votes to Clay's 105. If Clay had carried New York, he would have won. But Silas Wright, running several thousand votes ahead of Polk, brought enough strength to the Democratic ticket, while Clay lost enough to Birney, for Polk to finish with a five-thousand–vote advantage in the crucial state. "Had Polk been as hard a Swearer as Clay," was the solemn reflection of one New Englander, "he would have been beaten out & out." [18] Disconsolate minstrels sang in poignant melodies the sorrows of Whigs through the land, bewailing the defeat of their idol, glorious Harry Clay: —

> By little Jimmy Polk of Tennessee;
>   Oolah, a-lah, oolah ee
> Let's climb the wild persimmon tree! [19]

3

"Who is James K. Polk?" The question sounded incessantly with sarcastic inflection in Whig papers and Whig stump speeches till it created the familiar picture of a mediocre politician lifted, accidentally, from obscurity that has only recently been erased from the

---

[16] Greeley, *Recollections of a Busy Life*, 167.
[17] T. T. Munger, *Horace Bushnell: Preacher and Theologian*, 44–45.
[18] Samuel Lawrence to Amos Lawrence, November 12, 1844, Lawrence Papers.
[19] McCormac, *Polk*, chap. xiii.

histories.[20] Yet Polk's services in the Jacksonian struggles entitled him to a more illustrious name. As floor manager and as Speaker of the House, he had proved himself a keen and competent leader. Drafted into Tennessee politics to recover the state from the Whigs, he had two successful terms as Governor, almost became the vice-presidential nominee in 1840, and was slated to be Van Buren's running mate in 1844. He was well known far beyond his state. A Massachusetts paper, for example, predicted as early as 1839 that he would be President.[21]

Only forty-nine years old when elected, Polk was the youngest man up to that day to occupy the White House. Still the pleasant, unassuming, rather dignified man whom Washington remembered from the eighteen-thirties, he came to his new responsibilities with something of an inferiority complex, aware, as he confessed to Samuel J. Tilden, that he did not arrive with "the same personal strength" as some of his predecessors. But he was determined, as he put it, to be *locum tenens* for nobody; old Thomas Ritchie reported him "very sensitive to the idea of compulsion"; and he would not even be ruled by his hero and political benefactor, General Jackson. Polk stoutly disregarded, for example, Jackson's wish that the *Washington Globe* be continued as the organ of the administration; he ignored Jackson's warnings against Robert J. Walker; and he rejected Jackson's suggestion that Amos Kendall and W. B. Lewis be given government jobs.[22]

While not a statesman of the first rank, lacking the creative political capacities of a Jefferson or Jackson, Polk has been excelled by few Presidents in his ability to concentrate the energies of his administration toward the attainment of given ends. "There are four great measures," he early declared to George Bancroft, striking his thigh to emphasize his remarks, "which are to be the measures of my administration: one, a reduction of the tariff; another, the independent treasury; a third, the settlement of the Oregon boundary question; and lastly, the

[20] The rehabilitation of Polk still apparently has far to go before it reaches the general public, though it is to be hoped that Bernard De Voto's admirable portrait in *The Year of Decision: 1846* will have some effect. As recently as 1937, Mr. James Thurber, a highly intelligent layman, could exclaim with wonder at the sight of "a person who, eighty or more years after Polk's death, could actually give three facts about the man. . . . For of all our array of Presidents, there was none less memorable than James K. Polk." *Let Your Mind Alone!* (New York), 141.

[21] "Mr. Polk is yet a young man — but a little more than forty, we believe — and will by and by be President of these United States." *Plymouth Rock and County Advertiser*, May 9, 1839.

[22] Tilden to W. H. Havemeyer (?), March 4, 1845, to J. L. O'Sullivan, May 31, 1845, Tilden, *Letters and Literary Memorials*, John Bigelow, ed., 27–28, 34–35; McCormac, *Polk*, 306 ff.

acquisition of California." [23] He set out to realize these objectives with calm, implacable force, moving with steady determination to clear away all obstacles, and insisting on the subordination of all personal ambitions to these purposes.

Not anticipating this executive force, people had awaited his choice of cabinet with great concern as indicating the influence under which his administration would fall. The announcement had been unenlightening: Buchanan as Secretary of State, Walker in the Treasury, Marcy and Bancroft in War and Navy — a cabinet of prima donnas which severally dissatisfied the Van Buren, Cass and Calhoun factions, the three largest groups in the party, and gave little promise of a united and effective administration. But Polk's firm will and his lucid conception of what he wanted to do made him the master. Renouncing a second term for himself, he obliged each cabinet member similarly to renounce presidential aspirations. As Bancroft remarked many years later, he was always the center of his administration, always controlling his Secretaries so that they acted in unison.[24]

Secretive and suspicious, he kept his own counsel, and he possessed, as Gideon Welles rather irritably phrased it, "a trait of sly cunning which he thought shrewdness." [25] Moreover, an extremely hard worker himself, with a retentive memory and a mastery of detail, he was not a President to be overawed by the claims of cabinet members to dictate policy in their fields. Indeed, his inability to delegate responsibility was a major fault. "I prefer to supervise the whole operations of the Government myself rather than entrust the public business to subordinates," he declared, "and this makes my duties very great." [26] He actually left Washington only twice in the first eighteen months of his term, and then but for the day.[27] When he said in 1847, "though I occupy a very high position, I am the hardest working man in this country," he was probably speaking the literal truth.[28] He drove himself relentlessly, and his presidency so exhausted him that he died a few months after he left the White House. He knew what he wanted, and got it, but it killed him.

The first two items on his program — the reduction of the tariff and the re-establishment of the independent treasury — were high on the

[23] James Schouler, *History of the United States of America under the Constitution*, IV, 498.

[24] Bancroft to J. G. Wilson, March 8, 1888, J. G. Wilson, ed., *The Presidents of the United States*, 230.

[25] Welles, "Political History of the Forties," 33, Welles Papers.

[26] Polk, *Diary*, IV, 261.

[27] Polk to Buchanan, February 17, 1845, Curtis, *Buchanan*, I, 548; Polk, *Diary*, II, 84.

[28] Polk, *Diary*, II, 360.

radical agenda, and Polk's policy commanded the warm support of the radical Democrats. But they were prevented from assuming a proprietary attitude toward these reforms by the direct role of Robert J. Walker, as Secretary of the Treasury, in achieving them. Walker's erratic and checkered past, his part in defeating Van Buren at Baltimore, and Jackson's well-known distrust for him ruined him in the eyes of the radical wing. But he fought for Polk's program on good hard-money grounds, and executed it with great ability.

After setting the independent-treasury system into efficient operation, he turned to the problem of tariff revision. His Report of December 3, 1845, gave the classic statement of the Democratic case against protection. "It is deemed just," Walker wrote, "that taxation, whether direct or indirect, should be as nearly as practicable in proportion to property." From this premise he moved to a vigorous criticism of high tariffs as "a mere subtraction of so much money from the people, to increase the resources of the protected classes." Far from benefiting labor, it was a means of delivering the workingman into the power of capital by increasing the control of capital over wages.[29] Walker's own ideas were embodied in the tariff enacted after a bitter fight in 1846. (Polk's "range of vision extends only to the capitalist," charged Horace Greeley, ". . . him he teaches all other classes to envy and hate as a general oppressor.")[30] By the spring of 1847 Walker was so worn out that, with throat raw and bandaged, he could converse only by writing on a slate, and Polk was convinced he had not long to live.[31]

4

Yet, though Polk's financial policy was fully in the Jacksonian tradition, and though his management of the third item — Oregon — won the approval of the radicals, feelings between the administration and the Barnburners became nevertheless increasingly embittered. Polk's course on the fourth item — California — was to bring to maturity a discord whose seeds were already well sown.

Polk himself clearly perceived the origin of the conflict. "Mr. Van Buren became offended with me at the beginning of my administration," he wrote in 1847, "because I chose to exercise my own judgment in the selection of my own Cabinet."[32] The friends of Van

[29] F. W. Taussig, ed., *State Papers on Tariff*, 225, 231, 227.
[30] Greeley, "Pandora," *American Whig Review*, III, 103 (January, 1846).
[31] Polk, *Diary*, III, 18.
[32] Polk, *Diary*, III, 74.

Buren, feeling that their leader had been cheated out of the presidency, thought that Polk should serve more or less as his deputy. The federal patronage, they believed, should be used to strengthen the Barn-burners; and, when Polk used it to unite the whole party, they construed each rebuff as treachery. Disbelieving in Polk's independence, they concluded that he had sold out to the slaveholders.

Polk had actually made many attempts to placate them. At the start, he offered cabinet posts to Wright and Butler, both of whom declined. The next man in New York with a national reputation was Marcy, to whom Polk then proffered the War Department. Van Buren had recommended Flagg or Cambreleng, but someone more learned in the intricacies of New York politics than Polk might have been pardoned the selection of Marcy, who had never been distinctly anti-Jacksonian in state or national affairs, who was closely identified with Van Buren in national politics, and who indeed had carried on certain delicate negotiations for Van Buren (such as persuading Bancroft to write a campaign biography) just before the recent convention. In addition, Polk, at Van Buren's strong recommendation, tendered the Navy Department to George Bancroft. (The ex-President urged Polk not to be deceived, by Bancroft's literary reputation, into underestimating his practical ability: "the error consists in attaching to Yankees who are literary men the same disqualifications in business which almost invariably attach to those of other races, but from which they and the Scotch are very generally exempt, wanting only opportunity . . . to qualify themselves for everything.") [83]

But Marcy and Bancroft did not constitute in Barnburner eyes sufficient guarantees of their interests. Then Polk dismissed Frank Blair, closed up the *Globe* and installed Thomas Ritchie and the *Washington Union* as the new party organ. Polk had good grounds for objecting to Blair, whom he regarded as likely to be an obstacle both to party harmony and to his own freedom of action. The *Globe*, he correctly considered, would be the organ of Van Buren and Benton, not of the Polk administration. Blair was openly hostile to Calhoun, he was not trusted by Cass, and he had alienated most of the Democrats who dallied with Tyler. "It is impossible," Polk observed to Jackson, "for him to command the support of the whole party." He resented moreover Blair's attempts to run the government from the editorial rooms of the *Globe*. "I must be the head of my own adminis-

---

[83] Van Buren to Polk, March 1, 1845, Van Buren Papers. Marcy's candid guess was that Wright and Flagg would probably favor his appointment, Van Buren and "the whole *barnburning* interest" oppose it, and the Hunkers "would probably be moderately inclined towards me but not very actively." Marcy to P. M. Wetmore, November 10, 1844, Marcy Papers.

tration, and will not be controlled by any newspaper." And he suspected Blair of lukewarmness toward himself.[34] But the radical Democrats, unable to understand this treatment of the faithful champion of Jacksonian democracy, could only assume that he had been sold down the river as part of a deal with Calhoun.

The President's efforts to use the patronage in New York to heal the party split, instead of to build up the Barnburners, confirmed their conviction of his perfidy. Yet here again he was only seeking party unity. "Nothing could satisfy them," he remarked, "unless I were to identify myself with them, and proscribe all other branches of the Democratic party. I will do, as I have done, Mr. Martin Van Buren's friends full justice in the bestowal of public patronage, but I cannot proscribe all others of the Democratic party in order to gain their good will." [35] Actually Polk's policy dissatisfied Van Buren's opponents equally. One day Daniel Dickinson, the Hunker Senator from New York, stormed into the presidential office, threatening to resign if a Hunker were not immediately appointed to a certain office. "I felt very indignant at this attempt to bully," observed Polk characteristically, "but restrained my temper & said to him, when you get cooler you will probably think better of it. . . . I had become perfectly indifferent whether Mr. Dickinson and Mr. Marcy resigned or not." Polk would swear a plague on both the houses. "I am perfectly disgusted with the petty local strife between these factions. . . . I have in many cases refused to lend myself to either & have alternately given offense to both." [36]

Yet it remains true that the Barnburners had stronger claims to official favor than the Hunkers. They were much more reliable supporters of the administration's economic policy, for example, and they had hardly expected that men of unimpeachable Jacksonian orthodoxy would be put on a plane of equality with the descendants of the old Conservatives. Polk was undoubtedly misinformed about the extent to which the New York squabbles involved principles, and perhaps in part deliberately so, by men like Buchanan and Walker who were anxious to whittle down Silas Wright as a presidential possibility. Certainly Polk elsewhere demonstrated his basic sympathy with the radical position on Jacksonian issues, not only by his own program, but by his appointments in other states, such as Ohio and Massachusetts.

[34] Polk to Jackson, March 17, 26, 1845, Jackson, *Correspondence*, VI, 382, 390; Polk, *Diary*, I, 356–358; Smith, *Blair Family*, I, 163–183.

[35] Polk, *Diary*, I, 104.

[36] Polk, *Diary*, II, 404, 405. See also *Diary*, II, 20, and Marcy's angry letter listing Barnburner appointments in New York, to G. W. Newell, February 25, 1846, Marcy Papers.

He made Marcus Morton Collector of Boston, for example, and fought for his confirmation against the opposition of Southerners who were denouncing him (with some prompting from Henshaw, Hallett and Rantoul) as an abolitionist.[37]

In any case, the Barnburner theory that Polk was discriminating against them for the benefit of any other faction had no foundation. Polk's unswerving insistence on unity infuriated while it intimidated every section of the party. The private letters of anti-Barnburner Democrats in Polk's first year were filled with the familiar resentments, only they were directed against Polk for going over to Van Buren. Calhoun, angry at not being kept on as Secretary of State, could see but one explanation — "I stood in the way of the restoration of the old Jackson Regime." "Instead of an independent man," complained another Calhounite, "we have elected a Prest. bound hand and foot to the Van's." The refrain was inescapable. "Benton, Blair and the New York regency can command any thing." "Polk's administration is assuming almost an exclusive Van Buren character." [38]

Variations would ascribe the controlling influence to Walker or to Buchanan, but all the theories were based on the fallacy that James K. Polk was incapable of running his own administration. Yet even he could hold the factions together only by sheer force of will. The issues in the wake of Texas would transfigure faction and make party conflicts burst the political bonds.

5

The Jacksonian unity was breaking down. And Old Hickory himself? The old man still refused to die. His body was racked by the pain of old wounds, his constitution undermined by the hardships of the Creek campaign thirty years before, but his will was adamant, and on he lived. Years of tobacco chewing had left him with throbbing temples and shattering headaches. Tuberculosis had wasted away one lung and diseased the other. Dropsy and diarrhea had reduced him to helplessness, and his remedies were primitive — bleeding

[37] Weisenburger, *Passing of the Frontier*, 425; E. A. Holt, *Party Politics in Ohio, 1840–1850*, 221; Polk, *Diary*, I, 206–207, 371.

[38] Calhoun to R. M. T. Hunter, March 26, 1845, Hunter, *Correspondence*, 76; L. S. Coryell to Calhoun, May 27, 1845, *Correspondence Addressed to Calhoun*, 295; W. A. Harris to Calhoun, July 11, 1845, Calhoun, *Correspondence*, 1038; Aaron Hobart to Bancroft, April 14, 1845, Bancroft Papers. The son of President Tyler wrote three quarters of a century later, "So completely did Polk fall into the hands of Benton and the Van Buren faction that the friends of Mr. Calhoun shared just as badly as Mr. Tyler's." L. G. Tyler, "The Annexation of Texas," *Tyler's Quarterly Historical and Genealogical Magazine*, VI, 92.

to check hemorrhage, and calomel. Tall, ghostlike and fleshless, with his brush of snow-white hair, he could eat little more than rice and milk.

Yet he clung to life with unconquerable toughness. No stab of suffering could extract from him a word of irritation or self-pity. His intellect remained as keen and vigorous as ever, and his manner, as Paulding noted when visiting the Hermitage in 1842, "more kind, graceful, and benevolent, than that of any man who has ever fallen under my observation." [89] He ruled his plantation like a patriarch. In the morning, when he could rise, he would ride around the land, pausing to talk with his favorite groom about the colts, then to the fields, where the Negroes picking cotton gave three cheers for him. In the evening he conducted family prayers. And always he followed politics with avidity, never ceasing to make fierce and decisive suggestions about the destiny of his nation. . . . But death was irresistible, and even General Jackson could not stay its hand. [40]

The shadows fell longer over the Hermitage, and in the late afternoons the old General, leaning on his tall ebony cane, would walk up and down the long porch; then, in the last flare of sunset, he would stride, erect and steady, across the green lawns to his wife's grave. Eighteen-forty-four gave way to 1845, and Mr. Polk was safely installed in the presidency. June came, with the still, heavy heat of Tennessee summer. On the morning of Sunday, June 8, after a week of unusual feebleness, the General fell into dead-pale unconsciousness. A long wail of anguish rose up from the slaves in the house and echoed through the fields and stables. "Oh, Lord! Oh, Lord! Old Massa's dead! Old Massa's dead!" But soon the mists fell away, and the old man recovered consciousness. Major Lewis arrived at the bedside at noon to receive messages for Benton, for Blair, for Sam Houston.

On pressed the afternoon, and around the high bedstead with the tall mahogany posts his friends stood in tears. Outside the window the slaves clustered in lamentation, and his body servants joined the group in the room. "Do not cry," said the dying man, rousing himself for a moment, "I shall meet you in heaven, yes I hope to meet you all in heaven white and black." A new burst of moaning greeted his words. He looked around. "Why should you weep? I am in the hands of the Lord! who is about to relieve me, you should rejoice, not weep!" "Oh, do not cry. Be good children, and we will all meet in heaven." He was given an anodyne and did not speak again. At six

[89] W. I. Paulding, *Paulding*, 289.
[40] Parton, *Jackson*, III, 667–668; Rachel Jackson Lawrence, "Andrew Jackson at Home," *McClure's*, IX, 792–794 (July, 1897).

o'clock, with the evening sun flooding through the windows, he had a slight convulsion, his underjaw dropped, and his breathing faded so gently that they hardly knew when he died. Sarah Yorke Jackson, who was holding his hand, suddenly fainted, and they carried her away. Through the plantation spread the moan of death.[41]

The funeral was a great mass meeting, white and black jostling together in an agony of grief, cramming the house and waiting patiently outside to follow the body to its resting place in the shade beside his beloved Rachel. Between the funeral sermon and the burial a wildly twittering parrot, a household pet, broke into raucous profanity and was taken away. When the body was lowered into the grave, the stone was left off for all to look a last time. The slave women in their anguish pressed in among the friends of their old master, leaving the laces and shawls of white women wet with tears. "Death did not make all equal," said one observer, "more completely than did this funeral." [42]

Pondering a day later on Jackson's greatness, Justice Catron was tempted to ascribe it all to the magnificence of his leadership. "The way a thing should be done struck him plainly — & he adopted the plan." If it were not the best, it would still do, if well executed. "To the execution he brought a hardy industry, and a sleepless energy, few could equal." But most of all "his awful *will*, stood alone, & was made the will of all he commanded." "If he had fallen from the clouds into a city on fire, he would have been at the head of the extinguishing host in an hour, & would have blown up a palace to stop the fire with as little mis-giving as another would have torn down a board shed. In a moment he would have willed it proper — & in ten minutes the thing would have been done. Those who never worked before, who had hardly courage to cry, would have rushed to the execution, and applied the match."

"Hence it is," said Catron, "that timid men, and feeble women, have rushed to onslaught when he gave the command — fierce, fearless, and unwavering, for the first time." Hence it was that for fifty years he

[41] There are several eyewitness accounts of Jackson's death. I have drawn particularly on those printed in Parton, *Jackson*, III, 678–679; Rachel J. Lawrence, "Andrew Jackson at Home," *loc. cit.*; the statement of Old Hannah, Jackson, *Correspondence*, VI, 415; the statement of Elizabeth Martin Randolph Donelson, Pauline W. Burke, *Emily Donelson of Tennessee*, II, 18; the statements of G. P. A. Healy as given in his letter to Van Buren of July 7, 1857, Van Buren Papers, and in his *Reminiscences of a Portrait Painter*, 144–146. See also Marquis James's moving reconstruction in *Andrew Jackson: Portrait of a President*, 496–500.

[42] John Catron to Buchanan, June 11, 1845, McCormac, *Polk*, 7–8; W. M. Norment to S. G. Heiskell, February 18, 1921, Heiskell, *Jackson and Early Tennessee History*, III, 54.

had been followed by the broad land; hence it was that he had swept over all opposition, "terrible and clean as a prairie fire, leaving hardly a smoke of the ruin behind." [43]

The people felt an emptiness in their hearts. Michael Shiner, the poor free Negro of the Washington shipyards, set forth their aching sorrow. "the Hon Major General andrew Jackson is gone and his voice are heared no moore on earth. But his name still lives in the heart of the American people his spirit has takein its fligth it has gone to the one that first gave it and now i trust he is setting on the Right hand of god reaping his reward." [44]

[43] Catron to Buchanan, *loc. cit.*
[44] Michael Shiner, mss. Diary, 87, Library of Congress.

XXXIV FREE SOIL

TEXAS was annexed early in 1845 by joint congressional resolution, and in January, 1846, Polk ordered American troops under Zachary Taylor to advance through territory claimed by Mexico to the Rio Grande. Manifest Destiny was coming to a boil, and Van Buren, at ease in Lindenwald, deserved congratulation for clairvoyance. General Taylor waited at the head of the rabble army in the disputed land, while Polk tried vainly to buy the northern provinces of Mexico. Then, on April 24, Mexican and American soldiers clashed. The news arrived in Washington just in time to destroy all opposition to Polk's plan of gaining by war what he could not gain by negotiation. From South to North the common man lined up at recruiting offices and said farewell to his tearful family: in New England, far indeed from the Rio Grande, Seth Luther, the veteran agitator for the rights of labor, claimed to be the first Yankee volunteer.[1] The American democracy prepared to broaden the area of freedom. "It is for the interest of mankind," wrote Walter Whitman, the Brooklyn editor, "that its power and territory should be extended — the farther the better."[2]

1

Portrait of a radical Democrat: David Wilmot of Bradford County, Pennsylvania, thirty years old in 1844. In local politics he had fought against imprisonment for debt and for hard money. He had stood manfully by the independent treasury. He had borne himself gallantly in the rout of 1840. Elected to the House in 1845, he had registered the only Pennsylvania vote in favor of the Walker tariff. An ardent Van Buren man from the start, he had helped whip Pennsylvania into line in 1844. But, like other radicals, he had diverged to support the annexation of Texas.

[1] Marcus Morton to W. L. Marcy, June 2, 1846, Morton Letterbooks; Hartz, "Seth Luther: Working Class Rebel," *New England Quarterly*, XIII, 410. Luther never reached the front; he broke down a few weeks after enlistment and was confined to the East Cambridge asylum.

[2] *Brooklyn Eagle*, December 2, 1847, Whitman, *Gathering of the Forces*, I, 266. The best account of this year is Bernard DeVoto, *The Year of Decision: 1846.*

A plump, baby-faced man, slovenly in dress, a cud of tobacco in his mouth and hair tending to fall about his eyes, David Wilmot remained a thoroughgoing Jacksonian, conceiving his political duty to be the defense of the rights of labor. In terms of this duty he began to understand more and more, as the war progressed, the point which had stuck in Van Buren's throat in 1844. Would the new land acquired by the war become the property of the free workingman of the North, or would it be sequestered by the slaveholder of the South?

Preston King was already at work in his cheerful and persuasive way, seeking to unite the Northern Congressmen. Wilmot soon joined King, Jacob Brinkerhoff of Ohio, Hannibal Hamlin of Maine and other young antislavery Democrats in an informal Northern steering committee. Each supposed himself the leader of the group; but, as Gideon Welles observed, King, "without making pretensions, was the man, the hand, that bound this sheaf together." [3] They saw their chance in August, 1846, when Polk requested an appropriation of two million dollars in order to negotiate with Mexico.

Early in the evening of a humid August day, with candles and lamps burning brightly in the dark chamber of the House, while members sat about drinking ice water and fanning themselves with folded newspapers, David Wilmot moved that the appropriations bill be amended so as to exclude slavery from all territory acquired in the war. "I would preserve for free white labor," he later declared, "a fair country, a rich inheritance, where the sons of toil, of my own race and color, can live without the disgrace which association with negro slavery brings upon free labor." [4] Or, as Preston King put it when reintroducing the Wilmot Proviso in February, 1847, "The time has come when this republic should declare by law that it will not be made an instrument to the extension of slavery. . . . If slavery

[3] Welles, *Diary*, II, 385; Welles, "Political History of the Forties," 19–21.

[4] C. B. Going, *David Wilmot: Free Soiler*, 98–100, 174. Brinkerhoff, in later years, put in a claim for authorship of the Proviso; but the idea itself was not original, in fact only a revival of Jefferson's proposal for the Northwest Territory, and some such movement was inevitable. Wilmot's more prominent role in its introduction was sustained in the subsequent careers of both men. Going admirably weighs the rival claims, *Wilmot*, 117–141.

Welles suggested in his "Political History," 23, that Wilmot's action came in part from a desire to rehabilitate himself in the North after his vote on the Walker tariff, which was construed in the South as a pro-Southern vote. Actually Wilmot's tariff vote was popular in his district. The grounds for his resentment of the South went much deeper; and since his action was thoroughly consistent with his past course, thoroughly borne out by his course in the future, and along the same lines as most of the leading Van Buren Democrats, it seems idle, as certain modern writers have done, to reduce the Wilmot Proviso to a petty act of political finagling.

is not excluded by law, the presence of the slave will exclude the laboring white man." [5]

The Proviso failed of passage, but the free-soil issue was now formulated and laid before the country in terms which invoked deep Jacksonian sentiments. "The question," cried Walter Whitman, ". . . is a question between *the grand body of white workingmen, the millions of mechanics, farmers, and operatives of our country*, with their interests on the one side — and the interests of the few thousand rich, 'polished,' and aristocratic owners of slaves at the South, on the other side." [6]

But another Jacksonian thought differently. "The agitation of the slavery question is mischievous & wicked," declared James K. Polk, "and proceeds from no patriotic motive by its authors." The Wilmot Proviso appeared, to him, "mischievous & foolish,": and the whole movement seemed a gratuitous disturbance by which "demagogues & ambitious politicians hope to promote their own prospects." [7]

This hostility did not arise from any particular solicitude for slavery. Polk refused to be, in any active sense, proslavery or antislavery; he was simply trying to carry on in terms of the Jacksonian unity — to extend into the eighteen-forties the neutrality of the eighteen-thirties. His whole experience had assumed the social existence and political nonexistence of slavery, and, as a man, he flatly did not feel the moral urgencies which were tearing the Jacksonian unity apart. "Slavery," he would say, "was one of the questions adjusted in the compromises of the Constitution. It has, and can have no legitimate connection with the War with Mexico." [8] Why then should the Barnburners wantonly press a dangerous issue which would only split the party without accomplishing anything for the nation?

Polk's great defect was an inability to recognize the honesty of opposition. It was always selfish and factious, based on ambition or jealousy or disappointment over patronage. This dry assumption of infallibility gave his administration its peculiar strength — its decision, its firmness of purpose, its steady selection of ends, and its precise achievement of them. But it was also responsible for its peculiar weakness. As a result of misjudging the grounds of opposition, Polk consistently underestimated its moral force. His most signal failure was the refusal to perceive the moral irrepressibility of the slavery question.

For many, in the forties, neutrality seemed increasingly a hypocrisy.

---

[5] Hammond, *Wright*, 706–707.
[6] *Brooklyn Eagle*, September 1, 1847, Whitman, *Gathering of the Forces*, I, 208.
[7] Polk, *Diary*, IV, 251, II, 75.
[8] Polk, *Diary*, II, 305.

The passions of the day thus produced a theory, which later gained a brief currency among historians, that Polk was the agent of a slave-holders' conspiracy. This theory had two main sources — the historical writings of the Van Buren Democrats, especially Judge Hammond's life of Silas Wright and Benton's *Thirty Years' View*, and the polemics of the New England reformers, especially Theodore Parker's articles in the *Massachusetts Quarterly Review* and the *Biglow Papers* of James Russell Lowell.

Yet Polk was thoroughly honest when he told Wilmot that he had no desire to extend slavery; that the whole Proviso controversy was a fuss over "an abstract question," since slavery would almost certainly never exist in New Mexico or California.[9] He took care to avoid close relations with the ardent proslavery annexationists, and he never was on good terms with either of the groups which represented the planters, the Southern Whigs or the Calhoun Democrats. Indeed, the hysteria in defense of slavery appalled him as much as the hysteria against it. "There is no patriotism on either side," he curtly said, and he believed that Calhoun, grown "perfectly desperate in his aspirations to the Presidency," had seized on the sectional question "as the only means of sustaining himself in his present fallen conditions." The Barnburners, he feared, would accept this challenge with only too much delight in order to thrust forward Silas Wright. Both groups "desire to mount slavery as a hobby, and hope to secure the election of their favourite upon it. . . . I am utterly disgusted at such intriguing."[10] When Calhoun appealed to Polk's Southern blood in order to incite him against the North, Polk told him that "I gave no countenance to any movement which tended to violence or the disunion of the states," and he condemned the Calhoun Democrats who joined with Whigs to reject Northern Democrats of supposed antislavery leanings nominated by Polk for government posts. "I put my face alike," he said, "against southern agitators and Northern fanatics."[11]

2

But Northern anxiety over the question of slavery was increasing. The agitations of two decades were beginning to tell. The religious antislavery men, who were mostly conservative on economic issues, caring more about the Negro than about the white man at home, were infecting large sectors of the Whig party, while the political antislavery

[9] Polk, *Diary*, II, 308, 289; McCormac, *Polk*, 612–616.
[10] Polk, *Diary*, II, 348, 458–459.
[11] Polk, *Diary*, IV, 288, I, 369, IV, 299.

men, who were primarily concerned for the future of white labor, were having increasing influence among the Democrats.

Already there were signs that the two groups might join forces. John Greenleaf Whittier, one of the few ethical abolitionists with much instinct for practical politics, had earlier recognized that Van Buren, the master politician, erred in trying to make Texas the issue; the people were too much in favor of annexation. "But a large portion of our noisiest Democrats even, who are hoarse with hurras for Texas," Whittier observed, "would be glad if that ugly matter of slavery could [be] shown not to be after all an inevitable condition of annexation." The fight should be made, not against expansion ("let us not attempt impossibilities"), but against the admission of more slave states.[12] David Wilmot now supplied this fight with its exact issue.

For their leader the antislavery men were thinking more and more of Van Buren's lieutenant, the Governor of New York, Silas Wright. Wright had not wanted to become Governor, accepting the nomination only when the obligations of party, which for a member of the Regency superseded everything but personal honor, required his service. "Never has any incident in the course of my public life," he declared shortly afterward, "been so much against my interests, and feelings, and judgment." He did not think he would be defeated in the election, but he knew that "success will most effectually beat me"; and he confessed a deep conviction that "defeat would be the best thing."[13] This doomed sense surged through a naturally pessimistic temperament. He would remark in private conversation that, seeing no escape from the governorship, he had decided that it would end his political career.[14]

There was good reason for Wright's apprehensions. The New York political situation was insoluble in its intricate antagonisms. Wright knew he could not unite the party, whatever course he took, and, in becoming the leader of the Barnburners, he would expose himself to the full venom of the Hunkers. "His nomination is the fatality," observed W. H. Seward. "Election or defeat exhausts him."[15] Wright's

[12] Whittier to E. Wright, Jr., October 14 [1844], S. T. Pickard, ed., *Whittier as a Politician*, 34.

[13] Wright to Buchanan, September 23, 1844, Curtis, *Buchanan*, I, 522; Wright to D. S. Dickinson, October 9, 1844, J. R. Dickinson, *Speeches; Correspondence, Etc., of the Late Daniel S. Dickinson*, II, 371.

[14] G. W. Newell to Marcy, March 29, 1845, Marcy Papers.

[15] Seward remarked later that Wright was a strong man till the day of his nomination; "he fell far, and if left alone will be not what he might have been . . . lineal heir to Jackson." See Seward's letters of August 23 and September, 1844, Seward, *Seward*, 723, 725.

genius, moreover, was that of the parliamentarian, not that of the executive. Calhoun, who could not believe that Wright would accept the nomination, is supposed to have exclaimed that his place was in the Senate. "He wields a power there that few men can contend against. He has a logical mind, thoroughly understands the business of legislation, and leads a majority of the body with a degree of tact and skill unsurpassed in the history of Congress. He is an adroit advocate of other men's measures, but without power of origination. With Mr. Van Buren for a leader, he is almost irresistible; thrown upon his own resources, he is sure to fail." [16]

Whatever the reason, Wright went into every battle of his administration subconsciously prepared for defeat. "From all I can learn," wrote Marcy in 1846, he "acts as if he was *paralised*"; and in 1849 Marcy, looking back at a once strong admiration, declared that Wright was not himself after he went to Albany, "or he never was the man I supposed him to be." [17] Though not by ordinary standards a failure, Wright's governorship aroused his enemies without gaining any striking victories for his friends, and its general air was one of indecision. When his term expired in 1846, the Hunkers, angry at his radical economic policy, were determined to oust him. But the Barnburners, under the brilliant direction of John Van Buren, controlled the convention and insured his renomination.

Polk's attitude further confused the situation. In 1845 he had told John L. O'Sullivan that he considered Wright "the first man in the country for any place in it," and there can be no doubt that his personal feelings toward Wright continued friendly. [18] Yet he held to his theory that both wings of the New York party should be conciliated long after the Hunkers had marked Wright for destruction. As Bancroft told Wright in 1846, the problems of New York were simply not understood in Washington. The effect of Polk's policy was in the end to create the impression in New York that the administration opposed Wright. Some of the federal officeholders were hostile to him in 1846, and the Hunkers as a whole did their best to knife his candidacy. As a result, his vote declined fifty-four thousand, and he was beaten. "I doubt whether the President designed the result," observed Wright, who was a fair-minded man, "but it matters not in the effect, as those who have influenced him did." [19] When Polk

[16] T. N. Parmelee, "Recollections of an Old Stager," *Harper's*, XLVII, 758 (October, 1873).

[17] Marcy to P. M. Wetmore, January 21, 1846, endorsement by Marcy, June, 1849, on G. W. Newell to Marcy, March 29, 1845, Marcy Papers.

[18] O'Sullivan to Van Buren, March 28, 1845, Van Buren Papers.

[19] Wright to J. M. Niles, November 6, 1846, Miscellaneous Letters, New York

heard the news, he recognized that the main cause of Wright's defeat was the "lukewarmness and secret opposition" of the Hunkers. "This faction," Polk wrote in cold anger, "shall hereafter receive no favours at my hands if I know it." [20]

Convinced that his political career was over, plain Mr. Wright retired to his simple frame house in the little village of Canton. But the nation was not so certain. Far from discrediting him, defeat made him a martyr to the slave power. The cool and daring course pursued by Preston King in Congress reflected additional glory, for King, as Wright's protégé, and Representative of his district, was regarded as his spokesman, much as in past years Wright had been regarded the spokesman of Van Buren. When the Wilmot Proviso established the issue, no one could doubt Wright's position. "I shall regard a decision against Mr. King," he wrote in January, 1847, "as fatal to this administration." And again in April: "I am surprised that any one should suppose me capable of entertaining any other opinion, or giving any other answer, to such a proposition." "The question will be readily settled," he declared in private conversation, ". . . if all the free states should now act as an entire body in the defence and support of free territory, as the South in latter times have and will continue to act in efforts to extend slavery." [21]

3

Eighteen–forty-eight was drawing near, and, through the North, men were pondering how best to bring the free states to act as "an entire body" in defense of free territory. In May the leader of the antislavery men in Ohio, a keen young man named Salmon P. Chase, wrote an important letter to John P. Hale. Chase had been working with the Liberty party, and Hale seemed its probable nominee for 1848. But Chase was dubious about third-party prospects. "As fast as we can bring public sentiment right," he pointed out, "the other parties will approach our ground, and keep sufficiently close to it to prevent any great accession to our numbers. If this be so, the Liberty party can never hope to accomplish any thing as such, but only through it, an indirect action upon the other parties."

Public Library. For Wright's relations with Polk, see their correspondence of 1845–46, printed, along with other material, in Gillet, *Wright*, 1643–1702; see also Hammond, *Wright*, 693–698.

[20] Polk, *Diary*, II, 218.

[21] Wright to Dix, January 19, 1847, to J. H. Titus, April 15, 1847, Gillet, *Wright*, 1918, 1874; Hammond, *Wright*, 714; Titus to the Committee, April 24, 1856, *Proceedings of the Meeting . . . on the 29th of April, 1856, . . . Opposed to . . . the Extension of Slavery*, 28.

Would it not thus be better simply to support all antiextension men in the major parties? "To build up a new party is by no means so easy as to compel old parties to do a particular work." Some antislavery men looked with hope to the Whig party. "I do not. . . . I fear that the Whig party will always look upon the overthrow of slavery as a work to be taken up or laid aside . . . as expediency may suggest; whereas," continued Chase, himself a former Whig, "if we can once get the Democratic party in *motion* regarding the overthrow of slavery as a legitimate and necessary result of principles, I would have no apprehension at all of the work being laid aside until accomplished." If the Democrats nominated Silas Wright, should not the antislavery men go for him? [22]

Two months later Chase was writing to Preston King, promising Wright the support of the Liberty party on a Wilmot Proviso platform. "For myself," added Chase, who had been forced steadily to the left by his passion against slavery, "I sympathize strongly with the Dem. Party in almost everything except its submission to slaveholding leadership & dictation." [23] In August, Thomas Hart Benton, who had avoided endorsing the Proviso by a legal quibble but was increasingly enraged by Southern arrogance, declared that the Democratic party must meet the challenge of Calhoun and nominate Van Buren or Wright, even at the cost of an open breach.[24] Through the North Wright's name began to appear on the mastheads of newspapers as the people's candidate for 1848. (The South felt the pressure: a devout follower of Calhoun woke up from an uneasy sleep after an oyster dinner with a shriek, "I thought that D——d fellow Silas Wright was on my breast pommelling me.") [25]

But Wright lived on quietly in Canton. The fretfulness and rancor of politics gave way to the simplicities of farming. He totally stopped drinking, set the thought of public life aside and turned with relief to the fields. Soon he was laboring three times as long as he had at the start. A visitor on a sultry day in June, 1847, found him hoeing potatoes, like a common farmer, the sweat streaming down his face. The hours passed quickly in the remote village, with the long day's work and the short evenings when the family gathered around the plain mahogany center table in the living room. Heat settled like a blanket on Canton in July and August, but Wright continued hard at work,

[22] Chase to Hale, May 12, 1847, R. B. Warden, *An Account of the Private Life and Public Services of Salmon Portland Chase*, 313–314.

[23] Chase to King, July 15, 1847, Chase, *Diary and Correspondence*, 121.

[24] Benton to Dix, August 22, 1847, Flagg Papers.

[25] J. A. Seddon to R. M. T. Hunter, November 16, 1844, Hunter, *Correspondence*, 74.

clearing ditches, loading dirt into a wagon, and beginning to rake and bind grain. On the eighteenth and again on the twenty-first of August he had sudden spasms of pain in his chest, but, when he rested, they passed off after a few minutes of profuse sweat.

On August 26 he attended a funeral, then worked till late on an unexpectedly chilly evening to get in the last of his grain. Early the next morning he went, as was his custom, to the post office for his mail. He had barely opened a letter when an ashy pallor came over his naturally florid face. Someone found him sitting there and insisted, over his protest, on calling a doctor. He was clearly in great pain, his eyes bloodshot and glassy, his forehead deadly pale, his chest heaving, his head resting on his hands. As new people drifted in and asked him how he felt, Wright answered the same questions over and over with infinite patience. The doctor administered an anodyne and Wright walked calmly back to his house. Feeling no better, he lay down on his bed with his clothes on. At ten o'clock he suddenly died.[26]

The North had not realized till then how much it had come to depend on him. On that fatal morning a paper in far Missouri had hoisted his name for the presidency, and the news of his death brought a cold chill to antislavery men. (The South rejoiced. "Burnt out at last," said Calhoun at Pendleton, knowing, as a friend would soon write him, that "if Silas Wright had lived we could not have prevented his nomination.")[27] Polk called him, in the privacy of his diary, "a great and a good man. . . . I deeply regret his death."[28]

Silas Wright was gone. "Rarely has a sadder phrase fall'n on the ears of the people," wrote Walt Whitman, "than that which met us so appallingly this morning — and which yet passes, with an almost incredulous wonder, from man to man: 'Silas Wright is dead.' Ah, it has a crashing effect, still! and we can hardly write the words." Our hopes, he exclaimed, "were so identified with this man — relied so upon him in the future — were so accustomed to look upon him as our tower of strength, and as a shield for righteous principle — that we indeed feel pressed to the very earth by such an unexpected blow!"[29]

David Wilmot expressed the dismay among the political leaders. You and I, he told Preston King, could fight the small battles, "but we

[26] For Wright's last months and death, see Wright to Flagg, March 12, 1847, J. L. Russell to Flagg, August 27, 1847, Flagg Papers; the various statements in Gillet, *Wright*, 1963–1970; Hammond, *Wright*, 722–731; J. S. Jenkins, *Life of Silas Wright*, 248–249.

[27] Perry, *Reminiscences of Public Men: Second Series*, 187; J. A. Campbell to Calhoun, December 20, 1847, Calhoun, *Correspondence*, 1153.

[28] Polk, *Diary*, III, 153.

[29] *Brooklyn Eagle*, August 28, 1847, Whitman, *Gathering of the Forces*, II, 185

want a man whose voice can reach and electrify the Nation." "There was more moral and political power united in his person, than in that of any other American Citizen." What can we do now? "Silas Wright has left behind him no living man in whom is contained the same elements of strength and moral grandeur of character. He was the man for the crisis." [30]

John Greenleaf Whittier's "The Lost Statesman" spoke for the religious antislavery men: —

> Man of the millions, thou art lost too soon!
> Who now shall rally Freedom's scattering host?
> Who wear the mantle of the leader lost?
> Who stay the march of slavery? [31]

The psychological necessities of the day had transmuted Silas Wright into a symbol. It was inevitable that the North create a leader to voice its moral sentiments against slavery: a man of the people, humble in origin, modest in circumstance, plain in manner, given to hard physical labor himself, digging on a farm in New York (or splitting rails in the shadowed backwoods of Illinois), so that his very life might embody a challenge to the values of the slaveholder. Still the leader could be no extremist, no fanatic, but a man who would give the South every latitude until principle was clearly threatened, and even then would place the Union above everything else; yet whose steady awakening to danger would express the awakening of the free states, and whose stern loyalty to principle would prevent the compromise of conscience. He had to be capable of jovial exchanges with the men of the town, of telling the companionable tale around the smoking stove; but, in the darkness of the night, his own inner conflicts must prepare him to comprehend the agony of a nation divided against itself, and his somber perception of the mystery of experience must endow him with a tragic sense and equip him for a tragic destiny.

As no other political leader, Silas Wright filled these specifications. Men of all shades, from rabid abolitionists to average citizens troubled about slavery extensions, could trust him to bear the burden of their anxieties. His essential conservatism reflected the reluctance of the North to tear away the bonds of peace, but his firmness expressed the profounder reluctance to share the guilt of slavery. "One so great and of such simplicity, so choice and almost unique, and yet so entirely of the common people," said George Bancroft, "the leader and

---

[30] Wilmot to King, September 25, 1847, Van Buren Papers.
[31] Whittier, *Complete Poetical Works* (Cambridge ed.), 304–305.

teacher and guide of the mass, and yet so unaspiringly of the mass, I never knew." [32]

The words could apply to another and greater man. Indeed, Silas Wright was a preliminary sketch for Abraham Lincoln. The bitter shock, the wild sense of irretrievable loss, which swept the North in 1847, was a forecast of the terrible vacancy which followed the murder at Ford's Theatre in 1865. [33]

4

A month after Silas Wright's death the Democrats of New York gathered at Syracuse for their state convention. It was a stormy meeting, embittered by fights over contested seats, state economic policy and slavery. When, at one point, someone spoke of doing justice to Silas Wright, and a Hunker answered with a sneer, "It is too late; he is dead," James S. Wadsworth, a leading Barnburner, sprang on a table and declared in tones that thrilled the hall: "Though it may be too late to do justice to Silas Wright, it is not too late to do justice to his assassins." [34] The Hunkers, with their bare majority, voted down the resolutions against the extension of slavery, and the Barnburners, walking out of the party, issued a call for a convention of their own at Herkimer in October.

The men who met at the Herkimer railroad station, the largest building in town, were in a grim and zealous mood. C. C. Cambreleng came out of retirement to act as president, and David Wilmot, the hero of the Proviso, appeared to define the predicament of Jacksonian reform. "It is the mission of the party," Wilmot declared in a ringing appeal to the spirit of the thirties, "to elevate man, to vindicate his rights, to secure his happiness — and shall its progress be averted? Shall its high aims and purposes be defeated, because Slavery commands

[32] Bancroft to Bryant, November 3, 1847, Howe, *Bancroft*, II, 27.
[33] All the biographies of Wright were written by people who knew him and were under the influence of the Wright myth which grew up in 1847 and the few years following. Consequently they are severely denatured, presenting much more of a saint than a fallible but honest man. Hammond's life was written in the midst of partisan excitements which make it a much less valuable and discriminating work than the first two volumes which compose with it his political history of New York. Jenkins's life was a hack work, and Gillet's, though written many years after Wright's death, is marred by a tone of eulogy as well as by a tendency to make out that Gillet himself, in pursuing a conservative course on slavery, was not being disloyal to Wright. None of these biographies, for example, makes any honest attempt to treat his intemperance. Wright's letters tend to be crisp and racy, exhibiting a tolerant, humorous man, candid, sincere, adept in political management and without vanity.
[34] Stanton, *Random Recollections*, 160.

a halt? . . . If the South cannot keep pace with the age, and the progress of Democratic reform . . . let her not drag us down from the high destiny before us." [35]

John Van Buren, cool, incisive and unusually serious, delivered the main address, protesting "in behalf of the free white laborers of the North and South, in behalf of the Emigrant from abroad, in behalf of posterity, and in the name of freedom" against the further extension of slavery. In a set of glowing phrases, the convention crystallized the radical aspirations: "Free Trade, Free Labor, Free Soil, Free Speech and Free Men." [36]

John Van Buren had taken a good deal from the Hunkers in the past few years without striking back. "I have forborne much," he told his father late in 1847, "on your account and Mr. Wright's. Mr. W. is dead, and I assume that you are sincere in not wishing to return to public life. I can, therefore, hurt no one but myself." [37] Now he was on the warpath and fighting mad. Under his direction the Barnburners sabotaged the Syracuse ticket and tumbled it to defeat. Many New York Democrats cast ballots starkly inscribed in ominous letters: "Remember Silas Wright!" [38] And through the North the enemies of slavery watched New York with intense excitement. "I know of no event in the History of Parties in this Country," wrote Salmon P. Chase, describing to Charles Sumner the repercussions, in Ohio, of the Barnburner secession, "at all approaching, in sublimity and moment, the Herkimer Convention." [39]

Eighteen–forty-eight appeared a year of destiny. In Europe angry mobs demonstrated against despotism, and established governments trembled, tottered and fell. "If I do not err," said the elder Van Buren of the Italian upsurge in 1847, "this is but the beginning"; if the existing governments obstinately oppose necessary change, they will provoke "violent and bloody revolutions." [40] The revolution in France stimulated Frank Blair to plant trees designed to grow up and form a tricolor; he worked with such ardor as to bring on a hemorrhage. [41] Jacksonian Democrats, from Polk down, were delighted by the fall of despots, while Whigs and Calhoun Democrats were plunged further into melancholy by every dispatch from Paris. [42]

[35] O. C. Gardiner, *The Great Issue: or, the Three Presidential Candidates*, 62.
[36] *Herkimer Convention. The Voice of New York!*, 5.
[37] John Van Buren to Martin Van Buren, November 13, 1847, Van Buren Papers.
[38] C. H. Peck, "John Van Buren," *Magazine of American History*, XVII, 321.
[39] Chase to Sumner, December 2, 1847, Chase, *Diary and Correspondence*, 125.
[40] Van Buren to Robert Hogan, *et al.*, November 24, 1847, Van Buren Papers.
[41] Martin Van Buren, Jr., to Van Buren, April 17, 1848, Van Buren Papers.
[42] Curtis, "American Opinion of the French Nineteenth Century Revolutions," *American Historical Review*, XXIX, 263.

This series of outbreaks in the very citadel of tyranny heightened among the radicals a sense of their obligation to strike the last blows for liberty in its homeland. "Can we show ourselves lukewarm," exclaimed George Bancroft, now Minister to Britain, "while the old World is shaking off its chains and emancipating and enthroning the masses?"[43] An enthusiastic Barnburner pointed the moral: "*Shall we, in view of these struggles of all Europe, with our model before them, renounce the doctrine of our fathers, and the sentiment of the civilized world, that slavery is an evil?*"[44] It could not be, and Martin Van Buren roused himself to face the challenge.

Up to the spring of 1848 the ex-President had lingered in the background, but now he must speak. In April he wrote a long exposition of the Free Soil case, setting the war against slavery extension solidly in the Jacksonian tradition. With insignificant emendations by his son and Samuel J. Tilden, it was adopted as an address by the Barnburner members of the legislature. "From the first institution of government to the present time," Van Buren declared, "there has been a struggle going on between capital and labor for a fair distribution of the profits resulting from their joint capacities." At the beginning, the advantage was always on the side of capital, but lately men of good will have become increasingly concerned with "securing to him who labors a consideration in society and a reward in the distribution of the proceeds of industry more adequate than his class have heretofore received." The system which had worked in France for centuries "to impoverish and debase the children of industry, and enrich a favored few" was now overthrown by "the naked hands of the laboring masses." "Shall we," Van Buren asked, "whose government was instituted to elevate and ennoble the laboring man," pursue a policy in regard to slavery which tends toward his degradation?

The question of the relations of slavery and democracy had now arisen "in a practical form. It can no longer be evaded or postponed. It is upon us. We must decide it. Shall these vast communities [acquired from Mexico] be the creations of free or slave labor?" The two systems, he pointed out, could not coexist. Which to exclude, the planter or the free laboring man? "It is against the hundreds of thousands of our own descendants, who must earn their bread by the sweat of their brows, and hundreds of thousands of children of toil from other countries, who would annually seek a new home and a refuge from want and oppression in the vacant territories, that this unjust exclusion is sought to be enforced." Have the enemies of the

---

[43] Bancroft to Buchanan, March 24, 1848, Howe, *Bancroft*, II, 33.
[44] Gardiner, *The Great Issue*, 21.

Wilmot Proviso forgotten "the peculiar duty which our Government owes to the laboring masses, to protect whom, in their rights to political and social equality, and in the secure enjoyment of the fruits of their industry, is at once its object and its pride?" [45]

Equipped with this address as their platform, and furnished by Van Buren with a private memorandum on political tactics, a Barnburner delegation, led by Cambreleng, Tilden and Preston King, went south to Baltimore for the Democratic convention. When the gathering proposed to seat also a rival Hunker delegation and split the New York votes between them, the Barnburners withdrew. The Democrats remaining quickly nominated Lewis Cass, well known as a foe of the Proviso. Cass's alternative plan of "squatter sovereignty" was a new expression of the Western preference for home rule as against the larger issues of economic democracy. General Zachary Taylor, the Whig candidate, was no more satisfactory to the opponents of slavery extension.

The spontaneous burst of public support which greeted the returning Barnburner delegation spurred the leaders to plan a convention for June in Utica. Counsels were divided on the question of a separate presidential ticket. Theodore Sedgwick, Jr., had expressed himself against allowing slavery to become an issue in the presidential election. William Cullen Bryant was unenthusiastic about a new organization. Benton, Blair, Flagg and Dix were all opposed to an independent nomination. [46]

Yet the younger men — Preston King, David Wilmot, Gideon Welles, David Dudley Field and, above all, John Van Buren — pressed ardently for action. Moreover, Benjamin F. Butler, who had lagged behind in the earlier Barnburner movement, suddenly threw himself heart and soul into the fight. "I consider the prohibition of Slavery in the territories now free, the greatest question of the day," he declared. ". . . It will, ultimately, carry or revolutionize the country." [47] Behind the leaders spoke the people opposed to slavery. Letters poured

[45] "Address of the Democratic Members of the Legislature of the State of New York," Tilden, *Writings and Speeches*, II, 571, 572, 569. All the passages quoted were written by Martin Van Buren.

[46] For Sedgwick's position, see "The Present Position of the Democratic Party," *New York Evening Post*, December 3, 1847, which proposed leaving the question up to Congress. This editorial emerged from a conference attended by Marcus Morton, Bryant, F. B. Cutting, J. L. Stephens and D. D. Field, and expressed the views of Morton, Cutting, Stephens and Sedgwick. Field was definitely opposed, and Bryant uncertain. See Sedgwick to Van Buren, December 2, 1847, Van Buren Papers. For Bryant, see also Bryant to John Bryant, February 7, 1848, Godwin, *Bryant*, II, 40; for Benton, Blair and Dix, see Benton to Van Buren, May 29, 1848, and for Flagg, Flagg to Van Buren, June 19, 1848, Van Buren Papers.

[47] Butler to Van Buren, May 29, 30, 1848, Van Buren Papers.

in to the Van Burens and Butler setting forth popular sentiment. *Cass and Taylor are not fit candidates for Northern support. We can no longer brook Southern dictation. What can I do? You can depend on our county. Who else in my state is favorable to the movement? I must get in touch with them. What will New York do? We are behind you. We are awaiting your decision. The hopes of the North are centering on the Barnburners. We must have a Wilmot Proviso candidate. Will Mr. Van Buren come out of retirement? Above all, New York must act — ACT. The North will follow.*[48]

5

Preston King, B. F. Butler and John Van Buren made rousing speeches to open the Utica convention, and David Dudley Field then read a letter from Van Buren, praising the aims of the meeting but requesting that his own name not be considered for the nomination. By the second day the national excitement about the proceedings was becoming evident. A flurry of telegrams, one from the Mayor of Chicago, pledged support. A mass meeting in Lafayette, Indiana, wired: "WE HAVE OUR EYES UPON YOU. DESIRE PROMPT ACTION." One message, addressed to John Van Buren, declared tersely: "Nominate Nominate no postponement." [49] The convention responded, naming Martin Van Buren for President by acclamation. "I do not see anything in the Constitution," as John cheerfully told his father, "which enables you to forbid our voting for you." [50]

John Greenleaf Whittier, with quiet Quaker realism, had already envisaged the next step. In a letter to Charles Sumner, written two days before the Barnburners gathered at Utica, he asked, "Is there no hope of uniting with them? . . . Dare! *Dare! DARE!* as Danton told the French; that is the secret of successful revolt." But who should be the candidate? Whittier inclined toward John Van Buren, but Sumner would settle for his father. "With him we can break the slave power: that is our first aim." [51] In Ohio, Salmon P. Chase was laboring to bring the Liberty party together with Whittier's group of New England abolitionists and Sumner's Conscience Whigs.

As for the Barnburners, some still believed that the call for a national convention should exclude the more fanatical abolitionists.

[48] See letters, Van Buren Papers.
[49] Gardiner, *Great Issue*, 116; Dean Richmond, *et al.*, to John Van Buren, June 23, 1848, Van Buren Papers.
[50] John Van Buren to Martin Van Buren, June 26, 1848, Van Buren Papers.
[51] Whittier to Sumner, June 20, 1848, S. T. Pickard, *Life and Letters of John Greenleaf Whittier*, I, 331–332.

On July 2 and 3 conferences on this point became increasingly acrimonious till John Van Buren gave a sociable dinner to help restore harmony, and suggested that the group adjourn to Lindenwald on the Fourth for a talk with the ex-President. They were met by the aging statesman, still an active, sprightly man, who greeted his son with a delight, said an observer, which bespoke "a mutual love, warm, cheering, and unbroken." Through a delightful day the two Van Burens "hurled their shafts of wit at each other," and in the evening Sam Tilden set forth the case for a restricted call. "You must be very strong," the ex-President said in conclusive response, "if you are already picking and choosing. . . . I had supposed that we wanted every man who was opposed to the extension of slavery. . . . Is not the vote of Gerritt Smith just as weighty as that of Judge Martin Grover?" [52]

On August 9 antislavery men of every stripe gathered at Buffalo from all the free and three slave states to pack a large tent broiling under the August sun. For two days a succession of speakers, Democrats and Whigs and Liberty men, kept the sweltering crowd in a frenzy of excitement. On the second morning the sonorous tones of Benjamin F. Butler reported the platform, which he had written in collaboration with Salmon P. Chase. Each militant sentence was cheered, and some provoked shouts and screams, with the waving of hats and handkerchiefs.

In the meantime a special committee was considering the nominations in secret session. The Liberty party had come to Buffalo highly distrustful of Van Buren, but the frankness and honesty of Butler and the firmness of the platform had dispelled many misgivings. Nonetheless, the Liberty men voted mostly for Hale on the informal ballot, and the Democrats mostly for Van Buren. The result was still uncertain when Massachusetts was reached on the roll call. S. C. Phillips, a Whig, declared for Van Buren, Richard Henry Dana followed suit, and a few minutes later Salmon P. Chase of Ohio added his emphatic vote. The unofficial ballot ended with a decided majority for the ex-President.

At this moment, Joshua Leavitt, the veteran Massachusetts abolitionist, obtained the floor. His voice choked, his fine face filled with emotion, he began slowly to speak while a profound stillness came over the hall. "Mr. Chairman," he said, "this is the most solemn experience of my life. I feel as if in the immediate presence of the Divine Spirit." Standing as the incarnation of religious abolitionism, he now handed over his leadership in the very moment of success and

[52] L. E. Chittenden, *Personal Reminiscences, 1840–1890*, 15–16.

moved Van Buren's unanimous nomination. "The Liberty party is
not dead," he shouted in a voice of thunder, "but TRANSLATED."

A family of singers was performing before the main body of delegates when someone on the outskirts of the crowd announced that the
committee had made its choice. Voices cried out from all over the
tent: "Name! name!" The speaker replied: "MARTIN VAN BUREN."
Pandemonium followed, a storm of cheering, clapping, stamping and
shouting. . . . Few who took part in the great Free Soil convention
ever forgot the breathless, dedicated days. "Christian men of the
highest character," observed Leavitt later, "declared that they were
never more impressed with the manifest presence of the Divine Spirit."
George W. Julian, at the end of his long career, could remember no
convention equal to Buffalo in seriousness and idealism.[53]

6

At no time could the Free Soilers have had much hope of
carrying the election, but they swept into the campaign with as much
zeal as if victory lay around the corner. Conscience Whigs and abolitionists worked shoulder to shoulder with Van Buren Democrats.
In Massachusetts the Van Buren organization had been crippled by
the erratic behavior of George Bancroft, who, after joining Polk's
cabinet, effected an alliance with Henshaw and Hallett. But Amasa
Walker provided energetic leadership for the Free Soil Democrats,
and Marcus Morton strong moral support. Though the Conscience
Whigs, under Sumner and Charles Francis Adams, tended to dominate
the Massachusetts Free Soil party, and the party included more Whigs
than Democrats, the Whig representation was a much smaller proportion of the state Whig party.[54]

Through the North old Jacksonians began to rally to the Free Soil
banner. In Connecticut John M. Niles headed the Free Soil state
ticket, and in Pennsylvania David Wilmot once again led the campaign

[53] The chief source on the convention is Oliver Dyer, *Phonographic Report of
the Proceedings of the National Free Soil Convention.* See also Joshua Leavitt's
letter to the Liberty party, *Clarion of Freedom* (Indiana County, Pennsylvania),
September 13, 1848; *Campaign of Freedom* (New York), August 26, 1848; Adams,
Dana, I, 138–144; Julian, *Political Recollections,* 56–61; *Reunion of the Free-Soilers
of 1848, . . . August 9, 1847,* especially 59. Gardiner, *Great Issue,* is an invaluable
source book for the Barnburner revolt, and Donovan, *The Barnburners,* an admirable modern history.
[54] The Democratic vote in Massachusetts declined much more than the Whig
as a result of the Free Soil ticket. See the careful computations of W. G. Bean,
"Party Transformation in Massachusetts with Special Reference to the Antecedents
of Republicanism, 1848–1860," 31–33, unpublished doctoral thesis, Harvard University.

for Van Buren. In Ohio Benjamin Tappan, Jacob Brinkerhoff and Edwin M. Stanton joined with Chase in whipping up Free Soil enthusiasm. Frank Blair was converted to the Free Soil cause by Van Buren's letter to the Utica convention — "the greatest act of your life" — and his brilliant son, Frank Blair, Jr., led the Free Soil fight in Missouri.[55] In New York Bryant and the *Evening Post* swung enthusiastically into line. John A. Dix, if somewhat against his inclination, became the Free Soil nominee for Governor. The young editor of the *Daily Eagle* in Brooklyn, with his short beard and his indolent manner, not quite yet sounding his barbaric yawp, lost his job because of his Free Soil enthusiasms. "For a period of nearly twenty years I have been your political friend," wrote the old Jacksonian and labor editor Hobart Berrian to Van Buren. ". . . I have contributed my mite, in time and zeal, to advocacy of the principles of Radical and Progressive Democracy. . . . Your last letter, is the letter of your life." [56]

The hero of the Free Soil campaign was John Van Buren, now at the height of his power. Standing quietly before huge audiences, with his wit, his invective and his capacity suddenly to stir his hearers to their emotional depths, he was, as the *New York Times* said twenty years later, "by all odds the most popular stump speaker in the Northern States," and he won in this campaign "a more brilliant reputation than has ever been won in a single political campaign by any other man." [57] When a Pennsylvanian had moved, at Buffalo, that John Van Buren be invited to stump his state, the tent was filled with cries: "We want him in New York." "He must stump Ohio." "They need him in Mississippi." "Let him stump the world." A resolution was finally passed "inviting Mr. Van Buren to stump the United States generally." [58]

This he proceeded to do, as much as one man could, speaking night after night, dropping his jokes as lightly as a feather, then turning with relish to the savage, slashing passages he did so well. His fame and following increased as the months went on. A Massachusetts Free Soil paper announced the date of a forthcoming appearance: "Need any thing more be said, to induce the people to come to Boston on that day?" People would long remember him on a hot evening at Faneuil Hall, with collar and neckerchief off, his eloquence burning like a beacon in the night.[59]

[55] Blair to Van Buren, June 16, 26, 1848, Van Buren Papers.
[56] Berrian to Van Buren, June 26, 1848, Van Buren Papers.
[57] *New York Times*, October 17, 1866.
[58] Dyer, *Phonographic Report*, 27–28.
[59] *Boston Semi-Weekly Republican*, September 2, 1848; Congdon, *Reminiscences of a Journalist*, 133.

Not all radical Democrats could bring themselves to break **with** the party they had served so long; not all could accept the emergence of slavery and the fateful beginnings of the sectional division.[60] Benton, while concurring in principle with the Utica convention, refused to bolt the organization and actively supported Cass. Men like George Bancroft, Robert Rantoul, Frederick Robinson, Thomas W. Dorr, even Theodore Sedgwick, Jr., stayed with the party, and antislavery Whigs like W. H. Seward went down the line for Taylor. Horace Greeley, the great idealist, considered going Free Soil, but the flourish of a Whig congressional nomination changed his mind.[61]

November came, and the smoke cleared to show that Taylor and Fillmore had carried New York and consequently the election. The Free Soil ticket had polled nearly three hundred thousand votes, an almost fivefold increase in the antislavery vote from 1844. How much longer could the government ignore the question which its people were every year asking more insistently?

[60] John A. Bolles delivered the Free Soil answer to the charge of setting section against section: "In the Slave States now thousands of men . . . are looking towards us . . . the Sand-hillers of North Carolina . . . the Corn-crackers of Tennessee and Alabama — the poor white men, not owners of slaves, but poor mechanics and poor farmers, more trampled upon, if possible, than the very Africans themselves. . . . That is the quintessence of the slave doctrine; labor degraded, the laborer degraded, money exalted, and the owner of property exalted." *Boston Semi-Weekly Republican*, September 9, 1848.

[61] For Benton, Blair to Van Buren, June 26, 1848, Van Buren Papers; Bancroft to W. H. Prescott, September 15, 1848, Howe, *Bancroft*, II, 36; Rantoul, *Second Speech . . . on the Coalition in Massachusetts*, 5; (Robinson, Dorr) *Boston Post*, July 8, 15, 1848; Edwin Croswell to Sedgwick, December 27, 1857, Sedgwick Papers; R. M. Robbins, "Horace Greeley: Land Reform and Unemployment, 1837–1862," *Agricultural History*, VII, 30.

XXXV THE STORM APPROACHES

A S THE sectional tension increased, the sense of irrepressible differences, long buried in the national consciousness, began to burst into the clear. The growing pressure on the North had finally persuaded many Northerners that the slavery system embodied a fundamental threat to free society. The growing pressure on the South had finally persuaded many Southerners that democracy constituted a fundamental threat to slavery. On both sides the pressure compelled a reconsideration of political premises; and, as the reconsideration progressed, the conviction of irreconcilability became more intense and more alarming. "Slavery," declared David Wilmot, "is the deadly enemy of free labor." "*Democracy*," wrote a member of the Virginia constitutional convention, "*in its original philosophical sense, is, indeed, incompatible with slavery, and the whole system of Southern society.*" Inevitably, radical democracy and slavery were coming to find in each other the fatal obstacle to security and power.[1]

1

The increasing sharpness of the issue made Northern opponents of democracy look more longingly than ever before toward an alliance with the slave power. The business community dreaded

[1] David Wilmot, letter accepting the Republican nomination for Governor of Pennsylvania, April 22, 1857, Going, *Wilmot*, 499; M. R. H. Garnett to W. H. Trescott, May 3, 1851, Henry O'Rielly, *The Great Questions of the Times, Exemplified in the Antagonistic Principles Involved in the Slaveholders' Rebellion against Democratic Institutions as well as against the National Union*, 8. A convenient summary of Southern attacks on free society is to be found in Henry Wilson's speech in the Senate on March 20, 1858, *Congressional Globe*, 35 Congress 1 Session, Appendix, 168–174, later published under the title *Are Working-men 'Slaves'?* See also the works of H. O'Rielly, a former Barnburner, published during the Civil War: *The Great Questions* and *Origins and Objects of the Slaveholders' Conspiracy*. The speech of J. H. Hammond in the Senate on March 4, 1858, setting forth the "mudsill" theory of society, *Congressional Globe*, 35 Congress 1 Session, Appendix, 69–71, and the response of Abraham Lincoln in his Milwaukee speech of September 30, 1859, *Works* (Nicolay-Hay), V, 247–255, contain a good discussion of the issues. The writings of George Fitzhugh present the most devastating Southern attack on the principles of liberal capitalistic society.

sectional conflict lest the delicate and shimmering web of commerce and credit, spread wide across the country, be rudely broken, with consequent convulsions on the stock market, destruction of assets and dissolution of contracts. Many merchants were, in addition, bound specifically to the South by profitable economic ties. In any case, the avidity with which the South moved to rebuke Northern radicalism after the Free Soil activity of the radical Democrats in 1848 markedly increased conservative solicitude for the future of the slave power.

In August, 1849, the *American Whig Review*, the magazine set up in 1844 to chasten the *Democratic Review*, ran an article entitled "A Word to Southern Democrats. By a Northern Conservative." The union between Calhoun and the radical democracy, the author declared, was always "forced and unnatural." It had been based on common enmities, not on common principles. "In the South it was capital and aristocracy that naturally opposed the American system; in the North it was poverty and numbers. And thus by a forced combination, political extremes met, and Tammany Hall shook hands with the Charleston aristocrats." But since 1848 all had changed. *"Abolitionism in the North has leagued itself with radical democracy. That is the great fact of the age."* Let Southern Democrats now consider who would handle more tenderly the constitutional guarantees of slavery, "the conservative constitutional Whig, or the hot, wild, reckless body that is organizing out of loco-foco and abolition elements in the North and West." [2]

The union of property North and South seemed already to be in good working order by 1850. A Whig Congressman from Florida could assure the conservatives of the North that the slave power would save them from "Socialism, Agrarianism, Fanny Wrightism, Radicalism, Dorrism, and Abolitionism . . . [and] the thousand destructive *isms* infecting the social organization of your section," and in exchange the chairman of the Massachusetts Whig state committee could send around a circular just before the election requesting each businessman "to use all the influence he can over those in his employ, or in any way under his control," to defeat the Free Soil-Democratic coalition. [3] "The Money Power," charged Charles Sumner, "has joined hands with the Slave Power." [4]

[2] "A Word to Southern Democrats. By a Northern Conservative," *American Whig Review*, X, 190–194 (August, 1849).

[3] E. C. Cabell in the House, March 5, 1850, *Congressional Globe*, 31 Congress 1 Session, Appendix, 242; Cole, *Whig Party in the South*, 283; Whig circular of November 8, 1850, signed by George Morey, chairman of the Whig State Central Committee, *Boston Commonwealth*, October 31, 1851.

[4] Sumner, *Works*, II, 318.

Looking at the world through a haze of profit sheets and counting-houses, the Cotton Whigs could see only that property was in danger, a revelation which closed the discussion. But other Whigs had other values. Property, they felt, was not so much at stake as free society, and the maintenance of free society was as essential for business as for reform. The men in the party who cared about democracy and freedom began to cluster around William H. Seward, and through the North the Whigs began to split into antislavery and proslavery wings. In general, the division between Conscience and Cotton Whigs corresponded to earlier differences within the party on economic questions. Antislavery Whigs, everywhere, were more or less forced to the left on other issues, in part by the hostility to their cause of most wealthy merchants, but in great part because the Jacksonian tradition, rather than their own, supplied the most solid foundations for political antislavery.

This leftward drift was exhibited all the more clearly on the level of political philosophy. Antislavery conservatives found themselves obliged by the intellectual necessity of sustaining themselves as champions of freedom and democracy to abandon, increasingly, the premises of Hamilton. They had to continue, with new seriousness, the campaign to capture Jeffersonianism which the political genius of Seward had laid down in the thirties. Seward himself appealed to a "higher law" than the Constitution, the Conscience Whigs talked freely of "natural rights," and by 1859 a liberal Whig, like Abraham Lincoln of Illinois, could even refer to the principles of Jefferson as the "definitions and axioms of free society." [5]

The Cotton Whigs, their hands forced by these heresies, had finally to disclose their own fundamental aversion to the maxims of democracy. Webster thundered against the notion of the "higher law," and Rufus Choate spoke with contempt of the "glittering and sounding generalities of natural right which make up the Declaration of Independence." [6] Without accepting all the values of the slaveholders, the Northern conservatives yet collaborated earnestly in the ideological attack on radical democracy and in the repudiation of equalitarianism.

The conservatives of the North were thus compelled increasingly to decide whether, like Seward and Lincoln, they would move toward the politics and philosophy of Jefferson, or, like Webster and Choate, toward the politics and philosophy of the slave power. The pressures

---

[5] Lincoln to H. L. Pierce, *et. al.*, April 6, 1859, *Works* (Nicolay-Hay), V, 126.
[6] Choate to E. W. Farley, *et al.*, August 9, 1856, *The Old-Line Whigs for Buchanan!*, 4.

of the day permitted fewer and fewer alternatives between appeasement and resistance.[7]

2

The Compromise of 1850, though denounced by extremists on both sides, expressed the profound desire of moderates through the land to resolve peaceably the problems raised by the territory won from Mexico. The Missouri Compromise had banished the slavery question for a quarter of a century, and men hoped desperately that the new Compromise would produce another interlude of sectional harmony. Most of the Free Soilers opposed the Compromise, but they accepted its enactment as a settlement of the slavery issue, and were prepared to reunite with the Democratic party on the basis of the older questions.

Yet, for all their eventual assent to the Compromise, Free Soilers felt a natural reluctance to entrust the government to men who had fought for slavery extension. If the party were to be reunited, it ought to be reunited behind an old Jacksonian; and the old Jacksonian most clearly in the apostolic succession, with the retirement of Van Buren and the death of Wright, was Thomas Hart Benton.

Benton himself had not been a Free Soiler. He found technical reasons (later exploded by Calhoun) for regarding the Wilmot Proviso as unnecessary, and party regularity enlisted him behind Lewis Cass in 1848. Yet in the Senate he was becoming increasingly the pitiless critic of the slave power, even goading the gentleman from Mississippi on one occasion into drawing a gun on him. As a speaker Benton had never been so effective. In Jacksonian days, his massive figure, rising with sheaves of paper in hand, would often be the signal for the galleries to clear, and colleagues would yawn or rustle papers as he labored to recollect a prepared passage, or peered through his glasses for necessary statistics. Now he spoke without notes and with a passion and trenchancy which packed alike the galleries and the floor. In the past Frank Blair had preferred reading Benton to hearing him. "Now it is all the reverse — His printed speeches are not comparable." [8]

In these later years Benton was increasingly negligent as a politician,

[7] The condition of the modern Republican party before Pearl Harbor presented interesting resemblances to the condition of the Whig party in this period; see Arthur M. Schlesinger, Jr., "Can Willkie Save His Party?" *Nation*, December 6, 1941. Had the South gone to war in 1850, the Whig party would have been saved, in spite of itself, as war has saved the Republican party today.

[8] Blair to Van Buren, August 1, 1850, Van Buren Papers.

seldom mending fences back home and regarding his seat more or less as personal property. But Missouri was a slave state, and Benton's mounting hostility to Southern claims gave his enemies new ammunition. In 1849 he had to go back to carry his fight to the people in a series of caustic speeches. He was particularly severe on Calhoun whom he spoke of with scorn as John "Catiline" Calhoun, till the opposition press attacked him harshly for it. Then the old man unblinkingly denied the story, saying magnificently that he could not be "so unjust to the brave Roman conspirator as to compare the cowardly American plotter to him." [9] With the aid of Frank Blair's two able sons, Montgomery and Frank, Jr., Benton put on a wonderful fight against the busy local politicians, like a great bear, as the elder Blair said, surrounded by a yelping pack of whelps. "He slaps one down on this side — another on that — and grips a third with his teeth, then tosses him with his snout." [10] But the opposition was too well organized. When the Senate convened in 1851, another man sat in Benton's place.

The old man was sixty-eight in 1850, but no one could detect any lapse in energy or egotism. Once, at dinner, Lord Elgin, then Governor-general of Canada, asked Benton casually whether he had known Jackson. Jackson? "Yes, sir," Benton replied. "I knew him, sir. I shot him, sir. Afterwards he helped me in my battle with the United States Bank, sir." [11] He now turned to a history of his times, working away in shirt sleeves with his collar open to rescue the past from the Federalist distortions he discovered with horror in the pages of Tocqueville. ("See what a figure we are to make," he exclaimed to Van Buren, "if we do not write for ourselves.") "I never felt better, not even at 30 years of age," he declared exultantly in 1851, and increasingly he conceived of his *Thirty Years' View* as a means of purifying the Democratic tradition and restoring party unity in face of latter-day corruptions.[12] The Free Soil wing was already turning toward him for 1852. Preston King, Blair and Wilmot were prepared to set the Benton boom in motion, and through the North old Jacksonians like Van Buren, Gideon Welles, Marcus Morton and the Free Soilers watched with hope. But the old man honestly did not

[9] Meigs, *Benton*, 452.
[10] Blair to Van Buren, August 8, 1849, Van Buren Papers.
[11] Bigelow, *Retrospections*, IV, 56. A variant has Benton passing the Clark Mills statue of Jackson and commenting: "Yes, sir; General Jackson was a great man, sir — a very great man, sir. He was of great use to *me*, sir, in *my* war upon the United States Bank, sir." Dyer, *Great Senators*, 208–209. Actually, Benton's detached account of the Bank War in *Thirty Years' View* hardly justifies the anecdotes.
[12] Benton to Van Buren, June 16, 30, September 11, 25, 1851, Blair to Van Buren, July 23, 1851, Van Buren Papers.

want to be President. Even Blair, who had never really believed these protestations, was finally convinced.

Who then if not Benton? The old man's own suggestion was Levi Woodbury of the Supreme Court, a Northerner, a mild Jacksonian and a man uncommitted on slavery. Blair considered this "a sad nostrum, but I would take it rather than be physicked by Cass or Clay." [13] Van Buren, while preferring Taney, also acceded to the Woodbury scheme, but the campaign hardly got under way before Woodbury died. Blair, Dix and Welles then turned toward Sam Houston of Texas, but Benton demurred, and the radical group finally settled on William O. Butler, a Jackson protégé, docile and colorless, whom they hoped to be able to control. But early in 1852 Butler endorsed some proslavery resolutions passed by the Kentucky legislature, and Blair gave up President-making in disgust.

The others began to think rather desperately of William L. Marcy, whose rugged independence had finally alienated him from the Hunkers. But the Free Soilers were still unorganized when the convention met in June. After forty-nine ballots and an interminable contest among Cass, Buchanan and Stephen A. Douglas, Franklin Pierce of New Hampshire was nominated in another dark-horse upset. Most of the Free Soilers accepted this weak and amiable man, who had been a nominal Jacksonian and whom B. F. Butler had considered for a moment in 1848 for the Free Soil nomination.[14]

3

The Whigs nominated Winfield Scott on a platform endorsing the Compromise of 1850, and the unreconciled Free Soilers ran John P. Hale on a Free Democratic ticket. Salmon P. Chase in an open letter to Benjamin F. Butler forcibly presented the case against the regular Democratic nominations and for the Free Democrats. He reminded the Barnburners that their every step back to the Democratic fold had been accompanied by ringing pledges that they would stop short of any sacrifice of Free Soil principle — pledges uttered ordinarily by John Van Buren, "the Coeur de Lion of the free democracy . . .

---

[13] Blair to Van Buren, February 6, 1851, Van Buren Papers.
[14] See the letters among the two Van Burens, Benton, Blair, Dix, etc., in the Van Buren Papers, 1851–1852; R. F. Nichols, *The Democratic Machine, 1850–1854*, 79–98; Van Buren, *Political Parties*, 365; Butler to Pierce, June 16, 1848, W. L. Leech, *Calendar of the Papers of Franklin Pierce*, 18; Smith, *Blair Family*, I, 242–243, 265; Morton to John Van Buren, February 7, to Hamlin, February 29, 1852, Morton Letterbooks; Dix, *Dix*, I, 262–266; Preston King to Bigelow, February 24, 1851, Bigelow, *Retrospections*, I, 112; Welles to Tilden, September 24, 1851, Tilden, *Letters*, I, 79.

whose bold voice for freedom had rung throughout the land like a trumpet call." Then came the Compromise of 1850 and the Baltimore convention of 1852. If the pledges still held, how could Preston King, Butler and the Van Burens announce their support of the Baltimore nominations? [15]

Butler's defense was troubled. "So far as your letter is designed to explain and vindicate your rejection of the slavery resolutions of the Baltimore Convention," he said, "it expresses, substantially, my own convictions, and receives my entire concurrence." The resolutions, he further admitted, were "irreconcilable with the Buffalo platform" to which, he vigorously declared, "I yet hold, entirely and without reserve." "With the compromise resolutions of 1850 and 1851 I was wholly dissatisfied, and openly rejected them." But he had decided to vote for Pierce because he felt the slavery policy would be no worse under a Democratic than a Whig administration and the economic policy would be much better.[16] William Cullen Bryant tried, similarly, to fight the campaign on the old economic issues, reprinting in October a letter of Van Buren's with the hopeful comment that it "revives, in all their original freshness, those important lines of distinction between the party of equal rights and the party of privilege." [17] But these lines were not to be revived in their ancient form; and since the Compromise had technically eliminated slavery as an issue, the campaign was bound to be unreal. No canvass since 1820 had been so dull. Pierce won decisively with an electoral vote of 254 to 42.

Though the Compromise had actually caused some of the disquiet to subside, certain of its provisions, especially the Fugitive Slave Act, only increased the resentments of the extremists. An attempt to enforce the law in Boston in 1851, for example, brought to a head the hostility between the Free Soil and "doughface" or pro-Southern wings of the Democratic party. The Democratic and Free Soil organizations had formed a coalition in 1849 when the Democratic convention had declared its opposition to "slavery, in every form and color," and its support of "Freedom and free soil wherever man lives throughout God's heritage." [18] In 1851 the coalition sent Charles Sumner to the Senate, while putting a far-reaching program of social reform through the state legislature. But the support of the Fugitive Slave Law by Hunker Democrats, like B. F. Hallett and Charles Gordon

---

[15] Chase to Butler, July 15, 1852, *New York Herald*, July 20, 1852.
[16] Butler to Chase, July 31, 1852, *Boston Commonwealth*, August 10, 1852. See also W. A. Butler, *Retrospect of Forty Years*, 243.
[17] *New York Evening Post*, October 18, 1852.
[18] *Boston Post*, September 19, 1849.

Greene, ended the harmony, Frederick Robinson condemned the prosecutions in the state senate, and Robert Rantoul, Jr., now in the national House of Representatives, denounced the law as an infringement of State rights. At the 1852 convention Hallett as chairman of the Democratic national committee was faced with the problem of explaining away the attacks on slavery by Massachusetts Democrats. His solution was to launch a personal assault on Rantoul.[19]

In spite of himself Rantoul was in the end joining the radicals. His reformism of the thirties had faded considerably in the next decade when he began a career of Western investment and even served as lawyer for Eastern interests in Western railroad deals (in his attempt to get a charter for the Illinois Central from the state legislature he crossed swords with a shrewd local lawyer named Abraham Lincoln).[20] Now slavery was belatedly forcing him into open revolt, not in 1848 with the Free Soilers, but later on; and his courage, though tardy, was repaid. He now stood on the threshold of the national career he had so long coveted. Then in August, 1852, six days before his forty-seventh birthday, he died on the edge of his greatest fame. Whittier, an old friend, spoke the sorrow of the antislavery forces: —

> One day, along the electric wire,
>   His manly word for Freedom sped;
> We came next morn: that tongue of fire
>   Said only, "He who spoke is dead!"
>
>   *   *   *
>
> We saw his great powers misapplied
>   To poor ambitions; yet, through all,
> We saw him take the weaker side,
>   And right the wronged, and free the thrall.[21]

From the start the new President showed a marked tendency to defer to Southern opinion. In 1854 Stephen A. Douglas, the Democratic Senator from Illinois, anxious for a number of reasons to open the territories of Kansas and Nebraska to settlement, introduced with administration support what eventually became known as the Kansas-Nebraska Act. This bill included among its provisions an explicit repeal of the Missouri Compromise and thus would allow the advance of slavery into regions from which it was hitherto excluded. Its author, like Hugh L. White in the thirties and Lewis Cass in the forties, was a proponent of the dominant form of Mississippi Valley "democracy";

[19] Bean, "Party Transformation in Massachusetts," 91–129.
[20] *Proceedings of the Massachusetts Historical Society*, Third Series, II, 84.
[21] Whittier, "Rantoul," *Works*, IV, 84, 86.

he was a great champion of "popular sovereignty," home rule, speculation and August Belmont, the banker, but he cared little about the issues of economic democracy. For many Free Soilers the Kansas-Nebraska Act was the final betrayal.

Salmon P. Chase's "Appeal of the Independent Democrats," widely circulated through the free states, expressed the indignation of the antislavery North, and Chase, Sumner and Seward led the fight against the measure in the Senate. Thomas Hart Benton, elected to the House in 1852, attacked the bill savagely, declaring that its enactment would "run the Democratic party into the ground." [22] In New York in May, Benjamin F. Butler, making his first political appearance since the Free Soil campaign, denounced the "northern traitors" who backed the bill and declared he would rather support Seward than Douglas for the presidency. "I say you are immediately to rally and to organize," he told the cheering audience.[23] Later he described the act to Van Buren as "the most wanton, and the most inexcusable piece of folly and wickedness ever perpetrated in our country." [24] Van Buren himself was greatly shocked and indignant.[25] Younger men, like Preston King, David Wilmot and Gideon Welles, felt that there was no longer room for them in the Democratic party.

4

Francis P. Blair, the farmer of Silver Spring, never failed to drive over to Washington several times a month when Congress was in session. He was a mellow, bright-eyed old man (sixty-three in 1854), with his charming, ugly face, usually wearing an odd low-crowned broad-brimmed hat and looking on everyone with the utmost amiability. The old asperities had softened. In the winter of 1850, for example, he became reconciled with Henry Clay. The veteran editor's conversation was beguiling and his reminiscence instructive. But he was far from being simply a chatty ghost from a forgotten past. The younger Democrats from the North had infected him with their own zeal for Free Soil. Benton, whom age did not mellow, fired him with the necessity of resisting the slave power. His two sons were fighting the slavery extremists in Missouri. But still he lingered inactive on the sidelines. Then Congress passed the Kansas-Nebraska Act, and

---

[22] Butler to Van Buren, December 2, 1854, Van Buren Papers.
[23] *New York Evening Post*, May 15, 1854.
[24] Butler to Van Buren, December 2, 1854, Van Buren Papers.
[25] Van Buren, *Political Parties*, 355; Van Buren to Moses Tilden, September 1, 1856, Tilden, *Letters*, I, 119.

Blair rose in wrath. "I hope there will be honest patriots enough found to resist it," he declared, "and that the present aggression will be rebuked. I am willing to devote the balance of my life to this object." [26]

Through the free states men were turning against the party of Franklin Pierce and Stephen A. Douglas in anger at this last surrender to the South. Spontaneous meetings, led by Conscience Whigs and Free Soil Democrats, passed resolutions against the Kansas-Nebraska Act and asked for Representatives pledged against further appeasement. As evidence of their kinship to Jefferson, local groups began to revive the name of his old party, calling themselves "Republicans," and the word swept the North, as the inevitable designation for the new organization which would grapple directly with the question that now seemed the most urgent and terrible of the day. In the elections of 1854 the Republicans made striking inroads. By 1856 its leaders were laying plans for the coming presidential campaign.

Men gathered from every free state and eight slave states at Pittsburgh on Washington's birthday in 1856. Frank Blair was chosen president of the Republican convention, and old comrades with whom he had fought hard battles were among the delegates: Preston King, jovial and cool; plump rumpled David Wilmot; Jacob Brinkerhoff of Ohio and Kingsley Bingham of Michigan. Through the country other Jacksonians watched the proceedings: in New England lame, shambling John M. Niles of Connecticut and his friend Gideon Welles, Hannibal Hamlin of Maine, John P. Hale of New Hampshire, Amasa Walker and Marcus Morton, Jr., of Massachusetts; in New York, Benjamin F. Butler, David Dudley Field, William Cullen Bryant of the *Evening Post* and Walt Whitman, now growing into the poet of democracy. Through the free states, old followers of Jackson and Van Buren, raised in the creed of equal rights: all, from the men peering at the paper by warm stoves in New England to the people waiting patiently in country post offices in remote Missouri, looked for direction from the new party of liberty.

The Jacksonian alienation from the Democratic party was nearly complete. In April Blair, with something of the authority and passion of his editorials in the old *Globe*, set forth the radical case in a piece called *A Voice from the Grave of Jackson!* "To use a homely phrase," he declared, " 'the Democracy has been sold out' to Mr. Calhoun's nullifying party." The question now to be decided was whether "the Nullifiers who have thus usurped the name and organization of the Democratic party, but who have no principles in common with it, shall be allowed to carry out their designs in such disguise." "Against

[26] Blair to Dix, 1854, Dix, *Dix*, I, 284.

this spurious Democracy," Blair cried, "which has thus perfected its system in the Kansas act, and made it their test, I, as a Democrat of the Jefferson, Jackson, and Van Buren school, enter my protest." [27]

The *Voice of Walt Whitman to Each Young Man in the Nation, North, South, East, and West* expressed similar emotions. "What the so-called democracy are now sworn to perform would eat the faces off the succeeding generations of common people worse than the most horrible disease. . . . You young men! American mechanics, farmers, boatmen, manufacturers, and all work-people of the South, the same as North! you are either to abolish slavery, or it will abolish you." [28]

Events of the spring increased the anti-Southern feeling. In May Charles Sumner delivered his celebrated speech on the civil war in Kansas. His language wounded sensitive representatives of the slave states, who had come to regard invective as a Southern prerogative; and the next day one model of plantation chivalry, Preston Brooks of South Carolina, crept up on the Massachusetts Senator as he was working at his desk, addressed a brief sentence and then clubbed him with a heavy cane till Sumner fell unconscious. Other Southern gentlemen prevented interference. When Brooks finished, the group departed, leaving Sumner bleeding on the floor (perhaps to contemplate at leisure the instinct for chivalry developed in a society founded on human bondage). Sumner, who never fully recovered from this brutal assault, retired to the Blairs' at Silver Spring for the first stages of his convalescence.

The shock of horror which went through the North was intensified by the complacency with which many Southerners, such as Jefferson Davis, viewed Brooks's exploit. When the Republicans met at Philadelphia in June to name a presidential ticket, they rode on a swell of anti-Southern emotion. John C. Frémont, son-in-law of Benton, received the nomination, and the Republicans scattered to carry their candidates to the country.

[27] Blair, *Letter . . . to a Public Meeting in New York, Held April 29, 1856*, 1, 8, 11. Cf. Blair's earlier development of this argument in his *Letter . . . to the Republican Association of Washington, D.C.*, of December 1, 1855, where he charged that "the present Administration has departed from the Jeffersonian principles relative to the government of the Territories of the United States, and has become little better than a working model of John C. Calhoun's Nullification and Disunion doctrines."

[28] Whitman, "The Eighteenth Presidency," Furness, *Walt Whitman's Workshop*, 101, 110.

5

The departure of the Free Soilers from the Democratic organization was somewhat compensated for by the accession of great numbers of Whigs. This drift began in the South, where in 1849 the Whigs were faced by the fact that the Free Soil schism had pretty well purged the Democratic party of its antislavery leaders, while, under Seward's ascendancy, they remained strong in the Whig. A. H. Stephens and Robert Toombs of Georgia and T. L. Clingman of North Carolina accordingly walked out of the Whig party early in the Taylor administration. The nomination of Scott in 1852 moved many Southern Whigs to vote for Pierce, and the break-up of the Whig organization in the next two years left the Democratic party as the chief refuge for many, both South and North.[29]

For others the meteoric Know-Nothing party provided a halfway house. This astonishing political phenomenon appealed to the traditional conservative prejudice against the foreigner, recently intensified by the sharp increase in immigration in the late forties. When the Know-Nothing party disappeared after the election of 1856, most of its ex-Whig adherents moved on to the Democrats.

By 1856 Blair could ask: "Who are the leaders in the South who make such loud professions of Democracy? . . . Men who never were Democrats, but abhorred the name when it rallied the country around an Administration that was true . . . to the cause of free government." He named the most vociferous Southern Democrats: Henry Wise and R. M. T. Hunter of Virginia, Toombs, Stephens and Clingman, Butler, Yulee and Soulé. "Where did they study for their Democratic diploma? In the school of every opposition that ever assailed the party re-established by Jackson." [30]

A similar realignment took place in the North. After the elimination of the Barnburners in 1848, the Hunker Democratic party looked enough safer than a party run by Conscience Whigs for such rich merchants as James W. Gerard of New York to declare, "If my party gives itself up to leaders who will betray its principles, . . . I will go over to the old Democratic party." [31] At the same time Isaac Hill, who, a few years before, used to caution Franklin Pierce about visiting Webster, now began to do so himself. By 1851 Webster was exchang-

---

[29] Cole, *Whig Party in the South*, 152–153, 223, 264–265.
[30] Blair, *Letter . . . to a Public Meeting in New York*, 8–9.
[31] At the Union Safety meeting, October 23, 1850, Philip S. Foner, *Business and Slavery: the New York Merchants and the Irrepressible Conflict*, 48.

ing cordial letters with David Henshaw and advising Massachusetts Whigs to collaborate with conservative Democrats. Before his death in 1852 Webster urged his friends to vote for Pierce.[32]

Caleb Cushing had already gone over to the Democrats, and by 1856 he was joined by Rufus Choate, Amos A. Lawrence, Robert C. Winthrop, George Ticknor Curtis and the sons of Webster and Clay. Choate put the case for all of them. When someone asked him why he came out for Buchanan, he answered that he could go nowhere else. "But, Mr. Choate, what becomes of your long cherished Whig principles?" "Whig principles! I go to the Democrats to find them. They have assumed our principles, one after another, till there is little difference between us." [33] The situation through the North was much that described by Abraham Lincoln for Illinois. "Much of the plain old Democracy is with us, while nearly all the old exclusive silk-stocking Whiggery is against us. . . . And why not? There has been nothing in politics since the Revolution so congenial to their nature as the present position of the great Democratic party." [34]

Yet not all the Jackson Democrats were prepared to go over to Frémont and the Republicans. Ties of party loyalty were strong, ties of national loyalty stronger, and they restrained many from moving to a sectional party some of whose leaders were Whigs. For older men, like Benton and Van Buren, the preservation of the Union took precedence over almost every other issue. Moreover, Buchanan, the Democratic nominee, for all his Doughface past, was the choice of the Northern Democrats; and though he was felt to be lacking in executive energy, his abilities and experience commanded respect. Northern Democrats looked to him to end the Southern — in great part ex-Whig — influence which they felt had ruined Pierce's administration. Thus Benton accompanied his endorsement of Buchanan by savage onslaughts on the policy of the retiring government. Thus Van Buren, while "not a particular admirer of Mr. Buchanan," believed he might administer the Kansas-Nebraska Act efficiently enough to prevent outside interference with the organization of the territorial government, a policy which would make Kansas "a territory so decidedly free as to put an end to attempts to make it a slave State." [35]

[32] Harvey, *Reminiscences of Webster*, 203, 243, 254–255; Webster to T. B. Curtis, January 20, 1851, *Proceedings of the Massachusetts Historical Society*, XLV, 165 (1911–1912); Webster to Henshaw, June 11, 1851, Webster, *Writings and Speeches* (Memorial Ed.), XVI, 616.

[33] Joseph Nielson, *Memories of Rufus Choate*, 350–351.

[34] Lincoln to A. G. Henry, November 19, 1858, Lincoln, *Works* (Nicolay-Hay), V, 95.

[35] Van Buren to Moses Tilden, September 1, 1856, Tilden, *Letters*, I, 120.

George Bancroft was equally bitter over the Pierce administration. "He has got round him so many whigs that democrats are crowded out of an organisation pretending to the democratic name," he said with a vehemence which would have delighted Blair, going on to curse out "this bastard race that controls the organisation, this unproductive hybrid begot by southern arrogance upon northern subserviency." The only apology that posterity could find for Pierce, Bancroft added, will be the "feebleness of his intellect." "The cruel attempt to conquer Kansas into slavery is the worst thing ever projected in our history." Yet, like Van Buren, Bancroft clung to the hope that Buchanan would make everything right, clear out the Whigs and nullifiers, and bring in Kansas as a free state, "the only great healing measure, which can restore the country permanently to tranquility." [36] Lesser men, like John A. Dix, Samuel J. Tilden and Theodore Sedgwick, Jr., growing conservative with age and prosperity, dutifully supported Buchanan.

But where was the most brilliant antislavery leader of them all, the hero of the Free Soil crusade, the "Coeur de Lion of the free democracy"? Of all the men of '48, the one most clearly designed for greatness would have seemed beyond question to be John Van Buren. Most of the antislavery movement looked to him for leadership (a few perhaps made reservations for W. H. Seward; none looked west to Illinois). For a few years Prince John maintained his position. In 1849 he declared in ringing tones that he would "under no necessity whatever" support for President any person "who would not use the whole constitutional power of the government to abolish" slavery. (He went on to make a grimly prophetic joke, a few months before the death of President Taylor. "Experience teaches us," he observed of the Democratic party, "that that party, when they succeed, come in to stay [laughter]; their adversaries come in to die. [Laughter]") In 1850 he opposed the ratification of the Compromise at the Democratic state convention, remarking that he was unwilling to "walk arm in arm to the funeral." In 1851 in Vermont he advised popular resistance to the Fugitive Slave Law. "Within the limits of my constitution," he cried, "hostility to human slavery is the predominant sentiment of my heart. It is as natural to me as the air I breathe, and will perish only with my life." [37]

[36] Bancroft to Marcy, September 24, 1856, to Buchanan, February 21, 1857, Howe, *Bancroft*, II, 123-124, 125-126; Bancroft to Gilpin, December 29, 1856, Gilpin Papers.
[37] John Van Buren, "Speech . . . at Faneuil Hall," *New York Evening Post Extra*, November 8, 1849; "Speech of Mr. Van Buren," *Democratic Review*, XXIX,

Yet, for all his apparent devotion, people suspected his resolution. "I do not perceive in him," said one observer, "the slightest real sympathy with human nature. . . . All is hard and selfish." "I know no one," Charles Sumner declared, "who has spoken a stronger or more timely word for us than he has. I am much attached to him personally, I admire his abilities . . . but I feel that, if he would surrender himself more unreservedly to the cause, he would be more effective still. Few have such powers." [38]

Some inner weakness lurked underneath the charm and wit and magnetism. In 1853 he boiled at the Pierce administration but was persuaded to remain silent, and his first instinct in 1854 was to denounce the Kansas-Nebraska bill, but eventually he acceded to popular sovereignty in Kansas. When Preston King, Butler, Bryant, Field, John Worth Edmonds and lesser Barnburners went into the Republican party, Prince John remained behind. In 1856 his friends rebuked him for not joining them. "If you had, you would now have been where Frémont is." "Wait and let us see," said John Van Buren quizzically, "how Frémont turns out." [39] As usual he had the better of the repartee, but the worse of the situation. By campaigning for Buchanan in 1856 he perhaps hoped to regain his place in the Democratic party; but the slave power would never trust him with a position of authority. As Sumner had observed in 1851, "He is so completely committed to our cause that he can hope for nothing except by its triumph." [40]

---

74 (July, 1851); Peck, "John Van Buren," *Magazine of American History*, XVII, 327–329.

[38] William Kent to Sumner, August 31, 1849, E. L. Pierce, *Sumner*, III, 61; Sumner to Bigelow, October 24, 1851, Bigelow, *Retrospections*, I, 121.

[39] Stanton, *Random Recollections*, 175–176. Henry Wilson, who, as a former Whig, had no particular leanings toward John Van Buren, wrote: "Such was the brilliant record he then [1848] made, his popular talents, his prestige of name and position, that, had he remained true to the principles he then advocated, he would unquestionably have been one of the foremost men of the Republican party, if not its accepted leader." *History of the Rise and Fall of the Slave Power in America*, II, 142.

[40] Sumner to Bigelow, October 24, 1851, Bigelow, *Retrospections*, I, 121.

XXXVI "OUR FEDERAL UNION . . ."

BUCHANAN carried the election of 1856, and the last fateful days of uneasy peace set in. The Jacksonians who had voted for Buchanan now watched hopefully for signs of his delivery from Southern influence. Kansas — "Bleeding Kansas" — remained the critical issue, and the submission in 1857 of a proslavery constitution, drawn up at Lecompton by a small minority of the settlers, brought affairs to a test. When Buchanan recommended the admission of Kansas under the Lecompton constitution, no one could doubt his fidelity to Doughface principles. Even Stephen A. Douglas, the father of the Kansas-Nebraska bill, turned against the administration.

1

The policy of Robert J. Walker, whom Buchanan appointed Governor of the Kansas Territory, added strength to the revolt. The Barnburners, who never forgot Jackson's mistrust of Walker nor forgave Walker's course at Baltimore in 1844, had mistaken this able, devious, soft-spoken little man. His role as expansionist seemed to pronounce him a proslavery man; but, though a Southerner, he was no more a slavery extensionist than Polk or Jackson. By 1849, as Blair discovered to his surprise and passed on to Van Buren, Walker was "a more radical free soiler than you or I": he was proposing then to broaden the Monroe Doctrine in order to make it apply to all attempts "from home or abroad 'to *africanize*' any portion of the continent now free." [1] As Governor of Kansas he tried to assure the majority of settlers the deciding voice on slavery instead of delivering the state over to the South. When Buchanan refused to back him up, Walker resigned.

Through the free states Jacksonian Democrats who had voted for Buchanan now gathered to repudiate his Kansas policy, while conservatives rallied to his support. In New York George Bancroft and

[1] Blair to Van Buren, June 10, 1849. Van Buren Papers.

A. C. Flagg took the lead in an anti-Lecompton meeting. Significantly only one businessman signed the call, and business pressure on the directors of the Academy of Music resulted in denial of the hall to the opponents of the slave power. Later the business community sponsored its own Kansas meeting which listened enthusiastically to John A. Dix's defense of the administration and endorsed the Lecompton constitution.[2] The union of conservatism was still in good working order. But the general outcry in the North eventually forced a compromise which enabled the Kansans to reconsider (and reject) the proslavery instrument.

In the meantime an even more explosive issue increased the tension. The Supreme Court, in its decision in the Dred Scott case, declared in effect that slavery could exist anywhere in the territories — a ruling which, if it were to be binding, constituted a drastic assault on the premises of the Free Soil-Republican position. But was it binding? The Court, in the mind of the Free Soilers, had proceeded beyond the point of legal issue — the citizenship of Dred Scott — and was making a set of gratuitous political pronouncements concerning questions outside its purview.

The Jacksonian tradition had always been vigorously against aggression by the judiciary; and the political antislavery movement, in the general process of fortifying itself behind the main Jacksonian positions, had taken over the case against judicial usurpation. As early as 1852 Charles Sumner had invoked the Jacksonian theory which had so horrified Webster, that the decisions of the Supreme Court were not binding on men as legislators. "I adopt with entire assent," Sumner exclaimed (as a student of Justice Story, he had gone sadly astray), "the language of President Jackson, in his memorable veto, in 1832, of the Bank of the United States."[3]

[2] *New York Democratic Anti-Lecompton Meeting;* Foner, *Business and Slavery,* 150, 152.

[3] Jackson (or Taney) had written that the opinion of the Supreme Court "ought not to control the coordinate authorities of this Government. . . . Each public officer who takes an oath to support the Constitution swears that he will support it as he understands it, and not as it is understood by others. . . . The opinion of the judges has no more authority over Congress than the opinion of Congress has over the judges, and on that point the President is independent of both. The authority of the Supreme Court must not, therefore, be permitted to control the Congress or the Executive when acting in their legislative capacities, but to have only such influence as the force of their reasoning may deserve." Richardson, *Messages and Papers,* II, 582. This statement was powerfully attacked by Webster who construed it to mean that Jackson proposed to make up his own mind on whether he would carry out laws regardless of the decisions of the Court. Presumably all Jackson meant was that laws had not been adjudicated by the Court till they had been adjudicated by the Court, even if the Court had ruled on similar laws before; but his expression was certainly ambiguous. For comment, see Van

Now this language of President Jackson had undoubtedly been set down — or at least approved — by Roger B. Taney, who, ironically enough, was the author of the main Dred Scott decision thirty-five years later. This decision was profoundly disturbing to most old Jacksonians, as it was to neo-Jacksonians like Sumner. Few of Taney's supporters in his indictment of the overweening ambitions of the Marshall bench were prepared to accompany him in his own exercises in judicial imperialism — even under Taney's own hope that he was thereby removing a critical issue from politics. Montgomery Blair, as Dred Scott's chief counsel, argued the case in the tense, silent courtroom, while his father sat proudly in the audience. George Bancroft called it "a *most* latitudinarian construction of the constitution," pointing out that the same principles would justify "almost any interference with the relation of labour." [4] Other men through the North raised in the Jeffersonian school had similar misgivings; and the two who, along with Blair, had been perhaps the closest politically to Jackson, and who, unlike Blair, had refused to break with Jackson's party in 1856, could no longer suppress their contempt for the new doctrines of the so-called Democracy.

Thomas Hart Benton was an extremely sick man. His defeat the year before in the race for the governorship of Missouri had driven him finally from politics, and by 1857 he was dying slowly and agonizingly from cancer of the rectum. But he remained grim and courageous to the end, never uttering a word of complaint, working tirelessly on his abridgment of Congressional debates. Then he read the Dred Scott decision, and the aged fighter was roused to one last magnificent outburst. In a detailed and passionate pamphlet he expressed his monstrous scorn for the perversions of democracy licensed by this supposedly Democratic tribunal.

Then he went back to his work, lying on a bed in his library, the linen snow-white, hoarsely whispering dictation to his daughter, who in turn repeated it to a secretary. A former Barnburner, now Republican Senator from Wisconsin, reported after a visit that Benton was free in his denunciations of the "so-called Democratic Party which had neither a principle or a measure in common with the Demo-

---

Buren, *Political Parties*, 325; Swisher, *Taney*, 196–197; Boudin, *Government by Judiciary*, I, 466–468 (from which the Sumner quotation is taken). Jefferson had expressed himself similarly: "These are examples of my position, that each of the three departments has equally the right to decide for itself what is its duty under the constitution, without any regard to what the others may have decided for themselves under a similar question." Jefferson to Spencer Roane, September 6, 1819, Jefferson, *Writings* (P. L. Ford, ed.), X, 142.

[4] Bancroft to J. M. Mason, July 24, 1857, Howe, *Bancroft*, II, 127.

cratic party of Jefferson & Jackson's day." [5] Sinking slowly, the old man lingered on into the spring of 1858. In April he finished the abridgment. Two days later, his powerful will finally faltering, he beckoned Kitty, his black nurse, to his bedside and said, "I shall not trouble you much longer — Do you hear that?" She listened; Benton said, "Kitty that is the death rattle." Soon he was dead.[6]

Van Buren, aging gracefully beneath his elms at Lindenwald, was equally shocked by the Court's invasion of the realm of politics. In a lengthy, and precise, analysis he pointed out how, in defiance of the principles of the party, the notion of judicial supremacy had been quietly assumed by the Court and acquiesced in by the administration. How could this have taken place in the party of Jefferson and Jackson? The old ex-President noted sadly how many of the "Democrats" of 1857, from Buchanan and Taney down, had begun their political career as Federalists. The cabinet and the Court included probably a majority of each in the same category; and an "unprecedented number" of the administration supporters in Congress on the Kansas question were from conservative backgrounds. Of some of the present Democratic leaders, Van Buren remarked dryly, he had never heard "save as extreme partisans in the ranks of our opponents."

What was happening to the party of Jackson? Van Buren profoundly feared that it was bent on promoting "the selfish and contracted rule of a judicial oligarchy, which, sympathizing in feeling and acting in concert with the money power," would destroy the democratic foundations of American government.[7]

In 1858, visited by a former Free Soiler, now active in the Republican party, Van Buren declared that his views of '48 represented his mature convictions. "I have nothing to modify or change," he said; and then, after a moment, in a tone of great earnestness, he added, "The end of slavery will come — amid terrible convulsions, I fear, but it will come." [8]

[5] Letter of James R. Doolittle, fall 1857, quoted in Smith, *Blair Family*, I, 432. See also Benton, *Historical and Legal Examination of . . . the Dred Scott Case.*

[6] Blair to Van Buren, April 12, 1858, Van Buren Papers. A ghoulish controversy followed Benton's death as to what his dying opinions were on the Buchanan administration. For the best critical account, see Smith, *Blair Family*, I, 431–438.

[7] Van Buren, *Political Parties*, 370–371, 376.

[8] Stanton, *Random Recollections*, 192.

2

In the days of Jackson — indeed, till about 1850 — the bulk of the slaveholding aristocracy had been Whigs. Then why was the Democracy now the citadel of the slave power?

The answer to this question is complex. The Democratic party was paying the price of its own radicalism. It had been the first party to divide over slavery; and those remaining in control of the organization after the Free Soil exodus were, in the main, reliable on the slavery issue. The Whig party did not split in 1848. Consequently, from being the more dependable party in 1840, from the Southern viewpoint, it became the less dependable in 1850. As Seward and his followers gained in power, the Southern Whigs wondered increasingly what they were doing in that gallery — at the very moment that the Southern Democrats were for the first time breathing easily in the party of Jefferson.

Moreover, John C. Calhoun had prepared within the Democratic party a more elaborate and conclusive set of constitutional defenses for slavery than anything devised by the Whigs. Indeed, the Southern Whigs had sacrificed a good deal of the State-rights dogma as their price for an alliance with Northern conservatism. Thus the Democratic party was more quickly rid of its antislavery sections, and it had more formidable equipment for the protection of slavery: as a result, after 1848 it became increasingly attractive to the slave power.

But, though the South had finally settled on the party of Calhoun, this did not mean the victory of Calhoun's general strategy. Calhoun had favored an alliance with the radical democrats of the North against the business community, while the Southern Whigs had held out for their alliance with Northern conservatives against radicalism. Calhoun was correct in his perception of the underlying forces — the essential clash between a liberal capitalistic society, and one founded on slave labor. But he was wrong in his belief that the capitalists would be the active agents in the assault on slavery. The Free Soil movement showed clearly that the dynamic came from the radical democrats; and, when the Southern Whigs moved into the Democratic party after 1848, their views about an alliance with Northern conservatism were adopted without a struggle. Indeed, though the Democrats after 1850 clung to State rights as a defensive doctrine, they had absorbed enough from Southern Whiggery to take a vigorous anti-State-rights position when they thought they could get away with it, as in the case of the Fugitive Slave Act or of the Dred Scott decision.

The fact was that by the fifties both the old parties had disappeared. The election of 1844, as Gideon Welles observed many years later, was "the final struggle between the two opposing elements known as democrats and whigs" which had sprung into life over the great economic questions of the thirties. "The names of these two parties," Welles added, "were continued as rallying cries several years later, but little, save the prejudices growing out of former antagonisms, remained to stimulate action." [9] From the introduction of the Wilmot Proviso politics turned on the slavery issue. By 1856 General Sam Houston could testify that, not only were the old questions which engaged Whigs and Democrats gone, but the "parties themselves have no distinctive character. They have faded, become extinct, and expired." [10]

Whatever remained of the live Jacksonian tradition had in the main, by 1858, entered the Republican party. On March 23 of that year, Frank Blair, Jr., now a Representative from Missouri, rose in the House and proposed to discuss the slavery question from a point of view which, he said, had not been treated in that hall — that of "the non-slaveholding people" of the South (which, he might have added, made up the bulk of the Democratic party of the South in the forgotten days of Andrew Jackson). He then launched into a scornful attack on the Southern oligarchy. "I make no complaint . . . of having been read out of the party. I should as soon think of complaining of being read out of a chain-gang." What was the Democratic party anyway? "I have always understood," young Blair declared, "that Democracy concerns itself more about personal rights than about rights of property — the rights of individuals rather than those of monopolizing institutions." "Was the Government founded to protect rights of property in slave labor, and not to protect the rights of freemen to their own labor?"

What a position for the Democratic party to take! "There was a time when this Democratic party was not Democratic in name alone . . . when this party took ground against privileged classes, and against every attempt on the part of capitalists to usurp the power of this Government, and pervert it to their own purposes." Blair recalled the Bank War, the battles over the tariff; "now here is another question in which this struggle between capital and labor is presented in its most odious and revolting form." Here was "a colossal aggregation of wealth invested in negroes," undertaking to seize the govern-

---

[9] Welles, "Review of Political History of the United States and Presidential Contests," 1, Welles Papers.
[10] Houston, letter of July 21, 1856, *The Republican Scrap Book*, 13.

ment and prevent the freemen of the country from entering the territories except in competition with slave labor; "and the Democratic party, instead of standing where it used to stand, in opposition to these anti-Democratic measures, is as servile a tool of the oligarchy as are the negro slaves themselves." [11]

Abraham Lincoln was amused in 1859 to note that the party supposedly descended from Jefferson had stopped mentioning his name, while the party supposedly descended from his opponents was now draping itself in his mantle. It all reminded him, he said, of a fight between two drunken men with greatcoats on. After a long contest each had fought himself out of his own coat and into the coat of the other. "If the two leading parties of this day are really identical with the two in the days of Jefferson and Adams, they have performed the same feat as the two drunken men." [12]

3

Yet not all Jacksonians would accept Blair's analysis. Mike Walsh as a member of Congress in 1854 powerfully stated the opposing case. "The only difference between the negro slave of the South, and the white wages slave of the North," Mike exclaimed, "is, that the one has a master without asking for him, and the other has to beg for the privilege of becoming a slave. . . . The one is the slave of an individual; the other is the slave of an inexorable class." He demanded that the abolitionists produce "one single solitary degradation" heaped on the slave that a Northern free laborer was not liable to suffer through poverty. "It is all very well for gentlemen to get up here and clamor about the wrongs and outrages of the southern slaves," he observed bitterly; "but, sir, even in New York, during the last year, there have been over thirteen hundred people deprived of their liberty without any show or color of offense, but because they were poor, and too honest to commit a crime." The difference between the two systems, Mike went on, was simple. "If a dozen of us own a horse in common, we want to ride him as much as possible, and feed him as little as possible. [Laughter.] But if you or I own a horse

---

[11] Blair in the House, March 23, 1858, *Congressional Globe*, 35 Congress 1 Session, 1283–1284. This speech followed the argument developed by Hinton R. Helper, in *The Impending Crisis* (1857). Helper was in close touch with the elder Blair, who perhaps even compiled the widely reprinted compendium of *The Impending Crisis*. Later editions of the work were dedicated to Frank Blair, Jr. See D. R. Barbee, "Hinton Rowan Helper," *Tyler's Quarterly Magazine*, XV, 158–159.

[12] Lincoln to H. L. Pierce, *et al.*, April 6, 1859, *Works* (Nicolay-Hay), V, 125–126.

exclusively, we will take good care to feed him well, and not drive him too much to endanger his health, but just enough to keep him in good traveling order." [13]

(Poor Mike was nearing the end. He filled his days in Washington with wisecracks and horseplay, but observers noted that in moments of repose his face was profoundly sad. Defeated in 1854, he went to Europe, to negotiate some contracts for a shipyard owned by a friend, but his irresponsibility, the careful work of a lifetime, overtook him again, this time decisively. He toured around the continent on a prolonged binge and finally returned to New York in the steerage of a sailing vessel, broken down in health and morale. There he lived a scrappy and obscure existence for a few more years. On St. Patrick's Day in 1859 he spent the evening roistering with friends in Broadway saloons. Around two in the morning Mike began to reel home. They found him the next day, dead in the areaway of a store on Eighth Avenue, sprawled down the steep flight of stone steps, his head twisted unnaturally on the last step but one, the lower steps covered with blood. His gold watch and diamond ring were missing. The next morning, thousands peered curiously down the dirty cellarway in ironic tribute to one of America's first proletarian leaders.) [14]

Yet, whatever Mike's failings, there was something to be said for his argument. The Jacksonian impulse had, after all, sprung up to meet certain inadequacies of Northern society, and for all the hullabaloo over slavery, those inadequacies continued to exist. The Free Soilers might urge that the destruction of slavery was an indispensable preliminary to further reform; but the doctrinaire radicals could not but regard this as a confession of impotence, a compulsion on the part of a bankrupt reform party to escape its responsibilities at home by going on a crusade abroad. Their own sentiments, compounded of a strong sense of guilt over Northern conditions, an intellectual inflexibility and certainly a very intense desire on their own part to avoid responsibilities, drove them into sour opposition to the whole antislavery movement.

They were basically wrong. The slavery question did, in fact, embrace the Jacksonian issues of democracy and liberty: it probably did objectively, and it certainly did as soon as enough people, North and South, showed by their conduct that they felt these issues to be vitally involved. In earlier generations democratic aspirations had ex-

[13] Walsh in the House, May 19, 1854, *Congressional Globe*, 33 Congress 1 Session, 1224.

[14] *New York Herald*, March 18, 1859; *New York Times*, March 18, 1859; McLaughlin, *John Kelly*, 152; Forney, *Anecdotes*, I, 113; Breen, *Thirty Years of New York Politics*, 307.

pressed themselves in battles over the suffrage or banking or the tariff, but in the fifties they were definitely expressing themselves in the crusade against slavery, and in no other national issue. Thus men like Walsh, despite their evident sincerity, were casting themselves adrift in national politics. By refusing to see any danger in the slave power, they were in effect supporting it. They were putting themselves outside the main stream of democratic development.

Every economic reformer blind to the implications of slavery in the fifties was dooming himself to frustration. The Land Reform group, for example, shared Walsh's feelings about the antislavery movement. Their own special anxiety about homesteads, it is true, made this nonchalance over whether free or slave labor occupied the West somewhat remarkable. But, as doctrinaires, they achieved it without difficulty. John Commerford, for example, voted for Buchanan in 1856, and he and the other leaders asserted repeatedly that the masses (*i.e.*, themselves) cared not about slavery, only about land. When Commerford considered voting Republican in 1860, it was solely because of the Republican sponsorship of the homestead issue.[15]

Walsh, Commerford, the Land Reformers — the names were symbolic of the growing incoherence of social reform. Fitzwilliam Byrdsall, living on in New York till 1875 and presumably supporting Calhoun to the bitter end, represented another aspect of futility. John Windt's name did not disappear from the New York directory till 1865, and in 1862 a tract appeared entitled *The Honest Man's Book of Finance and Politics*, copyrighted by Windt and written perhaps by John H. Hunt. If Windt approved the argument, he had abandoned the faith in Land Reform for the old orthodoxies of radical democracy. The book rehearsed the familiar arguments against the American System and expounded the values of hard money; but it added strange spiritualistic and religious excursions, and it could not have carried much weight among the workingmen. The careers of George Lippard, John Pickering, Josiah Warren, Thomas Low Nichols, Clinton Roosevelt, each absorbed in eccentric and isolated activity, testify further to the splintering of the reform movement.

Locally there was still considerable progressive action, carried on generally (as in New York and Massachusetts, Ohio and Michigan) by men who nationally were determined enemies of the slave power. The trade-union movement was once again vigorous, but it was concerned with visible benefits for small groups, and not much with national organization. The Jacksonian unity had gone: the reform

---

[15] T. A. Devyr to Andrew Johnson, December 8, 1859, Commerford to Johnson, December 17, 1859, quoted in Zahler, *Eastern Workingmen and National Land Policy*, 103, 104, 172 n.

impulse had disintegrated under the crushing impact of the slavery question.

4

In the fall of 1860 Horace Greeley, trying to describe the fury of the business community against Lincoln, could not but recall an earlier political crisis. "Nothing like it has been seen since the Bank controversy of 1832–8," he wrote; "and even that did not compare in the intensity and unanimity of the commercial furor." [16] But it compared in ineffectiveness, and in November the Republicans triumphed at the polls amid gloom in the conservative clubs and mutterings of disunion from the South.

The mutterings too were reminiscent of an earlier crisis, and many Northerners began to wish that General Jackson might be once more in the White House. In December, as old Frank Blair looked down from the gallery, Charles Sumner in the midst of a speech on secession drew a letter from his pocket and held it aloft for all to recognize the free, bold scrawl. As the hall listened in uneasy silence, Sumner contemptuously hurled the blunt Jacksonian remarks about nullification at the Southern Senators. " 'Haman's gallows ought to be the fate of all such ambitious men, who would involve their country in civil war. . . . The Tariff was only the pretext, and Disunion and a Southern Confederacy the real object.' " Then, with sharp emphasis, the grim prophecy: " 'The next pretext will be the Negro or Slavery Question.' " [17] (But who among the Southern Democrats still cared for the words of Jackson?)

And secession? Charles Francis Adams, Van Buren's running mate on the Free Soil ticket in '48, believed that the government could do nothing if the fifteen slave states went out together. Preston King, now Republican Senator from New York, and Sumner came to dinner in January, and over wine and cigars tried to convince Adams that compromise was impossible. The argument grew angry, and Adams soon froze Sumner into silence. But he listened to King (his clever son Henry reported that King, "the most amiable, fat old fanatic that ever existed," was "never offensive . . . even when saying things that in Sumner's mouth would be unpardonable.") [18] Then secession came, and even Adams quickly accepted the necessity of coercion.

"Our Federal Union, it must be preserved." The obligation was as

[16] *New York Tribune*, November 8, 1860, quoted in Foner, *Business and Slavery*, 193.

[17] Jackson to A. J. Crawford, May 1, 1833, Sumner, *Works*, V, 434–435.

[18] Henry Adams to C. F. Adams, Jr., January 17, 1861, *Letters of Henry Adams (1858–1891)*, W. C. Ford, ed., 80.

binding in 1861 as in 1830. Jacksonians everywhere, even many from
the South, recognized the superior claims of nationality. All of Jackson's Southern appointments to the Supreme Court — Catron of
Tennessee, Wayne of Georgia, Taney of Maryland — remained loyal
to the Union. Martin Van Buren drew up resolutions for the New York
state Democratic convention so antisecessionist in tone that his son
felt there was no point in submitting them to the Hunker leadership.[19]
Frank Blair became one of the new President's most useful and faithful advisers. Gideon Welles, Montgomery Blair, Salmon P. Chase and
Edwin M. Stanton all joined the cabinet.

Old Amos Kendall had watched events with mounting apprehension during the fifties. In 1856 he supported Buchanan; in 1860, still
clinging to the dream of a national President, he hoped that the followers of Douglas, Breckinridge and Bell would unite on a single candidate. But the reality of disunion fired him to action, and in 1861 he
returned to political journalism, showing in his letters on *Secession*
that his pen had lost little of its skill and none of its force. For a man
used to the prompt measures of a Jackson, the uncertainty and vacillation of the Lincoln government were alarming. Kendall called for
the vigorous prosecution of the war and as an example offered two
of his houses for use as barracks. He pressed on Seward the need for
energy, wrote spirited articles for the papers, and in February, 1862,
remarked that if Jackson had been President, "the rebellion would
not have occurred, or if it had, the rebels would ere this have been
driven into the Gulf of Mexico." [20] By 1864 he had turned against
the administration and was writing essays, one series signed "Andrew
Jackson," denouncing Lincoln for incompetence and advocating the
election of McClellan, the determined waging of the war and a generous peace.

George Bancroft emerged as another leading private citizen using
his influence in favor of a vigorous war. By the summer of 1862 he
was urging emancipation, and in that fall he was boomed for Congress
on the Republican ticket. Declining, he reiterated the Jacksonian line:
"The party at the South which made this rebellion is not, and never
was, a Democratic party; it was, and is, the most embittered hater of
Democracy . . . by the very necessity of its nature, [it] seeks to ex-
tinguish the Democratic principles." [21] During the war years he served
as a kind of unofficial representative of loyal Democratic opinion,

[19] Van Buren, "Resolutions Drawn for the New York State Democratic Convention," Van Buren Papers.
[20] Kendall, *Autobiography*, 634.
[21] Bancroft to S. P. Chase, August 9, 1862, Chase, *Diary and Correspondence*,
511–512; *Voters of Massachusetts. . . . Letter from George Bancroft, Esq.*, 10.

and after Lincoln's death he was selected to pronounce the eulogy.

Orestes A. Brownson was another Jacksonian whom the war returned to public attention. After 1844 he had retreated vociferously into the Catholic community where he carried on his stormy existence, only emerging now and then to condemn Protestantism and its works. For some years he energetically explored those lines of Catholic dogma which reject democracy and sanctify authoritarianism. In 1853 he denounced equality as "an idle dream, and empty word" and assumed pretty much the Mike Walsh position on the antislavery movement. But the arrogance of the slave power became in the end too much for his thorny nature. By the time of the Dred Scott decision he saw clearly the fatal implications of the Southern attempt to rule the nation. In 1860 he supported Lincoln with a weary conviction that the problem of Southern domination must be settled once and for all.

War mobilized his old energies. From the start he harassed the administration for its timidity and want of decision, even visiting Washington to urge on Lincoln personally the importance of emancipation. In the fall of 1862 he accepted the Unionist nomination for Congress in the third district of New Jersey. Though defeated, he kept up his tireless work for the war, writing innumerable articles, making innumerable lectures, driving himself to any sacrifice of health and of his Catholic following in order to strengthen the country. In 1864 he was involved in the conspiracy of the Radical Republicans to replace Lincoln by Frémont. In the meantime political and theological deviations caused attacks upon him within the Church; and though the charges were dismissed at Rome, the promulgation in December, 1864, of the papal encyclical *Quanta Cura*, with its wholesale proscription of liberalism, placed his recent activities under official ban. This blow, added to the collapse of the Frémont boom and the death of two sons in the war, left him sick at heart. In 1865 he dedicated a book to Bancroft "as a sort of public atonement" for the invective he had heaped on his old friend; but shortly thereafter he returned to the orthodoxies, and the last few years before his death in 1876 found him defending with vigor the most reactionary Catholic positions on almost every issue.[22]

Frederick Robinson, the old Massachusetts radical, showed in another way how the antislavery crusade had absorbed the old Jacksonian fight. He still clung in 1862 to the basic Jacksonian convictions. "The world has always been separated into two classes. . . . and the people are divided into two parties, the aristocrats and the democrats, the conservatives and progressives." He recalled a remark he had made

[22] Schlesinger, *Brownson*, 240–275.

in the thirties — that so long as conservatism continued to denounce the Democratic party, calling it "radical, loco foco, leveller, agrarian, property dividers, setters of the poor against the rich," so long the Democratic party "would be the true rallying place of the people. But when all those vile epithets shall cease, and conservatism begins to heap its virulency upon some other name, it will be a sign that they have scented corruption in the democratic party, and have gone over into its ranks." Corruption had triumphed, and he traced its growth, apologizing for his own support of Cass in 1848, and declaring that after the Kansas-Nebraska Act "all democracy left the democratic party, and every true democrat that was too intelligent to be cheated by a name, deserted its ranks." [23]

Even Theophilus Fisk, for all his one-time devotion to Calhoun, could not swallow secession. In January, 1846, he had departed from the *Democratic Expositor*, setting forth in bitter valedictory his disillusionment with the working classes for their contentment in servitude. In 1845 and 1848 he attended meetings of the Industrial Congress, but after 1848 he dropped out of sight till he reappeared in the fifties, with an additional "e" in his name, as editorial writer for the *Philadelphia Argus* and later for the *Pennsylvanian*. In 1856 he held a clerkship in the Philadelphia Navy Yard.[24] During the campaign of 1860 he revived the *Democratic Expositor*, which he made a strident antiabolitionist and antisecessionist sheet. In August he tried to launch a compromise Democratic ticket, headed by Andrew Johnson, the "Mechanic Statesman of Tennessee," but when the boom got nowhere Fiske came out for Douglas and the Union and supported the war.[25]

Of the few real Jacksonians who favored the Confederacy, John L. O'Sullivan was perhaps the most unexpected. A Barnburner in 1848, he apparently supported Van Buren without taking an active part in the campaign.[26] But more and more his impractical imagination fed on the dreams of expansion set in motion by his own famous phrase. He tried to sell Polk the idea of buying Cuba, and during Taylor and Fillmore's administration he consorted with filibusters and vaguely conceived great imperialistic expeditions. In 1852 he was actually brought to trial for filibustering. In 1853 Pierce appointed him Minister

[23] Robinson, *An Address to the Voters of the Fifth Congressional District*, 2–4, 11.

[24] *Democratic Expositor*, January 24, 1846; Commons, *Documentary History*, VIII, 26, 27; E. B. Robinson, "The *Pennsylvanian*: Organ of the Democracy," *Pennsylvania Magazine of History and Biography*, LXII, 351.

[25] *Democratic Expositor*, 1860, *passim*.

[26] Polk, *Diary*, III, 480–481.

to Portugal, where he engaged in various doubtful activities until he was removed by Buchanan in 1858.

It was probably during his return to America in 1860 that he shocked John Bigelow of the *Evening Post* by declaring himself proslavery, adding that the American Negroes ought to erect a monument by voluntary subscription to the first slave trader. He returned to Lisbon in 1861 and went to London in 1863, entertaining himself by writing prorebel letters to friends in the North. "It is the South," he blandly told Sam Tilden, "which is now fighting in defence of all the principles and rights of American liberty, for self-government and the dignity of man." After the war his life became obscure. He was in Paris in 1871 and back in New York by the end of that decade. He finally died in a hotel on East Eleventh Street in 1895, his services for democracy as well as his services for slavery having long receded into the forgotten past.[27]

Ben Butler of Massachusetts, who had few convictions of his own but had a certain skill in expressing the convictions of the audience he happened at any moment to be addressing, probably uttered adequately enough the feelings of rank-and-file Jacksonian Democrats about their Northern comrades who opposed the war. "I should like to hear old Andrew Jackson say a few words about such politicians, who call themselves Democrats," Butler declared in 1863. "He'd hang them," shouted some enthusiast in the crowd. The crafty man on the platform twisted his ugly face. "No, my friend, I don't think he would hang them. I don't think he would ever catch them." The hall rang with laughter and applause.[28]

5

The agony of war passed, and in its wake came the eternal disquiet of peace. The federal Union had been preserved. Now, it must be made real again, and to this task the remaining Jacksonian Democrats addressed themselves.

The new President was a Jacksonian from Jackson's own state, Andrew Johnson, fifty-six years old when he entered the White House in 1865. Born in North Carolina, Johnson moved West in 1826. From pinched beginnings he gradually became a successful and rather fashionable tailor in Greenville, Tennessee. In 1828, the year that Jackson the General was elected President of the United States, Johnson the

[27] O'Sullivan to Tilden, June 5, 1861, Tilden, *Letters*, I, 161. See also Bigelow, *Retrospections*, I, 280; Pratt, "O'Sullivan," *New York History*, XXXI, 226–234.

[28] Butler, *Genuine and Bogus Democracy*, 8.

tailor became an alderman of Greenville. His powerful personality and his frank appeal to the farmers and workingmen as against the cotton aristocrats won him steady political advancement. In 1835 he went to the state House of Representatives, in 1841 to the state Senate, and from 1843 to 1853 he served in the federal House of Representatives. A man of middle height, with strong and massive head, swarthy face and sturdy shoulders, his eyes black and belligerent, his bearing defiant and resolute, Johnson made himself felt in Washington.

But the sufferings of childhood and youth, the painful flounderings of a tailor in a town which respected only the farmer and the merchant, had left their mark on him. He never forgave society for these earliest hardships. They bred in him a fierce envy toward those who had won easily what for Andrew Johnson had been a severe struggle. He automatically detested wealth and refinement, hated the institutions which created the great social differences, and would turn his heavy black scowl upon any he suspected of aristocratic airs. His sense of inferiority made him secretive and suspicious. Someone noted his characteristic expression as "vigilant intelligence," with his dark eyes seeming to observe everything, and his face covered with a "kindly but yet sinister look, displaying a lurking distrust." [29]

His harsh upbringing also gave him the calm and unfeeling brutality of which he was occasionally capable. He had only contempt for fair play in politics. Kindness from an opponent seemed to him evidence of weakness. When his Whig competitor in the Tennessee gubernatorial campaign of 1853, an accomplished gentleman, waived the use of personal invective, Johnson declared with grim satisfaction, "Then, I will give him hell to-day." He bore his grudges hard, and was an implacable enemy. In debate he could be stinging and merciless, and on the hustings his personal attacks were often cruel. This combination of envy, suspicion and brutality made him often appear as cold, disdainful and arrogant as the aristocrats for whom he had so much disgust.[30]

Yet Johnson was able, honest and utterly fearless. Regarding himself as the spokesman of the non-slaveholding people of eastern Tennessee, he fought their battles with vigor and courage. In Congress he followed for the most part the Polk line, supporting annexation and the Mexican War, the Walker tariff and the independent treasury, opposing the Wilmot Proviso but never in Congress advocating slavery

[29] Hilliard, *Politics and Pen Pictures*, 130.
[30] Temple, *Notable Men of Tennessee*, 361–364, 451–466; Andrew Johnson, *Speeches . . . with a Biographical Introduction*, Frank Moore, ed.

extension or defending the institution on abstract grounds.[31] His great political contribution was the Homestead bill, which he introduced in 1846 and for which he carried on over many years a persevering and often lonely battle. This brought him to the attention of the Northern workingmen. In 1851 he received some votes in the Industrial Congress as its nominee for President, and in May, 1852, he actually addressed a New York mass meeting arranged in part by George H. Evans. In 1853, gerrymandered out of his Congressional district, Johnson ran successfully for the governorship of Tennessee, holding that position for two terms. In 1857 Tennessee sent him to the Senate.

Though Johnson never had close personal ties with Jackson or any of his immediate circle — Polk, indeed, regarded him with marked distrust — Jackson was his political idol, and his speeches had the true Jacksonian ring. He followed Cass and Douglas in their endorsement of "popular sovereignty," but he never believed, as they appeared to believe, that the achievement of political democracy exhausted the responsibilities of the democratic politician. "If, through an iniquitous system, a vast amount of wealth has been accumulated in the hands of one man, or a few men," he declared in 1864, "then that result is wrong, and the sooner we can right it the better for all concerned." The attempt to right it consumed the main part of his life. "All, or nearly all of our legislation," he said, "is for corporations, for monopolies, for classes, and individuals; but the great mass who produce while we consume, are little cared for; their rights and interests are neglected and overlooked." In 1858, when most of the South had disavowed the Declaration of Independence and was denouncing democracy, Johnson reaffirmed his faith in Jefferson and popular government, casting back into the faces of his colleagues the talk of "mud-sills" and property. "I have referred to the Declaration of Independence, and to Mr. Jefferson's Inaugural Address, for the purpose of showing that democracy means something very different from what was laid down by the distinguished Senator from Alabama. I furthermore refer to these important documents to show that property is not the leading element of government and of society." [32]

What would war do to this faith in democracy? For Johnson there was no hesitation. Democracy had a stake in only one side of the conflict, and Jackson had charted the course for a Tennessee man to follow when the Union was in danger. Johnson boldly denounced

[31] Abernethy, *From Frontier to Plantation in Tennessee*, 312–313.

[32] Johnson, *Speeches*, xxxix, 76, 63–64. His faith extended to the doctrine of agricultural virtue. "Mr. Jefferson never said a truer thing than when he declared that large cities were eye-sores in the body-politic: in democracies they are consuming cancers." *Ibid.*, 36.

the seceding Senators, observing incidentally (without "intending to disparage others") that, if Jackson had been President, the rebellion would never have taken place.[33] As War Governor of Tennessee he did his mighty best to hold the state for freedom. By 1864 he was the leading War Democrat, and in June the Union convention nominated him to run for Vice-President with Abraham Lincoln. Johnson's letter of acceptance quoted the prophecy of Andrew Jackson which Sumner had read to the startled Senate in 1860.

Yet Johnson as champion of democracy was in a sense betrayed by his private bitternesses. His early life, true enough, had been hard. Still at twenty he was an alderman, at twenty-seven a member of the state House of Representatives, at thirty-five a Congressman, and others had worked up from equally desperate beginnings. But the experience was peculiarly drastic for Johnson, wounding him deeply and scarring him for life. Thus democracy was not simply for him, as it was for Jefferson and Jackson, a set of social ideals; it was that, but it was also an instrument of revenge for the grievances of childhood. His compulsions drove him relentlessly in a personal vendetta against wealth, and this often confused and complicated the war he was waging as a disinterested public man for Jeffersonianism. His speeches, for example, were adorned with boasts of his lowly origin and calling. These neurotic feelings of inferiority burst forth most pathetically in his drunken insistence on Johnson the "plebeian" in his tragic inaugural.

They were perhaps as responsible as anything for his failure as a democratic statesman. This violence of resentment, ordinarily suppressed, under his earnest and courteous demeanor, occasionally exploded into lurid demagoguery which always harmed his cause. He lacked the instinctive restraint of the great leader who never excites the people to want more than he is able to give them. Debauching his audiences by his own excesses, he left them all the more vulnerable to assaults by more unscrupulous rabble rousers. He never knew when to stop; that inner turbulence would never permit him; and in the end he paid the penalty.

6

With Johnson's accession the surviving Jacksonians made their last serious movement to recover their former influence. Old Frank Blair, of course, knew Johnson as he knew everyone; it was to Silver

[33] *Ibid.*, 275–276.

Spring that Johnson retired for recuperation after his disgraceful inaugural. Preston King had been a friend of Johnson's for twenty
years and was especially influential in putting him forward for the
vice-presidential nomination. Gideon Welles remained as a shrewd
and loyal adviser. George Bancroft wrote Johnson's first message to
Congress. Amos Kendall declared his support of the new administration. All these men urged him to continue Lincoln's policy of generous
reconstruction. (Theophilus Fiske, erratic to the end, congratulated
Providence on placing Andrew Johnson in a position to end the
policy of "criminal clemency to traitors." Fiske was now fancying
himself an expert on divine intention. When he died in New York,
he left behind him several volumes of theological and philosophical
inquiry. Like Kendall, and like their old butt Duff Green, he ended
his days in the consolations of faith.) [34]

But the Johnson administration was a failure, in large part because
of Johnson's own defects of leadership, and with its failure collapsed
the last drive of the Jacksonians. Men who had served under Old
Hickory were old now, and dying off rapidly. John M. Niles died in
1856, Benjamin F. Butler in 1858, James K. Paulding and Ely Moore in
1860, Martin Van Buren and C. C. Cambreleng in 1862, Marcus Morton in 1864. Early on a cold morning in November, 1865, Preston
King, now Collector of the Port of New York and in an acute stage
of breakdown, carefully buttoned his overcoat over two heavy bags
of gunshot, boarded a New Jersey ferryboat, and laying his black
silk felt hat on the deck, quietly jumped into the river.[35]

John Van Buren? Years of sickness and nervous collapse had made
him a broken man. During the war he seemed faded and tired, prematurely old; his friends barely recognized him in the street. "My
incapacity for business, and disposition to dwell on, and magnify
trifles," he wrote desperately in 1861, "seems, if possible, to increase.

[34] "A concerted movement had begun to rally the ante-bellum Jacksonian Democracy to the standard of the administration. The letter files of the President offer
abundant evidence of the strength and importance of this movement." W. A. Dunning, "More Light on Andrew Johnson," *American Historical Review*, XI, 575
(April, 1906). For Blair and Johnson, see A. K. McClure, *Recollections of Half a
Century*, 243; for Preston King, J. G. Blaine, *Twenty Years of Congress*, II, 11,
186–187. Professor Dunning demonstrated Bancroft's authorship of Johnson's first
message in the article cited above; his argument is confirmed by Mrs. Bancroft's
remark to John Bigelow on April 5, 1871, quoted from Bigelow's diary in *Retrospections*, IV, 486. For Fiske, see Fiske to Johnson, April 20, 1865, Carl Sandburg,
Abraham Lincoln: the War Years, IV, 338–339; W. A. Ellis, ed., *Norwich University, 1819–1911*, II, 110.

[35] *New York Times*, November 15, 16, 1865; *New York Tribune*, November 15,
16, 1865; Welles, *Diary*, II. 386; Weed, *Autobiography*, 475.

. . . The dashing of all my hopes in life keeps me of course in a state of despondency." [36] Though he recovered from this deep depression, he was never again the glittering Prince John. When people asked about 1848, he would explain away his youthful idealism in a flash of his old wit by telling the anecdote of the boy frantically removing a load of hay by the side of the road. Someone asked the reasons for his haste. The boy, wiping his dripping face as he pointed to the pile of hay, cried, "Stranger, *dad's under there!*" [37]

In 1866 he took a European trip for his health, and on the way home fell gravely ill. For many hours he lay in delirium, talking incessantly, repeating jokes, recollecting snatches of ancient speeches, entering into wild tirades against old opponents. During his moments of lucidity he denied that his sickness was serious and tried to reject medicine and food. Shortly after he died the skies darkened, and the cold Atlantic wind blew up a furious sea till a group of sailors demanded that his body be thrown overboard to appease the elements. A double watch guarded the corpse until the ship reached New York. [38] It was the end of one of the most talented, attractive and unfortunate men ever to appear in American politics.

David Wilmot died in 1868, Amos Kendall in 1869, Frank Blair in 1876, William Cullen Bryant and Gideon Welles in 1878.

Who were left? Mostly political weak sisters, adept at following the lines of least resistance: David Dudley Field, the ambitious lawyer, mouthpiece for Jubilee Jim Fisk, Jay Gould and Boss Tweed, his example doing almost as much to retard law reform as his writings to encourage it; Samuel J. Tilden, the wealthy corporation lawyer; John A. Dix, the respectable Republican politician; Banks and Boutwell, the careerists from Massachusetts. Some men, like William Allen of Ohio, continued the lonely fight, but without direction or support on a national scale. Others turned away from politics altogether: George Bancroft to his history, Orestes A. Brownson to his religion, Amasa Walker to economics. (Walker, indeed, gave in his *Science of Wealth* [1866] the most comprehensive summary of the Jacksonian position on economic issues, reshaping the hard-money theory to fit a more complex financial structure and restating the case against the banking system in a more temperate vein. Its manner and presuppositions were much influenced by William M. Gouge, to whom Walker paid tribute in his preface.)

---

[36] John Van Buren to Martin Van Buren, January 31, 1861, Van Buren Papers.
[37] DeAlva S. Alexander, *Political History of the State of New York*, II, 129.
[38] *New York Tribune*, October 17, 1866; Charles Edwards, *Pleasantries about Courts and Lawyers of the State of New York* (New York, 1867), 239.

And the younger men? The generation growing up in the forties and fifties tended to accept the Jacksonian victories as premises of political action. When Jacksonian results could be incorporated in state constitutions, as a good many were in the two decades before the Civil War, they no longer had the glow of radical reform.[39] The rise of the slavery controversy prevented the emergence of new economic issues. Thus few young men were schooled in Jacksonian enthusiasms, and the generation which came into power after the Civil War had scant training in the methods or objectives of liberalism.

Some of the Jacksonians had sons. John Van Buren, the ablest, burned out quickly. The Blair boys never realized their full promise. Others, like William Allen Butler, kept out of politics. Some, like Arthur G. Sedgwick, the son of Theodore Sedgwick, Jr., turned against Jeffersonianism (in *The Democratic Mistake*, 1912), and another member of the family succeeded even in discovering Christian heroes in the ranks of General Franco. On the other hand, William B. Greene, son of Nathaniel Greene and nephew of Charles Gordon Greene, shocked the Massachusetts constitutional convention of 1851 by advocating female suffrage (at which time Lord Acton described him as "a doctrinaire, a horrid-looking fellow") and ended up as a Proudhonite anarchist.[40]

The Democratic party meanwhile showed few signs of recovering from its misadventures of the eighteen-fifties, while the Republican party, captured during and after the war by a boarding party of bankers and industrialists, so hastily abandoned its aspirations toward freedom and democracy that some of its ablest leaders bolted in the Liberal Republican schism of 1872, eventually to rejoin the Democrats. The Democratic endorsement of the Liberal Republican candidate Horace Greeley, once one of the most active of Whigs, the inveterate foe of Jackson, Van Buren and Silas Wright, the powerful champion of the Bank of the United States, the high tariff and internal improvements, showed the evaporation of Jacksonian issues.

In 1874 John Bigelow predicted that "the original Democratical elements of the Republican party" would return to the Democratic party, with "the Whig elements" remaining as Republicans.[41] While this may have been likely enough, the Democrats did not go very far in regaining their past vigor. In 1876 the party ran Samuel J. Tilden on an honest-government issue, and for some years this cry served

[39] See F. L. Paxson, "A Constitution of Democracy — Wisconsin, 1847," *Mississippi Valley Historical Review*, II, 3–24.

[40] *Fortnightly Review*, DCCXI, New Series, 74 (January, 1922). See also W. B. Greene, *Socialistic, Communistic, Mutualistic, and Financial Fragments*.

[41] Bigelow to von Bunsen, November 8, 1874, Bigelow, *Retrospections*, V, 172.

as a substitute for more basic reform. Not till Grover Cleveland became President did much reform energy get in control of the Democratic party, and not till the rise of William Jennings Bryan, appealing in his Cross of Gold speech to the spirit of Jackson, did this energy assume a, very radical form.

XXXVII TRADITIONS OF DEMOC-RACY

THE TRADITION of Jefferson and Jackson might recede, but it could never disappear. It was bound to endure in America so long as liberal capitalistic society endured, for it was the creation of the internal necessities of such a society. American democracy has come to accept the struggle among competing groups for the control of the state as a positive virtue — indeed, as the only foundation for liberty. The business community has been ordinarily the most powerful of these groups, and liberalism in America has been ordinarily the movement on the part of the other sections of society to restrain the power of the business community. This was the tradition of Jefferson and Jackson, and it has been the basic meaning of American liberalism.

1

Yet the tradition clearly went into eclipse for some years after the Civil War. There had risen up before the war a party of industrial control, with smooth-running organization, energetic leadership, an active program and a solid economic base. Then the new and more terrible problem of slavery had burst forth, mobilizing the loyalties and capacities of men of good will. The antislavery crusade thus drained off the energies, diverted the enthusiasm and destroyed the party of Jacksonian democracy.

In part, this was simply the physical consequence of facing an agonizing question and fighting an exhausting war. But in part, too, it resulted from the ineffectiveness of the Jacksonian approach to the war. The Jacksonian analysis correctly made it imperative for the radical democracy to combat the slave power with all its will; but that analysis did not sufficiently embrace all the facts of the situation to gain strength and urgency from the war, or even to arm itself for the struggle of survival.

Frank Blair, Jr., well stated the Jacksonian theory as it was extended to cover the conflict arising over slavery: —

This is no question of North and South. It is a question between those who contend for caste and privilege, and those who neither have nor desire to have privileges beyond their fellows. It is the old question that has always, in all free countries, subsisted — the question of the wealthy and crafty few endeavoring to steal from the masses of the people all the political power of the Government.[1]

Now this was true only in part; for, in hard fact, the war *was* principally a question of North and South. Most of the humble people of the slave states rallied eagerly to the cause of slavery — the Andrew Johnsons were the exceptions — and most of the "wealthy and crafty few" in the North backed the Union. Thus many fought on Blair's side without his reasons, and many who should have accepted his reasons fought against him. In one aspect a "class" war, a war for democracy, the Civil War was primarily a sectional war; and, like all theories of war which skip the actuality of regional and national loyalties, the Jacksonian theory of the Civil War foundered on the facts.

Accordingly, as the conflict deepened, the sectional theory gained status and authority, partly because more facts and sentiments supported it; partly also because the class theory had to be soft-pedaled in the interests of national unity, and because many conservative Northerners, fearing the explosive possibilities of the class theory, did their best to destroy it. In the end, the Jacksonian analysis, powerfully expressed before the war by the Van Burens, Preston King, the Blairs, came out a fairly academic thesis, without having gained a strong emotional appeal or a wide following from the bitter years of conflict.[2]

The instinct of a conservative writer in the *Atlantic Monthly* in 1859 was truer than the hopes of Blair. This writer, perceiving that the slavery question had absorbed Jacksonian democracy while turning it from its main objects, observed that the emergence of the sectional issue had achieved "the freedom of our later party struggles from radical theories." "From about the year 1829 to 1841," he wrote, "there was in our politics a large infusion of Socialism," but now there

---

[1] Blair in the House, March 23, 1858, *Congressional Globe*, 35 Congress 1 Session, 1284.

[2] It is unnecessary to point out that liberal thought has suffered a similar fate in the current world conflict. Substitute "America" and "Germany" for "North" and "South" in Blair's statement, and you get a conventional liberal interpretation of the present war, and one with the same weakness as the original. Ever since liberalism "emancipated" itself from nationalism, it has found it hard to cope with the facts of war.

was far less of "the feeling known as Agrarianism" than there had been in 1833.[3]

This quiescence of the Jacksonian tradition, the breakup of the Jacksonian organization, the death of the Jacksonian leaders, disarmed liberalism for the postwar struggles. In the meantime the impulse of the business community toward protective coloration, begun by Seward, Weed and Greeley in the thirties, came to triumphant culmination. By capturing the Republican party the business community captured the prestige of representing freedom and democracy. The technique of "waving the bloody shirt" — that is, of freeing the slaves again every fourth year — enabled the Republicans long to submerge the fact that they were becoming the party of monopoly and wealth. Thus, for some time after the war, the pressing economic issues were kept out of national politics. When the country returned once more to the problems which had preoccupied the thirties, the radical democrats were forgotten, their experiments unknown, their philosophy sunk in oblivion. The continuities of reform had been broken.

2

At the same time new complexities, which the Jacksonians did not have to face, were weakening the faith of even some democrats in the efficacy of the radical democratic solution — in the efficacy, that is, of unlimited reliance on popular government. Of these, the most serious was the rise of a rootless, bewildered, unstable population, the creation, on the one hand, of the spread of industrialism, and, on the other, of the rapid increase of immigration. Starting on a large scale in the eighteen-forties, thousands of Europeans, ill-educated, tractable, used to low economic standards, unused to political liberty, began flocking to American shores. There they mingled with native Americans in the large cities and mill towns, all living a scanty and desperate life at day labor, all driven into a herd, imprinted with the same mold, and subjected to a barrage of insecurities which restricted their freedom of choice and undermined their responsibility. The "people" were being degraded into the "mass," bound together, not by common loyalties and aspirations, but by common anxieties and fears.

The political consequences of the rise of this new population were plain and terrifying. The "masses," huddled together in the slums, seemed no longer, in any real sense, to be free. As voters they were

[3] C. C. Hazewell, "Agrarianism," *Atlantic Monthly*, III, 397, 396, 393 (April, 1859).

either at the beck and call of their employers, or else the dupes of unscrupulous demagogues. "Bread and circuses" appeared to be once more the formula for political success. Mike Walsh was a symbolic figure, exhibiting the good and the evil in the new mass politician: on the one hand, an honest fervor for popular rights; on the other, the methods of an accomplished political gangster — the Spartan Band and brawls in the streets and corruption at the polls ("vote early and vote often").

Yet Mike Walsh at least did, in his erratic way, have the people on his mind; but what of the men who took over Walsh's methods without his saving honesty? The rise of bosses like Fernando Wood in New York was profoundly alarming to believers in democracy.

Even more alarming in the long run were the men who took over Walsh's fervor, trumpeting their love of democracy and liberty, mainly in order to gain the power to destroy it. In New York, George Wilkes, fancy man, gossip monger, salesman of obscene literature, became an ardent Communist and wrote pamphlets extolling the Internationale and the Paris Commune. Yet the lineage from William Leggett to Mike Walsh to Walsh's pal Wilkes was straight, and much of Wilkes's appeal was couched in almost Jacksonian language.[4] Similarly in Massachusetts the unscrupulous Ben Butler became a noisy "radical," in 1884 the presidential nominee of the Anti-Monopoly party, and he too was in direct line of descent from Jacksonianism.

Many Jacksonians, reading these portents, began to succumb to the old Jeffersonian fears of the city and the industrial proletariat. In 1864 Gideon Welles and Preston King, expressing to each other their disgust that New York City could send Fernando Wood to Congress, got into a discussion of the limits of radical democracy.

"The whole city of New York," exclaimed Welles, "is alike leprous and rotten. . . . How can such a place be regenerated and purified? What is the remedy?" He confessed a reluctant belief that "in such a vicious community free suffrage was abased, and it was becoming a problem whether there should not be an outside movement, or some restriction on voting to correct palpable evil in municipal government."

King, as Welles put it, maintained the old faith. "The evil will correct itself," the veteran radical stoutly declared. "After they have disgraced themselves sufficiently and loaded themselves with taxes and debt, they will finally rouse to a sense of duty, and retrieve the city from misrule."

---

[4] Wilkes, *Defence of the Paris Commune, with Some Account of the Internationale*, 44-45.

For a moment Welles felt the "old enthusiasm of former years" return with King's unquestioning conviction. He recalled those happy days "when in the security of youth I believed the popular voice was right, and that the majority would come to right results in every community; but alas! experience has shaken the confidence I once had. In an agricultural district, or a sparse population the old rule holds," he conceded; but in the large cities? The "floating mass" seemed to him no safe depository of power. "Some permanent element is wanting in our system." [5]

Even the superb confidence of Walt Whitman was faltering. As he looked out on the post-Civil War world, as he saw "the shallowness and miserable selfism of these crowds of men, with all their minds so blank of high humanity and aspiration — then comes the terrible query, and will not be denied, Is not Democracy of human rights humbug after all"? Did these people "with hearts of rags and souls of chalk" have the grandeur of vision for self-government? He did not know; he would not "gloss over the appaling dangers of universal suffrage," but at bottom he was still convinced that the people would save themselves; he too still maintained the old faith. [6]

Yet democracy was certainly facing a problem which no rhetoric of majority rule could assuage. The rise of the masses gave the democratic appeal a sinister ambivalence. It could be employed with as much passion, and with many fewer scruples, by the Fernando Woods, the Ben Butlers and the George Wilkeses, the corrupt bosses, the proto-fascists and the proto-communists, as by the honest democrat. If democratic leadership could not solve the crucial economic problems, would not the masses, seeking in despair everywhere for relief, turn in the end to the man who would provide apocalyptic promises of everything?

The returns are not yet in. But the tired liberalism of Gideon Welles clearly exaggerated the imminence of disaster. The faith of Preston King and Walt Whitman in the recuperative capacity of American democracy, in its tendency toward self-correction, was still justified (in great part, of course, because of the natural endowments of economic wealth and geographical isolation). The people have not yet altogether become the "floating mass," and the "floating mass" itself is not beyond redemption. The future thus became a race between the radical democracy, trying to build a society which would eliminate anxiety and despair, and the black infectious taint

[5] Welles, *Diary*, I, 524.
[6] Whitman, "Notes for Lectures on Democracy and 'Adhesiveness,'" Furness, *Whitman's Workshop*, 57; "Democratic Vistas," *Prose*, 198.

of fear, which would demoralize the people and create the drive toward security at any price — as Whitman saw it, "the battle advancing, retreating, between democracy's convictions, aspirations, and the people's crudeness, vice, caprices." [7] Three quarters of a century after Gideon Welles's forebodings, the radical democracy in America still preserved, by some herculean exertions, a small but important advantage.

3

We have seen how the growth of impersonality in economic relations enhanced the need for the intervention of government. As the private conscience grew increasingly powerless to impose effective restraints on the methods of business, the public conscience, in the form of the democratic government, had to step in to prevent the business community from tearing society apart in its pursuit of profit. The rise of the "mass," by increasing the proportion of society only fitfully capable of making responsible decisions, added to the compulsion for state action. Yet by origin and creed the tradition of Jefferson was vigorously antistatist; and the conflict raised new problems for democratic thought.

This mistrust of government had roots deep in the American past. Many of the colonists, as Van Buren pointed out, had arrived with vivid recollections of the persecutions suffered by Puritan, Huguenot, Hussite and Dutch ancestors, which, "gradually stimulated into maturity and shape by the persevering injustice of the mother country, became political opinions of the most tenacious and enduring character." The first motive of American democracy was hostility against what was felt to be insupportable tyranny, and the war with Britain confirmed democracy in its suspicion of the state. Moreover, for people in the shadow of the Middle Ages, the history of liberty had been the history of the capture of guarantees and immunities from the state; and in the American republic itself, most interference by the central government — United States Bank, internal improvements, tariff — had been for the benefit of the business community. The instinct of democrats was thus to insist on the constitutional bounds of the state. Their experience of government and their reading of history, as Van Buren put it, destroyed all hope that "political power could be vested in remote hands, without the certainty of its being abused." [8]

---

[7] Whitman, "Democratic Vistas," 198.
[8] Van Buren, *Political Parties*, 51, 54.

"That government is best, which governs least," "The world is too much governed" — the mottoes respectively of the *Democratic Review* and the *Washington Globe* — expressed forcibly the prevailing antigovernmental complex. The corollary was that what government was necessary should be in the hands of the states. "The man who chiefly desires to preserve the rights of the States, and he whose interests are concentrated in perpetuating the rule of the many," as the *Democratic Review* said in 1844, "must, under our political system, use the same means to attain their ends." [9] George Bancroft observed that it was Jackson's deep conviction that "strict construction is required by the lasting welfare of the great labouring classes of the United States." [10]

These emotions about State rights and the evil of government were absorbed into and fortified by what may be called the "Jeffersonian myth." Every great social movement, as Sorel has reminded us, generates its "social myth" — the "body of images capable of evoking instinctively all the sentiments which correspond to the different manifestations" of the movement. Such a myth, though it purports to deal with the future, is by no means to be taken as a blueprint. It "must be judged as a means of acting on the present; any attempt to discuss how far it can be taken literally as future history is devoid of sense." The myths are "not descriptions of things, but expressions of a determination to act." [11] It is thus idle to refute a myth, since it exists as an emotional entirety whose essential function is to mobilize men for action.

Jackson in his vindication of his presidency to the Senate displayed some of the resources of the Jeffersonian myth. It had been his purpose, he said, "to heal the wounds of the Constitution and preserve it from further violation; to persuade my countrymen, so far as I may, that it is not in a splendid government supported by powerful monopolies and aristocratical establishments that they will find happiness or their liberties protection, but in a plain system, void of pomp, protecting all and granting favors to none, dispensing its blessings, like the dews of Heaven, unseen and unfelt save in the freshness and beauty they contribute to produce." [12] The imagery discloses the underlying pattern: the Constitution undefiled vs. the Constitution

[9] "True Theory and Philosophy of Our System of Government," *Democratic Review*, XV, 232 (September, 1844).

[10] Bancroft's eulogy in B. M. Dusenberry, comp., *Monument to the Memory of General Andrew Jackson*, 44.

[11] Georges Sorel, *Reflections on Violence* (London, n.d.), 137, 135–136, 32.

[12] Jackson, "Protest to the Senate," April 15, 1834, Richardson, ed., *Messages and Papers*, II, 92–93.

violated; plain government vs. splendid government; equal rights vs. powerful monopolies; the dews of heaven, in freshness and beauty, vs. "aristocratical establishments," with their suggestions of monarchy, wealth and decadence.

The Jeffersonian myth thus implanted and sustained in the minds of its followers a whole set of social choices: simplicity vs. ostentation; frugality vs. extravagance; rectitude vs. laxity; moderation vs. luxury; country vs. city; virtuous farmer or mechanic vs. depraved capitalist or demoralized day laborer; plain homely government vs. sumptuous complicated government; economy vs. debt; strict construction vs. loose construction; State rights vs. huge federal power; decentralization vs. concentration; democracy vs. aristocracy; purity vs. corruption.

This body of values and images animated and deepened the appeals of Jefferson, John Taylor, Jackson, Van Buren and the other Jeffersonians. They were operating in terms of a great common vision, strong, simple and satisfying, evoking the emotions which hope, memory or experience had endeared to millions of Americans, and thrusting in sharp and ugly relief the invading armies of industrialism and aristocracy. The existence of this myth in the background of the mind gave its component parts — not least the belief in the evil of government — a strong and almost sacred status.

4

Yet change brought a growing divergence between the myth and the actuality. We have seen how the pat contrasts between country and city, honest farmer and demoralized laborer, were tripped up by the realities of Jacksonian politics. In the realm of government the divergence became acute with respect to the antigovernmental complex. The neat formulas of antistatism simply failed to work. Invented as protective doctrines against aristocratic despotism, they became an embarrassment when the radical party got into power itself. Jefferson ignored them when he felt strong executive action to be necessary, and in the quiet of his retirement he even developed a general rationale for overstepping the Jeffersonian limitations.[13]

[13] See Jefferson's important letter to J. B. Colvin, September 20, 1810, *Works*, XII, 418–422. "To lose our country by a scrupulous adherence to written law, would be to lose the law itself, with life, liberty, property and all those who are enjoying them with us; thus absurdly sacrificing the end to the means. . . . The line of discrimination between cases may be difficult; but the good officer is bound to draw it at his own peril, and throw himself on the justice of his country and the rectitude of his motives." Probably this statement describes accurately the

The administration of Jackson accentuated the complexities which underlay the deceptively simple maxims of the *Globe* and the *Democratic Review*. Granted that competition free from government intervention constituted the ideal economy, what was the Jeffersonian obligation when that freedom resulted in the growth of monopolies which destroyed competition? The Jacksonian answer was government intervention — to restore the conditions of competition; that is, to "heal the wounds of the Constitution" and re-establish the principles of government in their original purity. As John L. O'Sullivan put it, "A good deal of positive government may be yet wanted to undo the manifold mischiefs of past mis-government." [14] Thus, the Jacksonians, under the banner of antistatism, could carry on a vigorous program of government intervention, and Jackson, ruling in the name of weak government, ended up by leaving the presidency stronger than it had ever been before.

Some of the details of the Jacksonian policy, however, caused orthodox Jeffersonians distinct discomfort, even those who managed to swallow such deviations as the Nullification Proclamation or the removal of the deposits.

The struggle to reconcile the Jeffersonian myth and the Jacksonian fact was fought out most candidly in the pages of the *Democratic Review*. The first issue contained a glowing and trustful statement of the Jeffersonian position, with the theory of weak government imbedded as the keystone. But what was the status of this theory in face of an army of corporations hostile to democracy? O'Sullivan wrestled with this difficulty in a casuistical article in the second number, eventually confining the theory to the federal government alone and vehemently attacking the Supreme Court for limiting the power of state governments over business.

But was this much help? After the banks suspended in May, 1837, a trade-union meeting in Philadelphia had declared in a typical outburst, "On the question of the currency, we have no confidence in the State administrations generally. . . . we hereby call upon the national administration to take all such measures as it shall judge the most expedient." [15] Where did this leave O'Sullivan's revised theory?

---

necessities of leadership in a democracy. A kind of power is required in crises which would be dangerous normally and which rests ultimately on popular approval. In any case, Jefferson's statement certainly applies accurately to the behavior of himself, Jackson, Lincoln, Wilson and the Roosevelts in major crises. Jefferson evidently regarded the Constitution as an instrument to prevent bad action but not, in cases of emergency, to prevent good.

[14] O'Sullivan, "Note," *Democratic Review*, XII, 583 (May, 1843).
[15] *Washington Globe*, May 18, 1837.

He perceived the difficulty, and the third number carried a somewhat embarrassed article justifying the robustness of Jackson's presidency, but hoping devoutly that "those great powers resident in the Executive arm, may never again be called forth into activity." [16]

And so it went. Jeffersonian fundamentalists got off the bandwagon early. Even a Jacksonian like Orestes A. Brownson could in certain moods exclaim with alarm at Jackson's "tendency to Centralization and his evident leaning to *Bureaucraticy*. . . . We are making more rapid strides towards . . . Centralization and to the Bureaucratic system than even the most sensitive nullifier has yet suspected." [17]

It is no wonder that the attempt to defend Jacksonianism in terms of that government being best which governed least excited only the derision of the Whigs. To them Jacksonian policy consisted simply, as Caleb Cushing described it, of "the meddlesome interference of General Jackson in the business of the country, his prurient tampering with the currency under the pretext of reforming it," and so on.[18] The talk about restoring constitutional purity seemed a cynical pretext for reckless government intervention.

The vital point underlying this bandying of accusations is that "intervention" is not an absolute. It is always a question of whose ox is gored. Government *must* act; it cannot rest in Olympian impartiality. Even "governing least" is likely to be government for the benefit of the strongest group in the community. The crucial question is not, Is there "too much" government? but, Does the government promote "too much" the interests of a single group? In liberal capitalist society this question has ordinarily become in practice, Is the government serving the interests of the business community to the detriment of the nation as a whole? This has been the irrepressible conflict of capitalism: the struggle on the part of the business community to dominate the state, and on the part of the rest of society, under the leadership of "liberals," to check the political ambitions of business.

The real issue between the Whigs and Jackson was, thus, not freedom of enterprise. Both parties would concede that enterprise should be free, would claim always to be acting to protect this freedom,

---

[16] "Executive Usurpation," *Democratic Review*, I, 290 (February, 1838).

[17] *Boston Reformer*, August 4, 1837.

[18] Cushing in the House, September 25, 1837, *Register of Debates*, 25 Congress 1 Session, 889. In 1834 William Leggett complained, "The attempts of the democracy to reassume their rights are clamorously denounced as usurpations of the rights of others; and all their efforts to restore the government to its original purity, stigmatized as encroachments on its long established principles." *New York Evening Post*, October 23, 1834. The skepticism of the conservatives is understandable.

and each, when in possession of the state, would unhesitatingly intervene in business, on its own behalf and in the name of "freedom," by destroying United States Banks or establishing protective tariffs. The champions of Jeffersonianism were eager for government to suppress small notes and institute a ten-hour day, while the Hamiltonians would flourish free-trade principles when questions of trade-unionism or corporation control were brought up. If the men of the thirties and forties really accepted the antistatist maxims they constantly invoked, they would not have been in political parties at all, but in lonely huts around country ponds like the one man of the day who believed radically that that government was best which governed least.

The question was not principles but power: was a "liberal" government, in fact, strong enough to act contrary to the wishes of the business community? And in the struggle over this basic question conservatism or liberalism would adopt any myth, and has adopted most which promised to promote its cause. This is not to impugn the honesty of belief in the visions excited by the myth, for no great social movement can exist without such stimulus and support. The myth, it should never be forgotten, expresses only the "determination to act." The ends of action lie necessarily in an inscrutable future.

5

There were, in fact, certain "strong government" strains implicit in Jeffersonianism from the start. Jefferson himself could refer to "the protecting hand of the legislature." Speaking of the distresses caused by paper money, he would declare that they could not fail to "engage the interposition of the legislature."[19] The decisions of Marshall's Court, safeguarding corporations from the operations of state laws, intensified the Jeffersonian tendency to aggrandize the state governments. "The restoration of public supremacy," observed Charles Jared Ingersoll, arguing for legislative control over charters of incorporation, "is the great desideratum."[20] A Democratic Justice from Virginia, Philip P. Barbour, firmly and emphatically expanded the police power of the states against the disciples of Marshall.[21]

[19] Jefferson to W. C. Rives, November 28, 1819, Jefferson, *Writings* (Ford), X, 151 n., 150.
[20] "Speech of Charles J. Ingersoll. In the Convention of Pennsylvania," *Democratic Review*, V, 99 (January, 1839).
[21] See, especially, Barbour's opinion in *City of New York v. Miln*, 11 Peters 139.

Once government was conceded some virtue in the states, it was difficult not to extend a little of the exoneration to the federal government. Some functions were simply too important to be confided to the states. As Thomas Hart Benton remarked of the currency, it should not be trusted to any authority "but the highest and most responsible which was known to our form of government" — the people's government at Washington.[22] The experience of the eighteen-thirties, when, from a Jacksonian point of view, state governments were exceedingly unreliable and the federal government was the stronghold of democracy, increased the tendency toward tolerance.

The pivotal conception in this redirection of the liberal tradition was expressed very ably by Taney in his Charles River Bridge decision. "The object and end of all government," he declared, "is to promote the happiness and prosperity of the community by which it is established; and it can never be assumed, that the government intended to diminish its power of accomplishing the end for which it was created."[23]

Now this remark appalled no Jacksonians and delighted no Hamiltonians; yet it foreshadowed a basic shift in the Jeffersonian theory, in the direction of Hamiltonianism. For Taney's maxim could hardly be distinguished from observations made by Hamilton and Marshall: —

> Now it appears to the Secretary of the Treasury that this *general principle* is *inherent* in the very *definition* of government, and *essential* to every step of the progress to be made by that of the United States, namely: That every power vested in a government is in its nature *sovereign*, and includes, by *force* of the *term*, a right to employ all the *means* requisite and fairly applicable to the attainment of the *ends* of such power, and which are not precluded by restrictions and exceptions specified on the Constitution, or not immoral, or not contrary to the *essential ends* of political society.[24]
> Let the end be legitimate, let it be within the scope of the Constitution, and all means which are appropriate, which are plainly adapted to that end, which are not prohibited, but consist with the letter and spirit of the Constitution, are constitutional.[25]

Jeffersonianism, if it were to follow the lead of the Taney formula, must abandon a good deal of its abhorrence of the state. And what other lead could it follow? Was not Jackson's administration — was

[22] Benton, *Thirty Years' View*, I, 450.
[23] *Charles River Bridge v. Warren Bridge*, 11 Peters 547.
[24] Hamilton to Washington, February 23, 1791, Hamilton, *Works*, III, 446.
[25] *McCulloch v. Maryland*, 4 Wheaton 421.

not Taney's very decision — a confession that Jeffersonianism required Hamiltonian means to achieve its ends?

Jacksonian democracy lacked, however, a great creative political philosopher, who would perceive the essential drift of the Taney doctrine, formulate its implications and restate basically the principles of the liberal faith. The Jeffersonian myth was so persuasive, and Jacksonian action could be so plausibly explained as hewing the way back to original principles, that few were prepared to face the vital gap in the Jeffersonian argument. Yet this gap had to be faced. For if, in the ideal state, government was to be confined to the narrowest possible sphere, what was there to prevent the proliferation of the very monopolies that would, at some later date, require the active intervention of the government? Without a strong government, in other words, how could the people ever hope to deal with the business community? A Jeffersonian would answer that at least the "aristocracy" could do less harm in control of a weak government than a strong one. But under a weak government would not economic power gain the aristocracy all the control they needed? And was not the whole moral of the Jacksonian experience that only a strong people's government could break up the power of concentrated wealth?

But the Jeffersonians refused to admit this final step. Each energetic employment of the government for Jeffersonian ends was for them an exception, a transition stage, irrelevant to theory. In fact, they dared not acknowledge the true answer. They had to suppress it. The birth of democracy in revolt against tyranny had a traumatic effect on Jeffersonian democracy, coloring it with morbid fears of despotism, conditioning it to hate the state, inducing a whole complex of fantasies about government, which made it impossible for Jeffersonians to accept its necessity and drove them to hide what they were doing under a cabalistic repetition of the slogans of antistatism.

This persistence of the Jeffersonian myth during the Jacksonian period had, moreover, great immediate advantages. Indeed, the very fact of its persistence was presumptive proof of its necessity. It corresponded more accurately and profoundly to the needs of the people than any alteration could have. In particular, it united, for more or less harmonious action over a long period, two essentially unfriendly groups: on the one hand, those opposing the business community from the point of view of the *rentier* class, the landed aristocracy, North as well as South; and on the other, those opposing it from the point of view of the small farmer and workingman. Their differences in interest, social status and ultimate hopes were concealed by their common absorption in the slogans and images of Jeffersonianism.

Small points occasionally betrayed the basic divergence. The first group, for example, exulted in the word "conservative," like Calhoun, Cooper, Taney, Hawthorne, the middle Brownson, and regarded themselves primarily as guardians of the sacred flame, cherishing the purest essence of the Jeffersonian past. The other group exulted in the word "radical," like Van Buren, Bancroft, Blair, Benton, the early Brownson, and regarded themselves as crusaders, out to realize the full values of the Jeffersonian tradition. The first group was defensive in outlook, fundamentally oriented in favor of a vanishing order, and on its behalf assisting in assaults on the aggressive sections of the existing order, while the second was itself aggressive, interested above all in transforming the existing order according to the Jeffersonian faith. The alliance broke down when the emergence of slavery, presenting the basic challenge, called the bluff of the "conservative" Jeffersonians.

6

But, in the long run, the failure to codify the Jacksonian deviations was unfortunate for American liberalism. With Jackson's mighty personality removed and the lessons of his presidency unlearned, his party tended to relapse into the antistatist formulas. The Jeffersonian myth was allowed to linger on, gaining a certain venerability and sanctity; and as a strong government became more clearly the necessary instrument of greater democracy, the business community rushed to fortify itself behind the antigovernmental parts of the Jeffersonian tradition. Ever since, conservatives have been turning to the Jeffersonian myth for weapons to defeat Jefferson's essential purposes. When the antistatist formulas are invoked today, it is ordinarily in defense of the very interests which Jefferson was using them to attack.

After the Civil War, conservatism, draping itself in the mantle of Jefferson and assuming the credit for destroying slavery, stared down the pretensions of any other group to stand for "democracy." Liberalism, deprived of the social myth which had united and sustained it before the war, was left uncertain and incoherent. Men of liberal inclination had nothing with which to mobilize their forces against the rule of the business community.

It was this sense of democratic impotence, intensified by the cynicism of postwar politics, which caused Walt Whitman to define "our fundamental want to-day" — a new faith, "permeating the whole mass of American mentality, taste, belief, breathing into it a new breath of life, giving it decision . . . radiating, begetting appropriate teachers, schools, manners, and, as its grandest result, accomplishing . . . a religious and moral character beneath the political and productive and intellectual bases of the States."

Whitman was demanding, among other things, a new social myth, which would serve the liberal tradition as the Jeffersonian myth had served it before the war. He recognized keenly how "the great literature," as he called it, "penetrates all, gives hue to all, shapes aggregates and individuals, and, after subtle ways, with irresistible power, constructs, sustains, demolishes at will." Unless radical democracy could thus inaugurate "its own perennial sources, welling from the centre for ever, its strength will be defective, its growth doubtful, and its main charm wanting." He announced the time had come for "a native expression-spirit . . . sternly taking command, dissolving the old, sloughing off surfaces, and from its own interior and vital principles, reconstructing, democratizing society." Whitman himself made the greatest sustained attempt to create the "single image-making work," but the need he had perceived could be filled only secondarily by literature. As he saw at other times, "the exercise of Democracy" contained the greatest promise for salvation. The very struggle for liberty and equality was immensely valuable; "strength it makes & lessons it teaches," and from it would emerge the great men who would renew and incarnate democratic ideals.[26]

In the end, exercise rather than literature saved democracy. A century of bitter experience in the democratic fight finally led liberalism to uncover what the Jeffersonians had buried: the need for a strong government. The impotence of the Jeffersonian state to realize Jeffersonian ends first became clear in the economic field, as it grew increasingly apparent that workingmen required protection from the mercies of their employers. Jackson and Van Buren sponsored the ten-hour day and worried over the power of businessmen to drive wages below subsistence. As George Bancroft declared in 1854, *laissez faire* might solve problems of international trade, "but its abandonment of labor to the unmitigated effects of personal competition can never be accepted as the rule for the dealings of man to man. . . . The good time is coming, when humanity will recognise all members of its family as alike entitled to its care; when the heartless jargon of overproduction in the midst of want will end in a better science of distribution."[27]

Such aspirations, in last analysis, called for government to take

[26] Whitman, "Democratic Vistas," *Prose*, 199–200, 202, 236, 218; "Notes for Lectures on Democracy and 'Adhesiveness,'" Furness, *Whitman's Workshop*, 57, 58.
[27] Bancroft, *The Necessity, the Reality, and the Promise of the Progress of the Human Race*, 34.

a much more active role in economic life. One of the first to acknowledge the inadequacy of the Jeffersonian view was the rascally but
thoroughly intelligent Ben Butler of Massachusetts. While he had
been "dazzled with the brilliancy of Jackson's administration," he
wrote in his autobiography, "I early had sense enough to see that it
conflicted, in a very considerable degree, with the teachings of
Jefferson." The conclusion seemed obvious. "As to the powers and
duties of the government of the United States, I am a Hamiltonian
Federalist. As to the rights and privileges of the citizen, I am a
Jeffersonian Democrat." [28]

Slowly the liberal tradition was overhauled, and the twentieth century saw the final disappearance of the Jeffersonian inhibitions. The
Hamiltonian progressivism of Theodore Roosevelt ushered in a period
of energetic government. Woodrow Wilson understood even more
plainly the need for executive vigor and government action. Franklin D. Roosevelt carried out these tendencies more decisively than
Wilson, and the New Deal achieved the emancipation of liberalism
from this aspect of the Jeffersonian myth. By 1941 Roosevelt could
observe that the criteria of the liberal party were its beliefs in "the
wisdom and efficacy of the will of the great majority" and in the
"duty" of government intervention. [29]

7

The final rejection of the Jeffersonian case for weak government does not mean that liberalism must herewith commit itself in-
extricably to the philosophy of government intervention. That would
be to create a myth as misleading as Jeffersonian antistatism. Roosevelt himself has pointed to one obvious danger. "We have built up
new instruments of public power. In the hands of a people's Government this power is wholesome and proper. But in the hands of
political puppets of an economic autocracy such power would provide
shackles for the liberties of the people." [30]

Some who talk about the infallibility of "planning" should ponder
these words. So long as democracy continues, the government will
periodically change hands; and every accretion to the power of the
state must be accounted as a weapon of a future conservatism as

[28] Butler, *Butler's Book*, 85.
[29] Roosevelt went on to cite Lincoln's version of the remark we have noted in
Taney, Hamilton and Marshall: "the legitimate object of government is to do for
a community of people whatever they need to have done, but cannot do at all,
or cannot do so well, for themselves, in their separate and individual capacities."
Roosevelt, *Public Papers*, VII, xxix–xxx.
[30] Roosevelt, *Public Papers*, V, 16.

well as of a present liberalism. It is not too much to anticipate that the fortunes of interventionism may duplicate the fortunes of free enterprise, and what began as a faith for liberals end up as a philosophy for conservatives.[31]

The problem of liberalism is rather to preserve as much variety within the state as is consistent with energetic action by the government. The chief enemy of variety, and thus of liberty, is likely to be that group which is most powerful and consequently needs liberty least. In American history that group has ordinarily been (though it may not always be so in the future) the business community. The judgment of American liberalism has been that it was best for the whole society, including the capitalists, that their power be constantly checked and limited by the humble members of society. The Jacksonian attempt to carry out this judgment challenged two other theories of society, which had able advocates both a century ago and today.

One was the theory of Federalism: that, since this is a capitalistic society, the class most interested in its security and prosperity is the capitalist class, which thus should have the most power. The theory has survived every test but experience. It simply has not worked. Since the Federalist party the American business community appears to have lost its political capacity: it has not been, in the strict sense, a ruling class. In placid days political power naturally gravitates to it as the strongest economic group in the state; but through American history it has been unable to use that power very long for national purposes. Moved typically by personal and class, rarely by public, considerations, the business community has invariably brought national affairs to a state of crisis and exasperated the rest of society into dissatisfaction bordering on revolt.

It is this moment of crisis which can unite the weaker groups and frighten the business community sufficiently to bring "liberalism" into power. Every great crisis thus far in American history has produced a leader adequate to the occasion from the ranks of those who believe vigorously and seriously in liberty, democracy and the common man. The sense of public responsibility, the ability to inspire national confidence, the capacity to face imperative issues, seem in this country to have been largely the property of the great democratic leaders, while in England, for example, the people have been able in crises to turn to the aristocracy for truly national government.

---

[31] Now that a past liberalism has become a present conservatism, it will be of increasing interest to observe how much less outraged businessmen become over a bureaucracy under their own control.

In the past, when liberalism has resolved the crisis and restored tranquillity, conservatism has recovered power by the laws of political gravity; then it makes a new botch of things, and liberalism again must take over in the name of the nation. But the object of liberalism has never been to destroy capitalism, as conservatism invariably claims — only to keep the capitalists from destroying it.

This essential conservatism of American liberalism brings it into conflict with the second antagonistic theory: the theory of socialism, which in the Fourierite form excited so many intellectuals in the eighteen-forties. This theory would say that capitalism is hopelessly wrong in principle, and salvation can lie only in its total abolition and the formation of new collectivisms. In the century since Jackson, socialism has far outstripped Federalism as the hope of mankind. Yet the history of the past decade has perhaps made it harder to respond to its promise with enthusiasm. The search for a New Order is somewhat less inspiring now that we have seen in practice what such New Orders are likely to be. As yet, none have shown much capacity to reconcile liberty with their various forms of regimentation; indeed, all have dispensed quite cheerfully with the liberal virtues. Perhaps those may not be the virtues of the future, but that has not yet been demonstrated.

In a time like the middle of the twentieth century, when the pressures of insecurity have driven people to the extremes of hope and anxiety, the Jacksonian experience assumes special interest. Its details are, of course, obsolete, but its spirit may be instructive. In an age dominated by the compulsive race for easy solutions, it is well to remember that, if social catastrophe is to be avoided, it can only be by an earnest, tough-minded, pragmatic attempt to wrestle with new problems as they come, without being enslaved by a theory of the past, or by a theory of the future.

For Jefferson and Jackson the demands of the future — whatever readjustments they may compel for our government and our economy — will best be met by a society in which no single group is able to sacrifice democracy and liberty to its own interests. "It will never be possible for any length of time for any group of the American people, either by reason of wealth or learning or inheritance or economic power," declared Roosevelt in 1936, perhaps a trifle optimistically, "to retain any mandate, any permanent authority to arrogate to itself the political control of American public life. This heritage . . . we owe to Jacksonian democracy — the American doctrine that entrusts the general welfare to no one group or class, but dedicates itself to the end that the American people shall not be thwarted in their high purpose to remain the custodians of their own destiny." [32]

The Jacksonian attitude presumes a perpetual tension in society, a doubtful equilibrium, constantly breeding strife and struggle: it is, in essence, a rejection of easy solutions, and for this reason it is not always popular. One of the strongest pressures toward the extremes, whether of socialism or of conservatism, is the security from conflict they are supposed to insure. But one may wonder whether a society which eliminated struggle would possess much liberty (or even much real stability). Freedom does not last long when bestowed from above. It lasts only when it is arrived at competitively, out of the determination of groups which demand it as a general rule in order to increase the opportunities for themselves. To some the picture may not be consoling. But world without conflict is the world of fantasy; and practical attempts to realize society without conflict by confiding power to a single authority have generally resulted (when they have taken place on a larger stage than Brisbane's phalansteries) in producing a society where the means of suppressing conflict are rapid and efficient.

"Sometimes it is said that man can not be trusted with the government of himself," said Jefferson. "Can he, then, be trusted with the government of others? Or have we found angels in the forms of kings to govern him?" "The unfortunate thing," adds Pascal, "is that he who would act the angel acts the brute." [33] The great tradition of American liberalism regards man as neither brute nor angel.

[32] Roosevelt, *Public Papers*, V, 198.
[33] Jefferson's First Inaugural, Richardson, *Messages and Papers*, I, 322; Pascal, *Pensées* (Everyman), 99.

APPENDIX

THE ADVOCATES of the hard-money policy reiterated constantly that they had no intention, as their opponents charged, of doing away with the banking system and establishing an exclusively metallic currency. As Calhoun stated the issue with characteristic precision, "The question is, not between credit and no credit, as some would have us believe; but in what form credit can best perform the functions of a sound and safe currency." (Calhoun in the Senate, September 18, 1837, *Register of Debates*, 25 Congress 1 Session, 63.)

But the charge that the Jacksonians wanted to overthrow the banking system was politically potent, and conservatives rang all the changes on it. Even historians who have not written on this period exclusively out of the orations of Webster and Clay have sometimes been misled by this charge, because of the special meaning the period attached to the word "bank." Note issue was regarded as the characteristic function of banks, and an attack on the "banking system" or on "banks" meant generally an attack on the power of private note issue. It did not mean the elimination of the functions of discount or deposit. Cf. Albert Gallatin to A. C. Flagg, December 31, 1841, Flagg Papers: "I use the term, *banking*, in that sense in which it is universally understood in the U. States, that is to say, as implying the permission to issue a paper currency." Or Daniel Webster, arguing before the Supreme Court in the case of *Bank of the United States v. William D. Primrose*, February 9, 1839, Webster, *Writings and Speeches*, XI, 127: "What is that, then, without which any institution is not a bank, and with which it is a bank? It is a power to issue promissory notes with a view to their circulation as money." Or Orestes A. Brownson in the *Boston Reformer*, August 18, 1837: "Anti-bank men understand by a *bank an incorporated or chartered institution, chartered for the purpose*, among other things, of *issuing its notes to circulate among the people as money*. In this sense we are opposed to all banking . . . and in this sense the Anti-bank men generally have supposed General Jackson, president Van Buren, Mr. Benton and the Globe to be opposed to all banking." See also Miller, *Banking Theories*, 11–12.

A few typical statements of the objectives of the hard-money policy follow.

Roger B. Taney, Letter to the Ways and Means Committee, April 15, 1834, *Register of Debates*, 23 Congress 1 Session, Appendix, 160: "No commercial or manufacturing community could conduct its business to any advantage without a liberal system of credit. . . . This cannot be obtained without the aid of a paper circulation founded on credit. It is therefore not the interest of this country to put down the paper currency altogether. The great object should be to give to it a foundation on which it will safely stand. . . . The state of the currency, then, which is proposed in the foregoing observations, would provide silver and gold for ordinary domestic purposes, and the smaller payments; and the banks of the different states would easily be able to furnish exchanges between distant places according to the wants of commerce. . . . Funds are more conveniently and safely transferred from place to place by drafts and bills of exchange than by bank notes."

William M. Gouge, *Journal of Banking*, October 13, 1841: "We do not contend for an *exclusive metallic medium:* but we believe that THE MONEY of the country should be *exclusively metallic.* To this metallic money we would add bills of exchange, and such other devices as merchants might choose to adopt for economising the use of specie. To bank notes of such denominations as would make them *representatives of bona fide bills of exchange,* we would not particularly object."

Theophilus Fisk, *Labor the Only True Source of Wealth,* 22: "But it may be asked would you banish paper altogether, would you have a currency exclusively metalic, and if so how are we to make remittances to distant parts of the country? To this we answer let us have an exclusive metalic currency, for our *circulating* medium, and let paper be confined to commercial operations, such as drafts, bills of exchange, &c."

William Leggett, *Plaindealer,* June 24, 1837: "Mr. Tallmadge's pretended horrour of an 'exclusive metallick currency' is mere affectation. It is a hypocritical phrase, thrown in to divert attention from the true issue. No party, no faction, and we may almost say no individual, contends for a compulsory and exclusive metallick currency. The 'visionary theorists' at whom he turns up his senatorial nose ask only, not the annihilation of credit, but the separation of it from political control and intermeddling."

C. C. Cambreleng in the House, October 13, 1837, *Register of Debates,* 25 Congress 1 Session, 1629: "Banking, legitimate banking, is a trade, and should be as free as all other trades. . . . Currency, sir, is not a trade. Governments will be called upon to decide whether an attribute of sovereignty shall be exercised by trading companies, and, if so, to what extent."

Thomas H. Benton in the Senate, March 14, 1838, *Congressional Globe*, 25 Congress 2 Session, Appendix, 217–218: "Large mercantile payments always . . . will be made in bits of paper, representing masses of property. . . . So far as large mercantile operations are concerned, specie is but an inferior part of the means of payment. With the body of the community, it is different. Specie is, or should be, the main part of their payment, and with every government it should be the sole instrument of payments."

Robert J. Walker in the Senate, January 21, 1840, *Congressional Globe*, 26 Congress 1 Session, Appendix, 142: "Sir, in opposing the banks of circulation, I do not object to banks of exchange, of discount, and deposite, issuing no paper currency. The bill of exchange long preceded all banks of circulation, and will as certainly survive their downfall. This useful instrument of commerce should be encouraged."

BIBLIOGRAPHY

I. *Manuscripts*

Nathan Appleton Papers, Massachusetts Historical Society.
George Bancroft Papers, Massachusetts Historical Society.
F. P. Blair-John C. Rives Papers, Library of Congress.
Orestes A. Brownson Papers, Notre Dame University Library.
William Cullen Bryant Papers, New York Public Library.
Edward Everett Papers, Massachusetts Historical Society.
A. C. Flagg Papers, New York Public Library.
Henry D. Gilpin Papers, Pennsylvania Historical Society.
Andrew Jackson Papers, Library of Congress.
Andrew Jackson-W. B. Lewis Papers, New York Public Library.
A. A. Lawrence Papers, Massachusetts Historical Society.
William L. Marcy Papers, Library of Congress.
Marcus Morton Papers, Massachusetts Historical Society.
James K. Polk Papers, Library of Congress.
Theodore Sedgwick Papers, Massachusetts Historical Society.
Jared Sparks Papers, Harvard College Library.
Charles Sumner Papers, Harvard College Library.
Roger B. Taney Papers, Library of Congress.
Roger B. Taney Papers, Maryland Historical Society.
Martin Van Buren Papers, Library of Congress.
Gideon Welles Papers, Library of Congress.
Gideon Welles Papers, New York Public Library.

II. *The Jacksonian Tradition: Source Materials in Defense, Explanation and Reminiscence of Jacksonian Democracy*

1. Newspapers

Argus of Western America (Frankfort, Kentucky), 1828–1830.
Bay State Democrat (Boston), 1839–1843.
Boston Post, 1831–1848.
Boston Reformer, 1834–1838.
Boston Republican, 1848.
Commonwealth (Boston), 1849–1852.
Hampshire Republican (Northampton, Massachusetts), 1835.
National Laborer (Philadelphia), 1837.

New England Artisan, and Laboring Man's Repository (Pawtucket, Providence, Boston), 1832–1834.
New Era (New York), 1836–1840.
New York Democrat, 1836.
New York Evening Post, 1832–1852.
New York Independent Press, 1835.
New York Plebeian, 1843–1844.
Plymouth Rock and County Advertiser, 1839.
Union (New York), 1836.
Washington Globe, 1831–1844.
Working Man's Advocate (New York), 1830–1835, 1844–1845.

2. Magazines

Boston Investigator, 1832–1836.
Boston Quarterly Review, 1838–1842.
Campaign (New York), 1844.
Democratic Expositor (Washington), 1845–1846, 1860.
Democratic Review (Washington and New York), 1837–1846.
Free Trade Advocate and Journal of Political Economy (Philadelphia), 1829.
Journal of Banking (Philadelphia), 1841–1842.
Kendall's Expositor (Washington), 1841–1844.
People's Democratic Guide (New York), 1841–1842.
Plaindealer (New York), 1836–1837.
Priestcraft Unmasked (New York), 1830.
Radical Reformer & Working Man's Advocate (Philadelphia), 1835.
Rough-Hewer (Albany), 1840.
Subterranean (New York), 1843–1845.

3. Books and Pamphlets

Address of the Democratic Members of the Massachusetts Legislature to Their Constituents and the People, at the Close of the Session for 1841 (Boston, n.d.).
Allen, Samuel Clesson, *An Address Delivered . . . before the Hampshire, Franklin & Hampden Agricultural Society, October 27, 1830* (Northampton, 1830).
Allen, Samuel Clesson, *An Oration, Delivered at Petersham, July 4, 1806* (Boston, n.d.).
Bancroft, George, *Address at Hartford . . . Feb. 18, 1840* (n.p., n.d.).
Bancroft, George, "The Bank of the United States," *North American Review*, XXXII, 21–64 (January, 1831).
Bancroft, George, "Correspondence with Martin Van Buren," W. C. Ford, ed., *Proceedings of the Massachusetts Historical Society*, XLII, 381–442.
Bancroft, George, "Marcus Morton, of Massachusetts," *Democratic Review*, IX, 383–395 (October, 1841).

Bancroft, George, *Martin Van Buren* (New York, 1889).

Bancroft, George, *The Necessity, the Reality, and the Promise of the Progress of the Human Race* (New York, 1854).

Bancroft, George, *An Oration Delivered before the Democracy of Springfield and Neighboring Towns, July 4, 1836* (Springfield, 1836).

Bancroft, George, *An Oration Delivered on the Fourth of July, 1826, at Northampton, Mass.* (Northampton, 1826).

Beardsley, Levi, *Reminiscences* (New York, 1852).

Benton, Thomas Hart, *Historical and Legal Examination of That Part of . . . the Dred Scott Case, Which Declares the Unconstitutionality of the Missouri Compromise Act* (New York, 1857).

Benton, Thomas Hart, *Thirty Years' View* (New York, 1854).

Berrian, Hobart, *Brief Sketch of the Origin and Rise of the Workingmen's Party in the City of New York* (Washington, [1840]).

Bigelow, John, *Life of Samuel J. Tilden* (New York, 1895).

Bigelow, John, *Retrospections of an Active Life* (New York, 1909–1913).

Bigelow, John, *William Cullen Bryant* (Boston, 1890).

Blair, Francis P., *Gen. Jackson and James Buchanan* (n.p., [1856]).

Blair, Francis P., *Letter . . . to a Public Meeting in New York, Held April 29, 1856* (Washington, [1856]).

Blair, Francis P., *Letter . . . to the Republican Association of Washington, D.C.* (n.p., [1856]).

Blair, Francis P., *Republican Documents. Letter . . . to My Neighbors* (n.p., [1856]).

Blair, Francis P., Jr., *Speech . . . on the Kansas Question; Delivered in the House of Representatives, March 23, 1858* (Washington, 1858).

Bolles, John A., *Review of Dr. Wayland's Discourse on the Affairs of Rhode Island* (Boston, 1842).

Boutwell, George S., *Reminiscences of Sixty Years in Public Affairs* (New York, 1902).

Bradley, Cyrus P., *Biography of Isaac Hill* (Concord, New Hampshire, 1835).

Brownson, O. A., *Address of the Workingmen of Charlestown, Massachusetts, to Their Brethren throughout the Commonwealth and the Union* (n.p., [1840]).

Brownson, O. A., *Babylon Is Falling, a Discourse Preached . . . May 28, 1837* (Boston, 1837).

Brownson, O. A., "The Convert," *Works*, H. F. Brownson, ed., volume V (Detroit, 1884).

Brownson, O. A., *Oration before the Democracy of Worcester and Vicinity . . . July 4, 1840* (Boston, 1840).

Brownson, O. A., *Oration . . . Delivered at Washington Hall, July 5th, 1841* (New York, 1841).

Brownson, O. A., *Oration on the Scholar's Mission* (Boston, 1843).

Bryant, W. C., *Prose Writings*, Parke Godwin, ed. (New York, 1884).

Buchanan, James, *Works*, J. B. Moore, ed. (Philadelphia, 1908–1911).

Butler, Benjamin F., *Butler's Book* (Boston, 1892).

Butler, Benjamin F., *Genuine and Bogus Democracy* (n.p., [1863]).

Butler, W. A., *Martin Van Buren: Lawyer, Statesman and Man* (New York, 1862).

Butler, W. A., *Retrospect of Forty Years, 1825–1865*, Harriet A. Butler, ed. (New York, 1911).

Butler, W. A., *Revision of the Statutes of the State of New York* (New York, 1889).

Byllesby, L., *Observations on the Sources and Effects of Unequal Wealth* (New York, 1826).

Byrdsall, Fitzwilliam, *History of the Loco-Foco or Equal Rights Party* (New York, 1842).

Chase, Salmon P., *Diary and Correspondence*, American Historical Association, *Annual Report for the Year 1902*, II.

Clay, Thomas H., "Two Years with Old Hickory," *Atlantic Monthly*, LX, 187–199 (August, 1887).

Cobbett, William, *Life of Andrew Jackson* (London, 1834).

The Condition of Labor. An Address to the Members of the Labor Reform League of New England. By One of the Members (Boston, 1847).

The Conspiracy to Defeat the Liberation of Governor Dorr! or the Hunkers and Algerines Identified, and Their Policy Unveiled (New York, 1845).

Cooper, J. F., *The American Democrat*, with an introduction by H. L. Mencken (New York, 1931).

Cooper, J. F., *Correspondence*, J. F. Cooper, ed. (New Haven, 1922).

Cooper, J. F., *Excursions in Italy* (Paris, 1838).

Cooper, J. F., *Gleanings in Europe*, R. E. Spiller, ed. (New York, 1928–1930).

Cooper, J. F., *The Lake Gun*, R. E. Spiller, ed. (New York, 1932).

Cooper, J. F., *A Letter to His Countrymen* (New York, 1834).

Cooper, J. F., *New York* (New York, 1930).

Cooper, J. F., *Notions of the Americans: Picked Up by a Travelling Bachelor* (New York, 1852).

Cooper, J. F., *Novels*, Darley-Townsend edition (New York, 1859–1861).

Cooper, J. F., *Sketches of Switzerland* (Philadelphia, 1836).

The Crisis Met. A Reply to Junius (New York, 1840).

Devyr, Thomas A., *The Odd Book of the Nineteenth Century* (Greenpoint, New York, 1882).

Dix, John A., *Memoirs*, Morgan Dix, comp. (New York, 1883).

Dunlap, Andrew, *Speech . . . in Defence of Abner Kneeland* (Boston, 1834).

Dusenberry, B. M., comp., *Monument to the Memory of General Andrew Jackson* (Philadelphia, 1846).

Dyer, Oliver, *Phonographic Report of the Proceedings of the National Free Soil Convention at Buffalo, N. Y. August 9th and 10th, 1848* (Buffalo, [1848]).

Eaton, Peggy, *Autobiography*, C. F. Deems, ed. (New York, 1932).

Emmons, Richard, *Tecumseh; or, the Battle of the Thames, a National Drama, in Five Acts* (Philadelphia, 1836).

Emmons, William, *Address in Commemoration of the Battle of Bunker Hill!! . . . June 16th, 1825* (Boston, 1825).

Emmons, William, *Authentic Biography of Col. Richard M. Johnson, of Kentucky* (Boston, 1833).

Emmons, William, *Oration . . . Delivered Fourth of July, 1834, on Boston Common* (Boston, 1834).

Fairfield, John, *Letters*, A. G. Staples, ed. (Lewiston, Maine, 1922).

Field, H. M., *Life of David Dudley Field* (New York, 1898).

Fisk, Theophilus, *The Banking Bubble Burst; or the Mammoth Corruptions of the Paper Money System Relieved by Bleeding* (Charleston, 1837).

Fisk, Theophilus, *The Bulwark of Freedom* (Charleston, 1836).

Fisk, Theophilus, *Labor the Only True Source of Wealth. . . . An Oration on Banking, Education, &c.* (Charleston, 1837).

Fisk, Theophilus, *The Nation's Bulwark. An Oration, on the Freedom of the Press* (New Haven, [1833]).

Fisk, Theophilus, *Our Country; Its Dangers and Destiny* (Washington, 1845).

Flagg, A. C., *Banks and Banking in the State of New York* (Brooklyn, 1868).

Forrest, Edwin, *Oration Delivered . . . in the City of New-York, Fourth July, 1838* (New York, 1838).

Foster, William, *A Society for the Special Study of Political Economy, the Philosophy of History, and the Science of Government* (Boston, 1857).

Four Letters Respectfully Dedicated to the Working Men of America (n.p., [1840]).

Frémont, Jessie Benton, *Souvenirs of My Time* (Boston, 1887).

Gardiner, O. C., *The Great Issue: or, the Three Presidential Candidates* (New York, 1848).

Garland, Hugh A., *Life of John Randolph of Roanoke* (New York, 1850).

Gillet, R. H., *Life and Times of Silas Wright* (Albany, 1874).

Gilpin, H. D., *Speech Delivered . . . July 4th 1834* ([Philadelphia], [1834]).

Gouge, W. M., *Curse of Paper-Money and Banking*, with an introduction by William Cobbett (London, 1833).

Gouge, W. M., *Inquiry into the Expediency of Dispensing with Bank*

Agency and Bank Paper in the Fiscal Concerns of the United States (Philadelphia, 1837).

Gouge, W. M., *A Short History of Paper Money and Banking in the United States . . . to Which Is Prefixed an Inquiry into the Principles of the System, with Considerations of Its Effects on Morals and Happiness* (Philadelphia, 1833).

The Great Contest. What the Two Political Parties Are Struggling For (n.p., n.d.).

Greene, L. F., *Writings of the Late Elder John Leland* (New York, 1845).

Greene, W. B., *Socialistic, Communistic, Mutualistic, and Financial Fragments* (Boston, 1875).

Greenough, Horatio, *Letters . . . to His Brother, Henry Greenough,* F. B. Greenough, ed. (Boston, 1887).

Hale, William H., *Useful Knowledge for the Producers of Wealth* (New York, 1833).

Hallett, B. F., *Oration before the Democratic Citizens of Oxford . . . July 5, 1841* (Boston, 1841).

Hallett, B. F., *Oration before the Democratic Citizens of Worcester County . . . July 4, 1839* (Worcester, 1839).

Hallett, B. F., *Oration Delivered July 4, 1838, at the Plymouth County Democratic Celebration* (Boston, 1838).

Hallett, B. F., *The Right of the People to Establish Forms of Government. Mr. Hallett's Argument . . . before the Supreme Court of the United States, January, 1848* (Boston, 1848).

Hallett, B. F., *Three Letters to Col. C. G. Greene* (n.p., [1852]).

Hamilton, J. A., *Reminiscences* (New York, 1869).

Hamilton, Luther, *Memoirs, Speeches and Writings of Robert Rantoul, Jr.* (Boston, 1854).

Hammond, J. D., *History of Political Parties in the State of New-York* (Cooperstown, 1842–1848).

Hammond, J. D., *Life and Times of Silas Wright* (Syracuse, 1848).

Hawthorne, Julian, *Nathaniel Hawthorne and His Wife* (Boston, 1884).

Hawthorne, Nathaniel, *The American Notebooks,* Randall Stewart, ed. (New Haven, 1932).

Hawthorne, Nathaniel, *Love Letters,* Roswell Field, ed. (Chicago, 1907).

Hawthorne, Nathaniel, *Writings* (Boston, 1900).

Hayes, J. L., *A Reminiscence of the Free-Soil Movement in New Hampshire, 1845* (Cambridge, 1885).

Henshaw, David, *Address Delivered . . . at Faneuil Hall . . . July 4, 1836* (Boston, 1836).

Henshaw, David, *Remarks upon the Bank of the United States* (Boston, 1831).

Henshaw, David, *Remarks upon the Rights and Powers of Corporations* (Boston, 1837).

Henshaw, David, *Review of the Prosecution against Abner Kneeland, for Blasphemy* (1835).

Herkimer Convention. The Voice of New York! (Albany, 1847).

Hickey, John, *The Democratic Lute, and Minstrel* (Philadelphia, 1844).

Hill, Isaac, *Brief Sketch of the Life, Character and Services of Major General Andrew Jackson* (Concord, New Hampshire, 1828).

Holland, W. M., *Life and Political Opinions of Martin Van Buren,* second ed. (Hartford, 1836).

Hunt, John H., *The Honest Man's Book of Finance and Politics* (New York, 1862).

Ingersoll, C. J., *Historical Sketch of the Second War between the United States of America and Great Britain* (Philadelphia, 1845–1849).

Jackson, Andrew, *Correspondence,* J. S. Bassett, ed. (Washington, 1926–1933).

Jefferson, Thomas, *Writings,* Memorial Ed. (Washington, 1905).

Jefferson, Thomas, *Writings,* P. L. Ford, ed. (New York, 1892–1896).

"Jeffersonian," *Which Will You Have for President, Jackson or the Bank?* (n.p., [1832]).

Jenkins, J. S., *History of Political Parties in the State of New York,* second ed. (Auburn, 1849).

Jenkins, J. S., *Life of Silas Wright* (Auburn, 1847).

Johnson, Andrew, *Speeches . . . with a Biographical Introduction,* with introduction by Frank Moore (Boston, 1865).

Johnson, Charles W., *Proceedings of the First Three Republican National Conventions of 1856, 1860 and 1864* (Minneapolis, 1893).

Johnson, Richard M., *Report on the Transportation of the Mail on Sunday* (Boston, 1829).

Kendall, Amos, "Anecdotes of General Jackson," *Democratic Review,* XI, 270–274 (September, 1842).

Kendall, Amos, *Autobiography,* William Stickney, ed. (Boston, 1872).

Kendall, Amos, *Letters Exposing the Mismanagement of Public Affairs by Abraham Lincoln* (Washington, 1864).

Kendall, Amos, *Letters on Our Country's Crisis* (Washington, 1864).

Kendall, Amos, *Life of Andrew Jackson* (New York, 1843–1844).

Kendall, Amos, *Secession. Letters of Amos Kendall* (Washington, 1861).

King, Preston, *Oration Delivered at Canton . . . July 4, 1848* (Ogdensburgh, New York, 1848).

Kneeland, Abner, *Speech . . . Delivered before the Supreme Court of the City of Boston, in His Own Defence, on an Indictment for Blasphemy* (Boston, 1834).

Langworthy, Asahel, *Biographical Sketch of Col. Richard M. Johnson, of Kentucky* (New York, 1843).

Lawrence, Rachel Jackson, "Andrew Jackson at Home," *McClure's Magazine,* IX, 792–794 (July, 1897).

Leggett, William, *Political Writings*, Theodore Sedgwick, Jr., **ed.** (New York, 1839).

Luther, Seth, *Address on the Origin and Progress of Avarice, and Its Deleterious Effects on Human Happiness* (Boston, 1834).

Luther, Seth, *Address on the Right of Free Suffrage* (Providence, 1833).

Luther, Seth, *Address to the Working-Men of New-England* (Boston, 1832).

Masquerier, Lewis, *Sociology: or, the Reconstruction of Society, Government, and Property* (New York, 1877).

Moore, Ely, *Address Delivered before the General Trades' Union . . . December 2, 1833* (New York, 1833).

Moore, Ely, *Address on Civil Government: Delivered before the New York Typographical Society, February 25th, 1847* (New York, 1847).

Nelson, Anson and Fanny, *Memorials of Sarah Childress Polk* (New York, 1892). ·

A New System of Paper Money, by a Citizen of Boston (Boston, 1837).

New York Democratic Anti-Lecompton Meeting (New York, 1858).

Nichols, Thomas L., *Forty Years of American Life* (London, 1864).

O'Reilly, Henry, *The Great Questions of the Times, Exemplified in the Antagonistic Principles Involved in the Slaveholders' Rebellion against Democratic Institutions as well as against the National Union* (New York, 1862).

O'Reilly, Henry, *Origin and Objects of the Slaveholders' Conspiracy against Democratic Principles, as well as against the National Union* (New York, 1862).

Owen, Robert Dale, "An Earnest Sowing of Wild Oats," *Atlantic Monthly*, XXXIV, 67–78 (July, 1874).

Owen, Robert Dale, *Labor: Its History and Its Prospects* (Cincinnati, 1848).

Owen, Robert Dale, "My Experience of Community Life," *Atlantic Monthly*, XXXII, 336–348 (September, 1873).

Padgett, James A., ed., "Correspondence between Governor Joseph Desha and Amos Kendall — 1831–1835," *Register of the Kentucky State Historical Society*, XXXVIII, 5–24.

Parliamentary Observance of the Sabbath an Infringement of Public Right and Liberty of Conscience (London, 1853).

Parmelee, T. N., "Recollections of an Old Stager," *Harpers*, XLV–XLIX (August, 1872–June, 1874).

Parton, James, *Life of Andrew Jackson* (New York, 1859–1860).

Paulding, W. I., *Literary Life of James K. Paulding* (New York, 1867).

Perry, B. F., *Reminiscences of Public Men* (Philadelphia, 1883).

Perry, B. F., *Reminiscences of Public Men, Second Series* (Greenville, 1889).

Pickering, John, *The Working Man's Political Economy* (Cincinnati, 1847).

Pillow, Gideon J., "Letters . . . to James K. Polk, 1844," *American Historical Review*, XI, 832–843.

Polk, James K., *Diary . . . during His Presidency, 1845 to 1849*, M. M. Quaife, ed. (Chicago, 1910).

Polk, James K., "Letters . . . to Andrew J. Donelson, 1843–1848," *Tennessee Historical Magazine*, III, 51–73.

Polk, James K., "Letters . . . to Cave Johnson, 1833–1848," *Tennessee Historical Magazine*, I, 209–256.

Proceedings and Addresses on . . . the Death of Benjamin F. Butler, of New York (New York, 1859).

Proceedings of the Democratic Legislative Convention Held in Boston, March, 1840 (Boston, 1840).

Proceedings of the Meeting . . . in the City of New York on the 29th of April, 1856 . . . Opposed to . . . the Extension of Slavery (New York, 1856).

Reunion of the Free-Soilers of 1848 . . . August 9, 1877 (Boston, 1877).

Riell, Henry E., *An Appeal to the Voluntary Citizens of the United States . . . on the Exercise of Their Elective Franchise* (New York, 1844).

Robinson, Frederick, *Address to the Voters of the Fifth Congressional District* (n.p., [1862]).

Robinson, Frederick, *Letter to the Hon. Rufus Choate Containing a Brief Exposition of Law Craft* (Boston, 1831).

Robinson, Frederick, *Oration Delivered before the Trades Union of Boston and Vicinity* (Boston, 1834).

Roosevelt, Clinton, *The Mode of Protecting Domestic Industries. The Science of Government, Founded on Natural Law. Paradox of Political Economy* (New York, 1889).

Royall, Anne, *Letters from Alabama on Various Subjects* (Washington, 1830).

Royall, Anne, *Southern Tour, or Second Series of the Black Book* (Washington, 1830).

Sedgwick, Theodore, Sr., *Public and Private Economy* (New York, 1836–1839).

Sedgwick, Theodore, Jr., *Thoughts on the Proposed Annexation of Texas* (New York, 1844).

Sedgwick, Theodore, Jr., *What Is a Monopoly?* (New York, 1835).

Simpson, Stephen, *Biography of Stephen Girard* (Philadelphia, 1832).

Simpson, Stephen, *The Working Man's Manual: a New Theory of Political Economy, on the Principle of Production the Source of Wealth* (Philadelphia, 1831).

Skidmore, Thomas, *The Rights of Man to Property!* (New York, 1829).

Spalding, G. B., *Discourse Commemorative of . . . Hon. John Parker Hale* (Concord, New Hampshire, 1874).

Stanton, H. B., *Random Recollections,* third ed. (New York, 1887).

Tarbell, John P., *Oration Delivered . . . at Groton, July Fourth, 1839* (Lowell, 1839).

Taylor, John, *Construction Construed and Constitutions Vindicated* (Richmond, 1820).

Taylor, John, *Inquiry into the Principles and Policy of the Government of the United States* (Fredericksburg, 1814).

Taylor, John, "Letters of John Taylor," *John P. Branch Historical Papers,* II, 253–353.

Taylor, John, *New Views of the Constitution of the United States* (Washington, 1823).

Taylor, John, *Tyranny Unmasked* (Washington, 1822).

Tilden, Samuel J., *Letters and Literary Memorials,* John Bigelow, ed. (New York, 1908).

Tilden, Samuel J., *Writings and Speeches,* John Bigelow, ed. (New York, 1885).

Traubel, Horace, *With Walt Whitman in Camden* (New York, 1905–1912).

Van Buren, Martin, *Autobiography,* J. C. Fitzpatrick, ed., American Historical Association, *Annual Report for the Year 1918,* II.

Van Buren, Martin, *Inquiry into the Origin and Course of Political Parties in the United States* (New York, 1867).

Van Buren, Martin, *Opinions . . . Mr. Van Buren's Reply to the Democratic State Convention of Indiana* (New York, 1843).

A Voice from Old Tammany! Meeting of the People! (New York, 1838).

Voters of Massachusetts. Governor Andrew's Letter of Acceptance; Letter from George Bancroft, Esq.; Chas. Sumner as a Statesman (Boston, 1862).

Walker, Amasa, *Address Delivered on the Fiftyseventh Anniversary of American Independence* (Boston, 1833).

Walker, Amasa, *The Nature and Uses of Money and Mixed Currency* (Boston, 1857).

Walker, Amasa, *The Science of Wealth* (Boston, 1866).

Walker, Amasa, "*The Test of Experience,*" or the Working of the Ballot in the United States, E. C. Whitehurst, ed. (London, [1855]).

Walker, Robert J., *Speech . . . at the Banquet . . . to M. Lewis Kossuth* (London, 1851).

Walsh, Michael, *Sketches of the Speeches and Writings of Michael Walsh* (New York, 1843).

Welles, Gideon, *Diary,* J. T. Morse, Jr., ed. (Boston, 1911).

Wentworth, John, *Congressional Reminiscences* (Chicago, 1882).

Whitcomb, Samuel, Jr., *Address before the Working-Men's Society of Dedham* (Dedham, 1831).

Whitman, Walt, *Complete Prose Works* (Boston, 1898).

Whitman, Walt, *Gathering of the Forces,* Cleveland Rodgers and John Black, eds. (New York, 1920).

Whitman, Walt, *New York Dissected,* Emory Holloway and Ralph Adimari, eds. (New York, 1936).

Whitman, Walt, *Uncollected Poetry and Prose,* Emory Holloway, ed. (Garden City, 1921).

Wilkes, George, *Defence of the Paris Commune, with Some Account of the Internationale* (New York, 1872).

Williams, Henry, *Speech . . . in Vindication of the Right of the People of Rhode Island to Amend Their Form of Government* (Washington, 1845).

Woodbury, C. L., "Some Personal Recollections of Robert Rantoul, Junior," *Historical Collections of the Essex Institute,* XXXIV, 195–207.

Wright, Frances, *Biography, Notes, and Political Letters of Frances Wright D'Arusmont* (New York, 1845).

Wright, Frances, *What Is the Matter?* (New York, 1838).

Young, Samuel, *Oration Delivered . . . July Fourth, 1840* (New York, 1840).

III. *The Whig Tradition: Source Material in Opposition to Jacksonian Democracy*

1. Newspapers

Boston Advertiser, 1830–1840.

Boston Advocate, 1835–1836.

Boston Atlas, 1834–1840.

Boston Centinel & Gazette, 1836.

Boston Commercial Gazette, 1837.

Boston Courier, 1833–1840.

Bunker Hill Aurora & Boston Mirror, 1835.

Columbian Centinel (Boston), 1837.

Franklin Mercury (Greenfield, Massachusetts), 1834–1835.

Greenfield Gazette & Franklin Herald, 1830–1831.

Independent Chronicle & Boston Patriot, 1838.

Madisonian (Washington), 1837–1840.

National Intelligencer (Washington), 1829.

New York American, 1837.

New York Commercial Advertiser, 1837.

New York Herald, 1852.

New York Times, 1836–1838.

Northampton Courier, 1834.

United States Telegraph (Washington), 1829–1832.

2. Magazines

American Monthly Magazine (New York), 1834–1838.
American Quarterly Review (Philadelphia), 1827–1837.
American Whig Review (New York), 1845–1852.
Jeffersonian (Albany), 1838–1839.
Log Cabin (New York), 1840–1841.
New-England Magazine (Boston), 1831–1835.
New-York Review (New York), 1837–1842.
Niles' Register (Baltimore, Washington), 1829–1844.
North American Review (Boston), 1830–1844.
Southern Review (Charleston), 1828–1832.
Truth's Advocate & Monthly Anti-Jackson Expositor (Cincinnati), 1828.

3. Books and Pamphlets

Adams, John Quincy, "Letters . . . to Alexander H. Everett, 1811–1837," *American Historical Review*, XI, 88–116, 332–354.
Adams, John Quincy, *Memoirs*, C. F. Adams, ed. (Philadelphia, 1877).
Address of the General Union for Promoting the Observance of the Christian Sabbath, to the People of the United States (New York, 1828).
Address of the Whig Members of the Senate and House of Representatives of Massachusetts (Boston, 1843).
Appleton, Nathan, *Remarks on Currency and Banking* (Boston, 1841).
Barnard, D. D., *Address Delivered before the Philoclean and Peithessophian Societies of Rutgers College . . . July 18th, 1837* (Albany, 1837).
Barnard, D. D., *Plea for Social and Popular Repose* (New York, 1845).
Barnard, D. D., *The Social System* (Hartford, 1848).
Barnard, D. D., *Speeches and Reports in the Assembly of New-York, at the Annual Session of 1838* (Albany, 1838).
Baylies, Francis, *Speech . . . before the Whigs of Taunton, on the 13th of Sept., 1837* (Taunton, 1837).
Bemis, ——, *Whig Songs . . . September 19, 1844* (Boston, 1844).
Biddle, Nicholas, *Address before the Alumni Association of Nassau Hall . . . September 30, 1835* (Philadelphia, 1836).
Biddle, Nicholas, *Correspondence*, R. C. McGrane, ed. (Boston, 1919).
Bigelow, Josiah, *Review of Seth Luther's Address to the Working Men of New England* (Cambridge, 1832).
Brownlow, W. G., *A Political Register, Setting forth the Principles of the Whig and Locofoco Parties* (Jonesborough, Tennessee, 1844).
Buckingham, Joseph T., *Personal Memoirs and Recollections of Editorial Life* (Boston, 1852).
Clay, Henry, *Private Correspondence*, Calvin Colton, ed. (New York, 1855).

Clay, Henry, *Works,* Calvin Colton, ed. (New York, 1855–1857).

Colton, Calvin ("Junius"), *American Jacobinism* (New York, 1840).

Colton, Calvin ("Junius"), *Crisis of the Country* (New York, 1840).

Colton, Calvin ("Junius"), *Labor and Capital* (New York, 1844).

Colton, Calvin ("Junius"), *Sequel to the Crisis of the Country* (New York, 1840).

Colton, Calvin, *A Voice from America to England. By an American Gentleman* (London, 1839).

Conspiracy of the Office Holders Unmasked (Boston, 1840).

Cooper, Thomas, *Lectures on the Elements of Political Economy,* second ed. (Columbia, 1831).

Crockett, David, *Life of Colonel David Crockett, Written by Himself* (Philadelphia, 1859).

Crockett, David, *Life of Martin Van Buren* (Philadelphia, 1835).

Curtis, G. T., *The Merits of Thomas W. Dorr and George Bancroft as They Are Politically Connected* (Boston, 1844).

Cushing, Caleb, *Speeches Delivered in the House of Representatives of Massachusetts, on the Subject of the Currency and Public Deposites* (Salem, 1834).

Davies, C. S., "Constitutional Law," *North American Review,* XLVI, 126–156 (January, 1838).

Davis, C. A., *Letters of J. Downing, Major* (New York, 1834).

Davis, C. A., *Life of Andrew Jackson . . . by Major Jack Downing* (Philadelphia, 1834).

Derby, J. B., *Political Reminiscences, Including a Sketch of the Outline and History of the "Statesman Party" of Boston* (Boston, 1835).

Dickinson, J. R., *Speeches; Correspondence, Etc., of the Late Daniel S. Dickinson* (New York, 1867).

Duane, W. J., *Narrative and Correspondence Concerning the Removal of the Deposites* (Philadelphia, 1838).

Ely, Ezra S., *The Duty of Christian Freemen to Elect Christian Rulers* (Philadelphia, 1828).

Everett, A. H., *The Conduct of the Administration* (Boston, 1831).

Everett, A. H., *Discourse on the Progress and Limits of Social Improvement* (Boston, 1834).

Everett, Edward, *Address, Delivered before the Mercantile Library Association* (Boston, 1838).

Everett, Edward, *Lectures on the Working Men's Party* (Boston, 1830).

Everett, Edward, *Orations and Speeches on Various Occasions,* third ed. (Boston, 1853).

Frelinghuysen [?], Theodore, *An Inquiry into the Moral and Religious Character of the American Government* (New York, 1838).

Gallatin, Albert, *Writings,* Henry Adams, ed. (Philadelphia, 1879).

Gordon, T. F., *The War on the Bank of the United States* (Philadelphia, 1834).

Greeley, Horace, and Raymond, H. J., *Association Discussed; or, the Socialism of the Tribune Examined* (New York, 1847).

Greeley, Horace, *Hints toward Reforms*, second ed. (New York, 1853).

Greeley, Horace, *Recollections of a Busy Life* (New York, 1868).

Green, Duff, *Facts and Suggestions, Biographical, Historical, Financial and Political* (New York, 1866).

Hamilton, Alexander, *Works*, H. C. Lodge, ed. (New York, 1904).

Hare, Robert, *Suggestions Respecting the Reformation of the Banking System* (Philadelphia, 1837).

Harvey, Peter, *Reminiscences and Anecdotes of Daniel Webster* (Boston, 1877).

Hazewell, C. C., "Agrarianism," *Atlantic Monthly*, III, 393–403 (April, 1859).

Hildreth, Richard, *Banks, Banking and Paper Currencies* (Boston, 1840).

Hildreth, Richard, *The Contrast: or William Henry Harrison versus Martin Van Buren* (Boston, 1840).

Hildreth, Richard, *Despotism in America* (Boston, 1840).

Hildreth, Richard, *History of Banks: to Which Is Added, a Demonstration of the Advantages and Necessity of Free Competition in the Business of Banking* (Boston, 1837).

Hildreth, Richard, *History of the United States* (New York, 1849–1852).

Hildreth, Richard, *My Connection with the Atlas Newspaper* (Boston, 1839).

Hildreth, Richard, *The People's Presidential Candidate: or the Life of William Henry Harrison of Ohio* (Boston, 1839).

Hildreth, Richard, *Theory of Politics* (New York, 1853).

Hillard, G. S., *Life, Letters and Journals of George Ticknor* (Boston, 1876).

Hillard, G. S., *Memoir and Correspondence of Jeremiah Mason* (Cambridge, 1873).

Hone, Philip, *Diary . . . 1828–1851*, Allan Nevins, ed. (New York, 1927).

Hunt, Thomas P., *The Book of Wealth* (New York, 1836).

Journal of the Proceedings of the National Republican Convention, Held at Worcester, October 11, 1832 (Boston, 1832).

Kenney, Lucy, *History of the Present Cabinet. Benton in Ambush for the Next Presidency. Kendal Coming in Third Best. Gather All Your Strength and Oused the Cossacks* (Washington, 1840).

Kent, James, *Commentaries on American Law* (New York, 1826–1830).

Kent, William, *Memoirs and Letters of James Kent, LL.D.* (Boston, 1898).

Lieber, Francis, *Essays on Property and Labour* (New York, 1841).

Lieber, Francis, *Manual of Political Ethics* (Boston, 1838–1839).

Loco-Focoism; as Displayed in the Boston Magazine against Schools and Ministers, and in Favor of Robbing Children of the Property of Their Parents (Albany, 1840).

Lothrop, S. K., "Existing Commercial Embarrassments," *Christian Examiner*, XXII, 392–406 (July, 1837).

Lothrop, S. K., *Preparation for Death. A Sermon Preached . . . the Sunday after the Interment of Hon. Peter O. Thacher* (Boston, 1843).

MacKenzie, W. L., *Life and Times of Martin Van Buren* (Boston, 1846).

MacKenzie, W. L., *Lives and Opinions of Benj'n Franklin Butler and Jesse Hoyt* (Boston, 1845).

Mayo, Robert, *A Chapter of Sketches on Finance* (Baltimore, 1837).

Mayo, Robert, *Political Sketches of Eight Years in Washington* (Baltimore, 1839).

Memorials to Congress Respecting Sabbath Mails (New York, 1829).

Mines, Flavel S., *The Church the Pillar and Ground of the Truth* (New York, 1838).

Nielson, Joseph, *Memories of Rufus Choate* (Boston, 1884).

"Northampton," *To George Bancroft, Secretary of the Navy, the Traducer and Eulogist of General Andrew Jackson* (Washington, 1846).

Norton, A. B., *The Great Revolution of 1840* (Mt. Vernon, Ohio, 1888).

Ogle, Charles, *Pretended Democracy of Martin Van Buren* (Boston, 1840).

Ogle, Charles, *Speech . . . on the Regal Splendor of the President's Palace* (Boston, 1840).

The Old-Line Whigs for Buchanan! (n.p., [1856]).

Parker, S. D., and others, *Arguments for the Attorney of the Commonwealth in the Trials of Abner Kneeland for Blasphemy* (Boston, 1834).

Parsons, Theophilus, *Address Delivered before the Phi Beta Kappa Society of Harvard University . . . on the Duties of Educated Men in a Republic* (Boston, 1835).

Peabody, A. P., *Views of Duty Adapted to the Times. Sermon Preached . . . May 14, 1837* (Portsmouth, 1837).

Perry, T. S., *Life and Letters of Francis Lieber* (Boston, 1882).

Pitman, J., *Reply to the Letter of the Hon. Marcus Morton . . . on the Rhode-Island Question* (Providence, 1842).

The Political Mirror: or Review of Jacksonism (New York, 1835).

Potter, Alonzo, *Political Economy: Its Objects, Uses, and Principles* (New York, 1841).

Pugh, J. A., *Political Conservatism* (Oxford, Ohio, 1841).

Randall, Dexter, *Democracy Vindicated and Dorrism Unveiled* (Providence, 1846).

Review of the Proceedings in the Massachusetts Legislature for 1843 . . . by the Whig Minority (Boston, 1843).

Robinson, William S., *"Warrington" Pen-Portraits: a Collection of Personal and Political Reminiscences* (Boston, 1877).

The Sabbath Convention (n.p., [1844?]).

Scott, Nancy N., *Memoir of Hugh Lawson White* (Philadelphia, 1856).

Seward, F. W., *Autobiography of William H. Seward, from 1801 to 1834. With a Memoir of His Life* (New York, 1877).

Seward, F. W., *Seward at Washington* (New York, 1890).

Story, Joseph, *Miscellaneous Writings* (Boston, 1835).

Story, W. W., *Life and Letters of Joseph Story* (Boston, 1851).

Swammerdam, Eustacius, *The Lash; or Truths in Rhyme* (n.p., [1840]).

Thacher, Peter O., *Address . . . before the Members of the Bar of the County of Suffolk, Massachusetts* (Boston, 1831).

Thacher, Peter O., *Charge to the Grand Jury of the County of Suffolk* (Boston, 1832).

Thacher, Peter O., *Charge to the Grand Jury of the County of Suffolk* (Boston, 1834).

Thoughts on the Laws, Government, and Morals, by a Citizen of Boston (Boston, 1840).

Upshur, A. P., *A Brief Enquiry into the True Nature and Character of Our Federal Government* (Petersburg, Virginia, 1840).

Wainwright, Jonathan M., *Inequality of Individual Wealth the Ordinance of Providence, and Essential to Civilization* (Boston, 1835).

Warland, J. H., *The National Clay Melodist*, second ed. (Boston, 1844).

Wayland, Francis, *The Affairs of Rhode Island* (Boston, 1842).

Webster, Daniel, *Letters*, C. H. Van Tyne, ed. (New York, 1902).

Webster, Daniel, *Private Correspondence*, Fletcher Webster, ed. (Boston, 1856).

Webster, Daniel, *Speech at Saratoga, New York, August 19, 1840* (Boston, 1840).

Webster, Daniel, *Works* (Boston, 1853).

Webster, Daniel, *Writings and Speeches* (Boston, 1903).

Webster, Noah, *Letter to the Hon. Daniel Webster, on the Political Affairs of the United States* (Philadelphia, 1837).

Weed, Thurlow, *Autobiography*, Harriet A. Weed, ed. (Boston, 1883).

Whipple, F. H., *Might and Right; by a Rhode Islander* (Providence, 1844).

Whipple, John, and Webster, Daniel, *The Rhode-Island Question. Arguments . . . in the Supreme Court* (Providence, 1848).

Williams, J. M., *Proceedings . . . Occasioned by the Sudden Death of Hon. Peter O. Thacher* (Boston, 1843).

Winslow, Hubbard, *Oration Delivered . . . [in] the City of Boston, July 4, 1838* (Boston, 1838).

Winthrop, R. C., *Memoir of Henry Clay* (Cambridge, 1880).

Winthrop, R. C., "Memoir of Hon. Nathan Appleton," *Proceedings of the Massachusetts Historical Society*, V, 249–308.

Wise, Henry A., *Seven Decades of the Union* (Philadelphia, 1871).

Woodman, Horatio, *Reports of Criminal Cases, Tried . . . before Peter Oxenbridge Thacher* (Boston, 1845).

A Word in Season . . . by a Harrison Democrat (Washington, 1840).

IV. *Travelers' Accounts and Other Neutral Contemporary Writings*

1. Magazines

Christian Examiner (Boston), 1837–1841.

Christian Review (Boston), 1840.

Cobbett's Political Register (London), 1830–1836.

Examiner, and Journal of Political Economy (Philadelphia), 1833–1835.

Financial Register of the United States (Philadelphia), 1837–1838.

Harbinger (New York and Boston), 1845–1847.

Knickerbocker Magazine (New York), 1833–1840.

Methodist Quarterly Review (New York), 1840–1841.

Missionary Herald (Boston), 1829–1830.

Phalanx (West Roxbury, Massachusetts), 1843–1845.

Present (New York), 1843–1844.

Spirit of the Age (New York), 1849–1850.

Spirit of the Pilgrims (Boston), 1829–1830.

2. Books and Pamphlets

Abstract Exhibiting the Condition of the Banks in Massachusetts on the First Saturday of August, 1843 (Boston, 1843).

Adams, Henry, *Letters . . . (1858–1891)*, W. C. Ford, ed. (Boston, 1930).

Allen, George, *Reminiscences of the Rev. George Allen of Worcester*, F. P. Rice, ed. (Worcester, 1883).

Atwater, Caleb, *Remarks Made on a Tour to Prairie du Chien; thence to Washington City, in 1829* (Columbus, 1831).

Bacourt, Adolph de, *Souvenirs d'un Diplomate* (Paris, 1882).

Baldwin, C. C., *Diary . . . 1829–1835* (Worcester, 1901).

Bell, Andrew, *Men and Things in America* (Southampton, 1862).

Bentham, Jeremy, *Anti-Senatica*, C. W. Everett, ed., Smith College *Studies in History*, XI, no. 4.

Bentham, Jeremy, *Works*, John Bowring, ed. (Edinburgh, 1843).

Benton, N. S., *History of Herkimer County* (Albany, 1856).

Blaine, James G., *Twenty Years of Congress* (Norwich, 1886).

Brisbane, Albert, *Concise Expositor of the Doctrine of Association*, eighth ed. (New York, 1844).

Brisbane, Albert, *Social Destiny of Man: or, Association and Reorganization of Industry* (Philadelphia, 1840).

Brothers, Thomas, *The Senator Unmasked: Being a Letter to Mr. Daniel Webster* (Philadelphia, 1834).

Brothers, Thomas, *The United States of North America as They Are; Not as They Are Generally Described: Being a Cure for Radicalism* (London, 1840).

Buckingham, J. S., *America, Historical, Statistic, and Descriptive* (London, [1841]).

Bungay, George W., *Crayon Sketches and Off-hand Takings* (Boston, 1852).

Bungay, George W., *Off-hand Takings; or, Crayon Sketches of the Noticeable Men of our Age* (New York, 1854).

Bushnell, C. I., *Bushnell's American Tokens* (New York, 1858).

Calhoun, J. C., *Correspondence*, J. F. Jameson, ed., American Historical Association, *Annual Report for the Year 1899*, II.

(Calhoun, J. C.), *Correspondence Addressed to John C. Calhoun, 1837–1849*, C. S. Boucher and R. P. Brooks, eds., American Historical Association, *Annual Report for the Year 1929*, II.

Calhoun, J. C., *Works*, R. K. Crallé, ed. (New York, 1851–1856).

Carey, Mathew, *Appeal to the Wealthy of the Land*, third ed. (Philadelphia, 1833).

Carey, Mathew, *Letters on the Condition of the Poor*, second ed. (Philadelphia, 1835).

Chamberlin, J. F., *Answer . . . to the Complaint of George Wilkes* (New York, 1873).

Channing, W. E., *Lectures on the Elevation of the Labouring Portion of the Community* (Boston, 1840).

Channing, W. H., *Memoir of William Ellery Channing* (Boston, 1848).

Chase, Lucien B., *History of the Polk Administration* (New York, 1850).

Chittenden, L. E., *Personal Reminiscences, 1840–1890* (New York, 1893).

Claiborne, J. F. H., *Mississippi, as a Province, Territory and State* (Jackson, 1879).

Clibborn, Edward, *American Prosperity. An Outline of the American Debit or Banking System* (London, 1837).

Combe, George, *Notes on the United States of North America, during a Phrenological Visit in 1838–9–40* (Philadelphia, 1841).

Congdon, C. T., *Reminiscences of a Journalist* (Boston, 1880).

Curtis, G. T., *Life of James Buchanan* (New York, 1883).

Davis, Matthew L., *Memoirs of Aaron Burr* (New York, 1837).

Dyer, Oliver, *Great Senators of the United States Forty Years Ago* (New York, 1889).

Ellet, Mrs. E. F., *Court Circles of the Republic* (Philadelphia, n.d.).

Elliott, Richard S., *Notes Taken in Sixty Years* (Boston, 1884).

Emerson, R. W., *Complete Works* (Centenary Edition, Boston, 1883–1893).

Emerson, R. W., *Correspondence of Thomas Carlyle and Ralph Waldo Emerson, 1834–1872*, C. E. Norton, ed. (Boston, 1883).

Emerson, R. W., *Journals . . . 1820–1872*, E. W. Emerson and W. E. Forbes, eds. (Boston, 1909–1914).

Emerson, R. W., *Letters*, R. L. Rusk, ed. (New York, 1939).

The Federalist, E. M. Earle, ed. (Washington, 1937).

Field, M. B., *Memories of Many Men* (New York, 1873).

Foote, H. S., *Casket of Reminiscences* (Washington, 1874).

Forbes, A., and Greene, J. W., *The Rich Men of Massachusetts* (Boston, 1851).

Forney, J. W., *Anecdotes of Public Men* (New York, 1873, 1881).

Foster, G. G., *New York by Gas-Light* (New York, 1850).

Foster, G. G., *New York in Slices: by an Experienced Carver* (New York, 1849).

Frothingham, O. B., *Memoir of William Henry Channing* (Boston, 1886).

Garrison, W. P. and F. J., *William Lloyd Garrison* (New York, 1885–1889).

Gobright, L. A., *Recollections of Men and Things at Washington* (Philadelphia, 1869).

Godwin, Parke, *Biography of William Cullen Bryant* (New York, 1883).

Godwin, Parke, "Constructive and Pacific Democracy," *Present*, I, 181–196 (December 15, 1843), I, 338–349 (March 1, 1844).

Godwin, Parke, *Popular View of the Doctrines of Charles Fourier* (New York, 1844).

Grattan, T. C., *Civilized America* (London, 1859).

Griggs, W. N., *The Celebrated "Moon Story," Its Origin and Incidents* (New York, 1852).

Griswold, R. W., ed., *The Biographical Annual, Containing Memoirs of Eminent Persons, Recently Deceased* (New York, 1840).

Griswold, R. W., *Passages from the Correspondence of Rufus W. Griswold*, William Griswold, ed. (Cambridge, 1898).

Haswell, C. H., *Reminiscences of an Octogenarian* (New York, 1896).

Hayes, R. B., *Diary and Letters*, C. R. Williams, ed. (Columbus, 1922–1926).

Healy, G. P. A., *Reminiscences of a Portrait Painter* (Chicago, 1894).

Hilliard, H. W., *Politics and Pen Pictures* (New York, 1892).

Hudson, Frederic, *Journalism in the United States from 1690 to 1872* (New York, 1872).

Hunter, R. M. T., *Correspondence . . . 1826–1876*, C. H. Ambler, ed., American Historical Association, *Annual Report for the Year 1916*, II.

Irving, P. M., *Life and Letters of Washington Irving* (New York, 1862–1863).

Jenkins, J. S., *Life of John Caldwell Calhoun* (Auburn, 1850).

Journal of Debates and Proceedings in the Convention of Delegates, Chosen to Revise the Constitution of Massachusetts . . . [1820–1821] (Boston, 1853).

Julian, George W., *Political Recollections 1840 to 1872* (Chicago, 1883).

Kemble, Frances A., *Records of a Girlhood* (New York, 1879).

Kemble, Frances A., *Records of Later Life* (New York, 1882).

Koerner, Gustave, *Memoirs . . . 1801–1896*, T. J. McCormack, ed. (Cedar Rapids, 1909).

Lanman, Charles, *Haphazard Personalities* (Boston, 1885).

Lathrop, Rose H., *Memories of Hawthorne* (Boston, 1897).

Leech, W. L., *Calendar of the Papers of Franklin Pierce* (Washington, 1917).

Lincoln, Abraham, *Complete Works*, J. G. Nicolay and John Hay, eds. (New York, 1905).

Loring, J. S., *The Hundred Boston Orators* (Boston, 1852).

MacLure, William, *Opinions on Various Subjects, Dedicated to the Industrious Producers* (New Harmony, Indiana, 1831, 1837).

Mann, Mary P., *Life of Horace Mann* (Boston, 1865).

Mansfield, E. D., *Personal Memories . . . 1803–1843* (Cincinnati, 1879).

Martineau, Harriet, *Retrospect of Western Travel* (London, 1838).

Martineau, Harriet, *Society in America* (London, 1837).

Maury, Sarah M., *The Statesmen of America in 1846* (Philadelphia, 1847).

McClure, A. K., *Recollections of Half a Century* (Salem, 1902).

McSherry, James, *History of Maryland* (Baltimore, 1849).

Milburn, W. H., *Ten Years of Preacher-Life: Chapters from an Autobiography* (New York, 1859).

Moore, F. W., ed., "Calhoun by His Political Friends," *Publications of the Southern History Association*, VII, *passim*.

Morpeth, Lord, *Extracts from the Diary . . . of His Journey to the United States in 1841–1842*, Harvard College Library.

Parton, James, *Life of Horace Greeley* (New York, 1854).

Peabody, Elizabeth P., *Reminiscences of Rev. Wm. Ellery Channing* (Boston, 1880).

"A Peep at Washington," *Knickerbocker Magazine*, III, 439–446 (June, 1834).

Pickens, F. W., *Address, on the Great Points of Difference between Ancient and Modern Civilization* (Athens, Georgia, 1843).

Pierce, E. L., *Memoir and Letters of Charles Sumner* (Boston, 1877–1893).

Poe, Edgar Allan, *Works* (Chicago, 1895).

Poore, Ben: Perley, *Perley's Reminiscences of Sixty Years in the National Metropolis* (Philadelphia, 1886).

Power, Tyrone, *Impressions of America, during the Years 1833, 1834, and 1835* (London, 1836).

Prescott, W. H., *Correspondence . . . 1833–1847*, Roger Wolcott, ed. (Boston, 1925).

Proceedings and Debates of the Virginia State Convention of 1829–1830 (Richmond, 1830).

Quincy, Josiah, *Figures of the Past* (Boston, 1882).

Reports of the Proceedings and Debates of the Convention of 1821, Assembled for the Purpose of Amending the Constitution of the State of New-York (Albany, 1821).

Richards, Laura E., and Elliott, Maud H., *Julia Ward Howe, 1819–1890* (Boston, 1916).

Richardson, J. D., comp., *Compilation of the Messages and Papers of the Presidents, 1789–1907* (Washington, 1908).

Sargent, Nathan, *Public Men and Events* (Philadelphia, 1875).

Scoville, J. A. ("Walter Barrett"), *The Old Merchants of New York City* (New York, 1862–1864).

Sedgwick, Catharine M., *The Poor Rich Man and the Rich Poor Man* (New York, 1836).

Shillaber, Benjamin P., "Experiences during Many Years," *New England Magazine*, VIII, *passim*.

Simpson, Henry, *Lives of Eminent Philadelphians* (Philadelphia, 1859).

Smith, Margaret Bayard, *First Forty Years of Washington Society*, Gaillard Hunt, ed. (New York, 1906).

Southern State Rights, Free Trade and Anti-Abolition Tract No. 1 (Charleston, 1844).

Stevenson, A. E., *Something of Men I Have Known* (Chicago, 1909).

Sumner, Charles, *Works* (Boston, 1870–1873).

Tocqueville, Alexis de, *Democracy in America* (New York, 1855).

Tucker, George, *Progress of the United States in Population and Wealth in Fifty Years, as Exhibited by the Decennial Census* (New York, 1843).

Tucker, N. Beverley, *The Partisan Leader*, Carl Bridenbaugh, ed. (New York, 1933).

Waterston, R. C., *Address on Pauperism, its Extent, Causes, and the Best Means of Prevention* (Boston, 1844).

Weiss, John, *Life and Correspondence of Theodore Parker* (New York, 1863).

Wharton, Francis, "Banking and the Bank of the United States," *Christian Examiner*, XXXI, 1–28 (September, 1841).

Wikoff, Henry, *Reminiscences of an Idler* (New York, 1880).

William Winston Seaton of the "National Intelligencer" (Boston, 1871).

Willis, N. P., *Hurry-Graphs: or, Sketches of Scenery, Celebrities and Society* (Detroit, 1851).

Wilson, Henry, *History of the Rise and Fall of the Slave Power in America* (Boston, 1872–1877).

Wilson, J. G., *Bryant, and His Friends* (New York, 1885).

V. *Secondary Works*

Abernethy, T. P., "Andrew Jackson and the Rise of Southwestern Democracy," *American Historical Review*, XXXIII, 64–77.

Abernethy, T. P., *From Frontier to Plantation in Tennessee* (Chapel Hill, 1932).

Abernethy, T. P., "The Origin of the Whig Party in Tennessee," *Mississippi Valley Historical Review*, XII, 504–522.

Adam Smith, 1776–1926 (Chicago, 1928).

Adams, Charles Francis, *Richard Henry Dana* (Boston, 1890).

Adams, Henry, *Life of Albert Gallatin* (Philadelphia, 1879).

Alderman, E. A., and Gordon, A. C., *J. L. M. Curry: a Biography* (New York, 1911).

Alexander, DeAlva S., *Political History of the State of New York* (New York, 1906).

Alger, W. R., *Life of Edwin Forrest* (Philadelphia, 1877).

Ambler, C. H., *Life and Diary of John Floyd* (Richmond, 1918).

Ambler, C. H., *Thomas Ritchie: a Study in Virginia Politics* (Richmond, 1913).

Ambler, C. H., "Virginia and the Presidential Succession, 1840–1844," *Essays . . . Dedicated to Frederick Jackson Turner* (New York, 1912).

Andrews, M. P., *History of Maryland: Province and State* (Garden City, 1929).

Asbury, Herbert, *The Gangs of New York* (New York, 1927).

Barnes, G. H., *The Antislavery Impulse, 1830–1844* (New York, 1933).

Barnes, T. W., *Memoir of Thurlow Weed* (Boston, 1884).

Bartlett, M. G., *Chief Phases of Pennsylvania Politics in the Jacksonian Period* (Allentown, 1919).

Bassett, J. S., *Life of Andrew Jackson* (New York, 1928).

Bauer, G. P., "The Movement against Imprisonment for Debt in the United States," an unpublished thesis in the Harvard College Library.

Bean, W. G., "Party Transformation in Massachusetts with Special Reference to the Antecedents of Republicanism, 1848–1860," an unpublished thesis in the Harvard College Library.

Beard, Charles A., *Economic Origins of Jeffersonian Democracy* (New York, 1915).

Beveridge, A. J., *Life of John Marshall* (Boston, 1919).

Binney, C. C., *Life of Horace Binney* (Philadelphia, 1903).

Blair, Walter, "Six Davy Crocketts," *Southwest Review*, XXV, 443–462.

Blake, E. Vale, *History of the Tammany Society or Columbian Order* (New York, 1901).

Boudin, Louis B., *Government by Judiciary* (New York, 1932).

Bouglé, C., *Socialismes Français* (Paris, 1933).

Breen, M. P., *Thirty Years of New York Politics Up-to-date* (New York, 1899).

Brisbane, Redelia, *Albert Brisbane, a Mental Biography* (Boston, 1893).

Brown, Samuel G., *Life of Rufus Choate* (Boston, 1878).

Brownson, H. F., *Orestes A. Brownson's Early Life* (Detroit, 1898).

Bruce, W. C., *John Randolph of Roanoke* (New York, 1922).

Burke, Pauline W., *Emily Donelson of Tennessee* (Richmond, 1941).

Cabot, J. E., *Memoir of Ralph Waldo Emerson* (Boston, 1887).

Callender, G. S., "The Early Transportation and Banking Enterprises of the States in Relation to the Growth of Corporations," *Quarterly Journal of Economics*, XVII, 111–162.

Canby, Henry Seidel, *Thoreau* (Boston, 1939).

Canby, Henry Seidel, *Walt Whitman, an American* (Boston, 1943).

Carey, R. L., *Daniel Webster as an Economist* (New York, 1929).

Carlson, Oliver, *Brisbane: a Candid Biography* (New York, 1937).

Carlton, F. T., *Economic Influences upon Educational Progress in the United States, 1820–1850* (Madison, 1908).

Carlton, F. T., "The Workingmen's Party of New York," *Political Science Quarterly*, XXII, 401–415.

Carroll, E. M., *Origins of the Whig Party* (Durham, 1925).

Carsel, Wilfred, "The Slaveholders' Indictment of Northern Wage Slavery," *Journal of Southern History*, VI, 504–520.

Carson, H. L., *Sketch of Horace Binney* (Philadelphia, 1907).

Catterall, R. C. H., *Second Bank of the United States* (Chicago, 1903).

Chaddock, R. E., *The Safety Fund Banking System in New York, 1829–1866* (Washington, 1910).

Chase, F. H., *Lemuel Shaw* (Boston, 1918).

Chitwood, O. P., *John Tyler: Champion of the Old South* (New York, 1939).

Cleaves, Freeman, *Old Tippecanoe* (New York, 1939).

Coker, F. W., "American Traditions Concerning Property and Liberty," *American Political Science Review*, XXX, 1–23.

Cole, A. C., *The Whig Party in the South* (Washington, 1914).

Cole, A. H., *Wholesale Commodity Prices in the United States, 1700–1861* (Cambridge, 1938).

Commons, J. R., and others, eds., *Documentary History of American Industrial Society* (Cleveland, 1910).

Commons, J. R., and others, *History of Labour in the United States* (New York, 1918).

Commons, J. R., "Horace Greeley and the Working Class Origins of the Republican Party," *Political Science Quarterly*, XXIV, 468–488.

Commons, J. R., "Labor Organization and Labor Politics, 1827–1837," *Quarterly Journal of Economics*, XXI, 323–329.

Crandall, A. W., *Early History of the Republican Party, 1854–1856* (Boston, 1930).

Curti, Merle E., "Robert Rantoul, Jr., the Reformer in Politics," *New England Quarterly*, V, 264–280.

Curtis, E. N., "American Opinion of the French Nineteenth Century Revolutions," *American Historical Review*, XXIX, 249–270.

Curtis, E. N., "La Révolution de 1830 et l'Opinion Publique en Amérique," *La Révolution de 1848*, XVIII, 64–73, 81–118.

Darling, A. B., *Political Changes in Massachusetts, 1824–1848* (New Haven, 1925).

Davis, H. E., "Economic Basis of Ohio Politics, 1820–1840," *Ohio Archaeological and Historical Quarterly*, XLVII, 288–318.

DeVoto, Bernard, *The Year of Decision: 1846* (Boston, 1943).

Dewey, D. R., *The Second United States Bank* (Washington, 1910).

Dewey, D. R., *State Banking before the Civil War* (Washington, 1910).

Dewey, Mary E., *Life and Letters of Catharine M. Sedgwick* (New York, 1871).

Dodd, E. M., Jr., and Baker, R. J., *Cases on Business Associations* (Chicago, 1940).

Dodd, E. M., Jr., "The First Half Century of Statutory Regulation of Business Corporations in Massachusetts," *Harvard Legal Essays . . . Presented to Joseph Henry Beale and Samuel Williston* (Cambridge, 1934).

Donovan, H. D. A., *The Barnburners* (New York, 1925).

Du Bois, J. T., and Mathews, G. S., *Galusha A. Grow* (Boston, 1917).

Ellis, W. A., ed., *Norwich University, 1819–1911* (Montpelier, 1911).

Eriksson, E. M., "The Federal Civil Service under President Jackson," *Mississippi Valley Historical Review*, XIII, 517–540.

Eriksson, E. M., "Official Newspaper Organs and the Campaign of 1828," *Tennessee Historical Magazine*, VIII, 231–247.

Eriksson, E. M., "Official Newspaper Organs and Jackson's Re-election, 1832," *Tennessee Historical Magazine*, IX, 37–58.

Eriksson, E. M., "Official Newspaper Organs and the Presidential Election of 1836," *Tennessee Historical Magazine*, IX, 114–130.

Flick, A. C., "Samuel Jones Tilden," *New York History*, XXIX, 347–359.

Flick, A. C., *Samuel J. Tilden* (New York, 1939).

Foner, P. S., *Business and Slavery: the New York Merchants and the Irrepressible Conflict* (Chapel Hill, 1941).

Fox, D. R., *The Decline of Aristocracy in the Politics of New York* (New York, 1918).

Frankfurter, Felix, *The Commerce Clause under Marshall, Taney and Waite* (Chapel Hill, 1937).

Fraser, H. R., *Democracy in the Making.* (Indianapolis, 1938).

Frothingham, O. B., *George Ripley* (Boston, 1882).

Frothingham, P. R., *Edward Everett, Orator and Statesman* (Boston, 1925).

Furness, C. J., "Walt Whitman's Politics," *American Mercury*, XVI, 459–466 (April, 1929).

Furness, C. J., *Walt Whitman's Workshop* (Cambridge, 1928).

Gammon, S. R., Jr., *The Presidential Campaign of 1832* (Baltimore, 1922).

Ginzberg, Eli, *The House of Adam Smith* (New York, 1934).

Going, C. B., *David Wilmot, Free-Soiler* (New York, 1924).

Goodpasture, A. V., "John Bell's Political Revolt, and His Vauxhall Garden Speech," *Tennessee Historical Magazine*, II, 254–263.

Gordon, A. C., *William Fitzhugh Gordon* (New York, 1909).

Govan, T. P., "John M. Berrien and the Administration of Andrew Jackson," *Journal of Southern History*, V, 447–467.

Gover, W. C., *The Tammany Hall Democracy of the City of New York* (New York, 1875).

Hailperin, Herman, "Pro-Jackson Sentiment in Pennsylvania, 1820–1828," *Pennsylvania Magazine of History and Biography*, L, 193–240.

Hamlin, C. E., *Life and Times of Hannibal Hamlin* (Cambridge, 1899).

Hammond, Bray, "Free Banks and Corporations: the New York Free Banking Act of 1838," *Journal of Political Economy*, XLIV, 184–209.

Harrington, F. H., "Nathaniel Prentiss Banks," *New England Quarterly*, IX, 626–654.

Hartz, Louis, "Seth Luther: Working Class Rebel," *New England Quarterly*, XIII, 401–418.

Hazard, Blanche E., *Organization of the Boot and Shoe Industry in Massachusetts before 1875* (Cambridge, 1921).

Heiskell, S. G., *Andrew Jackson and Early Tennessee History* (Nashville, 1918–1921).

Henderson, G. C., *Position of Foreign Corporations in American Constitutional Law* (Cambridge, 1918).

Herring, E. Pendleton, *The Politics of Democracy: American Parties in Action* (New York, 1940).

Hill, H. A., *Memoir of Abbott Lawrence* (Boston, 1883).

Hoar, G. F., *Autobiography of Seventy Years* (New York, 1903).

Hofstadter, Richard, "Parrington and the Jeffersonian Tradition," *Journal of the History of Ideas*, II, 391–400.

Hofstadter, Richard, "William Leggett, Spokesman of Jacksonian Democracy," *Political Science Quarterly*, LVIII, 581–594.

Holden, V. F., *Early Years of Isaac Thomas Hecker* (1819–1844) (Washington, 1939).

Holmes, O. W., "Sunday Travel and Sunday Mails," *New York History*, XXXVII, 413–424.

Holt, E. A., *Party Politics in Ohio, 1840–1850* (Columbus, 1931).

Horton, J. T., *James Kent. A Study in Conservatism* (New York, 1939).

Howe, M. A. DeWolfe, *Life and Letters of George Bancroft* (New York, 1908).

Hubbart, H. C., *The Older Middle West, 1840–1880* (New York, 1936).

Huntington, C. C., "History of Banking and Currency in Ohio before the Civil War," *Ohio Archaeological and Historical Quarterly*, XXIV, 235–539.

Jackson, Joseph, "Bibliography of the Works of George Lippard," *Pennsylvania Magazine of History and Biography*, LIV, 131–154.

Jackson, Joseph, "George Lippard: Misunderstood Man of Letters," *Pennsylvania Magazine of History and Biography*, LIX, 376–391.

James, Marquis, *Andrew Jackson: Portrait of a President* (Indianapolis, 1937).

Jenkins, W. S., *Pro-Slavery Thought in the Old South* (Chapel Hill, 1935).

Jordan, H. D., "A Politician of Expansion: Robert J. Walker," *Mississippi Valley Historical Review*, XIX, 362–381.

Kinley, David, *The Independent Treasury of the United States* (Washington, 1910).

Klein, P. S., *Pennsylvania Politics, 1817–1832* (Philadelphia, 1940).

Knight, T. A., *Tippecanoe* (Cleveland, 1940).

Koch, Adrienne, *The Philosophy of Thomas Jefferson* (New York, 1943).

Koch, G. A., *Republican Religion* (New York, 1933).

Leftwich, G. J., "Robert J. Walker," *Publications of the Mississippi Historical Society*, VI, 359–371.

Leopold, Richard W., *Robert Dale Owen* (Cambridge, 1940).

Linn, W. A., *Horace Greeley* (New York, 1903).

Littlefield, N. W., "Governor Marcus Morton," *Collections of the Old Colony Historical Society*, VII, 75–93.

Livermore, Shaw, *Early American Land Companies: Their Influence in Corporate Development* (New York, 1939).

Livermore, Shaw, "Unlimited Liability in Early American Corporations," *Journal of Political Economy*, XLIII, 674–687.

Ludlum, D. M., *Social Ferment in Vermont, 1791–1850* (New York, 1939).

Madeleine, Sister M. Grace, *Monetary and Banking Theories of Jacksonian Democracy* (Philadelphia, 1943).

Mangold, G. B., *The Labor Argument in the American Protective Tariff Discussion* (Madison, 1906).

Matthiessen, F. O., *American Renaissance* (New York, 1941).

Mayo, Bernard, "The Man Who Killed Tecumseh," *American Mercury*, XIX, 446–453.

McClure, C. H., *Opposition in Missouri to Thomas Hart Benton* (Nashville, 1927).

McCormac, E. I., *James K. Polk* (Berkeley, 1922).

McGrane, R. C., *The Panic of 1837* (Chicago, 1924).

McLaughlin, J. F., *Life and Times of John Kelly, Tribune of the People* (New York, 1885).

Meigs, W. M., *Life of Charles Jared Ingersoll* (Philadelphia, 1897).

Meigs, W. M., *Life of John C. Calhoun* (New York, 1917).

Meigs, W. M., *Life of Thomas Hart Benton* (Philadelphia, 1904).

Menger, Anton, *The Right to the Whole Produce of Labour*, with Introduction and Bibliography by H. S. Foxwell (London, 1899).

Meyer, L. W., *Life and Times of Colonel Richard M. Johnson of Kentucky* (New York, 1932).

Miller, H. E., *Banking Theories in the United States before 1860* (Cambridge, 1927).

Milton, G. F., *The Eve of Conflict* (Boston, 1934).

Mims, Edwin, Jr., *The Majority of the People* (New York, 1941).

Mitchell, Stewart, *Horatio Seymour of New York* (Cambridge, 1938).

Moore, Powell, "The Revolt against Jackson in Tennessee," *Journal of Southern History*, II, 335–359.

Morse, J. M., *A Neglected Period of Connecticut's History, 1818–1850* (New Haven, 1933).

Morse, J. M., *Rise of Liberalism in Connecticut, 1828–1850* (New Haven, 1933).

Mott, F. L., *History of American Magazines*, I (New York, 1938).

Mowry, Arthur M., *The Dorr War* (Providence, 1901).

Mueller, H. R., *The Whig Party in Pennsylvania* (New York, 1922).

Munger, T. T., *Horace Bushnell: Preacher and Theologian* (Boston, 1899).

Munroe, J. P., *Life of Francis Amasa Walker* (New York, 1923).

Myers, Gustavus, *History of Tammany Hall* (New York, 1901).

Nelles, Walter, "Commonwealth v. Hunt," *Columbia Law Review*, XXXII, 1128–1169.

Nettels, Curtis, "The Mississippi Valley and the Federal Judiciary, 1807–1837," *Mississippi Valley Historical Review*, XII, 202–226.

Nevins, Allan, *The Evening Post. A Century of Journalism* (New York, 1922).

Nichols, R. F., *The Democratic Machine, 1850–1854* (New York, 1923).

Nichols, R. F., *Franklin Pierce* (Philadelphia, 1931).

O'Meara, James, *Broderick and Gwin* (San Francisco, 1881).

Outland, Ethel R., *The "Effingham" Libels on Cooper* (Madison, 1929).

Parsons, H. C., *A Puritan Outpost* (New York, 1937).

Paxson, F. L., "A Constitution of Democracy — Wisconsin, 1847," *Mississippi Valley Historical Review*, II, 3–24.

Pease, T. C., *The Frontier State, 1818–1848* (*Centennial History of Illinois*, II, Chicago, 1918).

Peck, C. H., "John Van Buren," *Magazine of American History*, XVII, *passim*.

Perkins, A. J. G., and Wolfson, Theresa, *Frances Wright: Free Enquirer* (New York, 1939).

Phillips, Catherine C., *Jessie Benton Frémont* (San Francisco, 1935).

Phillips, U. B., "The Southern Whigs, 1834–1854," *Turner Essays in American History* (New York, 1910).

Pickard, S. T., *Life and Letters of John Greenleaf Whittier* (Boston, 1894).

Pickard, S. T., *Whittier as a Politician* (Boston, 1900).

Pierce, F. C., *Foster Genealogy* (Chicago, 1899).

Pierson, G. W., *Tocqueville and Beaumont in America* (New York, 1938).

Poage, G. R., *Henry Clay and the Whig Party* (Chapel Hill, 1936).

Porter, S. H., *Life and Times of Anne Royall* (Cedar Rapids, 1908).

Pratt, J. W., "John L. O'Sullivan and Manifest Destiny," *New York History*, XXXI, 213–234.

Prime, S. I., *Life of Samuel F. B. Morse, LL.D.* (New York, 1875).

Rantoul, R. S., *Personal Recollections* (Cambridge, 1916).

Read, A. W., "The Evidence on 'O.K.,'" *Saturday Review of Literature*, July 19, 1941.

Rezneck, Samuel, "The Depression of 1819–1822, a Social History," *American Historical Review*, XXXIX, 28–47.

Rezneck, Samuel, "Rise and Early Development of Industrial Consciousness in the United States, 1760–1840," *Journal of Economic and Business History*, IV, 784–811.

Rezneck, Samuel, "Social History of an American Depression, 1837–1843," *American Historical Review*, XL, 662–687.

Riley, I. W., *The Founder of Mormonism* (New York, 1902).

Robbins, R. M., "Horace Greeley: Land Reform and Unemployment, 1837–1862," *Agricultural History*, VII, 18–41.

Robinson, E. B., "The *Pennsylvanian*: Organ of the Democracy," *Pennsylvania Magazine of History and Biography*, LXII, 350–360.

Robinson, W. A., *Jeffersonian Democracy in New England* (New Haven, 1916).

Roosevelt, Franklin D., *Public Papers and Addresses*, S. I. Rosenman, arr. (New York, 1938–   ).

Roosevelt, Theodore, *Thomas Hart Benton* (Boston, 1886).

Rourke, Constance, *Davy Crockett* (New York, 1934).

Sanborn, F. B., *Hawthorne and His Friends* (Cedar Rapids, 1908).

Sandburg, Carl, *Abraham Lincoln: the War Years* (New York, 1939).

Schlesinger, Arthur M., "Tides of American Politics," *Yale Review,* XXIX, 217–230.

Schlesinger, Arthur M., Jr., "Can Willkie Save His Party?" *Nation,* December 6, 1941.

Schlesinger, Arthur M., Jr., *Orestes A. Brownson: a Pilgrim's Progress* (Boston, 1939).

Schouler, James, *History of the United States of America under the Constitution* (New York, 1880–1913).

Sears, L. M., "Nicholas P. Trist, a Diplomat with Ideals," *Mississippi Valley Historical Review,* XI, 86–98.

Secrist, Horace, "The Anti-Auction Movement in the New York Workingmen's Party of 1829," *Transactions of the Wisconsin Academy of Science, Arts and Letters,* XVII, 149–166.

Sedgwick, Sarah C., and Marquand, Christina S., *Stockbridge, 1739–1939* (Great Barrington, 1939).

Semmes, J. E., *John H. B. Latrobe and His Times, 1803–1891* (Baltimore, 1917).

Shaw, Samuel S., *Lemuel Shaw* (Cambridge, 1885).

Shepard, Edward M., *Martin Van Buren* (New York, 1899).

Simms, H. H., *Life of John Taylor* (Richmond, 1932).

Simms, H. H., *Rise of the Whigs in Virginia, 1824–1840* (Richmond, 1929).

Sioussat, St. G. L., "Andrew Johnson and the Early Phases of the Homestead Bill," *Mississippi Valley Historical Review,* V, 253–287.

Sioussat, St. G. L., "Some Phases of Tennessee Politics in the Jackson Period," *American Historical Review,* XIV, 51–69.

Smith, C. W., Jr., *Roger B. Taney: Jacksonian Jurist* (Chapel Hill, 1936).

Smith, Goldwin, *Reminiscences,* Arnold Hautain, ed. (New York, 1910).

Smith, T. C., *The Liberty and Free Soil Parties in the Northwest* (New York, 1897).

Smith, W. B., and Cole, A. H., *Fluctuations in American Business, 1790–1860* (Cambridge, 1935).

Smith, W. E., *The Francis Preston Blair Family in Politics* (New York, 1933).

Spiller, R. E., *Fenimore Cooper: Critic of His Times* (New York, 1931).

Steiner, B. C., *Life of Roger Brooke Taney* (Baltimore, 1922).

Stewart, Randall, "Hawthorne and Politics," *New England Quarterly,* V, 237–263.

Stickles, A. M., *The Critical Court Struggle in Kentucky, 1819–1829* (Bloomington, Indiana, 1929).

Streeter, F. B., *Political Parties in Michigan, 1837–1860* (Lansing, 1918).

Sumner, W. G., *Andrew Jackson* (Boston, 1882).

Sumner, W. G., *History of Banking in the United States* (New York, 1896).

Swisher, C. B., *Roger B. Taney* (New York, 1935).

Taussig, F. W., ed., *State Papers and Speeches on the Tariff* (Cambridge, 1892).

Temple, O. P., *Notable Men of Tennessee from 1833 to 1875* (New York, 1912).

Thomas, B. F., *Sketch of the Life and Judicial Labors of Chief-Justice Shaw* (Boston, 1868).

Trimble, William, "Diverging Tendencies in New York Democracy in the Period of the Locofocos," *American Historical Review*, XXIV, 396–421.

Trimble, William, "The Social Philosophy of the Loco-Foco Democracy," *American Journal of Sociology*, XXVI, 705–715.

Turner, Frederick J., *The United States, 1830–1850* (New York, 1935).

Tyler, Lyon G., *Letters and Times of the Tylers* (Richmond, 1894–1896).

Tyler, Samuel, *Memoir of Roger Brooke Taney, LL.D.* (Baltimore, 1872).

Walker, F. A., "The Hon. Amasa Walker, LL.D.," *New England Historical and Genealogical Register*, XLII, 133–141.

Waples, Dorothy, *The Whig Myth of James Fenimore Cooper* (New Haven, 1938).

Ward, A. H., "David Henshaw," *Memorial Biographies of the New England Historic Genealogical Society*, I (Boston, 1880).

Warden, R. B., *Account of the Private Life and Public Services of Salmon Portland Chase* (Cincinnati, 1874).

Ware, Norman, *The Industrial Worker, 1840–1860* (Boston, 1924).

Warren, Charles, *History of the American Bar* (Boston, 1911).

Warren, Charles, *Old Byways in American History* (Cambridge, 1942).

Warren, Charles, *The Supreme Court in United States History*, revised ed. (Boston, 1926).

Waterman, W. R., *Frances Wright* (New York, 1924).

Weisenburger, F. P., *The Passing of the Frontier, 1825–1850* (Carl Wittke, ed., *The History of the State of Ohio*, III, Columbus, 1941).

Wellington, R. G., *Political and Sectional Influence of the Public Land, 1828–1842* (Cambridge, 1914).

Weston, Florence, *The Presidential Election of 1828* (Washington, 1938).

Williams, S. T., *Life of Washington Irving* (New York, 1935).

Wilson, J. G., ed., *The Presidents of the United States* (New York, 1894).

Wilson, Woodrow, *Division and Reunion, 1829–1889* (New York, 1893).

Wiltse, C. M., "Calhoun and the Modern State," *Virginia Quarterly Review*, XIII, 396–408.

Wise, B. H., *Life of Henry A. Wise of Virginia* (New York, 1899).

Witte, E. E., "Early American Labor Cases," *Yale Law Journal*, XXXV, 825–837.

Woodberry, G. E., *Life of Edgar Allan Poe* (Boston, 1909).

Woolf, Leonard, *After the Deluge*, II (New York, 1940).

Woollen, Evans, "Labor Troubles between 1834 and 1837," *Yale Review*, I, 87–100.

Wright, B. F., Jr., "American Democracy and the Frontier," *Yale Review*, XX, 349–365.

Wright, B. F., Jr., *The Contract Clause of the Constitution* (Cambridge, 1938).

Wright, B. F., Jr., "Political Institutions and the Frontier," *Sources of Culture in the Middle West*, D. R. Fox, ed. (New York, 1934).

Zahler, H. S., *Eastern Workingmen and National Land Policy, 1829–1862* (New York, 1941).

INDEX